•

LAW, FAMILY, AND WOMEN

•

Law, Family, & Women

•

TOWARD A LEGAL ANTHROPOLOGY OF RENAISSANCE ITALY

•

THOMAS KUEHN

The University of Chicago Press
Chicago and London

The University of Chicago Press, Chicago 60637
The University of Chicago Press, Ltd., London
© 1991 by The University of Chicago
All rights reserved. Published 1991
Paperback edition 1994
Printed in the United States of America

00 99 98 97 96 95 94   5 4 3 2

ISBN (cloth): 0-226-45762-1
ISBN (paperback): 0-226-45764-8

Library of Congress Cataloging-in-Publication Data

Kuehn, Thomas, 1950–
    Law, family & women : toward a legal anthropology of Renaissance
Italy / Thomas Kuehn.
        p. cm.
    Includes biographical references and index.
    1. Law—Italy—Florence—History and criticism.   2. Dispute
resolution (Law)—Italy—Florence—History.   3. Women—Legal status,
laws, etc.—Italy—Florence—History.   4. Family—Italy—Florence—
History.   I. Title.   II. Title: Law, family, and women.
KKH9851.K84   1991
349.45′51—dc20   91-13341

For Allison

CONTENTS

•

vii

PART THREE: WOMEN

TABLES

●

ACKNOWLEDGMENTS

With the exception of additions from subsequent research to the first, third, and ninth chapters, eight of these chapters have been previously published and are presented here substantially unchanged (except for the deletion of documentary appendixes where such occurred). Errors have been corrected and the notes have been adjusted to make them consistent. Redundancies have, I hope, been eliminated (with cross-references provided), so some passages of previously published papers have been slightly modified or cut out. Matters of style that seemed sensible at the time of publication, but that made less sense after the passage of as many as ten years, have been adjusted. Updated bibliographical references have been added in the notes where I thought such a change from the published version was warranted. Much excellent and important work has been published in the last decade and, for those papers that appeared in the early eighties, I believed it was worthwhile considering more recent historiography in those contexts. This seemed especially valuable for the two papers on women's legal rights and abilities (chapters 8 and 9), for a great deal has appeared on women in history in recent years.

The transfer of the Florentine State Archives from the Uffizi to a new building on Piazza Beccaria during 1988 was also the occasion for the reorganization of various archival *fondi*. The research behind this volume spans fifteen years. It has not proved possible to go back and adjust every archival citation to the new format, where there is one. As regards my research the main pertinent reorganization involved the Notarile antecosimiano. Both old and new citations appear in these papers; archival indexing makes tracing these citations possible.

The chapters already in print can stand on their own for the occasions they were written, and anyone interested can take the citations in them and find the original versions. They will be cited in the notes both by their position in this book and in their original forms.

I am grateful to the following journals for permission to reprint my essays. Part of chapter 1 appeared as "Arbitration and Law in Renaissance Florence," *Renaissance and Reformation,* n.s. 11 (1987): 289–319. Chapter 3 first appeared in *Quaderni fiorentini per la storia del pensiero giuridico moderno* 14 (1985): 303–72; chapter 4 in *Ricerche storiche* 10 (1980): 287–310; chapter 6 in *I Tatti Studies: Essays in the Renaissance* 1 (1985): 161–87; chapter 7 in *American Journal of Legal History* 29 (1985): 275–300; chapter 8 in *Tijdschrift voor Rechtsgeschiedenis* 49 (1981): 127–47; chapter 9 in *Viator* 13 (1982): 309–33; chapter 10 in *Continuity and Change* 2 (1987): 11–36.

In the course of the years I have accumulated numerous debts of gratitude, scholarly and personal, that made this volume possible. Some of those scholarly debts are evident in the essays themselves. More directly, I wish to thank the staffs of the Archivio di Stato, Florence, and the Biblioteca Nazionale Centrale, as well as the Library of Congress, St. Louis University Library, and Clemson University Library (especially the indispensable aid and generosity of the interlibrary loan staff). To the National Endowment for the Humanities I owe two summer research grants and a stipend to travel to St. Louis and examine the Vatican microfilm collection at St. Louis University. Clemson University provided two faculty research grants and a Provost Research Award, as well as a much-needed sabbatical. To my colleagues in the Clemson History Department I owe thanks for support and encouragement, and to present and former students Mike Sutton and Jonathan Fowler I owe thanks for research and computer assistance. Libby Steedly's help and friendship sustained me as I completed the book. Janet Leipelt typed the oldest three essays into a computer so I could rework them.

Elaine Rosenthal generously shared archival references and sources while we were both in Florence in 1987. I hope I have used the material well. Over a longer period of acquaintance David Herlihy similarly provided information and advice. His death as this book went to press was a deeply felt personal and professional loss. Gino Corti came to my aid on several occasions, especially in dealing with *catasto* texts for the third chapter. David Marsh read my essay on Alberti—a venture into his area of expertise—and saved me from various errors. Anthony Molho has been a constant friend and source of advice. It was his suggestion that sent me off to investigate the *mundualdus*. The late Eric Cochrane was an example of rigor in scholarship and audacity in historical interpretation. At various points over the past fifteen years Paolo Grossi of the Centro di Studi per la Storia del Pensiero Giuridico Moderno of the Facoltà di Giurisprudenza of the Università di Firenze has made available to me the use of studies and materials housed there. His warm hospitality is greatly appreciated; his interest in my work is returned with admiration for his. Finally, I can only begin to express my gratitude to Julius Kirshner, mentor and friend, whose intellectual imprint is all over these essays and who has provided help in all sorts of ways over the years. The faults and shortcomings of these essays, as a group and singly, are surely my own; what strengths they may have are just as surely attributable to him and to the others who have helped me.

•

INTRODUCTION

•

Of the ten chapters in this book seven and portions of another have been previously published. They have appeared at different moments and in different publications (not all of them readily available in U.S. libraries) during the past ten years. However, any resulting difficulties of access do not, themselves, justify assembling these essays into one volume. Even the opportunity to make needed additions and corrections is insufficient to account for a book. It is my belief that these essays constitute a whole because they share a number of common features, only the most obvious of which is their concentration on Italian, especially Florentine, history in the fourteenth and fifteenth centuries. Above all, they are the product of a particular historical perspective, itself the result of my encounters with the predominantly legal sources for Florentine social history and with the works of legal anthropologists as well as of historians of the Italian Renaissance. Because these essays arose from the use of certain types of sources and from a particular way of reading them, they have some degree of coherence to excuse their reincarnation in the form of a book.

These essays attempt to delineate problems about Renaissance history, especially social history. They spring from my sense that law (itself a multifaceted entity) was implicated throughout society in an Italian city-state. Awareness of legal rules and the operation of legal mechanisms were present on a regular (that is, daily) basis. Law's formative influence was not merely occasional. It came into play not only at moments of trouble—the criminal trial, the legislative debate—though it was powerfully present then. It informed most levels

1

of activity and discourse. As I try to show in the essay on Leon Battista Alberti, even when the law was not directly in play it informed the possibilities of a text or a social situation. As my title implies, law had a shaping influence on domestic life (itself conceptualized in the law's terms and made operative through legal mechanisms of property, dowry, inheritance, marriage, dispute settlements), including the lives of women and the men related to them.[1]

At the very least we have to confront the fact that our sources for Renaissance social history are predominantly legal texts, most notably the notarial instruments historians track down in archives to illuminate vital processes such as marriage and inheritance. I have endeavored to respect the complex "texture" of relations and meanings in these texts while keeping in view the peculiar fabric of their legal language. I have approached them not as "documents" describing past actions unequivocally but as portions of a dialectic interaction with the past—with their own "context"—as well as with the present. The historical agents who gave us these texts were themselves involved in attempts to make sense of them, to shape distinct understandings of events and texts.[2] These legal texts must be examined in light of and along with nonlegal texts. In fact it is necessary at times to recognize that the distinction between legal and nonlegal was and is nebulous. Account books in Florence, for example, were subject to summons as judicial evidence; Florentines knew that and could shape their accounts accordingly. In what sense then were accounts nonlegal? Likewise the fiscal census—the famous *catasto*—might be invoked in evidence of property claims or even perhaps of ages of individuals. Florentines seem to have been wary of what they put in their fiscal declarations and of how they put it.[3]

Some years ago Julius Kirshner urged the study of law upon social historians of the Renaissance. In forceful terms he demonstrated the pitfalls for historical understanding of uninformed reading of legal texts that were composed in an arcane and technical language and crafted to conceal as well as reveal actions and intentions.[4] To date, few have taken up the challenge. Gaining facility with even fairly circumscribed areas of law is not easy. Still, failure to do so leaves present the danger of deception and historical misinterpretation. Delusive impressions of self-executing testaments or unmitigated patriarchy have resulted.[5]

When one confronts the meaning and operation of law as disputants and practitioners did (and do), seemingly solid structures and clear rules dissolve. One is then free to appreciate the dimensions available for maneuver, for error, and for miscommunication. One is faced with another recurrent theme here—the prevalence of realms of ambiguity in society and law and, in consequence, the constant potential for conflict as these realms and their borders were tested and traversed. Several of the essays included here sample these ambiguities, conflicts, and the possible ways of composing them, even if only temporarily.

All of the chapters in this book concern the history of Florence. It is the rich deposits of materials in Florence that brought me to that lovely city originally and have brought me back several times. These materials make possible my analyses of the sorts of historical problems that I have wanted to tackle. It is largely in consequence of those interests that I have gained an interest in understanding the history of Florence itself during its era of cultural and artistic creativity.

Studying the history of Florence, however, has another advantage. As a fertile and important field for research, it has attracted the efforts of outstanding scholars, especially those interested in social historical topics, such as family and women. Their work has provided a sophisticated and enlightening context for my own. It has been indispensable to whatever insight I have been able to gain. At the same time, while developing an approach anchored in the law, using different sources or in different combinations, I have come to conclusions or developed perspectives that vary from those of other historians.

When I first came to Florentine social history, in the course of research on the legal emancipation of children in the fourteenth and fifteenth centuries, the focus of historical concern was the structure of the patrician family. The very different approaches of Richard Goldthwaite, Francis William Kent, David Herlihy, and Christiane Klapisch-Zuber were aimed at delineating the abiding and typical features of households and lineages.[6] My assumption as I began research on an institution by which children were removed from subjection to legal paternal control (*patria potestas*) was that emancipation could furnish further insight on these structural questions, which it did. Yet what struck me as I began my own reading in various sources was that structures were not necessarily and always fixed and certain. The city that has been celebrated as the home of the Renaissance was a dynamic social arena, marked by conflicts and accommodations, by ambiguities and attempts at precision, by strategies and manipulations. Along with and influenced by others, I have come to see that kinship and household were realms of cultural meaning and interaction in which social values were inscribed and through which they could be conceptualized, transacted, and attained.[7]

The single most influential book for Florentine social history, one which indeed has had ramifications far beyond that narrow field, has been *Les toscans et leurs familles* by David Herlihy and Christiane Klapisch-Zuber. This monumental work was made possible by the abundance of Florentine sources and especially by that city's unique fiscal census, the *catasto*. Herlihy and Klapisch's careful statistical analysis of this incomparable source yielded insights about the various household forms found in early fifteenth-century Tuscany and about the demographic structures and economic patterns that underlay those forms. That demographic and economic factors affected household forms and kinship practices cannot be denied. But they were not the only factors. They occupy pride of place in *Les toscans*. Only after their treatment did the authors go on to consider cultural expressions of kinship in literary and narrative sources.[8] Yet cultural constructs involving kinship and domestic life were also at play, including those that gained normative expression in the law, thus helping to shape the precise effect of demographic and economic factors. Rules governing formation of marriage, dowries, and *patria potestas,* for example, set the possibilities for Florentines. At times they made these rules operate in a rational and practical manner in the face of demographic and economic realities; at times they did not.[9]

In her own work Christiane Klapisch-Zuber has gone on to construct a provocative notion of the structures of meaning and practice in various dimensions of Florentine domestic life. Beyond her close acquaintance with the *catasto,* she has drawn heavily on another peculiarly Florentine source, the book of household *ricordi*. In a brilliant series of essays she has utilized these *ricordi* to delineate the relations between household, kin, and neighbors; the relations between spouses and between their families of origin; relations between biological parents and wet nurses; between families and their servants; and much more. The gathering of her essays into single volumes in English and Italian makes possible a more exact assessment of her work.[10] Hers is a nuanced sense of Florentine families in their structural elements. A common thread in her work has been her point of departure from a sense ("stupore" is her Italian term for it) that women occupied a secondary or even socially irrelevant place in the social images left us by Florentines.[11] She has endeavored to explain and correct this impression with the view that "the domestic group is the theater in which are put in question—at times by the women themselves—the roles and rules of behavior that tradition assigned to the sexes and to the different age groups."[12] Her attention has been focused on vocabulary and the most minute details (in artistic iconography or the color of conventional items in a woman's trousseau [*corredo*], for example). These details are revealed in her reading as elements of a "feminine discourse" or a discourse about women, who were otherwise lost in the interstices between the lineage of males who spawned them and the lineage of males who used them to provide sons and heirs.[13] It was the strategies of these lineages for self-perpetuation and self-aggrandizement that explained the treatment (often a form of neglect) shown women. Women, for example, were excluded from management of their dowry.[14] They were reduced to the image of Boccaccio's and Petrarch's Griselda, given by her father to a husband to whom she then owed everything. Perhaps most characteristic of Klapisch-Zuber's position is her celebrated essay on the "cruel mother"—the young widow with children whose family of origin arranged her remarriage, for their own purposes, removing her from her children, themselves members of the lineage of their dead father, whose family interest, of course, was to keep her a widow and active mother.[15] Here one confronts a woman torn from her own children but presented as weak-willed and cruel, abandoning them to the mercies of guardians who might steal their wealth, which was now diminished by the loss of their mother's dowry.

Klapisch-Zuber remains sensitive to the potential for conflict between lineages or even within lineages, as evidenced at moments when families adopted new names to distinguish themselves.[16] But though these conflicts might be because of women, always she sees these as matters for and by men. Means of accommodation of these conflicts, including a valued sense of cognatic, as opposed to patrilineal, kinship, existed. Her vision of the inalterable structural tension between lineages, for example, would not predict an event such as a son giving property to a mother who had remarried into another lineage. But such events could and did happen,[17] just as it was also true that for religious as well as practical reasons many widows never remarried.[18]

In his introduction to the English-language collection of Klapisch-Zuber's essays, Herlihy suggests that an examination of less formal networks and modes of meaning might make Florentine women "appear somewhat less marginal, and their experiences a little less harsh than they seem in Klapisch's hands."[19] That may indeed be, but I would also suggest that the same impression can emerge from looking at the even more formal, but less overtly ideological, realm of the law. While the case can be made that Roman law in conjunction with canon law institutionalized restrictions on women,[20] it also must be acknowledged that law institutionalized and protected rights in and through women.[21]

The *mundualdus,* an institution peculiar to Florence among the cities of Tuscany and northern Italy, is a case in point. The *mundualdus* was a male guardian provided for legal actions by women. Without his consent no legal action by a woman (with a few exceptions) was valid. As I attempt to demonstrate in chapter 9, despite the gender-related ideological bias behind the institution, its effectiveness in controlling women's legal actions is open to doubt. Depending on their circumstances, some women were able to have the *mundualdus* more or less reduced to a formality. This does not mean that all women were free social agents or that the *mundualdus* could not indeed be an effective control on women.[22] They were disadvantaged by the institution; their acts were voidable when subjected to challenge, while the *mundualdus* bore no liability for his role. In any case, I do not think that the picture regarding women was quite as neat as Klapisch-Zuber's analysis would make it seem.

Her approach to history closely parallels that of the *Annales* school, which neglects law generally. *Annalistes* see law as epiphenomenal; they downplay its importance and impact.[23] Legal history, in consequence, has been ousted from the mainstream of historical research and, especially in France, relegated to the periphery with ancillary disciplines such as paleography. But tracking the shifting and contingent operations of the law would also greatly complicate Klapisch-Zuber's neat analyses. There are no loose ends in her elegant studies; everything has its place in a structure, a function to fulfill and a meaning to express. The workings of law, on the other hand, reveal jarring notes of disharmony, incoherence, and even dysfunction. Some events, in their particularity, defy easy classification; some meanings are multiple or, alternatively, indecipherable. In contrast to hers, then, mine is an approach to Florentine social history that offers a poststructural space for the play of ambiguities.[24]

Another historian whose work has been of great influence is Francis William Kent. His sources have included letters, *ricordi,* notarial acts, and anything else that can carry him into the midst of familial life and expressions of it. Cultural constructs of domesticity and kinship among the patriciate have been the object of his attention. He has done the most to make us aware how the structure of patrician households and the practices of lineage membership were the functional outcome of the ideology of kinship these patricians embraced and celebrated in their lives, their words, and the words and artistic works of those they sponsored.[25] What I believe Kent's historical vision leaves out of account or, rather, minimizes, is the degree to which kinship was frought with ambiguities, the extent to which conflicts could and did occur even between kin and family members, and the fragility of familial continuity. Florentines crafted strategies in pursuit of culturally inscribed values, and sometimes those strategies failed. If nothing else, they could run headlong into the strategies of others. It was also true that successful strategy could have dysfunctional results.[26] Kent's own research reveals how the success of Giovanni Rucellai bred jealousy in lesser figures among the Rucellai.[27] Two of the chapters in the set of essays on Florentine family life explore fissures in domestic and lineage solidarity, both made more evident, paradoxically, by the cultural stress on such solidarity. It is easier to see these fractures in the facade of lineage solidarity under the lens of legal sources. There we find kin, most often in the guise of heirs, at odds over property. But property, as Kent has been most forceful in reminding us, was itself bound up with familial honor, and it is precisely on that score that one can also find Florentines at odds even with members of their own household. The chapters that concern disputes and law were all undertaken with a sense that these types of events provide a privileged access to the dynamic of familial life in Florence.

Kent's many important studies also have tended to neglect women. He has taken the Florentine ideology of patrilineage at face value—that the lineage was an association of related men who owned the property and directed the affairs of the group. My work is intended as a small part of a critical stance regarding that ideology (as are the works of Klapisch-Zuber and others). If only because various property rights and claims were inscribed in women's names, their male relatives could not pursue strategies without reference to them. Nor can historians follow those strategies, I think, without reference to these women and the nature of their legal position.

To bring law to bear in the reading of the generally legal sources for Florentine social history requires one to confront the work of legal historians. They are the experts in decoding the language of doctrinal writings, judicial records, and notarial charters. Unfortunately for social historians the legal historians can provide only limited guidance—because of an emphasis on normative structures and a disinterest in the law in practice. Because of the nature of their place in universities and the legal profession and because of the academic nature of the civil law in general, legal historians focus on legal thought, the doctrinal schools of important jurists, academic commentaries, glosses, lectures, and disputations. Only secondarily are they interested in legislative sources, such as the statutes of the late medieval communes, or in notarial formulas. Actual notarial charters escape their purview, as do most forms of documentation arising from processes of litigation, arbitration, or other modes of conflict resolution. Their attention is, rather, on the coming into being of grand normative structures based on broad legal philosophical principles, which are presumed to regulate social interaction.[28]

Symptomatic in this regard is the work of the foremost Italian historian of family law, Manlio Bellomo. The undoubted strength of his work lies in his awareness of the formative influence of urban structures, patrician lineages, and institutions such as the universities themselves on the normative formations generated in the schools (*ius commune*) and in civic statutes (*ius proprium*).[29] Because the *ius proprium*, however, appropriated the terms of *ius commune*, it was limited by its necessary correspondence to the meanings of the latter's terms and the power of jurists to interpret them. Thus, in his study of the rights and claims of sons in paternal property, Bellomo finds that the problem of a "dual ownership" by father and son was first raised within *ius commune* and had reverberations in penal statutes in various cities of Italy. But because law and urban society celebrated and perpetuated paternal power, there was no hope of sons exercising any such claims except in extraordinary critical moments. Jurists mined the texts of civil law for "ideas that bore them immediately and with ease to normative results that were congenial to everyone, to the head of a family who was acting for the power of his house and to the government that was trying new constitutional measures in the city and to the jurist who was called on to give a theoretical configuration to every phenomenon."[30] As long as these jurists operated with an eye to the utility of their doctrinal accommodations, they brought the benefits of law to their society. The heyday of juristic doctrinal formation culminated in the works of the great jurists Bartolo da Sassoferrato (d. 1357) and Baldo degli Ubaldi (1327–1400). By the fifteenth century, Bellomo maintains, jurists had merely become tools of local interests; and in professional terms they abused the methods of dialectic to manufacture long-winded doctrinal solutions to problems that no longer held any social resonance. The jurisprudential crisis was embodied in the mass of *consilia* that jurists crafted for parties or judges in the course of litigation. Sheer quantity, Bellomo claims, bred confusion while hamstringing the jurists who had to confront all the preexisting opinions on an issue.[31]

My own confrontation with texts generated by legal practice, as well as with doctrinal texts, has led me to a different conclusion. The fifteenth century was not a stagnant era for law, at least outside the lecture hall. The very mass of *consilia* Bellomo bemoans can also be taken as testimony to jurists' influence and creativity (and to that of litigants and their advocates or notaries, for that matter) in moments and situations where the import of law was not clear. The role of jurists, experts at managing social and legal constructs, in crafting or determining meaning where it was uncertain, was vital. That is why their *consilia*, which bridged academic doctrines and local norms and the particular interests of litigants, are such an interesting, revealing, and important—if consummately difficult—source. *Consilia* figure prominently in five of the chapters that follow. They provide a fruitful focal point for inquiry because in them conflicts of interest are articulated as normative conflicts. These *consilia* present moments where accommodations were invented for such conflicts.[32] As valuable as the *consilia* are, their value is limited if they are read to the exclusion of other types of sources (and they cannot be read without reference to doctrinal texts and legislation). So *consilia* are only one type of document used here. Other sources range from those of legal (notarial charters) and quasi-legal (*catasto* and *ricordanze*) practice to letters and even Leon Battista Alberti's famous humanist dialogue on the family. As a result, law comes off not as a level terrain with clearly demarcated features but as an indistinct landscape whose shadowy surface hides the quicksand of pervasive ambiguities. Litigants and jurists stumbled across that surface.

Jurists were conservative figures. Interested in the perpetuation of social order, they were intent on mapping that shadowy landscape. However, that does not mean they were single-mindedly wedded to

interests of a dominant social class of which they were members or
with which they were closely associated. For one thing, the interests
of that class were not always unambiguous. For instance, an inheritance case (such as those discussed in Chapter 10) could involve two
patrician families. The solution worked out in favor of one of them
need not be any more or less in the interests of their class than an
opposed solution that left the other party as winners. It would seem
to have been in the interests of patricians to protect family property
and to make sure that debts were paid. Yet doing the second could
jeopardize the first. Furthermore, jurists approached these problems
as professionals, believing in the law and trained in its use. Especially
in the area of private litigation, away from areas of public law and
"statecraft," jurists do not seem to have been so determinedly patrician or even male in their outlook.[33]

Legal historians such as Bellomo do not follow the doctrines of the
schools or the norms of statutes into the courtrooms or the notaries'
books. Law in practice is a missing dimension. Another case in point
is a historian whose work is crucial to my views about arbitration in
chapter 1. Luciano Martone's analysis of the meaning of the terms
arbiter and *arbitrator*, which he takes to the fringes of legal practice
by considering notarial formularies, is an exemplary piece of legal
historical scholarship. But because he never examines actual arbitrations, he concludes that the ultimate subsumption of arbitration into
law (by allowing appeals to court, against the statutory desire to keep
such matters out of court) was a result of doctrinal imperialism
pushed by new absolutist forces emanating from Spanish domination
in Italy in the seventeenth century.[34] In chapter 1 I have attempted a
preliminary sounding of arbitration in practice. The difficulty of the
issues in arbitration and the depth of the animosities played out
within it can become clear only in that manner. Here again we find
that arbitration, as so much else, did not always function well. One
reason was that the means of enforcement of rules and judgments
were weak. People's protection lay in amassing papers that stated
legal claims (or obfuscated them at times). Arbitration generated
such paper. It did not generate an efficacious means of enforcement.
Appeal to court judgment might be necessary, and even that was not
easy of enforcement. These problems existed in practice, independent
of any Spanish legal imperialism, and they remain in different forms
today. They are characteristic not only of Italy (where, for example,
one finds both some of the most stringent environmental laws and

standards but also some of the worst environmental problems in Europe) but of other countries, the litigious United States included.

In seeking to proceed beyond the limits of legal historical practice, I have taken cues from legal anthropology. In contrast to legal historians, legal anthropologists have developed sophisticated, fruitful approaches to the phenomenological dimension of legal language. Anthropologists have concentrated on disputes and elaborated the so-called extended case method, which delves into the backgrounds of relations between disputants and prevailing social and economic conditions, tracing a dispute over time, through various manifestations, to some form of settlement. More recent anthropologists, such as Sally Falk Moore, John Comaroff and Simon Roberts, and Carol Greenhouse, have devised approaches to the interests and norms invoked and articulated in the course of disputes. Based on research in tribal or village contexts, on modes of dispute-handling that operate in place of or alongside formal modes of adjudication, their work makes possible insights into social processes and into the meaning of norms that cannot be obtained by concentrating on courts, legal professions, and the technical and often arcane normative language of the law itself. Legal anthropology's findings thus act as a powerful corrective to the myopia of historians of Continental civil law. At the same time, however, legal anthropology's fixation on cases leaves it ill equipped to conceptualize law per se as a theoretical object or as a historical reality. Anthropologists have gone so far as to argue that law is not a valid analytical category, a conclusion a historian of Western history, even social history, can only find difficult to follow.[35]

What I have attempted in the studies in this volume is a truly legal anthropology of a historical society. Whatever the situation in an African tribe, in the Renaissance Italian city law was a sophisticated and professionalized body of knowledge, of rules and procedures, of concepts and symbols, which was actively present in society in the courts, jurists, and notaries of a city such as Florence and ultimately in the hands of her citizens and residents. The status of law as a theoretical object and as a historical institutional nexus in Renaissance Italy cannot be denied. My desire has been to understand how, or how much, the very sophisticated and complex apparatus of law could serve the interests of litigants and to see how law functioned in a context with other mechanisms of disputing and settling disputes, ranging from fairly formal arbitration to violence.

The title I have chosen reflects the movement of themes in these papers—from the fundamental social arena of law and the disputes that came to it and the means adopted to resolve them, on to family and then to women in the concluding chapters. However, all three themes figure more or less throughout the volume. Remigio Lanfredini's concern for family honor, discussed in chapter 4, for example, is matched by that of all the Florentines whose arbitrations, as parts of their familial strategies, are the basis for chapter 1. The first essay, in fact, combines a paper previously published in *Renaissance and Reformation* with an analysis of a sampling of arbitrations from a single notarial book. Even that sampling is sufficient to demonstrate, I think, the range of issues Florentines could bring into conflict and the flexibility they could exhibit in handling them. The book begins with arbitration because there both the legal and the extralegal came into play, because both norms and procedures were on display, and because moments of both kin solidarity and conflict were revealed. The second chapter similarly deals with conflict, but the sources utilized there are unquestionably not legal. The *ricordi* of Oderigo di Credi and of Bernardo Machiavelli allow us rare glimpses into the minds of people in conflict. In the third chapter, then, I follow a single conflict (in a case-method approach) through its various permutations, as far as the sources allow. Domenico di Zanobi Fraschi sought to recover judicially a house that had belonged to his father. His attempt to do so raised interesting conceptual issues about property, for fifteenth-century jurists and for twentieth-century historians. Property in that era was not the absolute standard of ownership that it would become in later liberal theories; it was a nexus of rights within a network of persons.[36] In Fraschi's case it was also embedded within a strategy whose final form was unknown to me when I completed the essay as published in 1985. The surprising twist provided by the birth of a son after the house had been reacquired is chronicled in extensive additions to the essay (in compensation, the original long appendix has been dropped, though anyone curious to see it can go to the *Quaderni fiorentini*).

Chapters 4 to 7 concern family, or, more properly, the extent of domestic and lineage solidarity brought to the forefront of research by Klapisch-Zuber and Kent. All these chapters examine intrafamilial or intralineage disputes. Taken together these essays introduce a variety of extralegal tactics in disputes, including Alberti's use of humanist writing to make subtle statements about the ways in which his illegitimate birth unfairly conditioned the treatment accorded him by other Alberti. His desire to be associated with the Alberti contrasts, however, with Remigio Lanfredini's desire to sever ties with his father and with Piero Peruzzi's failure to abide by the terms of the vendetta set out for him by his kinsmen. In all these cases familial honor was also at stake. Chapters 4 to 6 also provide a contrast to chapter 7, which reexamines the moral and legal issues of illegitimacy, but from the perspective of the formal theoretical accommodation worked out by a trained jurist in the course of litigation. One of the reasons for my research interest in bastards is that in them normative ambiguities were evidently heightened, the tensions (even in Alberti's carefully contrived dialogue) barely beneath the surface. The very social and cultural notion of personhood was overtly subject to negotiation and construction in the case of bastards, as I hope to demonstrate when I publish my findings more fully.

Chapter 7 also introduces the themes of chapters 8–10—women, their property rights, and their legal capabilities. The three essays in these chapters explore some of the gender distinctions in law, notably regarding male legal controls over females and the privileging of male property claims in inheritance over those of females. My intent in these chapters is to offer a more nuanced sense of the historical understanding of gender. Against the simple assertion that a woman passed legally and effectively from control of her father to that of her husband at the time of marriage, I wanted to point out the ambiguity of continued paternal control in the *patria potestas*. Against the un-deniable preference in Florence and elsewhere to patrilocal marriage practices, at least among the elites, the father of the bride still held a residual control, which could become of more active significance on occasions when the woman's property rights acquired importance.

These matters of control were greatly complicated and acquired urgency through the practice of dowry. The bride's family furnished a dowry to the husband to support the "burdens of matrimony," which was also the girl's share of her father's patrimony. Thus her father and family of origin continued to have an interest in her, which might (as James Casey has argued) undercut household authority of the husband, but she also had attached to her legal *persona* property that, by rules of its devolution and control, could leave her more closely tied to the interests and survival of her husband and children. The problems posed by dowry were enormously complicated.[37]

Alongside, and at times part of, paternal and spousal control was the more general masculine dominance, legally available in Florence by means of the *mundualdus,* among other legal institutions. No woman could undertake a legal action without the consent of a male guardian. On face of it there would seem no more complete expression of male dominance than in this peculiar Florentine legal institution derived from Lombard precedents. (That females at times would take control of their lives and property is one perhaps surprising, certainly important implication of my very limited excursion into this area of law.) But there were also limits and real dimensions to male power. To clarify this point, I have made some changes in this chapter from the original version, adding consideration of two *consilia* that hinged on the provision of a *mundualdus.* Chapters 8 and 9 point out that women had property rights and interests but were not free to dispose of them (in theory at least) without reference to men, who also had interests in property rights held by and through women. Chapter 10 more directly addresses the provenance of these rights in inheritance, specifically by examining cases arising under the Florentine statute (typical of other Italian cities) governing inheritance by women. This statute was erected upon the *exclusio propter dotem,* the exclusion of dowered women from further inheritance from male agnates. The cases examined in the paper contribute some sense of the difficulties in the statute's meanings brought forth by the varying familial circumstances of inheritances. The possibilities of women pressing inheritance rights or of men pressing rights through women raised difficult issues of the meaning of agnation and gender as Florentines pursued familial strategies.

As a corrective to a too simplistic acceptance of realities of patriarchy in consequence of openly patriarchal rules and attitudes, some historians have tended to stress women's range of self-control and independence. Gene Brucker's *Giovanni and Lusanna* went so far as to present a Florentine woman as acting on her own prerogative against prevailing social prejudices to express and obtain her love. I have elsewhere expressed doubts as to this reading of the evidence.[38] It is important to note how powerful a case Lusanna had, to remember that she won the initial verdict in the archiepiscopal court; but it is equally important to remember that she lost in the end and that, throughout, the language of the sources portrayed her with gender stereotypes. Women were precluded from the arenas of power, from the shops and offices where material wealth and prestige values were made and transacted. The undeniably important roles of women in the home and in raising children, while on one level giving the lie to the stereotypes men advanced (one need think only of the renowned Alessandra Macinghi negli Strozzi), also gave credence and substance to male-oriented values and prerogatives.[39] Brucker's Lusanna, for example, may have moved against prevailing views and asserted her prerogatives by suing her lover (especially if she took a monetary settlement to drop the matter, as Giovanni accused her of doing at one point), but she also accepted those views when she acceded to a secret wedding ceremony without notarial record or dowry. She left herself open to the charges that were hurled at her, to the conspiracy of witnesses that faced her. The entire issue of what it was she would have "won" from the conflict confronts us with the sorts of limits a woman faced. I would maintain that only by reading such complex source texts against a wide array of other texts that afford insight into normative and ideological structures and a variety of social practices can we begin to have confidence in our reading of history.

It is the reading of source texts that also provides another form of coherence, I hope, to these essays. Many of the texts used in these papers have also been used by others, whose perceptiveness surpasses mine. But these readings at times have also been launched from singular perspectives that have not, perhaps, grasped as much as they should. Samuel Cohn and Steven Epstein have both written books based on study of testaments.[40] They have described, categorized, and counted inheritance practices as found in those texts. Both, however, operate on the legally naive presumption that a will by its nature was designed to withstand challenge and did. In fact the will was the beginning and basis of challenge, in comparison to intestacy, for both the testator and the heirs and legatees. To complete the picture derived from counting the types of clauses in wills requires counting, as well, the types of challenges, settlements, and modifications. Even without contesting a will in formal adjudication, an heir could ignore or modify its terms, unless perhaps challenged by some other interested party. For that matter, nothing legal constrained the heir to become heir and accept the inheritance.[41] A testament was another legal part of the process (itself legal in good part, but also social and economic, cultural and political) that was the family for Florentines and other Italians in the Renaissance.

The essays in this book constitute only a beginning, or even less than that. Legal materials for Florentine history (let alone other Italian cities) are incredibly rich. Many dimensions of political, economic, and social history remain to be explored through these materials. Simply what there is to learn about familial life from testaments, dowry and marriage contracts, or the most nondescript bill of sale leaves an enormous area for future research. But that research will have to await the development of some basic tools, or at least be greatly hampered until that time. The fundamental statute redactions of 1355 (itself of historical importance for evidence of reaction and adjustment to the plague of 1348) and 1415 have yet to be edited critically. There is no published register of Florentine legislation, not even so much as a detailed index to the most prominent of the numerous legislative sources, like the registers of *Provvisioni*. A legal gateway to Florentine history will find few daring to enter as long as it is so poorly marked. I can only hope that these essays give some small indication of the possible benefits of exploring it.

PART ONE

Law

1

•

LAW AND ARBITRATION IN
RENAISSANCE FLORENCE

•

Long relegated to an intermediate position in the presumed progression from violent self-help to the sophisticated machinery of a state-run judicial system, arbitration seemed to hold little historical interest. It lacked formal procedures and conceptual sophistication. Its contribution to legal history, therefore, was minimal, so arbitration received only brief treatment in histories of civil procedure.[1] Political and social historians also neglected arbitration, which was seen as contributing little to the formation of effective government and social order. Arbitration, it was assumed, flourished only where and when government was too weak to provide truly effective order.[2]

Now the picture is changing, however. Historians have begun to take stock of the persistence and vitality of arbitration alongside the law. This persistence is taken as indicative not so much of shortcomings in the formal judicial system but of "a vigorous and durable tradition of extra-judicial settlement."[3] It has also become apparent that litigation and arbitration were not mutually exclusive. Many suits were initiated to culminate not in formal adjudication but in a compromise settlement. The lawsuit was not an end in itself but a form of leverage to force a settlement, at times with the encouragement of the judge.[4]

Anthropology has powerfully informed this historical revision of arbitration. Important is the anthropological concept of dispute as a normal, not pathological, stage in ongoing social relationships. The anthropological approach itself, however, is deeply influenced by the legalistic distinction between law and arbitration. With an emphasis on conflict resolution and social control, utilizing an "extended case" method, anthropologists have given largely functional accounts of arbitration, in contrast to formal adjudication. Arbitration, they claim, maintains social relationships, especially the "multiplex" relations between kin in tribal and traditional societies. Legal anthropologists have thus erected typologies of dispute-settlement mechanisms and social structures.[5] The presence of a third party in the dispute process and the extent and origin of his authority are integral to these typologies. But in tribal or "traditional" societies parties have "multiplex" relationships. Insofar as a dispute is part of a relationship, it has origins and implications far beyond any one factual or normative issue. Mediation and arbitration provide means of striking a new "balance," of continuing a relationship important to both parties and to others close to them. The imposition of rules, the achievement of some abstract ideal of justice that grounds a normative order are not desirable here, according to anthropologists. Rather the maintenance of social order demands compromise. The winner-takes-all of formal adjudication is considered to fit the situation of modern capitalistic society in which relationships are one-dimensional, utilitarian, oriented to an impersonal market—the sort of relationships that can be sacrificed in litigation.[6]

In court the judge subordinates everything to a simple issue of law; he does not inquire broadly into the relationship before him. In arbitration, on the other hand, a third party compromises disputes by removing them from a normative to a factual basis, while at the same time allowing an entire context of interests and relationships, rather than a narrow and rigidly defined issue, to come into consideration. Study of the processing of disputes replaces an ethnocentric assumption (modeled on the role of judges in Western courtrooms) of a clear relationship between "legal" rule and outcome. The result is a salutary corrective tendency to think in terms of effects of a dispute, to reduce the determining power of laws or judges. But there is no lessening of the theoretical distinction between law and arbitration (or between the law and even less-formal modes of dispute processing). For anthropologists, instead of law subsuming arbitration, the politicized processes of dispute settlement subsume the law and empty it of meaning as a theoretical construct.[7] Historians utilizing these anthropological insights have stated that the more flexible, less rule-bound procedures of arbitration could "perform functions to which the courts could not aspire: they could settle feuds, make peace and restore harmonious social relations between disputing neighbors." Arbitration "might often be more effective than the legal process in reaching a final settlement which both sides regarded as equitable."[8] The arbitrators'

> function was not that of a law court, to decide in favor of one party or another on the basis of a body of legal rules and principles. Legal thinking might influence their deliberations, but . . . arbitrators were concerned less to apply objective rules of decision than to ensure that both parties were satisfied and that no one left empty-handed.[9]

Because arbitration took into account whole relationships and their contexts, rather than just a few relevant rules, it served to reconcile the parties and re-create durable social ties. "Such compromises were therefore regarded as being if anything, firmer, more binding and more just than the court judgments that might sometimes have been rendered in the same cases."[10] According to Robert Davidsohn, the magisterial historian of Florence, even the guild courts there took cognizance of simple cases in an arbitral manner to avoid coming to conclusive, resentment-raising sentences.[11]

Arbitration and law thus end up, or remain, in both ethnographic and historical analyses, as functional opposites: one intent on restoring peace, the other on doing justice. The functional explanations of anthropology, brought wholesale into legal and social history, leave one wondering not how arbitration was able to persist but how law was able to make any headway against it, until social structure changed independently. Careful examination of the historical record—or at least the part of it presented below—will show, however, that the dichotomy between law and arbitration was not so great, especially in the late Middle Ages. To do justice could also be to restore peace, or to take an effective step in that direction. In distinguishing between justice and peace, we must be on guard against an ethnocentric assumption. It was a medieval maxim that "an agreement overcomes law and love overcomes judgment" ("pactum legem vincit et amor judicium").[12] The distinction between agreement and law, between love and judgment, animated a good deal of medieval theorization of and recourse to arbitration, to be sure. But the same set of distinctions does not necessarily apply to dispute processing in non-Western societies, and it does not imply a thorough separation of law and arbitration in Western history.[13]

Historians of European societies have also revised the anthropological dichotomies. The societies they have studied had both formal and informal means of dispute processing. So they have found that litigation and arbitration often alternated or coincided within the same "case." Lawsuits had the effect frequently, by design or not, of pushing parties to mediated or arbitrated settlements.[14] Nor was arbitration antithetical to law. Clothed in legal formulas, arbitration agreements nested ultimately in the normative repertoire and enforcement mechanisms of law courts.[15]

It may be that law contributed to arbitration. At least one anthropologist, noting that those who wish to avoid agents of the state avail themselves of arbitrators, has been moved to remark that "arbitration generally grows up in the shadow of adjudication, rather than the other way round."[16] Only "once state procedures were crystallized, private agreements could be seen as more flexible."[17] Certainly in the Middle Ages arbitration was formalized in canon law and bore the "unmistakable imprint of legal thought and practice."[18] At least one legal historian has argued that the inadequacies of academic law led to the use of arbitration and subsequent doctrinal developments that attempted to keep up with practice.[19] Oral arguments and written proof, testimony of witnesses, bonds for performance, setting of dates for awards, and other aspects of arbitration processes testify to the successful influence of law. Nor was, and is, arbitration played out without reference to norms, even highly complex ones of professional law.

> In negotiatory processes, as in those of adjudication, disputants and third parties organize their arguments around normative propositions. These may be more or less explicit and clear-cut, and are unlikely rigidly to determine an outcome; but they will inform the arguments and play some part in the outcome that is reached.[20]

The parties have to make their dispute intelligible in normative terms to others. They may mask the true nature of their dispute, or they may be incapable of giving it an accurate formulation; but they must make the effort. As Jenny Wormald has it,

> We may be too ready to contrast cases which came before the courts with private settlements, seeing in the first a formality and an authoritative quality which was lacking in the second. It is a false distinction. There was nothing casual about the private settlement. . . . The point in common between the justice of the courts and of the private settle-

ment is that both offered the chance to resolve dispute. The distinction, insofar as one can be drawn with any confidence, lay in the fact that the private settlement might be more effective.[21]

It is important to note her qualifier—it *might* be. Some disputes could not be settled, or at least not until after a protracted and complex set of processes had been tried. Functionality in any one context was not assured or predictable.

Here is where the functionalist account of arbitration and law most clearly reveals its shortcomings. The litigants'/disputants' circumstances, their interests, and pertinent norms were not clear cut at all times. They were riddled with indeterminacies, ambiguities, uncertainties. Ambiguities made for disputes, and they were not always easily resolvable. Some were just too complex.[22] We have to be attuned to the possible dysfunctions or even total failures of arbitration, in addition to its undoubted functional potential in the culture in which it operated. Finally, it has to be acknowledged that the sanctions available to enforce observance of the provisions of an arbitration included court intervention. An arbitration agreement did not necessarily mean the end of a dispute.

> The widespread imitation of the precise legalistic formulae of canon-law arbitration, suitably adapted for the requirements of the common law [but also of civil law and local statutes], implies a recognition on the part of disputants that a settlement made out of court would only endure if it proved unassailable to a subsequent challenge in court. The resources of the law were thus harnessed to provide support and protection for arbitration.[23]

Arbitration may have been more appropriate to restore a state of peace between parties, but more formal public procedures could fashion a more comprehensive conclusion to a dispute.[24] So arbitrations were written down with all the notarial solemnities of contracts, testaments, and other legal acts to establish the terms of compliance and their actionability, if needed, in a court of law.[25] This point—the contesting of an arbitrated settlement in a Florentine court—will be among the subjects of this chapter. My intent in the chapter is to investigate the relationship between arbitration and law in Florence, focusing in the end on a judicial case concerning arbitration, but examining along the way the relevant norms of academic law and of statutory law as well as a limited sampling of Florentine arbitration practices from the early fifteenth century. The value of working on

Florentine materials—beyond the economic, political, and cultural importance of the city—lies in the fact that, as a civil law jurisdiction, Florentine statutory law provides a context as yet unexamined with regard to arbitration.[26]

Arbitration in Academic Legal Doctrine

Legal historical studies of arbitration have based their interpretations almost solely on legal doctrinal sources—glosses, commentaries—of civil and canon law. The questions that historians have posed to these sources arose from within doctrinal traditions. Medieval legal doctrines (what legal historians refer to as the *ius commune*) approached the process of arbitration through two closely related terms—*arbiter* and *arbitrator*. The prevailing view has been that the two terms simply represented different procedural forms always present in the law. The *arbiter* decided according to law, following a judicially imitative procedure. The *arbitrator,* on the other hand, was an *amicabilis compositor* who operated without reference to norms or set procedures but solely on the basis of a more vague but flexible equity.[27] Recent research by Luciano Martone has revealed that, contrary to previous views these two terms did not arise simultaneously and were not simply facets of a dialectic between law and equity.[28] *Arbitrator* was not a term known to or explored by the glossators, whereas *arbiter* had been part of Roman law and was visible in the texts of the *Corpus iuris civilis. Arbitrator* came to prominence only with the postglossators, such as Guglielmo Durante (d. 1295), whose enormously influential *Speculum iudiciale* set the tone followed by jurists like Giovanni d'Andrea (d. 1348), Bartolo da Sassoferrato (d. 1357), and Baldo degli Ubaldi (1327–1400) in discussion of arbitration. To Durante the *arbitrator* differed from the *arbiter* not only on the basis of a distinction between equity and law but also from the fact that he did not have the decisional powers of the *arbiter* to consider the merits of the case but merely could arrange certain factual matters committed to him by the parties—contractual matters generally—in the interests of peace between them.[29] The *arbitrator* first arose in practice. It was the notaries who took the lead in establishing legal formulas that distinguished the *arbitrator* from the *arbiter.*

The powers of both *arbitri* and *arbitratores* were voluntary. They were chosen by the parties, who placed themselves under their determination at the time of "election" in a contract of *compromissum.* In

all cases the person to whom the parties had committed their differences was bound to decide on his own; he could not delegate the task
to another.[30] There were no firm procedural guidelines, though the
expectation was that the *arbiter* would imitate formal judicial proceedings, while the *arbitrator* would operate more informally—"an
arbitrator is one who decides a controversy by his own judgment, in
good faith and by good intuition, observing no formality of law and
without the noise of a trial," in the formulation of Bartolo.[31] Enforcement of the settlement lay with the parties. In the contract of
compromissum, in which they agreed to submit to binding arbitration
and named the arbitrators, the parties also established a monetary
penalty on each other for noncompliance. Provision of a penalty was
an important validating device. If no penalty had been set, the arbitration was valid only if the parties agreed to it in writing or kept
silence for ten days. In essence, enforcement mechanisms and problems were similar to those for most other forms of contract.

Aside from enforcement was the problem of the validity of the
arbiter's or arbitrator's determination and the admissibility of means
to modify or annul it. There was in theory no recourse from an
inequitable decision of an arbiter. The parties had, by choosing him,
an obligation to accede to his decision, which was limited to the
matter placed before him by them.[32] Only an *exceptio doli* on the
grounds of the arbiter's malfeasance was allowed against a sentence.[33]
An arbiter was thus an agent in a generally private and voluntary
context; he had no jurisdiction and so his *sententia* had no binding
force.[34] It could not stand as a precedent for others or affect the legal
rights or abilities of those not party to it.[35] It could not even bind the
parties themselves, except insofar as they had bound themselves by
the monetary penalty for noncompliance. Thus there could be no
appeal, in the strict sense, although some jurists were willing to con-
template appeals of arbitration on the grounds of violation of law, if
not of equity (*contra ius*).[36]

In contrast to the inappellability of the *arbitrium* of an arbiter, the
findings of an arbitrator could undergo a sort of appeal. The informality of the arbitrator tended to push the arbiter, in the minds of
jurists, into the same camp with the *iudex*—as operating within *stric-
tum ius* and with a formalized and largely written procedure utilizing
a *libellus* of charges or claims, the hearing of witnesses, granting
delays, and resolving all normative and factual elements. The arbitrator, however, sought a more indefinite *aequitas* with no set proce-

dure, and, though his competence was supposedly limited to narrow factual questions, any resulting inequity had to be remedied. So here a disgruntled party could appeal to another's judgment—*arbitrium boni viri*.[37] The arbitrator issued not a *sententia,* not an *arbitrium,* but a *laudum* or *arbitramentum*—a form of transaction.[38] The parties had sought an equitable basis to their relationship, so they were entitled to reascertain that basis by appeal to a "good man."[39] In the manner of a sindication by citizens of a communal officeholder following his term of office, the *bonus vir* could not modify the act of the arbitrator, he could only annul it after examining the relation between contents of the *compromissum* and the *laudum*.[40] The parties' expressed desire for equitable concord, rather than their previous state of conflict, became the basis for arbitration in the eyes of jurists, so "the *reductio* constituted a final guarantee of the intentions embodied in the recourse to arbitration."[41]

While scholastic legal doctrines kept the distinction between arbiter and arbitrator, notarial and statutory practice elided them.[42] Notaries, who also often served as arbitrators, ran the terms together in their redactions of arbitrated settlements.[43] As Linda Fowler has argued, this may have allowed for maximum flexibility: the parties left procedure to the mediating third party, and only after the fact, if one of them chose to challenge the outcome, was it necessary to distinguish and define, on the basis of the procedures followed, whether the third party had acted as an arbiter or as an arbitrator.[44] Or it may also be, as Martone has it, that the procedural and equitative flexibility of the arbitrator was enlarged over the areas of wider than factual competence belonging to the arbiter.[45]

Arbitration in Florentine Statutory Law

In hopes of peaceful settlement of differences among citizens, many Italian cities inserted arbitration into the range of statutorily available legal procedures.[46] While indiscriminately using terms like *sententia* and *laudum,* cities' statutes were nonetheless giving arbitrated settlements legal sanction. Arbitration was generally made available to all and anyone with full legal capacity (therefore, not minors, women, or slaves) could serve as arbiter or arbitrator.[47] Generally, statutory concerns were two. One was to extend the use of arbitration to disputes between kin so as to defuse potentially explosive situations before they came to litigation. This was the so-called arbitration *ex necessi-*

tate statuti.[48] Such statutes typically required that disputes between kin go to arbitration rather than adjudication. It was not, however, as Martone explains, jurisdictionally imposed; one of the parties had to request arbitration by invoking kinship, and both the parties still controlled the choice of arbitrator(s).[49] That disputes would arise between relatives would not be surprising, because property rights and obligations, as well as honor, were implicated in such relationships. The statutes did not visualize atomistic individuals but molecular groups held together by blood and law. The ideology of kinship solidarity made it imperative that disputes between close kin not get out of hand—not become violent and public (some, of course, did).[50] The government, through its laws, was supposed to promote the continued existence and well-being of families, which were seen as its structural basis and, in governmental paternalism, as its functional model.[51] The second legislative concern was to preclude appeals of arbitrations in the interest of public order—to bring an end to disputes.[52] However, if there were discontents with arbitration decisions, they were unlikely to be mollified by a law forbidding appeals. The effectiveness of arbitration was not alone a matter of legislation. In arbitration the parties, the arbitrators, and the issues had full play.

The statutes of Florence were fairly typical in their treatment of arbitration, typical even in their confusion. The core of Florentine legislation concerning arbitration, and the point where it most directly touched the judicial apparatus, lay in a statute entitled "That kin and relations having a problem or conflict must compromise it" ("Quod consanguinei et consortes habentes questionem vel controversiam teneantur ipsam commictere") in the 1355 statutes of the Podestà.[53] A smorgasbord of relatives in male and female lines, including bastards, within about four degrees of relationship (cousins, grandparents) but even "usque in infinitum," were judicially enjoined "at the request of the other party" to elect "arbitros et arbitratores." They had eight days, no right to cite exceptions or seek the *consilium* of a *sapiens,* and faced a fine of 300 *lire* for failure to make the elections. Each party chose one (or more if they had so agreed) and gave guarantees that he/they would abide by the subsequent ruling.[54] The *arbitri* or *arbitratores* (presumed usually to be other *consanguinei*) had two months to reach a decision or face a 100 *lire* fine levied on them by the Podestà; and even then they still had to pronounce a judgment. The Podestà could, after two months, give the arbitrators another month to name a third, thus breaking the tie and establishing majority rule. The third could thus be seen as an arbitrator between two discordant arbitrators.[55] The judge was to safeguard against inequality or deception in the selection process, and, if the parties could not agree in formulating the charge to the arbitrators to be embodied in a written *compromissum*, he was to appoint a "iurisperitus" to do so, whose formulation could not be opposed or appealed.

Judges were enjoined to enforce all such *compromissa, lauda,* and *sententiae,* even to the point of jailing someone at the bidding of the other party. Nonperformance of stipulated payments was to meet with a fine of two *soldi* per *lira* (10 percent). Women could not be forced to arbitration concerning their dowries. And no one could be compelled to compromise the same matter twice. But neither could a mere promise not to go to arbitration keep one from enjoying the benefit of this statute (according to an addition first enacted in 1324). Such a promise was invalid.

The legislative situation prevailing from 1355 reveals several interesting things. The lack of definition of terms shows an assumed reliance on prevailing norms of the "common law" of the schools. Arbitration was also set into the statutes only in the context of disputes among kin, seeking to ease such disputes out of court and to confine them (in their formulation, if not in their total enforcement) to kin. Notions of equity surface in the statute, not notions of strict literalistic legality. The resulting *laudum* was thus distinguished from the decision that would have been rendered had the case remained in court.[56] Peace, or at least reestablishing a working relationship among the parties, seemed to underwrite this law. Above all, as Martone has pointed out, this and other statutes like it did not change the essentially private nature of arbitration. Statutes could demand a move from litigation to arbitration only when one of the parties made kinship to the other an issue. Naming the arbitrators always lay with the parties themselves, as did setting the issue(s) for them. The statutes set fines and time limits to hurry along the process, allowed maximum flexibility and speed by conjoining the powers of arbiter and arbitrator, and inserted it all into the judicial order by guaranteeing enforcement.[57] In seeking a speedy conclusion to conflicts the statute also foreclosed appeals of arbitrators' *lauda,* except in the form of the *reductio.* To allow new evidence and issues to be introduced in a full-blown appeal would not further the cause of equity.[58]

The fact that arbitration was more generally part of the legal system, a permanent part of notarial practice, and an increasingly useful institution hardly seems evident from the 1355 statutes. In 1415 the institution was legislatively decked out in a very different and more comprehensive manner. The jurists Paolo di Castro (c. 1360–1441) and Bartolomeo Vulpi da Soncino (c. 1359–1435) reworked the existing statute and legislative provisions from the intervening years in light of judicial practice. The rubric "De compromissis fiendis inter consortes" substantially resembled the 1355 statute, but it also contained important revisions as well as a careful tightening up of its language.[59] Gone was the lengthy spelling out of the process by which a third arbitrator would be selected. In its place was simply a brief reference to the fact that one would be chosen "a principio simul." Also omitted was reference to the fine for nonpayment. Added to the statute were clauses specifying that the move out of litigation into arbitration had to come before the probative stages of the judicial procedure (once into the evidence, one could not be forced to arbitration), that no one could be forced to arbitrate what had been judged by any civic or guild official, that no one could deny kinship to avoid a compromise.[60] Also there was a provision that no one could move against a decision by renunciation of the agreement to compromise unless he did so by a public instrument. This was followed by the general observation: "And by the form of the present statute a compromise may be sought and must be sought once and many times and as often as will be opportune, until the questions and controversies thus compromised will be decided and terminated, save always the already disposed."

This preservation of existing judgments and the setting of limits as to when a case could be removed into arbitration from litigation were designed to preclude undue delays and shady tactics. Di Castro and Vulpi may have been familiar with a case handled by the noted Bolognese lawyers Pietro d'Ancarano (c. 1330–1416) and Floriano da San Pietro (fl. 1400), a copy of which is preserved in a Florentine manuscript. In that case a father and his son had repudiated the grandfather's estate in favor of the brother/uncle, but with a condition attached to the repudiation that they could later return and seek their legitim (one-quarter of the portion owed to a son on intestacy) from the estate. The jurists denied any validity to this condition.[61] Not satisfied with this result, the father then emancipated the son and entered into a *compromissum*, the resulting *laudum* handing to the son all right of the father in the estate in question. Alleging this *laudum* as his right, the son then gained judicial tenure (*tenuta*) to the property, but the uncle responded with sufficient proof to have the property returned. Then the son tried to have his uncle forced to compromise, by terms of a statute very similar to that of Florence. The uncle responded that the issue had to be resolved by a judge, that it was not compromisable in law. Floriano da San Pietro and Pietro d'Ancarano agreed with him. The issue of fact had been resolved. The issue now was one of law, and that was not something for compromise.[62] To reopen the case was both illegal and, in view of the intent of the statute for rapid and peaceful settlements, inequitable.[63]

The following five rubrics of the 1415 statutes also concerned arbitration, and only one of them had any overt grounding in the texts of 1355. Rubric 67 forbade the Priors and Gonfaloniere di Giustizia to force anyone to compromise with them during their terms of office. Rubric 69 established that those not subject to Florentine jurisdiction could not hope to see their *lauda* judicially enforced unless they first paid their *gabelle*.[64] Rubric 71 allowed exceptions and appeals from any *laudum* rendered by a magnate to the court of the Podestà.

The other two rubrics took great strides in generalizing the *compromissum* and *laudum* as legal situations. Rubric 68, "De notificatione laudorum," set procedures by which the terms of a settlement were to be published. No *laudum* was valid unless formally published to both parties in their presence, or at least unless they had been hailed to hear the decision at a designated time and place. Ratification in the presence of the other party within thirty days was considered to constitute notification, as was notification by a herald of the Podestà or Capitano with the leaving of a note detailing the names of the parties, arbitrators, notary, and herald.[65] With formal notification any time periods set in the *laudum* for payments or such began to run. Rubric 70, "De generali executione laudorum," reaffirmed that any validly contrived and notified *laudum* received full legal protection "as if it were a guaranteed instrument," with no appeals, exceptions, or contradictions allowed (except for *restitutio in integrum* to a minor). Proof that obligations arising from a *laudum* had been settled was to be taken only in the form of public written instruments. The changes made evident in 1415 show that legal doctrines regarding arbitration, spurred it seems, by problems arising in practice, were still in the process of formation in the fifteenth century.

Arbitration in Renaissance Florence

For whatever reason—the greater procedural informality, the ultimate judicial sanctions—legal forms of arbitration seem to have
flourished in Florence. Neighbors or partners might find it useful to
resolve differences, for example. It was also extraordinarily useful in
dealing with disputes among kin, notably in fraternal divisions of
inheritance, in which case other kin, often affinal, were likely to be
called upon as arbitrators.[66]

Florentines undertook arbitration with a number of motives and
expectations. Lapo di Giovanni Niccolini undertook an arbitration as
guardian for his young nephew "for the well-being and peace and
repose of the parties . . . so it would not be necessary to litigate."[67]
His comments reveal a distinguishing between arbitration and litigation that in terms of peace between the parties gave preference to the
former. But how widely were his views shared?

The initiative in arbitration, as in vendetta, which retained a carefully circumscribed legality, lay with the parties themselves.[68] The
arbitrators in some cases had little to do but make a decision, and
sometimes not even that. Occasionally private *ricordi* afford us a
glimpse of such collusion. Lapo Niccolini, for instance, wrote in his
of a *compromissum* lasting ten years, where the parties in fact had an
agreement from the start on the payments eventually to be stipulated
by the arbitrators.[69] He also noted a *compromissum* with his son
Niccolaio, made for purposes of property division prior to arranging
his marriage. "Thereafter [the arbitrators] did not issue any sentence,
as the compromise expired [its term was two months], because we
had not yet come to the completion of our intention."[70]

The language employed in these documents tried to cover all contingencies. Arbitrators were almost always described as *arbiter* and
arbitrator. The documents also tended simply to give the basic terms
worked out by the arbitrator(s) with little justification or expansion
into the relationship between the parties. The settlements themselves
might be simply framed or they might contain a number of conditions and options giving either greater precision or greater flexibility
to the relationship between the parties.

It is impossible to tell from a *laudum* how real and intense was any
conflict between the parties. *Lauda* were at times clearly treated as
just another contract, noted in records with the same diffidence as
any other legal transaction.[71] Where there was actual conflict, a

laudum might only provoke further resentment. That was what happened in 1391 when Salamone di Carlo Strozzi's father-in-law, Filippo Corsini, served as arbitrator for his cousins. The dispute between Matteo di Niccolò Corsini and Neri di Giovanni Corsini concerned their business ventures. Matteo complained that Neri had siphoned some 6,500 florins out of the business between 1385 and 1389, mainly by taking on accounts without informing him. Besieged by creditors, Matteo went to the Podestà and received a judgment for 5,613 florins. Messer Filippo and other kinsmen pressured him to reach a compromise with Neri. Filippo as arbitrator then gave Matteo ownership of Neri's *poderi* in Nerzano and Valifico, with, however, a lifetime usufruct remaining with Neri. Matteo complained bitterly about this: "This false *laudum*, falsely given by the arbiters, and especially by messer Filippo, who wanted it thus, and the others, that is Jacopo and Stefano Corsini, did not dare to contradict his malevolence and pronounced sentence in that manner along with him."[72]

Such coercion may or may not have been frequent; only much more systematic research can reveal that. But clearly it did happen. Nor was coercion the only reason there might be discontent. Even a fully agreed-to arbitration might later be deemed inadequate or insufferable. Bartolomeo di Tommaso Sassetti by arbitration gained a farm from his brother Federigo in 1436. "The said *laudum* was given as a precaution," he claimed, "because Federigo had many debts with the commune regarding his *gravezze* and because I might protect him and thus I did while I could and I assigned him an account on his things as appears in our old books." Years later, however, and despite reconfirmation in another *laudum* given in 1446, Federigo attempted to claim the farm, alleging that Bartolomeo had promised it to him.[73] Fraud came into play in some arbitrations. One finds mention of a fictitious *compromissum* and *laudum* between Giovanni di Matteo Corsini and his sister in order to disguise ownership of a farm and protect it from creditors.[74] Likewise Lapo Niccolini used arbitration with his sister to retrieve through her credits he had relinquished but on which he felt cheated. She promised verbally to deliver to him any money realized from pursuit of these claims, which promise she fulfilled.[75] He also several years later used arbitration to sell part of a *podere* to his brother Filippo in order to avoid the *gabelle*.[76]

At least once in the fifteenth century the governing councils of Florence saw the need to pass a law dealing with fraudulent use of arbitration settlements. And jurists would be called on to deal with such cases. In one such case Antonio di Vanni Strozzi (1455–1523) defended a *laudum* between brothers from accusations of fraud that were based in part on the argument that the *laudum*'s following immediately on the *compromissum* implied collusion. Strozzi, however, defended the work of an arbitrator from such a presumption; evidence would have to be produced and, in this case, documentary evidence seemed to substantiate that there was a debt claim to be settled.[77] Such varied uses of arbitration threw up conceptual and practical problems for jurists.

Arbitration in Practice

By expanding the range of sources he considers, to include statutes of different Italian city-states and notarial formularies (but not actual arbitrations), Martone claims a basis to speak to practices as well as law. The social forces leading to this legal development were anchored in political and economic developments. The redefinition of politically privileged groups in the late thirteenth century left some "*clans* familiari" on the margins of power and intent on preserving their position and patrimony. Arbitration was to their advantage. Even in the guise of arbitration *ex necessitate statuti* (laws mandating that disputes between kin be taken to arbitration rather than adjudication), the families were able to protect themselves against the encroachment of the state. The move to arbitration was the result of a recognition of kinship, which was entirely within their control, made in order to safeguard their privileges.[78] It also facilitated transactions with a speed suited to economic needs of "the small and great landed proprietors, the artisans, the merchants," groups for whom commerce seemed to dissolve the link between property and the *patria potestas* that controlled it. These folk could set very limited issues of fact for their arbitrators to resolve quickly. "In the *arbitrator*'s activity were thus exalted the commercial strengths of the merchant class. Economic value and no longer the law alone imposed new schemes of legal solution endowed with greater elasticity and suited to the requirements of this new activity."[79] And use of arbitration increased greatly after 1350, both because legal doctrines then developed to allow appeals of arbitrations and because there was a growing distrust of the quality of justice flowing from the courts of the aristocratic communal governments.[80]

Martone's assertions, however, stand uncorroborated without further investigation into actual arbitration practices. Such historical studies utilizing actual arbitration records are, in fact, few and very recent. None of them have been even mildly statistical; they have been based on narrative descriptions of one case or a handful of cases. And there is no study I know of that considers arbitration practices in an Italian context. Yet records of arbitrations, at least for the late Middle Ages, are abundant, especially in Italian archives. It will not be possible to determine how much the anthropological perspective must be modified—and how complex the historical reality was—until more of the historical record has been exposed to examination. Who used arbitration? Who acted as arbitrators? What issues were put to them? How were these issues handled? How lasting and satisfactory were arbitration settlements? Were arbitrations open-ended, as the anthropologists have it, or narrow and factual, as Martone insists? Was arbitration especially geared to mercantile interests? Was it especially effective for kin-based problems? These and other questions have to be taken to a number of examples—that is, to the sorts of materials legal historians neglect and to more of them than other historians have looked at. This is what I propose to do, albeit still on a modest scale and in a tentative manner.

My source is a single notarial cartulary covering the years 1422 to 1429 (1430 modern style—the Florentine year beginning on March 25). It is one of several surviving cartularies of the Florentine notary ser Francesco di Piero Giacomini.[81] In it, in different forms, are the records of 123 arbitration agreements or settlements. No other materials have been brought to bear. Only the legal, public, formal notarized documents are under scrutiny. Thus my sense of whether parties or arbitrators were related is carried entirely by evidence internal to the cartulary (e.g., surnames or stated relationships, as marriage), as is my sense of the monetary and other interests being transacted. Obviously much more could be learned by searching across different sources to flesh out each case. Just as obviously many more cases could be considered over a much broader span of time, thus allowing for the tracking of changes in the use of arbitration by, in this instance, Florentines. Still, as I hope to show, important conclusions of at least a tentative nature can be drawn.

The relevant documents in the cartulary are of two types—the *compromissum* and the *laudum*. The import of the *compromissum* was to set out the competence of the arbitrator(s)—that is, the specific issue(s) committed to arbitral resolution. By law the arbitrators' competence extended only to what had been committed to them by the parties. In actual fact, however, most *compromissa* did not designate a specific issue but remained content with the vague legal formulas commissioning arbitrators to look into "all and every" matter bringing the parties into conflict.[82] The *laudum* was the arbitral decision formally laid out by a notary, often the same one who had recorded the *compromissum*. Our notary, Giacomini, served also as notary for the *laudum* on about half (57 percent) of the *compromissa* he enrolled.[83] But he further notarized a number of *lauda* whose enabling *compromissa* were the work of other notaries. The *laudum* was set out in first-person plural (the *compromissum* was in narrative third person) as the statement of the arbitrator(s). It began by recapitulating the *compromissum*, then moved to the formulaic assurance that both parties had been heard, evidence had been gathered, time had been spent carefully weighing issues:

> And having seen the petitions, responses, rights and allegations of the said parties and whatever said parties wanted to say and allege before us, and having had in and about all and every of these herein written matters information and solemn deliberation for the good of the peace and concord of the aforesaid parties, and in every manner, way, right, and form by which we can, to greater and better effect, sitting as a tribunal for security in the herein said place, electing the way of the arbitrator we decide. . . .[84]

These formulas certainly portray a thoughtful, independent, judge-like arbitrator, although the reality might be very different from the formulaic assertion. Nothing in these formulas declared that the arbitrator was following a full judicial procedure, demanding that claims be couched in the terms and texts of the learned or statutory law. They claimed only a certain fairness, impartiality, and factualness.

Next, the subsequent decision was given some rationale. It might simply be said that there were reasons, unspecified. Or reasons might be briefly laid out—for example, one party was in debt to the other for a certain amount, with no indication of when or how the debt arose. However, reasons were sometimes spelled out in great detail (interesting examples will be considered below). Then followed the decision itself, in its necessary detail and with all the formulaic clauses required—as, for example, to affect a full formal transfer of owner-ship. Finally the information as to time, place, and who was present completed the document. If the parties, or one of them, were not present at the formal reading of the *laudum*, they were required to indicate later, in notarized form, their recognition and acceptance (*ratificatio*) of the *laudum*.[85]

The arbitrators themselves could be anyone. Martone's view, echo-ing that of most historians, is that arbitrators simply came from the same social groups as the parties whose interests were being trans-acted. They were not a class of specialists (unlike judges or even notaries). The usual legal incapacities applied—minors, slaves, women, the insane could not act as arbitrators. Otherwise the arbi-trator need only be a *vir bonus*, which according to Martone meant in effect "anyone who by whatever title possessed that certain eco-nomic capacity needed to resolve issues of voluntary jurisdiction."[86] Whether and how much such men may have been paid is uncertain. I know of no statement by a Florentine of having received direct compensation for arbitrating. But general goodwill, indirect compen-sation, a later reciprocal favor—none of these can be ruled out.

Whether the arbitrators were limited by the information supplied to them by the parties or could inquire independently into matters seems to have depended on what the parties expected in the way of procedure. There were cases where arbitration was in fact a formality. The parties arranged everything but put it in the form of an arbitra-tion for the record, to establish a debt or title over against any other claims.[87] They could thus arrange things to fit their purposes, even fraudulent ones. But there were also cases where the arbitrators worked hard to bring about an agreement and had to sift through numerous facts and considerations. As we will see below, it is difficult to generalize about the power and influence of arbitrators over deci-sions that, in terms of notarial syntax, were put in their mouths.

AN OVERVIEW

From our notary we know the identities of 123 pairs of disputing parties and their arbitrators.[88] *Lauda* for 83 of these pairs allow a further probing of what issues were at stake. Table 1.1 presents a categorization of these arbitration situations in terms of the kin rela-tionships between the parties (as recoverable from the arbitration records themselves). Arbitrations between unrelated parties have been further subdivided into urban or rural and by gender. Clearly some of the "unrelateds" could have a kin relationship not mentioned in their texts, so there is a likelihood that the table understates the proportion of arbitrations involving kin.

Interestingly, the data break down almost evenly between arbitrations involving kin and those not involving kin (61 to 62). Of kin relationships in arbitrations, brothers were far and away dominant, and when one factors in the seven brother-sister arbitrations, one is looking at almost half the kin-based arbitrations centering on sibling relationships. As for arbitration between nonkin, it is important to note that Giacomini's clients were almost all individuals. They were neighbors, business partners, or just people seeking or supplying certain goods or services. On rare occasions he faced a group of men who represented an institution, such as the seven residents of Castro Franco who represented their *comune* in arbitration against the powerful Florentines Luca and Rinaldo degli Albizzi.[89]

The chronological content of the table raises only a few interesting points, and no conclusions can be firm on the basis of such a small amount of data. The prominence of rural arbitrations in 1422 is hard to explain. Giacomini may simply, as it seems, have spent some time

Table 1.1 Relationships of Arbitrating Parties

Type	1422	1423	1424	1425	1426	1427	1428	1429	Totals
1	2	3		2	1	4	5	5	22
2				1					1
3	2	1			2		1	2	8
4	1	1		1	1	1		2	7
5	1	1			2	3	1	1	9
6		1	1		2		3		7
7		1			3	2	1		7
								Subtotal	61
10	5	1	2	3	4	9	4	4	32
11	8	2			1	1	2	3	17
12	1	2		1		1	2	1	8
13	1			2	1		1		5
Total	21	13	3	10	17	21	20	18	123

1 Brothers
2 Spouses
3 Father/Child
4 Uncle/Nephew
5 Cousins (agnatic)
6 Sister/Brother
7 Mother/Child

10 Unrelated, city
11 Unrelated, contado
12 Unrelated, city (one female)
13 Unrelated, contado (one female)

outside Florence that year and the data reflect that, just as the absence of either his records or of any professional activity is reflected for 1424. On the other hand, in most of those arbitrations one party was in fact an urban dweller, and in two of the eight cases wealthy Florentines stood as one party against numerous men of a single rural community. The year 1422 may have presented a good opportunity for Florentines to recover debts and adjust their relations with rural clients.[90] But the same could be said for all arbitrations categorized herein as "rural."[91]

This table gives some indication of the impact of Florentine fiscal reform in 1427. In that year one finds the highest number of arbitrations between unrelated Florentines, and most sibling-based arbitrations (17 of 29) occur in or after that year, which also inaugurates a slight increase in arbitral activity in general (59 of 123 come in those three years, though clearly 1424–25 is underrepresented in Giacomini's records). However, it is not possible, when looking at the *lauda* themselves, to say that arbitrations between unrelated folk were in any direct way stimulated by the near or past occurrence of the passage of the *catasto* law, though at least one between brothers (mentioned below) was.[92]

Table 1.2 Relationships of Arbitrators to Arbitrating Parties

Type	1422	1423	1424	1425	1426	1427	1428	1429	Totals
1	1	2			1	1	3	2	10
2	7	4		4	7	6	7	3	38
3	11	5	2	2	5	6	6	6	43
4		1				3			4
								Subtotal	95
10				2		2	3	4	11
11					3				3
12	1	1	1	2	1	3	1	3	13
Total	20*	13	3	10	17	21	20	18	122

1 One arbitrator, legal professional
2 One arbitrator, unrelated to either party
3 Multiple arbitrators, unrelated to either party
4 Multiple arbitrators, one a legal professional
10 One arbitrator, related to one or both parties
11 Multiple arbitrators, related to one or both parties
12 Multiple arbitrators, some related to one party

*Total of 21 in table 1.1 includes one renunciation of arbitration that does not name the arbitrators.

Table 1.2 categorizes the arbitrations by the number of arbitrators and their relationships, if any, to the parties (again, as recoverable solely on the basis of internal evidence). There was no significant bias toward using one or several arbitrators (59 using one, 63 more than one). Here the significant finding is that most arbitrators were not related to either of the parties (95 of 122). The ideal arbitrators would be neutral enough to be acceptable to both parties. Most of the time, it appears, that ideal was met by looking outside the kindred of either party. Even when both parties were related, the overwhelming bias was toward unrelated arbitrators (see table 1.3). (Though again, one must be aware that relationships, especially through marriage, are not necessarily recoverable from the sorts of information in the texts.) Unsurprisingly, most of the situations in which the arbitrators were related to one of the parties were situations in which the parties themselves were kin (18 of 27). Yet even then, in almost half the cases, the related arbitrator or arbitrators were also joined by one or more who were not (or whose relationship cannot be reconstructed from the notarial text). So Martone's anticipations as to who served as arbitrators cannot be uncritically accepted. Kin in arbitration on occasion sought nonkin arbitrators, and it cannot be established on Giacomini's evidence that commercial colleagues were often chosen as arbitrators. One suspects that there were ties between parties and their arbitrators, but they need not have been close or predictable in a simple fashion.

Also of some significance is the number of times (over 10 percent) that the arbitrator or one of several arbitrators was a lawyer or notary. Seemingly, in this sort of person both neutrality and legal expertise were manifest. Messer Stefano Buonaccorsi (1353–1433) was espe-

Table 1.3 Arbitrators, Where Parties Were Related

| | Arbitrators | |
Type	Unrelated	Related
1	15	7
2	1	
3	6	2
4	4	3
5	8	1
6	5	2
7	4	3
Total	43	18

cially active in Giacomini's pages. He arbitrated between Michele di Bartolomeo Buonaiuti and his uncle Jacopo in 1423, between two brothers from Monte Albino and Giovanni di Francesco di ser Giovanni of Florence that same year, along with two other arbitrators between Modesto di Chele and Bernardo and Giovanni d'Andrea di Maso in 1427, and between Simone di Salvi di Filippo Bencivenni and his brother Stefano and their brother's three sons in 1429. Also appearing more than once were the jurist Nello da San Gimignano (b. 1373) and the notary ser Michele di Giovanni di Jacopo Banchi.[93] These professionals were asked to deal with a variety of problems. Ser Michele Banchi resolved some business and property matters between members of the Peruzzi lineage. Similarly Buonaccorsi resolved a small business debt between the Buonaiuti by giving one a small house "that needed not a little repair" belonging to the other. For the Bencivenni he divided an estate between the brothers Stefano and Simone and their nephews—an estate the first two did not have to share with their brother's sons according to Florence's statutes.

On the presupposition that significant findings would emerge, I also constructed table 1.4 dealing with arbitrations in which one of the parties, or both, was female. It is indeed interesting to note that in 31 arbitrations only six had one or more arbitrators related to the woman, whereas the arbitrators were unrelated to either party in 23 arbitrations. Also, in some contrast to the overall numbers, women's arbitrations were more likely to involve kin as the other party—18 of

Table 1.4 Arbitrators, Where One Party Was Female

Type of Arbitrator	Other Party Child	Spouse	Sibling	Cousin	Father	Unrelated	Totals
1			2				2
2							
3	4		2	1	1	4	12
4	2		1		1		4
5						3	3
6	1	1	2			6	10
Total	7	1	7	1	2	13	31

1 One arbitrator, related to her
2 One arbitrator, related to other
3 One arbitrator, related to neither
4 Multiple arbitrators, one related to her
5 Multiple arbitrators, one related to other
6 Multiple arbitrators, related to neither

31 (58 percent) versus 61 of 123 (49 percent). On the other hand, this is not surprising in view of the relative seclusion of Florentine women and their exclusion from commercial and legal arenas, except through male intervention.[94] But it is also a further reminder of the potential importance of their legal property rights to their male kin and also to their female kin. As for these kin, they were the women's children and siblings, by and large. But nonkin, too, clearly could also find their interests implicated in the property rights of women or transmitted through them.

Table 1.5 attempts in a schematic fashion to categorize the contents of the 83 *lauda* in Giacomini's book. This categorization is necessarily loose and can be subjected to various searching criticisms. Inheritance and dowry, for example, were not neatly separable. "Debts" is especially vague, and could include such issues as dowry and inheritance where they were not otherwise spelled out. It is at least interesting how debt operated between kin as well as between unrelated persons. In fact, only division of inheritance shows a high correlation between content of the dispute and the relationship between parties. Either from marital or other relations not retrievable from these sources or from business investments, kin-based matters like dowry and inheritance also came to involve not obviously related persons in arbitrations against each other. Strozza di ser Piero di Benedetto da Linari, for example, had to resort to arbitration to get messer Pietro Gaetani to pay up and relinquish the property that was his through inheritance from his wife.[95] It was not explained how Gaetani came into possession. In another instance Giuliano di Matteo Pezzati brought suit before the Podestà against Giovanni di Guccio Nucci. Back in 1393 Giovanni's father had been involved in giving surety for the dowry of 970 florins of monna Dianora, wife of Matteo di Miniato Nucci. In 1422 the son and heir of that marriage, Miniato, had ceded most of that dowry to Giuliano (actually in two installments of 435 and 250 florins). Giuliano wanted to capitalize the dowry against the obligation of suretyship, which had fallen to Giovanni as his father's heir. Arbitration was quickly arranged before the suit was heard. Giovanni argued that he was not his father's heir and so did not have to restore that portion of the dowry touching Guccio's obligation. Giuliano, on the other hand, claimed that Giovanni's inventory of his father's property, the day following his death, indicated a desire to be his heir and a sense of ownership. Giovanni replied that the inventory was drawn up at the behest of his uncle Antonio and for the benefit of his younger brother Guarneri. For his part Giovanni had never wanted the estate and had formally repudiated it. The arbitrators, in fact, went through the uncle's accounts and determined he had "cunningly and maliciously seduced" the minor (at that time) Giovanni into making the inventory. They, therefore, released him from any obligation for the dowry, leaving Giuliano to seek redress from the heirs of the other guarantors.[96]

PROCEDURAL COMPLEXITIES

Before considering the types of issues Florentines and other Tuscans brought to arbitration before ser Francesco di Piero Giacomini, we should look at some of the complications revealed by these arbitrations.

One emergent fact is that some individuals, households, and lineages were more frequent users of arbitration and, therefore, perhaps more likely to resort to it than to litigation. They would also have been more familiar with arbitration's myriad capabilities and more able to exploit them. Take the Bardi. The Bardi were a large clan, one of the oldest and most prominent in Florence. Of Giacomini's 123 arbitrations one or more Bardi were participants in 15. That they had numerous interests transactable in arbitration is in itself hardly surprising.[97] The Bardi, however, had a decided penchant for choosing arbitrators from among themselves. In only four of the fifteen arbitrations were the arbitrators unrelated, one of those involving a woman married to a Bardi in arbitration with a monastery.[98] Another involved a wife of a Bardi against her son. In only two instances, then, one between brothers, did Bardi males choose unrelated arbitrators.[99] There were two further instances in which a female member of the lineage, who had been married into the Brancacci, went to arbitration in close succession with her daughter and her brothers, and in both cases the arbitrators were Brancacci.[100] For the rest, six of the Bardi arbitrations involved brothers. In three of them, in 1429, the four sons of the deceased Benedetto di Lipaccio worked out their inheritance and finances with the aid of Bernardo di Ciandrello Bardi as arbitrator. In a first arbitration with their uncles Andrea and Larione, the four were awarded one-third in common of their grandmother's estate. In the second arbitration between the two eldest, it was determined that management of the bank and all profits and losses fell to Lipaccio. Finally, in arbitration between Lipaccio

and the two youngest, Bernardo di Ciandrello awarded their money
as deposit or business capital to Lipaccio, who had to pay 8 percent
annually.[101]

Even within the confines of Giacomini's pages one sees the same
parties drawn into arbitration more than once. Andrea di Domenico
had to renew his *compromissum* with Michele di Simone of San Andrea a Botonaccio. After this renewal the three unrelated arbitrators
decreed that Andrea owed Michele 25 florins and had two months to
pay. Following that time, however, the arbitrators produced a second
laudum in view of the fact "that we arbiters and arbitrators could not
examine all the rights of the said parties as we should, due to lack of
time" ("quod nos arbitri et arbitratores non potuimus propter
brevitatem temporis omnia jura dictarum partium ut decet ex-
aminare") and ordered the parties to enact a new *compromissum*
within five days with Donato d'Aldobrando as one of three arbitrators. Failure to do so would leave the previous *laudum* in force.[102] It
took three *lauda* by Averardo da Castiglionchio and Bartolomeo
Gualterotti to settle matters (so far as can be gleaned from one cartulary) between monna Piera di Bartolo della Valle, widow of Maso
di Bartolo remarried to Giovanni di Stefano, on the one hand, and
Domenico di Pietro, priest at San Giorgio di Ruballa, on the other.
Piera's husband had a testamentary substitution to the church if, as
occurred, his young son died. She wanted from the priest her 80
florin dowry and the "legitima et trebellianica" due her dead son. The
arbitrators concurred and set her credit on the estate at 230 florins.
This was 24 August 1425. The priest was given until 15 September
to pay 100 florins and a year for the rest. He was to use the money to
purchase shares in the Florentine *monte comune* in her name. The
interest would be paid to her husband, and he would own the shares
if he outlived her, while she would come into full ownership by
outliving him. This first *laudum* stumbled on ser Domenico's inability to pay, which occasioned a second *laudum* of 6 January 1425
(1426). The arbitrators reaffirmed his obligation to buy the shares
but added a long list of *res mobiles* from the estate that were to remain
with Piera. Immediately following this *laudum* the two arbitrators
renounced the *compromissum* made in them, but they nevertheless
found it necessary in September 1426 to reopen the issue. They
found Piera had more *masserizie* than they had been led to believe,
so, as "it is not fitting that the church be defrauded by the aforesaid

facts" ("nec est conveniens quod predictis ipsa ecclesia fraudetur"), they ordered her to pay 12 florins to a bank against the sum of 230 owed her.[103]

As a final example, Lodovico di Piero Ricoveri and Giovanni di Francesco Ferrantini, business associates, entered into two different *compromissa* on the same day (27 February 1427 [1428]), each with five unrelated arbitrators (ten men in all). Giacomini's book contains a *laudum* only for the first *compromissum*, and it did not come until a year later. The *laudum* reproduced a private agreement between the men. Ferrantini had actually run the bank of the brothers Jacopo (since dead) and Lodovico, because Jacopo was blind and Lodovico was not good at business ("a ciò era poco pratico"). By agreement between them, then, Giovanni was declared the owner of the bank's assets, except for what Lodovico was directly indebted for. The two *compromissa* were part of the arrangement. Each was to last five years. The men in the first were to look after "questa scripta" insofar as it touched Lodovico and in the second after Giovanni's interests. The arbitration resulted from Lodovico's claim that Giovanni Ferrantini had manipulated the books against him and had not satisfied creditors so that Lodovico was cited in three pieces of litigation against the firm, which still bore his name. Only one of the five arbitrators was present, and he was Lodovico's distant cousin Francesco d'Angelo Ricoveri. He had to review the tangled events of the intervening year. Lodovico wanted a third independent accounting "quia natura est acta ad dissentiendum" and indemnity against the three lawsuits, all of which had been lost, and still other cases. Giovanni, meanwhile, had disappeared, and the Mercanzia, at Lodovico's request, had examined the firm's books. Lodovico was assessed the remainder of a sum he owed to Stefano di Vanni Ricoveri. Giovanni had to abide by the agreement, present the firm's books, and, because he had caused Lodovico "dampna, expensas, verecundias et incommoda," pay the *gabelle* for the *laudum*.[104]

Individual *lauda* themselves also reveal at times a complicated prehistory leading up to them—a history of negotiations, arbitrations, even litigation. A simple case is that involving Bartolomeo Gualterotti and his brother Gualterotto. In 1421 Bartolomeo had won from Gualterotto by arbitration various properties worth over 1,174 florins. But the property awarded to Bartolomeo had been designated in the *catasto* as belonging to Gualterotto. So the same arbitrator spoke again to reaffirm that, notwithstanding the *catasto,* Bartolomeo was owner and, therefore, responsible for the fiscal duties.[105]

An arbitration between the same Bartolomeo and Gherardo di Pagolo Davizi really began with a suit in the court of the Mercanzia between Piero di Neri Ardinghelli and Orsino Lanfredini, on one side, and Gualterotto Gualterotti and Gherardo, on the other, for the sum of 10,000 florins.[106] One of the most complex cases involved Tommaso di Guido Monaldi against his emancipated nephew Piero d'Antonio, also acting for his brother Giovanni. The three arbitrators, Giovanni di Francesco Caccini, Lodovico di Piero di Bonaventura, Lorenzo di Giovanni del Grasso, had to unravel a mess. Tommaso, with his father and brothers Antonio and Francesco, had back in 1380 "confessed" the 1,325 florin dowry of Antonio's wife. In 1390 Antonio's sons had been left 1,500 florins by Guido. In 1407 they had been emancipated and formally accepted the estate of their mother. In 1420 arbitrators from the Arte de' Medici e Speziali had acted between Tommaso and his nephews, on the one hand, and the other nephews, Piero and Carlo di fu Francesco. Tommaso and Piero on that occasion, to cover the maternal dowry and the legacy in Guido's will, received Guido's *domus magna* and five other houses. Back in 1393 arbitration, by members of the same guild, between the brothers Francesco, Antonio, and Tommaso had assigned those same houses to Antonio and Tommaso "in partem divisionis" along with two others. Now the arbitrators found that all that property barely sufficed to meet the *dos* and *legatum* owed to Piero and Giovanni and that the second *laudum* of 1393 had merely been intended to see to those debts. So they gave it all outright to Piero and Giovanni. In a second *laudum* then, with only Caccini acting as arbitrator, Piero and Giovanni split the property because a yet previous *laudum* between them was revoked.[107] Nor did the story end there. Antonio di Guido later went to arbitration against his two sons, with Lorenzo di Giovanni del Grasso as arbitrator. This *laudum* spelled out that 3,494 florins had been assessed as Tommaso's and Antonio's and his sons' in 1393. The property awarded then amounted to 3,260 florins—1,058 of which was for Tommaso. It also went into more detail about the *laudum* of 1420, and added reference to the *laudum* of May 1422. In detail, now, the property of Antonio was handed to his sons.[108]

In some arbitrations one might suspect collusion between the parties and arbitrators. That is, the parties actually worked out the settlement—or had no real dispute in the first place—but wanted a disposition of rights in the form of a *laudum*. The arbitrators, then, were not independent. What, for example, is one to make of an arbitration following immediately upon the *compromissum*?—as in the case where Tedaldo di Bartolo Tedaldi could immediately divide property between the brothers Piero and Nofri di Maffeo Tedaldi.[109] Jurists were inclined to presume such an arbitration collusive if a question of fraud arose.[110] And in other cases the suspicion of collusion, even to the point of fraud, mounts to a conviction. In January 1426 (1427) monna Paola, wife of Ridolfo Bardi, with him as her *mundualdus*, went to arbitration against her newly emancipated (for this purpose, in part) son Leonardo. The arbitrator was Bartolomeo Gualterotti. He found immediately that Leonardo "by his own money and effort" ("ex sua propria pecunia et ex sua propria industria") had bought a *podere* next to one his father owned. Leonardo, however, as a precaution, had placed the title to this property in his mother's name. One presumes that in his prior unemancipated state Leonardo did not want the property in his name (thus in his father's), for there was still reciprocal liability between them.[111] But it is also not clear how an unemancipated son was able to buy the property, except by posing it as a purchase by his mother. There were no references to documents or dates for this purchase. The whole transaction was accepted by the arbitrator on the word of parties, who were also admitting collusion as to ownership of the farm in the first place. Also, the arbitrator appended a unique condition to Leonardo's ownership. If his father should ever fail to provide for his insane ("mente capti") brother Luca, Leonardo was to take on the obligation to feed and house him.[112] Leonardo was assuming a place of responsibility in his family's affairs.[113]

Where *lauda* following immediately on their enabling *compromissum* carry some presumption of collusion, those that came at a later date seem to bear the opposite presumption—not ironclad, to be sure—that the arbitrators operated on their own. One assumes that some time was necessary to give reality and substance to the formulas describing the arbitrators as sifting through evidence, testimony, and arguments. But above all one assumes that there were indeed times when the parties truly needed the arbitrators to devise a solution they themselves could not find. These solutions might not always work; hence one sees the sorts of complicated, prolonged disputes as mentioned above, where the matter moved through several arbitrations or even back and forth from arbitration to litigation. One even sees a case where, following an arbitrator's decision, the parties renounced their *compromissum*.[114] An interesting example concerns Niccolò da Uzzano and Mariotto Banchi, arbitrating between Michele and Francesco di Simone, on the one hand, and Antonio and Duccio di Dino Canacci, on the other. The problem was the vendetta going on between these parties. They issued an immediate decision that the Canacci owed the others 600 florins and had eight days to pay. But they also reserved the right during the not yet expired term of the *compromissum* to correct, emend, or revoke, and arbitrate anew. By the next month they were issuing summonses to the Canacci to appear before them at the Arte di Calimala. A new *laudum* demanded the Canacci make a formal peace (*pax*), for which they would be freed from the terms of the previous *laudum*.[115] One can easily imagine that vendettas would be difficult to resolve, and the resolution would depend on the arbitrators to at least some degree. In any case, it can be said that some *lauda* were not the result of collusion.[116]

When the arbitrator was a jurist or notary, he may more consistently have shaped the resolution than did other arbitrators. Messer Giuliano Davanzati's one excursion into Giacomini's pages displayed him grappling with complex legal issues between Niccolò Manovelli and Boldro di Lorenzo Boldri. In 1380 Tedicio Manovelli in his last illness designated a farm as equivalent for his wife's dowry, leaving her a legacy of its *fructus* for the duration of her widowhood, and livestock worth 37 florins and *masserizie* worth 150 *lire*. His wife enjoyed the property for twenty years, to her death in 1400. She left as heir her son, Merlino, by her first husband Benvenuto, who took possession of the farm. Merlino died in 1411, and Lorenzo Boldri, as closest agnate to Merlino, acceded to his estate and took possession of the farm. Boldro di Lorenzo came into it, in turn, as his father's heir. Only in 1421 did Niccolò Manovelli formally accede to the estate of the long-deceased Tedicio and press a case in the Arte de' Beccai for the value of the property left by Tedicio to his wife. The arguments and documents produced there were also reproduced for Davanzati, who was reminded that Tedicio's desire had been for the property to be distributed as alms for the benefit of his soul following his wife's death. Davanzati ordered Boldro to pay Manovelli 40 florins. Manovelli, however, had to use the money to dower Sandra, daughter of Niccolò d'Antonio Manovelli. Or Boldro could show

that funds had been paid "amore dei" in accord with Tedicio's desires, and then he was not bound by the judgment. He could also
escape it if he could show (means unspecified) that the dowry Tedicio
had received from his wife was other than he had claimed in his will.
Apparently there were suspicions.[117] Collusion between the parties,
in this case at least, seems impossible.

ISSUES IN ARBITRATION

The foregoing discussion has already implicitly presented an idea of
the range of issues coming into play in arbitrations. No one case was
like any other. All was *particolare,* as Francesco Guicciardini would
later have it.[118] Still, I have attempted a loose categorization of issues
according to the status of the parties as related or unrelated. The
results appear in table 1.5. Slightly over half the arbitrations involved
"debts." This category includes both those arbitrations where the
origin and nature of the debt were spelled out and those where a debt
simply was asserted and an order to pay was given.[119] But in a real
sense, a broad category is meaningless, for all issues in arbitration
were "debts" in some sense. A mother's dowry, for example, constituted a debt against her husband's estate. All the cases of vendetta
arose in two installments, the first the levying of a monetary "debt"
and the second the ordering of a *pax.* When Antonio di Giovanni
Mozi was said to owe his sister 100 florins and ordered to give her
certain property, was he just satisfying a debt or dividing an inheritance with her?[120] I called it a debt. But when the five sons of
Lorenzo di Marco Benvenuti went to arbitration to determine who
was responsible for a 600-florin obligation on their father's estate, I
called it division of inheritance, mainly because the three eldest, who
had to repay the business loans, were compensated with ownership of
their father's properties near Casentino.[121] In other cases where a
man was said to owe his brother some amount, it was impossible to
know if that debt was from transactions or from an accounting toward division of the patrimony.[122] I called them debts.

The ones I have labeled debts are those where the issue, even
between kin, was not clear, as well as all those where commercial
transactions were in question. Distinguishing between the other categories is no less difficult. Certainly, as a dowry was nominally a
woman's share of the patrimony, an arbitration concerning it could
also be termed a division of inheritance. Take the example of monna
Bice d'Antonio Strozzi and her brothers. When her first marriage

ended, she returned her dowry, which had evidently been repaid, to her brothers. At her second marriage she needed the dowry back. Kinsmen Francesco di Benedetto di Caroccio and Benedetto di Piero Strozzi acted as *fideiussores* and furnished the cash.[123] Or take the case of Ginevra di Francesco di Domenico d'Andrea. She won a dowry by arbitration from her brothers, but in compensation her share of her mother's estate went to them.[124] And, as a final complication, some *lauda* dealt with several very different issues. Mariotto di messer Albizzo de' Roselesi was found to owe his uterine brother Francesco Quaratesi both 400 florins from the maternal *bona hereditaria* and 600 florins from business.[125] As the business relationship was here seemingly based on kinship, I counted this an inheritance issue.

In general table 1.5 can only underestimate the degree to which inheritance and dowry figured as core issues in arbitrations, not just between disputants who were related but also between those who were not. As it stands, I have identified 32 (of 85) arbitrations as unquestionably involving inheritance and dowry.[126] Those involving division of inheritance were aimed generally at equitable distribution. Tedaldo di Bartolo Tedaldi saw to the division between his kinsmen Nofri and Piero di Maffeo. Tedaldo carefully divided houses and lands, leaving the winemaking apparatus in common, and ordering Piero, whose share was worth slightly more, to pay a small balance of 10 florins to his brother within a month.[127] Those involving dowry were aimed at several possible results, depending on whose dowry was in question. There was the problem of retrieving a woman's

Table 1.5 Issues under Arbitration

| | Arbitrators | | |
Issues	Related	Unrelated	Total
Debts	20	28	48
Division	10	2	12
Mother's *Dos*	4	4	8
Sister's *Dos*	3		3
Own *Dos*	3	3	6
Daughter's *Dos*	1		1
Wife's *Dos*	1	1	2
Vendetta		3	3
Miscellaneous	1	1	2
Total	43	42	85

dowry from her husband's kin and heirs. An arbitration between Piero di Riccio del Buglesso of Castelfiorentino and Guido di Lazeri was occasioned by the dowry of monna Filippa, Piero's widowed stepmother. Guido's father had stood surety on that dowry. "Said monna Filippa for her dowry and pursuant rights molested said sons of said Lazeri as heirs obligated for the dowry of the said monna Filippa and, therefore, said Guido and Luca [his brother] molested said Piero, saying he is the heir of said Riccio, his father, and for Piero's part it was alleged that he is not his father's heir." The upshot was that Guido and Luca were ordered to pay her 44 *lire*, without compensation from Piero, who in turn had to pay her the unspecified *residuum* of the dowry.[128] There were also problems of simply supplying a dowry from the patrimony of a woman's family. Francesco di messer Arnaldo Manelli in 1429 was concerned to provide dowries for two daughters while he was in the midst of financial problems.[129]

As for the "debts," they came in all varieties. A few examples can only begin to spell out this category. The kinsman Bernardo and Jacopo di Gerozzo di Francesco Bardi, on the one hand, and Bardo di Francesco Bardi, on the other, went to arbitration because the brothers owed Averardo de' Medici's bank 500 florins and Bardo was *fideiussor* on that sum. Bardo's *fideiussio* told Averardo de' Medici that if he failed to realize his money from Bernardo and Jacopo, he could get it from Bardo. The arbitration, on the other hand, told Bardo that his nephews had to keep him *indempnis*. If he had to pay their debt for them, he was entitled to a house in Prato and two *poderi* in different corners of the Tuscan countryside.[130] In the second example one finds that the monastery of San Salvatore di Vaiaio owed Francesco di Berto Busini 375 florins. The arbitration resulted in a payment schedule to liquidate the debt over two years. For his part, Francesco had three days to vacate any monastery properties he then occupied. It would seem Francesco had forced the issue to settlement by taking control of some of the monastery's lands.[131] A final example of debt involved two Pisan merchants. Giovanni di Cristofano Cirione owed Zacheria di Giovanni Vannicelli 700 florins. The arbitrator, the Florentine Donato di Piero Velluti, was told Giovanni lacked sufficient cash. The *laudum* then launched into a survey of Giovanni's assets: a *fondaco* and house in Piombino (in fact his, though under Zacheria's name), 102 florins owed him by Niccolò Tinucci according to a *scriptura privata*, 100 florins owed by Perone di Castro. The arbitrator awarded these assets to Zacheria, as well as whatever was realized from the sale of 200 sacks of grain Giovanni had sent to Corsica, and 202 he had sent to Genoa.[132] In these cases, as in the other debt cases in Giacomini's cartulary, it is interesting to note that the fact of a debt was rarely, if ever, in doubt. These matters were established at the outset. The arbitrators were being asked to figure out how, and to a lesser extent when, repayment could occur. On some occasions they were asked to fix the sum of the obligation itself. But without some degree of prior agreement between the parties that there was an issue (debt) to be settled, there would have been no arbitration.[133]

The range of issues arising in arbitration also provokes contemplation of the role of norms in arbitration. These issues were jurally defined. Terms like *hereditas* and *dos* had very complex meanings. That these meanings were all present, in precise fashion, in any arbitration is impossible to say. Arbitrations, unlike judicial *sententiae* and jurisprudential *consilia,* did not contain exact references to statutes, passages of civil or canon law, or even to other decisions (involving other parties) that might be utilized as precedents, even when the arbitrators were lawyers or notaries. But that does not mean that there was no normative content to *lauda,* that there was no awareness of norms on the part of arbitrators and disputants, that norms—at least of a broad, ideological nature—did not play a role in shaping settlements.

In the course of the discussion to this point, we have already encountered examples. There was, of course, the overriding ideology that underwrote arbitration, namely, the need to avoid scandals and put an end to conflicts, bringing peace between parties. Pursuant to that end, *lauda* disclose a willingness to determine people's obligations and make them live up to them, along with a corollary of not tolerating fraud or malice in avoiding obligations. But the normative sensibility exhibited in *lauda* could also be much more refined and detailed. Three arbitrators gave voice to the sense that "it is not just nor convenient that anyone feel loss from the deed of another and it is a very equitable principle to preserve unharmed the sureties who are obligated for him."[134] Also, as an example to be seen later, arbitrators (one of them a lawyer) revealed a knowledge of the prescription of legal rights in civil law—or at least acceded to one party's presentation of those rights.[135] Arbitrators also worked with a general sense of equity, a desire to be fair to the parties in a way that took into account their rights and economic resources.[136] When one considers that they at times took into account the most minute nuances of contractual language and the most intricate details of account books and also the most general senses of fairness and the condition of the parties, one realizes that arbitrators could respond to a range of norms as they sifted through the stuff of the case before them. The parties also could operate with a normative sense and invoke norms, though the nature of the *laudum* makes it almost impossible to recover that dimension.

A MICROHISTORICAL APPROACH

To this point this chapter has attempted to categorize and count. Examples have been adduced along the way as illustrations of the various categories, although the uniqueness and peculiarity of these examples cannot help but shine through. I want to consider some arbitrations in all the glory of their uniqueness. There has been a fashion in historical studies, though not without its severe critics, to focus on exciting, atypical events and persons. Often these are found in judicial records. In these studies the event then shapes the context the historian tries to reconstruct for it. "When successful, this microcosmic focus conveys a sense of immediacy, intimacy, and concreteness that is often absent from analytical histories."[137] But it also tends to dwarf the general and structural. Here, with some sense of the structures of arbitration, we can encounter these unique events in a way that beginning with them in isolation and seeking only to comprehend them will not allow.[138] Also, these events do no more than stand out to the historian from the full range of events in Giacomini's ledger. They are not indicative of full-bore social anomalies. They are indicative of the flexible range of arbitration. They are also frank, in some cases, about the ideology of arbitration—how it was viewed by the Florentines associated with it.

Case 1. An emancipated son, Giovanni, went to arbitration against his father, ser Piero di ser Tommaso di ser Francesco in 1428. Giovanni had a dowry of 315 florins for his wife, Pippa, which had been sought for him by his brother Salvi from the heirs of Pippa's first husband. But in fact Giovanni, according to the *laudum,* had only received 115 florins. Of the remaining 200, Rinieri del Pace had 137, and ser Piero had a lien (*pignus*) on a farm. The arbitrator, Stefano di Salvi Bencivenni, ordered the debt transfered to Giovanni, with repayment to be sought immediately. The money was to be put in *Monte* credits as security for the dowry, and the credits were not to be alienated in any manner. Their interest, however, was to accrue to Giovanni. At the end of the marriage, what they were then worth was to be considered part of Pippa's dowry "just as in similar conditions it is customary, and with other forms and conditions in similar cases it is customary, to be counted according to the style of the scribes and notaries of the *monte* of the said commune." Giovanni's father was to make good the remainder of the dowry, first, by paying off a debt Giovanni had for 24 florins and, second, by assigning him either *bona immobilia* or *monte* credits worth 39, plus one *modius* of grain and one *cingium* of wine. Finally, it was deemed *inconveniens* that the brother, Salvi, might "molest" his father about that property, for if Salvi sought relief from ser Piero, he in turn would go to Giovanni "and thus it would go in a circle" ("et sic res esset in circulo"). So Giovanni was ordered to cover any loss ser Piero might sustain as a result of any action by Salvi. Just what Salvi was concerned about is not clear, but the language of the text dealing with him would seem to indicate he had a grievance and was threatening to act on it.[139] Even though he acted as his brother's agent to retrieve Pippa's dowry, Salvi was not going to lose sight of his own interests. The dowry mattered to him both as *procurator* at its *confessio* and as property that had obviously been handled by his father, prior to Giovanni's emancipation, as his own.

Case 2. Division of inheritance lurked beneath the previous case. It was the overt issue in the next one, which will be treated briefly. There were three parties to this arbitration, each entitled to one-third of the estate of Andrea di Chimente di Stefano. They were the monastery of San Benedetto (from the deceased's brother, a monk there), his widow Lisa, and his brother Angnolo, who also acted for his brother Taddeo and nephew Andrea. Angnolo held a *podere* opposite the monastery, concerning which *scandala* had already arisen and, doubtless, said the arbitrators (Averardo di Lapo da Castiglionchio and Cresci di Lorenzo Cresci, who was Lisa's brother), would arise again. The problem was that this particular *podere* and its appurtenances could not be easily divided because the houses for lord and worker could not be easily divided. Here the arbitrators had real work to do. They gave the monastery 30 *staiora* of land, but with the proviso that if Lisa or Angnolo paid 300 florins within two days the monastery had to relinquish title at that price. The monastery could thereafter continue to rent the land at 40 *soldi* per *staia* and was still entitled to one-third the *fructus* through the fall harvest. Still more clauses were intended to protect the monastery. The thrust of what could have been a three-sided *laudum,* and that in its formal two-sidedness posed the monastery and the brothers against Lisa, ended up in fact posing family interests against the monastery. Rights and prerogatives between Lisa and her brothers-in-law were not really spelled out. One wonders if the Florentine archive does not harbor another arbitration to that end.[140]

Case 3. The previous case's difficulties revolved around the nature of the property to be divided. The problems in our next case revolved around a long and complicated legal background. In 1349 Bino di Ceccho gave certain properties to a Bartola di Nuto Carcherelli; there was also a *reconductio* of these properties to her in 1361. Years later, in 1418, Bino's son Jacopo, party to the present arbitration, and Cristofano di ser Bernardo Carcherelli, also party to the present arbitration, and his brother Giovanni, entered a *compromissum* in ser Paolo Pagni. Jacopo and Giovanni had their own arbitration in messer Tommaso Salvetti three months later, as did Jacopo and Cristofano. Their arbitration was to be decided by ten different men, allowing any two of them to determine the issue. That seems to have been a procedural error, for two, ser Paolo Pagni and a priest, Tommaso, decided against Jacopo, while two others decided against Cristofano. A final piece of procedure was a release of claims (*finis*) by Cristofano and Giovanni to Jacopo in 1419, and another in May 1422. Now on 6 May 1422 the sole arbitrator, Baldassare d'Antonio Santi, determined that the gifts of 1349 " were fictitious and made as a precaution of the late Bino and for protection of the goods of the said Bino and because Bino himself had great confidence in the said Bartola who was the maternal aunt of monna Bartolomea wife of the said Bino." Supposedly Bino had rented back these properties, but in actual fact no money had ever changed hands. Bino possessed it all "ut sua propria" for thirty-six years. He even alienated it *per laudum* to his sons in 1377, and it had been Bartola's relative, Giovanni di messer Jacopo Carcherelli, as arbitrator, who designated that the property belonged to Jacopo di Bino. Yet Cristofano on his own behalf and for his nephews advanced a claim to the said goods and even tried to recover the revenue (*fructus et redditus*) from them as heir to Bartola, although the arbitrator noted that Jacopo's sister Filippa stood in closer relation to Bartola than did Cristofano. The arbitrator's decision was that, as the donation of 1349 had been fictitious, the property was Jacopo's. The previous *compromissa* and *lauda* were all left standing. Because Jacopo had been "non iuridice et contra iustitiam vexatus" and had suffered expenses amounting to 150 florins, Cristofano was commanded to repay this sum. In view of his *paupertas,* however, payment was made contingent on his filing suit or otherwise molesting Jacopo, in which case he would have to pay immediately.[141]

One sees in this case an interesting, if desperate, set of attempts by a man in financial straits to resurrect himself by legal means. The best weapon he had was the legal presumption in favor of paper evidence. Jacopo, who also had some paper and the facts of possession on his side, had to defend his interests at considerable cost.[142] One would like to know if these two had any relationship prior to 1418 and if it was hostile. One cannot imagine they were friendly at the time of this seemingly conclusive *laudum* in 1422. Here, as in all the *lauda,* one would like to know much more than made the notary's page, even while recognizing that a great deal of suggestive material did. One suggestive bit is the presentation of *lauda* as partial in the last analysis. They could be said, and were, to come out against one party. They could be perceived as one-sided, like judicial decisions.

Case 4. Another case with a long and complex prehistory came near the end of Giacomini's cartulary. The initiating incident, as the arbitrator saw it, was the will of Migliore di Jacopo Covoni of 1413. In it were *legata* to his daughters, born and unborn, for dowries of 1,000 florins. If only one married, she got 1,200. As his universal heirs he designated any future sons, with substitution to his uncle Antonio di Paolo Covoni. When Migliore died later that year, he left no sons, but one daughter, Giovanna. His widow's pregnancy resulted in a second daughter, Lucretia, so in July 1414 Antonio took the inheritance. In 1417 he then produced his own will, leaving each niece 1,200 florins as dowry and designating his two sons, Alessandro and Loysio, as heirs. Antonio soon died in that plague year, as did his little niece Lucretia, to whom Giovanna was heir on intestacy. So when Giovanna was later married to Lorenzo di Crescio Cresci, her dowry was set at 1,337 florins. The couple then found themselves in conflict with Antonio Covoni's sons, and that conflict generated the *laudum* of 1429. Cresci pressed that his wife was due not only her own dowry of 1,200 florins but Lucretia's estate, said to amount to 800. He claimed Migliore's estate was worth 4,800 and so easily could cover it. Alessandro responded that the estate was worth only 4,100 and reminded one and all that Giovanna's *dos* had been 1,337 florins. His argument was that the amount over 1,200 had to be considered Lucretia's estate. Cresci responded legalistically that a father could leave his daughter more than her mere legitimate portion ("quod pater potest etiam ultra legitimam legare filiabus"), protecting Giovanna's primary right, and that her rights from Lucretia were separate. The arbitrator, Michele di Fruosino, *hospitalarius* of Santa Maria Nuova, found that Lucretia's *legitima* was not worth even 700, but that Cresci was still owed some of his wife's dowry, 137 florins of which had to be imputed to Lucretia's *legitima*. But Michele, as arbitrator, also had to take into consideration the poor financial position of the brothers Alessandro and Loysio in view of the latter's bankruptcy (*cessatio*). Citing finally the touching concern of Giovanna, her husband, and her father-in-law for Alessandro and the little sons of Loysio, the arbitrator ordered payment to Giovanna of 300 florins over five years. Apparently her concern was not sufficient to cancel the debt, but it was also possible that her claim was prior in law to that of any business creditors, so she was just making sure that, in some way, some of the capital remained in the family. But from indications in the *laudum* that both sides presented lengthy and detailed arguments in support of their rights, it seems hard to believe that the settlement was easily reached.[143]

Case 5. The last two cases involved guardianship (*tutela*) and the problem of rendering accounts when the *tutor* stepped aside as the *pupillus* came of age. A man named Modesto di Chele went to arbitration in 1427 against Bernardo and Giovanni d'Andrea di Maso. Modesto's father had been under *tutela* to their grandfather and even over thirty years after Maso's death Modesto wanted to review the accounts of his guardianship ("revidere rationem sue tutele"). He even argued that the division of property between Andrea di Maso and Chele's three sons was invalid because he had still been a minor at the time. He nowhere, however, alleged that his *tutor* had cheated him. Bernardo and Giovanni replied to the arbitrators (messer Stefano Buonaccorsi, along with Alessandro Alessandri and Niccolò Carducci), that it was not so. Modesto was fifty-four, "and therefore was and is prescribed from all right of seeking an account of the said *tutela*" because he had let it stand unchallenged for over thirty years. The arbitrators agreed with them and ordered Modesto to drop the matter.

The arbitrators were not finished, however. There was another issue. In June 1385 Girolamo di Chele had married Bartolomea Corsini, and along with Andrea di Maso had acknowledged the 500-florin dowry. Modesto and his brother Giovanni had promised, on the pages of Andrea's account book, to pay him 300 florins if he had to pay out on this contingent obligation. When Bartolomea died she left a granddaughter, Ermellina di Piero di Filippo Porcellini, and her husband, who had since died. Ermellina, through her *procurator,* brought suit in the court of the Podestà to gain *tenuta* on Andrea's property in execution of this obligation, so she could retrieve her grandmother's *dos.* The arbitrator wanted to make Modesto shoulder the obligation he had signed in Andrea's book, but he also took account, as did other arbitrators in other cases, of the debtor's relative *paupertas.* So his 300-florin obligation came out as 150 in the arbitration, and the final payment was not due until the end of 1433. The payment's first installment was moved up if Ermellina married in 1429 or 1430, or if her *dos* of 475 florins had to be returned during that time. The brothers Bernardo and Giovanni also wanted to stick Modesto for the return of Bartolomea's dowry by claiming he was his brother Girolamo's heir. Modesto denied that, and in this matter the arbitrators found for his side.[144] It is hard to say if Modesto was really satisfied with the results; his financial plight was little alleviated.

Case 6. Modesto brought no clear charges or proof of impropriety in guardianship. Such was not the case in the last arbitration we will look at. The parties were Filippa, with her husband and son, against Giovanni di Bartolomeo di ser Spinello. The arbitrators were Tommaso di Pazzino Alberti and Bartolomeo di ser Giovanni Neri. In 1396 Riccardo di Tommaso Bardi, *curator* for Giovanni di Bartolomeo di ser Spinello, took, without his ward's consent and "nulla necessitate cogente," 490 florins and gave them to Chiricho di Giotto as the dowry of his wife, Filippa di Guido di Giovanni of Castelfiorentino, one of the parties to the arbitration. There had been an understanding among these parties, however—or at least it was so put to the arbitrator—that a list of properties (a house and two pieces of land) belonged to the ward Giovanni. To give effect to this agree-

ment there had been a *compromissum* between Chiricho and his wife
(with Giovanni's mother), the arbitrators being the jurist Filippo
Corsini and Andrea di Niccolò Minerbetti. This *compromissum* was
issued in favor of Giovanni evidently because the arbitrators were
"attached" to him—both being fathers-in-law to Giovanni's sisters.
But because of Riccardo's negligence the term of the *compromissum*
expired. In 1406, having come of age, Giovanni discovered the loss
and brought suit before the Ufficiali dei Pupilli. They ordered
Chiricho's father to pay the estate of Bartolomeo di ser Spinello 200
florins, though payment could be avoided by a second *compromissum*
in Filippo Corsini. This was never done; no money was paid nor were
the properties ever surrendered. That was where the matter stood
when the arbitrators stated, rather formulaically, "it is not just nor
convenient that anyone perceive profit from the loss of another"
("non est iustum nec conveniens quod aliquis cum dampno alterius
lucrum sentiat"). They ordered Filippa to pay 400 florins within two
months or give Giovanni the properties in one month, along with
300 florins in compensation for the *fructus* he had lost.[145] In this case
there had been no contesting that Giovanni had a claim against the
cura, only that the obligation had not been paid. This instance also
is indicative of yet further uses of arbitration, stacking it in favor of
one party as a form of surety on an obligation. However, it is also
clear that the young Giovanni was taken advantage of. Why it took
him over twenty years after 1406 to achieve a settlement cannot be
determined from the evidence we have here. We know only that he
finally used arbitration to get back what another arbitration had been
supposed to give him.

Legal Problems of Arbitration

One window into the problems of arbitration in Florence is the statute commentary of Alessandro Bencivenni (1385–1423) written in
the early 1420s.[146] The allegations prior to formal *litis contestatio*
could set the terms for arbitration, as well as adjudication, so
Bencivenni cautioned litigants to set out their cases clearly, to stick to
true issues and not raise fictive ones.[147] They could not seek a second
laudum on the same matter, even if its resolution had come in court
and not by way of arbitration. However, if the nature of the case
changed in any significant way (in the type of action or its cause, in

the person of the plaintiff or defendant, or otherwise), then, on the authority of Angelo degli Ubaldi (d. 1400), a *compromissum* could be sought even in the face of a previous *laudum*. The basic rule, however, according to Bencivenni, was that the *compromissum* was to be general in form, directing the arbitrators to look into any and every angle of the specific differences between the parties. The arbitration itself was to stick to issues of fact, it was not competent to deal with matters of law. In fact, except for what the statute directed regarding kin (by extension the high advisibility of employing arbitration in dealing with valid or invalid wills), the rules of "common law" were to apply.[148]

Bencivenni's gloss to "De notificatione laudorum" reveals that there were few major problems with this statute. He denied that minor omissions of detail, like the date of the *compromissum*, would invalidate a *laudum*, but he reaffirmed that sufficient notice of the arbitrators' findings be given to an absent party. Some parties would be more difficult to notify, that was all. The statute "De generali executione laudorum" also raised few problems, but it did pose the interesting issue of the date of effect of an arbitration, which Bencivenni concluded was the date of the *compromissum*.[149] Learned legal authorities disagreed on the question of the temporal term of the *laudum*, but the course actually taken in court had supported the procedural guarantee by which the creditor could move against the debtor's property without first having to establish the fact of the debt. The resolution lay in linking the *laudum* to the *compromissum* that necessarily preceded it.

Nello da San Gimignano ran into the problem more than once. In a *consilium* that survives in a sealed original in a Florentine manuscript he confronted the following case. Two men, Piero and Paolo, had entered into a *compromissum*. Paolo pledged to have a monna Antonia ratify the agreement. She did not ratify the *compromissum*, she did ratify the *laudum*. Ratification of the *laudum*, however, occurred after the time limit on the *compromissum* had expired. Piero, therefore, argued that Paolo had failed to perform the condition set out in the *compromissum* and laid claim to the penalty for noncompliance. Nello took the case as *sapiens* at the behest of the court and found in favor of Paolo. It was absurd, he said, to claim that, though the *laudum* was framed within the requisite time and could be ratified, the *compromissum*, on the other hand, could not. Dionigi de'

Barigiani of Perugia, who joined Nello on this case, concurred, adding the logical observation that the force of the *compromissum* had
not indeed expired but continued in the *laudum*.[150]

The parallels between the *compromissum/laudum* and the general
procedure in formal civil litigation are striking, especially in the more
widely used summary procedure. Recourse to an arbitrator was parallel in many ways to the recourse to a legal expert, *doctor sapiens*,
from the midst of litigation.[151] Either the two parties agreed to put
the case to a jurist, or the judge perceived the need for expert legal
advice and, with the consent of both parties, approached a jurist with
specific legal questions.[152] The jurist(s) had to be acceptable to both
parties. The *sapiens* had to arrive at a fully valid legal result; he could
not be as flexible in theory as an arbitrator could.[153] Notification of
the *laudum* paralleled the process of summons of a defendant to
court to respond to a complaint. Above all, even in the courtroom
much was dependent on the initiative of the parties—what issues to
raise, how, when, and in what order.[154] The pleadings of the parties
set the case in law, just as what they chose to lay before the arbitrator
set the limits of his competence. The arbitrator himself could adopt
a very formal procedure.[155]

The parallels are even more striking when we examine a case in full.
Among the surviving Florentine *consilia* is one by Nello da San
Gimignano and others concerning a *laudum*. Nello clearly was actively involved in such cases and had to confront conceptual issues
revolving around arbitration as practiced by Florentines. And the
passage from arbitration to the context of formal litigation, in which
we find Nello's text, is itself revealing of how interconnected the two
procedures were.

A CONSILIUM OF NELLO DA SAN GIMIGNANO

The facts of the case were these: Monna Antonia wrote a testament
in which she left to a Giovanni di messer Simone her houses and
furnishings located in Florence. She also named him and his brother
Francesco as her universal heirs. These two had three nephews,
Simone, Berto, and Marco, sons of their deceased brother Antonio,
who were not named in monna Antonia's testament.

> And said Francesco and Giovanni, wanting to make adequate provision
> for their nephews in the estate of the said Antonia, made among them-
> selves a private document and agreement in which it is established that
> all possessions, things, money, credits and debts that are acquired and

found in the estate of said monna Antonia belong to Giovanni for a third part and to Francesco for another third and to Simone and his brothers for the other third, not withstanding the testament and bequest. . . .[156]

Later, however, disagreement arose and a *compromissum* was arranged with two men (unnamed) chosen as arbitrators. These "arbitri et arbitratores" affirmed that the private written agreement dividing Antonia's estate into three equal parts was indeed valid and should be executed as if it were an instrument with a guarantee for seizure of property to cover the debt without need of judicial sentence allowing the seizure ("ac si esset instrumentum guarentigiatum"). These arbitrators later reversed themselves, however, annulling the first *laudum* and issuing a second. They had since learned that the three nephews had been under the guardianship (*tutela*) of their uncles and had grievances about the tutorial management of their affairs. So the arbitrators ordered the uncles to turn their thirds over to the nephews. Any amount remaining after settling this debt would then be split into thirds.

The nephews went to court to get this second *laudum* enforced. The uncles (or their legal representative) countered that the arbitrators had not had that issue committed to them. They had been told to deal with Antonia's estate and not with the *tutela*. There was a *defectum potestatis* on this matter. The nephews' response (or, again, that of their representative) was that the *laudum* was valid because the language of the *compromissum* not only pointed to a specific issue but to a general state of controversy and the need to resolve it. The dispute and its resolution were separate.

There are many questions to which the historian cannot find an answer. We do not know what the families were, for no surnames were given. The relationship between Antonia and these men is never specified. The value of her estate and the amount in question from the *tutela* are not revealed. The identity of the arbitrators and their relationship to the parties are other bits of information that are lacking. These matters did not have a bearing on the legal status of the case, so they were not transmitted to the *sapiens*. It is also not certain what court handled the case, though presumably it was that of the Podestà, nor on whose initiative the case went to the *sapiens*—the judge's or the parties'.[157] But what is clear is that by no matter whose initiative the parties had to agree and that they had to set the legal issue for the jurist as a result of their arguments.

Nello di Giuliano Martini Cetti da San Gimignano was an excellent choice. He was a prominent figure in the ruling councils and elite circles of Florence. He was also a highly esteemed jurist, a writer of incisive legal treatises, frequently called upon to render *consilia* in cases that arose in the various courts and political bodies of Florence.[158] According to Lauro Martines, Nello held a high opinion of city government in Florence, as *sibi princeps,* and of the grounding of statutes in the public utility.[159] In 1427 he would actively advocate adoption of the sweeping fiscal reform of the *catasto* as an appropriate measure of public utility.[160]

Nello began his *consilium* by noting that the contentiousness of the litigants and the complex issues required learned intervention.

> If everyone would be easily pleased with the truth for a decision on this case there would be little to do, but because such matters rarely transpire without extended treatment of the question, it is necessary to reach the truth of the article not with a few words but by a full examination.[161]

In this case a "full examination" meant a formal pro-et-contra presentation.

First he rehearsed the arguments in favor of the validity of the *laudum.* It had been rendered in the form prescribed by "common" and municipal law. All the affairs between the parties had been committed to the arbitrators "as if special mention had been made of them, the force of which general clause silences anyone trying to have the *laudum* negated."[162] Support for these arguments came from the *Digest,* as did the corroboration for the next point—that by statute the *laudum* was an *instrumentum guarentigiatum,* a point also made by Bartolo da Sassoferrato (d. 1357).[163] By statute one could not oppose execution of such an instrument, for the intent of the guarantee was to allow the creditor to realize his money without having to prove the existence of the debt first. Furthermore, additional legislation (to be incorporated in the statutes of 1415 as "De generali executione laudorum") seemed to preclude any procedure for nullifying a *laudum* by a discontented party. Even if the arbitrators had exceeded their authority by considering the tutelary obligations, it had been in their competence to dispose of Antonia's estate, and that part of the *laudum* should stand. Here the added authority of Bartolo was again invoked. In his commentary on the *lex Quid tamen § Intra* of the title *De receptis: qui arbitrium receperint* (commonly designated simply by *De arbitris* in medieval law) (D. 4.8.21,12), Bartolo provided an example of the discretion of an arbitrator. The civil-law text concerned whether an agreed penalty could be exacted from a party who failed to act by the specified day as ordered by an arbitrator. Bartolo had determined that an arbitrator could exact a penalty only if the *compromissum* said so, but he could set a time limit and reduce the penalty.[164] The point in the present case was that the treatment of the estate and of the *tutela* had to be seen as separate. On this basis the *laudum* in favor of the three nephews had to stand.

The issues raised in the case thus touched on an area in the legal landscape that was still in formation in the early fifteenth century—the problem of appeal of a *laudum* given *ex necessitate statuti* in a dispute between kin. The *reductio ad arbitrium boni viri* did not provide for the correction of errors in the *laudum*.[165] Jurisprudence, as opposed to statutory law, was very concerned "with the possible harm caused by an arbitral decision based on equity not conditioned or limited by the *compromissum*—in this case the *laudum* would not have been an expression of the parties' autonomy but the direct result of an act of judgment exclusively bound to the arbitrator's will."[166] Doctrinal statements, formulated now in the courtroom more than in the classroom, tended to line up on the side of appellability. No less a figure than Paolo di Castro, who a few years later would be involved in revising Florence's statutes, stated in a *consilium* that a bad *laudum* had to be reworked, no matter what the statutes seemed to say.[167] So perhaps it is not surprising that, in Nello's case, it was the contrary position—that the *laudum* was not valid—that carried the day.

In the first place, and most importantly, the arbitrators had exceeded the powers vested in them by the parties: "the powers of the arbiters or arbitrators depend on the *compromissum* such that those arbitrating beyond the *compromissum* do nothing, rather the arbitration is null by defect of power or investigation."[168] Clear legal support for this position lay in three texts of the *Digest* cited by Nello, especially the *lex Diligenter* (D. 17.1.5), which required that one acting by authority of a *mandatum* remain within its terms, and by the *lex Non distinguemus* § *De officio* (D. 4.8.32,15), which directly required an arbitrator to address only the issue set forth for him in the *compromissum*. In the case before him, said Nello, the arbitrators had been asked to deal with Antonia's estate, not with the *tutela*. Their actions could not be justified (and the *laudum* validated) on the grounds that they were merely setting a condition to the settlement of Antonia's estate, for what was not entrusted to their disposition could not be treated conditionally. The arbitrators also could not order a second *laudum*. No less an authority than Baldo degli Ubaldi had taught that "it is certain that an arbiter cannot command a second compromise with him as arbitrator, unless it be by an act of the parties deferring to him."[169] The arbitrators had acted *in fraudem* by breaking the rules enjoining them to remain within the terms of the *compromissum*. The only reason Nello could find for their decision to favor the three nephews in the division of Antonia's estate was to generate fear in Francesco and Giovanni so that they would make restitution for the *tutela*.[170] It would be a dangerous principle to allow arbitrators to do what they were not directly permitted. The problem was to demonstrate just what was allowed to arbitrators by the language of the notarially encoded *compromissum*. The standard formula stating that arbitrators were to look into "omni et toto eo" causing controversy between the parties did not expand their competence beyond what had been expressly mentioned. In actuality, however, many *compromissa* did not state a specific issue, so Nello was effectively leaving the competence of the arbitrators to a verbal understanding reached before drawing up the *compromissum* and not necessarily specifically embodied in it.

> That general clause ["de omni et toto eo"] is restricted by what is specified so that it may not be extended to thoroughly different and separate matters, as is set forth in the *lex Sed et siquis § quesitum, ff. si quis cautionibus* (D. 2.11.4,4), in *lex Emptor § lutius, ff. de pactis* (D. 2.14.47,1). If we should say otherwise it would be purposeless to specify any matter in a *compromissum* if, notwithstanding that expression, that clause that "of all and everything etc." be understood as general for all matters; but because by that expression the *compromissum* is called special, not general, it would appear that that expression of specifics operates notwithstanding that clause. So that clause then makes a *compromissum* full and special, but it does not make it general. It is the case if one rightly considers *lex Si cum dies § plenum, ff. de arbitris* (D. 4.8.21,5,6).[171]

By thus resting the argument on the *compromissum*, Nello did not have to confront the problem of whether these arbitrators had acted as *arbitri* or *arbitratores*, for in either case their competence was still set by the *compromissum*.

Circumstances also restricted the scope of the *compromissum* according to texts of both civil and canon law. In addition the clause "de omni et toto eo" could not license proceeding beyond the terms of the *compromissum* anymore than an illicit agreement not to oppose anything resolved *extra compromissum*. Here Nello could cite in support the commentary of Guillaume de Cunh to D. 15.1.3,8, Baldo to the *Peace of Constance,* and *consilia* of the Florentine jurist Francesco Albergotti d'Arezzo (1304–76). Baldo certainly provided crucial support here. In no uncertain terms, with reference to canon law, he denied validity to any *sententia* that went beyond the *compromissum.*[172] It is also interesting that Nello dealt with the phrase "de omni et toto eo," which could be read, as he read it, more or less in the singular. Many *compromissa* also declared that the arbiter was commissioned "generaliter" to look into "omnes lites, causas, et questiones" that had arisen between the parties. That there was a plurality of disputes would admit a greater possibility of allowing what the arbitrators had done in this case in order to achieve a lasting and peaceful settlement between the parties. That Nello did not see a plurality of disputes, however, seems to have been fully consistent with prevailing jurisprudential practice. Angelo degli Ubaldi had on several occasions confirmed in *consilia* that arbitrators were limited to the issues set forth in *compromissa* and that general language did not give them license to inquire broadly into all facets of the relationship between parties.[173] Angelo had further argued in at least one case that a *laudum iniquum* could be appealed to the *arbitrium boni viri* even if a clause renouncing appeals had been included in the *compromissum.*[174] Clearly, despite the principle of inappellability of arbitration, the arbitrators were not given a blank check.

A second line of argument against the second *laudum* was that the statute concerning *instrumenta guarentigiata* did not preclude recourse to an *exceptio nullitatis* against a *laudum*. Here Bartolo in both his *consilia* and his commentary in D. 29.1.24 provided corroboration.[175] The Florentine statute forbidding that one seek nullification of a *laudum* also did not apply in this case: "it is especially true because, as appears in the beginning of the legislation, it requires the *laudum* be given *ex compromisso,* so it is clear that it does not prevent [seeking nullification in this case]."[176] By a more complex process of reasoning Nello further concluded that one could not divide the *laudum* into two clauses, one dispositive and the other conditional, and permit the latter to stand. What could not be done dispositively could not be done conditionally with regard to *iuris effectum.* Here he found support in Baldo and Bartolo.[177] "Nor does it matter that there are two sections, because they are connected and one depends on the other."[178] Bartolo himself had concluded in a *consilium* that "when an arbitration is invalid in one part it is invalid in total."[179]

Finally Nello had to interpret a passage from Bartolo's commentaries that seemed to support the *laudum*. In examining the *lex Quid tamen* (D. 4.8.21,12), Bartolo had allowed that "if there are different sections [in the *compromissum*], they can be separately pronounced upon, unless it is enacted otherwise."[180] An arbiter or arbitrator could resolve all issues at once, or do some at one time and the rest later, however he pleased, said Bartolo. Nello insisted that that did not mean Bartolo approved of the *laudum* but that if he seemed to it was because in his commentary the arbitrator did not act in an area where he could not. And one need not conjecture on what was in the arbitrator's mind in this case, said Nello, for he clearly had arbitrated on what had not been committed to him.[181] Interestingly, though he hinted that Bartolo was not as pliant on this point as it might seem at first glance, Nello did not fully explicate the Bartolist text. At the end of his commentary on *Quid tamen* Bartolo directly said that an arbitrator could correct his judgment only if the *compromissum* expressly allowed it. The principle behind this position was the same one that Nello had embraced in framing his opinion: "For an arbitrator does not have this power by common law. . . . But I think it can be attributed to him by the consent of the parties."[182]

Nello subscribed his opinion on 12 December 1411. It passed then to the hands of Filippo di messer Tommaso Corsini (1334–1421)—the same man whose arbitration provoked the ire of his kinsman seen above. Corsini found nothing to dissent from and nothing to add. He had reached the same conclusion in a similar case, as had his colleagues on that occasion, Pietro d'Ancarano (1330–1416), Onofrio and Marco da Perugia. The next day Roggeri d'Antignalla (fl. 1390s) reviewed the case and added some arguments to Nello's. He was especially concerned that legislation denying all recourse against an arbitration seemed too harsh. To temper this he pointed to the principle that no sin could be allowed by law. "Therefore such general terms contained in the statute must be taken reasonably so that nothing is done against the intent of the statute, otherwise fraud may be done to the law, that is, to that statute."[183] So it could not be maintained that one could not proceed against a *laudum* that exceeded the arbitrator's authority. Antignalla's argument, however, seems weak. There was no real question of fraud or *dolus* in this case. There were no doubts about the arbitrators' intentions. What was in question was if they had exceeded the licit bounds of authority given them by the parties—a separable issue. Antignalla was effectively only explaining one reason in general why arbitrators should be held to such limits.

It was two weeks later that a fourth jurist, Rosso d'Andreozzo degl'Orlandi (fl. 1400–1420s) penned his signature on the document. He added no further arguments or citations. Why at that comparatively late date his corroboration was seen as necessary or desirable one cannot say. What one can say is that the jurists, most especially Nello, had constructed a careful opinion that reaffirmed the voluntary nature of the *laudum* and *compromissum* while overturning a *laudum* in the name of legal principle, which was absolute and not at all voluntary.

Conclusions

Decisions like Nello's helped solidify the place of arbitration in the regularly functioning legal institutions of Florence. He helped to define the procedures and competence of arbitrators and thus the entire connection between arbitration and other processes. At the same time it was conceded that arbitrators had effective power within the limits set for them by the parties and even had latitude in how they chose to exercise their powers. As Angelo degli Ubaldi had put it in overturning a *laudum* where the arbitrator had been compelled to find in a certain fashion, "the nature of arbiting [arbitrium] is this, that the faculty of arbiting is free to make the judgment it wants."[184]

Nello's *consilium* did not resolve the dispute between the two uncles and their three nephews. All it did was overturn the second *laudum*. Where the matter went from there was up to the litigants. Division of monna Antonia's estate was probably resubmitted to arbitration. The grievances over the uncles' administration of the *tutela* were another issue. The nephews could let it drop, negotiate it directly with their uncles, submit it to arbitration, or formally litigate, depending on their desires, the strength of their case, and the determination of the opposition.

Unless the uncles conceded that there had been maladministration, the nephews would probably have to go to court to establish their right to *restitutio in integrum*. Where the existence or nature of a right was in question or where the nature of a relationship or personal status was open to doubt, litigation provided the best forum. Arbitration was best suited to issues of property, where facts or amounts were at issue, or to instances where relationships or status had been posed in terms of property.[185] In the arbitration's original form there seemed no question of right to the estate, the specifics of division were all that mattered. The nephews treated the matter of monna Antonia's estate as a property issue, as did the arbitrators. But the normative basis of the claim shifted between the first and second *laudum*—from the uncles' grant to their tutorial administration. In the process the relationship between the parties was also thrown open, as ward/guardian overlaid nephew/uncle. The relationships were partly defined by and made operable in rights over property.

Thus the nature of the dispute, its form and precise object, was not fixed. It varied by procedural context; given one form in the first *laudum*, it became something else the second time around. In court it was further redefined; now they were parties to an arbitration and the matter in dispute was the validity of the settlement, contested on the grounds of the competence of the arbitrators.

Arbitration had been designed to avoid litigation. At least it was broadly understood as a means to bring peace between the parties. But in this case, as in others, it had clearly failed to do so.[186] Rather than defusing animosities it had exacerbated them. Unilateral reformulation of the matter by the arbitrators was the problem. If arbitration was to succeed it had to be accepted by both parties. But why should the uncles (short of occupying a politically weak and untenable position) accept a *laudum* that left them with far less than they anticipated—and on the basis of something not submitted by them to the arbitrators? Their litigious protest makes sense (maybe especially if their division with the nephews was intended by them to make up for any shortcomings in the administration of their estate). So too does the attempt of the nephews to change the nature of the claim— that is, perhaps they were worried that by accepting the division in the first *laudum* they were relinquishing their right to claims arising from the *tutela,* and shortchanging themselves in the process. Why the arbitrators did this—other than, perhaps, from a sense of fairness—is hard to say.

Where the arbitration failed to make peace, the formal machinery of the law could step in, but not without regard to the arbitration. Here lies the legal ambiguity highlighted by our investigation. How did supposedly informal arbitration fit into formal law? In one sense by producing a transaction, a contract, whose enforcement was actionable in the courts. But also by being beyond appeal. Contracts could be judicially invalidated for a number of reasons, to be sure, and *lauda* too could be contested and in that sense, if not in a strict sense, appealed. A *laudum,* however, had to be contested on a point of law.[187] If right was conceded, the *laudum* could not be contested on an issue of fact. There it could indeed be "arbitrary." Its essential "rightness" was not then in question. Where it was, the law posed remedies. These formally presented remedies, especially in contrast to the greater informality of arbitration, could render the issues of right "true" and "unquestionable" and downplay any uncertainty in the law.[188] Yet such uncertainty existed. In the case we have considered, and in others, the problem lay in the factual and situational specificity of arbitration, on the one hand, and the (notarially enshrined) general charge to the arbitrator(s) to inquire broadly into the causes of dispute between the parties and do whatever it took to bring them peace, on the other. Nello, however, found it necessary to restrict arbitrators to a very narrow sense of the issue—at least to make clear that they could not unilaterally change the nature of the rights to which they were theoretically providing equitable redress. Uncertainty also existed on the problem of appeals. Martone has argued, based on a reading of Luigi Lombardi's work on forensic jurisprudence, that jurists were only responding to clients' interests in permitting appeals of *lauda.*[189] However, for every party seeking to overturn a *laudum,* there was also one seeking to uphold it. While allowing litigation on these points may have played into the hands and pockets of practicing jurists, they were also offering "logical" solutions (*verus conceptual exegesis*) that fit their sense of justice. In the last analysis, their allegiance was to the just legal order of society; and the best guarantee of that was the law in all its formality and texts. So *lauda* could not be appealed, and they could. So equity stood in contrast to legality, and it was subsumed within the latter.

Jurists like Nello and the others who have been mentioned were professionally wedded to notions of justice and right (*ius* and *iustitia*). Their training suited them for contested and doubtful issues of law as emerge in formal litigation. They may have been as happy to leave legally insignificant issues of "fact" to arbitration. But in so doing they were also according enforceable standing to findings whose justice was open to doubt. On the other hand, the jurists also

embraced notions of equity and the goal of social peace and order
fostered by arbitration.[190] Jurists were also familiar with arbitration
at first hand. They served as arbitrators for kin and friends. They had
problems of their own arbitrated. As members of the property-own-
ing elite they could see the utility of arbitration's speedy and informal
procedure. What we see taking shape in the opinions before us is an
interesting intermediary procedure. By holding down the scope of
the arbitration to the issue(s) assembled by the parties, while giving
the arbitrator power to inquire into all aspects of the parties' relationship and actions touching on the issue(s), the jurists were placing
arbitration midway between the formal and abstract, or arbitration
designed "to reduce the infinite variety of individual conflict cases to
standard uniform units so that they may be handled with dispatch and
with demonstrable fairness," and the informal, or arbitration that
attempts "to deal with the total relationships and total social personalities of the parties, thereby admitting the unique nature of every
case."[191] The "equity" arrived at in every case could thus be
grounded in "right" and mask any fundamental inequities between
the parties. The outcome of arbitration need not be any fairer; a party
with an advantage could still use it.[192] But the ideology of fairness in
the arbitration would survive, especially as the courts posed as the
guarantors of it.

With the enhancement of enforcement and validation by the formal law of courts and jurists, arbitration grew as a thriving legal
institution in Florence and elsewhere. As "facts" were resolved in
arbitration, people could become more aware of the rights defining
them, especially as *lauda* clothed them in proper notarial legal language, so that their sources and terms could become apparent. Here
too arbitration was an intermediate form—not as rule-centered as
litigation but not as fact-oriented as more informal mechanisms.
Rules were always implicit, even if not explicitly abstracted from
events (any more than the arbiter was usually fully abstracted from
prior ties to the parties). They could be made explicit in contesting a
laudum. Rules and facts are never fully separate in disputes.[193] Exchange of claims and allegations can reveal what the rules are, what
facts are important, and what are not.

Arbitration, finally, may have played an important role in the
growth of law and the decline, never linear, of violent self-help. The
effectiveness of legal procedures in medieval Europe "was dependent

less on the coercive powers of officials, than on the preparedness of parties to accept the procedures of the court, and on their willingness to accept court judgements or to come to terms informally."[194] The more frequently people resorted to arbitration the more familiar and comfortable they would be with the law and the more they might escalate their legal tactics to the field of formal litigation, and the more likely would be their success there.[195] Nor is it true that norms invoked in arbitration were always general and imprecise, in contrast to the precise rules at play in litigation.[196] The object in dispute and the normative language to encapsulate it were both negotiated as a dispute moved along.[197] We have seen examples. The matters in arbitration were fairly precise.[198] Rights and interests could be clearly identified, including interests of others who might bring pressure to keep the parties to the peace. Even where they did not succeed—and in the last analysis, terminating the dispute lay with the parties, as did framing it in the first place—and did not reestablish social relationships, they could bring some sort of closure to the immediate issue and provide time, a delay, during which a real settlement might be arranged.[199] In sum, arbitration was not one-dimensional, especially not in its crucial intermediary position as a form of dispute processing appended to the legal system of a city like Florence.

Notarial evidence suggests that Florentines let themselves be caught between contradictory norms. On the one hand, impelled by an ideology of honor, they identified and defended their interests by a variety of means, most of them public and legal. These actions had led at least one prominent historian of Renaissance Florence to label the society "litigious."[200] On the other hand, as the formulas of arbitrations state, they were also concerned to avoid "scandals" and to keep themselves from being "molested" by suits. This sentiment was captured perhaps best by the humanist Leon Battista Alberti:

> Lawsuits are types of enmities. Wise men say that he who needs a doctor is not well, he who needs a judge is worse. Such needs would occur rarely where there is good rule. Often seeking back a debt with rigor and too much diligence makes the ingrate man become an enemy. Lawsuits have in themselves nothing but vexation, expense, care, anger, and suspicions, perhaps also shame. All know you are litigating: few understand which of you speak the truth. And what reasonable man will not judge it better sometime to lose part of his property than to consume time, thoughts, savings, efforts only to obtain the victory?[201]

Where does arbitration fit in? Was it really an alternative to the enmity of litigation? Or was it only a more quiet manner of disputing?

Most simply put, arbitration was extremely flexible. Florentines filled it with complex problems and relationships; they coaxed a range of functions from it. So it was both another way to litigate, and a way to avoid litigating. It was used by all sorts of people. And, while not all legal or other issues entered its purview, it handled more problems, and more difficult ones, than legal historians or anthropologists have suspected.

The relationships that came into arbitration under Giacomini's pen varied widely—from close kin to nonkin, including, occasionally, institutions (rural communes or monasteries). It is hard to imagine that the type of relationship was a sole determinant driving parties to arbitration rather than litigation.[202] The quality of relationship also varied greatly—from amicable (and so issuing at times in collusive judgments) to outright hostility, as in the Peruzzi and Canacci vendettas. If there was a common denominator, it was simply the desire to avoid more public means of managing conflict. That desire was partially motivated by the nature of a relationship; kin had more reason to keep things quiet.[203] By statute they could be constrained to arbitration. But as the quote above from Alberti indicates, the major factor was a calculation of the "costs" of litigating, or fighting. The eventual costs of arbitration, as some examples show, might still be too high, but they may have been more tolerable as a rule.[204] Nor does it necessarily appear that arbitration, as a less formal mode of procedure, considered the total relationship between the parties as opposed to a narrow legal issue, as some anthropologists maintain.[205]

There was also no simple or small list of issues that were placed before arbitrators. There were limits. Some matters were precluded, by their nature or by law, from being submitted to arbitration—marital status, for example.[206] According to legal historians like Martone, arbitration was suited to factual issues; matters of status and the determination of norms, or of priority among them, did not come to arbitration. While it seems certain that the professional and political mechanisms monopolized the formulation and interpretation of norms, matters of status were not so clearly beyond the purview of arbitrators, at least indirectly. Property and status were not, and are not, so easily separable in practice. When an arbitrator or arbitrators determined someone had a property right as consequence of being someone else's heir, he or they were also effectively making that person an heir, consecrating a status.[207] Is that not what happened when arbitrators said that Giovanni di Guccio was in no way heir to his father and so had no obligations for return of a dowry?[208] Nor were parties always putting the real issue before their arbitrators. When Michele di messer Lapo da Castiglionchio went to arbitration with his wife, Antonia, was the issue simply her *alimenta* or was it the entire nature of their marital relationship? To say, with the legal level of the text, that a particular arbitration entailed a "debt" (and we have seen how ambiguous that category must be) is not to say that it, therefore, did not concern status and relationships. As Comaroff and Roberts point out, a debt may precisely be the relationship. To pay off the debt would thus be to constrain the relationship, to close off certain avenues. So Antonia's pressing of her credit over Michele defined their relationship, for some time at least, as one of separation.[209] Issues brought to arbitration were also obviously complex in many cases and were designed as, or became, part of a series of moves and strategies, in litigation and other arbitrations. Complex issues were not easily resolvable, despite the ideology of peaceful settlement that pervaded the notarial language and legal rules of arbitration. Arbitration settlement might also still seem too costly to abide by.

Even the legal language investigated by Martone reveals that arbitration transcended the simple dichotomies of law vs. equity, normative interest vs. fact, formality vs. informality, inappealability vs. reduction to reasonable judgment. Though these categories pervaded the early procedural description of Guglielmo Durante, they were elided in notarial formularies. So it was that Bartolo, while perpetuating the distinctions between formality and informality, and law and equity, left out any distinction between normative interests (*ius*) and facts.[210] And while there was no direct citation of the particular norms of civil and canon law in arbitrations, the law still lurked in the background. Issues could still be reformulated for treatment in litigation and *lauda* were contested in Florentine courts.

Martone emphasizes the "familiarity" of arbitration—of the parties to each other, of the arbitrators to them, and the "familial" basis of the interests and strategies transacted. But just as clearly nonkin were involved in arbitration. Close relationships were not always in question, as has already been pointed out. Distant, even unknown arbitrators (e.g., lawyers) might be more evidently neutral than closely related persons who, after all, had their own view of matters and their own interests. But Martone's point goes deeper. It is that the spheres of public and private were being delineated in Renaissance cities. In that context arbitration could safeguard familial interests of both parties, whether or not they were of the same family (in his terms a solidary lineage aligned with a patrimony).[211] However, in its uses arbitration also severed or attenuated elements of that familial solidarity—collective liability for debts and penal matters, the holding of property in common between brothers. In establishing debts and ordering payment, arbitration also eroded the patrimonies of debtors. Generally only one person represented his family in arbitration. The family's interests were what, and as, he, or she, saw them. Arbitration had too many possible uses for one to say it functioned unilaterally for the good of families, even of those families with greater resources who had recourse to arbitration more frequently than others. Arbitration provided a peaceful outlet for managing disputes, one that remained relatively close to the parties and in their control but that also put a third party between them to take the decision-making (though not enforcing) onus off them, at least in appearance. Because its theoretical basis was transactional, however, it also could function as little more than a contract.

Arbitration was thus, at least at the beginning of the fifteenth century, a creative moment in legal and social practice.[212] The locus of creativity was at times the arbitrator(s), at times the parties. The range of creativity in form and content was great. As in all areas of creativity, there were some failed efforts and many cases of following a known tried path when it was perhaps not appropriate. But by and large arbitration worked, if not to settle matters always, then at least to give expression to them in some form.

2

•

DISPUTE PROCESSING IN
THE RENAISSANCE
Some Florentine Examples

•

Anthropological Conceptualization of Disputes

An anthropologist can interrogate the social actors. A historian, except for the most recent events, can "interrogate" only documents and other, equally passive forms of evidence. Anthropologists see this difference as an advantage for their discipline, as well as the rationale for their methodological reliance on fieldwork to uncover cultural meanings and social relationships that lie behind, beneath, and beyond the largely documentary material the historian is left with.[1] The result for anthropology has been an expansion of the weight accorded to culture, with fruitful (at times, also fruitless) debates on the relative force of culture in the face of social structure and material conditions.

Historians have eagerly—perhaps too eagerly—plundered their sister discipline for insights and methods, especially in the study of family and kinship.[2] Increasingly, anthropological influences can also be detected in legal history.[3] And legal anthropology may be one of the subfields most fruitful of theoretical insight within the present discipline of anthropology.[4] One result has been the formulation of the concept of dispute as the object of study, and the processing of disputes as the empirical center of research.[5] Dispute is no longer construed, on the model furnished by Western jurisprudence, as a pathological outcome of broken rules but as a concomitant of social life.[6] A related development is the attention paid to modes of redress of grievances or even expression of them other than in formal litigation. This is a consequence both of the fact that formal legal methods are not always evident in societies anthropologists study and of the fact that the processing of a dispute often occurs in nonlegal or quasi-legal arenas, even when formal law is available.[7] Here is also where historians have made most frequent use of legal anthropology. They can rarely reconstruct disputes in the manner of the extended case method. Left largely with legal records, they can only surmise the motives, meanings, and emotions that would fill the gaps. So the functional dimensions as outlined by anthropologists have been invoked to supply the missing information. Another consequence has been the investigation of dispute modes other than litigation. The omnipresence of such alternatives during the "traditional" premodern period of Western history that ended with the formation of the modern nation-state with its bureaucratic apparatus has especially prompted anthropological interest on the part of medieval, Renaissance, and early modern historians.[8]

Even as anthropology has broken down distinctions between courts and other forms of settlement, between litigation and other aspects of dispute, it has arrived at a thorough criticism of the category of law itself.[9] Indeed, law as such is not the object of study, dispute processes are. Norms are reduced to epiphenomenal status or are seen to function as instruments of power, manipulated by disputants.[10] Law is treated as a language laden with potential meanings and ambiguities.[11] Disputants contrive a "paradigm of argument" in which actions are rendered in terms of normative referents, explicit or implicit. The plaintiff usually sets the paradigm; the defendant may accept and use it or assert a competing one. Success can be seen as a matter of construing as much of the history of a dispute over the widest set of normative referents possible.[12]

Legal historians, usually possessed of legal training and often on the faculties of law schools, have not called the category of law into question.[13] At most, some scholars have challenged any rigid distinction between justice and peace, between legal and extralegal means of settlement. Legal history has remained largely within what anthropologists term a "rule-centered paradigm," where law is related to social control and rules are seen to be decisive in the resolution of conflict.[14] The advantage ascribed to law over less formal dispute-settlement processes, then, can be said to be its laying out of a normative basis for decisions and thus a degree of certainty and predictability toward the future.[15] For legal historians it is more crucial to establish that law, and state mechanisms articulating it, came to replace and put down modes of self-help in dealing with disputes.

The process paradigm of legal anthropology resulted, in part, from inadequacies in the rule paradigm, and powerful criticisms have been launched against the latter by it, mainly to the effect that rules do not constrain or determine behavior or judicial settlements. But the process paradigm also has shortcomings. For one thing it reduces human motivation to a simple principle of maximizing and reduces the sociocultural order to a "given" within which strategizing behavior occurs.[16] For another, it does not adequately take rules into account. Rules do indeed figure in disputes, in all sorts of processes—from the formal to the very informal. Norms may not be separable from the processes in which they emerge. They are a form of power, codes manipulated in argument. But "a particular weakness of many recent anthropological approaches is the tendency to reduce law to dispute settlement and to view legal and social processes as not simply inseparable but identical" and thus to be "unable to conceptualise law as a theoretical object."[17] Not only for lawyers and sociologists, but for historians of Western societies, where law was (or was emerging as) a "separate" realm, this is a serious shortcoming. Even if one's object of study is extralegal dispute processes, the presence of legal (strictly speaking) means in the same society would seem to alter and circumscribe them.[18] More broadly, the functionalist assumptions of most legal anthropology (for all that they may owe to the functional assumptions of modern Western legal ideologies) preclude dealing with the legal in terms of the society under study, of its desires and sense of justice, guilt or innocence, and so forth.[19]

For the historian intent on reconstructing processes of dispute settlement in a society as distant as that of Renaissance Florence, anthropology provides useful warnings and corrections and much that is suggestive. Litigants—their values, thoughts, interests, and circumstances—will always remain elusive. But occasionally a corner of the veil shrouding them from the historian's sight is lifted. At odd moments a letter or an account in that peculiarly Florentine source, a *ricordanza*, will offer nonlegal insight into a dispute. Such fragmentary sources, read carefully and critically, can yield a new sense of disputing, legal and extralegal, in a city such as Florence. These

sources too have epistemological problems. No more than legal records were they concocted to meet the needs of historians; their
authors wished to present themselves in a certain light to contemporaries and/or posterity. Nor were these records totally nonlegal, for
by statute in Florence account books were admissible in evidence,
sometimes demanded, in cases of debt and contract or even in more
general property matters.[20] More simply, they contain the viewpoint
of only one of the parties; what is known of the other's position,
interests, and arguments is only paraphrased, at best.

Cultural Conceptualization of Disputes in Florence

One basis from which Florentines regarded disputes was the undeniable principle that one had a right to seek redress or revenge against
perceived injuries. The initiative lay with the offended party. Urban
communes, families, the church, and others could all seek to discour-
age violent self-help in the visible and dangerous form of armed
vendetta, but they could not deny one's ultimate right to it.[21] The
traditional historical view, richly nourished on a progressive positivis-
tic bias, considered the failure of governments to forbid all vendettas
and effectively eradicate them as a sign of weakness in the state that
would be remedied finally only in the nineteenth century. It seems
rather that there was no conceptualization within governing classes
or on the part of their learned advisers, such as the legal profession,
of governmental function encompassing and preempting the private
grievances of individuals.

However, the government tried to set limits in the name of the
public welfare. Vendettas were not to be conducted widely against an
enemy's kin, nor were they supposed to be carried out in any circumstances. Allowing a vendetta between relatives, for example, was seen
to carry a grave danger of potential chaos, so by statute kin were
enjoined to submit their disputes to arbitration.[22] Vendettas were
supposed to occur between kindreds; disputes within a kindred were
to be handled differently. One's revenge also need not result in
bloodshed. A formally arbitrated peace ending the conflict (with both
sides renouncing further right of vendetta, and the offended party
being awarded an appropriate monetary compensation, the whole
being guaranteed with sureties and oaths) could also work. So city
statutes underwrote enforcement of arbitrated settlements and formal acts of *pace*. They also enforced truces (*tregua*) where vendetta

was not to rage for a determined period. Thus it can be said that, though vendetta was a private prerogative, "on the other hand, these relations among private persons did not form completely outside the action of the 'State' itself, which influenced them and recognized and regulated the peaces and truces, protected them and imposed its laws on them, and often employed coercion."[23]

Vendetta was not well grounded in Roman law, so it could not be elevated to an extension of its principles of justice. It received no grounding in canon law. It could not be elevated to a principal mechanism in the maintenance of public order as it could be seen in a Germanic law book such as the *Lombarda,* which still had some play as a customary source of statutory law in some cities, including Florence. Rather vendetta seems to have been rooted in what were seen as individualistic or familial issues of honor. That was the level on which vendetta was accepted into academic and practical jurisprudence, the level where one finds expressed the sense that a man who does not look to his *fama* is insane and, though living, might as well be dead.[24] It is on that level that Florentines crafted their views and advice on the subject.

Anthropologists have come to see feud as another form of exchange relationship, analogous to kinship and friendship, in which debts and credits are calculated and paid back at some later moment. Reciprocity is not immediate or automatic; and thus political interests and strategizing can operate in the interval.[25] Certainly Florentines were aware of the time factor and of the need to weigh options and assess one's relative strengths. Not seldom, in Florence and elsewhere, does one run across advice to those who have suffered injury to bide their time, plan quietly, and seize the opportunity with whatever means are then at hand to enjoy their revenge. In the cynical formulation of the humanist Leon Battista Alberti in the mid-fifteenth century, "taking revenge is a lengthy experience, often deceptive, always linked to many dangers and the growth of even more harmful possibilities. For vendetta one must use caution, reason, time, and manner. Therefore one needs prudence much more than courage, advice more than arms."[26] Yet the advice of the fourteenth-century proverbial moralist Paolo da Certaldo was not much different: "Never make vendetta or have it made, because vendettas destroy the soul and the body and possessions. If you are injured, help yourself with reason and you will overcome every obstacle."[27] Of course, "reason" was also a common synonym for justice and law, so this is a

nicely multivalent statement. In accord with it was the thinking of
Francesco di Tommaso Giovanni, a Florentine who recorded numerous favors and slights to keep memory of them alive and to pay them
back as opportunity offered, though "not in order to start a vendetta."[28]

For all these warnings about the difficulty of vendetta and the need
for patience, men like Paolo da Certaldo still found that "the first joy
is making vendetta; sorrow is to be offended by one's enemy."[29]
Florentines' first thoughts were of revenge. Those thoughts might be
quickly dismissed, but they were there, redolent with the cultural
demands of offended honor.[30]

Vendetta was not something to rush into over any slight, nor was
it for everybody. Notoriously it was matters of personal injury, grave
insult, or physical harm, most especially killing, that generated vendettas.[31] Still, there was certainly nothing to prevent one from seeking peace and compensation in the face of a murder (or even suffering
the insult without retaliating, that being the lot of the poor and
powerless), nor, on the other hand, was there anything to prevent a
property issue from escalating into a point of honor. Then if, as at
least one historian has maintained, armed vendetta was accorded less
esteem in the fifteenth century, it must be because it did not prove as
useful in contrast to other means of processing disputes.[32] Inaction
("lumping it"), private settlement means (negotiation or mediation),
forms of third-party arbitration, and litigation flourished instead.
Litigation could also be a means of revenge. The legal process can be
visualized, according to Marc Galanter, as a game whose rules can
both attract and repel potential "players." Those who repeatedly use
the system stand a better chance of winning, and they are likely to be
wealthier and in a position to hire the quintessential "repeat player"
and broker, the lawyer.[33] In part perhaps to ease the use of law in
Florence, and simply from shared assumptions, legal procedure in
fact tended to mimic vendetta. Initiative lay largely with the litigants
as to when and how to press a complaint. They could break off
proceedings, and they could negotiate or compromise on the enforcement of judgments.[34]

Florentines harbored no illusions about courts and legal procedures, in which they might participate as judges as well as litigants.
They displayed a healthy wariness before the law's labyrinthine and
mystical ways, even as they weighed its use to them as a weapon in
their vendettas.[35] Not only would litigation possibly raise the other

party's enmity and create public scandal, once one got into court there was no guarantee the process would be fair and impartial. The *Decameron* had railed against judges "who in order to convey the impression that they are zealously seeking the truth, often have recourse to cruelty and cause falsehood to be accepted as proven fact, hence demonstrating, for all their proud claim to be the ministers of God's justice, that their true allegiance is to the devil and his iniquities."[36]

The complex system of justice, conducted in legal Latin by academically trained jurists and experienced notaries was, as Gene Brucker has noted, prone to manipulation.[37] Alberti, for one, despaired before the mass of mutable legislation drafted by Florentines, which he contrasted to the mere twelve tables that had sufficed in the early Roman republic.[38] Further, by one count there were some thirty-eight different courts of first instance in fifteenth-century Florence. Even though not all of them were available to any one litigant in any one instance, there were still a number available, with no hierarchy among them and with a range of procedures from fully judicial to more executive bodies with some judicial authority.[39] Use of money and friends was especially effective, if only because the judges themselves were not legal professionals in every case.[40] Jurists were also subject to criticism. In the early sixteenth century Francesco Guicciardini, himself a university-educated and practicing jurist, penned both criticisms and defenses of his profession. A general distrust of the lawyers' subtle expertise was his target.[41] He defended the variability of judgments and the variety of opinions among jurists on the grounds that general rules could not comprehend all cases, and that resulting judicial discretion was not therefore arbitrary.[42] On the other hand he scored jurists' tendency to present a phalanx of authorities rather than cogent arguments.[43] He was even led to speculate whether the supposed Turkish practice of quick judgment was not as just or even more just than the result of the slower and more deliberate procedure employed in his land.[44] He chose to ignore, however, the allegations that lawyers succumbed to the interests and pressures of leading citizens like the Medici.[45]

The legal system could indeed be employed as a weapon against one's enemies, but one had to beware of it backfiring, just as one had to fear retaliation from the opposition. Like vendetta, litigation carried risks, notably the risk of losing. The case might also drag on too long. Delaying tactics could force the opponent to surrender, concede, or compromise short of a final judicial disposition of the case (as often happens today). In a revealing statement, Guicciardini explains

> In my various administrative posts I have observed that whenever disputes came before me which for one reason or another I wanted to settle, I never mentioned a settlement. Instead by proposing various postponements and delays, I caused the parties to seek a settlement themselves. And thus, a proposal which would have been refused had I made it at the start, came to appear so attractive at the proper time that they would beg me to make it.[46]

The delays and circuitous goings-on of the legal process could thus also be conducive to reaching a peaceful, mutually agreeable out-of-court settlement.

The historian finds a certain apprehension among Florentines at leaving their fate to others. Lapo di Giovanni Niccolini, for example, entered into a compromise "for prosperity and peace and repose of the said parties . . . so that they do not have to litigate." The arbitrator in this case was a notary whom Lapo considered "my kinsman and intimate and friend and well-wisher" ("mio compare e intimo e amicho e benivolo"). Lapo also acknowledged an obligation in this particular matter and so simply recorded the amount arising "when monna Tancia . . . defeated me and took it."[47] Similarly, when stuck for perhaps 500 florins as a result of going surety naively on one of his son's business deals, Lapo pursued an agreement (through the good offices of the same friend) that was only ratified by the court of the Mercanzia to which the case had gone.[48] Lapo had been canny enough to extract a verbal promise before witnesses, showing that he was aware of the sorts of evidence that carried weight in a court. But he had still reached an understanding before letting the legal process finish.

Yet even less formal arbitrated settlements could be unfair.[49] It was the motives and interests of the third parties that were in doubt and thus dangerous. Matteo Corsini ascribed to one arbitrator a mysterious, but damning, malevolence, to another greed and deceptiveness (*inganno*), ostensibly to facilitate the greed.[50] Deception is also what Giovanni di Pagolo Morelli claimed worked against his father in legal proceedings regarding usury in the episcopal court. "Everyone," including the bishop, cheated poor Pagolo, who found recourse "not by force of money but by reason and his diligence" only in Rome.[51]

Beyond possible inequities or downright fraudulent and deceptive practices, there was always the problem of having one's affairs become the center of public attention and scandal. One of the formulaic functions of *lauda* redacted by notaries was "obviare scandala oriri." Similar sentiments were expressed frequently as justification for various legislative enactments. But it was not just a formula. Florentines feared scandal.

The evidence garnered to this point—a limited sampling of the sorts of material found in *ricordi* and letters—can be summarized. They give voice to the language of revenge, of right and justice versus malevolence, deceit, greed, treachery. They betray an awareness of options for the expression and settlement of grievances, which were furthered or frustrated, depending on the individual's perspective, by the use of friends. From these materials, then, we can determine something of the interests and passions that fed disputes. But to see the connection between the parties' motivations and the way a dispute worked itself out, it is necessary to observe carefully the way some disputes unfolded.

Bernardo Machiavelli's Pregnant Servant

The first of two disputes we will consider in some detail is set down in the *ricordi* of Bernardo Machiavelli, a lawyer and the father of the famous Niccolò. Because of the son, Bernardo's *ricordi* were edited and published over thirty years ago, thus making them, and this incident, more widely known. Gene Brucker translated this segment of the *ricordi*.[52] The matter did not make it into court. The only document it generated remained private. Everything was deliberately kept quiet. Hence this dispute affords us a rare glimpse into a difficult nonlegal settlement involving, as it happens, blood kin related in the male line. This account in Bernardo's *ricordi* concentrates on his efforts to salvage his honor, rectify an insult, without escalating to scandalous proportions his quarrel with a kinsman. The terms he used to record his perceptions and the order in which he proceeded reveal a great deal about one Florentine's mode of dispute resolution.

In 1475 Bernardo's servant girl, Nencia, became pregnant. The matter came to Bernardo's attention on Wednesday, 17 October, by way of his wife, who had become suspicious. Giving her the opportunity to be alone with the girl, Bernardo returned to learn that his wife's flatteries, alternating with threats, had garnered admissions of pregnancy and the naming of Bernardo's relative, Niccolò d'Alessandro

Machiavelli, as the culprit. Nencia described her nocturnal trips across the roof to Alessandro's house while Bernardo's wife was pregnant and later, when Niccolò's wife was sick, how he had "used her" on the kitchen hearth in Bernardo's own house. Bernardo's reaction was to seek out his wife's brother, Giovanni Nelli, who had arranged for the girl's stay in his home. Over breakfast the next morning he informed Giovanni and his brother Carlo. Then the three men and Bernardo's wife confronted Nencia again. They expressed their doubts to her, wondering why Niccolò would have anything to do with her when he had a young and beautiful wife. She stuck by her story and added details of staying with Niccolò two or three times a week when they were "in villa."

To this point Bernardo had established the substance of the allegations of paternity, including the fact that this had not been a casual or brief encounter. He had also enlisted the presence of his brother-in-law, Giovanni, who was also insulted by these acts, for he had given assurances to the girl's father, who was a "friend" of his. Giovanni and Carlo agreed that Bernardo should confront Niccolò with this.[53] Bernardo in the meantime insisted that the girl leave his house immediately. Her pregnancy, when visible, would bring shame on him. The brothers, however, advised that Bernardo deal with Niccolò first and then worry about the girl. So on Saturday Bernardo encountered Niccolò in Piazza Santa Felicita. By Bernardo's account, Niccolò claimed that he had wanted to say something for six months. The truth, according to Niccolò, was that the father was really Francesco Renzi, who often stayed by himself in Niccolò's villa. Niccolò declared that his only fault lay in not telling Bernardo.

Bernardo was not buying any of it. His anger was scarcely concealed:

> Whence I answered complaining bitterly of the injury [*ingiuria*] he had done me, which was grave in itself but worse in that he was a neighbor with a common wall and a close relative; and that I had never done anything to him or his father, and that I did not know how he could hold me in so little esteem [*sí poco conto di me*] that if it had truly been Francesco, he was often with me both here and in villa and yet he had not made it known so that I might take steps that my home not become a bordello; and that he well consider the nature of this matter, that this girl was not a whore but was of good but poor folk from Pistoia, and that her father and brothers could be such that one had to take account of them and that I no longer wanted her in my house; and that I could honorably do no other than tell Giovanni Nelli who had given her to

me or make her father and mother come for her; and that I did not know what they might do with the girl, who said it was Niccolò her father would want to retaliate against, and that he think about that.[54]

Niccolò still claimed it had been Francesco Renzi; it was no concern (*peso*) to him to have sex with the servant, as he had a wife with sisters. But he had also tacitly accepted the normative framework Bernardo implicitly referred to. He agreed Bernardo had cause for complaint and redress, he disagreed only that the complaint should be lodged against him.[55]

The next day Bernardo saw Giovanni Nelli, who advised patience. The following day Bernardo once again ran into Niccolò, who this time revealed that he had not told Bernardo about Nencia and Francesco because Francesco had helped Niccolò get at a beautiful girl in the house of Francesco's uncle, maestro Raffaello da Terranuova. So Niccolò was "consenziente" in Francesco's liaisons with Nencia, but he claimed he was now free of the grasp of the devil that had possessed him. Bernardo termed this a "fine cover" ("bella coverta"). The girl had not said anything about Francesco and if what Niccolò said now was true that only made matters worse, since he had seen fit to pander (*ruffianare*) Bernardo's servant to a friend and make Bernardo's house into a bordello so "that all night my house stood open and people entered and left." Bernardo told Niccolò that Giovanni Nelli knew of the pregnancy, and before he sent for the girl's father he wanted to talk to Niccolò "to see if he could do something to get out of scandal." And Bernardo warned that Niccolò not put on an act ("qualche forma") with Giovanni.

Three evenings later Giovanni came to dine and spend the night with Bernardo and revealed that he had just spoken with Niccolò. Though Niccolò stuck to the same story, Giovanni suggested that the way to avoid the scandal of the girl's father finding out was to find a woman to take her in until the birth and provide 25 florins for a dowry "to save his honor" (Giovanni's). Still protesting innocence, Niccolò nonetheless seemed receptive to the proposal. Indeed three days later Niccolò sought out Bernardo in his villa and said he had decided to say nothing to Francesco, on the pretext that it would be a waste of time, and carry this loss (*danno*) by himself since he had made a great error in allowing Francesco to do what Niccolò claimed he had done. He asked that Giovanni, Bernardo, and his wife not say anything to anyone about the matter.

So it was that on the twelfth day of November[56] the three men drew up a document by which Niccolò promised to pay Giovanni by the end of March 100 *lire* for Nencia's marriage.[57] There were no other witnesses "so that the matter might not become public." Six days later Giovanni reported that he and Niccolò had arranged for a monna Lisa "who raises babies" to take Nencia in at Niccolò's expense, and so she left Bernardo's. The following June Nencia's marriage was arranged.[58]

It had taken a month to settle the affair to everyone's satisfaction. That Bernardo saw it as over shows from the termination of the continuous narrative he devoted to it. Twice Bernardo spoke directly to Niccolò; then Giovanni spoke to him; then the three met to draw up and sign their agreement; thereafter Niccolò and Giovanni made arrangements for the girl. In effect Bernardo on the first occasion lodged an accusation against Niccolò and received a preliminary "not guilty" plea. On the second Bernardo got and rejected an explanation in defense. Niccolò gave in, though admitting nothing and giving in not to Bernardo but to Giovanni Nelli. Interestingly, the men then wrote up the settlement—in three copies with all three signing each. True, this was not a formal notarial instrument with seals and witnesses but a mere *scriptura privata*. The legality of the language may easily have been challenged, sanctions and contingencies uncovered. But the document was a record of a moral obligation, and a potential sanction lay to hand in communicating its substance to other kin.[59] It was something of an admission of guilt on Niccolò's part and proof of steps by Bernardo and Giovanni to repair their honor. And in practical terms, it was unlikely that anyone would challenge the agreement; Niccolò held up his end of the bargain. No outside help had been enlisted, other than the brother-in-law Giovanni Nelli, who was as much a party to the injury as Bernardo. No other relatives had even been called in, much less neighbors or friends, or judges, jurists, and notaries. The principals were paternal cousins and neighbors (along with the brother-in-law of one). The matter at issue was the nature of their relations, called into question by an event of personal injury and honor. The process utilized for settlement was direct negotiation. The personal wrong was turned into (imprecise) monetary form; the relationship was preserved, even if not unscarred.

Here there was such a potential for scandal, such a concern for honor and reputation, that it all had to be hushed up. Honor demanded that Bernardo not overlook the insult of invasion of his house, by a kinsman he should have been able to trust, to compromise a nubile young woman who had been entrusted to his care. On the other hand, that these events had occurred did not speak well for his honor; they had to be kept quiet. Interestingly, all the dealings with Niccolò, who had violated Bernardo's house, took place in public thoroughfares and *piazze*—the arenas where male honor was asserted—not in the house (except for the final private agreement, when Niccolò might honorably be readmitted to it). As long as what had happened was not public knowledge and adequate redress could be arranged by private means, it was possible for Bernardo to operate in that manner. His was a vendetta that had to be private, that had to steer clear of the ways of the law, even of mechanisms such as arbitration. And Bernardo, it must be remembered, was himself a jurist. Laws and courts held no mystery for him; they apparently just were not appropriate for this matter. But law's brooding presence, as an institutional mechanism and as a body of rules, had a shaping hand in the dispute (as a negative, something to be avoided). His was the anguish of a wronged kinsman, but he also worked to maintain some semblance of normal kin ties with Niccolò. Bernardo had, however, also alluded to the vengeful wrath of the girl's father in seeking to put pressure on Niccolò, who notably did not change his story (his honor too was at stake!) but acted as if guilty (and certainly seems circumstantially guilty, as he did to Bernardo and Giovanni). For his part Niccolò shifted the blame to a friend of his who was in no way kin to Bernardo. However, this attempt to lessen Bernardo's sense of "injury" backfired when Niccolò amplified the story into a swap of nocturnal visits to serving girls, for then he was admitting to complicity in Francesco's alleged actions and to giving Francesco something that belonged to Bernardo.

The terms used in this affair display "paradigms of argument" at work. Each party tried to array things according to a particular range of meaning. To Bernardo the sexual affair was entirely illicit. Niccolò had "used" the girl like a whore (*mugea*) and turned his house into a bordello, or according to the second version of Niccolò's story, had "pandered." The image of the house as open all night to strangers especially reeks of a sense of violation of one's "being," a sense reinforced by the insistence on getting the girl out.[60] In contrast Niccolò had stated that there had been not a calculated violation of a relative's home but an infatuation (for the girl at maestro Raffaello's) that came of the *diavolo*, that gripped him and overcame reason. Bernardo's general characterization of the affair also differed from his cousin's. To Bernardo (and his perception was seconded by Giovanni Nelli) the matter amounted to *ingiuria*. *Ingiuria* is an ambiguous term, to say the least. In the context in which we encounter it, it is hard to say what all it encompassed. Even in the terminologically overburdened realm of law *ingiuria* (*iniuria* in Latin) was an indeterminate category.[61] Against this sense of injury Niccolò invoked two terms, the *peso* of the affair and the loss (*danno*) that he claimed belonged to Francesco Renzi but that he would take on. Niccolò's terms relate more to material or monetary quantity; he would not admit to doing *ingiuria* to his cousin, to violating his home, but he would make things right in terms of monetary compensation. *Ingiuria,* it would seem, went beyond material *danno* to matters of personal honor and status.

Finally it is worth noting that Bernardo's terms for Niccolò's story denied that it was true but did not accuse him directly of lying. The Renzi business was termed a *bella coverta*. He warned Niccolò not to employ *qualche forma* with Giovanni Nelli. These terms reveal an awareness that Niccolò needed a facade, a "cover," and show a reluctance to push Niccolò too far by accusing him of dishonesty.[62] The reality behind that cover was denied by Bernardo, but it seems he had to put up with it as part of the mechanism filtering the turbid waters of the case, in the absence of conclusive proof or confession that would lift the cover.

Oderigo di Credi's Adventures in Florentine Litigation

The Machiavelli episode was handled so as to prevent violent vendetta and public adjudication. Negotiation between the principals kept anger from growing and kept the girl's father uninformed. Earlier in the fifteenth century, however, the goldsmith Oderigo di Credi saw a property claim cycle through various litigious steps as direct negotiation failed from the start. This case, then, gives us a view of attitudes behind legal actions, in a matter between kin, where honor and property were interlaced from the outset.[63]

Oderigo characterized the set of events as litigation (*piato*). His attention was focused on the law. He began a process in the court of the Podestà on 1 December 1405 against Niccolò di Lotto degli Agli, nephew of Oderigo's father-in-law, Nofri di Simone degli Agli, and administrator of Nofri's estate. The Agli were an old magnate family. By the early fifteenth century their wealth was diminished and their political clout was minimal. But they still had a proud familial tradition and clearly commanded respect. The marriage of the relatively humble goldsmith Oderigo to an Agli heiress is indicative of how low the fortunes of one branch had fallen. Oderigo sought a *poderetto* near San Casciano, a house in the Agli neighborhood of San Michele Berteldi in Florence, and the house next to it where Niccolò currently lived, but two-thirds of which belonged to Nofri by the terms of Simone degli Agli's will and by a *laudum* dividing the inheritance. Nofri had leased these properties on a five-year lease when he left Florence in 1398, and Oderigo had the leases and account books to prove it. Oderigo was clearly well informed of the pertinent legalities and could name the notaries who had redacted the relevant transactions.

The one house had been rented originally to Lotto and later, after Nofri had established himself in Padua, had to be rented again to his son Niccolò. Niccolò in turn had pressed a suit against his uncle. Oderigo di Credi could not conceal his intense dislike for Niccolò in describing how he "unjustly and malevolently and like an evil man" acted "without any reason" and without informing Nofri beforehand ("senza mai niente fargliene a sapere") but only after he won the judgment (by a letter in Oderigo's possession).[64]

The judgment was invalid, claimed Oderigo, because it was contrary to the statutes of Florence, which required the presence and summoning of the other party to litigation. Faced with Niccolò's betrayal (*tradimento*), Nofri had intended to return to Florence to recover his rights, when war broke out between Padua and Venice. During the war Nofri, his second wife, and his son Mone, died of plague. Nofri's daughter Caterina was Oderigo's (second) wife. Before her death in 1404 she left him a son and a daughter.

Florentines, like most Italian urban dwellers, thought that property, especially real estate, should pass to sons. Nofri degli Agli had no son. His property went to his daughter (and thence to his son-in-law). The close domestic relationship and agnation to his girl won out over a more general agnation and male orientation that might have placed the property in Niccolò di Lotto's hands. Nofri's will overrode the Florentine statute on intestate inheritance (similar to those of many other Italian cities) that would have directed the bulk of the estate to Niccolò.[65] Kinship and honor were not (and are not) separable from property, especially the kinds of property most closely associated by Florentines with the entire meaning of *casa*.[66] For Nofri not to pass his property to Niccolò was, if not to deny kinship, certainly to devalue the relationship. The previous dispute between Nofri and Niccolò may have anticipated the will and already have gone a long way to devalue the relationship. Likewise Niccolò's attempt to keep the property from Oderigo was also a denial of kinship to this Paduan goldsmith.[67]

Personal relations, not just property rights, were at stake. Indeed prior property management, including the lawsuit, "locked" Oderigo into certain steps as he began to certify his rights. Previous judgment regarding the Agli houses, if nothing else, seems to have deterred Oderigo from pursuing his claims on them. The legal machinations he undertook were all aimed at securing title to the *poderetto* of Macia Lunga near San Casciano. In any event, following his wife's burial, Oderigo moved to Florence, a newcomer intent on "seeking to have my rights [*ragione*] and reacquire the dowry of Caterina's mother . . . which belonged to my son Andrea by inheritance." He began by gathering all the written evidence and documents he could and then going to Niccolò with the material "showing him plainly my every intent" (which Niccolò had obviously not done to Nofri). Niccolò was not pleased. "Like one long corrupted [*per adietro magagnato*], with little charity or love, and even less patience, he began to call me a villain and threatened me, believing by these means to turn his will into right [*ragione*], as he had done with Nofri."[68] Oderigo retreated in the face of Niccolò's *fellonità* and the solid support his kin gave him. He turned instead to the courts, produced his evidence, and won an immediate judgment of *tenuta*.[69]

Now Oderigo's problems really began. Niccolò, "lacking honor and a desire for it, like an unjust man," went to the Sei delle Vendite and put it to them that the property should be sold to cover Nofri's *prestanze*. The Sei, a body "authorized to confiscate and sell the patrimonies of tax delinquents,"[70] published their intent to do so regarding Nofri's property and Oderigo rushed "humbly" to place himself under their *balia* and told them of his case against Niccolò. The Sei then began to act judicially, summoning Niccolò, confronting him with Oderigo's arguments and listening to his response (again depicted in highly negative terms by Oderigo). The Sei constrained the parties to a formal compromise "to see who had the right, he or the Commune or I." Oderigo was content that right was on his side, but "not being informed how they live in Florence" he did not realize that among the Sei, who were the arbitrators, Niccolò had a friend, Francesco di Giorgio Canigiani.[71] Niccolò's preemptive move to the Sei had thus cleverly kept the case away from the more professional and impartial court of the Podestà, a natural venue for it and the place where Oderigo therefore had begun. The Sei set a procedure giving the parties three days to assemble their arguments and evidence, intending to turn it all over to a jurist (*savio*) whose determination would become their sentence. And so they did, giving the case to Antonio da Romena, a relatively modest figure among jurists active in Florence at the time and not himself of a Florentine family.[72] He returned a sealed *consilium* in three days (at the litigants' expense). Niccolò's friend violated the sworn secrecy of the committee and revealed the contents of the *consilium* to him prior to its formal reading into the sentence. The jurist had found in Oderigo's favor, so Niccolò went out to the *poderetto* (now promoted to a *villa* by Oderigo) and vandalized it, the buildings, furnishings, and tools. Then the Sei added as a condition to the judgment in Oderigo's favor that he pay 40 florins for Nofri's *prestanze* within ten months (only 20 if he paid in six months)—something Oderigo termed "fuori d'ogni ragione e consiglio" and "fuori d'ogni compromesso." Oderigo's refusal to pay led to his being summoned back by the Sei and condemned for 200 *lire* by Niccolò's friend Canigiani. The ostensible reason for this payment was that Nofri had two children by his second wife and they were left with nothing. Oderigo, however, protested that Niccolò's machinations had in fact defrauded the children of at least 600 florins, that the houses in Niccolò's possession half-belonged to these two.[73] Oderigo protested that the Sei had no authority to do this to him, neither by the instrument of *compromissum* nor by institutional jurisdiction.[74] "But in truth, because I was not used to Florence, and not seeing myself supported by any friend, I decided to go ahead and pay the 20 florins rather than litigate with them." Later when he confronted Niccolò for the *masserizie* he had carried off from the farm, he got only ridicule ("fessi beffe di me"). Again Oderigo decided on silence "because I had had too many misadventures."

Niccolò, however, had more torment in store for Oderigo. He went to the archdiocesan court and claimed that the conditional bequests of monna Taddea, the sister of Nofri and Lotto, by terms of whose will the farm had come to the brothers (Nofri later buying out Lotto), had never been fulfilled. By the will the farm should revert to the hospital of Santa Maria Nuova. Oderigo responded to the suit by pleading ignorance but a willingness to comply, noting that it had been thirty years since Taddea's death. The vicar seemed sympathetic to the fact that Oderigo was facing a nuisance suit from an enemy, but he gave him fifteen days to respond with evidence of payment, which Oderigo quickly secured. He made his proofs to the episcopal court and received a written release of all claims (*finis*).

Niccolò then went to the Gabelle officials and claimed that Oderigo had had two wives but paid no *gabelle* on their dowries, the penalty for which would hit Oderigo hard. He defended himself in this forum now and on matters seemingly far removed from the property rights initially at issue. He claimed he had never received a dowry for Caterina, though he had made public confession of one. The Gabelle officials set a tax of 100 florins with a penalty of 5 florins, 3 quattrini. Then they wanted him to pay the *gabelles* for his two married sisters.

> Finally after so much, by the grace of God, I got out of the hands of them and the maddened Niccolò di Lotto, who wanted to see the end of what I could do and ingeniously sought every way and means to do me every evil that he could, with no right or reason but to want my goods; he had done this to me, by merit of the good I did to Caterina, who was his blood cousin and my wife, and for whom I bore that love one must have for a creature, and likewise for all of them [the Agli], as seen before. And so, seeing him employ so many cruelties on me, and not being deceived, none of them [the Agli] thought to be sorry for me and beyond measure they harden their hearts; but, not wanting to waste my substance, and having more regard for my family than for him, I bore myself with that patience I thought best. But if ever the time come that I can pay it back, I will do whatever is possible, and so I have written this memory of it to have it always before my mind.

The spirit of vendetta burned brightly in Oderigo. He had seen Niccolò use every means available, judicial or not, to attack him. He would bide his time. To make sure the wounds were fresh and tender, he then appended an itemized and annotated list of the expenses he had incurred in these various processes with Niccolò. The list is instructive of how expensive litigation (seen by some historians as one of Florentines' favorite sports) could be. Most of the expense was for documents, such as two florins for a copy of Caterina's mother's dotal instrument and two more for a copy of the compromise of division between Nofri and Lotto degli Agli, and another five for a copy of the *laudum*. Oderigo's annotations concerned the legal value of these papers; Simone degli Agli's will, for example, allowed one to see "that Niccolò di Lotto was not telling the truth that everything he had was his but that he had usurped it." In sum Oderigo spent fourteen florins for copies of documents relating to Nofri's ownership rights and copies of the previous *piato* between Niccolò and the absent Nofri, as well as a further two florins to the son of the notary to search through his father's *imbreviaturae* and two florins to persons living in the vicinity of the *villa* for *informazioni* prior to litigation.

His own litigation had also cost Oderigo dearly. His narrative neglects to mention, but his expense list does not, the services of his *procurator*, ser Guido di ser Tommaso, who presented his case in court, and of his notary, ser Piero, "who wrote up my *processi* when I litigated." The services of these two cost Oderigo five florins, six *lire*, and fifteen and a half soldi (most of it going to ser Guido). He also paid ser Vanni Stefani one *lira*, thirteen soldi to stay out of the case "so that he would not act as *procurator* against me." The services of a herald, required at various points in the procedures, ran to one florin, three soldi; and twice examining six witnesses cost one florin, two *lire*, and two and a half soldi. But in his narrative these elements were neglected. There the story was Oderigo resisting Niccolò, and no intermediaries were mentioned.

Then the process before the Sei delle Vendite ran up the costs. There was, of course, the twenty florins Oderigo had to pay on the final judgment. But there was also an expenditure of one *lira*, ten soldi for ser Piero and ser Guido to put the issue before the Sei: "thus, when we made a compromise in them, it was first necessary to give them a question, which cost me, between ser Piero who made it and ser Guido who saw that it stood well, and also to come to speak to the Sei on my behalf." It cost four florins for the Sei's notary to draw up the *compromissum* and *laudum*, plus twenty soldi to the notary and six *grossi* for the cost of the *consilium* of Antonio da Romena (presumably Niccolò also paid six). The releases from the episcopal court (two florins) and the Gabelle officials also cost dearly (seven florins, three *lire*, one and a half soldi). The total ran to 56 florins, 22 *lire*, 78 and a half soldi—all not counting the subsequent list of expenses incurred to make good the damage caused to the *villa* by Niccolò.[75]

In the long term this money resulted in a decent investment. Much of the rest of Oderigo's *ricordi* were taken up with details of receipts from the farm. It occupied pride of place at the top of his list of properties in the 1427 *catasto,* with a value of over 182 florins. Oderigo possessed a modest patrimony in that year to provide support for a household of five; the returns from the farm of Macia Lunga were vital.[76]

In this set of affairs face-to-face negotiation failed. Indeed in gathering his documents, and with awareness of the previous process Niccolò had conducted against Nofri, Oderigo seems to have anticipated its failure, though he also may thereby have promoted its failure. What he did not expect was Niccolò's vindictive use of legal procedures, hauling him before the Sei, the episcopal court, and the Gabelle officials. Niccolò was more willing to let outside institutions have the family's property than to let it fall into the hands of his cousin's husband and son. To this end he enlisted the aid of the other Agli and of his friends. For his part, Oderigo did not have any real preexisting relationship with his wife's cousin and so had nothing in that realm to lose by pressing his case, especially when the rest of her kin lined up with Niccolò.

Also interesting in this episode is Oderigo di Credi's colorful language. It stands in such contrast to the formal legality of the documents he gathered, to the terms that must have been used in the *procurator*'s arguments, and to the terms in which the jurist Antonio da Romena must have put his decision. The jurist had to be coldly principled and stay close to the legally relevant facts. He had to look at both sides of the issue in normative terms. Da Romena's *consilium* in Oderigo's case has not survived, to my knowledge, but a good idea of how he proceeded can be derived from another *consilium* that deals with the problem, common with Oderigo's case, of succession to a mother.

> Whether a son may transmit to his sons a maternal inheritance not formally entered into, it seems so at first by the matter in the penultimate *lex* of the Codex, "On legitimate heirs" [C. 6.58.14], where it is said that an estate is sought for sons by the same right. The contrary is true that it is not transmitted and thus Bartolo expressly determines in the *lex Ventre* of the Digest, "On acquiring an inheritance" [D. 29.2.84], by the matter in the *lex* ii of the Codex, "On the senatus consultum Orfitianum" [C. 6.57.2], and by the *novella § In novissimo* of the sole *lex* in Codex, "On taking up fallen legacies" [C. 6.51.1,5]. To the penultimate *lex* of the Codex, "On legitimate heirs" [C. 6.58.14], Bartolo responds in the afore-alleged place that a son suc-

ceeds his mother by right. "By right" is understood, namely, if it is entered into by a man as we said in compensation, as in Codex, "On compensation," *lex* ii [C. 4.31.2], and it is therefore the conclusion according to Bartolo that the estate of a mother not entered into is not transmitted.[77]

There are no parties here or, rather they have been reduced to legal rights and allegations. Every statement is brought back to a text of the commentary of an authoritative jurist (here Bartolo).

A sense of this legal landscape informs part of Oderigo's presentation of himself—his sense of the justice and rightness of his case. It cannot help but be part of the thinking of a man who took his case to court, who seems from the outset to have thought in terms of *piato*. But Niccolò's resistance to these "just" claims met only with Oderigo's opprobrium. Niccolò's vengeful pursuit of the case in different venues, not seeking a judgment for himself but merely to damage his enemy, and his vandalism of the *villa* seem to confirm Oderigo's judgment; but Oderigo never conceded any right, much less sympathy for Niccolò, who, after all, stood to lose sizable resources to a man he did not know and who was not even a Florentine. In any case Oderigo unleashed an unremitting verbal barrage on Niccolò. He described the latter or his actions as *iniquo, malvagia, cattivo, magagnato, arrabiato, falso e bugiardo, disposto di seguire il più male.* Niccolò, he said, operated *senza niuna ragione* (and as God was the *mantenitore della ragione,* Niccolò was clearly on the wrong side), *con poco onore* (one of several variants to the same effect), and *sotto coverta.* He perpetrated *tradimento, fellonità, cattive malizie, villania, rubalderia, tante crudeltà, inganno,* and simply wanted to *dare noia* to Oderigo. An obvious hatred set this avalanche of pejoratives cascading down on Niccolò's head. In contrast to legal citations and documents, Oderigo's private language appealed to a broad moral sensibility. Reason, honesty, goodness were the normative referents in the *ricordanze,* where the paradigm of argument was directed to elicit action from his son, not a decision from a judge. But Oderigo was also faced with an opponent who, in contrast to Niccolò d'Alessandro Machiavelli, conceded no basis of normative agreement. This hatred was not abated by events. Gaining the *villa* did not fully assuage Oderigo. The passages quoted above show a man worn down, exhausted, and lacking a means to strike back immediately. But they also show a man determined to strike back or leave a record of the quarrel for someone else, probably his son, to take up. His legal rights had been won, but at the cost of personal insult and great monetary expense. A case whose legal record consisted of precise property rights was, in fact, a matter of honor and relationship.

Concluding Reflections

Because historians have only official records of disputes, they face enormous difficulty in getting behind the formal facade of a dispute or even in recognizing that there was more than the record contains, for what it contains suited the compiler's purposes only. One of the insights of legal anthropology, therefore, has been that

> in any culture we must expect some disparity between the form in which a dispute appears in court and the "real" substance of the quarrel which gives rise to it. Even in the absence of specialization which characterizes the courts of contemporary legal systems, there is likely to be some gap between the way in which the parties conceive of their quarrel and the manner in which it is seen by interveners. The disputants will probably know this and thus present the matter in such a way that the court will be prepared to hear it.[78]

Parties may also go to court as a matter of honor, to publicize something, or just to cause problems for an enemy (as Niccolò degli Agli did to Oderigo di Credi). The advantage, therefore, in the sources utilized here is they are not formal records. The authors of these accounts simply wanted to retain a memory of the situation, including their emotions, for themselves and their children. Their accounts still have biases and shortcomings, to be sure, but at least we can get beyond a facade of formal records.

The two disputes took very opposite courses. One remained distinctly private, hidden, and informal; the other took place by the most public and formal legal means. Yet they share certain features. In both, wealth and honor were at stake. An analysis that stuck too closely to the supposedly cross-culturally valid construct of dispute would perhaps miss the historically specific resonances of the values and interests of these Florentines. It might also downplay the brooding presence of law—as an institution staffed with trained professional personnel, as a language, as a sophisticated and isolable body of norms. Even in the Machiavelli case where law did not overtly participate in the framing and resolving of the issue, the recording of the episode, the drawing up of a *scriptura privata*, the use of legalisms like *ingiuria* display an awareness of law and the possibility of turning to it. There were negative aspects to the use of the courts—publicity for Bernardo Machiavelli, cost and corruption and delays for Oderigo di Credi. But there were also benefits. At least the courts used the norms that privileged Oderigo's claims and ultimately awarded him the property, despite his lower social status and foreign birth. He could win the property issue. As for the rest, he could only stack up pejoratives in his *ricordi*. Politically he had no support.[79]

The problem Oderigo faced in securing a maternal inheritance for his son was no doubt a much more common one than the problem of violation Bernardo Machiavelli faced. Oderigo confronted what was, loosely construed, a species of dowry restitution or acquisition. Remarks and advice on these sorts of matters are common in surviving Florentine sources. Oderigo came simply to the same point as one of Leon Battista Alberti's interlocutors in his *Libri della famiglia:* "Finally you will be put in a position where you must either suffer the loss in silence or enter upon expensive litigation."[80] No such sense of the inevitability of litigation seems to have motivated Machiavelli, a lawyer.

But law cannot be seen in isolation; the result of a dispute (even one taken to court) cannot be tied solely to norms. The norms themselves were not always clear. The fact that both parties could cite norms in their support shows that norms could conflict.[81] The norms provided ranges of discourse within which a comprehensible picture might be constructed, either by two parties directly negotiating (Machiavelli) or by a third party. In court, normative references tended to be precise and substantive, because (at least in Credi's case) the object of dispute was rendered as very specific. In *ricordi,* however, one sees more generalized ethical precepts invoked, directly or indirectly, because there (beyond specific matter or acts) the nature of relationships was being exposed. Relationships also were an object of dispute. They too were transacted. The Machiavelli reestablished their relationship; Credi and Agli found no way to get along, and escalated hostilities. So it is not easy simply to peg the nature of a relationship (especially as kinship or not) and thereby determine how a dispute would be handled. True, the Machiavelli were patrikin, Credi and Agli were affinal kin; and in Florence the presumption was the former would be stronger. But by anthropology neither relationship would predict the litigiousness of the second case.

In the Machiavelli case the two kinsmen began from basic points of normative agreement (at least tacitly accepted by Niccolò when he crafted his lie about Renzi). Thus they could keep the matter out of public notice by using kin as go-betweens and concentrating on monetary arrangements. Their dispute was a matter of words among themselves, an expression of their sense of honor. Credi and Agli had no basis of normative agreement except enmity. Their dispute played out in others' language; notaries and officials (even if friends of Agli) were their go-betweens. Not a mere wounded sense of honor but deep moral indignation oozed from Credi's pen; he only gave up when the costs became intolerable. Third parties were distrustful; litigation was revenge, not justice.

Certainly the individuals involved in these disputes had a sense of their rights—a sense barely distinguishable from their sense of their (culturally inscribed) interests. "The individual's sense of entitlement to enjoy certain experiences and be free from others is a function of the prevailing ideology, of which law is simply a component."[82] But in Florence law was indeed a component and its effects cannot be neglected. A vague, ambiguous, broad, but no less powerful sense of honor could issue by a continuous process in very precise legal norms if needed. Dispute both gave pragmatic content and conceptual form to those rights. There could hardly have been an apprehension of dispute without norms, and clearly both authors of our sources perceived these as coherent episodes, initiating with perception of right, expression of this to the other party, and culminating (however temporarily) in a settlement of the normative issue. There was no assurance that matters would hold where the parties perceived them as settled or finished, but what defined the dispute as narrative episode was its normative content as well as procedure. Bernardo Machiavelli did not limit his account to his own conversations with Niccolò or just to Giovanni Nelli's dealings with him; Oderigo di Credi followed the *villa* issue through a number of forums and even into immediate spinoffs regarding legacies and *gabelles*.

We do not have all the information we need to do a full extended case analysis, such as anthropologists do. We are unable to illuminate the shadowy perimeters; and we are saddled with one-sided accounts. Still, extended cases are cases; the normative content of a dispute is still definitional, whether those norms are simple or complex, precise or general, legal or not. And these norms did set certain constraints to behavior, most especially in the Credi case.[83] In both cases something fairly specific was at issue—a pregnant servant, a *villa*, and houses. There was some range of choice of how to array the matter normatively; there was choice as to how, if at all, to proceed. But in neither case was the range of choice absolute or open-ended. Bernardo Machiavelli was very aware of that as he looked at the options before him. Oderigo di Credi knew at least that, after a point, he was no longer defending the title to the property but its monetary value—as did Niccolò degli Agli, who went from claiming the property to diminishing it so as to lose less honor, while also using his power in kin and friends.

Courts were available as only one strategy at whatever stage of a dispute. But recourse to courts carried a special quality. As several historians have jointly concluded,

> courts were everywhere seen . . . as the major *locus* for the climax of dispute. And, if that is so, then courts must have been of some use for disputants; we should not assume that people went to court out of a disinterested love for the law. The key advantage of going to court was the width of support potentially available to a party there.[84]

Public procedure could thus bring a more comprehensive end to a dispute through the involvement of others, whose support hinged on a sense that the matter would end there. Rules of law would also come into play. The two disputes seen above, however, demonstrate that publicity and rules of law were not always the answer. The Machiavelli case avoided both, lest the scandal get out and lest one cousin expose the other as a false kinsman. The Credi case shows that even the utilization of formal litigation seen to its conclusion does not guarantee closure; there is always the possibility of further litigation, at least for nuisance value. The courts could absorb feud, not abolish it.[85] The narratives of Machiavelli and Credi reveal that each man drew his own closure to the case at the point where he was normatively satisfied and/or procedurally exhausted, at the point where, in other words, for whatever reason, he was willing to live with what had been gained. Insight into that point for the historian cannot come from the legal record, but it also cannot come apart from it.

In the context of a dispute, whether in present-day tribal societies or advanced ones, or in Renaissance Florence, more was at stake and more was in play than law. But in Florence, as in modern societies, law was a specialized realm, more properly distinguishable from other normative domains, perhaps, than is the category of an economy from all other transactions. Certainly the boundary between the legal and the nonlegal is not always clear, nor is it impermeable and unchanging. The law never operates in isolation. To litigants it is a means—one among others—and not an end. So they may also refuse to abide by a decision imposed on them (rather than one worked out with their participation). But it is also not possible to reduce the distance between law and the nonlegal. In the cases we have seen that distance was marked by the intervention of judges, notaries, and a jurist; by the purchase and formulation of documents; by reference to norms articulated in jurisprudential writings and communal statutes in Latin; by costs and delays. To label both episodes simply as disputes is to elide major differences in tone, manner, and content. It is especially to undervalue the disputants' own appreciation of the special status and form of law as a category of norms and dispute intervention.

3

•

CONFLICTING CONCEPTIONS OF PROPERTY IN QUATTROCENTO FLORENCE
A Dispute over Ownership in 1425–26

•

As everyone knows, in private affairs it is an advantage to be in possession,
even though the legal right is not affected, and even though judicial proce-
dures for determining ownership of property are well known and fixed. But
it is an incomparably greater advantage in matters that depend on the policy
of the state or on the will of those who rule. For not having to fight against
immutable principles of reason or against established decisions, you can easily
use the thousands of accidents that happen every day against anyone who
seeks to remove you from possession.
Francesco Guicciardini, *Maxims and Reflections of a Renaissance Statesman*,
trans. Mario Domandi (New York, 1965), 131

The meanings and uses of property were of intense concern in early
Quattrocento Florence. As Hans Baron, in a seminal essay, and others
following him have argued, humanists like Leonardo Bruni, Matteo
Palmieri, and Poggio Bracciolini reexamined the ethical meaning of
property as a feature of civic life.[1]

Accompanying this conceptual reexamination were new challenges
to the sources of wealth and important, even disturbing, uses of it.
Wars, recurrent plagues, and other problems contributed to a deteri-
orating economy and worsening fiscal situation. Complaints of fraud,

fiscal inequities, tax evasion, and maladministration were frequent.[2] In response there emerged important legislative initiatives: the registration of emancipations and the magistracy of the Sea Consuls in 1421, the *Monte delle doti* in 1425, the ambitious *catasto* in 1427, and the *Conservatori delle Leggi* in 1429.[3]

Finally this legislation itself rested on a vital legal infrastructure. The wealth that circulated in Florence moved in the guise of legally defined categories, like dowry and patrimony, and by means of legal instruments and procedures, like contracts and wills. The basic legal concepts of property that underlay these categories and instruments and that were, therefore, vital for the management of wealth and the conceptualization of the social and economic order were themselves undergoing a parallel process of reexamination at the hands of professional jurists in canon and civil law.[4]

It was in the midst of this context of conceptual ferment, economic stagnation, and legislative innovation in Florence that a dispute in law arose in 1425 over the ownership of a house. Surviving documentation allows for a fairly thorough reconstruction of the dispute. The issues raised in this dispute and their treatment in a legal opinion by five prominent Florentine jurists provide a unique perspective on the meanings and uses of property in this crucial period.[5]

Facts of the Case

The suit first came before the court of the Podestà in July 1425. On 3 July Domenico di Zanobi di Ceccho Fraschi of the *popolo* of Santa Maria sopr'Arno emancipated his daughter Francesca, called Checcha. As an emancipation gift Domenico gave his daughter the estate of his grandmother. Checcha immediately had appointed a

Table 3.1 Genealogy of the Fraschi Litigants

```
                       Cecco = Francesca
        ┌─────────────────────┴────────────────────────┐
  Zanobi = first wife              = second wife    Guidaccio
      │                                 │
  Francesco  Caterina = DOMENICO = Antonia
                         │                │
                      Zanobi          CHECCHA   =   JACOPO TANI
```

notary, ser Loisio di ser Michele Guidi, as her *procurator* (an agent-attorney) to secure possession of the property through the court.[6] Checcha herself was married a few days later, on 9 July, to Jacopo di Tommaso Tani.[7] On 10 July, ser Loisio obtained from the court of the Podestà a decree of eviction (*preceptum de disgombrando tenutam*) against the current holder of the property, a monna Antonia, widow of Francesco di Daldo Cantini.[8]

The crux of the matter for Domenico and his daughter was that (contrary to the advice later given by Francesco Guicciardini) they were not in possession of the property. The gift to Checcha rested on a claim to ownership, but Domenico Fraschi had never been in actual possession of the property at any time in the forty-three years since he had acquired title to it.

Ownership and possession had a complicated history that went back to 8 July 1358, when possession was first separated from ownership. This complicated history is best presented schematically.[9]

- 8 July 1358: Domenico Fraschi's father and uncle were involved in arbitration with their mother. The sons were obligated to support her with 13 florins yearly for *alimenta,* in return for which they received possession of the family's house near the baptistry and cathedral of Florence.
- 1363: The uncle died without heirs.
- 1381: Domenico and his half-brother Francesco fell heir to the house following their grandmother's death.
- 1382: Domenico formally took title to the inheritance (*adire hereditatem*). He was not then in Florence.
- 1387: Francesco, the half-brother, while in France, sold his rights as heir to the 350-florin dowry of his mother, Zanobi's first wife.[10] The purchaser, Francesco Cantini, returned to Florence and obtained the requisite judicial decree giving him tenure (*tenuta*) of the house as security (*hypotheca*) for the value of the dowry. As the house was seemingly vacant, he took up residence there.
- 1392: Cantini married Antonia, daughter of Luigi Quaratesi, with a dowry of 650 florins, and brought her to live with him in the Fraschi house.
- 1400: Francesco, the brother, died without heirs.
- October 1424: Cantini died and his widow in turn judicially obtained tenure of his property, including the house, which had been obligated for her dowry.[11]

Less than a year later, the widow Antonia was faced with an eviction order in favor of Fraschi, who had done nothing to assert ownership or retrieve possession in all the years between 1382 and 1425. So far as we can tell, Domenico Fraschi had not set foot in the house since 1380. He had in the meantime spent eighteen years in foreign lands, presumably on business, and, after returning to Florence, had set up residence across the Arno.[12] Between 1380 and 1425, Domenico Fraschi had accumulated a modest patrimony and had acquired some prominent friends. Indeed his fortunes and his friends went hand in hand. In the estimation of the chronicler Giovanni Cavalcanti, Fraschi was an *amico* of none other than Cosimo de' Medici and "although virtually a nobody, he acquired great wealth under Cosimo's sponsorship."[13]

Despite Cavalcanti's assessment it can be said that Domenico Fraschi did not exactly start from nothing and was not totally dependent on the Medici. Some, though not all, the documents pertaining to the case gave him the cognomen Adimari ("Aldimari"). The Adimari were an old, prominent lineage whose fortunes had greatly declined since the early fourteenth century. Still, there were some wealthy and prestigious members of this prepotent magnate lineage, some of whom were active in the anti-Medicean political circles in the 1420s and 1430s.[14] The house in dispute was located in the midst of the ancestral enclave of the Adimari along the south flank of the cathedral and baptistry. Domenico's grandmother had been of the prominent Giugni lineage, members of which had ties to the Medici in the 1420s.[15] Fraschi also gained the patronage and affinal connections to his powerful, wealthy, and numerous neighbors, the Bardi. He rented his residence in Santa Maria sopr'Arno from one of them.[16] More to the point, his first wife, Checcha's mother, was a Bardi—Antonia di Lipaccio. Domenico's Bardi brothers-in-law, Andrea and Larione, figured as important collaborators in his patrimonial strategies, as we will see below.

The name by which Domenico was best known in Florence, however, was Fraschi.[17] At the least he did not stress his Adimari ties. He notably settled among the Bardi on his return to Florence and had not tried to retrieve the house among the Adimari. His fortunes were modest. By the *catasto* of 1427 he possessed only two *poderi* in the Mugello (one of them only for his life) and various credits in Florence's funded public debt (the *Monte comune*). Against this modest patrimony said to be worth about 1,225 florins stood debts totaling over 1,300.[18] This was a man from a relatively poor, disaffected branch of the Adimari who was pursuing aid and identity elsewhere. Notably he pursued social standing among the partisans of the Medici rather than among the Adimari's aristocratic allies. Domenico owed the 1,300 florins to Averardo de' Medici, and the debt was a substantial one for a man of limited resources. His Bardi brothers-in-law were active supporters and business associates of the Medici.[19] His son-in-law, Jacopo di Tommaso Tani, represented an unusually attractive social alliance for a man of Fraschi's financial stature, and was an important Medici employee who possessed a considerable fortune when he took Checcha as his second wife.[20] It was also her second marriage. Previously she had had a son, Niccolò, and a daughter, Madalena, by Bartolino di Niccolò Bartolini, member of another lineage with Medici ties.[21]

Only at the time of his daughter's second marriage did Domenico Fraschi move through her to recover the property. Why did he act in 1425? Several possible answers suggest themselves. In the first place, Fraschi was not a young man. At the relatively advanced age of at least sixty-two, he may have thought he had little time left to arrange his affairs.[22] Less than two years later, as his wife declared her intent to die intestate, Fraschi had his (first) will drawn up, indicating concerns on his part along these lines.[23] Securing the property and turning it over to his daughter could have been intended to provide for himself and his wife in their old age.[24] The property might also have figured in his daughter's dowry.[25] Perhaps above all, in the midst of a clouded commercial atmosphere in 1425, and in the midst of personal financial difficulties, Fraschi may have decided to retrieve a neglected asset of considerable value.[26]

A more intriguing question, however, is why Fraschi would still consider the property his after all those years. From the perspective of the twentieth century and from Anglo-American law, it is hard to understand why Fraschi would try to reclaim possession after almost forty years of peaceful possession by others, without so much as a token payment of rent or any other recognition of his ownership. From the perspective of Quattrocento Florence, however, Fraschi's attachment to family property, especially a house, does not seem so peculiar. Florentines' attachment to family property was strong. Numerous strategies existed to preserve family control and to pass such property through the generations.[27] Florentines who had been absent from their homes and lands for a long time, for whatever reason, still considered ancestral property theirs and would pursue various avenues to regain it.[28]

Pursuit of property claims after a long time was also fully consistent with the qualities of a vendetta.[29] Moralists like Paolo da Certaldo in the fourteenth century and the humanist Leon Battista Alberti in the fifteenth, while cautioning against physical violence, advised patience in waiting for the right opportunity for revenge of family honor and recovery of family interests.[30] Countless plots of *novelle* were constructed around patient and cunning acts of revenge.[31] The lawsuit initiated by Fraschi was a bloodless surrogate for revenge. The suit provided a forum for the processing of family moral and political, as well as economic, claims. So an abiding attachment to family property might be processed through a dispute, even (or perhaps especially) after a long time. Furthermore, when one was not in possession and able to use "the thousands of accidents that happen every day," the judicial process offered the only remedy. That there were reasons for revenge in Fraschi's case is hard to establish. Francesco Cantini may have been an Adimari too.[32] His acquisition of the property by purchasing a dowry right was consistent with the acts of a kinsman, especially toward a property in that part of town. Fraschi's actions showed no affection for the Adimari, but we cannot (yet) say why.

Pursuit of these claims through the courts also required some sense of the law. Ser Loisio's legal expertise, therefore, was very important. Certainly the emancipation and lawsuit in 1425 displayed a sense of legal timing. Fraschi could not have waited much longer, for time was against him. Fraschi and his son-in-law Tani also had had experience with legal procedures. Tani's *catasto* declaration, at least, reveals that judicial proceedings had been undertaken against some substantial debtors.[33] So in the last analysis, as his claims were legal, rather than factual, Fraschi tried to use emancipation and the skills of ser Loisio to manipulate the law in his favor.[34] This manipulation consisted partly in the initiation of proceedings and partly in the presentation of claims therein. These claims, in turn, rested on interpretation of legal norms. Ser Loisio presented this interpretation in his arguments of 10 July 1425. He claimed, on the basis of the history of the property, that Domenico held title and that the debt to Francesco Cantini had been settled by the return (*redditus*) on the house during the intervening years, so that Cantini's widow had no right to stay there any longer.[35]

By the terms of the applicable Florentine statute, these arguments were sufficient to obtain the decree.[36] By the same statute, however, monna Antonia had thirty days to respond, to show cause why she should not be evicted. If she could demonstrate continuous possession of the property for the four previous years and that she had possession by title or just cause, or otherwise treated the property as her own ("pro suis vel tanquam sua bona"), then it was up to the court to "discuss and determine the priority and strength of the right of both parties."[37]

Antonia was not a poor widow, she was a Quaratesi with a substantial dowry tied up in the house.[38] She was not about to let Fraschi suddenly assert what was from her perspective a moribund claim. She retained her own *procurator* (as she had to as a woman), ser Davanzato di Jacopo. He forcefully and skillfully presented her case, mounting a three-pronged counterattack. The first and most important argument was that Domenico's title, which went back to the arbitration of 1358, had been legally prescribed by the passage of time. Prescription (about which more will be said below) was an institution of civil and canon law that had been admitted into Florentine statutory law. It allowed that a title or right not acted upon for a period of thirty years was lost to the person(s) who had exercised the right during that period. Time and fact of possession, in other words, could change the legal fact of title. Because Cantini had been in continuous possession of the house for thirty-eight years, ser Davanzato argued that time, in the form of legal prescription, made his client the sole owner of the house.[39]

Ser Davanzato's second argument established Antonia's just title to the property: that "peacefully and quietly and in good faith by reason, title, and cause" Francesco Cantini had acquired the house— and so did his widow after him. Ser Davanzato even produced three neighbors to testify that Cantini had lived there for over thirty years. None of the witnesses could say what title Cantini had, but they all affirmed that he had treated the property as his own, even making structural improvements and additions "just as true owners and possessors do with their own property." Ser Davanzato also reminded the court that Antonia now held the house under judicial decree for her dowry.[40] But the major contention was that "Francesco held the property as his own for so long a time, namely 30 and more years, that he prescribed it."

The third argument raised a technicality. Ceccha's emancipation had not been registered with the Signoria as required by law since December 1421.[41] By the terms of the law, therefore, her emancipation and the gift that gave her title to the house were invalid—so too was the suit being pressed in her name by ser Loisio.

Property Law and Prescription

The crux of ser Davanzato's presentation was that prescription had occurred in favor of his client. This appeal to prescription rested, in turn, on an underlying sense of property. Ser Davanzato was arguing that relations between persons and things (legally describable in terms of ownership) were established, in the last analysis, not by abstract notions of title but by the objective facts of uncontested possession and use over a long period.

This "objective" view of property enjoyed wide support in medieval jurisprudence, for the outstanding feature of medieval property law was its "conditioning by the facts."[42] In the works of medieval jurists, property—the legal relations between human subjects and real things—was predicated on the autonomous existence and value of the real. So relations between persons and things were dialectical, and property took on an objective quality.[43] In contrast, property in modern law is essentially subjective and voluntaristic. The real has simply become a passive extension of the owner's *persona*. Rather than being conditioned and limited by the real, the owner endowed with modern "possessive individualism" dominates it and others through it.[44]

The objective nature of medieval property law is revealed above all by the development of the notion of *dominium utile*. Roman ownership, *dominium,* was absolute. Roman law hesitated to attribute even possession to anyone but the owner, so where property was actually in the hands of another (e.g., a tenant, a borrower) the other was usually attributed with mere detention (*detentio*) or use, as distinct from possession.[45] In the Middle Ages, however, land was often in the hands of people other than the putative owner. The fact of enjoyment by others and the quality of this enjoyment over a long period came to separate the owner (*dominus*) from his property and instead to vest a form of autonomous useful ownership (*dominium utile*) in the possessor.[46] The outstanding example of this medieval objective sense of property was the *locatio ad longum tempus* (rental for long term). This uniquely medieval institution attributed *dominium utile* to one who rented a property for a long time and is the most evident example of how a lasting objective state of facts acquired a normative power and issued in an adjustment of the normative order.[47]

Dominium utile drew limits around the formerly absolute ownership (termed *dominium directum*) of Roman law. *Dominium utile* marked the concrete, temporal, utilitarian relations between persons and things. *Dominium directum* became a mere residue of formal and personal qualities of ownership.[48] However, while *dominium utile* ordinarily stood alongside *dominium directum* or even in nominal subordination to it, in prescription *dominium utile* opposed and denied any *dominium directum*.[49] Because of this frontal assault on *dominium directum,* medieval jurisprudence, despite its evident regard for the objective facts of use and enjoyment, was reluctant to admit prescription and conceded only *dominium utile,* not full *dominium directum* to a successful *praescribens*.[50]

Subjective and voluntaristic dimensions of ownership embedded in the notion of *dominium directum* became unavoidably prominent in prescription. *Directum* was seen as a personal quality inhering naturally in an owner.[51] It was in his very bones. Prescription, therefore, not only stripped him of the effects of ownership but struck at his very personality.[52]

So ser Davanzato's case, while strong, was not airtight. It could not avoid a clarifying contrast with a subjective and voluntaristic sense of property that also had wide, if not complete, support in the early fifteenth century. Voluntaristic notions of property had gained adherence among Franciscan theologians, moralists, and preachers; and they had entered into discussions of usury in Florence and elsewhere.[53] Humanists in Florence were also developing and propounding a subjective sense of property in their works on civic life.[54] And finally, by means of canon lawyers, some of this subjectivism was entering juristic discussions of prescription.

One of the legal requirements for prescription was good faith (*bona fides*) on the part of the *praescribens*.[55] In Roman law prescription was both extinctive of obligations and acquisitive of title to real property.[56] Where ownership of real property was in question not only was legal action debarred but title itself passed to the possessor. In order for acquisitive prescription to take effect, the *praescribens* had to be in continuous possession of the property by a legal means (*iusta causa*) and be in good faith when gaining possession.[57] Canonists saw all prescription as acquisitive, if only because extinction of actions still had undeniable substantive effects.[58] So canonists broadened the requirement for good faith to all forms of prescription and to all moments during the prescription-accruing period. Canonists demanded that any bad faith must return the property to the owner, that there could be no prescription whatever in the absence of good faith.[59]

At its simplest, good faith amounted to a belief that a property was truly one's own or that a debt had been settled. Thus the knowledge that title lay elsewhere precluded good faith. However, what civil law emphasized in good faith was a lack of intent to harm the other, whereas canon law saw good faith as lack of sin in the person acquiring ownership; to canonists it was not enough that there merely be no harm to the owner, and negligence on the owner's part did not excuse bad faith in the *praescribens*.[60] To them, good faith was a positive subjective force.

The major problem for legal practice was whether the canonists' sense of prescription and good faith should prevail over that of the civilians. Florentine statutory law provided no clear guidance. By the rubric *De prescriptionibus civilium actionum* of 1355, actions could be prescribed after thirty years (fifteen for *locationes ad longum tempus*). Prescription was not allowed against certain categories of persons: creditors in possession of their debtor's property, minors, and those absent from Florence (except those officially exiled).[61] The statutes of 1415, revised by the jurists Paolo di Castro (1360–1441) and Bartolomeo Vulpi (1359–1435), under the rubric *De prescriptione*, reaffirmed the 1355 law—with one crucial addition. It allowed prescription of *dominium*, not just extinction of actions: "If anyone should hold or possess real property by himself or his antecedents for thirty years or more peacefully and quietly, he cannot be molested or disturbed but should be defended."[62] In neither version was the question of good faith raised; that was left to the courts. The statute, it would seem, was more concerned with the establishment of civic order in property relations than it was with abstract ethical notions of good faith. Jurists, however, were concerned with such abstract notions and with the relationship between statutes and the *ius commune* of the schools. So the Florentine lawyer Alessandro Bencivenni (1385–1423) in his commentary on the statute *De prescriptione* claimed that prescription against absent owners fell to the terms of the *ius commune* and that debtors in bad faith could not prescribe.[63]

Several areas of uncertainty thus existed in the law applicable to the case before us. There was jurisprudential disagreement on the good faith issue. There was also the problem of the relationship between statute and learned law. Above all there was the problem of the objective ownership manifest in enjoyment over time against subjective ownership manifest in title. All else was subordinate to this problem.

In his reply to the arguments of ser Davanzato, then, ser Loisio highlighted these uncertainties.[64] Against the argument that prescription had occurred, ser Loisio countered, first, that prescription had been interrupted in 1380 by Zanobi di Ceccho's death and, second, that thereafter Domenico Fraschi had been absent for eighteen years and prescription time could not be calculated against him during that period. Ser Davanzato had argued that Domenico's absence had been voluntary and, therefore, did not protect him; but ser Loisio suggested that the statute be interpreted as exempting even voluntary absences from prescription.

Against the second argument that Cantini had treated and held the property like an owner, ser Loisio argued that at the statutory rate of 5 percent the debt had been satisfied and, as a result, Cantini and his widow had no right to the house. Ser Loisio also argued that Cantini's claim was self-contradictory: he could not say the property was "pro suis" when he clearly had acknowledged it was a security belonging to another and held for a debt. At most Cantini had had detention, not possession.

Finally ser Loisio conceded the third point about emancipation. He had to. A jurist had already advised that the emancipation and all actions in Checcha's name were void because of the failure to register the emancipation; and a court had so pronounced. However, Domenico Fraschi was ready to emancipate his daughter again—this time carefully observing all requirements. So this third point was no real obstacle to resumption of proceedings.

The Consilium

Ser Loisio's counterarguments had clothed a subjective and voluntaristic conception of property—one that allowed for voluntary absence, for the desire to alienate title to another, and for the denial of possession to a creditor. His counterarguments had also isolated the key legal questions to be addressed by the court. Yet his opponents still had a strong case. To sway the court to adopt the subjective and voluntaristic side, ser Loisio and his clients employed some heavier artillery. They purchased the services of a Florentine jurist to draw up a *consilium* to be submitted as additional and authoritative argumentation on their behalf.[65] The jurist they approached, Buonaccorso di messer Giovanni da Montemagno (ca. 1392–1429), proved to be an excellent choice. As a humanist as well as a jurist, Montemagno was actively involved in discussions of the meaning and use of wealth in Florence at that time. In his dialogue *De nobilitate* he produced a subjective vision of wealth, and in the *consilium* he drafted on commission for Checcha he provided a legal equivalent. Humanistic views of property emphasized its moral dimensions in civic and familial contexts. It was a view of property marked by dominative voluntarism. External goods were seen as a medium for displaying one's virtue and nobility (to prove moral as opposed to economic worth).[66] On the level of the city, the beauty of its buildings, its size, its control and use of the wealth of an extensive domain revealed the full flowering of its energies. Acquisition and consumption of wealth from the *contado* were presented by Leonardo Bruni as testimony to Florence's inner greatness.[67] The actual practical expression of this "inner greatness" was, in fact, greatly aided by law. Not only did the law provide the titles of ownership, bills of sale, rental and loan contracts, but it provided the framework for city-country relations in treaties and statutes (themselves formulated, redacted, and interpreted by jurists).[68]

In the familial context explored by Alberti, a provident *paterfamilias* had to cultivate the proper virtue to use property properly, at proper times, for the good of the entire family. Wealth, power, and position were only gifts of fortune, and "the things of fortune are ours insofar as fortune permits, and also insofar as we know how to use them."[69] Such constantly threatened goods required care and diligence. Even body, soul, and time could be "lost" by unwise use. Only one firm possession governed all the rest (as a wise priest supposedly taught past noble members of the Alberti, including some lawyers—"nothing is properly ours except a certain will and force of mind."[70] This will could secure the unstable goods of fortune by judicious use of time, money, and written instruments.[71] Property was envisioned as inert, indifferent, subject to the will, whose use of property mattered more than possession.[72] Time also figured as a quantity to be exploited—as it was in prescription—and not as a shaping quality transforming one's relations with the real.[73] Clear possession and title to property were part of this process, the results and tools of prudent management, lest one's family lose the fruits of its labor and investment to someone else.[74]

Buonaccorso da Montemagno embraced a similar form of subjectivism by which he stressed inner virtue as the essence of nobility, rather than just birth or wealth.[75] In a succession of civic orations, he echoed Bruni's emphasis on the Florentine will and virtue behind the city's expanding dominion and reputation.[76] Montemagno's *De nobilitate*, fictionally presented as a quasi-legal proceeding, drove a wedge between inner virtue and external wealth, on the level of individual ethics. However, the entire tenor of Montemagno's dialogue does not dismiss the importance of wealth—properly received and used. The balance to be struck between the two competing views of nobility would dismiss ill-gotten wealth, or excessive wealth; but claims to nobility would not have been recognized without some degree of wealth and birth.[77] One needed not an overabundance of property but a "mezzana masserizia" (to cite the Italian version) suited to one's needs.[78] Wealth made possible the time for pursuit and display of virtue. This property might then be lost to fortune, but virtue could not; and virtue had a thousand ways to reacquire the conveniences of life.[79] It would acquire these conveniences by moral and legal means. As in Alberti's scheme, so too in Montemagno's, wealth and time became quantities in the service of the qualities of noble virtue.[80]

In his *consilium* on Checcha's behalf, Montemagno moved beyond the rhetorical and theoretical elaboration of this civic humanist view of wealth to participate in its practical expression. Montemagno signed and sealed his opinion on 16 January 1426.[81] In it he treated the questions more or less in the order presented to him, but the first problem, prescription, drew much more of his attention. This first problem was, in fact, two problems: had the property been prescribed by Zanobi di Ceccho, such that Domenico had not gained ownership as his grandmother's heir? And had it been prescribed by Cantini against Domenico, even in view of the latter's absence from Florence? Montemagno pointed out that Zanobi had been present at the arbitration of 1358, so he knew of it and could not have pleaded ignorance.[82] It followed that "if Zanobi wanted in his life to prescribe against the debt set up in the arbitration, he would always have been in bad faith, since he is presumed to have known of the debt."[83] This much was clear. The problem was whether prescription in bad faith of a personal obligation was allowable. Bartolo of Sassoferrato (d. 1357) had argued that it was. As he had seen it, possession was not required in prescription of obligations so neither was good faith. Prescription of obligations arose from the negligence of the one party, not the good faith of the other. Having linked good faith and possession, Bartolo had concluded that canon law's requirement of good faith did not carry over to civil law.[84]

Montemagno, however, intent on denying prescription to Zanobi di Ceccho, noted that canonists "commonly," Giovanni d'Andrea (d. 1348) specifically, argued the opposite.[85] What was contrary to good faith was sin, and the law should not be soft on sin.[86] At the heart of the disagreement between Bartolo and Giovanni d'Andrea lay differing perspectives. As defined by d'Andrea, prescription was "a right arising from time, embodying the authority of laws, bringing punishment to the negligent, and putting an end to disputes."[87] Civil law might not require good faith

> because civil law intends for its ultimate end to conserve civil society, to which end punishment of negligence and termination of disputes is necessary, therefore it must intend to punish the negligent and put an end to disputes rather than to correct or remove the iniquity of the prescribing party, for to it belongs the equity of this double end [punishing negligence and ending disputes] rather than the correction of the iniquity of the prescribing party. From all of which it appears immediately why in prescription in bad faith canon law disagrees with civil law.[88]

Canon law, in other words, directed its attention to the subjective state of the *praescribens* rather than to the objective condition of social relations. It was concerned not with a procedural remedy for disputes but with the acquisition of *dominium*.[89] Acquisition of *dominium* meant the subjection of something to a human will,[90] and in prescription this acquisition was seen to proceed with the tacit consent of the former owner.[91]

Montemagno came down firmly on the side of the canonists, citing the important authoritative support of Baldo degli Ubaldi (1327–1400), who was both a civilian and a canonist.[92] He reproduced Baldo's argument that, if good faith was required for prescription with possession, so much the more should it be required when possession was not.[93] He leaned heavily on Baldo's point that an obligation rested on a promise, itself a matter of good faith, so that good faith was more to be expected from a promissor than from a possessor.[94] On the other hand, Montemagno made absolutely no reference to negligence on the part of his client and suppressed any mention of jurisprudential support for Bartolo's view.[95]

Having assembled sufficient authorities to conclude that good faith was required in prescription of personal obligations, Montemagno produced the "liquida responsio" that Zanobi di Ceccho could in no way have prescribed the obligation to his mother; he would have been in bad faith. So the property remained in the mother's name and passed from her to her grandson and heir, Domenico.

The second part of the first question involved Domenico's absence. Here Montemagno had to interpret the Florentine statute. This statute did not allow prescription against *absentes*. The problem was whether it meant only those absent for a necessary reason. By referring to a prominent rule of statute interpretation—that a statute should be construed so that it least deviated from or corrected *ius commune*—it would seem that only necessary absence should be allowed, because *ius commune* did not exempt any *absentes* from prescription.[96] Ser Davanzato had implicitly so argued, and he may have had interpretive precedents on his side.[97] Montemagno, however, mounted an internal literalistic argument: the statute referred indistinctly to *absentes* in the plural, all of whom—necessary or voluntary—faced prescription in "common law." Thus all were accorded the protection of this statute. Montemagno further argued that, according to the rules of statute interpretation enunciated by Baldo, a statute that "corrected" *ius commune* or went beyond it was to be interpreted not according to *ius commune* but "simply just as it reads."[98] Thus, he concluded, Domenico's voluntary absence could not count toward prescription.[99] As a result there had not been sufficient time for prescription.

Montemagno did not rest content with these arguments. He also erected an argument against Cantini's claim. Cantini had held the house as a security (*hypotheca*) for the dowry debt. According to Roman law, such a security involved neither transfer of title nor possession but merely a right of detention. The holder could not possess the property as an owner; he could only count the proceeds against the debt. The debtor's interest in the property was protected.[100] So

Cantini had not, legally speaking, had possession, which was necessary for prescription. Also, as Baldo had pointed out, a *hypotheca* was never sufficient for prescription.[101] Finally, it could not be claimed that Cantini held the security "pro suo," because it clearly belonged to another. "So those general words 'he held and possessed for his own and as his own etc.' do not display an attitude for prescribing as his own but denote that he possessed them as if they were his and not another's."[102] The witnesses' descriptions of his treatment of the house were entirely subordinate to the nature of the legal *causa* by which he had entered into possession of it. And this *causa* was insufficiently subjective for him to have the "attitude" of an owner.

The remaining problems for Montemagno were largely procedural, though they were technically important. Suffice it to say that he declared that all testimony submitted to the court in the procedure that was aborted by the invalidity of Checcha's emancipation would carry over to another procedure on the same issues between the same parties. In a similar vein, should Antonia subsequently alienate the property, fraudulently or otherwise, the entire proceedings could be entered in evidence against the third party.[103] Finally, Montemagno pointed out that the debt had been satisfied; Cantini's *hypotheca* had been extinguished and the property could no longer be held by Antonia.[104]

Montemagno's juristic reasoning was not allowed to stand alone. Whether by his suggestion or by desire of the Fraschi party, Montemagno's *consilium* was submitted to other important jurists for their comment and signature. So, less than a month after Montemagno signed the document, on 13 February 1426, Nello da San Gimignano (b. 1373), perhaps the foremost legal mind in Florence, added his signature. And the very next day Giovanni di Girolamo Buongirolami (1381–1454) also signed.[105] These two, however, added little to the arguments advanced by Montemagno. They affirmed the simple legal point that as holder of a *hypotheca* Cantini merely had detention of the house, not the possession of it needed for prescription. But they declined to comment on the more subjective elements of Montemagno's work—the arguments about good faith and voluntary absence.

On 15 March a fourth jurist, a canonist, Guasparre del maestro Lodovico Accorambuoni (b. 1381), made a substantial contribution to the document. He addressed the good faith issue shied away from by San Gimignano and Buongirolami. Accorambuoni rehashed and quickly dismissed Bartolo's arguments with the observation that "the creditor's negligence does not cleanse the debtor's bad conscience." And the statute of Florence could not be presumed to have permitted prescriptions with sin, only those in good faith. So, again, there could not have been any prescription of Zanobi's obligation to his mother. Accorambuoni also agreed with Montemagno's interpretation of the statute regarding absence, though for different reasons. He claimed it did not matter if absence was necessary or voluntary; the statute protected *absentes* from prescription because of the inconveniences of distance, which applied to all *absentes.* If those necessarily absent could easily contest prescription through an agent, but were protected by statute, then so too must those voluntarily absent. As a final flourish in the margin of his opinion, he hinted that Cantini might have been guilty of usury by indistinctly appropriating all proceeds from the property beyond the principal of the debt.[106]

Accorambuoni's opinion, in turn, was endorsed by a fifth jurist, the civilian Michele di Santi Accolti (fl. 1415). Accolti also expressly agreed that bad faith prescription was not legal. The passage of time not only did not exonerate one in bad faith from sin, it made the sin worse.[107] Thus these last two jurists reconfirmed and strengthened the set of arguments on bad faith and voluntary absence.

Outcome

What began as a conflict of interests and perceptions between litigants was treated by the five lawyers as a conflict between legal norms. The dispute between Fraschi and Cantini was refracted through the law into a special set of words. These words, however, were simply another instrument in the dispute (though a powerful weapon, it would appear). The real resolution occurred outside the court, though not outside the law and not without the influence of the judicial process.

In anticipation of reopening proceedings, on 7 March 1426—eight days before Accorambuoni signed his opinion—Domenico Fraschi once again emancipated his daughter. This time the emancipation was properly registered.[108] With a valid emancipation and its accompanying alienation of title to Checcha, and with a *consilium* in his favor endorsed by five jurists, Fraschi was then in a position to pursue his case in earnest.

In fact he pursued it on two fronts. He won the house—at least it appeared among his possessions in his *catasto* declaration in 1427. But he also won a judgment against Cantini's widow in the Arte of Por Santa Maria for 150 florins—an asset he listed right after the house in his *catasto* declaration. The judgment in this separate but related action amounted approximately to the possibly usurious surplus Cantini and his wife had realized over the original 350-florin debt during their detention of the house.[109]

The widow Antonia left the house alongside the cathedral in 1427, for it was rented that year to ser Buonaccorso di Piero. She had lost the house and faced the 150-florin judgment in Fraschi's favor, but she had whatever was left of her husband's estate and her dowry. Back on 2 May 1426, however, monna Antonia had sold her dowry right to Piero di Jacopo Martini, who had stood surety on her dowry. Although the dowry was 650 florins, she sold it to Piero for 416 florins—the amount Antonia said was still owed her. This dowry had been secured against Cantini's property after his death, and, as the *consilium* reveals, the contested house had been part of the secured property. Antonia's desire to turn her dowry right into cash is not surprising, but what happened to her dowry right is. On 14 January 1427, seven months later, Domenico Fraschi bought her dowry from Martini, reimbursing him all 416 florins, plus 26 more to cover the *ius petendi fructus*.[110] Then on 16 January, "wanting to recognize the good faith" (an interesting phrase) of his daughter, who allegedly had provided him with the 442 florins paid to Martini, Fraschi deeded it over to her.[111]

This purchase of Antonia's dowry by Fraschi, through Martini, presents a perplexing finish to the legal interaction between them. There seems to be more here than meets the eye. It is, for example, curious that Fraschi held one debt from the Medici for precisely 442 florins, even though the purchase supposedly had been made with his daughter's money.[112] Even more curious was the role of Martini in the transaction. His *catasto* declaration reveals that he owed Fraschi (from his daughter supposedly) 150 florins to cover a debt of a Matteo di Domenico.[113] This Matteo had been Antonia's *procurator* when she established her dowry claim on her deceased husband's property in 1424. The 26 florins for *fructus* in the sale may only have been part of this loan. But it is also possible that the loan was in addition to the 442-florin purchase price.

What was this transaction for and how did it relate to the legal process? The interests of Martini are not hard to fathom. He got a loan and was released from any further obligation on the dowry. Matteo di Domenico too had had an obligation covered. So the two men associated with Antonia's interests extricated themselves, and with some profit.[114] Antonia, of course, appears to have recovered most of her dowry. And, if the entire two-part transaction had been carefully negotiated in advance, she turned over her husband's property and any rights to the house Fraschi claimed without having to deal directly with her old adversary.

What is much less clear is what Fraschi gained by purchasing this dowry, beyond the assurance it would not be used to take his house away from him. Of all the assets listed by Fraschi and Tani (since the purchase was in Checcha's name) none, and no obvious combination of them, was worth exactly 416 florins, or 442, or carried an income of 26 florins. Fraschi did have a large *Monte* credit with a discounted value of 452 florins that was enrolled in the San Giovanni quarter and may have come from Cantini's widow. He also had a large *podere* he claimed to have bought; and, although its value was much more than 442 florins, it cannot be ruled out that he paid less than full value. It is also entirely possible that Fraschi liquidated any assets and used the proceeds to purchase other holdings or even to diminish his debts. In sum, the purchase of the dowry from Cantini's widow, which may even have resulted in the acquisition of assets of greater or lesser value than the purchase price, operated as a nice compromise that could finally bring an end to the dispute. This particular outcome would not have been the same without the entire legal process, including the efforts of the five jurists, but a few finishing touches remained to the parties themselves. They had to reconcile themselves and adjust to the results of the legal process.

As for the house itself and the subsequent affairs of the Fraschi, there is an interesting anticlimax to relate.[115] Soon after the purchase of Cantini's widow's dowry right, on 1 May 1427, Fraschi composed his will. He left a bequest (*legatum*) to his daughter of her dowry, said here to be worth 700 florins. As his *heredes universales* he chose *pauperes Christi* to be designated by his wife and by his brothers-in-law.[116] He did not leave anything to his Bartolini grandson, nor did he leave everything to his daughter. In the absence of a legitimate (or even illegitimate) son he preferred to have his property liquidated and dispersed.

Fraschi did not die then, and the house did not long remain in his daughter's hands. On 3 June 1430, with her father acting as her *mundualdus,* she sold the house to her uncles, Andrea and Larione Bardi, for 500 florins.[117] So it passed from Fraschi hands, an asset capitalized into a dowry rather than a cherished ancestral property. This is the first irony of the subsequent events.

The second irony emerges before our eyes in a text generated several years later. By 7 February 1436 Checcha's mother had died, for on that day Checcha, with her husband as *mundualdus* and her father present, formally accepted her mother's estate. Her father had also remarried in the meantime to Caterina di Scolaio di Nepo degli Spini. This was another good match for the aged Domenico Fraschi; the Spini were a large clan, much diminished in wealth (as Alberti lamented in his *Della famiglia*) but still prestigious.[118] Their connections to anti-Medici families were perhaps countered to some small degree by marriage to the Medicean Fraschi. What he gained was the chance with a young wife finally to procreate a male heir. The chance paid off. Thus that same 7 February Checcha turned around and gave to her young half-brother Zanobi her mother's dowry right.[119] She also gave him the dowry right of Francesco Cantini's widow.[120] She and her father then made a mutual release (*finis*) of all claims against each other on the properties/assets given to Zanobi. Domenico also issued a *finis* regarding any obligations to him from his grandchildren by Checcha's first marriage.[121] With a son, Fraschi's entire inheritance strategy was changed, and his daughter dutifully went along with the new strategy.

This strategy was fully encoded in Fraschi's new will of 7 October 1437. By it he left his young second wife assurances of furnishings and sustenance (*alimenta*). He left his estate to Zanobi; if he died without heirs, his mother Caterina received life usufruct of a *podere* in the Mugello (listed in Fraschi's 1427 *catasto* report). Fraschi also took the precaution to name guardians (*tutores*) for Zanobi. He chose ser Michele Fruosini of the hospital of Santa Maria Nuova. If he declined the honor, then the boy's mother would act as his guardian along with Larione Bardi's wife, Fraschi's daughter Checcha (if she declined, her son Niccolò Bartolini would replace her), Agnolo Spini (Zanobi's maternal uncle), Niccolò di Domenico Giugni, Oddo di Vieri de' Tanti, and Amerigo di Filippo Antellesi. This inheritance strategy took effect on 19 March 1442, at least on that date Fraschi's widow became the boy's guardian, along with Bartolini, Spini, Giugni, and Tanti. The tutelary inventory of Zanobi's property revealed that his father's estate amounted to 306 florins in *monte* credits, various *masserizie*, 120 florins owed by Stagio Buonaguisi, some articles held by Antonio Attavianti, and the *podere* in the Mugello.[122] That *podere* would remain in Zanobi's hands until 1468, when he sold it to Tommaso d'Ubertino Risaliti for 265 florins.[123] At least in selling that property, as in his half-sister's selling of the house, he was exercising the prerogatives of ownership. But Zanobi's involvement of his son in the sale, like his half-sister's need to involve her father in hers, also indicated the degree to which ownership had social and so objective dimensions.

In 1457 Zanobi (incorrectly said to be only twenty-eight) filed his *portata* with *catasto* officials; it showed him as then married, with a four-year-old son dutifully named Domenico (his mother and a slave also lived with him). He listed *sustanze* of 705 florins (with only a bit over 14 florins in obligations), including the ancestral *podere* and some recent land purchases. Zanobi had moved from the Oltrarno, however, to the *gonfalone* of Drago in the quarter of San Giovanni. There he was nearer his mother's family and the Adimari house whose central role in the controversy of 1425–26 could have entirely escaped his notice. He was also closer to his half-sister Checcha, who had played such a crucial role in the controversy, and who was still alive, with her husband, two sons, one son's wife and son, and the other son's bastard and the freed slave who was its mother. Jacopo Tani showed a net wealth of around 3,700 florins (*sustanze* of 5,273) and so could have been a valuable asset for the young Zanobi.[124]

Conclusions: Property in Quattrocento Florence

The dispute had isolated and made visible areas of indeterminacy in the complex of norms governing prescription of property. The norms operated at an intermediate level, linking the particular interests of the litigants to the wider conceptual level of notions of ownership behind prescription.[125] The jurists linked these levels by professional means, in conformity with the most noted authorities and the best opinions of law. Corroboration by five jurists added persuasive weight to the legal findings.[126]

In the context of the dispute, the jurists offered determinateness and certainty. Constrained to a degree by rules and procedures, and above all by the needs of the court and the litigants for a resolution to an actual conflict, the jurists were not free to engage in academic speculation.[127] Nevertheless, by establishing the need for good faith, the admissibility of voluntary absence, and the power of title as against mere detention, they were able to conclude that Fraschi owned the property. In doing so they put forth a subjective conception of ownership—a conception of ownership in which the expansive and dominating will of the *dominus* over his *res* excluded any rights over the same *res* vested in others. The actual situation of use did not matter. Despite all the "factual" evidence of Cantini's "ownership," the jurists supported Fraschi's title.

One very important element in establishing this subjective conception of ownership was the canon law's invocation of *bona fides*. This construct opened up issues of persons' knowledge and intent. Domenico Fraschi's father and his adversary Cantini were both denied prescription on this basis. Montemagno's arguments on this matter were echoed elsewhere. His contemporary, the Paduan jurist Raffaele Fulgosio (1367–1427), addressed the issue of prescription of an obligation in a hypothetical *consilium* and drew conclusions similar to those of Montemagno. Against the findings of Bartolo, Fulgosio had invoked the authority of Angelo degli Ubaldi and his own teachers in canon law to determine that a debtor could not prescribe against an obligation he had sworn to uphold "perpetuo firma et rata et nunquam contrafacere."[128]

That such a subjective view would prevail in court cannot be seen as a foregone conclusion. There was a great weight of authority against a subjective view. Even the voluntarism of the Franciscans left no real imprint on conservative, traditionalistic medieval law with its objective view of "real situations." Facts of use continued to matter.[129] Statutory law would also seem to have favored prescription to punish a proprietor who had neglected his property for thirty-eight years. Prescription in such a case would serve the *bonum publicum* and put an end to the suit. The very admission by the same statute of both prescription and *locatio ad longum tempus* would argue that the statute might have justifiably been interpreted in an objective sense. Moreover, prescription had indeed been allowed by jurists in other cases. If these other cases did not involve *hypotheca* and voluntary absence, they nonetheless established a certain willingness in Florentine jurisprudence to accede to the "facts."[130] Finally, and above all, the uncontested facts of use and time militated in Cantini's favor.

Certainly it remained possible for another Florentine jurist, Antonio di Vanni Strozzi (1455–1523),[131] almost a century after Montemagno (in April 1522), to argue that facts of possession resulted in prescription. In the case before him a man had held a piece of property for fourteen years, by purchase, and that resulted in the extinction by prescription of the neighbors' statutory right to pre-empt his purchase and purchase it for themselves instead. Strozzi upheld this prescription, which was based on mere possession and not title, according to him, even against statutory language requiring the possessor to offer expressly to the neighbors the opportunity to purchase the property.[132]

There simply was no single triumphant view of property in the universe of discourse of the early Quattrocento. The bonds between individual virtue and legal title had not been conceptually forged into a coherent vision. A considerable gap remained to be conceptually bridged between the quasi-ascetic virtue advocated by Montemagno and Alberti and the possession of external wealth. Competing legal definitions of ownership left unclear the connection between the legal order and individual ownership and needs.[133] There was not yet the sort of essential connection between an individual and his property that would mark the "possessive individualism" of later law and philosophy. Subjective dimensions of the *consilium*'s arguments, therefore, required reinforcement from some of the jurists who followed Montemagno. Purchase of Antonia's dowry right by Fraschi was also a prudent precaution in this situation.

Within the *consilium* itself, however, we find a subjective vision of property wedded to the legal notion of title. By the *consilium*'s account, time could be used by a provident owner to secure his livelihood; property could be used to dower a daughter or as collateral for a debt; and bad faith actions or other blows of misfortune were blunted by the armor of the law shielding the bones of the proprietor. As the jurists' *consilium* reveals, there were also elements of law in Fraschi's favor. *Dominium directum,* as *proprietas,* inhered too deeply in a person to be easily lost to others.[134] *Dominium* also implied the right to enjoy and dispose of a thing,[135] to "use and abuse," which Fraschi did by seeing his house pledged as a security and then neglecting it for so long. The arguments presented in favor of Fraschi turned crucially around these senses of *dominium,* contrasted to the mere detention attributable to Cantini. In a manner similar to the Franciscan notion of use, Cantini's "possession" issued in no legal effects or prerogatives regarding ownership. Detention was reducible essentially to economic value alone (note how Cantini's claims boiled down to a calculation of monetary value).[136]

Conceptions of forms of use or holding of property that did not lead to *dominium* were familiar enough to Florentine jurists and surfaced elsewhere in their work.[137] Such distinctions issued in the firm denial that an objective state of affairs could of itself produce justiciable claims to *dominium,* even after a long time. Thus Cantini could not effectively alienate the property to a third party, as Montemagno affirmed at the end of his opinion. Alienation was a manifestation of (subjective) ownership; it was through alienation that Fraschi had asserted his title. He could even voluntarily leave his property. Whereas Cantini, as mere detainer, was denied any ownerly "attitude" with regard to the property, so any excessive or unauthorized use verged on usury and alienation on fraud.

In this conflict between norms and litigants, the political and ideological dimensions of the *consilium* cannot be ignored. The *consilium* was inextricably linked to the context in which it was situated, although it is not deducible from, nor reducible to, that context. Yet, within its context the *consilium* and the arguments and actions of the litigants assuredly occupied a political space. It constituted a creative moment in legal and social practice.[138] It forged a connection between a complex of legal norms, on the one hand, and a range of ideological and practical interests, on the other—all the while appearing to be formally consistent and rational.[139] It spoke to the needs of proprietors like Fraschi pursuing patrimonial strategies in Quattrocento Florence.

In a large sense, a family was constituted by the passage of the patrimony through the generations. The patrimony was the family's capital, its means of production of social values and of reproduction of itself. The family house especially (and the family was equated with and termed *casa*) was a visible sign of family honor.[140] Legislation and jurisprudence were supposed to aid in the preservation of family property.[141] While the law might grant a jurist discretion to deal creatively with legal problems, to a lawyer like Francesco Guicciardini that still meant "it does not empower him to give away other people's property."[142] Montemagno, of course, had to determine precisely whose property the house was, but his response spoke with clear meaning to certain types of owners. It spoke to the international merchant who needed to be away "voluntarily" on business.[143] It spoke to the proprietor who might have to use revenue-producing property to secure and/or satisfy a debt. At the very moment when the *catasto* was being debated and the death penalty was proposed for tax delinquency, in a difficult economic climate where debts were mounting, and in the wake of the *Monte delle doti* and concerns for putting together and securing dowries, the ideas contained in the *consilium* could assure Florentines who had to place property under *hypotheca* to meet their obligations that they would not lose their titles. They could trust that legal notions of title and the city's statutes would carry more weight with jurists than the activities of a creditor and the testimony of neighbors.[144] Knowing that their titles were protected, even from their own negligence (within broad limits of time), Florentines may have been encouraged to pledge their property so as to assemble dowries, invest in the public debt, and undertake business ventures. At the same time, they were assured of the necessity of fulfilling obligations.

This ideology embedded in the *consilium* tended to preserve the power and wealth of the more substantial proprietors, who were also the people who could best afford to hire jurists. And the jurists, as proprietors and family members themselves, could sympathize with the plight of a man like Fraschi. On various occasions, for example, both Accorambuoni and San Gimignano voiced their concern in legislative deliberative councils over economic conditions, inequitable fiscal policies, and mounting indebtedness.[145] Several of these jurists were also active in Florentine humanist circles, especially Montemagno.[146] Humanist expression of Florentine ideology, if not humanist rhetorical and philological methods, seems to have played a role in shaping the subjective and voluntaristic sense of property in the *consilium*.[147] That such a connection might be forged between humanism and law in practice, moreover, should not be surprising.[148] There were points of both ideological and social convergence between humanism and law. Humanists were acutely aware of the role of law in maintaining order in social life, as the basis for familial, corporate, and civic bodies. They could and did lavish praise on the laws of Florence and on the diligent jurists who interpreted them in practice.[149] Humanists and jurists in early Quattrocento Florence also tended to share a partially similar educational background.[150] And in the early Quattrocento the most prominent jurists and the most prominent humanists could almost all be classed as social newcomers or outsiders—men of non-Florentine origin and at least originally not among the social elite. All five jurists in the Fraschi case fall into the category of outsiders.[151] These men seem to have been sensitive to the struggles of those whose resources and social standing were limited.

Finally the *consilium* displays a tendency to connect personal virtue with legal title, not with possession. Title was to be acquired by honorable and voluntary legal mechanisms, like inheritance or purchase, by one's own desire and effort or by those of an ancestor or friend. Only with difficulty would title come to one by judicial decree, the passage of time, and another's negligence. Attention shifted to the moral qualities of the putative *praescribens*, whose concern to acquire property away from another's family smacked of a lack of virtue. Within the legal notion of title, then, the subjective ethic coming into being in humanist Florentine ideology could find practical expression. It is thus possible to see how Florentine attitudes toward wealth rested on faith in a functioning legal apparatus, in addition to faith in one's own abilities while in possession to use or avoid the "thousands of accidents" of time.

PART TWO

·

Family

·

4

•

HONOR AND CONFLICT
IN A FIFTEENTH-CENTURY
FLORENTINE FAMILY

•

On 23 September 1405 Remigio di Lanfredino Lanfredini, a member
of a Florentine family of some distinction and antiquity, wrote a letter
to his brother Orsino in Florence.[1] This, in itself, ordinarily, was an
event of little significance—except that Remigio's letter was not simply a report on business conditions in Venice, where he was at the
time, nor was it a description of mundane domestic affairs. This
particular letter was quite out of the ordinary. Remigio was writing
to inform his brother of the fact that he (Remigio) had had a fight
with their father Lanfredino. And it was no ordinary quarrel either,
for it had culminated in a complete and violent estrangement between Remigio and Lanfredino.

Remigio's letter offers a rare glimpse into the internal relations
and even drama of family life in the Renaissance; and it has, therefore, been the object of attention of historians of Florentine society.
Gene Brucker has translated part of the text of the letter in his book
The Society of Renaissance Florence: A Documentary Study; and he
has commented on it in his invaluable survey of Renaissance Florence.[2] William Kent has also offered remarks on the quarrel between Remigio and his father in his important study of family life
in Florence.[3] Their discussions of the text, however, have proceeded
from a shared set of assumptions about family life in the Renaissance. In this chapter I hope to clarify what their assumptions are

129

and to offer a complementary reading of the letter from another perspective.

Brucker sees the quarrel between Remigio Lanfredini and his father as proof of the fact that "where personal bonds were closest, as in the family, the possibility of friction was greatest."[4] After describing in some detail the facts presented by Remigio in his letter as evidence of his "poisonous hatred" for his father, Brucker concludes that Remigio was "apparently unable to bear" these indignities and thus broke with Lanfredino. Kent approaches the quarrel after closely studying the father-son relationship, which he calls the "pivotal" relationship in the family.[5] The quarrel, he concludes, is proof of the fact that "in emphasizing the central position of the father-son relationship, and its implications for household organization, there is no need (even if our sources allowed it) to idealize that passionate and deeply ambiguous bond." Fathers and sons could and did quarrel, he finds; after all, they were only human. The confrontation between Remigio and Lanfredino, therefore, means the same thing to Kent that it means to Brucker. It is an example of the fact that "the closer the tie between an adult son and his father could be, the greater the hatred, perhaps really a form of self-disgust, when a parent and child seriously fell out."[6] Such friction arose, says Kent, because "love and hate were different sides of the same coin."[7]

Both Brucker and Kent see the quarrel between the Lanfredini as an example of the types of serious disagreements and personal animosities that could develop within the Florentine family—as the obverse, in other words, of the sort of affection that otherwise should have governed relations between father and son. In that they see the quarrel as marking a failure to observe the norms governing the patterns of behavior of parent and child, the view Brucker and Kent take of the quarrel is the product of their conception of the nature of the Florentine family in the Renaissance, a conception they share with other historians.

According to this view, the family in the Renaissance was a corporate unit which lay at the heart of the social structure. With regard to Florence it has been argued that the family was "the most cohesive force in Florentine society"[8] and that the blood tie, therefore, was "the most powerful cohesive agent" in that society.[9] From the point of view of the individual, kinship obligations were primary, not only because "the family bond was a source of material and psychic support, a measure of security in a dangerous world,"[10] but because, as

Lauro Martines puts it, "the family in fifteenth-century Florence stands between the individual and society. It mediates and determines his relations with the world at large, for he confronts the social system conditioned by his family's position in society, and his place in public life is governed by the political place of his family."[11]

As the essential unit in Renaissance Italian society, the family has been studied from a variety of perspectives—demographic, economic, social, legal.[12] The essence of the family, no matter which perspective one takes, is seen to be the union of a group of people, related by blood, residing together on the patrimony. It was this fact of living together and sharing the patrimony that gave the family its stable, corporate character and its unity. The familial ideology embedded in the culture is seen by historians, then, as a reflection of the nature of the family and of the historical patterns of family activity.[13] This activity, in turn, is seen as conforming to a set of cultural norms clustering about the central figure of the father, who was the corporate officer of the family (in a manner of speaking).

The normal state of affairs in Renaissance families was that close paternal kinsmen lived with or near one another. Behind this norm and its expression in injunctions for family members to live together "lay the belief, common in patrilineal kinship systems, that the father-son relationship was a pivotal one."[14] The unity of the family was thus safeguarded by this close identity of father and son. The father held an autocratic position in the family; he alone controlled the disposition of the patrimony. His sons were to show respect and obedience to his sacred authority.[15] The identity of interests and spirit of cooperation between family members was also symbolized by the family home, retained through the generations with the aid of binding legal restrictions, as a symbol of family unity.[16]

Having established this vision of the organic structural solidarity of the family and the central position of the father-son relationship within it, historians are faced with the difficulty of explaining changes in family composition and structure (changes in the living arrangements of family members, in other words, such as the change revealed in Remigio Lanfredini's letter). Kent, for one, has turned to the important anthropological notion of the domestic developmental cycle to explain such changes. According to this explanation families as "organisms" were subject to the unavoidable rhythms of biological growth; so the limited physical size of the house could become inadequate for its numbers. On the other hand fathers eventually grew old and feeble or simply died, while children came of age, married, and succeeded to their fathers' wealth and authority (in the case of sons). When a change of living arrangements occurred otherwise, when families did not follow through on the ideal of living in common "under the shadow of a common will," it was the result of forces like "the sense of emotional claustrophobia" from living communally in small houses, even if overt disputes did not arise.[17]

Although historians of Renaissance Italian society and of Florence in particular have greatly enriched our understanding of that society and of the place of the family in it, there is a problem, I believe, in the interpretation they have given us. This interpretation is not wholly adequate for dealing with change of the type one encounters in the Lanfredini letter. There change was not solely a matter of external demographic or economic forces, nor was it solely a matter of personal animosities and the transformation of love into hate. In a family quarrel like that of the Lanfredini, it was a matter of external forces leading to differing perceptions as to the nature of the problems and the appropriate strategies to cope with them on the part of the historical actors. A too-static model that stresses, on the one hand, the ideological solidarity of the family and, on the other, the externality of the forces affecting it, does not provide sufficient room for the multiform dynamic of Renaissance family life, of which the Lanfredini case offers just one among countless forms. To dismiss a quarrel like that between Remigio and Lanfredino Lanfredini as a matter of personal animosities, to dismiss the separation of households under circumstances of strain as a manifestation of "emotional claustrophobia" begs a number of interesting facts contained in the documents. It is not that this explanation is necessarily wrong, it is that its explanatory power is not sufficient to comprehend fully an event like that in the Lanfredini family in September 1405.

If, as historians have described it, the Florentine family was marked by solidarity and cohesion, by common values and a common patrimony, inculcated and transmitted by the central relationship between father and son, what would have made Remigio Lanfredini quarrel with his father? Why would he have violated the norms clustering about this central relationship? Why would he have disrupted the peace and unity of the family and have detached himself from his father, his family, and its patrimony? To answer that his rupture with his father is a manifestation of hatred begs the question. The relationship between Remigio and Lanfredino as father and son was mediated by a cultural logic. The strategies and interests of the two men in this confrontation derived their meaning from this logic. To understand the conflict in all its dimensions, to grasp its causes and meanings, we must analyze the terms used by the two men—or, rather, in this case, the terms used by Remigio—to symbolize their relationship. Only then will we see that their quarrel was much more than an irrational emotional outburst rending the harmony of the family.

The quarrel between Remigio and his father Lanfredino arose as a result of the fact that Lanfredino had reconciled with an enemy of the family, one Giacomo Pascilocha. As Remigio explained to his brother Orsino, Giacomo had dined one evening with a friend, Basilio Baldini. After dinner they sent for Lanfredino and offered him drinks. Baldini acted as an intermediary, interceding with Lanfredino to put aside his family's dispute with Giacomo. He prevailed on him with arguments to the effect that Giacomo had never meddled in his affairs and had always considered himself his friend. Lanfredino gave in to these arguments. In Remigio's description of the scene, "Lanfredino replied that he was willing, but that he didn't want this settlement to become public knowledge for ten days, because he knew that we would not be so eager to make peace, but he would arrange the matter himself. Giacomo then said that he would like to seal this agreement by drinking with me. Lanfredino replied that he should not be afraid, and then, in the presence of honorable witnesses, he promised that none of us would offend him. In summary, they drank together and made peace without the knowledge of wife or sons or relatives or friends."

Unfortunately for Lanfredino, his son stumbled upon his secret. Upon returning from a trip to Ferrara, Remigio ran into Giacomo, who tried to approach him. When Remigio replied with a threat to run him through, Giacomo stated that such a rash act would destroy Remigio's family forever because Lanfredino had made peace with him.

It is not clear what Giacomo had done to incur the enmity of the Lanfredini, especially that of Remigio. Whatever the transgression, it was a stunned Remigio who went home to confront his father. Lanfredino did not reply to his son's account of how Giacomo had tried "to disgrace me before the whole world." His reaction was to break down in tears. It was Remigio's mother who attempted to comfort her son, asking him to suffer the injury, "for God will so arrange matters that we will have a just vendetta." Lanfredino merely continued his tears every time Remigio broached the subject with him, and Remigio, as a result, cursed his father in the following words: "I will never regard him as anything but a traitor and an evil man, and if I were to see him collapse at my feet, I wouldn't give him a penny!"

In Remigio's eyes, then, his father was a "traitor" (*traditore*). What did the term mean? In what sense was Lanfredino treacherous? In the first place, there was the fact that he had acted covertly. He had not informed his son of his actions, which left Remigio in some sense exposed and betrayed when he encountered Giacomo. But *traditore* in this context meant above all one who had done betrayals (*tradimenti*) to the family or one or more of its members. The *traditore* was one who had failed in his familial role and responsibility. The term could apply to sons as well as to fathers. In 1380, for example, Simone di Rinieri de' Peruzzi branded his son Benedetto a *traditore* when he disinherited him for his "many disobediences, falsities, deceits, betrayals, and torments." Among Benedetto's failings was an act of rebellion against the commune which exposed his family to reprisals on his account.[18] Remigio's use of such language was intentional. As he saw it, his father had betrayed him and the family. His response about not giving his father a penny was a statement of his intention to betray Lanfredino in turn. Lanfredino did not deserve his loyalty.

Remigio's opinion of his father gained confirmation from his mother. When Lanfredino later went to her and pleaded that she intercede and explain to the boy that he had been ordered by the Marquis of Ferrara to make peace with Giacomo, she replied, "O, Lanfredino, traitor to yourself, since you have brought such shame to so many sons, because you have made peace that neither they nor I knew about. Now you have taken away their property and their honor with everything in this world."

Her statement makes clear what was the substance of Remigio's complaint against his father. Lanfredino had betrayed the family's interests by not seeing to its honor. In Remigio's terms his father was shameful (*verghognoso*), in his mother's words his father had done shameful things to his sons. Of all the terms used by Remigio to describe and explain his fight with Lanfredino, terms like *onore*, *vergogna*, and *honestamente* are the most important and the most slippery.

Honor was both an individual and a group possession.[19] The vendetta between the Lanfredini and Giacomo Pascilocha was a point of honor for Remigio and for all the Lanfredini. Lanfredino's secret settlement with Giacomo had not upheld the family's honor. It was first of all a betrayal of Remigio—"All day there are the miseries and betrayals I see of Lanfredino saying he is a friend of the greatest enemy I have in the world." But the dishonor redounded on all. "I'm not even telling you the half of his cruelty," Remigio assured his brother in the letter, "toward me first of all, and then toward you, then toward all the rest." In summing up the incident Remigio said,

> Now we can see clearly that Lanfredino does not care about us and does not think us worth a fig, and he doesn't care about honor or shame, though he has daily need of them in his scheming. He doesn't care about anything. But as for me, if he doesn't care about me, I'll care less about him. If I were to see him cut to pieces I wouldn't get up from my seat.

Honor was something that could be challenged, as it had been by Giacomo; and it was incumbent on an honorable man to meet the challenge.[20] Honor was the basis from which one defended the family and its interests. Remigio's mother claimed that Lanfredino had deprived his family of its patrimony—its property (*roba*) and honor (*onore*). He had failed to act as the family's protector (hence he was a *traditore*). By his failure in his family role as husband and father (as seen in the complaints of his wife and son), Lanfredino had cost the family its honor, and with it the power and wealth an honorable man could hope to command. Honor was part of the symbolic patrimony. The men of the group had to defend the family and see to the security of its dominance and self-interest. The standing of the family in the eyes of others rested on its capability of defending familial honor. Lanfredino had besmirched the honor of his family, he had failed to safeguard the patrimony.[21]

To Florentines "life without honor [was] a living death."[22] Honor gave life and property meaning. Perhaps the most complete, certainly the most eloquent, statement on honor was offered by Alberti in his dialogue on the family:

> [Honor is] the most important thing in anyone's life. It is one thing without which no enterprise deserves praise or has real value. It is the ultimate source of all the splendor our work may have, the most beautiful and shining part of our life now and our life hereafter, the most lasting and eternal part—I speak of honor. . . . Satisfying the standards

of honor, we shall grow rich and well praised, admired, and esteemed among men. The man who scorns to hear or obey that sense of honor which seeks to advise and to command him grows full of vice and will never be contented even if he is rich. Men will neither admire nor love him. Being, unhappy, he often feels he would sooner live in poverty than in a splendor accompanied by bitter regrets: bitter regrets feed on the heart of the dishonest man. Remember always that poverty does us less injury than dishonor. Fame and men's favor help us more than all the riches in the world.[23]

Honor was the very foundation of status and wealth. Is it any wonder that Remigio was angered at his father's blatant disregard of the family's honor?

Honor, however, was not the only thing at stake in the quarrel. When one looks closely, one sees that the possession of authority within the household was also in question. The quarrel, in other words, was a product of the familial structure in which it occurred— the very structure it would change, a structure in which grown sons were subordinate to and dependent upon their fathers in good part for inheritance and reputation.

The Florentine father was generally extolled as the autocratic ruler of the household. Marsilio Ficino went so far as to compare the father to God and to call him a second god. Like God, the father could expect reverence, respect, and obedience from his children. This respect was to be exhibited in polite forms of address, in naming one's son after one's father, and in supporting one's aged parents.[24]

The father had duties to perform that justified his authority. He was responsible for providing the necessities of life, for expanding and maintaining the patrimony (material and symbolic). It was especially important that the father be *massaio,* that he prudently manage family affairs so as to conserve the patrimony. Among his duties was that of instructing his children, especially the males, in the management of affairs, to teach them how to treat people and property so as to conserve both (for working relations with others counted as an important part of a family's symbolic patrimony). The net result was, as Alberti stated, that sons owed everything to their fathers—their property, their status, their very being and name.[25]

In an operative sense, however, authority in the family lay in being able to impose one's definition of a situation so as to mobilize the group by universalizing a particular and private incident (such as an insult) into a matter of familial interest. Conversely, authority also involved the ability to demobilize the group by disowning a person who failed to identify his particular interest with the general, familial interest and to reduce him to the status of an individual unreasonably seeking to impose his private reason. Simone Peruzzi's disinheritance of his son is a graphic example of the latter aspect of familial authority.

The conflict between Remigio and Lanfredino was played out in precisely these terms. Lanfredino's authority in the family was shaky because he was timid in asserting it. We can see that weakness in his authority in his need for a period of time to mobilize family opinion with regard to the rapprochement with Giacomo Pascilocha. Ultimately Lanfredino could only fall back on his position in the family (on his titular authority as father, in other words) to defend his action and assert himself. At one point he stopped crying long enough to say to his son, "Look, Remigio, you are my son and you should be content with what I do. I did it for the best." As father he was supposedly the spokesman for the family, the sole font of authority, and the family's representative in the outside world. Remigio was supposed to trust his judgment as being for the best interests of all.

Remigio, though, did not buy his father's argument. As he saw it, his father had not acted in the best interests of the family and certainly not in his best interests. If anything, it was Remigio who succeeded in putting across his definition of the situation, for his mother agreed with him. His letter to his brother describing the quarrel was his attempt to convince Orsino, to justify himself.

For some time Remigio had been sceptical of his father's abilities and his handling of family matters. On 6 December 1404, some ten months before the incident which led to his falling-out with his father, Remigio had written to Orsino concerning Lanfredino's inept handling of the dowry negotiations for the marriage of their sister Lippa and concerning his fears that Lanfredino would cave in to pressure and make peace with the family's enemy.[26]

> But in order to warn you, I have great fear because our father works under his shade (that is, secretly). It may please my father that he come to be his friend, and he does not look after our honor. You will do well honestly to write about it to our father, not showing that you know anything of what I write. I have this fear because I know our father is a strange man.

Remigio went on to describe to his brother a conversation he had had with the Podestà of Ferrara (where Remigio and his father were at the time), in which he complained to that official about his father's lackadaisical conduct of the family's affairs, both its affairs of money and its affairs of honor. With some pride Remigio reported to Orsino that, as a result of his stature and conduct in Ferrara, "our friend has great admiration of the place I have here," and that "every day new people are attesting me as a father." It was Remigio who had had to assure the family's friends that his father had indeed been insulted by the family's enemy and that the family's honor would be preserved.

Remigio's assessment of his father's business acumen may not have been inaccurate. Certainly it took Lanfredino a long time to arrange his daughter's marriage, and he needed outside help to raise the funds for the girl's dowry.[27] In 1412, when he emancipated Orsino, Lanfredino was constrained by an arbitration process to give his son a farm in return for the 80 florins Orsino had provided from his own funds toward his sister's dowry and in return for other loans totaling over 600 florins.[28]

In his letter to Orsino concerning the quarrel, Remigio was again attempting to place his father beyond the pale, to characterize him as unreasonable. Alongside the fact that Lanfredino had made peace with Giacomo, which was proof of how he did not care about the family and was a traitor, Remigio presented the latest information about their father's handling of the dowry matter. "It seems to me that they [the rest of the family] will suffer together by reason of the fact that Lanfredino wants things beyond reason, and he will be held an evil man by what will result." Again Remigio claimed, "to tell you the truth, Lanfredino does not seem to me to be a wise man, rather he seems beside himself in the words and things he does all day." In some sense the competition for authority between Remigio and Lanfredino resolved itself into a contest for Orsino's allegiance.

> Lanfredino begged me very much that I not write to you about any of this. Yet I wanted to write to warn you of what hope we can ever have from that man. Still I tell you I will be very happy should you write him something about it. You also esteem too little our words and deeds, but God knows I cannot. But maybe he might show you that he is an evil man.

Such conflicts as that between Remigio and his father lay at the heart of the Florentine system of power over domestic affairs. The competition between father and son was a feature of a system that subordinated the son to the father for the duration of the father's life. Control by one person meant he alone would reap the material and symbolic profits of familial activities (e.g., Florentine fathers might pocket their sons' earnings for family expenses). A failure of historical studies of the Florentine family lies in not having taken account of the endemic nature of this competitive tension and, even more, in not having noted its causes.[29]

The fourteenth-century collector of proverbs and moral aphorisms, Paolo da Certaldo, saw that there was a constant danger of jealousies within the family, and he cautioned fathers to love all their children equally.[30] Alberti also stated that the dissimilarity between the desires of the young and those of the old "prohibits and denies that complete union which is required in true love."[31] Perceived imbalances in the distribution of favor or of responsibility could lead to domestic friction. Kent himself notes that there were two schools of thought in Florence on how to raise children—one characterized by him as strict and the other as moderate.[32] People like Paolo da Certaldo argued that fathers should not give their sons any independence or responsibility. As soon as a father let his son take over he would find himself out in the cold.[33] Others, like Giovanni Rucellai, believed that sons should be given increasing responsibility with age. But this divergence of contemporary opinion also marked a potentially dysfunctional point in the system. The disagreement over the way to treat one's son was the result of the fact that whichever path a father chose there were hazards to be faced. Paternal power might be lost; or it might become the object of dispute, vituperation, or even ridicule. In either case the solidarity of the family was on the line. The numerous injunctions to sons to obey their fathers and to fathers to treat their sons with consideration and respect were cultural means of trying to lessen or remove the potentially disastrous consequences generated by that very structure of familial power which was designed to preserve the family.

The relationship between father and son, however, was only potentially dysfunctional. Other factors, notably economic ones, entered into the picture to make the relationship actually dysfunctional. The competition between father and son revolved around the question of the profitability of remaining united to the group versus the profitability of separation. In Remigio's case the choice was clear. His father had forfeited his right to his authority and to the obedience and respect due him, because he had not seen to the family's interests. Remigio found that the only way he could regain his honor and hope to enjoy prosperity in his life was to affect change in the network of kinship ties surrounding him. Bitterly he left the house—the family, that is, for the family was the *casa*—and left Florence. He went to Venice and established himself in business there with the help of a generous patron. His physical separation from his father was completed by the symbolic act of changing his name. As he explained to his brother,

> when I left the *casa*, I made up my mind definitely never to be considered his son and to change my name. And so I have been calling myself Bellini from Florence, and I have nothing else in mind than to conduct myself as a merchant in order to regain my reputation and to show that I want to do well, and to restore past losses.

Both in fact and in name Remigio was no longer part of the Lanfredini *casa*. He could not have honor and reputation as long as he was associated with his father, so he broke with him materially and symbolically. Family goods and family members were held together by honor. In the absence of honor Remigio lost both.

In Remigio's case, economic prospects at home were not bright in view of his father's ineptitude, whereas he could hope to seize the economic opportunities available by moving to Venice. The fact that Remigio had available the opportunity to go to Venice and seek his fortune and honor placed him in a more powerful position in dealing with his father. Lanfredino, for his part, was vulnerable because he did not have a secure economic basis behind his paternal authority, and because his son could quite independently take advantage of business opportunities beyond paternal control. It was the presence of economic opportunity elsewhere and, even more, the lack of economic opportunity at home (as seen in Lanfredino's poor management of family resources and his squandering of its honor) that provoked Remigio to leave. Lacking an economic basis for his authority, Lanfredino could rely only on the moral sanctions contained in the father-son relationship; and these sanctions were insufficient in the face of those sanctions concerning honor which Remigio could and did advance in his defense.[34]

The quarrel between Remigio and Lanfredino was much more than an instance of intrafamilial hatred. It was an eruption along a fissure in the social geography. The fissure consisted of the potentially dysfunctional competition between father and son; the eruption was due to the father's lack of real power (both material and symbolic) to control the situation; and the eruption occurred in the form of conflicting interpretations of honor and family interest.

No matter from what angle historians have approached the history of the family—demographic, legal, economic, or sociocultural—there has been a general assumption that the various behavioral patterns and individual practices revealed by the sources represent attempts to follow a prescriptive norm. Law in the strict sense and culture in the more general sense have been treated as the sources of rules for conduct. This legalistic approach is conceived of as an explanatory device to cover all the myriad practices revealed by the society. An event like the one I have examined here, however, reveals, in my opinion, that culture (and the same is true for law as a cultural system) provides a set of symbols and values that social actors can and do interpret and manipulate for their own ends. Kinship, as an aspect of culture, is no less immune from such manipulation. Kin relations form a network of relationships which may or may not be used. Those that are used are those that are profitable in some way. They are the ones that are cultivated—kept in working order in a sense. If they are not cultivated, they can disappear into the brush like a path no longer traveled. Remigio Lanfredini, as a result of the fight with his father, opted not to travel the path of paternal relations anymore. In his eyes it led nowhere.

The conception of the family as a corporate unit marked by solidarity (created and carried by legalistic norms) and of society as erected on the basis of family units is a conception that is, at times, not capable of describing and explaining change, especially change resulting from conflict. In this regard the Lanfredini family dispute is instructive. The problems someone like Kent has in interpreting the Lanfredini incident are the same problems that cause him and others to avoid the issues of the role of females in the family and of the role of legal emancipation of children from paternal control.[35] These aspects of familial life are discordant notes in a symphony on the family as a functioning, unified whole. But if all was so stable and harmonious in the family, why do the archives overflow with documents describing contractual relations between kinsmen, why are these contracts safeguarded by legal sanctions, and why do they cover almost every aspect of domestic life? We will never know the answers to these questions by insisting on looking at the family as a rigid, self-contained entity rather than as a social process in which ideology and practice were not always and everywhere convergent.[36]

The Lanfredini family and the solution hit upon by one of its members to his problems with his father may indeed not have been typical of all Florentine families, but this very lack of typicality is not, therefore, meaningless. Not all families succeeded in adapting to, much less in overcoming, all of the problems and pressures thrown up before them by life in a Renaissance city-state. Families could and did fail, as the complaints and warnings of Alberti and Sacchetti remind us.[37] Recent research into the family in Florence has made great strides in broadening our appreciation of the demographic, economic, political, and other factors which played a part in shaping and reshaping the family. Kent, Herlihy and Klapisch, and Kirshner and Molho have made outstanding contributions in this regard.[38] My intent here has been to move both beyond and within the aggregate economic and social data and the analysis of cultural conceptions to detail how problems were dealt with by a single family. Similar and more exhaustive analyses can and should be worked out for other families of all types and all social strata. Only by gathering a number of such studies and placing them within the overall cultural, economic, and demographic context will it become possible to appreciate the diverse points of contact between families and the society within which they lived and to perceive the interface between familial success and familial failure. Ultimately, for all the similarities in beliefs and patterns of behavior, there was no Florentine family of the Renaissance, there were only families, like the Lanfredini, each with its own resources, problems, and strategies.

5

•

A RECONSIDERATION OF SELF-DISCIPLINING PACTS AMONG THE PERUZZI OF FLORENCE

•

In 1981 *Renaissance Quarterly* published an article concerning the important but difficult historical problems of family vendetta and political factionalism in Renaissance Florence. The authors, D. V. and F. W. Kent, presented an analysis and transcription of an intriguing fifteenth-century text (preserved in a seventeenth-century copy) that contained, as the article's title indicated, a self-disciplining pact among members of the Peruzzi lineage.[1] What I propose to do in the following pages is expand on the Kents' elegant treatment of the Peruzzi text by bringing to bear on it another text I have come across in the course of research on legal procedures and dispute settlements in Renaissance Florence. Actually what I have stumbled upon is a set of three texts dating from 1425, 1428, and 1429. They concern a vendetta between some of the Peruzzi and members of the Brancacci lineage. As was the case with the text the Kents brought to light, these texts have unique historical qualities that bear on the nature of kinship among the Florentine elite during a very turbulent period in the city's history.

We must begin with a summation of what the Kents found. During "the intense communal concern throughout 1429 to root out faction," the Peruzzi assembled in June to preserve themselves against both internal dissensions and outside enmities.[2] Four years later, soon after a *provvisione* imposing political disabilities on all paternal

143

kinsmen of murderers, nine Peruzzi assembled again. They established a council of three prominent Peruzzi, including Ridolfo di Bonifazio, second only to Rinaldo degli Albizzi among those opposed to the Medici, along with Rinieri di Niccolò and Bartolomeo di Verano Peruzzi. These men, or their designated alternates, were to deal with anyone whose crimes threatened the group.[3] The group of nine accorded these three "piena balia, autorità e potestà" to demand payment of compensation to victims or even to imprison and hand malefactors among them over to the courts. The others swore not to aid the perpetrator of "such horrible and unsuitable things" ("sifatte cose abhominevoli e sconvenevoli"). This meeting took place in Ridolfo's house on 25 June. His son Luigi drew up the text. On July 3 Ridolfo and Bartolomeo signed it; on July 4 Rinieri signed; on July 5 six others to be governed by it signed, including the thirty-year-old Piero di Giovanni, the protagonist of the texts discussed below.

The Kents approach this text largely from a political perspective. Seeing that its composition dated from June 1433, and that it was based on the earlier agreement of 1429, they are sensitive to those features of the text that indicate it was "a response to the factional manoeuvering of the years 1426–34."[4] In their eyes the text is a rare example "of a family meeting privately and solemnly to prepare itself for a political battle." "The persistence of lineage solidarity in politics" leads them to presume such meetings must have been relatively common, although written evidence of them does not survive (they claim, because of the "sensitive and even incriminating information" that would be left behind). The authors also see historical value in the differences between their text and earlier agreements of *consorteria*. As a pact governing kin, the Peruzzi agreement resembled or even derived from earlier consorterial pacts. Its meaning lay in part in both its similarities to and differences from them. The Peruzzi compact was "an agreement within one patrilineage, not an alliance between a number of individuals or families"; it was also private, not a notarized act. The Kents' text figures in a context of familial agreements and of legislation imposing political penalties on those involved in vendettas and factionalism.[5]

Also important to the Kents is establishing the solidarity of the Peruzzi lineage. "The overriding concern among this numerous kindred had become, one might suggest, to provide the machinery with which to restrain or discipline, for the sake of the family and of the regime (*stato*), the activities of foolish or perhaps impulsive kinsmen who shared a common cause."[6] They find no evidence of division among the Peruzzi, or at least note that reference to internal division in 1429 seems to have been lacking in 1433. The Kents invoke a vision of the clan living in homes clustered about their piazza near Santa Croce; they invoke the evidence of property-holding in common and mutual contracts as revealed in Peruzzi household heads' *catasto* declarations.[7] The men who assembled at Ridolfo Peruzzi's house in June 1433 represented all but two of the family's branches and came from three generations. "The nine men at the meeting in June 1433 could genuinely be said to speak for most of the seventy-five men and boys, as it were the Peruzzi republic."[8]

The Kents' insightful reading of their texts thus rests on several types of evidence. There is the date of the text. There is its similarity to other evidence of lineage solidarity, both within the Peruzzi and from other lineages. And there is the absence of evidence "that the Peruzzi of this period were particularly prone to violence against each other or outsiders."[9] The texts I have uncovered, on the other hand, do in fact reveal acts of violence toward outsiders by one of the Peruzzi signatories of 1433. Possible "internal" divisions and evident "external" vendetta surface alongside any concerns with the consequences of political factionalism. Knowledge of these acts and of their treatment by the Peruzzi cannot help but make us reformulate the reading of the text of 1433. Peruzzi solidarity and the intermingling, or separation, of private and public, familial and political, can be reexamined.

The three texts I have located are all formal, notarized, therefore public, acts. The first two (chronologically) provide limited insight into events. The first records an agreement to submit to binding arbitration (*compromissum*).[10] Ridolfo di Bonifazio and Bartolomeo di Verano Peruzzi, on 13 March 1425 (1426, new style), with the concurrence of Lorenzo and Giotto Peruzzi, acted as agents for Piero, Bartolomeo, Mariano, and Guido, the four sons of the late Giovanni di Bartolomeo Peruzzi. The other party to the *compromissum* was Guasparre di Salvestro Brancacci, acting for himself and for Lippaccio di Bartolomeo Brancacci and for all the other Brancacci ("et omnium et singulorum hominum et personarum de dicta domo et familia et seu consorteria de Brancaccis"). The arbiters chosen were Matteo di Piero di Banco degli Albizzi, Michele di Giovanni Riccialbani, Domenico di Zanobi di Cecco Aldimari [Fraschi], and Piero di Francesco di ser Gino (Ginori). The temporal term of the *compromissum* was a relatively lengthy three years and two months. The four sons of Giovanni Peruzzi had eight days to ratify the contract, which they in fact did almost immediately, on the same day.[11]

It is difficult to get behind the opaque, highly abbreviated legal formulas of this text. It says nothing about why there was any dispute between these parties or why over three years were required to resolve it. Looking at this text with the sort of lens the Kents provide, we can be struck, however, by two things. Both the Peruzzi and the Brancacci were generally on the same side—the anti-Medicean side—in the factional squabbles of 1426–34. Members of both lineages would be exiled after the Medici triumph of 1434, including Ridolfo and Bartolomeo Peruzzi, the young Mariano di Giovanni, and Salvestro di Guasparre Brancacci.[12] On the other hand, some of the four arbitrators appear among the pro-Medicean faction, according to Dale Kent's evidence. Domenico Fraschi figured among Medici supporters.[13] Piero Ginori was also a Medicean and was married to a sister of another arbitrator, Michele Albizzi.[14] Above all, with relation to the interests of the Peruzzi and the Brancacci, this was a neutral group. The relative powerlessness and obscurity of these men seems to have been desirable in these circumstances as a guarantee of neutrality.

The second text, the arbitration judgment (*laudum*) of 11 March 1428 (1429) furnishes little further insight. Formulas report that the parties' evidence and allegations had been considered. The "certis iustis et rationabilibus causis" that had moved the arbitrators were not spelled out, other than to state that the four Peruzzi were truly debtors of Lippaccio Brancacci and his brother Giovanni for the hefty sum of 1,500 florins, which they were given five days to pay.[15] The arbitrators expressly reserved the power to revise, amend, or annul their judgment within the remainder of the term set forth in the *compromissum*, namely two months. The parties were not present or represented when this *laudum* was drawn up in Domenico Fraschi's house.

Unexpressive though they are, these first two texts constitute the procedural background and historical confirmation to the highly revealing third text. Exactly two months after the first *laudum*, the arbitrators (this time minus Piero di Francesco di ser Gino), convened at an unspecified location in the *popolo* of Sant'Appollinare and modified their judgment. This time they spelled out the background of the dispute between the Peruzzi and Brancacci in order to justify their determinations. In the course of doing so they revealed to posterity how the Peruzzi more or less as a whole had tried to deal with this dispute.

Three and a half years before, while in Barcelona, Piero di Giovanni Peruzzi knifed Lippaccio Brancacci, wounding him in the left arm and side "to the grave loss and prejudice" ("in grave dampnum et preiudicium") of Lippaccio and "contra formam statutorum."[16] Why he did this—what issue was in dispute, what was the previous relationship between the two men, what was the immediate provocation—we have no way of telling at present. Subsequently, on 13 March 1425 (1426), as we have seen, they entered into formal arbitration with the help of kin as intermediaries. However, on that same day they also entered into a private agreement, drawn up in the vernacular (as was the Kents' text). The arbitrators were intended as an insurance against future actions if the private agreement failed to work.[17] Considering the nature of the private agreement, it is little wonder it did not work. But, because its failure necessitated the arbitrators' stepping in, the text of the agreement was transcribed into the second *laudum*.

The agreement, in line with other examples one can find in the archives, turned Piero Peruzzi into a moving target for the Brancacci. Two outsiders, Vannozzo di Giovanni and Niccolò d'Agnolo Serragli, helped negotiate.[18] Lippaccio Brancacci "and any of his kin" ("et qualunque de' suoi consorti"), and even outsiders acting for him, had three years in which "to avenge the said offense done to Lippaccio solely in the person of the said Piero" ("vendicarsi di decta offesa facta a Lippaccio solo nella persona propria del decto Piero"). He was allowed to strike back against Piero by inflicting some sort of physical injury, in return for the wounds he had received. Should Piero otherwise die within that period, the vendetta fell on whichever of Piero's brothers Lippaccio Brancacci chose (notifying them within fifteen days of his choice). Piero (or the designated target) was required to live those three years in Florence, except for four sojourns "in villa" of no more than eight days each in each year. Time over that amount was simply added to the time allowed the Brancacci to pursue their vendetta. Piero had to sally forth once every eight days, unarmed and unaccompanied, on the streets of Florence and go at least as far as the Mercato Vecchio. This itinerary drew him away from Santa Croce, but not across the Arno into the Brancacci neighborhood near Santo Spirito. In the event Lippaccio achieved his vendetta (whether that meant an equivalent wounding or what, is never specified), someone among the rulers of the city ("qualunque de' rectori della città di Firenze") would step in to affirm that Piero and his brothers had to let the matter rest there and not strike back at Lippaccio or the Brancacci. If Lippaccio failed to get even, both parties were to conclude a formal peace agreement—hence the *compromissum* and its long duration. The arbitrators effectively had an umpiring function, to determine if the vendetta had been achieved and to be notified as to the new target in the event Piero died.[19]

Though Piero, along with Bartolomeo and Mariano, signed the *scripta privata*, he did not abide by it. The arbitrators had learned that, even before the wounding of Lippaccio, Piero had struck Lippaccio's brother Serotino with a piece of wood. A truce (*tregua*) had resulted from that incident, so the wounding of Lippaccio was also a violation of the truce. In harsh language the arbitrators noted Piero's lack of penitence for his acts and his contempt for the agreement he had signed and, therefore, for the Brancacci. He avoided the Mercato Vecchio, indeed he had avoided Florence for long periods. When he went about he carried weapons. One consequence of this disdain for the Brancacci was that Piero's brother Bartolomeo, unmindful ("inmemor") of his brother's actions, often passed before Lippaccio's house, "which is contrary to the custom and good habits of the city of Florence" ("quod est contra usum et bonos mores civitatis Florentie"). Lippaccio's brother Giovanni, "moved by heat of anger" ("calore iracundie motus"), wounded Bartolomeo with a small knife one day in June 1428. Bartolomeo had later pressed charges; the case was still pending in the court of the Esecutore degli ordinamenti di giustizia.[20]

The arbitrators gave the brothers six months, to 10 November, to enter a full formal peace agreement (*pax*) with the Brancacci. They also had to drop the case against Giovanni Brancacci within two months or pay any fine levied against him by the court. The *laudum* of March was cancelled. Apparently the wounding of a Peruzzi, which must have been unknown to the arbitrators on the occasion of the first *laudum*, was worth 1,500 florins.

Is it farfetched to consider this set of incidents, settled only on 11 May, as the immediate background and concern of the Peruzzi on the occasion of the first "self-disciplining pact" in 1429? That was the year, unlike 1433, when express mention was made of internal divisions and external enemies. May the vague reference in the Kents' text to a "bullettino impetrato da nostri M[agnifici] S[ignori]" indicate the intervention by a "rector" mentioned in the final *laudum*?[21] Is the meeting of June 1429 perhaps an indication that a formal *pax* with the Brancacci, textual evidence for which has yet to surface, did take place? On larger themes, however, what does all this say about kinship solidarity, vendetta, and politics?

There can be no doubt these texts concern a vendetta. Their language is clear. The Brancacci's right to vendetta was expressly recognized as the terms of the game were set out. The Peruzzi certainly were no strangers to vendetta. Piero's grandfather Bartolomeo had a vendetta with the Tolosini in 1382 and openly marshalled his friends to protect him against retaliation. Ridolfo Peruzzi's political stances, especially in collaboration with the Ricasoli, were taken as vindictive by the Pitti.[22] The Peruzzi may not have been notably violent—they certainly moved to curb Piero's violence, or at least its consequences—but they were not total strangers to violence.

The Peruzzi-Brancacci dispute also followed the morphology of vendetta as laid out by anthropologists and historians.[23] It began with the point of honor—an act seen as sufficiently insulting to raise questions about the worth of the offended person. Wounding would be a classic example. Piero's failure to abide by the private agreement that made him a target for retaliation was depicted as a continuation of the initial insult, as further shaming the Brancacci. The one who took offense, however, then had the position of initiative, if not power. The other was in his "debt" (note the language and monetary compensation of the first *laudum*).[24] He could collect when and how he could. The "collection" had to be public, however, to proclaim to everyone, not just the new victim and his kin, that an act of revenge had been undertaken. So it was that Piero was a target only when he was on the streets, and he was notably ordered to appear in the market, a highly public place. The vengeance exacted on his brother came in the street.[25] It was in the interest of the other party, of course, to deny the debt or, failing that, to minimize the loss. In our case, if Piero's behavior constituted denial of the debt, it flew in the face of his own and his kinsmen's express recognition of the debt in writing back in 1425 (1426).[26] In those cultures where it flourishes, vendetta is part of the language of kinship. It sets an exclusionary principle to membership by establishing who is obligated to seek revenge or is subject to vengeance. It should thus contribute to an active sense of kin solidarity.[27] But vendetta is also expansive. Ideally the victim struck back at his offender.[28] If the perpetrator could not be had, another victim from among his relatives would do—just as Bartolomeo ended up receiving Piero's wounds. If the primary victim could not retaliate, then those closest to him should—just as Giovanni, not Lippaccio, inflicted the wounds. Innocent, uninvolved, fairly distant kin could thus get sucked into the vortex of vendetta. The nature of the retaliation could also easily escalate; blows delivered in anger could kill, rather than just wound. And each blow required a counter blow, so vendetta threatened to be perpetual. There was no statute of limitations on retaliation. One could bide one's time, as Florentines advised one another, and strike at the best moment. Grudges were carried across generations, sometimes in the pages of paternal *ricordi* where historians can find them.[29]

It was the tendency of vendetta to escalate and expand. It was also necessary that it be public, and take place in a public manner and place, so as to be recognized for what it was. It was on the thoroughfares and public spaces, like the marketplace where Piero Peruzzi was to appear every eight days, that one's reputation was on display. That was where the strongest personalities among the rich and prominent emerged.[30] Vendetta, therefore, could endanger public order, and that called forth intervention by communal authorities. The right to seek revenge was never denied. But laws and courts attempted to limit who could pursue vendetta and who could be subject to it.[31] The Florentine statutes of 1415, for example, defined circumstances involving physical wounding where vendetta was "allowed."[32] They also set penalties for pursuing a vendetta against someone other than the principal.[33] It seems clear from the wording, moreover, that these statutes only came into play effectively if one party brought the other to trial (presumably on assault or homicide) and the other alleged vendetta as a defense. The commune was not refereeing from the start. A parallel process took place with communally sanctioned reprisals undertaken by Florentines against citizens of foreign governments to redress grievances, usually relating to trade.[34]

Mechanisms also existed to bring vendetta to an end, even if only temporarily. Monetary or other compensation could be encouraged as against further blows. Truces, peace settlements, and arbitrated arrangements were all sanctified and supported by communal machinery in Florence and elsewhere. According to statute, breaking a *pax* was not an act of just vendetta, the peacebreaker lost the benefit of the statute allowing vendetta. Later, in 1471, the penalty for breaking a peace would be expanded into designation as a rebel and loss of property to the fisc.[35] In this way, from an explicit desire to preserve public order, the government played a policing function, though not a judicial role, as one historian has it, regarding vendetta.[36]

The role of the state in regard to vendetta is an area of historical concern and controversy. The Burckhardtian position, recently endorsed by Randolph Starn, is that the centralizing Renaissance state tended to curb violence and self-help, to redirect peoples' energies and conflicts to judicial arenas.[37] The continued existence of recourse to violent self-help, even in the privately arranged manner of the Peruzzi-Brancacci dispute, shows that it was a more complex matter than an expansive state power meeting resistance from private interests. Room remained for private initiative and strategizing; the state could figure as an obstacle to it. The *provvisione* of 1433, which the Kents see as crucial to the Peruzzi instrument of the same year, raised the price of vendetta for politically active men like those Peruzzi who signed their agreement, but it did not abolish vendetta. The state had control not by physical force—one sees no such compulsion operating on the Peruzzi—but by virtue of its function as an arbitrating element or as a basis for arbitrations worked out by private citizens.[38] As one historian has it, "feud implies the presence of arbitrators, it generates them, and imposes on them the difficult task of resolution desired by the participants in the conflict."[39]

Government did not exert overwhelming force on vendettas' participants; it did not have to. It was not only the interest of the broader community (tribe, village, city) to limit vendetta. The kin, who bore the risk most directly, clearly had an interest in limiting the consequences of acts of any one of them, especially when they were in a position of awaiting retaliation—as were the Peruzzi.[40] The kin hastened to set up alternatives to vendetta, such as arbitration, and appealed if need be to religious grounds for foreswearing enmity.[41] They also clarified, as did the Peruzzi, who the principal was and who among the kin was liable for the vendetta. Even the actions of women and enmities among them, though they might not be graced with the term vendetta, were potentially dangerous to a family and open to the same means of settlement as quarrels among men.[42] Ideally the goal of these efforts, as in the case of the Peruzzi, was the swearing of peace between the parties, thus signaling the end of vendetta.[43]

The arrangement of 1425 with the Brancacci, negotiated with the aid of the Serragli, attempted to limit vendetta in two ways. It designated only one target for retaliation, Piero, who was guilty himself of starting the problem. Substitution for him was limited to his brothers, those with the most immediate obligation to revenge him. The other Peruzzi, many of whom were Piero's close neighbors, were off-limits to the Brancacci, who also did not have to venture into the Peruzzi enclave to find their target. The intervention of the two most powerful and prominent of the Peruzzi, Ridolfo and Bartolomeo, probably aimed at just this result. To that end, they distinguished in the notarial texts as to who spoke for whom. Never were all the Peruzzi expressly drawn into the net. The wounded and offended Brancacci, on the other hand, were designated by general phrases. Only Piero (or one of his brothers) could be the target, but any Brancacci could deliver the blow.

The arrangement also set a time limit on vendetta.[44] Either one took compensation for a matter of honor, or one took one's revenge, whenever possible, sooner or later. Here vengeance was allowed only for a three-year period, to be followed by an arbitrated conclusion. Afterward things could return to normal, for further blows were given up in advance. In effect, the Peruzzi recognized that Piero had wronged the Brancacci and that they had to expect the Brancacci, as honorable men, to collect the debt. They had three years to collect in blood—the "coin" in which it had been paid. If they did not, then the designated arbitrators would impose a final peaceful settlement and would set a monetary compensation. The Brancacci could thus choose their weapon. As it happened, events took the course they might have in an unregulated vendetta—brother attacked brother. In 1429 and again in 1433 the Peruzzi moved to do just that—limit vendetta. Political considerations, strictly speaking, played a role also, to be sure, but the limitation of the "costs" of vendetta, of the collection of the "debt" by the Brancacci, was clearly in the thoughts of these Peruzzi.

Piero's rash acts, the acts of a headstrong young man, posed serious problems for those bearing the Peruzzi name. They were vulnerable to retaliation and to an obligation to contribute to compensation (and how could Piero and his brothers have come up with the entire 1,500 florins set out in the first *laudum?*). More important, the retaliation would come from a lineage they were otherwise sympathetic to, if not closely allied to, politically. Here the kinds of political considerations the Kents pointed to enter in, I have to agree, very directly. The recognition of the Brancacci claim, the means to pursue it, and the physical and temporal restrictions on it were all concessions of a political nature. The Peruzzi seem not to have accorded any similar concessions to their personal enemies among the pro-Medici ranks.[45]

The willingness of the Brancacci to abide by the arrangement of 1425 may indicate similar sentiments on their side. They too could hope to keep intact political ties, however indirect, to the Peruzzi. They received assurance that they could retaliate for the injury to Lippaccio without having to fear the consequent counter-retaliation of the Peruzzi.

The one who did not want to abide by it, understandably, was Piero. His sense of self-preservation evidently won out over lineage loyalty when it came to putting himself up as a duck in a shooting gallery that was the streets of Florence. Of course, he had also put his own honor and anger ahead of the interests of his brothers and the rest of the Peruzzi, in some ways, at least, by wounding two of the Brancacci in the first place.[46] In any case, the problem of lineage solidarity is clearly exposed in the relations between him, and his brother, and the other Peruzzi—both in 1425 and thereafter.

The other Peruzzi, notably Ridolfo and Bartolomeo, had to accede to Brancacci claims without seeming to be disloyal to their kinsmen. To draw up the arrangement, to stand effectively as guarantors of it,[47] was to make a declaration of common interests and a recognition of implication in a kinsman's acts. It was an affirmation of kinship. In the circumstances of the lived-in world of the Peruzzi, as depicted by the Kents, it is hard to see how they could have repudiated ties to Piero and his brothers. They held in common a portion of a Peruzzi *palazzo* along with four other family branches.[48] Peruzzi also interacted constantly in financial and other matters, and they arbitrated disputes among themselves.[49] Piero was one of them. By the same token he could not easily disassociate himself from his kin and neighbors. Still, their rights and liabilities, including property ownership, were not collective and equal for each. There was a constant accounting of assets and there were divisions of property. A proud man like Ridolfo could desire sole ownership of his *palazzo* against the rights even of his own brother.[50] Disputes inevitably arose. Implication in matters of honor and liability for them were also not evenly distributed. The consequences of Piero's acts rippled out from him along lines of relationship, diminishing in intensity, at least nominally. But it was the wealthy and prominent, those like Ridolfo and Bartolomeo, who had the most to lose—more than those less prominent but more closely related to Piero. It was men like these, therefore, as the Kents note, who took the lead in heading off vendetta in the self-disciplining pacts of 1429 and 1433.[51] And it should be remembered that they did not assemble all the Peruzzi. That the nine could speak for many of the other seventy-five Peruzzi males makes sense. Still, they directly represented only one-third of Peruzzi households, one-third of which were located away from the piazza around which the rest clustered. It was a particular cross section of the lineage that assembled at Ridolfo's house in 1433. It was the Peruzzi on whom vendetta liability could fall. It was, therefore, an active and largely effective kin group at the intersection of cultural conceptions and functional interaction. And again, much the same could be said for the Brancacci. Salvestro di Guasparre represented Lippaccio. There was no direct reference to the branch of Felice di Michele. Salvestro feared loss—of life, property, honor—if he did or if he did not support his kinsman. Piero Peruzzi, spokesman for all the households in the *palazzo* where he lived,[52] was one of only three younger men at the meeting in 1433.[53] The message to him and those like him was clear. In the future, any acts such as those he had committed in Barcelona years before would call down on him the wrath of the three older and wealthier Peruzzi who were entrusted with safeguarding the interests of all the signatories. The next time, if need be, they would seize him and deliver him over to judicial authorities. The arrangement with the Brancacci, coming on the heels of Piero's failure to follow through on the rules of vendetta negotiated in 1425, seems to form the immediate background to the pact of June 1429. It cannot have been far out of mind in the restatement of the pact in June 1433.

The arrangement of 1425, the pacts of 1429 and 1433, were not declarations of unilateral kinship solidarity. Rather they sought to remind the signatories that perceptions of collective solidarity were common outside the Peruzzi (at least as much as within), enshrined even in communal laws; that, therefore, an individual's acts implicated others and they, in turn, might perceive a greater line of solidarity in abandoning him to his fate than in standing with him. Lineage solidarity was not clear cut, simple, or automatic. Solidarity among the Peruzzi, for example, emerged most evidently precisely when it was threatened. It was expressed paradoxically as a willingness to remove or expose one of their number. Kinship solidarity was ambiguous because it was a multivalent, multifaceted construct. Situations, relationships, physical proximity—all could affect responses to given cases. The Peruzzi seem even to have changed their response in the years between 1425 and 1433. In the first instance they had acted to keep matters away from the courts and communal authorities. At most they would look to outside arbitrators, of their choosing, who could offer functional, effective, and satisfactory agreements, rather than justice in the abstract.[54] Otherwise they would handle their own honor. The government would step in only to guarantee the final peace—a laudable goal of government that even the Peruzzi recognized.[55] Legislation of 1433 setting political penalties on kin harboring a murderer, as well as the undoubtedly heightened political tensions of that pivotal year in Florentine history, produced very direct threats to turn malefactors over to the authorities. Familial or lineage solidarity had its limits.

Even where norms of kin solidarity are most ingrained and forcefully stated, as they were in Renaissance Florence (as seen by the presumptions underlying the Peruzzi maneuvers), not all kin got along. Material and symbolic interests could collide as well as coincide in the perceptions of social actors. So it happened, and was recognized, that family lines did not always act together. Most obviously, weaker and poorer branches might drift away, as did some among the Peruzzi.[56] As Dale Kent notes in her fundamental study of the Medici rise to power, family lines did not act in unison, nor were they assumed to, since some were not punished by the Medici.[57] Piero Peruzzi, for example, was not exiled, whereas his brother Mariano was. The incessant encoding of kinship obligations in legal form also indicates, I have argued elsewhere, a need to remind persons of these obligations, give them specific content, and provide means of enforcement (as did the Peruzzi pacts).[58] Of course there were also the notorious incidents of intralineage and intrafamilial disputes, decried to be sure but also regular in appearance.[59]

Beyond genetics and social functions, kinship is a cultural construct—a language, an idiom.[60] Parts of this idiom, including vendetta, are also normatively inscribed. Meanings are often ambiguous because the terms are multivalent and susceptible to metaphoric extension. In 1425 the Peruzzi and Brancacci negotiated as to who was a Peruzzi for the purposes of the Brancacci's revenge. In 1429 and again in 1433 nine men bearing the name Peruzzi privileged three of their number as interpreters of the meaning of kinship—the meaning of being Peruzzi. It was this power—to determine meaning—that was the essence of political power. Here was the incentive of a positive nature for men like Ridolfo and Bartolomeo Peruzzi, Salvestro Brancacci, or the four designated arbitrators to become involved. The principal figures in a kindred could exploit their role as mediators to the outside world. Interestingly, lesser members of a lineage, poorer, younger, could also exploit the situation to realign their kinship position, even if only as a threat to others.[61]

All dimensions of meaning were in the purview of such men ultimately, but it was the political dimension in the broadest sense—that is, the standing of the group in relation to the rest of society—that was to be the starting point of their interpretive journeys. This standing with the outside world, however, also could not be construed without reference to the dynamic of relations within the group. Kin solidarity seemed strongest in its passive voice. Piero Peruzzi wounded the Brancacci, all of them, in some sense. It was when one Peruzzi committed such an act that there was worry about "nostra famiglia," that "loss, burden, and inconvenience" ("danno, incarico e gravezza") could result for the rest of the family.[62] The older, more experienced heads, those who were—more than others—kin because they took the lead, were best entrusted with the task of determining meanings of kinship and strategies to deal with it. Ridolfo Peruzzi had more of the Peruzzi, of their interests, and of Florence—their stage—in his gaze than did the relatively myopic young Piero di Giovanni.

6

•

READING BETWEEN THE PATRILINES
Leon Battista Alberti's *Della Famiglia* in Light of His Illegitimacy

•

Leon Battista Alberti's *Della Famiglia* has become a fixture in historical studies of the early Renaissance.[1] Despite all the attention directed to it, however, *Della Famiglia* remains an ambiguous text. It is seen as an apology for the "bourgeois" or "civic" mentality of the patriciate that ruled Florence.[2] It is also seen as a "humanistic" text, the result of the intellectual and aesthetic inclinations of its versatile author.[3] Each view of *Della Famiglia*—as bourgeois or humanistic—has to confront textual problems. For example, although the dialogue's contents seem to "respond to the need to resolve theoretically problems that concern humanity in general,"[4] it does this only in the context and perspective of the urban patriciate. On the other hand, curiously, if it is an apology for the Florentine patriciate, it provides few precise references to Florence, and the family in the dialogue remains isolated, enclosed, self-sufficient—a very idealized vision with respect to the fifteenth century.[5]

The fundamentally ambiguous character of much of *Della Famiglia* has been ascribed to various factors. The dialogue form itself heightens ambiguities already present in Alberti's text.[6] His attempt at a "fusion of classical learning with the affairs and the very language of daily life,"[7] of the "best of the past civic traditions of Florence and of the precepts of the ancients,"[8] could result only in

157

rich and complex ambiguities as the inevitable by-product of defining and discussing difficult ethical issues and seeking to harmonize theory and practice. It has also been suggested that the idealized and "centripetal" image of the family created an unavoidable tension between this predominantly internal perspective on the family and the largely unexplored external perspective of the reality of fifteenth-century family life.[9] This ambiguity has also been related to another explanatory grid constituted by Alberti's personal experiences. To quote Alberti's modern editor: "His thought . . . is both a record of personal experience and a reflection of a need to reconcile old and new, ideal and real, that is an essential critical issue of early Quattrocento humanism."[10]

There were intense ambiguities in these personal experiences. Although he wrote about the Alberti, explored the duties of fathers and children, the formation of marriage, the acquisition and management of property, Battista Alberti was himself illegitimate, celibate, and a beneficed cleric.[11] Of all these conditions, the one most often cited, but also the least explored or understood, is that of illegitimacy. Cecil Grayson points to Battista's illegitimate birth, along with the family's exile from Florence, as a major formative influence on the man and his writings. Renée Watkins also has hinted that Alberti's illegitimacy lay behind the "assertive sense of family membership" that marks *Della Famiglia* and the appearance in it of the young Battista.[12] Ruggiero Romano wonders if the text was not the attempt of an illegitimate person to erect a bridge to his family, thus moving him to idealize it.[13] Eugenio Garin has embraced a similar view.[14] There are suggestions as well that in the course of the dialogue resentment at the treatment Alberti received from relatives boiled over into irony in discussion of issues like education and the division of family property on inheritance.[15]

Nevertheless, to my knowledge there has not been an attempt to interpret *Della Famiglia* systematically and consistently from the vantage point of its author's illegitimacy. It has been brought to bear only occasionally and haphazardly to account for isolated features of the dialogue. This chapter will attempt a reading that invokes the social and legal context of illegitimacy. It will treat the text neither as entirely "bourgeois" nor "civic" nor "humanistic" but as a unique distillation of these contexts around the organizing center of the author's own ambiguous familial status.

I do not mean to imply that biographical perspectives have not been brought to bear on Alberti's text. Girolamo Mancini, Joan Kelly Gadol, Grayson, and Garin have formulated biographical readings. For that matter, I am singling out only one facet of Alberti's life. My reading must remain tentative, yielding partial (though perhaps valuable) insights. The meanings of a text cannot be reduced to its genesis in the supposedly controlling intention of its author.[16] Authorial intent plays a formative part, but this intent may also be ambivalent and uncertain, and the text can and does carry other meanings for its readers. What we know of the history of Alberti's text itself confirms the limitations of a reductionistic reading based on a presumed intention or a presumed unity or identity between the author's life and his text. By Alberti's own account other Alberti reacted negatively to his work, if they deigned to read it at all.[17] It was also read by others in only partial form and in other contexts, being excerpted into various *rifacimenti,* like the pseudo-Pandolfini that served as a source for Giovanni Rucellai's *Zibaldone.*

Mine is an interpretation, I hope, that avoids seeing the text as a sign of the life and rather treats the relationship between text and life-process as problematic. Rather than reducing the text to a simple interpretative key in the author's life, such a reading opens complexities by demanding a cogent mapping out of the relations between the written text and the text of the life. Suffice it to say I see some relationship in the case of *Della Famiglia,* a relationship that hinges on illegitimacy and that is carried less, perhaps, by what is said than by what is left unsaid.

Historical readings of *Della Famiglia* must also take account of the type of text it is—a humanistic moral dialogue based largely on Ciceronian models. Such a dialogue juxtaposed extreme views in the mouths of interlocutors. The reader was left to determine where the normative mean implicitly lay or which of the explicit viewpoints contained the appropriate middle way.[18] The dialogue was not dictatorial, rather it aimed at persuasion of a rhetorical and subjective nature. Even the final reconciliation of the opposed views in any dialogue was not advanced as a conclusion. Readers were invited to carry on the discussion. It was because "humanist dialogues present their discussions not as definitive treatments but rather as bases for further examination of the subjects discussed" that the author "intentionally seeks to create ambiguities."[19] The reader had to locate the *via media* through these tensions.

Alberti's dialogues pose especially strong polarities in issues.

Whether or not these polarities spring from his own inner conflicts,[20] Alberti's forceful presentation of extremes generated a more pressing sense of the need for moderation. So too does the reader's inability consistently to identify Alberti the author with any of the speakers in his dialogues.[21] "The *Libri della Famiglia* exemplify the household discussion as an intellectual and social realization of Alberti's moral ideal of moderation. The interlocutors of *Libri della Famiglia* conceive their household discussion as a mean between the ignorance of the masses and the subtleties of the humanists."[22] It is my contention that among the "common sense" moderate solutions rendered by experience were some that related to the treatment of illegitimate children.

The Life

The first step in this reading must be at least partial recovery of the meaning of illegitimacy in the Quattrocento. All children born out of wedlock bore a social stigma from the circumstances of their procreation. Bastards were dishonorable creatures, scarcely better than beasts. But all bastards were not created equal. While all illegitimate children faced legal disabilities and diminished rights in comparison to legitimate children, the extent of these disabilities and the availability of means to overcome or lessen them varied according to a scheme of legal classifications and according to the social status of the parents. Lowest on the moral and legal scale were those *nati ex damnato coitu,* including those born in incest, from clerical concubinage or fornication, in adultery, or from casual illicit unions (including master-slave or master-servant relations). On the other hand there were *naturales,* who were the result of longstanding unions of concubinage between two marriageable people, unions that differed from marriages largely only because they had not been solemnized. Concubinage and its progeny were more easily tolerated in society and its law. The paternity of *naturales* was certain; their rights to use a family name and bear its coat of arms were more readily conceded, as were limited rights to inherit in the absence or even along with legitimate children. And *naturales* could be made fully legitimate simply by the subsequent marriage of their parents.[23]

On this scale of illegitimacy Battista Alberti stood at the top, among the *naturales.* He was born in 1404, the second son of concubinage established in exile by his father, Lorenzo, with Bianca di

Carlo Fieschi, daughter of a Genoese patrician family and widow of a Grimaldi, another powerful clan of that city.[24] The relatively favorable legal conditions of his birth were also further mitigated by social circumstances. His father's recognition of paternity was immediate and automatic. Battista grew up with a name and identity. He was accepted into the household and not abandoned to the sort of harsh fate considered usual, if not appropriate, for illegitimate children. He was fed, clothed, and educated, in good part because his father, despite the exile of the Alberti from Florence, was still a wealthy man who could afford to raise his two sons.[25] Lorenzo Alberti cared enough about Battista and Carlo to flee with them from the plague that ravaged Genoa in 1406 and killed their mother. As far as bastards went, then, Battista Alberti was rather fortunate.

Of course, as an illegitimate child Battista remained technically outside his father's family because he was not subject to *patria potestas,* which arose only in marriage.[26] Though he could bear the name and other symbolic identities of the lineage to which his father belonged, his effective rights to property and his status within the rest of the lineage were minimal. In a sense he was of, but not in, the family. In one important respect, then, Battista remained unfortunate: he was never made legitimate—though he could have been. Legitimation would have made him a full member of the family, subject to his father's *patria potestas.*

Lorenzo could have married Bianca Fieschi before her death—that would have legitimated Battista. Maybe, however, he had had no intention of marrying a Genoese but wanted to do eventually what he did in 1408—marry a Florentine. This marriage at least explains why Lorenzo did not legitimate his sons as long as he was married and had the hope of fathering legitimate, fully Florentine, sons. In the event, however, by the time of his death in Padua in 1421, Lorenzo had had no other children. He could then have legitimated his boys by a last minute judicial declaration or merely by his express desire to do so communicated in his testament (by designating them his universal heirs)—a privilege available only to *naturales.*[27] But, for whatever reason, Lorenzo chose not to. He merely left them a substantial legacy entrusted to the boys' uncle Ricciardo.

The subsequent fate of the vulnerable Battista has become familiar. Lorenzo's failure to legitimate his sons left them dependent on others for the payment of the legacy and, when their uncle Ricciardo soon died, responsibility for payment passed to Benedetto di Bernardo and

Antonio di Ricciardo. These two cousins procrastinated in paying the bequest. Nine years after Lorenzo's death they had paid only about half, mainly for educational expenses, and were pleading straitened financial circumstances. The fact that Battista and Carlo were illegitimate played some part here—the cousins could claim to be withholding family property from those who were not part of the family.[28] There is good evidence that the young Battista took their treatment of him as familial rejection. In his autobiography written in 1438, he looked back on the years following 1421 as a time of sorrow and pain.[29]

By 1432 Battista's fortunes had recovered. He was employed at the papal court, and in that year he was given a dispensation by Eugenius IV from the canonical disabilities of his illegitimate birth, thus allowing him to hold a lucrative benefice in Gangalandi. It was in this period, 1433–34, that Battista composed the first three books of *Della Famiglia* "for the sake of his kin."[30] This first version was hardly finished when Eugenius IV and his court fled Rome in June 1434 and came to Florence.[31] The dialogue itself, however, is situated in the past, at what seemed the last time he had known domestic and economic peace and security, but at what was also the time when the threat to that peace and security first emerged—the eve of Lorenzo's death in Padua in 1421.

The time of writing and the setting of *Della Famiglia,* then, were personally significant. Nevertheless, the themes treated in the book were not unusual.[32] As an "outsider" to his family, his lineage, and his city, however, Alberti enjoyed a unique perspective to bring these themes together in a coherent manner.[33] The themes could also suit personal interests and concerns in their manner and order of treatment.

The Text

The Prologue, the one place in the version of 1433–34 where Alberti spoke in his own voice to his Alberti audience, poses the general theme of the decline of great families in numbers, wealth, and glory. The fragility of families, the tenuousness of their survival, was a common and pressing concern in the Quattrocento.[34] The problem Alberti singles out is how to avoid malevolent Fortune that brings families down. The fortitude and integrity of the Alberti, he says, convince him that human conduct and reason can overcome Fortune. Displaying the fruits of his classical studies, Alberti demonstrates that good traditions and nobility of soul produced the success of Rome and all other successful governments. The same stands true for families. Management, restraint, good habits—factors fully in human control keep Fortune from destroying the family. Here, then, is the rationale and justification behind *Della Famiglia*. Alberti has investigated the writings of the authoritative figures of antiquity, and the customs of past Alberti *padri*, assembling the resulting bits of wisdom so that the present and future Alberti *padri* might see "how the family may multiply, by what means it might become fortunate and blessed, by what reasons favor, popularity, and friendship are gained, by what arrangements the family's honor, fame, and glory grow and spread, and how the family name may be commended to everlasting praise and immortality."[35] Presenting himself as equally implicated in the common fate of all Alberti, a fate carried by the themes of numbers, wealth, and fame raised in the Prologue, Battista offers his writing as a contribution to family honor that may also bring results in wealth and numbers. Battista is also trying to contribute to the increase in the family's numbers by asserting his membership in "*nostra* [my emphasis] famiglia Alberta." Indeed, all other claims to help the family rested on this one. In addition, according to the autobiography of 1438, the dialogue was a subtle and learned form of vendetta against those Alberti members who had harmed him. Rather than responding with hatred and violence, the long-suffering Battista claims to have returned benevolence.[36] Unity and continuity, not bitter divisiveness, were his overt themes.

The Prologue thus raises general issues of family survival and happiness, the need for good character and careful effort to resist the blows of Fortune, but it also situates these issues within the interests and experiences of the Alberti. The discussion is carried by three main speakers: Lionardo, Adovardo, and Giannozzo Alberti, with two lesser speakers, the young Battista and his mortally ill father, Lorenzo. These men span the generations—Battista being seventeen, Lionardo twenty-nine, Adovardo forty-five, Giannozzo sixty-four. The older ones tend to present the practical insights of experience, the younger ones the theoretical insights of a classical education, with Adovardo occupying a middle position.[37] There is more than logical coherence, however, between these themes and interlocutors. There is a movement among them that sets up certain questions, highlights certain themes, and directs responses to them. From this movement Book Two emerges as the pivotal one in the dialogue.

Book Two shares several formal and thematic features with the others. Notably, Lionardo is the one interlocutor who is active in all three books. Another formal similarity is the insertion of an interruption due to concern for Lorenzo's health. The speakers are excluded from his presence by order of his doctors near the beginning of Book One and near the end of Book Three. The departure of Lorenzo from the circle of speakers in Book One (actually their departure from him) is also mirrored by the return of Adovardo in Book Three. Symmetrically, around the middle of Book Two Battista departs to check on his father. Various common themes also circulate through all three books, notably that of the meaning of kinship. It is raised in Lorenzo's words to his sons in Book One as the relationship between kinship and friendship—between blood and virtuous efforts or activities.[38] This theme resurfaces in Book Three. It is the crux of disagreement between Lionardo and Giannozzo (also between Adovardo and Giannozzo). Giannozzo, for example (though in his later statements he contradicts himself), favors kin over friends and would go so far as to excuse theft by kin because the property does not leave the family and there would still be a sense of obligation.[39] Yet Book Two offers the most forceful statement, through Lionardo, about the value of blood, even over against other familiar relations: "Much more honorable and pleasing to you will be the company of your own than that of strangers; much more useful and productive for you will be the work of dear and faithful coresidents [*domestici*] than that of friends conduced and practically bought."[40]

However, Book Two differs in profound ways from the others. The movement of its argument runs opposite to that in Books One and Three. Those books begin with the establishment of uncontested values and principles, the consequences of which are then probed and debated for the benefit of the young Battista and his brother Carlo.[41] In Book One the boys' father, repeating the wisdom of his own father, displays his love for his sons and concern for their upbringing. His words establish a principle of paternal love reciprocated by filial respect and obedience. Acknowledging that he leaves his sons "in exile and fatherless, beyond your *patria* and your *casa*," the dying man urges them to cultivate a virtuous and honorable character and also to use the wealth he leaves them to endear themselves to their kin and others (and here there certainly is irony). In Book Three the equally undeniable principle of *mezzana masserizia* is established at the outset.[42] By this principle, one who knows that he truly possesses only body, soul, and time should deal moderately, virtuously, and prudently with material possessions, avoiding senseless waste and useless avarice. Thereafter, in both books, occurs a give-and-take that results from problematizing otherwise "obvious" issues—the necessity of marriage and the joys of fatherhood in Book One, the necessity of friends in Book Three.

Contrarily, rather than proceeding from consensus to debate, Book Two moves from debate to consensus about the consequences of the "current" opinion. The opening disputation on the nature of love leads to an exposition on marriage and related issues. Also this book differs because here the young Battista is the only other speaker and is active for the only time in the discussions. There is no older experienced voice such as that of Adovardo or Giannozzo; the two youngest speakers carry the dialogue. Why? The progression of themes from Book One through Book Three might seem chronologically pegged to the life cycle: one begins as a child under paternal discipline, then marries, then manages property. Chronology, however, would also argue for another arrangement: marriage is first, before one becomes a father and manages a patrimony. Reserving the subject of marriage until after fatherhood also curiously parallels the course of Lorenzo Alberti's life—a de facto father before he was a de iure husband.

Book One's discussion of paternal duties in the context of an argument to convince Lionardo to wed also provokes the memory that the dying Lorenzo did not observe the niceties of marriage before committing himself to fatherhood. Lorenzo had chosen a love match before, or in place of, following familial dictates in marriage. Book Two begins with a debate about love in which the young Battista espouses—"For the sake of argument"—the view that "[love] is a force and law not, in total, worthy of hatred and disdain but rather imposed by divine nature herself on each living creature born to reproduce itself and increase its line."[43] Lionardo, on the other hand, argues that passion is animalistic and that only rational friendship such as that between husband and wife is honorable and truly human.[44] Here then Book Two looks at the sort of friendship that produces blood, rather than at the friendship produced by blood, and returns most closely to the issues raised in the Prologue, especially the problem of the decline and disappearance of great families like the Alberti. In so doing Book Two comes closest to the touchy subject of Battista's illegitimacy.

Conceivably there are personal overtones to the otherwise fairly conventional juxtaposition of passionate love and rational affection in the debate between Battista and Lionardo. Certainly likening lovers to brutes can bring to mind that the offspring of illicit unions were also brutish. Bastards were no better than dogs.[45] But the nature of Lorenzo Alberti's affair with Bianca Fieschi remains ambiguous in terms of this debate. Theirs may have been a passionate affair, but it also seems to have been stable and perhaps rational in Lionardo's terms. It was not technically a marriage, however, and it is precisely the subject of marriage that the speakers turn to next.

Battista abruptly concludes the debate on love out of reverence for the older Lionardo and the authority of his arguments and resumes the role of passive but enthusiastic student. The older Lionardo becomes the teacher.

Asked to address the good and honor of the family, Lionardo declares, "we may call happy that family in which will be a supply of men wealthy, esteemed and loved, and that we will term unhappy will have but few infamous, poor, and disliked men."[46] The first problem is how to increase or maintain its numbers (the same problem raised at the outset of the Prologue). Nature, Lionardo claims, has decreed the necessity of monogamous marriage, which is for the good of the family and its "legitimate and honorable growth" ("il legittimo e onestissimo accrescere della famiglia").[47] By nature a man cannot care "for several women and families" at once. Young men, however, like Lionardo before his "conversion" at the end of Book One, are often reluctant to marry, fearing the loss of their freedom, the burdens of family life, or the loss of a lover. To prevent the decline of the family, its young men must be persuaded to marry. They must see that "to him who will have worked to acquire riches, powers, estates, will weigh very heavily not having after himself a true heir and preserver of his name and memory," whereas "he of whom such heirs remain cannot consider himself entirely spent and gone, because his sons take his place in the family and are the true image of the father."[48]

The first matter to be considered is the careful choice of a wife. Of the factors in this choice—beauty, breeding, wealth—Lionardo clarifies that the wife's parentage is most important because one acquires her kinsmen along with her.[49] Advice is then offered on when and how to procreate so as to produce healthy children, followed by instruction on protecting their health. Disease, especially the plague, constitutes one grave threat to family survival. Divisions and quarrels are a second source of threats to the family.[50]

Then comes the crucial turn in Lionardo's arguments in Book Two, and in *Della Famiglia* as a whole. Despite every precaution, Lionardo warns, it still might happen that one is left without children. It suddenly appears that Fortune might win; one's children might die or one's wife might be sterile—as Lorenzo Alberti's had been. "But it seems necessary here again to consider how it may be licit to keep the family populous."[51] With that statement Lionardo pulls one last rabbit from the hat of human effort. Among the ancients, Lionardo informs his listeners, divorce had been "a licit and legitimate custom." Canon law, however, saw marriage as more than a mating for the purposes of procreation, it was a sacramental union of souls that could not be broken for reasons of sterility.[52] But there was another ancient custom to consider—adoption. Lionardo claims that Roman soldiers (he cites the example of Scipio Africanus' son), when retiring from service, wanting to preserve their families, "did as some do today" and turned to "this very useful, licit custom of adopting sons already born of others when they cannot be born to you."[53] The advantages of adoption were clear. It provided an heir where nature had not, and it allowed one to see what one's son would be like before being legally bound to him. But there were also some potential disadvantages:

> Because this adoption is nothing other than adding a new cousin to your nephews and a kinsman to your relatives, one wants to select such a person as those of the *casa* willingly accept. One wants to confer with everyone, so that no one then denigrates him whom they have praised and accepted; one wants to take care to adopt those born of good blood and good disposition, of gentle visage, and such as in other matters the *casa* may never have reason to regret. . . . And he who adopts should consider that if he will not love him as a son the others of the *casa* will not hold him as a kinsman, so he will not only be like a stranger in the house but will live burdened by envy and perhaps not be free of injuries and loss. And everyone knows how in families discords are to be avoided.[54]

Precisely at this point Battista breaks in to thank Lionardo for his elegant and ordered presentation. Battista then displays his filial piety by going to check on his father and returns with Lorenzo's injunction to leave behind everything else in order to acquire virtue and honor. "Go, my son," are Lorenzo's last words in the dialogue.[55]

Battista then urges Lionardo to proceed. Lionardo goes on to condemn idleness (which breeds adultery, murder, and other forms of disrespect for law and custom), to discuss the nature of happiness, the choice of careers, the accumulation of wealth. Book Two ends with an eloquent invocation to honor as the moral guide in human affairs, the end to which all efforts are directed, the impenetrable shield against Fortune.

This brief consideration of adoption, at the very center of the middle book, is a hinge on which much of the dialogue turns. The entire structure and tone of the few pages that raise the issue of adoption distinguish this part from the rest of *Della Famiglia,* lift it out from the very center of the work. Even the abrupt interruption that thrusts Battista forward and sends him off to look in on his dying father formally sets off this section.

Here, as elsewhere in his writings, an unexpected and surprising image compels reflection on the subject at hand.[56] This is the only segment of *Della Famiglia* where law is explicitly handled and legal institutions, here marriage and adoption, are glimpsed at least briefly as legal. To be sure, law lurks just below the surface of the text in many areas, notably in the frequent injunctions to keep careful records of family and business affairs. But only here can one see what law has done to the family, what law has added to nature. "Natural" monogamy has been solemnized by law, and so sacramentalized by canon law that divorce is forbidden, even when the procreative function has been thwarted by sterility. But law also has provided a remedy for sterility in adoption, a remedy, moreover, that has room for choice and selection not otherwise present when acquiring legitimate blood descendants in marriage. So the natural imperative to secure blood descent of one's line ("legitimate" descent) ends ironically in the admission of the possible necessity to secure heirs without blood, by means of law. Effort, virtue, and honor triumph.

Or do they? The key to the passage is the assertion that some men in the fifteenth century used adoption. In fact, full legal adoption was extremely rare in the Quattrocento.[57] My own examination of notarial and other records in Florence turned up few examples of adoption.[58] And Battista's Alberti audience must have known this, especially when adoption was presented to them as a laudable custom from antiquity. A much more common practice in the fifteenth century was to secure legitimate heirs by the legitimation of bastards—of sons like Battista and Carlo.

Adoption was a classical institution. Legitimation was a later development of Roman law dating from the fourth century. Reference to adoption, therefore, was in keeping with the classical tenor of Alberti's other references. On the other hand, prior to the establishment of legitimation, adoption was the only method available in civil law for effectively legitimating a bastard.[59] So the reference to adoption in a classical context could include legitimation. Also, in contrast to adoption, legitimation was closely associated with marriage. The first form of legitimation in civil law was that provided by subsequent marriage of the parents. The later form of legitimation by imperial rescript was intended to cover situations where marriage was no longer possible (as when one partner had since died). By the end of the fourteenth century, jurisprudence and juristic practice, influenced by the revival of legitimation in canon law, had expanded the range of legitimation by rescript and made it easily available through local counts palatine.[60] The attractiveness and viability of legitimation in the Quattrocento lay in the fact that it was seen to have a basis in nature, to operate on and purify an existing natural tie between parent and child. In contrast adoption was seen as the quintessential legal fiction, "imitating" nature in manufacturing a father-son relationship but not working through nature.[61] So jurists, including the ever authoritative Bartolo of Sassoferrato (d. 1357), maintained that legitimation rendered one truly, not fictively, legitimate.[62] There were others, notably Baldo degli Ubaldi (1323–1400), who maintained that legitimation was also a fiction, pointing often to the commonsense distinction between being legitimate and being legitimated.[63] But these men too could not deny that there was a natural link present in legitimation. Even the classical example of adoption cited by Lionardo—that of Scipio Aemelianus—invokes blood relatedness, because he was first cousin to his adoptive father.[64]

Insofar as Alberti's Florentine audience, especially his family, may have been familiar with adoption, they would hardly have considered the context—continuing a single patriline within the wider lineage—to have called for so drastic a solution. Adoption figured as a last resort when the continuance of an entire lineage was threatened. In contrast a single patriline could be allowed to lapse, or be continued by legitimation.[65] In brief, legitimation occupied the legal middle ground between marriage, normal and frequent, and adoption, highly abnormal and infrequent. In looking for a middle way between extremes, where else were Alberti's readers to be led?

Alberti would have known from his legal studies that adoption and legitimation were closely linked in jurisprudence. The immediately preceding presentation of marriage as a "natural" institution for "legitimate" procreation could provoke reflection on the very meaning of legitimacy. Battista, as a "natural" son, bore a certain natural, if not legal, legitimacy. In terms of custom he was a member of his father's family. After all he bore the Alberti name and had been raised in his father's house. Even in terms of civil law his rights to bear the family name and to be raised and supported by his kin were recognized and protected. But in the eyes of the law he still was not a member of his father's *familia*. He had never been subject to his father's *potestas*. It would have been simple—hardly a great step at all—to manufacture a bit of legal writing to make him legitimate (as Eugenius IV had just given him a canonical dispensation from the disabilities of illegitimacy, which ordinarily precluded ordination and the holding of benefices). He was already blood-related, so the sort of prejudice that kept adoption from being widely used did not apply in his case.[66]

However, it did not necessarily serve Alberti's interests to overstress the legality of his condition. To do so might imply a criticism of his father for failing to "adopt" him. And in 1434 the opportunity for legal action had become an impossibility, so he was forced to stress his blood-relatedness and his good character to win acceptance by the other Alberti. The discussion of adoption, therefore, stresses the advantages of knowing the new son's character, upon which depended membership in the family. Treatment of a son as one's own was also important. Could any Alberti doubt that Lorenzo had so treated Battista? True, he had not formally made Battista his *filiusfamilias* and heir, but he was his son by nature and by social habit, if not by law. Were there not limits to law? Did law not rest on nature and custom? What better way could there be to avoid a bad choice in adoption, and avoid discord in the family, than to "adopt" a bastard in whose veins the family's blood flowed?

The circumstances of Battista's upbringing lurk behind this presentation of "adoption"; their reality undercuts the meaning of legitimacy in law and makes a mockery of any sense that Battista was anything less than an Alberti. To be sure there are no specific references to Battista's past; he does not explicitly argue his own case. But the specifics are not far out of view. They haunt the shadows and fill the silences of the text. Their lurking presence may have been more effective than bringing them into the open. His case alone might be dismantled or stymied by quibbles on specifics (why had Lorenzo not married Bianca or legitimated his sons?). Treating the matter the way he did allowed Alberti to merge his case into a full canvas of rationally arrayed principles, idealized familial nature, in full perspective. Then it might appear how fully he measured up to the ideal, despite a few insignificant blemishes or deviations. And his ability to see this perspective rested on the fact that he stood to some extent outside the picture of the family. To craft an ethical argument he had to choose and arrange into a coherent image (of family) the ethical principles that served to get his message across.

That *Della Famiglia* was read by the Alberti as a criticism of some of them has long been known.[67] The hostility provoked by the work may have been responsible for the attempt on Battista's life later ascribed by him to some of his kin.[68] What is uncertain, however, is whether any of the Alberti read the work as a directive on the treatment of illegitimate children, as I have suggested. We cannot give a definitive answer. We do know that Francesco d'Altobianco Alberti, a close friend of Battista, and colleague in the Roman Curia, to whom the prologue to Book Three (a later addition) was dedicated, was one member of the clan who received *Della Famiglia* warmly. In May 1434, soon after the completion of the first version, and while in Florence in advance of the papal arrival, Francesco legitimated his two sons. He also then emancipated them and gave them two houses, a wool shop, and lands in the Florentine contado.[69] By these acts he unequivocally took these boys into his family and gave them full ownership of family property. He could manage the property for them, but as *emancipati* their claims to it were real and effective against others.[70] With legitimation and the *premortem* inheritance made possible by emancipation Francesco seems to have spared his boys from the fate suffered by Carlo and Battista. Whether he did so in response to Battista's writing or even in response to Battista's own hardship is impossible to say. However, his benevolent legal treatment of his two young bastard sons certainly stands out in clear contrast to the actions of Lorenzo Alberti toward his sons.

The Patriline

When Alberti returned to *Della Famiglia* in 1440, it was to add a fourth book on the theme of friendship, as opposed to kinship. In the meantime his hopes of wide acceptance by the rest of the Alberti were dashed, at least by the testimony of his autobiography. The autobiography itself was perhaps a last attempt to explain himself to those Alberti sympathetic to him.[71] Interestingly, in that work too he does not overtly raise the issue of his illegitimacy. The date, place, and circumstances of his birth are treated with silence. He mentions only his hard studies, subsequent illnesses, and the fact that "in his misery he endured his kin who were neither dutiful nor even humane."[72] And the word he uses for kin here and throughout the autobiography is *affines*. It is a good classical word, of course, but it more literally designates kin by marriage, as opposed to blood kin. He seems almost to be denying any blood tie by his choice of terms.

What remains to be considered about *Della Famiglia* is the meaning of *famiglia* to Alberti and the role of his illegitimacy in formulating it. In Book Three, as Francis William Kent has noted, Giannozzo offers two senses of *famiglia* within a few pages.[73] The first equates family with *casa*—in the sense of household: "E' figliuoli, la moglie, e gli altri domestici, famigli, servi."[74] The second extends the *casa* metaphorically to cover a more extended group of kin (brothers, cousins, grandchildren, and so forth), who, if they cannot fit into a single dwelling, should at least reside in the shadow of a single will.[75] Giannozzo could unselfconsciously propose both definitions because they represented points on a continuum of familial experience. In Kent's terms these are the household and the lineage, although the second, strictly speaking, is the patriline—a branch of the lineage, which, as Giannozzo's shifting definition reveals, can encompass one or more households. The lineage, in turn, would consist of one or more patrilines, all of whom would share a common name if nothing else. The distinction between patriline and lineage comes clearest in Book One, where the widest sense of *famiglia*, to indicate all the Alberti, is in constant tension with a narrower sense of *famiglia* to designate fathers and their sons.[76]

Underlying these shifting senses of *famiglia*—household, patriline, lineage—are shifting criteria of membership. In Book Three the criteria are functional. A large household is more economical than two small ones. Thus Giannozzo did not want his brother Antonio to live apart.[77] The reason a household would divide is equally functional. It could simply become too large for the available space. Book One, on the other hand, stresses blood and upbringing. The natural connection between fathers and sons (a number of such connections building back into a lineage) involves more than just blood. Fathers naturally see to the education of their sons, and the lineage provides a storehouse of customs and examples that inculcate a certain habit of deportment that also identifies its members.[78] For that reason, in Book One failure in the family, division and loss of members, is ascribed to the failure of sons to maintain virtuous family traditions. "If your son does not want you for his father, do not have him as a son."[79] Just as in Book Three Giannozzo urges patrilines to live together but grudgingly recognizes that this is not always possible, so in Book One Lionardo wants them to stay together but grudgingly recognizes that some sons turn out dishonest, disobedient, and undeserving and so must be removed for the good of the family.[80]

Book Two, again, is crucial because it not only brings to bear all three senses of *famiglia/casa* but it also brings in other criteria of membership and clarifies the connections among household, lineage, and patriline. Lineages like the Alberti increase by the procreation of children, for which the monogamous household is "naturally" necessary. For the good of the lineage young men must be persuaded to marry and take on the burdens of managing a household. The instrument of persuasion is the image of the patriline—sons as one's own heirs and images. Having sons endows one with dignity and authority (and old-age care).[81] The divisive danger to the family singled out in Book Two is the father's mad infatuation with his power and authority, to preserve which he would thrust away sons who challenge him—and thus achieve the opposite effect, a loss of respect and esteem.[82] "Adoption," on the other hand, constitutes a proper use of authority to achieve patrilineal continuity, just as marriage does. Book Two thus brings together new criteria of membership and the constitution of families—conjugal love, symbolic values like honor and name, and law—as well as the criteria of blood, family tradition, and wealth.

So *famiglia* corresponds to various criteria—residential, symbolic, legal—as well as to functional and consanguineal (agnatic) criteria that mark *famiglia* to some extent in all senses in which the term is used. The patriline, the *famiglia* built around *patria potestas,* is the pivotal intermediate unit. In Battista's experience he had been part of a residential *famiglia* that was dissolving at the time depicted in the dialogue. He claimed to be a member of the symbolic *famiglia* of the lineage. But he had never been a member of a jural *famiglia*. It was membership in this jural *famiglia* that was in question when the issue of "adoption" was raised at the center of Book Two. Without clear membership in the jural *famiglia*, Alberti's membership in the wider *casa* of "nostra famiglia Alberta" was open to doubt. Not part of the jural *famiglia*, Alberti was prevented from transmitting membership in it to any children. Perhaps for that reason, at least in part, he never married or had children (although Carlo did). He could still claim to make effective contributions to the *famiglia*. *Della Famiglia* itself was one such contribution. So was the house in Bologna he left after his death for the use of any Alberti who chose to take up studies there.[83] The other Alberti did not have to accept him. Lacking legitimation, his effective treatment as a member of the smaller residential *famiglia* only made more apparent the problem of his distance from the wider *famiglia* and raised the distinctions between blood, law, and virtue. Thus the different senses of *famiglia* and of criteria of membership came to inhabit *Della Famiglia*.

Given his situation, Battista downplayed the jural dimension of *famiglia* as he crafted his idealized vision of the patrician *casa*. Except at the crucial central passage on "adoption," the symbolic (blood, name, honor) and practical (residence, wealth) elements of family life predominated. Even in the "adoption" section these utilities and symbolic values draw much attention. Yet Alberti and his contemporaries were very aware of the legal realities. Florentines confidently married, emancipated, legitimated, inherited—even occasionally adopted. They used *patria potestas* and manipulated kin relations, and they litigated their differing interests almost as frequently. They expressed their legal understanding of *famiglia* in such actions, in keeping notarial copies of them, and in entries in their private accounts. In our continuing reliance on Alberti's systematic presentation of *famiglia*, we should not be led astray by this almost total absence of the jural. Indeed its one central intrusion can indicate how potentially important it was.

Family membership, to Alberti, was not a natural given.[84] Family was more than a natural organism, it was a work of art. Like any other work of art, as Alberti and other humanists well knew, it involved the imitation of nature, even its enhancement and perfection.[85] This nature, moreover, was to be captured from one perspective set by the artist and to be interpreted by an audience.[86] From the perspective of an illegitimate son, with one foot in the *famiglia* and one out, the family took on a particular complex form. Its ambiguities to him might be reduced but they could hardly be eliminated. What held the lineage together as a coherent composition was a number of patrilines converging on a vanishing point in a supposedly eponymous ancestor. But these patrilines did not just radiate from the center and organize the entire composition. It took a certain geometry of crossing lines imposed upon them to bind them together and place the various figures precisely in the lineage's space. So Adovardo, from yet another patriline married his distant cousin, Ricciardo's daughter. So, even as Battista and Carlo were commended to their uncle as his "children," it was Lionardo who was called father by Battista. So the elders of the lineage—the heads of the various branches—visited (as had Giannozzo in the dialogue) and conferred on important issues, and in them was the genealogy of the lineage manifest. The others took shape in light of all of them and benefited from their efforts (as Battista and Carlo did in the dialogue).[87] The outlines of the figure of Battista, however, were blurred and not distinct. In a *sfumato* effect it was not certain where he stood or even if he belonged in the composition. Only in the idealized artistic presentation might there be a place for him. There the artist could use a symbolic and ethical geometry to suggest the extension of a patriline to him. The reality of social and legal geometry was another matter.

7

•

"AS IF CONCEIVED WITHIN A LEGITIMATE MARRIAGE"
A Dispute Concerning Legitimation in Quattrocento Florence

•

"Fine Word—Legitimate!"

In Florence, sometime in late 1408 perhaps, Domenico di Pietro di Giovanni went before a count palatine. To this count Domenico revealed that he had an illegitimate son, Simone, who had been fathered by Domenico in adultery with an unnamed woman. Domenico asked the count palatine to legitimate this son. Legitimation was one of those acts for which the count had been empowered by privilege of the Holy Roman Emperor. With the "stain" of birth removed by legitimation, Simone was thus "restored" to a "pristine state"—"as if he had been conceived within a legitimate marriage." Further, as the legal charter drawn up to record this event stated, Simone was thus enabled to all legitimate rights and legal capacities, including the right to inherit from his father.[1]

Legitimation was a legal device used with some regularity in fifteenth-century Florence. It could provide a means to continue a family line through a bastard when a legitimate male heir was lacking. Simone's legitimation fit that pattern, for his father, who soon died, unmarried and otherwise childless, clearly intended that Simone be

176

his heir. Simone was only one of many Florentine children who were born illegitimate but later experienced judicial legitimation.[2]

This legitimation thus seems a straightforward and insignificant event. However, when carefully considered, it in fact raises a number of large and important historical questions. At first sight, one might wonder why such favor would, or even could, be shown to a bastard. The very word still carries a wide range of pejorative connotations, many of which continue to punctuate colloquial discourse. Legitimacy was both a moral and a legal category. It set the role of the family in transmitting status and property in social reproduction, crucially so since the twelfth century.[3] Illegitimacy, on the other hand, marked those who stood outside the usual, legitimate social relations. These persons could be considered a threat to family life and to the rest of the social order. Especially, they could threaten the inheritance claims of legitimate relatives. The bastard Edmund in *King Lear* conveys in dramatic fashion an example of the threat of illegitimacy to family and society. Edmund's defrauding of his legitimate brother and his manipulation of his father were comprehensible to Shakespeare and his audience as the immoral acts of a remarkably unscrupulous bastard. In Florence itself, only three years before Simone's legitimation, the bastard Lorenzotto di messer Thome Soderini had been executed for his unscrupulous, not to say illegal, machinations on his father's estate. Even in failure he brought shame and disgrace on the rest of the family.[4] Acknowledging and keeping a bastard could be a risky business. Legitimating a bastard, moreover, gave him (more rarely her) a legal means to threaten others' inheritance claims. Someone who stood to inherit—a legitimate daughter, a legitimate but more distant relative—was faced with partial or total disinheritance. Disputes and lawsuits erupted from these thwarted claims. Yet some Florentines preferred to risk this prospect and opted for legitimation, rather than allow daughters or distant relations to inherit. Why?

I can hope only to suggest a partial answer to this important question. A more detailed answer awaits further research. Yet this preliminary investigation of legitimation can still yield significant results. Legitimation implicates the broader issue of the social assimilation of bastards. It is an issue about which we know surprisingly little. Most recent historical work on illegitimacy has focused almost exclusively on illicit sexual activity. Its goal has been to measure the amount of illicit sexuality occurring in the past despite the principle of legitimacy and its conjoined ethic of licit sexuality. Thus Edward Shorter has argued that the statistical "explosion" of illegitimate births in the early nineteenth century spelled the end of "traditional" sexual ethics and brought on a crisis in familial relations.[5] Others have argued that "traditional" norms could coexist with fairly high rates of illegitimacy,[6] or even that social deviance as manifested in illegitimacy only served to reinforce social rules.[7] Yet, whatever position is taken, the fact remains that a statistical study of illegitimate births "has nothing to contribute with regard to the assimilation of the child in society."[8] Other historians, whose approach has not been quantitative so much as normative, have also offered little insight into the process by which society came to tolerate and assimilate illegitimate and legitimated persons. Historians of law and social customs have been content to list and describe legal and moral norms in isolation from the social context in which those norms took on reality and meaning. They treat norms as self-contained and self-evident, ignoring their adaptation and use in social life and conflicts over their effects.[9]

For all the moral and legal stigmata attached to them, bastards like Simone di Domenico did exist. A society like that of Florence, therefore, faced the problem of accommodating them without appearing to compromise the overriding principle of legitimacy, which held out an idealized process of social reproduction and not just a model of sexual behavior. It is assumed that such accommodation presented few problems, however, in view of the open presence and acknowledgment of bastards in Italy that has frequently caught the eyes of Renaissance historians. The fifteenth and sixteenth centuries, teeming with bastard Este, Medici, and Borgias, among others, has even been termed a "golden age" for bastards.[10] Tuscany and Florence in particular have been cited for liberalized treatment of illegitimates.[11] Although Florentine illegitimacy has not been subjected to statistical analysis,[12] undeniably major figures there, such as Giovanni Boccaccio and Leon Battista Alberti, seem to have found illegitimate birth little or no obstacle to the achievement of social prominence.[13]

Until further research is completed, a full discussion of the social assimilation of bastards is not possible. The degree to which they were a threat to social order or, conversely, enjoyed a golden age must remain unknown for now. However, legitimation also implicates— what is another dimension of the assimilation of bastards—a conceptual process. Whatever else may have been behind legitimation, a conceptual accommodation had to be the foundation that allowed illegitimate blood to displace legitimate. Some form of accommodation is implied even in cases like those of Boccaccio and Alberti. Certainly these examples show that the categorization of bastards in morally negative terms was not always thorough or universal. A certain ambiguity formed around such children. They were seen as morally and legally dangerous and in theory were not part of a family; but in reality they were in (if not of) society, at times were part of a household, lived off its resources and bore its name. Bastards were also potentially useful to society and family. Legitimation might be part of this utility. Artificially legitimate children, like artificially "created" citizens, could provide continuity in socially useful and valuable positions.

"Fine word—legitimate!" Shakespeare's Edmund thunders.[14] He reminds us that legitimation and legitimacy were words. Legitimation resulted in words. The encapsulation of the event in the notary's charter further reminds us that words like legitimate had precise technical meanings as well as broader social implications. This is not to say that these meanings and implications were always and everywhere different from each other, but that they were not always the same. The social and legal meanings of legitimation were inextricably intertwined. It was in legal language that the fiction "as if conceived within a legitimate marriage" was enshrined; and it was in legal language that the theoretical effects of this fiction were spelled out, as well as its very possibility and the requirements and conditions for it.

It is the conceptual dimension of legitimation, the use and meaning of words, that will be examined here. The best focal point for the examination of such meanings is a dispute.[15] A dispute can reveal conflicting constructions placed upon social reality. The historical importance of the legitimation of Simone di Domenico is that it led to a suit, a record of which survives in the *consilium* submitted to the court by three jurists. The negotiation of meanings in this dispute can reveal the conceptual foundations of legitimacy and family and the linguistic strategies involved in assimilation of a legitimated bastard. What follows, then, is an analysis of this dispute.

Lena di Francesco v. Simone di Domenico

Simone's father Domenico died in May 1409. Before his death, perhaps in anticipation of his son's later legal difficulties, Domenico had appointed his brother, Antonio, as his agent to see to a second legitimation of Simone—this time before the archbishop of Florence (ex officio empowered to legitimate since 1364).[16] This legitimation was performed after Domenico's death. Soon thereafter Antonio also died, without heirs, leaving Simone in the care of his grandmother, monna Agnola. The legitimated Simone thus stood as heir to both his father and his paternal uncle.

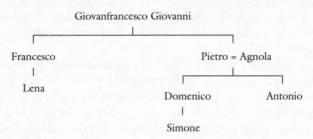

Table 7.1 Genealogy of the Litigants

At this point, however, another "heir" stepped forward: Lena di Francesco, a paternal cousin. On her behalf a notary, acting as her *procurator* before the court, advanced several telling legal arguments disputing Simone's claims to inheritance. The fact underlying Lena's suit was that the property Simone would inherit was actually the patrimony of Lena's father, Francesco. In 1395, Francesco, having no son of his own, left all his property—minus a 300-florin dowry for Lena—to his nephews, Domenico and Antonio. In his testament, however, Francesco had included a stipulation (*substitutio*) that should Domenico and Antonio die without "legitimate and natural sons" ("sine filiis legitimis et naturalibus") the estate was then to be divided equally between the hospital of San Francesco and his daughter Lena.[17] If Lena could successfully contest the validity of Simone's legitimation, she might then hope to invoke this testamentary clause in her favor.[18]

Lena's status and claims, however, were also unclear, for although she was legitimate, she was a woman. Both bastards and women were discriminated against in Florentine inheritance laws. Neither women nor illegitimates qualified as legitimate male agnates, as the *proles masculina,* which was the crucial ingredient in the preservation of family, property, and honor.[19] If not dowered, women could inherit only a portion of an estate; if dowered, they were excluded from inheritance by agnates "born of a legitimate marriage."[20] This last phrase militated against the claims of someone like Simone; but the entire thrust of the statute at hand militated against Lena. Such statutes, in fact, were common in Italian cities, and Lena's own father had merely been following their spirit in the dispositions contained in his will.[21] Equally common was the Florentine statutory discrimination against bastards. Florence recognized inheritance claims for illegitimates only in default of any other heirs, and even then these rights were allowed only for *naturales* (i.e., those born of a steady relationship of concubinage) and not for adulterous bastards and other *spurii* like Simone.[22]

Beyond specific legal disabilities, women and bastards were both classes of persons subject to powerful cultural prejudices. Women were considered weak and incapable of managing their own affairs or property.[23] Their sexuality, if uncontrolled, was a source of concern for the shame it could bring to them and their kin.[24] This dishonor would "stain" a woman's body and soul, and this "stain" was transmitted to her bastard child.[25] Bastards were thus classified among the animals, as nonhuman and incapable of honor. The dishonorable status of the bastard called down upon him (but especially her) not only severe legal disabilities but also a generally harsh fate.[26] Life itself was not assured. Infanticide and abandonment of bastards appear to have been often practiced in Florence, for such dishonorable creatures had no place in the human community.[27] Lena's suit against Simone sprang from and appealed to this diffuse prejudice against illegitimates.

Simone, however, did not fully fit this prejudicial stereotype of a bastard. Not only was he alive, but his father had recognized his paternity. Few Florentine bastard children were so lucky; those who were, tended to come from the wealthiest segment of the population.[28] As a result of recognition, moreover, Simone was assured of alimentary support, a name, and a familial identity.[29] He was implicated in a network of material and symbolic support among kin—support in his case made evident through his uncle Antonio and, after him, his grandmother monna Agnola, who must have taken up Simone's defense against Lena's claims. Simone's status in society, therefore, was ambiguous in part. Culturally and legally excluded from family membership, he was nonetheless part of a family. Finally and most important, Simone was fortunate in not having legitimate half-brothers and, therefore, in being formally, legally, and ritually legitimated to be his father's heir. In short, though a bastard, Simone was favorably treated because his father was of sufficient wealth and/or status to be able to "afford" to so treat him—or to be unable to afford not to when on the verge of dying without a legitimate son and heir.[30] Legitimation, in other words, figured—along with dispensation in canon law—as one means by which people could circumvent by purchase the prejudicial norms and principles regarding illegitimacy, while leaving those underlying ideological premises intact.[31] Legitimation above all would seem to have resolved the ambiguities surrounding Simone—definitively moving him over the line to full legitimate status "as if conceived within a legitimate marriage."

Lauro Martines has pointed out that "bastardy was no substitute for the guarantees of legitimacy."[32] Nor was legitimation it seems. At least legitimation did not prevent Lena from disputing inheritance by Simone. Simone's legitimation, after all, was a fiction, an artificial contrivance of law and ritual. Lena's case, on the other hand, was geared to recall to mind Simone's original, dishonorable, and "natural" status. Only by doing so could she hope to claim the estate. Had Simone been fully legitimate by birth, she would have had no case. In this situation, then, as a result of the arguments made on Lena's behalf, legitimation had not fully resolved the ambiguities of Simone's status. Far from it—the suit intensified those ambiguities. Even the guarantee provided by legitimation was in question.

Broadly conceived, Lena's arguments operated along two fronts. One set of attacks disputed the validity of Simone's legitimation— both legitimations. Legal technicalities were raised against the circumstances and procedures employed in these two legitimations. As will be seen below, however, these technicalities had enormous implications in the law, and they were worthy points of argument. Lena's legal counsel served her well by pinpointing aspects of the case that touched on uncertainties in the rules. A second set of arguments held that Simone, even if legally legitimated, still was not truly born of a legitimate marriage and so did not exclude Lena from the inheritance either by statute or by the terms of her father's will. In effect, Lena's claims were that Simone had not been legitimated and that, if he had, he still did not qualify as a legitimate heir.

These sets of arguments were distilled through the initial process of argumentation into eight questions of law. These questions were then submitted by the court[33] to three jurists: Signorino degli Omodei (d. 1419?), Raffaele Fulgosio (1367–1427), and Prosdocimo

Conti (fl. 1420s).[34] None of these men was a native Florentine or even practiced law in Florence for any appreciable length of time. Fulgosio was renowned in the legal profession in Italy and was most closely associated with Padua, as was Conti, who was of the comital family of that city. Omodei was from an illustrious Milanese family of jurists. These men may simply have been passing through Florence when asked to submit their collective opinion on the case to the court in the form of a *consilium*.[35] Their collective stature as jurists, as experts in civil and canon law, and their status as foreigners may have been taken as guarantees of their impartiality in handling the matter. In fact, they approached the case with the interests and conceptions of legal professionals (if not those of native Florentines) operating in a discrete social world. These interests and conceptions colored their treatment of the case—or, more correctly, Omodei's treatment of the case, for the other two merely appended their concurring signatures, substantively adding only one authoritative citation to the many employed by Omodei.[36]

Legal Issues

The procedure of legitimation used in both instances for the young Simone was known as *legitimatio per rescriptum principis*. The procedure had been instituted in the sixth century by Justinian to make legitimation available, through direct imperial intervention, for *naturales* for whom legitimation through subsequent marriage was not possible. The procedure had been revived by Innocent III and figured in the jurisdictional claims of the papacy enshrined in his famous decretal *Per venerabilem*. The medieval emperors had quickly claimed the power to legitimate by imperial rescript, even as they acquiesced in its extension beyond *naturales* to all forms of *spurii*. The emperors in the fourteenth century further broadened the use of legitimation through the counts palatine, who routinely received full authorization to issue imperial rescripts in legitimations, emancipations, and other acts.[37]

Almost from the start, therefore, legitimation by rescript had been implicated in the celebrated polemics about papal and imperial (and later civic) prerogatives. This issue of imperial jurisdiction was familiar and also of great interest to the jurists who handled Lena's and Simone's case. It was commonly taught in juristic glosses and commentaries that legitimation in temporal matters (such as inheritance)

was an act of voluntary jurisdiction, which ordinarily flowed ultimately from the emperor through those acting in his name.[38] In
principle, then, legitimation thus belonged to the emperor and to
civil law (the domain of the learned lawyers) and not to the cities and
their statutes.[39] When jurists discussed imperial prerogatives in legitimation, therefore, they were also discussing their own prerogatives
as the expert interpreters and "priests" of the law.[40] And the first
objection raised by the plaintiff against Simone di Domenico's legitimation forced Signorino degli Omodei precisely to defend imperial
prerogatives.

The objection was that the count palatine who officiated at the
first legitimation of Simone did not in fact have the power to legitimate because his palatine privileges had been issued by an emperor
who had only been elected and not yet crowned and officially in-
stalled in office. Invalidating this act, then, might have very far-reach-
ing consequences, because all acts of this count palatine and all others
like him would be voidable. And given the infrequency of late medieval imperial coronations, there were many like this count; the emperor himself would have to be considered unable to act until coronation. Omodei, therefore, rehearsed the variety of doctrinal
positions represented by authoritative doctors of civil and canon law
and arrived at the (foregone?) conclusion that election of an emperor
by the *barones* of Germany was commonly held by jurists to constitute installation in imperial administration—even before coronation.
On this basis he defended the validity of the comital privileges and
the consequent power to legitimate.[41]

Other legal issues affected both the first and second legitimations.
The court had asked Omodei a number of questions about it: Was
postmortem legitimation possible, so that it was retroactive to the
moment of death? Did the consent and active participation of Antonio the uncle, "to whom the estate would fall if this son had not been
legitimated," affect this second legitimation? Could legitimation be
performed through an agent (*procurator*)? And could an *infans* like
Simone be legitimated, since legally he did not have the capacity to
understand and consent to the proceedings? Omodei rearranged the
order of these questions, beginning his treatment of them with the
legally important issue of consent.

Consent was a crucial ingredient in a valid legitimation in the view
of the jurists. The father and son (or daughter) in question had to
consent, if only because legitimation redefined the relationship be-

tween them by the creation of *patria potestas*.[42] There was judicial disagreement, however, as to whether consent of other interested parties—agnates and those who stood to inherit on intestacy (*venientes ab intestato*)—was similarly required. Certainly these people had interests that were affected by legitimation, which gave them a new legitimate relative and postponed (or deprived them of) their inheritance claims. In the case at hand, then, Lena's complaint was that Domenico's brother Antonio had not been involved in the first legitimation as he had been in the second.

A number of jurists, mainly canonists, had argued that agnates and prospective heirs should have a place in legitimation.[43] However, Omodei ignored all these arguments when he simply argued the opposite, resting his case on the most illustrious civilian authorities: Bartolo da Sassoferrato (d. 1357), Baldo degli Ubaldi (1327–1400), and Cino da Pistoia (d. 1336/37). "The father," repeated Omodei, "is owner of his property and in its disposition no other consent is required than his own."[44] As a later Florentine lawyer, Filippo Decio (1454–1535), would put it—in an image calculated to send chills through an expectant heir—a father could deprive heirs by legitimating a bastard just as he could by throwing all his property into the sea.[45] The fact, then, that Antonio (as next in line) had not been consulted in the first legitimation of Simone did not matter.

Having restricted consent in the first legitimation to father and son, Omodei still had to respond to the charge that the necessary filial consent was lacking, because as an *infans* Simone could not legally consent. Here Omodei pointed out the analogy to emancipation of an *infans*, which also proceeded by means of imperial rescript.[46] In both cases, for an *infans*, the legal act was still available but consent was not required, thanks to the rescript.[47]

It had also been objected on Lena's behalf that legitimation could not be performed through a third party acting as a *procurator*, especially not post mortem. There were, in fact, good legal arguments on Lena's side—more than those admitted by Omodei—and the issue was, to say the least, controversial.[48] Omodei, however, chose to follow the arguments of the *Glossa ordinaria* that *procuratores* could be used to obtain a *rescriptum principis*. He also invoked the argument of Bartolo and Baldo (though without attribution to them) that the father did not legitimate, the emperor did (so the father's presence was not required).[49] Thus it was also possible for the father's agent to fulfill his responsibility after the father's death.[50]

As a reprise in defense of the second legitimation, finally, Omodei returned to the theme of the involvement of *venientes ab intestato* in legitimation and the consent of the son.[51] Some jurists had argued that in a post mortem legitimation, agnates who were prospective heirs and whose interests, therefore, were immediate in the wake of the death, had to be present and consenting.[52] Without letting on that such legal arguments existed, Omodei noted that in Simone's second legitimation, the prospective heir, Antonio, had indeed been present and consenting. His consent meant not only that the legitimation was valid but also, as Omodei pointed out at the end of his *consilium*, that Antonio presumably agreed to the consequence that Simone might be his heir.[53] As for the consent of the son, Omodei stated that in a legitimation during a father's life a son faced both benefits and inconvenience (he became legitimate and an heir, but he also was subjected to *patria potestas*), and, therefore, his consent was needed. But in a post-mortem legitimation there were no inconveniences, so consent was not necessary, even after the fact. With that flourish, he concluded that "the first legitimation is valid and, if it is not valid, the second is, beyond a doubt."[54]

Having established the validity of Simone's status as *legitimatus*, Omodei then had to face the second and more perplexing set of issues—inheritance. Here again, the jurist imposed his own order on the questions transmitted to him by the court. The court had directly singled out the problem of fiction in legitimation and had asked about Simone's status in relation to the Florentine statute excluding women from inheritance in favor of agnates "born of legitimate marriage."[55] Omodei, however, approached the inheritance issues as three successive patrimonial transmissions. The first was that of Francesco, who had chosen his nephews and not his daughter as his heirs. Omodei determined that this preference to keep property in the hands of male agnates was safeguarded by Florentine law.[56] Domenico and Antonio had been and ought to have been Francesco's heirs.

Only after this did Omodei advance to the crucial and tricky question: Was Simone truly or fictively legitimate? Did he obviate the condition of the *fideicommissum* in Francesco's will that directed the estate to Lena and the hospital if Domenico and Antonio died "sine filiis legiptimis et naturalibus"? Omodei affirmed that he did obviate the *fideicommissum*.

The jurist began his argument with basic legal definitions of legitimation. To be legitimated was to be made legitimate in all respects ("quo ad omnia").[57] "Moreover," he continued, "a *legitimatus* is restored to his old nature and free birth in which by law of nature all are born free."[58]

> And so through legitimation the stain of illegitimacy is totally eradicated so that a legitimated person is considered as if he were legitimate in all ways, . . . And so he is said to have been restored to his original nature rather than newly made legitimate. . . . Furthermore, just as concupiscence and illicit coitus were the occasion for concealing original legitimate descent, so legitimation removes the stains and repairs the original legitimacy.[59]

A cascade of citations to legal authorities then demonstrated that Omodei's assertions nestled comfortably in the realm of legal doctrine. And indeed common legal definitions of legitimation affirmed that it removed the "stain" of illegitimate birth, restored the nature and *fama* of an illegitimate, and fully enabled him legally.[60]

From this basis Omodei addressed the main problem: Was not all of this merely a fiction? Here he reproduced the argument of the fourteenth-century jurist Jacopo Bottrigari (d. 1348) that legitimation did not confer legitimacy per se but merely the rights of legitimacy (*iura legitimationis*).[61] He also added the argument that by definition a legitimate son was one born within marriage ("ex viro et uxore")—something a legitimated son like Simone could not claim.[62] On these points, then, rested the assertion of Baldo that a statement such as that in Francesco's will referring to legitimate sons "should be understood of legitimates properly and naturally and not of legitimates civilly by imperial privilege."[63] As Baldo had pointed out, *legitimati* were not "naturally" legitimate but fictively.[64] And why would Francesco have wanted his own legitimate daughter to be effectively disinherited by a grandnephew "born of damned coitus"?

Thus Omodei had set up the pros and cons. The law by definition claimed that legitimation made one fully legitimate. On the other hand, legitimation seemed to be a fiction—one, therefore, to be kept distinct from the "real" or "natural" thing. This was the position endorsed in Lena's arguments, and there seemed good reason for it. Was there not a verbal distinction between legitimate (*legitimus*) and legitimated (*legitimatus*)? A jurist like Baldo might turn this verbal distinction into a philosophical distinction between nature and fiction (or art).[65] But to others it was merely "common sense" that argued for a difference between legitimate and legitimated. This "common sense" (*communis usus loquendi*) figured in judicial discourse: "there are two species of legitimates, because some are original and some are not, and between them there is much difference in common usage, so that each is distinguished by its own terms."[66]

Omodei was faced with the task of hacking a conceptual path through this legal thicket. He chose to argue, contrary to Baldo and Jacopo Bottrigari, that a *legitimatus* was truly legitimate. He also chose, however, not to confront directly the arguments of as authoritative a figure as Baldo—not even with the considerable weight of a Bartolo, who had argued that legitimation was not a fiction but juristic truth.[67] Instead Omodei returned to an old juristic analogy, embedded in the texts of the *Corpus iuris civilis*,[68] between manumission of slaves and legitimation—an analogy that served as the basis of Bartolo's position and for the semantics of legitimation in terms of "restoration" to a pristine state of nature.

In the civil law all humans were said to be born free, but accidental social attributes resulting from circumstances of birth, captivity in war, and so forth, made some slaves, whose status was then set in the civil law. Manumission thus returned a slave, according to this view, to his "natural" and innate freedom; manumission did not give freedom so much as detect and reveal it beneath the servitude. To use Omodei's metaphor, the dispersal of clouds did not make the sky blue, it revealed the qualities naturally inherent in the heavens. To use the metaphor he borrowed from the *Glossa ordinaria*, threshing did not make grain, it revealed what had always been hidden beneath the husk.[69]

Just as there was a fundamental and natural human freedom, Omodei pointed out, there was a fundamental and natural legitimacy. He appealed to the juristic notion of a primeval natural law, by the terms of which—and other jurists could agree with him—all were innately legitimate.[70] It was civil and canon law that defined bastardy and removed the exercise of innate legitimacy with regard to succession and familial and civic honors.[71] The primitive legitimacy remained effective in such things as self-defense, mating, and being raised and raising one's own children.[72] Parallel to manumission, therefore, it was possible to argue that legitimation merely revealed innate natural legitimacy by removing the obfuscating qualities of bastardy. The legitimacy was real. It was the same legitimacy acquired by those legitimately born.[73] Thus Omodei argued, sweeping away all objections and concluding that, in terms of Francesco's will, Simone was indeed a naturally legitimate son. This natural—not civil or merely fictive—legitimacy meant that the substitution of Lena and the hospital did not go into effect. The second patrimony, that of Simone's father, Domenico, was transmitted to Simone.

With this argument Omodei attempted to dismiss a considerable problem in the law of legitimation (and in the case at hand), and thus dismiss any semantic distinction between legitimate and legitimated. Moreover, he denied that any semantic distinction could exist, not only in the law but also in the mind of a testator like Lena's father. But Baldo had raised an important objection when he argued that legitimation was fictive. Other lawyers would continue to agree with Baldo, pointing out as well that proper interpretation of the testator's intent should refer to the "common usage" of words, which did indeed see a difference between legitimate and legitimated.[74]

In adjudicating this problem later, jurists in Florence and elsewhere would point to the importance of a temporal distinction not explicitly made by Omodei. If the testator's words were taken—as they were by Baldo and others—as referring to legitimacy at the time of birth, then a *legitimatus* did not satisfy a *fideicommissum* to "legitimate" heirs. If, however, the crucial moment was that of death, then an already legitimated son had to be considered "legitimate" at that moment.[75] This temporal distinction allowed jurists to have doctrine both ways—to claim that legitimation was both fiction and truth. It was fictive toward the past, prior to legitimation (including birth), but it was true in the present and future.[76]

Whereas Omodei did not explicitly articulate this later distinction, he basically followed it in his arguments about the third patrimony, that of Simone's uncle Antonio. Curiously, then, after affirming the validity and truth of Simone's legitimacy, Omodei had to concede tacitly its temporal fictiveness. The immediate problem was whether Simone excluded his grandmother Agnola from inheritance from her son Antonio. Lena, who was in the fourth degree of consanguinity, was clearly excluded by Simone, who was in the third degree.[77] According to the Florentine statute, a woman like Agnola would be excluded by an agnate legitimately born.[78] Because Simone had not, in fact, been born in wedlock, he did not exclude Agnola, and this despite all of the language to the effect that legitimation meant that a bastard should be treated as if born in wedlock.[79] Paradoxically, then, after defending the validity of legitimation and its "reality,"

Omodei could not or would not remain consistent. Faced with statutory language that referred to the moment of birth, he had to treat legitimation as a fiction (although he avoided using that term) that could not change the past—and thus could not exclude a woman from inheriting from her son. Such statutory language would later force other jurists similarly to conclude that legitimation of males should not result in the statutory exclusion of legitimate females.[80]

Practically speaking, however, the nonexclusion of Agnola did not greatly damage Simone or his family. In the first place, Simone did inherit from Antonio—along with Agnola—so the intent of the statute to maintain property in the hands of agnates was not fully frustrated.[81] Secondly, Agnola's share of Antonio's estate was still limited by statute to one-quarter (and that not to exceed 500 *lire*), exclusive of houses and urban real estate. Simone still received the lion's share: Domenico's half of Francesco's estate and three-quarters of Antonio's half. And Lena got nothing.[82]

Conclusions

Omodei's *consilium* did not—could not in a civil law system—become a legal precedent. It is not even very likely that it was ever widely invoked elsewhere as a persuasive example.[83] All one can say with some degree of certainty is that the judge who heard the case probably followed the *consilium* in formulating the official decision. Still, as a historical document, the *consilium* and the entire case provide a valuable vantage point on the conceptual dynamics behind the social assimilation of bastards. In proposing a resolution to the problem of Simone's status, the jurist had to examine principles of legitimacy and nature that formed the conceptual foundation of the family. Only on this basis could a relationship (here between Simone and Lena) be legitimated.[84]

The litigants had pinpointed indeterminacies in the meanings of norms and corresponding uncertainties in their social situations.[85] Their perception of interests, values, and meanings thus triggered the conceptual problem for the jurists. The jurists, in turn, operated within a different epistemological framework. They applied to the case the concepts they had learned in their professional training and activity, concepts that furnished a view of social reality with which they were comfortable. Legitimate status to these jurists was not simply a result of descent (in the imprecise sense of being conceived within marriage) but descent itself operated through consent as a legitimating factor. Contractual, legal consent figured formatively in familial relationships. Therefore it was essential for acts like marriage, emancipation, adoption, and legitimation.[86] Consent rearranged the civil-law superstructure that channeled the workings of primordial legitimacy.

Omodei invoked the jurisprudential concept of an immutable and universal primordial nature that implied a natural legitimacy was inherent in all people. Against this concept was posed a notion of individual nature (or types of individual nature) to which Lena's arguments (and those of Jacopo Bottrigari and Baldo) appealed. This view saw nature fixed in the circumstances of procreation.[87] This nature might be "changed" only by fiction, by erecting the image of another possible nature.[88] At best this image might result in a semblance of legitimacy (a *habitus* with regard to *iura legitimationis*), made effective only with the knowledge and acquiescence of all agnates and *venientes ab intestato* (as was argued on Lena's behalf), who would engage to treat the newcomer as if legitimate. Here legitimation could only appear as artificial, contrived, and fictive. The departure from a simple model of descent by birth was made fully apparent. In contrast, by invoking an immutable primordial natural legitimacy (in parallel with the primordial natural freedom of a slave), Omodei could disguise the fictiveness of legitimation. Rather than making apparent the departure from legitimacy by birth, Omodei could stress the "natural" tie between father and son (which distinguished legitimation, however fictive, from adoption, which was universally seen as legal fiction) and restrict the range of consent in legitimation. Legitimation could then seem natural.[89]

Meanings were not simple and direct. In determining meaning, furthermore, Omodei was not only operating as a professional jurist, he was taking a political and ideological position.[90] He approved of the manipulation of kinship in pursuit of family-centered, socially defined interests. Specifically legitimation altered the consequences of descent to preserve family wealth and honor through a male heir. The alternative was inheritance by a more distant, though legitimate, female agnate and the extinction of the family as a *linea masculina*.[91] In the absence of legitimate males, legitimated natural sons might solve the dilemma of familial extinction—a dilemma that could potentially face any Florentine family. As members and heads of families themselves, Omodei and his fellow jurists were sensitive to the problems families faced and to the need for means to cope with them. Their insistence on the "naturalness" of legitimation supported one strategy available for pursuit of family interests.[92]

Legitimation aimed at providing familial continuity while not thoroughly denaturing familial identity. Omodei and his fellow jurists sought to maintain a fit between the continuity of a given family through legitimation and the "natural" legitimacy on which family identity was seen to rest. This fit was managed linguistically. It provided for the insertion of a single "stained" illegitimate into a social order normally perceived in terms of legitimate descent. Restored to a pristine legitimacy, "as if conceived within a legitimate marriage," Simone di Domenico ceased to be a threat to familial order and instead became the means for its continued survival.

Juristic treatment of legitimation, the acquisition of family membership, had much in common with the treatment of acquired citizenship. For both families and cities, an ideology of descent figured as the basis for identifying members. Jurists who sought to defend the rights of those who had acquired legitimacy or citizenship legally had to do so without seeming to denature descent, upon which social order was seen to rest. By crafting metaphors (Omodei's parting clouds and threshed grain), fabricating fictions, drawing equivalences to other institutions (manumission), and by other interpretive strategies, jurists could retain the naturalness of descent, while allowing families and cities to coopt new members.[93] These problems, however, were not to be put to rest by any one proposed resolution. Omodei had stretched norms and principles to a shape suited to the case before him. But these retained their flexibility and snapped back to their general (theoretical) shape, to be reshaped in turn by later jurists, who might fully cast legitimation as a fiction. No single future "Simone" was assured a similar fate. Law and legal opinion did not always support the claims of legitimated offspring.[94] Legitimation would continue to be termed a fiction of law. So too, in acquired citizenship, jurists like Bartolo, Baldo, and Paolo di Castro could arrive at differing determinations by reference to the same constructs, even in the face of previous determinations. But in both areas of law, whatever subsequent jurists and litigants might do, they would do it with the same terms playing across the same field of variant meanings.

As the case of Simone demonstrates, prejudices against bastards did not disappear, especially when they stood to inherit considerable wealth that would not have been theirs had there been legitimate heirs. These prejudices remained deeply woven in the cultural fabric and could be invoked by those, like Lena, interested in keeping honor and wealth from bastards. Even after legitimation, a bastard like Simone was not assured the same treatment as a legitimate child, any more than a new citizen could expect the same treatment as a native citizen in an Italian city-state like Florence.

How many others there were like Simone and how they were dealt with by the law remains to be determined. The economic circumstances of these people, the success or failure of *legitimati* in propagating a family line and patrimony—in short, the entire practical value of legitimation in Quattrocento Florence—cannot be deduced from a single case. But in every case a conceptual accommodation was needed. The case at hand demonstrates that the practical value of legitimation did not simply flow from a father's strategic desires for his family; nor were his desires assured automatic acceptance by legal officials. The fate of legitimated bastards lay in the hands of jurists whose judgments could seem unfathomable to others. Simone and those like him might well have echoed the prayer of Edmund in *Lear:* "Now gods stand up for bastards!"

PART THREE

·

Women

·

8

•

WOMEN, MARRIAGE, AND *PATRIA POTESTAS* IN LATE MEDIEVAL FLORENCE

•

In the third book of his dialogue on the family, Leon Battista Alberti presents Giannozzo Alberti's account of how he instructed his new wife in her duties as governess of the household, a task he undertook only "after my wife had been settled in my house a few days, and after her first pangs of longing for her mother and family had begun to fade."[1] In all he taught her Giannozzo found his bride to be as willing to obey him as she had formerly obeyed her parents. Her submission to her husband was recognition of the fact that she was no longer subject to her parents but that, by marriage, she had been taken from her family and placed under the tutelage of her husband.[2] The husband, meanwhile, found his marriage doubly useful, for as revealed in the second book of the dialogue, marriage allowed a man "first to perpetuate himself in his children, and second to have a steady and constant companion all of his life."[3] As another Florentine humanist, Poggio Bracciolini, noted, marriage allowed a man to propagate a line of descendants that was certain and not promiscuous, a line that bore his image.[4] The line's very existence was founded upon that sacrament which was itself the image of peace and harmony, by which "two wills, two souls are joined into one," by which a woman was joined to her husband "so that by the testimony of Truth the two in flesh might be considered as one."[5]

The conception of marriage shared by these two Florentine hu-

197

manists was one in which there was a close connection between husband and wife, a connection in which the husband was dominant and active and the wife was submissive and passive. While marriage could become the occasion to unite two families, it certainly also was the occasion for the male to propagate his image in children begotten on a lawful wife who had been taken from her family and given to him for that very purpose.[6]

This vision of male dominance in marriage has been a powerful force in shaping historians' interpretations of marriage in the late Middle Ages. Legal historians have located a basis for the husband's dominance in two closely related legal aspects of marriage. On the one hand, the woman's property, in the form of a dowry, was transmitted to her husband at marriage. The dowry carried with it the exclusion of the woman from any further portion of the patrimony of her natal family.[7] On the other hand, marriage also removed the woman from the legal control of her father—from his *patria potestas,* in legal terms—and placed her under the legal control of her husband. Marriage, in other words, consisted (in part, at least) of a dual process of separation and transferal of control over a woman and her property from her natal to her marital family—from her father to her husband.

It is this second aspect of marriage involving the fate of the *patria potestas* that I wish to focus upon. Dowry, quite naturally, was a variable quantity in a marriage. Its size and importance varied from marriage to marriage, from place to place, and from one era to the next. The *patria potestas,* however, had legal importance in every marriage, or at least every marriage of a woman whose father was still alive.

The medieval *patria potestas,* like that of ancient Rome, was normally a perpetual power that a father exercised over his legitimate children. This power over them lasted as long as the father lived, unless he emancipated them, either by an expressed legal act or tacitly.[8] According to the Italian legal historian Enrico Besta, the key to this latter, tacit form of emancipation was cohabitation with the father. In his words, "the *filiusfamilias,* therefore, was not every son whose father remained alive but every son who was not separated from his father. It was living together with the father that gave rise to the limitations which usually resulted from the *patria potestas.*"[9] In accord with this principle, says Besta, marriage automatically emancipated a woman from her father's *potestas,* for it was incumbent upon her to leave her father's house and take up residence with her husband's family. As Besta put it, and he was not the first or the only legal historian to make this observation, "marriage released the woman from paternal power; and she did not fall subject to it again, even if the marriage had been dissolved."[10]

This position of the legal historians regarding the fate of the *patria potestas* at a woman's marriage has been widely accepted and repeated by nonlegal historians of society. Generally marriage in the late Middle Ages is seen as the occasion of a woman's departure from her family (and from subjection to her father) into that of her husband (and into subjection to him).[11] The dowry, of course, accompanied the woman in this passage and served as the justification for her exclusion from any further access to her father's property.[12] Because the prevailing ideology of the fourteenth and fifteenth centuries stipulated that a family's property (*substantia*) was preserved and perpetuated through males, social historians have generally concluded that this ideology dictated that women be transferred to their conjugal lineages and excluded from their natal lineages.[13] A woman fulfilled her social role when through marriage she became the means of perpetuation of her husband's lineage, which was an agnatic association. In this social situation, it is believed by some, widowhood could free women from subjection to males,[14] although even widowhood could in some situations become a way of life that served the interests of the lineage into which the woman had married.[15]

Unlike legal historians, however, social historians have in some cases been anxious to demonstrate that marriage did not terminate all ties between a woman and her family of origin.

> Not all sense of kinship with women disappeared. The exclusion of sisters and married daughters did not place them totally beyond the collective memory [of the lineage], and, above all, it did not sever the sentimental and emotional ties which connected the women with their fathers and their brothers, or their children [and] after them with their grandparents and their maternal uncles.[16]

It was this sort of sentimental attachment which, according to some historians, lay behind the fact that women often made testamentary bequests to members both of the natal and conjugal lineages.[17]

Women, then, are seen by legal and social historians alike as having lost any legal-institutional ties to their families of origin with marriage and the establishment of a dowry. What connection remained was largely affective and occasional, because a woman's rights in inheritance were resolved by the dowry and her father's *patria potestas* over her was dissolved at marriage.

If, however, one looks at marriage not solely from the point of view of males or from the point of view of a single agnatic lineage, one runs across some interesting problems that are not resolved by the insistence on a lack of institutional ties after marriage between a woman and her family of origin. What, for instance, is one to make of the relationship of *parentado* created between families connected by marriage? These relationships were carefully recorded by Alberti's contemporaries, who thoughtfully weighed the advantages and disadvantages of such relationships.[18] Alberti himself urged that a young man carefully inspect not only the character of his wife but that of his prospective in-laws, his "nuovi coniunti."[19] Similarly, what is one to make of the ritual return of a new bride to her father's house, accompanied by feasting and celebration?[20] Such a ritual certainly demonstrates that ties between a woman and her family were more than merely occasional and affective. Through this ritual these ties were given public status and sanction in a manner similar to the ritual celebration of the new ties between wife and husband a few days before. Finally there are various legal doctrines circulating, for example, about the dowry or about alimentary law that indicate that legal-institutional ties persisted after marriage.[21]

The historical interpretation of the ritual and legal ties between a married woman and her family of origin must begin, I believe, with a reexamination of the legal effects of marriage. Such a reexamination will lead to a revision of the assertion that marriage terminated the *patria potestas* over a woman. According to the celebrated jurist of the late fifteenth and early sixteenth centuries, Filippo Decio (1454–1535), in a commentary on the *lex Foeminae* concerned with the rights of married women,

> the most true conclusion seems to be that a married daughter enjoys the privilege given her father and his daughters, because, although the woman is married, she remains in her father's *potestas*. . . . And she retains the origin and family of her father. . . . And, therefore, goods whose alienation outside the family is prohibited are not prohibited from alienation to a married daughter.[22]

Decio's statements clearly reveal that marriage did not bring to an end the *patria potestas* over the woman. So too the early glossator

Martino (d. 1166) recognized that women were not emancipated by marriage, when he composed a famous gloss dealing with the problem of the restitution of dowry.[23] There he treated emancipation of women as an institution separate from marriage and dowry.

It is evident from this brief consideration of Decio and Martino, which will be amplified by statements of other jurists treated below, that emancipation for women did not necessarily result from marriage. The emancipation of women, in fact, was no different from that of men.[24] That this aspect of medieval legal doctrine has not been grasped before is attributable to the fact that insufficient attention has been paid to the variances between the different legal systems then in use, and especially to the variances between civil and canon law. A tract attributed by some to Bartolo of Sassoferrato (d. 1357), on the other hand, noted that one of the many differences between civil and canon law lay in the fact that "in civil law the *patria potestas* lasts in every age of a child, but in canon law *patria potestas* comes to an end at adulthood, at marriage, whether carnal or spiritual, and at the taking of orders."[25] Similarly, it was only in accordance with the tenets of Lombard law, not civil law, that one could speak of a husband's *potestas* over his wife and treat that *potestas* as the equivalent of the *patria potestas*, according to some medieval jurists.[26] Yet even in this area some jurists carefully distinguished between the Lombard *mundium* and the Roman *patria potestas* (the confusion of the two being another source for the view that *patria potestas* over a woman ceased at her marriage). A commentator of the Lombard law, Carlo di Tocco (fl. 1200), kept the two distinct. The *mundium,* according to him, was a power over a daughter only (not over a son), and it passed to her husband. It was this transference of the *mundium* that also distinguished it from the Roman *patria potestas,* for the "*patria potestas* is not transferred to another, and its value is not estimable," while the *mundium* could be given a value, assigned, sold, and alienated.[27]

The fact that, at least in terms of the civil law, the *patria potestas* survived marriage leads to the consideration of just what the relationship between father and son-in-law was in terms of power and control over the wife-daughter. It has been asserted by one legal historian, Manlio Bellomo, who has recognized that the *patria potestas* remained after a woman's marriage, that this *potestas* was practically meaningless. "In reality," he says, "and by the norms of canon law and of the diverse local statutes, her life was totally absorbed into the life of her new family."[28] It is my contention, however, that the remnant *patria potestas* could and did have important legal consequences and that people in late medieval Italy were aware of these consequences and used them to their benefit—to the benefit, that is, not only of a woman's marital family but of her original family as well. The persistence of the *patria potestas* was not meaningless.

Just exactly what rights, then, did a husband gain over his wife and what was left to the father? According to the commentator Angelo degli Ubaldi (1325–1400), "a married and dowered daughter does not pass from her father's *potestas* . . . but as for *servitia* she does pass from it, because she is obligated to labor in her husband's house."[29] Similarly Paolo di Castro (ca. 1360–1441) stated, allowing himself an amount of freedom in the use of the legal terminology, that

> a married woman does not leave the *potestas* of her father, although she enters into the *potestas* of her husband with regard to the *obsequia* of matrimony, but with regard to the effect of the law and of the *patria potestas* she remains subject to the father, and this in matrimony of the flesh; but in spiritual matrimony, as if she were made a bishop or entered a monastery (like a man) she does leave the *patria potestas*.[30]

In the formula worked out by Angelo degli Ubaldi and Paolo di Castro, the married woman was in a position with regard to her husband that was analogous to that defined by the civil law as existing between a freedman (*libertus*) and his patron (*patronus*). Both a freedman and a married woman owed their respective legal counterparts *servitia* and *obsequium*. Other medieval jurists depicted the relationship between husband and wife in the same terms. Odofredo (d. 1265) and Jacopo d'Arena (c. 1253–96) following him said that the wife served her husband ("uxor viro servit") and was obedient to him ("in obsequio mariti").[31] It was the fact that a wife was in the *obsequium* of her husband that formed the basis of the civil-law obligation of a husband to provide *alimenta* for his wife.[32]

At his daughter's marriage, therefore, a father surrendered not his *patria potestas* but the right to the girl's service and labor. But if the husband gained the benefit of his wife's labor, and if he enjoyed the right to expect compliance and submission from her (as Giannozzo Alberti did), then what power remained with the father? What did his *patria potestas* represent after marriage? In this regard the following comment of Angelo Ubaldi's brother Baldo (1327–1400) is instructive.

Note that by marriage a daughter does not cease to be in her father's *potestas*. . . . In opposition [one might claim] that rather she is in the *potestas* of her husband, since he can claim her from her father. . . . The solution [is that] in three respects she is in the *potestas* of her husband, namely in residence, which she must take up with him; in works, because she must work for her husband; and in jurisdiction because she must obey the court and laws and statutes of the husband. . . . But in other respects she is in the power of her father, whence she cannot write a will. And she cannot choose her tomb unless her father agrees. . . . And she cannot make donations *causa mortis*, unless her father takes part [in them] . . . which gift she cannot make to her father, because one cannot interpose authority on one's own behalf.[33]

One could characterize the husband's control over his wife as active and the father's control over his married daughter as passive. The *patria potestas* over a married daughter imposed on her a succession of legal restraints that prevented her from undertaking any one of a number of legal acts. She could not write a will, alienate property, take part in legal proceedings without, at least, the knowledge and consent of her father.[34] This legal restraint on the daughter was most evident with regard to the dowry.[35] But the *patria potestas* also placed legal constraints and liabilities on the father. As long as his *potestas* lasted, a father could not deal with his daughter as a legal equal; he could not form a contractual relationship with her directly. Property could not pass between them, and the legal obligations incumbent upon one were also incumbent upon the other in most cases.

The establishment of the existence of a legal-institutional link between a father and his married daughter in the form of the survival of the *patria potestas* forms only half of the task of historical analysis. One must descend from the realm of doctrines and norms into that of *events* in order to locate the norms in their historical setting and determine the variety of effects they had on behavior. The answer to the question "What did the *patria potestas* over a married daughter mean?" is not complete until we look at the uses to which this *potestas* was put by people who used and manipulated the law to their own ends. In this regard, various examples located among the archival treasures of Florence provide the means for assessing the importance of the *patria potestas* over married women. Florence, it should be added, functions as a test case not only because a wealth of documentation survives but also because the statutes of the city generally followed the Roman law with regard to the *patria potestas*.[36]

Florentine statutory law did, however, create a somewhat different legal situation for women as opposed to that for men. Florentine law, like the civil law, held that a married daughter was not liable for her father's debts and other obligations.[37] With regard to men, however, and contrary to the doctrines of the civil law propounded in the schools, the Florentine statutes established such a liability for the debts and obligations of one's father.[38] In matters of debt and liability, then, marriage did indeed function as the equivalent of emancipation for women, for the men were released from liability for their fathers' debts only through emancipation. Yet even here it was not marriage that freed a woman from liability so much as the transfer of property rights in the dowry, for if a married woman was an heir to her father, she was then liable for his debts, her marriage not withstanding.[39] As Florentine law exempted a married and dowered woman from liability for the debts of her father (and for those of her husband), emancipation of married women was not a matter of creating such an exemption, as it often was for men.[40] Rather emancipation of married women was an enabling act, a means of creating legal capabilities and situations that could be used and exploited by those involved in them.

While Florentine law established a clear difference between women and men in matters of liability, it also created a clear distinction between their respective legal capabilities. Women were always, at least nominally, under the control of men. In Florence the law established that a woman, married or not, was in need of a guardian in order to take part in legal transactions. She had to have a *mundualdus,* who could be any designated male; although, in the case of a married woman, her husband could be assumed to be her *mundualdus.*[41]

As I have already noted, the *patria potestas* over a married woman was largely a passive and negative power. It allowed the father to prevent a number of legal actions on the part of his daughter without his knowledge and consent. This control could, of course, become more broad and active in the case of a widow, for then the father was the only male who could claim to control her (unless the marriage had produced children, in which case the dowry and the care of the children were of interest to the deceased husband's kin). On the other hand, in order for the married daughter to perform any of the legal acts for which she lacked legal capacity while subject to her father's *potestas,* whether she or her husband or her father wanted such an act performed, she had first to be emancipated from that *potestas.* It was only with the termination of the *patria potestas* that the control it represented could acquire active form and substance (and come under the purview of the historian in documentation). A woman freed from *patria potestas* by an act of emancipation could undertake contractual obligations, stand as a legal party in arbitration, or write a will, provided, of course, that she first had appointed for her some male guardian (normally a *mundualdus,* though occasionally a *curator, tutor,* or *procurator* was also appointed).[42] The termination of the *patria potestas,* in other words, gained meaning from the legal capacities that might replace it.

When one turns to the notarial documents of the fourteenth and fifteenth centuries, one finds a great variety of legal acts involving married and widowed women in emancipations and subsequent contracts. In some cases the legal capabilities conferred by emancipation were used by the women for the benefit of their children. One finds, for example, instances in which widows were emancipated in order that they might then apply for and receive guardianship over their children.[43] Other women, married and widowed, were emancipated so that they might write their wills, in which they stipulated how their property, including their dowry, was to be divided among their children or, should none of them survive, among their brothers and sisters.[44] By means such as these women were able to provide for their children, but quite often these provisions were dependent on the cooperation of male relatives. Certainly the cooperation and consent of the woman's father were already necessary for the emancipation and such legal acts as resulted from it. But women also relied even more directly on males. For example, monna Agostina, a widow and daughter of the Florentine lawyer messer Simone di Bernardo Uguccioni, was emancipated in 1497. With the consent of her father, she then gave her property to her son Francesco. Included in this property was a dowry set aside (by whom we are not told) for her daughter Alessandra. With receipt of the property Francesco was required to provide a dowry of 10 florins to Alessandra when she subsequently either married or entered a convent; and he was obligated to provide another dowry for monna Agostina's other daughter as well. The immediate reason for this legal maneuver is not apparent from the documents, but it is clear that the widow Agostina was attempting to safeguard her daughters through the agency of her son and/or his guardians.[45]

Legal devices such as wills and guardianships were intended to benefit a woman's children, though a will could also be written so as to benefit her brothers, sisters, or even her father (her family of origin, in other words). But her legal connection to her father could also work to her own benefit through emancipation. Emancipation gave the woman legal status as a *persona* (albeit burdened with the legal disabilities incumbent upon her sex) separate from her father. As a separate legal *persona* she could enter into contracts with her father and receive property from him.[46] So, for example, one might note the emancipation of monna Bartholomea, wife of Gheri Talducci della Casa, in March 1386. She received from her father a gift (*praemium emancipationis*) of ten *lire* and a further gift of a house and a piece of land.[47] Thirty-nine years later monna Checcha, daughter of Domenico di Zanobi di Ceccho Fraschi, was emancipated in order to receive from her father the complete estate of her paternal grandmother. She then, with the consent of her husband, appointed a notary to act as her agent on the property in question.[48]

In some few cases donations of property to married daughters carried stipulations that such property was not to accrue to the benefit of the woman's husband, that he was not to acquire any rights of ownership or disposal over the property. In such cases it was made clear that the property in question was both the result and the symbol of the attachment of the wife to her family of origin. An example of such a donation occurred at the time of the emancipation of monna Bella by her father Tommaso di Marco di Nuto in 1417. Bella was given a house with all its appurtenances on the condition that

> Tommaso does not want or intend that by the aforesaid goods or any of them any right should accrue to or be understood to accrue to said Piero, husband of the same monna Bella . . . and also Tommaso reserved to himself for all of his life and as long as he should live the use and usufruct of said house and goods.[49]

Considering that Bella, according to the documents, was about forty years of age, her father must have been rather old.[50] This particular transfer of property may have been a form of pre-mortem inheritance.

This last example leads to an important observation. The sort of residual *patria potestas* that endured past marriage often could and did benefit not the woman or her children but her family of origin, and, in all likelihood, the benefits to her family of origin were those perceived by her father. Stipulations placed on property given to a married daughter were one means of seeing to the family's interests, but there were other means as well. In the case of monna Lisabetta, daughter of Matteo di Ceccho di Feo da Linari, emancipation paved the way not for a gift of property from her father but for Lisabetta's standing as a party in arbitration with her mother Cara. As a result of this arbitration, Lisabetta took on the obligation to support and care for her aged parents, although, in return, she was given title to her parents' house.[51] The arbitration thus served as the means to spell out the obligations of parents and child and, by so doing, to establish a contractual relationship in which the daughter served her parents in accordance with prevailing cultural conceptions. According to the cartulary, Lisabetta accepted the obligation to care for her parents out of a sense of honor and natural obligation ("ex natura") to her aged, sick, and weak parents. Above all she promised "not to cease to honor them as her father and mother." Here culturally dictated sentiments and their symbolic expression coalesced in a legal relationship made possible by the father's willful dispensing with his *patria potestas* over his daughter. The transaction mentioned above between monna Bella and her father Tommaso may also have been intended to set up such a relationship, though there we find only the transfer of property to the daughter and not the corresponding obligations on her part to care for Tommaso.

There were other ways of using *potestas* over a daughter in order to acquire something of value. A daughter had the right to a share of her mother's dowry equivalent to that of each of her siblings. This right could become very important, especially to a father who found himself in dire financial straits. A father, then, might emancipate his daughter so that she could renounce her right to the maternal dowry or give it to her brothers and sisters, which is what occurred in the case of monna Nannena in 1496.[52] In some cases the emancipated married daughter renounced her right to her mother's dowry because she acknowledged that she had received some adequate form of compensation—like her own dowry,[53] or the assurance that she could return to her family home in case of widowhood.[54] Furthermore, if a woman did not renounce her mother's dowry, it was important that she at least declare that her claims to it had been satisfied. In 1412, for example, ser Giovanni di Neri da Castrofranco emancipated his daughter so that she could then acknowledge that her portion of her deceased mother's dowry had been paid to her and that she had no further legal claims in this regard.[55] Occasionally women went so far as to renounce a portion of their own dowries, in the event of the dissolution of their marriage and the restitution of the dowry, in favor of a sister or brother.[56]

Such renunciations of property rights on the part of married women were designed to help their brothers and sisters, but often they were also designed to bail out a father in financial difficulty who turned to his daughter and his legal relationship with her to find a way out of his problems. This use of legal relations with female kin in order to avoid financial difficulties was rather common in Florence. There are instances in which Florentines more or less admitted that they were using their women in this fashion.[57] In this vein there is the emancipation of monna Francesca, married daughter of Andrea di Guido Lippacci in 1407. In arbitration with her father following emancipation, she received four farms, two houses, and twenty-three pieces of land. These properties were accompanied by an obligation to return her mother's dowry to her and to pay three creditors of her father (one of whom was her grandfather). For his part Andrea was constrained by the arbitrator to repay his daughter within eight days.[58] It would seem that the father had found arbitration a means of preventing the total loss of his property by giving it to his daughter while, at the same time, providing a way of meeting his debts. Perhaps the motivation was similar in the case of the widow monna Selvaggia, who received a farm by arbitration but had to hand over to her father her dowry of 600 florins.[59] It appears that a need for ready cash forced both fathers to exchange land with their daughters. Ordinarily Florentine fathers sought to keep real property in their own hands while dowering their daughters with liquid assets, so the number of transfers of real property to married daughters is striking.[60] Perhaps, like Giovanni Corsini, who gave real property to his sister to keep it from falling into the hands of his creditors, these men were trying to use their daughters as shields to protect the patrimony.[61] In other cases, however, they may simply have sought an end to a legal obligation.

Clearly a daughter's dowry could provide an important and even vital financial boost to a hard-pressed family, although not all daughters were willing to see their dowries devoured for familial purposes. Also fathers sometimes wanted the daughters' claims to be recognized so that creditors could not lay claim to that part of the patrimony. In 1497 Matteo di Francesco di Geri Ferrini emancipated his two sons and his widowed daughter monna Piera. In a subsequent arbitration, in which she opposed her father and brothers, the male members of the family admitted that her dowry had been returned to them after the death of her husband. They had used the dowry for their own purposes and, therefore, they acknowledged that they were Piera's debtors. This debt was then satisfied by the arbitrator, who awarded Piera one-seventh of a farm.[62] Since there is no evidence that Piera was soon to remarry, it is possible that the emancipations and arbitration may have been the result of a desire to set aside as hers property that then would not be subject to the claims of creditors. In a similar case which occurred in 1410, the arbitrator demanded that the woman's father return the restituted dowry to his widowed daughter not in designated parcels of land but in cash (*pecunia numerata*).[63] In both of these instances the prior claim of a widowed daughter to the content and/or value of her dowry was established over the father's property.

But such arbitrations encompassed married daughters as well. To cite but one example, messer Pietro di messer Benedetto de' Gatani of Pisa entered into arbitration with his daughter Margherita, wife of the canon lawyer Agostino di messer Pietro da Lante, following her emancipation. The arbitrator awarded her a mill and a country estate, giving no reason for his judgment. The arbitration, however, occurred immediately after the emancipation, and one is led to suspect that messer Pietro had worked the whole business out beforehand, perhaps, again, to transfer property to his daughter so as to prevent its falling into the hands of creditors.[64]

Not all such emancipations worked to the advantage of fathers who had mishandled or misappropriated the family's wealth. Sometimes fathers were more concerned with the problems and liabilities created by others. Donations to daughters with restrictions on their husband's rights in the property may have been due to a recognition that sons-in-law were capable of mismanaging the property, and daughters too could be a potential source of financial embarrassment. While Florentine law removed a married woman from liability for her father's debts, it provided no such termination of liability in the other direction. Emancipation could present the opportunity to limit expenses incurred on behalf of a daughter *in potestate*, whatever her marital status.[65] In this way a father might avoid problems resulting from a daughter's prodigality or even from onerous, if necessary, expenses on her behalf. The emancipation in 1437 of monna Lisa, wife of Bernardo di ser Giovanni Ghini, led to an arbitration between her and her father, Taddeo di Giovanni Antellesi, in which it was determined that Taddeo had gone to great expense on behalf of Lisa and her husband and that, therefore, he was not obligated to give her any part of her mother's dowry, especially since he had other children to provide for.[66] At the time of the emancipation of the widow monna Nanna di Christofano di Niccolò di Rufino, nine years earlier, her father was simply awarded her dowry by arbitration with no explanation offered as to the reason for the award.[67] Perhaps the award was based on the fact that she had returned to live with her father in her widowhood and that he was entitled to the dowry as compensation for housing and feeding her.[68] In any case, it is clear from these examples that daughters represented an expense, both because of their dowries and because of their rights to other forms of property and to support, and it was an expense which their fathers sought to hold to a minimum or within reasonable (to them) limits.

Conclusion

Contrary to the generally held opinions of historians of law, a father retained his *potestas* over a married daughter. This *potestas* was a residual and negative power that coexisted with the active and positive control over the daughter exercised by her husband. The husband's control consisted of the legal right to demand obedience and service from his wife, but the control of the husband did not mean that the father's *potestas* was not or could not be significant. Seen in the socioeconomic context of Florence in the fourteenth and fifteenth centuries, and examined at the point of its dissolution in the legal act of emancipation, the *patria potestas* over a married daughter emerges as a meaningful part of that society, serving to maintain and transmit property rights in accordance with prevailing norms relating to honor and the family.

The *patria potestas* and property, especially a woman's dowry and that of her mother, constituted a strong legal link between a father and his married daughter. This legal connection was paralleled, in turn, by continuing social ties symbolized in the postwedding return ritual and in the rituals of bride-capture and rivalry at the time of the wedding.[69] This legally and symbolically expressed structural link, moreover, became at times the focus of intense legal activity. At such times it became an important, meaningful, and functional moment in a complex system of legal and cultural norms.

This study has located a structural reality and suggested some of the vicissitudes and manipulations this structure underwent in practice. A complete documentation of the historical features of this structural reality must await further research into events: not only emancipations but testaments, letters, diaries, account books, secular and religious literature, and pictorial representations. And this further research, aimed at historical reconstruction, must proceed by a cross-fertilization of approaches to the past. The historian must realize that the dynamics and the norms of the social structure of fourteenth- and fifteenth-century Italy were most often, if not always, worked out within recognized legal mechanisms and encoded in the legal language of the surviving texts. The full, multidimensional meaning of such legal acts is not available to the historian without a knowledge of the law.

By the same token, while it is incumbent upon the historian not to reduce to meaninglessness the legal terms, format, and rules of his documents, it is also necessary that the complex reality behind a text not be reduced to the legal principles enshrined within it. One cannot ignore socioeconomic factors or reduce them to expressions of legal maxims (as has occurred in the case of the research into the relations between married women and their families of origin). The historian must see the legal text from a variety of viewpoints (available from other types of texts) to arrive at a sense of what happened in its multidimensional character (as both legal and socioeconomic, as both normative and creative). Peculiar features of law, like the continuance of the *patria potestas* after a woman's marriage, and the many permutations of practice, as revealed, for example, in emancipations, will continue to elude historians who operate without a coherent theory of textuality and without adequate tools for the complete deconstruction of the texts.

9

•

"CUM CONSENSU MUNDUALDI" LEGAL GUARDIANSHIP OF WOMEN IN QUATTROCENTO FLORENCE

•

In 1481 monna Angelica, widow of Guasparre dal Lama, entered into an agreement with the Dominicans of Santa Maria Novella of Florence. This agreement is of historical interest because her husband's estate endowed the Cappella de' Magi in Santa Maria Novella, the crowning monument of which was a famous painting, *The Adoration of the Magi,* by Sandro Botticelli.[1] However, before the agreement could be formally concluded and codified into legal Latin by a notary, monna Angelica had to have a male guardian, a *mundualdus,* appointed for her by the notary. Whereas the endowment of a chapel— and one that bore such artistic fruit—was certainly not an everyday occurrence in fifteenth-century Florence, the appointment of a *mundualdus* for a woman was decidedly quotidian. Florentine women were obliged by statute to have some adult male associated with them in their legal transactions. The *mundualdus* might be a brother, as he was in monna Angelica's case, or he might be a father, son, husband, or anyone else, provided it was a male. The appointment of a *mundualdus* for monna Angelica may not, therefore, have been an event of singular historical significance, but it was one instance of a venerable and important Florentine legal institution. This institution, moreover, has received scant attention from historians. I present here the results of a limited foray into the subject of the

212

mundualdus: what it reveals about the role of women in Quattro-cento Florence.

The Legal Shape of the *Mundualdus*

Unlike many features of Florentine law, the institution of the *mundualdus* did not derive from the Roman civil law. The *mundualdus* and his power (*mundium*) were of Lombard provenance. Originally the *mundium* had been a patrimonial power over women. As such it was distinct from the protective and authoritative power that men held over women by virtue of personal relationships (that is, father-daughter, brother-sister, husband-wife).[2] As a patrimonial power the *mundium* could be treated like any right in property; it could be sold or given away or passed on in inheritance. A man's *mundium* over his wife, therefore, could conceivably end up in the possession of an infant son. In time the distinction between the *mundium* and other powers over a woman became blurred, largely because the holder of the *mundium* was usually also a family member. The *mundium* became confused with duties of care and guardianship which inhered in familial roles; and the resurgence of Roman law introduced further notions of guardianship in the *tutela* over minors.[3] The *mundium* remained a power distinct from familial relationships, but the holder of it had to be someone capable of acting as a guardian; no longer could an infant son hold his mother's *mundium*.[4]

The tutelary function of the *mundualdus* ultimately centered around the act of consenting to the woman's legal transactions, making the *mundualdus* into a *mundualdus ad negotium*, the equivalent for women of the *tutor ad singulam causam datus* for minors in Roman law. The *mundualdus* had to be appointed or confirmed by a judge, and his possession of the *mundium* lasted only for a single day or for the duration of a sequence of legal actions in a given day. In a judicial proceeding the judge appointed the *mundualdus;* in simple contracts and voluntary legal activities a woman could designate her *mundualdus,* subject to a judge's confirmation.[5] In either case the presence of a *mundualdus* and his consent to a woman's legal activities were considered necessary "because a woman does not have the legitimate *persona* to act in law without a *mundualdus.*"[6] Only an adult male could make up for a woman's gender-related legal incapacities.[7]

The Florentine *mundualdus* essentially corresponded with the form of the institution as elaborated in the scientific development of Lombard law in the eleventh and twelfth centuries. The context in which one encounters the *mundualdus* among the Florentine statutes of 1415 reveals that the *mundualdus* was clearly considered to be a woman's guardian.

> Any *mundualdus* selected by a woman, the fact that she has another guardian notwithstanding, even her father or her husband, should be given to her. And no woman may obligate herself in any way without consent of her *mundualdus*, or without her husband's consent if she has a husband. Any judge . . . matriculated in the guild of judges and notaries of the city of Florence has ordinary jurisdiction in giving *tutores, curatores, actores,* and *mundualdos.* . . . And any notary at least twenty years of age, matriculated in said guild, can give *mundualdos* to any woman seeking [one].[8]

Judges and notaries could appoint a *mundualdus* by virtue of the same authority by which they could appoint trustees and guardians for minors. The legal positions of women and minors were often equated in Florentine law, in fact, and treated under a single rubric in the city's statutes.[9]

One interesting feature of Florentine law is the assumption or bias in favor of the husband's functioning as *mundualdus*. If a husband was present at his wife's legal action and gave his consent to it, he was assumed to be her *mundualdus;* and her contract or obligation was valid as a result.[10] Florentine law also maintained a distinction between judicial proceedings and ordinary contracts. For the former a woman needed more than a *mundualdus*: she needed a *procurator*.[11] The *procurator* could also be almost any male, but the role was generally filled by notaries, who were versed in the law and could argue in court on behalf of their clients (male or female). Legal expertise was not nearly so crucial for a *mundualdus*, whose business it was to see to a woman's welfare and not to the legal correctness of proceedings.

The institution of the *mundualdus*, then, as established in Florentine statutory law, largely followed the contours provided for it by Lombard law. What made the Florentine institution peculiar was the fact that Florence was the only major Tuscan city to preserve the Lombard institution with regard to women. The statutes of cities like

Siena and Pisa did not use the word in any sense, or, when the term *mundualdus* appeared, it was used solely as a synonym for *tutor*, a guardian for children.[12] Only Florence used the *mundualdus* in a more precise sense as a guardian over women in the area of civil contracts, although the Florentine statutes of 1415 finally extended the institution to all of Florentine territory.

Being of Lombard origin, the institution of the *mundualdus* entered Florentine statutory law as an element of prevailing legal custom. Within the statutory law, however, it occupied a place beside other legal institutions, many of them of Roman origin, with which it was not always conceptually congruent. The institution of the *mundualdus*, therefore, raised difficulties for Florentine legal experts, who had been trained in the civil and canon law traditions developed in the universities.[13] Their ability to interpret the legal meaning of the *mundualdus* and to assimilate the institution into the linguistic structures of the legal tradition of the universities was dependent upon the notions of guardianship and of female legal incapacity found in civil and canon law. Their task was greatly complicated, moreover, by the fact that there was nothing similar to the *mundualdus* and the *mundium* in Roman and canon law.

Canon law was especially unhelpful. On the one hand, it gave seemingly contradictory signals regarding female legal capacities, and on the other hand, it tended to leave to the civil law all questions involving ordinary civil contracts. Canon law did, of course, have a great deal to say about marriage. The church was concerned with marriage as a sacrament, as the initiation into a particular form of Christian life, with all its consequences for the souls of those involved. This concern resulted in numerous canons and decretals, beginning with Pope Alexander III, which asserted that a valid marriage was based on the free consent of husband *and* wife and that parental consent was *not* necessary.[14] Similarly a woman's entry into the religious life had to be based on her free consent.[15] These provisions regarding marriage and the religious life gave an image of women acting legally on their own, on an equal footing with men. The woman's legal autonomy in the formation of marriage also issued in a corresponding control in its voluntary "dissolution"—that is, if a husband or wife wished to take a vow of continence or leave the married for the religious life, his or her partner had to consent. In this regard, then, within the marriage a woman could even be said to have exercised a form of legal control over her husband.[16] In their legislative and jurisprudential activities, popes and canonists consistently reaffirmed women's rights and abilities in these matters.

When canon law looked at women within the order of nature (as opposed to the order of grace), however, it seemingly opened the door to legal guardianship of women in certain areas. While affirming the necessity of the wife's free consent for a valid marriage, some canon lawyers were willing to admit a limited degree of familial guidance or even pressure in dictating the choice of a husband.[17] Canon law also gave vague or general indications that, within marriage and in regard to the normal day-to-day functioning of the household, the wife was subject to her husband. Such infrequent expressions concerning a wife's "servitude" remained legally vague, however, and were even at times used by jurists in order to enjoin various duties on the husband toward his wife.[18] In general, canon law left the ordering of domestic life alone. Domestic order remained largely a moral issue, left to theologians and confessors.[19] The legal dimensions of domestic life (that is, the validity of contracts and problems of civil status) were left to the civil law.[20]

The Roman law, however, provided no easy means for Florentine lawyers, intent on interpreting the Florentine statutes concerning the *mundualdus*, to assimilate the practices clustering about the institution to the scholastic legal tradition. By the time of the compilation of the *Corpus iuris civilis*, almost all trace of female legal incapacity or of guardianship over women had disappeared.[21] According to the Bolognese jurist Rolandino Passaggieri (d. 1300), a woman was not

> among those persons who cannot obligate themselves, because she can regularly celebrate all contracts in her own name. . . . nor by reason of her gender is she prohibited from entering into contracts . . . with a third party, and she does not need her husband's consent, for she has nothing to do with her husband when it comes to making obligations and contracts.[22]

This utter denial that legal incapacity was inherent in a woman could have made the lawyers' efforts to comprehend the *mundualdus* very difficult. However, there was one important female legal disability that the lawyers could make use of in assimilating existing practices with legal theory.

In the Roman law women could not effectively (*efficicaciter*) obligate themselves on behalf of others by standing surety for them (*fideiussio*). Passaggieri could not deny that, while women could obligate themselves in cases in which the obligation would be activated by their own deeds, they could not obligate themselves when the occasion for the activation rested with others. Under the provision of the *Senatusconsultum Velleianum,* women could waive their protection from obligation on behalf of others; but the existence of this protection in the law provided a point of departure from which the great civilian jurists, like Bartolo of Sassoferrato (d. 1357), Baldo degli Ubaldi (d. 1400), and Paolo di Castro (d. 1441), could begin to discuss statutory restrictions on the legal capacities of women.[23]

Bartolo, for one, drew a connection between the legal disability of women under the *Velleianum* and the existing statutes "which forbid women or minors from being obligated unless certain solemnities are observed."[24] Statutes demanding consent of others in the legal actions of a woman were to be found throughout Italy, and Bartolo elaborated some of the conditions that he saw attached to them. No one could consent to a woman's actions, he said, if that person stood to gain directly from her action.[25] To be truly protective of the woman, the guardian had to be disinterested. Clearly a woman's legal transactions were envisioned as a means of obtaining perceived benefits for her, and a self-interested guardian could stand in the way of any potential utility for the woman. The notion of the potential profit to women from legal activities was such that Bartolo argued that the inability to find an appropriate or suitable guardian should not prevent a woman from taking advantage of legal mechanisms. If a statute required consent of relatives, for example, and they refused their consent, Bartolo directed that a judge should examine the reasons for their refusal. If these reasons were not just, the woman should be permitted by the judge to do whatever it was she had proposed.[26] Bartolo did not contest the justice or legality of statutes requiring consent of others in a woman's acts. He even came out against an argument that attempted to exempt the acceptance of an inheritance from the requirement on the grounds that an acceptance was not a contract but only a quasi-contract.[27]

There were also relevant norms still to be found within canon law. Gratian had declared that women should be subject to their husbands and that they possessed no legal capacity to stand as surety, to give testimony or judgment in court. Subsequent papal decretals and juristic glosses and commentaries built on this base. Canon law's un-

questionable position within the learned *ius commune* of the late
Middle Ages meant that it was available to jurists and legislators to
buttress, especially with natural law arguments, norms encoding legal
incapacities by gender.[28]

The willingness of jurists like Bartolo to accept statutory restrictions on the legal capacities of women lay in the fact that they saw
these restrictions as protective of women. Their desire to protect
women derived in part from their adherence to the innate reason and
justice of the civil law, as they understood it, and in part from an overt
shared cultural bias against women. Baldo gave a clear expression to
this sentiment when he said that "a woman and a minor, on account
of their incapacity and weakness, cannot renounce [rights] unless
they are vouched for."[29] This notion of female weakness was elevated
to the level of legal truth by lawyers and to the level of philosophical
truth by theologians like Aquinas.[30] The defense of statutes like that
of Florence, then, rested on the sexual ideology that women were
inherently weak in mind and body and, therefore, should be subject
to perpetual guardianship ("sub perpetua cura").[31]

In at least one case, however, a lawyer was not willing to take a
position consistent with the logic of this vision of the weakness of
women. Paolo di Castro openly disagreed with Bartolo, who had
declared that a woman's legal actions were null and void if the statutory requirement for consent of another had not been met. Di Castro
contended that because the requirement for consent "is neither contrary to good customs nor to public utility, nor does it tend to prejudice [the rights of] another," there was no good legal reason for a
woman not to comply with the statute by obtaining the required
consent. If the statute took the position that noncompliance carried
the presumption of fraudulent or criminal intent, a woman could not
be released from a legally binding oath, even if the canon law and the
arguments of Bartolo claimed that her observance of the oath would
involve her in sin. "And this is the truth," said Paolo, "although the
jurists commonly do not want to admit such exceptions, and instead
such statutes are in fact observed."[32] Bartolo's argument, by Paolo's
admission, appears to have conformed with prevailing practice; but
Paolo himself was willing to entertain the notion of a woman con-
sciously committing fraud by taking advantage of her presumed
weakness.

Florentine lawyers who expounded on the legal practice and
meaning of the *mundualdus* did so from the perspective given them

by the tradition shaped so powerfully by figures like Bartolo and Baldo. They also approached the local statutes from the standpoint of the legal practitioner rather than that of the teacher. One issue they faced concerned the jurisdictional applicability of the laws requiring male guardians for women—both the *mundualdus* and the *procurator*. Because the institution of *mundualdus* was an element of custom and statutory law and not, therefore, an element of *ius commune*, there was doubt as to whether the requirement of a *procurator* or *mundualdus* extended to women who lived outside Florence, in areas subject to Florentine rule yet having no indigenous *mundualdus* or *procurator* law. Alessandro Bencivenni (1385–1423), in a commentary on the Florentine statutes, thought not. The custom in Florentine territory, he said, was not displaced by the contrary custom of Florence itself.[33] Tommaso Salvetti (1390–1472) in a later statute commentary, however, found the problem more complex. He recognized that Bencivenni was correct "de rigore iuris," but he did not want to deny Florence's ability to extend its legal institutions into its territory. Salvetti's solution was that courts established by Florence in the territory should operate on the basis of Florentine law: in those courts a woman would need a *procurator*. In the indigenous tribunals, however, local custom would be observed, because, even though the Florentine law was "reasonable and introduced for the sake of honesty" ("rationabile et indictum favore honestatis"), outside of Florence it could only be considered burdensome or hateful ("hodiosum") because it was contrary to prevailing custom.[34]

The geographic extent of the institution of *mundualdus* did not remain a problem for Bencivenni and Salvetti only because the problem had been rendered moot by a clause inserted into the statute redaction of 1415 (supervised by Paolo di Castro). This clause explicitly extended the requirement of a *mundualdus* to all of Florentine territory and even beyond, in cases involving a Florentine notary and a woman who was a legal resident of Florentine territory and thus subject to Florentine law.[35] According to Bencivenni this clause put to rest the ongoing discussion about the jurisdiction of the *mundualdus* legislation.[36]

The major problem with regard to the *mundualdus* (as distinct from the *procurator*) lay in determining the legal circumstances in which the requirement took effect. Bencivenni's determinations in this matter were based on those of Bartolo. Like Bartolo, he too declared that a woman needed a *mundualdus* to accept an inheritance and that she could not ordinarily obligate herself without the consent of a *mundualdus*. The *mundualdus* also could not be in a position to gain by giving his consent.[37] Bencivenni also demanded that a woman have a *mundualdus* in order to bind herself to the dispositions of any arbitration settlement involving her rights.[38] Likewise she needed a *mundualdus* in order to give her consent to any alienation of her property made by her husband, and she was legally bound to observe that alienation if she gave her consent.[39] In general, any alienation of property by a woman was valid if she had the consent required by law, even if that consent was not forthcoming immediately, because such alienations were allowed under the *ius commune*.[40] Obligations arising from the law itself and that were not voluntary were in force without the need for the consent of the *mundualdus*.[41] Such obligations were considered natural obligations, and for women these would include, for example, the obligation to feed their children.[42]

The justification for the restrictive and protective nature of the *mundualdus*'s guardianship was the same as that formulated by Baldo: "woman is of the weaker sex than the male . . . and the laws have less confidence in a woman."[43] Therefore, according to Antonio Strozzi (1455–1523) in a notation in his personal legal glossary, there had to be some legal mechanism, like the *mundualdus*, to protect women and to make sure they knew what they were doing, "since the simplicity of such persons persuades one that this act would arise rather from the faculty [of simplicity] than from a free generosity."[44] In accordance with this perceived need to protect women, Strozzi declared that any statute affecting men that was contrary to the *ius commune* should not be extended to cover women, his assumption being that the *ius commune* was a more accurate standard of justice and more apt to protect women properly.[45] On the other hand, Strozzi did not contest the validity of statutes requiring the consent of men in women's legal acts, which statutes were contrary to the *ius commune*, because they were designed to be protective of women. Only if a woman had no relations or neighbors to turn to, said Strozzi (and only if the statute limited consensual capacity to those categories, which the Florentine statute did not), could she act without their consent, and then only by permission of a judge.[46]

The Florentine *Mundualdus* in Practice

The ideological justification for guardianship over women on the part of the jurists corresponded to the general view of women in Florence. Women were widely considered to be weaker than men, especially weaker mentally. According to Paolo da Certaldo, a collector of proverbial Tuscan wisdom, women were empty-headed and easily swayed. They had to be kept at home, closely watched and never idle.[47] Leon Battista Alberti gave vent to similar misogynistic sentiments. "They are crazy who think there is any true prudence or right counsel in a woman's head," declared Giannozzo Alberti in his dialogue on the family.[48] Male guardianship over women was rooted in the idea that men ruled women and directed their activities.[49]

The supposed natural inferiority of women justified not only a legal inferiority but a social inferiority. Men were considered to be the true basis of the family; through them the patrimony and the family name were preserved. Women, on the other hand, spelled the end of the family. They married and moved away, bearing children for others. They were the occasion for financial hardship in accumulating their dowries, which were to consist of cash and other liquid assets and not the real property (*substantia*), which went to males.[50] The dowry, therefore, was to be their fair share of the patrimony; they were excluded by law from seeking anything further.[51] Any claims by women beyond the dowry would only endanger the integrity of the patrimony.

The pervasiveness of these beliefs is indicated by the Florentines' tendency to forget girls when counting family members, to abandon them as infants, or to expend less for their care and nurture. Women, however, also occupied an undeniably important place in the social structure. They were a means by which men could attain or maintain socially desired relationships and resources. The material and symbolic interests of a family, interests largely defined and pursued by its male members, could be realized through women.[52]

Marriage was one important point at which women figured prominently in familial strategies. Men stood to gain directly or indirectly by the judicious use of women in matrimonial alliances. Marriage provided the husband with the means for procreation of legitimate family members, especially male members, for direct material gain (that is, the dowry), for the establishment of useful alliances with other families, and for the increase in honor and prestige deriving from all of these.[53] For the woman's family marriage also could mean valuable ties with another family; and the burden of providing a dowry was compensated by the fact that it underwrote the woman's honorable existence as wife and mother and reflected honor and respect back on her family.[54]

Following her marriage, a woman continued to be a vital figure in familial strategies in her private, domestic role as wife and mother in her husband's house. Women were relegated to a domestic space, the *casa,* which was itself feminine. Women and *casa* were both to be protected from defilement and shame by men, whose standing in the community rested in good part on their fulfillment of their roles as provider for a *casa* and its women, as protector of female virginity and chastity, and as master over women and the *casa.* It was important, therefore, to a Florentine like Alberti to determine how a husband was to treat his wife. The man's space was "nelle piazze, in publico," there to traffic among men ("nelle cose virili tra gli uomini, co' cittadini, ancora e con buoni e onesti forestieri convivere e conversare"), and not in the house among the women ("chiuso in casa tra le femine").[55] But within the *casa* were things of value, and the wife had direct oversight over the sanctuary. She had to see to the preservation of the family wealth, using what her husband acquired for the needs of the *casa.*[56] The wife had to behave honorably for the good of her husband and her children. She had to obey and revere her husband (but Alberti also recognized that the husband had to fulfill his role toward her to be worthy of her obedience and respect).[57] She had to maintain peace and tranquillity in the house, and she had to learn from her husband how best to use the family's resources.[58] By these and other means she would both aid the family and be a source of pride for her husband, who, in his greater wisdom, had instructed her in her duties.[59]

So both as bride and as *madre di famiglia* a woman played important roles. In general these roles were engineered so as to be compatible with the sexual division of labor, and with the woman's supposed inherent inferiority and need for protection. But these roles also demanded that the woman have rights and access to property and that she be able to use these rights and property to care for herself and her children, especially if her husband was absent due to death, business, or banishment. Her right to her dowry, for example, underwrote her role as wife and mother, because the dowry was intended

to support the burdens of married life ("sustinere onera matrimonii"). Transaction of these rights, however, involved going out into
the *piazze* and public places reserved for men and engaging in "cose
virili." The conceptual threat posed by the image of women engaging
in familial business in a public forum could be obviated if the women
went into the *piazze* only with the corrective and protective presence
of a man.[60] Here is where the *mundualdus* operated in theory as a
practical moment in a conceptual complex revolving about notions of
honor and sexual differences. A woman's rights could be involved in
transactions, from which some material gain might result, while no
symbolic loss was incurred because the woman formally lacked any
authority or decision-making power. Even if a woman disposed of a
de facto power to arrange her affairs, she could do so only under the
guise of a fiction which insisted that power belonged to men.[61] In this
way the *mundualdus* could protect men both from the material losses
that were sure to arise when timid and weak women ventured into the
male world, where they could be taken advantage of, and from the
loss of honor that would arise if the women were to seem to have a
public and official authority.[62]

The advantage to be gained from the legal transactions of a woman
could accrue to almost anyone, but the one most likely to profit was
the person who instigated the activity. In the case of monna Angelica
mentioned above, the arrangement between her and the clergy of
Santa Maria Novella was generated by an intent whose origin and
nature are not easily divined. Guasparre dal Lama had revoked the
provisions of his earlier wills providing for the endowment of the
Cappella de' Magi. His widow, however, with the assistance of her
brother as *mundualdus*, undertook to carry out those revoked provisions.[63] The gain for the church was obvious; but she too stood to
gain from an action made possible only by the absence of her husband
and the presence of her brother. She stood to gain spiritual benefits,
and like a good widow she was providing for the spiritual and ritual
well-being of the family.

Monna Angelica operated independently of her husband's ultimate testamentary dispositions (though in accord with his earlier
ones). Other women acted in strict conformity with the desires of
their husbands, even to their own material detriment. In his *Ricordi*
Giovanni Morelli angrily complained that his sister had been too
obedient to her husband, eventually alienating all of her property at
his insistence to help bail him (and the family) out of financial diffi-

culty. He claimed that she had done so under pressure, that her husband would suddenly appear at home with a notary and witnesses in tow, explaining that she must consent to some deal. From a sense of shame she could not refuse in front of strangers. Morelli had cause for his complaint, because his sister had lost all of her dowry and had had to return to live with him, at his expense, after her husband's death.[64]

Whereas Morelli's sister's husband had made use of his wife, another Florentine, Giovanni di Matteo Corsini, in 1430, made use of his sister Checa, who was married to Luca del maestro Niccolò de' Falcucci. By means of arbitration settlements, which had in fact been dictated in accord with Giovanni's wishes and not by the arbitrator acting independently, Checa received title to Giovanni's house, to a farm located near Castello (which Giovanni called "il principale podere dela posesione"), and to 200 florins. Checa became titular owner in order to remove the property from Giovanni's ownership and thus safely away from the claims of his creditors. He wanted the property to go to his sons, or at least to be available to them, because it was "salvamento nostro." He found in that faith which brothers ought to have in their sisters ("come debo avere fratello con sirochia") the means to his end.[65]

Not all women were as compliant as these sisters. Francesco Guicciardini recounted how, in a similar situation to that of Morelli's sister with her husband, when Piero di messer Luigi Guicciardini was verging on bankruptcy and wanted to sell his house, his wife, for whose dowry the house had been pledged as security, refused to consent to the sale. "Rather she chased the notary and the buyer from the house, and in view of her obstinacy and perhaps pleased by that show of anger [Piero] had patience with her."[66] There could hardly be a more graphic example of a Florentine patrician woman's decisive independence in the face of a husband's legal demands. Still, before we are incautiously carried away, we must recognize that her role here was passive; her only prerogative was to consent to the sale (and that right arose only from the obligation her husband had to return the dowry), not to arrange it. In other situations a woman could move to reclaim her dowry in the face of her husband's financial problems, but then the question was open as to whether she was saving her rights or protecting her husband.[67]

At certain moments in the course of a family's fortunes, the legal actions of its female members could take on great importance, as the dal Lama, Morelli, Guicciardini, and Corsini examples demonstrate. In conjunction with a consenting *mundualdus,* they could act for their own benefit or for that of husbands, brothers, or others. In order to determine what role the *mundualdus* played and who he usually was, one must confront some set of data pertaining to the institution.

The remarks that follow are based on the examination of a small sample of the legal actions of women, those contained in a single notarial cartulary. These documents cover a seven-year period from 1422 to 1429 (1430 modern style). The legal actions are of all types, except for testaments, which this notary, ser Francesco di Piero Giacomini, kept in a separate cartulary, following a practice common among Florentine notaries. The period during which these actions took place was one of great economic and political difficulties in Florence.[68] These difficulties may have provided a stimulus to female legal activity, but the detection of any abnormalities must await a more ambitious study. For the moment the evidence of this cartulary can provide a basis for advancing some tentative positions regarding the *mundualdus* in Florence.

The cartulary contains 179 instances in which a woman took a *mundualdus*. Most often these women were widows (see tables 9.1 and 9.2); the rest were married (some for the second time). In only about 5 percent of these instances was there no indication that the woman was married. Another interesting statistical revelation is that these women frequently took a *mundualdus* who was not related to them. Twenty-six of the *mundualdi* were notaries and ninety-two

Table 9.1 Categorization of *Mundualdi* by Florentine Year

Year	Father or Husband	Consanguineal Kinsmen	Affinal Kinsmen	Notary	Unrelated	Total
1422	5		1	1	1	8
1423	2	3	2	5	23	35
1424	2	2			14	18
1425	4	3	2	5	5	19
1426	2	7	2	2	17	30
1427	2	7	2	3	13	27
1428	5	2	2	8	8	25
1429	2	1	1	2	11	17
Total	24	25	12	26	92	179

were men who had no apparent consanguineal or marital relationship to the woman (a total of 120, or 67 percent of the 179). Any male would do as a *mundualdus* according to the law, and in many cases it appears that the *mundualdus* was just that—any male.[69]

What one would most like to determine is why women engaged in the activities recorded by Giacomini and to what degree men actually controlled these activities by means of the position of *mundualdus*. From the fact that two-thirds of the *mundualdi* were not related to the woman, one's initial impression is that males exercised an effective control in only the remaining one-third of the cases. It must be cautioned, however, that this initial impression is deceptive to a degree. For one thing, it is quite possible that some of these seemingly unrelated *mundualdi* in fact had some relationship with the woman for whom they stood as a consensual guardian—some tie of kinship not readily retrievable from their names, perhaps, or some unspecified tie to her or to her husband or to either's family. One must also take cognizance of the prohibition against men acting as *mundualdi* if they themselves were in a position to profit from doing so. A good number of married women took a *mundualdus* who was neither their husband nor a relative; but some husbands were excluded because they stood to gain or because they acted along with their wives.[70] Similarly, twenty-five widows who were given a *mundualdus* who possessed no apparent prior relationship to them participated in legal actions with other males who did (sons mainly, but also brothers, marital kin, an uncle, a father, and the guardians of the children). In the presence of an ideology of male dominance and of a legal means of enforcing that dominance, one is best advised to assume male control and see if the truth was otherwise.

When married women took a *mundualdus* related to them, they took their husbands or their husbands' kin (though among the num-

Table 9.2 Categorization of *Mundualdi* by Female Marital Status

Female Marital Status	Father or Husband	Consanguineal Kinsmen	Affinal Kinsmen	Notary	Unrelated	Total
Widow	3	19	5	15	63	105
Married	19		7	7	23	56
Not Married		5			4	9
Remarried	2	1		4	2	9
Total	24	25	12	26	92	179

bers of men related by marriage is one instance in which a woman took her son-in-law). Widows turned more to blood relations—their brothers, paternal uncles, and sons. Interestingly, in the seventeen cases (involving both married and widowed women) in which the father was designated as still living, the woman chose him as *mundualdus* only four times; but in most of the remaining cases the father was either passed over in favor of the husband or the father was excluded as an interested and otherwise active party.[71]

The types of activity undertaken by women also varied somewhat according to marital status. Married women were less involved in buying, selling, or giving property, in renouncing economic rights, or in acknowledging formally the satisfaction of their claims (*finis*, a form of receipt). They were called upon a number of times to consent to property alienations made by their husbands. Widows were more active in selling or renting property; they had more occasions to declare that their claims had been met; and they were more involved in arbitration settlements with kin. On rare occasions widows participated in tutelary actions as guardians for their children or stood as sureties in acts involving others (for example, the receipt of a dowry by a son). A common legal action for both married and widowed women and the most frequent single legal action by women was the designation of *procuratores*. Women who had remarried shared both widowed and married status in a sense; and they seem to have undertaken actions common to both groups, although there are too few examples of remarried women to draw any firm conclusions. Of the few women appearing in the cartulary who had not married at all (or yet), some were associated in legal actions with their mothers, usually sharing the *mundualdus*, and others acted alone, in which case they sold or rented property.[72]

The legal and economic right that seems to have been most responsible for women's appearance in the legal arena was the dowry. The predominance of widows among the women in need of a *mundualdus*, especially, is explicable by the fact that the husband's demise created a legal situation in which the recovery and arrangement of the dowry became imperative.[73] But imperative for whom?

Many of the widows who sold or rented property may have thus been turning dotal assets into cash. The sale of a large portion of Piero d'Amario Gianfigliazzi's patrimony by his widow, for example, was intended to pay off the debts on the estate and to capitalize the remaining 600 florins owed her for her dowry.[74] In addition, many of the *procuratores* appointed by widows or by women who had remarried were directed to retrieve dowries from the estates of the deceased husbands. The return of the dowry and its transformation into liquid assets could be of great value to the woman herself, but in at least some cases there were also men who had an interest in the dowry and who made their interests felt. In 1424, for example, monna Gemma, whose second husband was Bernardo di Tommaso Baldovini, appointed him one of her *procuratores* to seek the return of her first dowry and the acquisition of legacies left her by her first husband.[75] The widow Caterina acted with her father, Jacopo di Cenne, as her *mundualdus* when she appointed two notaries and her paternal uncle as her agents in obtaining the return of her dowry.[76] In rare cases even married women sought the restitution of their dowries, and this act was one in which their husbands had no little interest. The wives of Benedetto di Marco d'Uberto Strozzi and of Bastiano di Paolo di Lorenzo directed agents to obtain the *consignatio* (the designation of property of equivalent value and recognition of a prior claim to that property) of their dowries from husbands who, it was alleged, "had begun to use their substance and goods badly and were verging on poverty" ("incepisse male uti substantia et bonis suis et ad inopiam vergere").[77] These women, however, may have been doing more than protecting themselves; they may have been doing their husbands an invaluable service by having specified amounts of property set aside as dowry, safe from the demands of creditors.

Arbitration settlements between women and their male relatives are revealing of the interests men could have in the property owned by widows. In one instance an arbitrator awarded the widow Caterina a number of credits in the bank of her son, Giovanni di fu Bartolomeo di ser Spinello, as compensation for the fact that he had made use of her lands near Poggibonsi. The credits, amounting to 5,000 florins, were given in lieu of cash because Giovanni had none.[78] Similarly another widow, daughter of Carlo Strozzi, was given by an arbitrator (Palla di Nofri Strozzi) a house currently in her brother's possession as satisfaction for the 1,000 florins he owed her.[79] Both of the male relatives in these arbitrations had taken advantage of the property rights of their female counterparts, either to use the property or to transfer and disguise property ownership in them (as Giovanni Corsini did with his sister). In other cases women lost their dowries as a result of arbitration. Bonda, the widow of Bartolomeo di

Salvestro Brancacci, saw an arbitrator hand her dowry to her brother, Larione di Lipaccio Bardi, as compensation for a debt she allegedly owed him.[80] Margherita, widow of Antonio d'Alessandro degli Alessandri, was found to be in debt to her daughters; and her dowry and a further 200 florins were awarded to them, while their husbands consented to the whole proceeding as *mundualdi* for the three women.[81]

The active disposition of women's property rights was of great interest to men, of course. Their presence and consent in the disposition of these rights is conspicuous, especially in the case of married women. Lorenzo di Giovanni di Grasso served as *mundualdus* when his wife rented a house in the neighborhood of San Frediano for five years.[82] When his wife sold a farm in 1423, Matteo di messer Donato Adimari and his sons were present to express their agreement to the transaction; and a daughter-in-law was made to renounce any rights she might have in the property.[83] In these instances, it appears, the husbands had an interest in the sale or rental of the property in question and wanted to see the proceeds come into their hands. In other instances, however, women, notably widows, disposed of their property without any evident guidance by men. A widow could take an unrelated *mundualdus* and, without the presence or consent of any male relations, sell a piece of property.[84] Either there were no living male relations, or they were not interested in the transaction, or the woman was acting on her own, with the conscious or unconscious complicity of the *mundualdus* she chose.

In many instances in which a woman was accompanied by a *mundualdus* not related to her and in which she did not deal with a relative, it is very difficult to pinpoint any active male control over her. The activities of these women, however, need not have been contrary to male interests. One could point to the example of a widow from the Florentine contado who, in an act of piety for the benefit of her soul and that of her husband, assisted by an unrelated *mundualdus,* gave away a quantity of household furnishings to provide a small dowry for a poor girl whose marriage she had arranged.[85] Not all interests were material, and not all control over women was necessarily direct. The husband may have expected such widowly regard for his soul. Another example of an act that can be interpreted as being in accordance with the interests of male relatives is that of Piera, a widow, who in 1424 acknowledged receipt of 400 florins toward the return of her dowry. At the same time she renounced the guardianship over her son, which had been left to her by her husband, stating that she intended to remarry, which she later did. Her remarriage may have been in the interests of her natal family, although it is difficult to tell for sure, because her father was dead and no relative stood as her *mundualdus*.[86] In contrast, the remarriage of Antonia, widow of Francesco di Niccolò Danti, which followed her receipt of a bequest of 200 florins from a dead brother, was entered into with the presence and consent of another brother.[87]

Nonetheless, it must be granted that in a number of cases in which there is no male relative in sight it is impossible to detect male influence on women. When widows dealt with their children in the absence of an adult male relation, one might suspect that they were free to influence the course of events. One widow, for example, used her dowry to arrange a form of security for herself and her offspring, but on her terms. She gave the dowry to her young son, but she attached a number of conditions he had to fulfill, which involved the dowering of his sisters and the mother's rights to enjoyment and support.[88] In yet another action, Roba, widow of Matteo di Rayneri de' Ricci, took a notary as her *mundualdus* and gave 150 florins to Bernardo di Filippo de' Ciari, her daughter's son, along with all the bedding in her home. The gift was to take effect at her death, and in the meantime she would retain usufruct. She also held usufruct on the gift of cloths (*pannos*) to the wife of Simone di Bancho di Guido, to whom she also left all wine, grain, and oil remaining after her death. The gifts formed together a rearrangement of her estate, for she then renounced the will she had drawn up in favor of the friars of Santa Maria Novella, declaring that she wished to die intestate instead because she had been deceived by them ("reputat se multum deceptam esse a dictis fratribus").[89] This alleged deception on the part of the friars, moreover, is an important item. It indicates that the men with whom women dealt in their legal business had substantial interests of their own and that they were willing to manipulate these women for their ends, with the compliance of a willing *mundualdus*.

The most frequent legal actions of women, the selection of *procuratores* and the formal receipt of claims (*finis*) were also marked by an absence of male relatives, especially when widows were involved.[90] Women often took notaries as their *procuratores*. Some notaries specialized in this role, and their legal skills and knowledge could be of great benefit when the property rights in question were complex, requiring prolonged legal inquiry. The gift of property in emancipation to one woman, for instance, led to a suit brought by her *procurator* (a notary) against another woman (also represented by a notary) who held the property. The clever arguments advanced on both sides produced significant legal problems, so that the issue was not resolved until five prominent jurists had looked into it and concurred in their judgment.[91] Women's legal rights were not directly at stake in *fines* and *procurationes,* however, and men may have been under little compulsion to get involved in such activities, even as a *mundualdus* simply voicing consent. Whatever the reasons for the absence of male kin in these and other activities, their absence indicates that the *mundualdus* was not always and unquestionably an instrument by which men imposed a legal guardianship and control over women. The guardianship of the *mundualdus* was part of a system of male dominance, but it could be short-circuited or switched off.

Juristic Problems Raised by the *Mundualdus*

What of occasions when male dominance was shorted out, so to speak? Did the women, or the men who stood to profit as well from their actions, get away with it? The survival of case materials, especially *consilia* from litigation, is evidence that challenges were raised. What these challenges were, who raised them, and how jurists and courts handled them are important components in a thorough understanding of the institution of the *mundualdus.*

The Florentine patrician jurist Antonio di Vanni Strozzi (1455–1523) tackled the *mundualdus* on occasions. One challenge to the actions of a woman who had proceeded without a *mundualdus* provoked Strozzi to examine the basic rationale of the institution. Was the *mundualdus* there to make whole (*ad integrandum*) the woman's legal *persona,* or was he present in answer to the prejudice of the one contracting with the woman? Strozzi quickly dismissed the second possibility. It did not matter to a *mundualdus,* even husband or kinsman, whether a woman made a contract or not, he said. It was, rather, the *imbecillitas intellectus* of the woman that required consent of a *mundualdus.*[92] If that consent had been limited by the statute to close kin, then the presumption of *imbecillitas* would fail, according to the teachings of Bartolo, Baldo, and numerous other *moderni.* But in leaving consent to any male, the statute vouched concern about the weakness of women's understanding.[93] Furthermore, such consent had to be expressed publicly and formally at the time of the contract, not later.[94]

In the case before Strozzi a man had acted as *mundualdus* for a woman who gave *bona adventitia* to his sons. They acquired title, but the father gained usufruct. So the point of legal doubt was whether the father could give consent "in suam utilitatem." Strozzi argued that he could. For one thing, usufruct was only a secondary consequence; the main purpose had been to make his sons owners. So the father had not been acting in his own interest, according to Strozzi.[95] A second argument Strozzi culled from a *consilium* of Francesco Albergotti of Arezzo (1304–76). This argument was that consent of a *mundualdus* was not required for a *donatio*, "for the statute presumes that a woman can be more easily deceived when she must obligate herself than when she actually must give something, because the *genus* of women is very greedy."[96] By thus slandering women Strozzi conceded them some freedom of maneuver.

In a different case alluded to by Strozzi at the end of his *consilium*, however, he argued to limit this feminine freedom to give away title to property.[97] If the woman gave something but reserved usufruct, she was obligating herself to deliver something (namely, usufruct) at a later date. Thus she was obligating herself as well as giving, and it was as protection in the face of obligations that the *mundualdus* existed. The case in question involved a woman of the Castellani lineage and arose in November 1513. Strozzi came to it not as principal *consulens* but to affirm the prior findings of Lodovico Acciaiuoli (1471–1527), whose *consilium* I have been unable to find. There were in fact two issues. The first resulted in dismissing the validity of the woman's *mundualdus,* a monk. Thereafter her *donatio* had to be treated as occurring in the absence of a *mundualdus.* Strozzi revealed himself as more hostile to any form of gift without a *mundualdus,* observing at one point, for example, that any form of *donatio* was "damnosa" to a woman.[98] Mainly, however, he argued that a *donatio* with reservation of usufruct constituted an obligation on the woman that required the consent of a *mundualdus* by the terms of the statute.

The principle that a woman could not obligate herself without a *mundualdus* was thus worked out differently depending on the type of act in question—if it could be said to entail an obligation. In another case, for example, Otto di Lapo Niccolini (1410–70) invalidated a woman's *aditio hereditatis* performed without a *mundualdus* because, as Bartolo and others had affirmed, declaring oneself another's heir made one liable for all sorts of claims on the estate.[99] Such a casuistic approach, however, could rarely breach the principle behind the *mundualdus*. For any party interested in contesting a woman's legal action, her failure (if such there was) to secure a valid *mundualdus*'s consent presented a strong weapon.

Reflections

In Florence, as elsewhere in Italy and Europe throughout the Middle Ages and Renaissance, women were in theory the weaker sex, always subject to male dominance and guidance. They were relegated to private, domestic spaces; and their energies were to be confined to mothering and housekeeping. A number of historians have hastened to point out the fallacy of this ideological vision of women. They have demonstrated how in practice women played important and active roles both within and outside the house, displaying social and economic influence, especially among urban patriciates.[100] Undeniably women in Florence were important economic and social figures—not the least so, and most regularly, in their crucial, if denigrated, domestic roles. Florentine women also possessed potentially formidable economic rights, most notably in their dowries. Occasions calling for the disposition or transmission of those rights arose, and various circumstances resulted in the absence of a husband or other male relatives, so that women emerged in public and their influence was felt beyond the *casa*.[101]

Florentine women, however, moved into the public arena only in the company of a male *mundualdus*. The fact that the *mundualdus* was not always and everywhere a practical instrument of male dominance over women should not blind one to the related fact that women exercised their economic and social influence within the realms left to them by the men. Given the existence of the institution of the *mundualdus* within a cultural complex that bestowed formal and official power, authority, and control on men, one must begin from the assumption that women did not freely, self-consciously, and self-interestedly exercise their important rights and roles. Directly or indirectly men, or some man, often stood to gain from a woman's activities; and these activities could be tolerated as a result. Women's possession and legal exercise of rights did not necessarily mean control over them. Institutions and structures were dominated by men, and any influence held by a woman remained informal and was effective only in certain circumstances.[102]

The *mundualdus* in some sense amounted to a formal recognition of the occasional importance of women's rights and of the need to transact them.[103] It provided, in allowing women to act legally, a means by which they could become instrumental—beyond their evident instrumentality in marriage alliances and in purely domestic roles—in familial strategies. It was from the familial context that male control or direction of female legal actions arose. The *mundualdus* was not the locus of male control, though he was the expression of it. That the law and ideology relating to women did not always play out in practice—that, in other words, women could be found doing what the law said they could not, acting in a manner more forcefully and independently than ideology allowed—should not be surprising.[104] The practical constraint posed by the *mundualdus* on a woman need not have been very great or immediate, but it was there in some way.[105] At the same time, by stipulating the need for male consent, the institution of the *mundualdus* ensured that, at the very least, the ideology of male dominance and superiority remained intact as a vital "truth."

The power of this ideology is even more apparent when one realizes that in a legal sense the institution of the *mundualdus* was trivial—that is, there were no sanctions falling on the *mundualdus* if the acts he consented to were not in the woman's interest.[106] The willingness of total strangers to act as *mundualdus* would seem to hinge on their sense of security in not being called to account. Although the Roman law of guardianship of minors (*tutela*) was cited in the Lombard jurisprudence, there were no penalties falling on the *mundualdus* or mechanisms for retrieval of lost property or income such as fell on the negligent *tutor*.[107] For all the concern about protecting women expressed by jurists and legislators, protection boiled down entirely to provision of an adult male as *mundualdus*. No other competencies were demanded. No penalties were set. No controls were erected other than that the *mundualdus* could not consent to his own advantage (and Strozzi's judgments show that even this could be limited). Other institutions that were justified as protective of women's property and rights had enforcement mechanisms and functioned to that effect at least some of the time. Most of these gravitated around the dowry.[108] The patrimonial character of the *mundium*, as originally laid out in Lombard law (a power exercised for the benefit of its holder rather than for the one over whom it was held) would seem to have been an important factor to explain this.[109] A more genuine form of guardianship for women would have been the *curatela* of civil law, but this would operate only by deliberate establishment over fatherless younger women and it was not gender-specific (indeed *tutela* and *curatela* were more intended as protection for young male heirs).

The peculiar survival of this Lombard institution in Florence raises important questions that are not easily answerable until someone undertakes full-blown comparative research in other Italian cities. It would seem that, in contrast to cities where consent to women's legal acts was limited to spouses or *consanguinei*, the Florentine *mundualdus* was more accommodating of women and their needs for legal transactions, or perhaps it was more accommodating to their husbands, who did not need to consult their wives' kin. The *mundualdus* was a requirement but not much of a barrier. More pointedly, control over women was more a practical problem than a matter of ideology. Women had property rights, and there were men who had interests in those rights.

Ordinarily the implementation of the ideology of male dominance lay in the hands of the father and the husband. Legally and culturally fathers controlled the economic and sexual capacities of their daughters. They disposed of this control (and of the primary obligation to feed and support their daughters) at the time of marriage and transfer of the dowry. It was then that control over a woman's economic and sexual capacities passed to her husband.[110] Marriage, however, also tended to coincide with legal adulthood for women, and it was the point at which anticipated rights to a dowry and responsibilities in a husband's *casa* attained specific content and form. These rights and responsibilities, as has been mentioned, could then become the reason for the appearance of women in legal processes. Certainly all but a handful of the women who received a *mundualdus* from ser Francesco Giacomini were or had been married.

Marital status emerges as one of the main factors both in incidence of use of the institution of the *mundualdus* and in the degree to which its use seems to have been consonant with the ideology of male dominance. Married women used it less and were seemingly more subject to direction from men, especially their husbands. Husbands often took an active part in any legal transactions of their wives (for example, acting as *procurator*) or provoked such transactions (for example, the wife's consent to an alienation of property); and otherwise husbands took on a consensual role as *mundualdus*.[111] Widows, on the other hand, who were not subject to a husband and who most often did not have a living father, acted more often and sometimes more freely.

There were, in fact, many widows in Florence and Tuscany, largely because husbands were usually much older than their wives.[112] The lack of a father or husband made these women something of an anomaly in terms of the ideology of male dominance, because the ideology was less "practical" with regard to them. There was no one male charged with control over them or necessarily closely interested in their affairs.[113] Widows also had important economic and symbolic functions that militated against their remarriage and, therefore, against the reimposition of direct male control over them in the form of a second husband. Widows could bring honor and spiritual benefit to a *casa* by living a pious and chaste existence, while their continued care for their children was of great practical importance.[114] Their dowries could be an important source of capital for their sons and of dowries for their daughters. Yet there was always the danger that the interests of a widow's natal family might dictate her remarriage (and abandonment of the children of the first marriage) or the dispersal of all or part of her dowry into the hands of her natal kin. In the absence of male control, widows were also perceived to be threatening figures capable of dishonorable sexual mischief, unfortunate economic decisions, and ruinously unbalanced upbringing of children.[115] One solution to the problem of control over widows may have been located in a tendency to larger and more complex households, where some male would always be available to keep an eye on things.[116] The legal ability of such males to exercise control over widows may have been further facilitated by the existence of the *mundualdus*. A number of widows who appeared before Giacomini either took a kinsman as *mundualdus* or transacted business with a kinsman, indicating some degree of control by brothers, sons, and brothers-in-law. Otherwise control over widows seems to have been less prevalent than over married women, at least insofar as widows' *mundualdi* were often unrelated men who probably had little real influence and only nominal tutelage over them. The relatively weak economic circumstances of widows, especially aged ones, may have held little attraction for males in those cases in which potentially interested kinsmen did not come forth.[117]

What this chapter has attempted to demonstrate is that the Florentine institution of the *mundualdus* provided a means of dealing with those potentially dysfunctional moments in the structure of male dominance when women entered the public arena. The limits of this inquiry should be fairly obvious. More research needs to be done on male control of women's legal activities in the late Middle Ages. Such research must range broadly in time and space to test the hypotheses offered here by placing them in a broader historical context. How did the use of the institution of the *mundualdus* in Florence in the 1420s differ from its use in the 1320s or the 1520s? And what factors contributed to these differences? One would also like to know how male control over women's legal activities in Florence compared with that control in other cities not having the *mundualdus* or an equivalent form of guardianship. In such other cities women were either officially forbidden to act legally (as was the case in Ragusa, according to Stuard) or they were allowed to do so without male interference. But in the former case (as Stuard has demonstrated) the law could be circumvented or ignored; and in the latter case the lack of formal legal control may have only disguised the de facto domestic power and moral suasion exercised by men over women. Only after such comparative research is completed can it truly be determined to what degree the institution of the *mundualdus* succeeded in placing women and their interests under the control of men.

10

•

SOME AMBIGUITIES OF
FEMALE INHERITANCE IDEOLOGY
IN THE RENAISSANCE

•

The *exclusio propter dotem*, the exclusion of dowered women from further inheritance from their natal families, represented a functional adjustment to the dysfunctional possibilities of the dowry system in medieval and Renaissance society. As the British anthropologist Jack Goody has said recently, the limited loss of familial resources represented by the dowry was tolerable and useful. It could preserve or extend familial interests by alliance with others, to whose familial propagation one's daughter now contributed. What had to be prevented was the total dissipation of wealth—a possibility in a system in which property of both parents passed to children of both sexes.[1]

Insights of anthropologists such as Goody have proven useful to social historians. They direct us to confront the issue of social functions of an institution like dowry. They also point us at the problem of rules, of seeing what they were and how they governed behavior. At this point anthropology meshes well with an old historical field, legal history. Legal historians too have studied the *exclusio propter dotem*.

In the city-states of Italy the *exclusio propter dotem* was not only customary it was explicitly canonized in municipal statutes embodying a general preference for males (*favor agnationis, favor masculinitatis*) in inheritance. Some fifty years ago Franco Niccolai gathered a number of these statutes.[2] His work affords the advantage

238

of seeing how similar the statutes were. In intestate succession women always stood well after certain categories of agnatic relationship to the deceased—sons, grandsons, great-grandsons, father, paternal grandfather, paternal uncle, brother. A woman had an enforceable right to a "suitable" dowry, to *alimenta* prior to marriage, and to support in widowhood if she returned to her natal family.[3] That was all. Nothing said that women's shares had to be equal to those of their male relatives.[4] Indeed, even if there were no close agnates to exclude them from an inheritance, women were limited to only a portion, generally described as "one quarter" of the estate (the Falcidian quarter of Roman law), with the rest going to any distant agnates within eight degrees of relationship.[5] The bulk of the patrimony was destined for sons, grandsons, or other direct lineal male descendants in equal shares.

These statutes could be explicit about their function: to quote from that of Trent, "so that agnatic masculine ties may be preserved, and that goods may stay in families through males and families and agnatic ties may long be preserved."[6] Manlio Bellomo's classic study of marital property law examines the *exclusio* in the context of the political and economic interests of families in the intense atmosphere of the twelfth- and thirteenth-century communes.[7] The *capo di famiglia* needed to control his property and so control his sons, to whom patrimonial continuity was entrusted. Claims of women had to be curtailed. So the dowry replaced the *legitima portio* of Roman law, ending any necessary proportionality between a woman's share and other shares of the patrimony.

> With the *exclusio propter dotem* the great communal families intended to pursue the goal of preserving undivided the greater part of the patrimony and of assuring temporal continuity. Sons were considered the true heirs and sole continuators of the family fortunes, and in their favor was enacted the statutory regulation, which was still respectful of the interests of daughters—but only within viable limits.[8]

Patrimonial continuity was to take place in the relationship between fathers and sons.[9]

Anthropology and rule-centered legal history, however, have crucial limitations. Between any set of rules and their consequent social functions lies the realm of individual strategies. These, in fact, may not be nearly so rule-bound as they seem. Their functions may not be apparent. And, above all, their functions may be more symbolic or ideological than material or practical. Indeed practical interests are expressed and validated in terms of cultural constructs whose meanings cannot be reduced to the socially or materially functional, even if a single function can be identified in every case. Kinship can neither be reduced to property qualifications nor separated from them.[10] Even in the face of the fifteenth-century juristic maxim "Familia, id est substantia," we cannot afford to neglect the realm of ideological cultural constructs and the ambiguities they could inject into social reality.[11]

It is too easy to downplay the dysfunctional aspects of the dowry and overemphasize the functional adjustments seemingly contained in the *exclusio propter dotem*. We may be placing excessive emphasis on the degree to which marriage severed a woman from her natal patriline and terminated her claims on it, or ended any continued interest in her on the part of her male relatives.[12] Statutory exclusions and limitations did not mean that a woman's father was unconcerned to dower her suitably and make provisions for her possible widowhood.[13] Those same statutes also clearly guaranteed daughters' rights to a dowry.

One problem is that the workings of the statutes have not been thoroughly investigated. Such an investigation is not simple. Statutes did not govern all legal matters in Florence.[14] As the *ius proprium* of that city, they also took for granted principles, definitions, terms, and rules enshrined in the *ius commune*, which consisted mainly of civil and canon law, but also included the academic feudal law and even Lombard law. These statutes could come into play in some forty different legal arenas in a city like Florence. Although the statutes were supposed to govern in cases within a given city or other jurisdiction, their import was not always clear. Clarification could be sought through new legislation, but on a case-by-case basis it could be rendered by jurists, trained in civil and canon law in the universities, called on by parties or judges and even required by statute to honor such requests. They would determine how statutes fit into the framework of the *ius commune* that they assumed, most notably in property and familial matters. Such contextualized interpretation makes it difficult to assume that the text of a statute (even if its meaning can be considered "clear") determined all outcomes without reference to *ius commune* or overriding it.[15] Jurisprudence remained a vibrant force in the fifteenth and sixteenth centuries, and its forceful collisions with statutory law were often played out in the neglected (by historians) arena of litigation. Opportunities for dispute were numerous. The effect of these statutes was regularly called into question because a sufficient proportion of married couples (around 40 percent) would have no heirs or have only daughters.[16] Inheritance was not predictable. In the fourteenth and fifteenth centuries especially, the recurrent plagues and economic disturbances only increased the element of chance threatening the biological and patrimonial survival of patrilines. Female succession was a statistically frequent possibility, and it provoked conflicting legal claims and a consequent collision of jurisprudential and statutory principles.[17] Nor were the statutes' implications always obvious. Gaps and ambiguities plagued litigants and their advocates while supplying jurists ample latitude to display their technical skills and collect the requisite fees.

It is the juristic interpretation of the *exclusio propter dotem* that I want to investigate a bit further. Operating between principles constitutive of social order (like agnation) and the actual devolution of property (with its competitive strategic activity), the processes of juristic interpretation allow us to map a small part of the ordering of Italian urban society.[18] For purposes of coherence and brevity I will limit myself to Florentine materials. In this way some of the ambiguities surrounding female inheritance might emerge.

Florentine Statutory Law

Rules affecting female inheritance were not set down once and for all. They were reworked and renegotiated, at times under the influence of doctrinal pronouncements or difficulties issuing from or identified by jurists. Such was the case in Florence and elsewhere. The essential pattern and content of the *exclusio propter dotem* was in place in the 1325 statutes of the Podestà, under the rubric *De modo successionis mulierum ab intestato de ipsorum materia*. It reappeared in the redactions of 1355 and 1415, commissioned by the commune from prominent jurists.[19] Both redactions were thus in some degree the product of jurisprudence as well as of legislation.

Within a common framework, however, there are some interesting variations between the versions: some minor (as the change of the rubric to *Qualiter mulier ab intestato succedat*, in 1355 and 1415) some quite significant.[20] All versions retain the essential features of the key first section: on intestacy a mother cannot succeed her children if there are still alive any legitimate and natural children, grandchildren, or great grandchildren of her child, or the child's father, paternal grandfather, paternal uncle, brother, sister, or nephew (brother's son). She was entitled to *alimenta* and that only in case of need. If there were no such survivors, she could claim one quarter, up to a value of 500 *lire,* not to include houses and such.[21] The rest was to go to male agnates within eight degrees of consanguinity. The 1415 version added that in case there were only houses or such in the estate she could claim an *extimatio* of one quarter of their value, again not to exceed 500 *lire.* This qualification clearly seemed to strengthen her limited claim. There was, however, also a progressive exclusion of the female line, beyond the mother, over the course of the statute's history. The 1325 version said grandmothers were also excluded (since 1295 [1294 o.s.]). The 1355 version added that, as of June 1351, the exclusion extended to the entire maternal line. This extension, as we will see, was in fact the result of an interpretive clarification provided by the famous jurist Bartolo da Sassoferrato (d. 1357) at the request of the commune. It was maintained in the 1415 version.

A mother, of course, was not agnatically related to her children. Sisters were agnatically related to brothers and daughters to fathers; nonetheless, the vertically descending exclusion of mothers was matched by a lateral exclusion of sisters from their intestate brother's estate in favor of his children or grandchildren, brothers, brothers' sons, or paternal uncles, and a vertically ascending exclusion of daughters from succeeding their intestate fathers, paternal grandfathers or great-grandfathers—or any other male paternal ascendant.[22]

A woman's right to a dowry was guaranteed. The addition of the term *competenter* in 1415, however, seemed to be a better guarantee that the dowry would be roughly appropriate to the size of the estate in question. Significant differences among the three versions concerned the rights of unmarried and widowed women to alimentary support. In 1325 and 1355 the right of an undowered daughter to *alimenta* had been expanded wherever the estate of the deceased fell not to a son or other direct lineal descendant but to a brother or a fraternal line. In that case she was given usufruct over the entire paternal estate. The same usufruct was given to widows who returned to a paternal estate that was not in the hands of their brothers but paternal uncles. Usufruct constituted a *ius in re aliena* that offered greater protection. It was a charge on the estate—not a personal obligation of its holder—that also restricted its value and free disposition.[23] The 1415 version removed any mention of usufruct, replacing it with simple *al-*

imenta competentia et decentia.[24] Thereafter these alimentary rights prior to marriage and in widowhood were personal, "natural," non-transferable rights of consumption only. They were limited material interests with symbolic import; but they admitted no proprietary interest or transferable real right on a woman's part.

Finally in 1325 and 1355 it was affirmed that in testamentary succession a woman who could succeed *iure romano* had to remain content with what was left her, which could be more or less than what she would have received on intestacy. The Podestà and Capitano had to dismiss any suits by women against a will. In 1415, on the other hand, it was admitted that women with a Roman law right of succession who had been left nothing in a will had a right to what they would have received in intestacy, but no more, and even then a paternal testament should not be voided totally. All three versions affirmed that relationships mentioned referred only to those "legitimate and natural born of a legitimate marriage" ("legitimis et naturalibus ex legitimo matrimonio natis").

The thrust of the different revisions was to provide clarification and precision in language, but it also resulted in some readjustment of a woman's inheritance rights. So, while the Florentine statute, in all three versions, treated female inheritance rights in a manner Niccolai and others have indicated, it did not treat these rights as fixed. In particular, the replacement of usufructuary rights by alimentary rights tended to stress increasingly the notion of a woman's right to support that was also embedded in the reigning juristic conception of the dowry as sustenance for the *onera matrimonii*. It broadened her dependence as a woman on support coming from property controlled by a man.

Commentary and Interpretation

Interpretive problems constantly arose in applying such an important statute. For example, in 1351, soon after the plague had riddled the population of Florence, attenuating numerous lines of relationship with gaps that made a shambles of inheritance plans, the question arose whether the exclusion of a mother and grandmother also implied the exclusion of the other maternal relations. The resolution of this important question was left to the most influential jurist of the day, Bartolo.[25] He reiterated his opinion in his commentary on the *lex Sive ingenua* in the Digest. There he revealed that, as the *ratio statuti* was to leave the estate "apud agnatos," the exclusion of the mother meant the exclusion of all following her in line of intestate succession by civil law.[26] The same went for a daughter's son. The agnate males who excluded them were called to succession instead.

Bartolo's opinion touched on a general and pressing problem. He was asked by the governing bodies of Florence to address this issue, and his solution was incorporated in the new statute redaction four years later. On occasion other general problems that emerged in practice were also committed to a general, that is, legislative treatment. In 1486 an emendation to the statute declared that women were limited by the terms of a will not only when the testator had direct descendants but also when he left his estate to any agnates who would have excluded the women on intestacy.[27] By and large, however, these practical problems that were first flushed out of hiding by jurists remained in their hands. Statutes such as the Florentine one we are considering clearly teased their juristic talents.[28] Bartolo, for example, also discussed the Florentine statute elsewhere. He treated the "valde difficilis" question of whether a son whom his father considered unworthy of the inheritance still excluded his mother or sister, in favor of other male agnates. Bartolo's conclusion was that the women were not excluded because the son was fictively dead in this case.[29] He did not inherit, so he could not exclude. Another problem concerned a woman's rights in the face of a paternal testament neglecting her. Baldo degli Ubaldi (1327–1400), the most authoritative jurist after Bartolo, declared that a dowered daughter so neglected could not exercise her civil-law right to have the will voided for passing over her. Municipal law here overrode civil law. To say otherwise was "absurd."[30] As we have seen, this desire to maintain a paternal will intact, even in the face of the neglect of a daughter, was incorporated into the language of the 1415 version of the Florentine statute.

It was not only the major academics who toyed with these issues. They were most acute for those who confronted them regularly—the jurists practicing in a city like Florence. Fortunately we possess an excellent source for surveying these difficulties in the statute commentary of Alessandro Bencivenni (1385–1423), written between 1415 and his death in 1423.[31] Six pages of this commentary were devoted to the statute *Qualiter mulier.* In these six pages Bencivenni discussed or at least raised twenty-five different issues. Some of these posed out-of-the-ordinary situations, even hypothetical ones. But most were raised by judicial practice, as seen in Bencivenni's continual reference to *consilia* by himself and others. He offered clarifications of important terms: as that in the phrase "agnate males within the eighth degree" ("agnatis masculis infra octavum gradum") "within" was to be taken inclusively, not exclusively, and that it covered eight degrees according to civil, not canonical, computation. He mentioned tacit conditions and qualifications: as that brothers had to formally accede to the estate (*adire hereditatem*) to exclude their sisters; that the dowry right guaranteed by the statute also included dowries for the purpose of monacation; and that "competenter" in reference to the dowry was to be estimated for the time of the death that gave rise to the inheritance and not for the time at which the dowry was established.

Several times Bencivenni was at pains to point out that the *ius commune* still prevailed where the statute did not explicitly cover certain contingencies, for example, in succession to a sister. Recourse to *ius commune* broadened female inheritance rights, as in this example:

> Although it seems that, if the mother is excluded by an agnate within the eighth degree, the father's sister [her sister-in-law] is also excluded by greater reason [*a maioritate rationis*], still I responded to the contrary because the statute does not provide for a father's sister, so here it remains in the disposition of common law and thus those within the eighth degree are excluded by her, especially those born of a bastard and thus of a nonagnate, such that lacking a branch they are not called agnates . . . as in the case of monna Papera and ser Cetti.[32]

These assertions of the continued relevance of *ius commune,* often made while also invoking case opinions, are emblematic of the university-trained jurist.

Also redolent of jurisprudence were the areas of disagreement that emerge from Bencivenni's commentary. Three are of interest. Were paternal grandmothers excluded? Bencivenni noted that the eminent Florentine jurist Nello da San Gimignano (b. 1373) had adopted the negative. Bencivenni, however, saw the statute as favoring agnate *males,* in which case both paternal and maternal grandmothers should be excluded, and so he had advised in cases, as had the renowned Bolognese jurist Bartolomeo da Saliceto (d. 1412).[33] He took a similar position, again extending the statute's preference for *agnati masculi,* on the exclusion of women from fraternal estates by a father, since fathers were not explicitly listed in that section of the statute. To Bencivenni an exclusion in favor of the sons of brothers or paternal uncles, who were named, necessarily extended itself to a father.[34] On the other hand, exclusion by a brother did not extend to exclusion by one's cousin (*frater patruelis*).[35] Finally was a woman excluded by a brother who had taken vows? Bencivenni simply noted that there was disagreement on this question.[36]

This brief tour through Bencivenni's pages demonstrates two things. Statute interpretation could be difficult, no matter how clear a principle seemed to be.[37] Nuances of meaning, inclusions, omissions, and contingencies raised doubts, the resolution of which was not easy. Also certain issues seem to have been especially vexing. The jurists acceded to the principle of lineal descent, but they seem to have been less certain about the effect of gender itself. Women clearly had rights of inheritance, however limited or contingent. Amplifying the openings for recourse to *ius commune,* limiting exclusion to those actually inheriting and not to all those occupying specified niches of agnatic relationship, and repeated examination of the problem of contesting a paternal will—all seem to indicate a willingness to consider protection of female inheritance and the limited inclusion of cognatic relationships. Because these problems came to light and acquired particular urgency in the context of cases, it seems advisable to pursue this topic to another level—to a sampling of the work of jurists in litigation. Even a limited sample of five cases, spread across the fifteenth century, is revealing of the "functional" possibilities of the *exclusio propter dotem.*

CASE ONE: INTESTATE SUCCESSION TO A WOMAN

The first *consilium* hails, I believe, from the end of the fourteenth century or the first years of the fifteenth.[38] Its author, Filippo di messer Tommaso Corsini (1334–1421), had been called on to determine who was heir to monna Antonia di Giovanni. At her death she left a husband, Giovanni, and an infant daughter, Ginevra, both of whom soon also died. Her father, therefore, sought the inheritance, but was opposed by her husband's brother. Bartolo's exclusion of the entire maternal line dictated that the paternal uncle (Giovanni's brother) was the heir, not the maternal grandfather.[39] The grandfather had argued, however, that the infant Ginevra had not formally taken the inheritance from her mother. As an infant she was legally incapable. Therefore, the estate in question was that of Antonia, not of Ginevra; and the relationships in question were those of father and brother-in-law, not maternal grandfather and paternal uncle. But

Corsini dismissed this argument, relying instead on the teachings of Jacopo d'Arena (fl. 1253–96), Bartolo, Jacopo Bottrigari (d. 1347), and Oldrado da Ponte (d. 1335) regarding *restitutio in integrum*. He also noted another argument of his Florentine colleague Giovanni de' Ricci (ca. 1342–1402) that formal *aditio* was not required in inheritance of a dowry, but "another doctor, also of great authority" had argued the opposite, so Corsini did not rest his conclusion on Ricci's view. In place of the fiction put forth by the grandfather, that the estate be treated as if the infant Ginevra had never lived, Corsini inserted the fiction that it be treated as if she had indeed formally taken possession.

Corsini might better have argued to excuse the incapacity of the infant, something done, for instance, in emancipation law.[40] The effect of his judgment is interesting in any case. Antonia's dowry, property that had first belonged to her father, passed not back to him but to her husband's brother through the crucial medium of the infant daughter, with the aid of the statute.

CASE TWO: SUCCESSION BY A MALE COUSIN OR A NIECE?

Some ten to fifteen years later, Nello da San Gimignano faced another case.[41] Pietro had died intestate in 1411. Nente, his mother, Caterina, his niece, and Filippo, his paternal cousin, were his only surviving relatives. Who was his heir?

Here the case differed from Corsini's in that instead of two males, one tracing his claims solely through a woman, there were a male and two females, the male tracing claims through males alone, the niece through a female. On the face of it one would anticipate that Nello would exclude the niece in favor of a male agnate in the fourth degree. But he did not.

Table 10.1 Genealogy of Litigants in Case Two

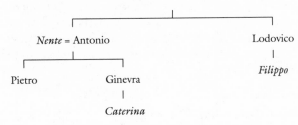

(Names of those living at the time of the case are italicized.)

In his statute commentary Bencivenni maintained that a sister should not be excluded by a cousin such as Filippo (a *frater patruelis*).[42] In Nello's *consilium* we see at greater length the juristic reasoning behind this position. Employing the pro-et-contra style, Nello recorded the arguments in favor of exclusion: that the statute excluded those related through their mother, that the statute plainly "was made in favor of agnates so that the dignities of families might be preserved," that the statute was *favorabile* and so to be interpreted freely, giving full play to the cousin's claims, that agnates by statute were to be prefered over cognates, and that generally *fratres* came before those *ex linea feminina*. The counterarguments began with a sweeping statement of principle: "For the aforesaid statute is corrective of common law, which, as said above, makes no distinction in the last instance between cognates and agnates. Therefore it must be understood not amply but strictly so that it corrects common law the least it can."[43] Although the statute was "favorable" to agnates, it was "odious" to cognates and so had to be construed narrowly. Such a strict construction resulted, for example, in the statement that the statute excluded those related through the mother of the deceased, not all those claiming to inherit (as did Caterina) through their mothers. So Nello concluded that Caterina was due half of Pietro's estate, not a mere statutory quarter but a full half as under civil law. Filippo got the other half, less a quarter (one-eighth of the whole) that went to Nente, who was excluded from Caterina's portion but not from Filippo's, according to Nello's construction of the statute. Nente, Pietro's mother, came out on the short end, Nello confessed, "because there may be found no [statutory] disposition in her favor that may seem to add to her portion."[44]

His was a masterful job of argumentation that paid close attention to the statute's wording. Especially revealing is the overall appraisal of the statute—something missing from Bencivenni's commentary— as *odiosum*. The rule of interpretation in jurisprudence was strict interpretation of an "odious" statute, so the labeling was important.[45] At least to Nello, as long as the statute disadvantaged *cognati* it was odious, even if it otherwise was favorable to agnates and to the public welfare.

CASE THREE: WOMEN CONTESTING A WILL

Sometime between 1440 and 1454 a case arose in Prato, which was subject to Florentine rule.[46] The case required the combined talents

of four Florentine jurists: Benedetto di messer Michele Accolti
(1415–64), Giovanni di Girolamo Buongirolami (1381–1454),
Pietro Ambrosini da Iesi (1403–72), and Tommaso Salvetti (1390–
1472).[47] Giovanni di Nuto, who had died without male descendants,
had designated as his heir an unrelated man (*extraneus*), Antonio di
Pietro. To three agnatically related women—unnamed in the case
materials—he left only dowries. Had Giovanni di Nuto died intestate
these three women would have split his property. They therefore
contested this will on the grounds that Giovanni had neglected his
mother in the will—she had been alive when it was drawn up but had
died before her son. Clearly there was no question of actual inheritance by the dead mother, who had never contested the will during
her lifetime. Her putative rights were championed as a pretext for
breaking the will, which would allow the women to inherit in the
resulting intestacy. Antonio's reply was that, in view of the mother's
statutory exclusion, failure to name her in the testament did not
militate against the will. And since she had predeceased her son, it all
did not matter. The response by the women's advocate was that a will
invalid at its inception did not later acquire validity.

Accolti, first of the four to confront the case, had to agree that
there were good arguments favoring Antonio di Pietro. Because the
mother was excluded by statute from inheriting from her son, it
seemed she would have had no right to break the will. Giving the
right to void a will to someone who could not inherit was the sort of
absurdity the law should not allow.[48] Nonetheless, Accolti proceeded
to support such an "absurdity" by carefully examining the "spirit and
letter" (*mens et verba*) of the statute. Its purpose (*ratio*) was the
exclusion of women in favor of men "so that the honor of the family
might be conserved." But there were no male descendants in this
case, so the *ratio* did not come into play. The mother could have
contested the will, for this situation fell under the terms of *ius commune* and not statutory law.[49] The will did not come back into force
when she predeceased, because the heir it named was an *extraneus*
and not someone who would have succeeded on intestacy. Voiding
the will meant that the three *agnatae* would split the estate and gain
more than the dowries left them.

One cannot help but think that Accolti's arguments were weakly
contrived. Certainly the fact remained that the mother had *not* contested the will. Though it was clear what the three women had to
gain, it was not clear by what right they pressed a useless claim for the

dead mother. Yet Accolti seems genuinely to have balked at letting a statute embodying *favor agnationis* become in this instance a mechanism by which agnates, albeit female, were deprived for the benefit of an *extraneus*. Buongirolami and Ambrosini shared his sentiments and contributed the observation that the mother's right to overturn the will was venal—that is, it resulted in someone's profit, if not her own—so that she might even have been paid by the three *agnatae* to contest the will.[50]

Salvetti's more extensive corroboration drew heavily on *consilia* of other jurists and on his evident familiarity with Florentine statutes. Three times he affirmed that the "common and undoubted conclusion" was that a mother who was left nothing in her son's will could render it null. The statute did not change this aspect of common law. The statute wanted a mother's exclusion only for sons or male descendants. The proof of this, he said, was the fact that the redactors of the 1415 version, skilled and experienced lawyers themselves, had not amplified the extent of the statute or tinkered with its wording on this point. In addition the right of close female agnates to have a will voided for neglecting them had been confirmed numerous times in practice in Florence and Bologna, and Salvetti hastened to list all the jurists who had done so.[51]

In this case, then, the *mens statuentium* was used to override the *mens testatoris*, to pass property to female agnates and not to an *extraneus*. The jurists slipped around that passage in the statute that said a testament was not to be voided for passing over a woman otherwise eligible to succeed on intestacy (not to mention slipping around her death). Yet they also clearly kept before them a sense of the statute that precluded harming agnates, even women.

CASE FOUR: FIDEICOMMISSARY SUCCESSION

In 1475 Manfredo Squarcialupi drew up his testament. He named his three sons, Antonio, Piero, and Jacopo, as his heirs, substituting them for one another by means of fideicommissary stipulations if any should die without male issue. If all three died before age twenty-five and without legitimate male descendants, the patrimony was to be divided between two hospitals, a monna Alessia Santi, and the descendants of Mino Squarcialupi. For any daughters yet to be born there was provision for a 1,200-florin dowry in the *Monte delle doti* for each girl. For granddaughters, in case there were no grandsons, there were to be similar 1,200-florin dowries.[52]

The youngest, Jacopo, fathered two legitimate daughters before his death. His two elder brothers then invoked the fideicommissary substitution in Manfredo's will to claim Jacopo's portion of the patrimony. Jacopo's daughters, Katerina and Margherita, did not contest this substitution; both their grandfather's will and Florentine law stood against them. But they did advance claims to dowries and *alimenta*. The girls cited the provision of dowries in the testament, the guarantee of dowries in the statute, and the presumed intent of the testator to provide in accordance with the law. The uncles responded that these girls had been born after Manfredo's death and so were not granted dowries by the will. They further argued that Manfredo had clearly favored even strangers over unborn granddaughters when he had stipulated for the estate to pass to hospitals rather than to females if there were no legitimate males. The prominent lawyer Antonio di Vanni Strozzi (1455–1523) was commissioned by the uncles to draw up an opinion in support of their position.[53]

Table 10.2 Genealogy of Litigants in Squarcialupi Case

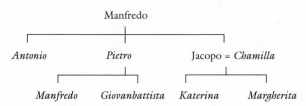

(Names of those living at the time of the case are italicized.)

The arguments of the parties appealed to the ambiguous intent of the testator Manfredo. Strozzi's problem was to give shape to the *mens testatoris* and delineate the contours of the legal landscape on which it stood. Manfredo had clearly favored males over females "for the preservation of the family." He had even favored *loca pia* over females. But the dowry problem was not so easy to resolve. It was commonly held by jurists, on the authority of Bartolo, that property subject to a *fideicommissum* was liable for the dowries of anyone whose *legitim* was insufficient and to whom the *fideicommissarius* was obligated for a dowry. Bartolo also maintained that a grandfather was obligated for a granddaughter's dowry, and others agreed with him. However, some of them also pointed out that the grandfather's obligation ceased at his death, and Baldo degli Ubaldi had weakened this obligation by making it contingent on the father's inability to provide the dowry himself. Strozzi concluded, therefore, that the grandfather's liability for a granddaughter's dowry ceased at his death and was not inherited by all his heirs.[54] It passed only to the girl's father. And in the case before him Strozzi found no basis for the grandfather's dotal obligation, because the girls had been born after his death. "I consider these granddaughters conceived and born after the grandfather's death are in no way said to be related [*coniuncte*] to him and as unknown persons [*incognite*] they are not admitted to his estate." Strozzi's teachers, Giovanbattista da San Severino and Bartolomeo Sozzini, had reached similar conclusions.[55]

Finally Strozzi disposed of the Florentine statute with two ingenious interpretations. The dotal guarantee, he said, went to those excluded because of the statute, but the two girls had been excluded not just by the statute but by their post-mortem conception.[56] Secondly, he argued that this case dealt with testacy, not intestacy, which was what the statute dealt with. (He thus ignored Accolti's argument from years earlier that the statute also covered testamentary succession, despite its rubric.)

One wonders how convincing Strozzi's arguments were—whether they swayed the court. His closing arguments attempting to read the statute away strike me as weak. But his opinion did not go forward on its own. At least it also carried the signatures of Niccolò di Pancrazio Rucellai (1467–1527), Francesco di Chirico Pepi (1451–1513), and Lodovico Amidei (?). In contrast to Accolti et al., who had explored the outer limits of the exclusion of women—for an *extraneus*—Strozzi explored closer to the inner limits where uncles excluded nieces. His seems an extreme formulation that would have jeopardized these girls' dowries in the name of male inheritance. However, moral suasion may have produced dowries for them anyway. Strozzi's decision freed the uncles from the 1,200-florin sum; they might still provide dowries, though of lesser value.

CASE FIVE: A BASTARD SON

Our last example arose at the very end of the fifteenth century.[57] In it Filippo Decio (1454–1535) and Ormannozzo Deti (b. 1464) showed themselves much more sympathetic to female inheritance claims than did Antonio Strozzi. When Rinieri Dei died, he left a will in which he named as his heir his legitimated son, Piero. He left nothing to his daughters beyond dowries (though these were considerable—3,000 florins, that being the sum of the dowry of the already married Caterina). The girls contested their exclusion from the will on the grounds that Piero was only legitimated, not born legitimate, as specified by the language of the statute.

Decio, basing himself on the canonist Antonio da Butrio (1338–1408), agreed that a *legitimatus* like Piero could not exclude the girls on intestacy, especially in view of the wording of the statute.[58] Having defended the statute's working, Decio then turned on it, rejecting the face value of the other pertinent clause that required women to remain content with the terms of a will. The statute, he said, defended the will of one who left his property to legitimate and natural heirs, which was not the case with Rinieri's will. The girls' civil-law right to contest the will thus remained in force, and the testament was void for neglecting them. The girls would split the estate in equal shares along with their legitimated half-brother Piero, whose right to inherit was not questioned, just his right to exclude his sisters.

Most of Decio's *consilium* was devoted to a consequent problem: as the will was now broken, Rinieri's estate devolved through intestacy, and then did not his brother's sons, again by the terms of the statute, exclude the daughters? Clearly the cousins would have excluded the girls if it were simple intestacy, but in this case intestacy arose from voiding a will in favor of Piero. What then? Decio rehearsed at length four arguments in favor of the cousins. Then he overturned them all: "because loss of succession on account of males is understood where the males in whose favor the loss occurred are admitted to succession, so if others are instituted as heirs the statute does not apply. . . ."[59]

From Decio the case went to Matteo Niccolini (1473–1542). Unfortunately I have not been able to locate his *consilium,* which is mentioned by Deti.[60] Deti's lengthy reexamination of the case came next and provided full corroboration for Decio's views, which had also been seconded by Niccolini. Deti agreed with Decio that the statute did not apply because Piero was merely *legitimatus.* Because the testament was in favor of an *extraneus* and did not name the fraternal cousins as heirs, the *reformatio* to the statute enacted in 1486 also did not apply.[61] Generally, "in terms of the statute a father could not neglect a daughter with impunity except to the benefit of a legitimate son or agnates."[62] The Dei will did not meet this test.

Furthermore, this was not a "simple" case of daughters and cousins; it was a "casus mixtus" involving daughters, cousins, *and* a legitimated son—a case not covered by the statute. By this exceedingly narrow interpretation, *ius commune*, not the statute, came to bear. That being the case, the *legitimatus*, being of the same degree of relationship as the girls, received an equal portion with each of them.

An important prop to this conclusion was the fact that Decio and Deti loosely labeled Piero an *extraneus* rather than an *agnatus*. In fact the status of a bastard with regard to agnation was an area of controversy, and in view of Piero's legitimation his agnation could have been maintained fairly easily. But by categorizing him an *extraneus*, the jurists could deny that Rinieri's will fell under the statute (just as Bencivenni had in his commentary).[63] If the statute did not apply, then civil law did. The girls were not excluded and, in fact, they excluded the cousins.

Both men covered themselves in case references, especially to Florentine jurists who had dealt with the statutory exclusion of women. It is an instructive decision. Neither the statute, which would have excluded the girls, nor the civil law, which would have disadvantaged Piero, nor Rinieri Dei's will ended up governing the settlement. Rather, the intersection of the three on the jurisprudential plain constructed by Decio and Deti produced a fourth dimension unforeseen by the trajectory of any one of them alone.

Conclusions

Clearly a statute like *Qualiter mulier* in Florence did not remove all female inheritance rights. It limited and postponed them. The statute was unequivocal in the simple cases—sons took preference over daughters, brothers over sisters. When there were no such males women could inherit.[64] The cases considered here, however, were not simple. Yet, though statistically in the minority, these cases were not insignificant—not in terms of the law and not in terms of statistics. They and others like them abound in the surviving *consilia*. The problems they generated were familiar to jurists and to provident *capi di famiglia*. Florentines would have known similar circumstances, if not in their own lives then in those of relatives, friends, and neighbors.

In these troublesome situations the statute's implications were ambiguous. It was never a self-contained discourse. It operated in relation to other rule complexes, as seen in the jurists' invocation of *ius commune* and their interpretive devices: *mens testatoris, mens statuentium,* strict construction of "odious" rules, and so forth. Within itself it contained and invoked rule complexes: intestacy, testamentary succession, dowry, agnation, legitimacy, and *alimenta*. The statute focused their subsequent discourse, but it did not determine it. It was another discourse, though a privileged one, in a context of discourses on inheritance. And these discourses were not limited to the legal. Florentines broadly held to the principles of family preservation through agnation. They could and did formulate strategies of familial aggrandizement and preservation. These strategies could reveal and take advantage of indeterminacies in the rule. Jurists had to interpret the statute and eliminate these indeterminacies. We have seen an imposing array of such texts and devices in the limited sampling before us. They do not seem to have always been invoked consistently. Yet this seeming inconsistency has its explanations and can mask an underlying consistency. Circumstances varied. Judges and clients differed. In each case, moreover, the jurists had to adjudicate between arguments advanced by and for the litigants, whose allegations determined the areas of law over which the jurist had to roam. It is hard to imagine detailed consistency as a result. The jurists had to accommodate these circumstances and arguments while saving all general legal principles as valid.[65] The circumstances they faced were not fully envisioned by the legislators and compilers of the statutes. So their intervention marked a creative moment, an adaptation of an existing principle to changing developments.

These jurists operated as professionals intent on saving the ideological principles of law relating to succession, including the ideology of agnatic descent. It was to the ideology itself, not the litigants' interests, that they were wedded.[66] To that end it is interesting to note how frequently the lawyers in fact limited the freedom of testators and restricted the scope of the statute in the name of what they saw as proper succession.[67] The result is that in a number of cases the women litigants won. Only agnate males of the categories named in the statute were permitted to exclude women. The women we have seen failing to get a favorable response—from a lawyer who was working for the other side—were faced with opposition from their father's brothers, not from cousins or more distant male agnates, much less *extranei*. But this gets us to the heart of the matter. Women's interests were not easily separable from men's. The protection of female rights meant that property was available for a woman's children and for use by her husband or brother.[68] All of these cases serve to demonstrate that the jurists were less concerned with female (or even male) control of property than with the proper and appropriate devolution of property within webs of relationship (themselves defined with agnatic emphasis). Here as elsewhere in civil law, property was not a matter of the rights of a willing individual over an object but a complex of rights shared among persons in relation to something of value (measured by standards of money or honor).[69]

Fundamentally the meaning of agnation was not inalterably fixed. Legally agnation could be lost (as by emancipation) or acquired (as by adoption).[70] Legitimation produced agnation, and yet it did not, at least according to Decio and Deti.[71] Even matters like the timing of conception and birth (the Squarcialupi case) and age at death (Corsini's) could call agnation into question, at least for certain relationships. Identities were manipulable, by litigants, both in their actions and in their judicial arguments, and by jurists.[72] Identity was manipulable because between the ideology of identities (agnation, linked in turn to *honor familiae* and cognation) and social realities was an intervening level of operable rules, enshrined in this statute and others, that set conditions, tests of validity, and so forth. Emphasis on the direct agnatic line could have the effect of favoring females in that line over males in collateral lines.[73] Certainly Nello da San Gimignano had favored a female in a closer, though cognatic, line over a collateral male. Above all agnation was finally established by the devolution of property. Those who got it could be considered agnates, those who did not (as the Squarcialupi girls, according to Strozzi) could not.[74] There was no prior, single, unchanging meaning to a cultural construct like agnation such that we can assume it in order to go on and map social functions. Only a historical approach to the process by which meaning was negotiated, derived, created, not a synchronous anthropological approach, can reveal such ambiguities and their momentary functional resolutions.

These cases also demonstrate that there was not a clear dichotomy between a male sense of kinship as agnation in competition with a female sense of kinship as consanguinity.[75] Here again between agnation and cognation lay ambiguity. Women were also agnates and used this sense of relationship, at least, or especially so, in the legal arena where agnation was privileged. Their cognation was sufficient against agnates of roughly fourth degree or beyond (as in Nello's case). Even if there were a clear difference between male and female senses of kinship, in the legal arena, which in Florence belonged to men by definition, one would expect to find the male sense predominate in argumentation.[76] A simply functional explanation, then, even if it could adequately account for the existence of *Qualiter mulier* and similar legislation elsewhere (which I doubt), cannot provide adequate explanation of the interpretive adventures of the statute and their possible dysfunctional results for some patrilines. We are not dealing only with situations in which the preservation of male honor required women—an obvious social phenomenon. It is not just that there were no male heirs in these cases and so women stepped in, as they stepped in to manage property in a husband's absence. Paternal cousins, nephews, and even a legitimated son received nothing or less than they had hoped. Women disposed nominally of more wealth than their relatives, including their own fathers, had desired them to.[77] They disposed of enough wealth that, if we do not wish to go so far as to question whether this was an agnatic system of inheritance, we must see that there were limits to the power of agnation.[78]

Law provided a language by which lawyers, legislators, and litigants framed the discourses by which they attempted to manage strategic resources and social order. As the focus of discourse fell on the social relationships derived from males, women who stood in such relationships acquired meaning. They were never forgotten, nor merely banished to another's house along with their dowry. They always had potential claims. At times these became real, with varying effects on the material and symbolic interests of men.

•

APPENDIX
Examples of Arbitration

•

Madalena di Carlo Strozzi
(ASF, Notarile 9040 [formerly G 212], fols. 378r–79r)

Item postea dictis anno [1428] et indictione [7th] et die [23 November].
Actum Florentie in populo Sancti Pancratii, presentibus testibus ad hec
vocatis, habitis et rogatis Jacopo Ticci populi Sancte Lucie Omnium Sanctorum de Florentia et Piero olim Francisci Palmerini de Castro Florentino co-
mitatus Florentie et aliis subscriptis.

Egregia domina domina Madalena filia olim nobilis viri Caroli de Strozzis
et uxor nobilis et egregii militis domini Luchini de Vice Comitibus de
Mediolano, que domina hodie habitat in dicto populo Sancti Pancratii de
Florentia, constituta etc. petiit suum mundualdum etc. ser Benedictum filium
mei Francisci notarii infrascripti ibidem presentem et acceptantem, cuius consensu possit se obligare etc. quem dedi etc. autoritatem interposui etc.

Item postea dictis anno, indictione, die et loco, et coram dictis suprascriptis testibus ad hec vocatis, habitis et rogatis.

Prefata domina Madalena cum legitimo consensu dicti ser Benedicti eius
mundualdi etc. certificata etc. ex parte una et Pierus eius frater et filius olim
dicti Caroli pro et vice et nomine Salamonis fratris carnalis dicte domine
Madalene et dicti Pieri ex parte alia et filii olim dicti Caroli de Strozzis de
Florentia ex parte alia generaliter omnes lites etc. compromiserunt etc. in
egregium militem dominum Pallam olim Nofri Palle de Strozzis presentem et
acceptantem tanquam in arbitrum et arbitratorem etc. Dantes etc. plenam
baliam duraturam hinc ad tres dies laudandi etc. de iure et de facto etc. Cum
pacto etc. quod de laudatis intelligatur litem fuisse etc. Promictentes parere

laudatum etc. Sub pena florenorum mille auri etc. Et sub refecto dampnorum etc. et obligationum bonorum etc. Renuntiantes etc. guarentigia etc. Item postea dictis anno et indictione et die. Actum Florentie in domo seu palatio universitatis Mercantie civitatis Florentie, presentibus testibus ad hec vocatis et rogatis Jacopo Ticci populi Sancte Lucie Omnium Sanctorum de Florentia et Piero Francisci Palmerini de Castro Florentino et aliis subscriptis.

Salamon olim Caroli de Strozzis, audito dicto compromisso hodie supra eius nomine facto per dictum Pierum eius fratrem cum dicta domina Madalena etc., dictum compromissum et omnia in eo contenta ratificavit etc. Rogans etc. guarentigia etc.

In dei nomine, amen. Nos Palla olim Nofri Palle milex de Strozzis de Florentia, arbiter et arbitrator et amicus communis electus et assumptus a nobili domina domina Madalena vidua, filia olim Caroli de Strozzis de Florentia et uxore olim egregii militis domini Luchini de Vicecomitibus de Mediolano, ex parte una, et a Salamone eius fratre carnali et filio dicti olim Caroli de Strozzis de Florentia ex parte alia, ut de compromisso in nos facto constat et apparet manu ser Francisci Pieri Giacomini notarii florentini, viso igitur dicto compromisso in nos facto et balia et potestate nobis a dictis partibus attributa, et visis et examinatis petitionibus et responsionibus, iuribus et allegationibus dictarum partium et quicquid dicte partis coram nobis dicere, proponere et allegare voluerunt, et habita super his omnibus et singulis infrascriptis informatis et deliberatis solempnibus pro bono pacis et concordie partium predictarum et omni modo, via, iure et forma quibus magis et melius possumus pro tribunali sede ad cautelam in loco infrascripto, viam arbitratoris eligentes, laudamus, pronuntiamus, sententiamus et arbitramur inter dictas partes in hunc modum et formam, videlicet: Imprimis quidem viso et reperto qualiter dictus Salamon fuit et est debitor dicte domine Madalene eius sororis in florenis mille auri ponderis et conii. Et viso quod dictus Salamon ad presens non habet pecunias preter quibus ex qua dicte domine commode satisfacere possit, et volentes inter dictas partes benigne agere et eas ad concordiam reducere laudamus, sententiamus, diffinimus, decernimus, declaramus et arbitramur [378v] quod una domus cum voltis super terram, puteo, salis, cameris et aliis hedifitiis, et in qua ad presens habitat dictus Salamon, posita in populo Sancti Pancratii de Florentia, cui a i° via que dicitur dal pozo a San Sisti, a ii° filiorum et heredum Cardinalis Pieri de Oricellariis de Florentia, a iii° via que dicitur la vigna, a iiii° Laurentii domini Jacopi del Biada de Florentia, infra predictos confines vel alios si qui fuerint plures aut veriores de cetero, sit et esse debeat dicte domine Madalene et ad ipsam dominam Madalenam pertineat et spectet pleno iure dominii et proprietatis, et eidem domine Madalene hoc nostro presenti laudo et arbitramento damus, concedimus et adiudicamus pleno iure dominii et proprietatis. Ad habendum, tenendum et istud usque ad per totum capitulum de defensione extende ut in libro exc. c. 3 possidendum, vendendum, pignorandum et alienandum et quicquid dicte domine Madalene et eius heredibus deinceps placuerit proprio faciendum cum omnibus et singulis que infra predictos continere confines etc. Et cum omni iure et actione etc. Et ex causa predicta adiudicamus dicte domine Madalene omnia iura et actiones dicto Salamoni competentia etc. contra suos et dictorum bonorum autores etc. Et facimus dictam dominam nomine dicti Salamonis procuratricem in rem suam etc.

Item laudamus quod dictus Salamon de cetero teneat dicta bona pro dicta domina Madalena etc. et eidem de fructibus respondeat donec dicta domina possessionem et tenutam intraverit etc. Et quod ipsa domina possit propria autoritate intrare tenutam dictorum bonorum etc.

Item laudamus etc. quod dictus Salamon non possit aliquam litem movere super dictis bonis etc. sed teneatur ipse et eius heredes defendere etc. ab omni homine et persona etc. suis expensis etc. et dare tenutam vacuam etc. Et si lix moveretur etc. in se suscipere etc. infra quintam diem post notificationem etc. etiam semel domi factam etc. Et quod facta notificatione etc. domina Madalena vel eius heredes non teneantur in adiudicium etc. Et si pronuntiari contingent super evictione etc. dictus Salamon teneatur dicte domine restituere pretium dictorum florenorum mille auri cum pena duppli etc. infra octo dies post evictionem etc. et post notificationem semel domi factam etc. remissa appellandi necessitate etc. et quod non possit dici quod facta sit iniuria etc. sed bona evincerentur etc. omnia extende ut in similibus cum omnibus preciis utilibus etc. quod extendi in libro ex carta 3.

Item laudamus, sententiamus et arbitramur quod si casus evenerit quod dicta domus per dictam dominam Madalenam venderetur et pro pretio dicte domus haberetur minus florenorum mille auri quod totum illud quod minus florenorum mille auri, videlicet illud quod deesset usque ad summam florenorum mille auri, dictus Salamon infra octo dies tunc proximos futuros dicte domine Madalene restituere et solvere teneatur ad hoc ut ipsa domina integre habeat et percipiat dictos florenos mille auri sibi ut prefertur debitos sine aliqua diminutione vel retentione. Et similiter si dictus Salamon reperiret emptorem dicte domus laudamus et arbitramur quod dicta domina Madalena teneatur ad omnem requisitionem dicti Salamonis in quantum tunc temporis dicta domus alii vendita non esset ipsam domum vendere cui dictus Salamon voluerit. Ita tamen quod tempore talis venditionis pretium quod ex dicta domo haberetur sit dicte domine Madalene et eidem domine persolvatur. Ac etiam primo et ante omnia et ante dictam venditionem et seu in ipsa huiusmodi venditione dictus Salamon integre det et solvat dicte domine Madalene totum illud quod ex dicto pretio deerit usque ad dictam summam florenorum mille auri quandocunque dicta domus quomodolibet venderetur, pignoraretur vel alienaretur sed interim stet contenta habere dictam domum pro dictis florenis mille auri. Hoc etiam in predictis addito et declarato ad hoc ne ipsi domine Madalene propter pendentiam dicte conditionis in locando dictam domum fieri possit aliquod preiudicium quod tempore huiusmodi venditionis ad instantiam dicti Salamonis fiende non rumpatur per venditionem predictam aliqua locatio per dictam dominam facta nec eidem domine in locando fiat preiudicium sed teneatur in casu predicto dictus Salamon ipsam dominam conservare indempnem ab omni locatione per eam fienda et que tunc duraret et ab omnibus promissionibus que ipsa domina in aliqua huiusmodi locationis fecisset vel per eam facta esse contingeret. Et predicta omnia et singula volumus et mandamus a dictis partibus observari et executioni mandari cum effectu sub pena in compromisso in nos facto apposita et adiecta.

Latum, datum, pronuntiatum et factum fuit suprascriptum laudum, sententia, arbitrium et arbitramentum per dictum dominum Pallam militem et arbitrum et arbitratorem predictum pro tribunali sede ad cautelam in populo Sancti Pancratii de Florentia, absente dicto Salamone et presente et predicta fieri petente et dictum laudum et omnia suprascripta ratificante et acceptante dicta domina Madalena. Sub anno domini ab eius incarnatione [379r] mccccxx octavo, indictione septima et die vigesima quarta Novembris, presentibus testibus ad hec vocatis, habitis et rogatis ser Piero ser Antonii Laurentii, ser Bartolo Fruosini de Albagnano, notariis florentinis et aliis.

Item postea dictis anno et indictione et die et coram dictis suprascriptis testibus ad hec vocatis, habitis et rogatis.

Domina Ghita filia olim domini Filippi de Corsinis de Florentia et uxor suprascripti Salamonis Caroli de Strozzis, constituta etc. petiit sibi dari in mundualdum etc. ser Bonifatium Bartolomei de Marinaris de Prato, notarium florentinum presentem etc. quem dedi etc. autoritatem interposui etc.

Item postea eisdem anno, indictione et die et loco et presentibus testibus ad hec vocatis et rogatis etc.

Prefata domina Ghita, cum consensu dicti mundualdi etc. prius dicto laudo et arbitramento etc. et audito et sibi per me lecto dicto laudo etc. certificata etc., asserens se habere notitiam etc. et certificata esse etc. dicto laudo et adiudicata consensit etc. et renuntiavit omni iuri ypotecario sibi competenti in dicta suprascripta domo adiudicata etc. pro dotibus suis vel alia quacunque de causa ipsum ius dicte domine Madalene presens, remictens etc. promictens etc. dicte domine Madalene presenti etc. firma habere etc. sub pena florenorum mille auri etc. et sub obligatione sibi et bonorum etc. Renuntians etc. et maxime benefitio velleiano etc. guarentigia etc.

Item postea dictis anno et indictione et die et in domo Mercantie, presentibus dictis testibus.

Dictus Salamon ratificavit dictum laudum etc.

Manovelli and Boldri
(ibid., fols. 281r–82v)

In dei nomine, amen. Nos Julianus Niccholai de Davanzatis legum doctor, arbiter et arbitrator et amicus communis electus et assumptus a Niccholao Manovellozzi de Manovellis de Florentia ex parte una, et a Boldro olim Laurentii Boldri beccarii populi Sancti Niccholai de Florentia ex parte alia, ut de compromisso in nos facto constet et apparet manu ser Antonii ser Luce notarii florentini, viso igitur dicto compromisso et balia et potestate nobis a dictis partibus attributa, et visa postea prorogatione dicti compromissi et seu novo compromisso in nos facto per dictum Boldrum ex parte una et Bernardum Andree Masi pro et vice et nomine dicti Niccholai Manovellozzi ex parte alia, nec non ratificatione et adceptatione dicte prorogationis et novi compromissi facti per dictum Niccholaum, de qua prorogatione et ratificatione constat manu ser Pieri ser Antonii Laurentii notarii [281v] florentini. Et visis petitionibus et responsionibus, iuribus et allegationibus dictarum partium et quicquid dicte partes coram nobis dicere et allegare voluerunt, et habita in his et super his omnibus et singulis infrascriptis informatione et deliberatione solempni pro bono pacis et concordie partium predictarum et omni modo, via, iure et forma quibus magis et melius possumus pro tribunali sede ad cautelam in loco infrascripto, viam arbitratoris eligentes, laudamus, sententiamus, pronuntiamus, decernimus, declaramus et arbitramur inter dictas partes in hunc modum, videlicet: Imprimis quidem viso et reperto qualiter de anno domini millesimo trecentesimo octuagesimo, indictione sexta et die primo mensis Augusti, et alio veriori tempore Tedicius olim Johannis de Manovellis existens infirmitate gravatus, de qua infirmitate infra paucos dies decessit, confessus fuit domine Filippe uxoris sue se habuisse pro dote dicte domine Filippe et a dicta domina Filippa pro extimatione unum podere positum a Monte Caroso, et subsequenter eadem die suos condidit codicillos in quibus plura disposuit et inter alia in effectu legavit dicte domine Filippe eius uxori pro omni et toto eo quod petere poterat dictum podere in dicta datione dicte dotis contentum et confinatum, si et in quantum sibi domine placuerit, supradictum podere et terram habere et quod dictus Tedicius dixit se recepisse ab eadem pro dicta extimatione, et insuper iura legati reliquit dicte domine Filippe eius uxori quamdiu ipsa domina Filippa vixeat vitam vidualem servando omne lucrum et fructus et fetus quod erat et tunc de cetero haberetur de quibusdam vaccis, pecudibus et capris quas idem Tedicius dixit locavisse ad soccidam Valori Nuccini populi Sancti Clementis de Monte Caroso pro extimatione et valuta florenorum quindecim auri, ac etiam omne lucrum quod haberetur et esset in et de quodam pari bovum quos tenebat ad soccidam pro dicto Tedicio Johanni vocato Riccio dicti populi Sancti Clementis pro extimatione florenorum viginti duorum auri, et ultra predicta reliquit dicte eius uxori tot masseritias lectorum et panni et aliorum que sint valoris librarum centumquinquaginta sp. que sibi domine magis placuerint ad ipsius domine usum toto tempore sue viduetatis. Quas bestias et seu earum extimationem predictam et dictas masseritias et res seu extimationem tunc temporis restitutionis fiende voluit et mandavit dictus Tedicius dari et distribui post mortem dicte domine Filippe illis pauperibus personis et piis locis pro anima dicti Tedicii quibus videbitur infrascriptis Antonio et Merlino, executoribus suis et executores suos et dicte sue ultime voluntatis reliquit et esse voluit dictam dominam Filippam eius uxorem et

Antonium Laurentii de Manovellis et Stefanum vocatum Merlino quondam Laurentii habitatorem in castro Burgi ad Sanctum Laurentium de Mucello, cum balia et potestate in dictis codicillis contenta prout predicta et alia in publico instrumento dictorum codicillorum inde rogatorum manu ser Mactei Lippi de Scarperia notarii florentini plenius contenta. Et viso et reperto qualiter postea inde ad paucos dies dictus Tedicius decessit relicta et supervivente dicta domina Filippa eius uxore predicta, et viso et reperto qualiter dicta domina Filippa a tempore mortis dicti Tedicii citra continue usque ad tempus et tempore mortis dicte domine Filippe et per totum dictum tempus continue habuit, tenuit et possedit pro suis et tanquam sua bona propria dictum podere de Monte Caroso sibi domine per dictum Tedicium legatum et in hereditate et bonis dicte domine Filippe remansit dictum predium. Ac etiam reperto qualiter dicta domina Filippa etiam habuit et possedit dictas res sibi ad usum ut prefertur legatas. Et viso et reperto qualiter dicta domina Filippa postea mortua est et decessit de anno domini mcccc vel circa, superstite et supervivente Merlino filio dicte domine, nato ex dicta domina Filippa et Benvenuto olim primo viro dicte domine Filippe, qui Merlinus fuit heres dicte domine Filippe eius matris et se pro herede dicte domine Filippe gessit et bona hereditaria dicte domine Filippe et maxime dictum predium et seu podere positum a Monte Caroso tanquam bona hereditaria dicte domine Filippe tenuit et possedit a morte dicte domine Filippe citra continue usque ad tempus et tempore mortis dicti Merlini et in hereditate dicti Merlini remansit dictum podere. Et viso quod dictus Merlinus postea mortuus est et decessit de anno domini mccccxi et ante diem decimam nonam mensis Maii dicti anni, et reperto [282r] qualiter postea de dicto anno domini mccccxi et die decimanona Maii Laurentius Boldri beccarius populi Sancti Niccholai de Florentia ut tanquam proximior agnatus et seu coniunctus dicti Merlini adivit hereditatem dicti Merlini in solidum ab intestato, de qua aditione constat manu ser Christofani Andree de Laterino notarii florentini. Et viso et reperto qualiter dictus Laurentius a tempore mortis dicti Merlini citra usque ad tempus et tempore mortis dicti Laurentii habuit, tenuit et possedit dictum podere de Monte Caroso et in ipsius Laurentii hereditate remansit dictum podere. Et reperto qualiter postea dictus Laurentius mortuus est et decessit iam sunt plures anni elapxi, superstite et supervivente Boldro filio dicti Laurentii et qui Boldrus filius et heres dicti Laurentii a tempore mortis dicti Laurentii citra tenuit et possedit dictum podere de Monte Caroso et alia bona hereditaria dicti olim Merlini et domine Filippe et dicti Laurentii eius patris et fuit et est heres dicti Laurentii eius patris. Et viso qualiter dictus Niccholaus de anno domini mccccxxp[0] et mense Aprilis dicti anni adivit hereditatem dicti olim Tedicii Johannis. Et visa quadam petitione et seu reclamo exibita in curia consulum Artis Beccariorum contra ipsum Boldrum in qua dictus Niccholaus heres predictus petebat a dicto Boldro herede predicto dictam extimationem dictarum rerum per dictum olim Tedicium ad usum relictarum dicte domine Filippe. Et visis exceptionibus in dicta causa factis et probationibus factis in dicta curia consulum cum productione iurium ad predicta facientium. Que omnia coram nobis arbitro predicto dicta proposita et repetita fuerunt et omnibus visis que videnda fuerunt, volentes partes ad concordiam reducere et considerantes etiam quod ex forma dictorum codicillorum dicti Tedicii dicta extimatio dictarum rerum ad usum dicte domine Filippe relictarum distribui debet amore dei pro anima dicti olim Tedicii, et aliis iustis et rationabilibus causis moti que nos merito movere debuerunt, laudamus, pronuntiamus, sententiamus et arbitramur quod pro omni et toto eo quod dictus Boldrus ut heres, suprascriptis occaxione, causa vel pretextu instrumentorum et iurium et pro causis de quibus supra fit mentio, quomodolibet dare vel solvere teneretur, det et solvat et restituat et dare et solvere teneatur et debeat dicto Niccholao Manovellozzi florenos quadraginta auri ponderis et conii florentini hinc ad unum annum proximum futurum, et ad sic dandum et solvendum dictum Boldrum hinc ad unum annum proximum futurum dictam quantitatem florenorum quadraginta auri hoc nostro laudo, sententia et arbitramento condempnamus cum hoc honere et gravamine dicto Niccholao iniuncto et adiecto quod dictus Niccholaus teneatur et debeat dictam quantitatem, deductis tamen expensis factis vel fiendis pro dicta quantitate habenda vel exigenda per dictum Niccholaum, dare et erogare in subsidium nuptus et auxilium dotis Sandre filie Niccholi Antonii de Manovellis de Florentia. Cum hoc tamen in predictis omnibus et singulis suprascriptis salvo, expresso et reservato quod si dictus Boldrus infra unum annum proximum futurum ostendiderit et fidem legitimam fecerit quod executores codicillorum dicti Tedicii habuerint et distribuerint amore dei dictas quantitates dicte domine Filippe ad usum legati ut prefertur prout disponitur ex forma dictorum codicillorum, de quo an dicta quantitas distributa fuerit amore dei secundum formam dictorum codicillorum nec ne stetur et stari volumus declarationi infra dictum annum fiende per consules Artis Spetiariorum, quod tunc et in dicto casu dictus Boldrus ad solutionem dictorum florenorum quadraginta auri minime teneatur.

Item laudamus, sententiamus et arbitramur quod si et in quantum dictus Boldrus infra unum annum proximum futurum ad declarationem dictorum consulum Artis Spetiariorum predictorum qui pro tempore fuerint infra dictum annum fiendam ostendiderit et probaverit dictam dominam Filippam aliam dotem dedisse dicto Tedicio quam dictam dotem per dictum Tedicium receptam et seu confessatam et dicte domine Filippe ut prefertur in dictis codicillis legatam, quod tunc et in dicto casu dictus Boldrus pro dicta alia tali dote quam de novo probaret ad declarationem predictam ut prefertur possit super dicta extimatione dictarum rerum ad usum dicte domine Filippe [282v] legatarie et super dictis florenis quadraginta auri in quibus eum supra condempnavimus prosequi omne ius suum ac si presens laudum latum non esset contra dictum Boldrum.

Item laudamus, sententiamus et arbitramur quod dictus Boldrus teneatur et debeat pro gabella presentis laudi et arbitramenti secundum formam ordinamenti gabelle contractuum et ab ipsa gabella dictus Boldrus teneatur et debeat conservare dictum Niccholaum indempnem et penitus sine dampno omnibus sumptibus et expensis dicti Boldri. Et predicta omnia et singula volumus et mandamus a dictis partibus observari et executioni mandari sub pena in compromisso in nos facto apposita et inserta.

Latum, datum, pronuntiatum et factum fuit suprascriptum laudum, sententia, arbitrium et arbitramentum per suprascriptum dominum Julianum arbitrum et arbitratorem suprascriptum pro tribunali sede ad cautelam in populo Sancte Trinitatis de Florentia, presentibus, audientibus et intelligentibus et consentientibus dictis Niccholao et Boldro partibus predictis et dictum laudum ratificantibus, adceptantibus et emologantibus. Et presentibus testibus ad hec vocatis, habitis et rogatis Bernardo Silvestri Michaelis Nardi populi Sancti Petri Scheradii de Florentia et Papi Juliani Raynerii del Forese de Florentia et ser Christofano Andree de Laterino notario florentino et aliis. Sub annis domini ab incarnatione millesimo quadringentesimo vigesimo septimo, indictione quinta et die vigesima nona Martii.

•

NOTES

•

Abbreviations

ASF   Archivio di Stato, Florence
           Carte strozziane
           Catasto
           Manoscritti
           Mercanzia
           Notarile antecosimiano
           Notificazioni di atti di emancipazione
           Provv.   Provvisioni, registri
           Podestà 1355   Statuti del comune di Firenze, 16
BNF   Biblioteca Nazionale, Florence
           Landau-Finaly
           Magliabechiano
           Panciatichiano
           Principale
BAV   Biblioteca Apostolica Vaticana
           Urb. Lat.
           Vat. Lat.
Statuta 1415 *Statuta populi et communis Florentiae, anno alutis mccccxv*,
           3 vols. Freiburg [Florence], 1778–83

Introduction

1. An issue I have addressed in my "Il diritto e l'uso del diritto nelle famiglie fiorentine nel Rinascimento," in *Palazzo Strozzi, Metà Millenio, 1489–1989: Atti del Convegno di Studi* (Rome, 1991), 108-25.

2. On this issue of historical reading of texts, though not directly con-

cerned with legal texts, see Dominick LaCapra, *Rethinking Intellectual History: Texts, Contexts, Language* (Ithaca, 1983), 17–19.

3. Here note the essential discussion of David Herlihy and Christiane Klapisch-Zuber on the compiling of the *catasto* records, *Les toscans et leurs familles* (Paris, 1978), 77–106; also Anthony Molho, "Deception and Marriage Strategy in Renaissance Florence: The Case of Women's Ages," *Renaissance Quarterly* 41 (1988): 193–217.

4. Cf. Julius Kirshner, "Some Problems in the Interpretation of Legal Texts *re* the Italian City-States," *Archiv für Begriffsgeschichte* 19 (1975): 16–27.

5. Cf. Samuel Kline Cohn, Jr., *Death and Property in Siena, 1205–1800: Strategies for the Afterlife* (Baltimore, 1988); id., "Donne in piazza e donne in tribunale a Firenze nel Rinascimento, *Studi storici* 22 (1981): 515–33; Romeo de Maio, *Donna e Rinascimento* (Milan, 1987), esp. 86–122.

6. To cite only the most important works now: Richard Goldthwaite, *Private Wealth in Renaissance Florence* (Princeton, 1968); Francis William Kent, *Household and Lineage in Renaissance Florence: The Family Life of the Capponi, Ginori, and Rucellai* (Princeton, 1977); Herlihy and Klapisch-Zuber, *Les toscans*, to be read in conjunction with more recent works such as Herlihy's *Medieval Households* (Cambridge, Mass., 1985) and Klapisch-Zuber's *Women, Family, and Ritual in Renaissance Italy* (Chicago, 1985); also Diane Owen Hughes, "Urban Growth and Family Structure in Medieval Genoa," *Past and Present* 66 (Feb. 1975): 1–28; Paolo Cammarosano, "Aspetti delle strutture familiari nelle città dell'Italia comunale (secoli xii–xiv)," *Studi medievali*, 3rd ser., 16 (1975): 417–35; Leonida Pandimiglio, "Giovanni di Pagolo Morelli e le strutture familiari," *Archivio storico italiano* 136 (1978): 3–88; Charles M. de la Roncière, "Une famille florentine au xiv^c siècle: Les Velluti," in *Famille et parenté dans l'Occident médiéval*, ed. Georges Duby and Jacques Le Goff (Rome, 1977), 227–48; Marzio Barbagli, *Sotto lo stesso tetto: Mutamenti della famiglia in Italia dal xv al xx secolo* (Bologna, 1984).

7. Cf. the sense of family arrived at by James Casey in his insightful *The History of the Family* (Oxford, 1989).

8. They even went so far as to eliminate much of this material in the later abridged English translation, *Tuscans and Their Families: A Study of the Florentine Catasto of 1427*, Yale Series in Economic History (New Haven and London, 1985). What was kept of the final chapters of the French, however, was integrated into the text at different points, with the corresponding effect of lessening a too great distinction between demographic and economic, on the one hand, and cultural, on the other.

9. Cf. my *Emancipation in Late Medieval Florence* (New Brunswick, 1982), 6. Herlihy's subsequent synthetic treatments of family and women over the entire Middle Ages similarly emphasize the effect of economic factors on developments, especially male dominance over women and the exclusion

of the latter from economic production. In these works, however, he accords some influence to general legal change, such as the reception of Roman law and the acceptance of ecclesiastical rules of marriage. See his *Medieval Households* (note 6 above) and *Opera Muliebria: Women and Work in Medieval Europe* (New York, 1990). As will emerge in this volume, in my own work I have emphasized not women's possibilities of guild membership but their rights and claims in familial property.

10. *Women, Family, and Ritual* (note 6 above) and a different, though overlapping, set of essays in Italian translation, *La famiglia e le donne nel Rinascimento a Firenze* (Bari, 1988).

11. In her words, Introduzione, in *La famiglia e le donne*, v: "la constatazione cioè della debolezza numerica e della irrilevanza sociale delle donne in una società che pure ci ha lasciato di esse le immagine più sensibili e raffinate."

12. Ibid., xv.

13. "'Le *zane* della sposa: La donna fiorentina e il suo corredo nel Rinascimento," in *La famiglia e le donne*, 210.

14. "Le genealogie fiorentine," in *La famiglia e le donne*, 55; "Childhood in Tuscany at the Beginning of the Fifteenth Century," in *Women, Family, and Ritual*, 106.

15. "The 'Cruel Mother': Maternity, Widowhood, and Dowry in Florence in the Fourteenth and Fifteenth Centuries," in *Women, Family, and Ritual*, 117–31 (original French version in *Annales* 38 [1983]: 1097–1109).

16. "Le genealogie fiorentine," 46; and her recent "Ruptures de parenté et changements d'identité chez les magnats florentins du xive siècle," *Annales* 43 (1988): 1205–40.

17. ASF, Notarile G 616 (1458–59), fol. 119r–v (31 January 1458 [1459]), where Lazero di Lotto Lazeri gave a house to his mother, twice widowed.

18. Cf. Herlihy and Klapisch-Zuber, *Les toscans*, 404–19; Julius Kirshner, *Pursuing Honor While Avoiding Sin: The "Monte delle doti" of Florence* (Milan, 1978), 7–8; Jacques Pluss, "Reading Case Law Historically: A *Consilium* of Baldus de Ubaldis on Widows and Dowries," *American Journal of Legal History* 30 (1986): 241–65; Isabelle Chabot, "Widowhood and Poverty in Late Medieval Florence," *Continuity and Change* 3 (1988): 291–311.

19. *Women, Family, and Ritual*, x.

20. Cf. Susan Mosher Stuard, "From Women to Woman: New Thinking about Gender c. 1140," *Thought* 64 (1989): 208–19.

21. For example, Julius Kirshner, "Wives' Claims against Insolvent Husbands in Late Medieval Italy," in *Women of the Medieval World: Essays in Honor of John H. Mundy*, ed. Julius Kirshner and Suzanne F. Wemple (Oxford, 1985), 256–303.

22. Cf. Elaine Rosenthal, "The Position of Women in Renaissance Florence: Neither Autonomy nor Subjection," in *Florence and Italy: Renaissance*

Studies in Honour of Nicolai Rubinstein, ed. Peter Denley and Caroline Elam (London, 1989), 369–81. On these themes note also the comments of Julius Kirshner, "Materials for a Gilded Cage: Non-Dotal Assets in Florence (1300– 1500)," in *The Family in Italy from Antiquity to the Present,* ed. David I. Kertzer and Richard P. Saller (New Haven and London, 1991), 184–207.

23. For example, Jacques Le Goff, "Histoire médiévale et histoire du droit: Un dialogue difficile," in *Storia sociale e dimensione giuridica: Strumenti d'indagine e ipotesi di lavoro,* ed. Paolo Grossi (Milan, 1986), 23–63, which offers a very instructive viewpoint from the leading *Annaliste* of the 1980s.

24. In a parallel fashion, see Ronald F. E. Weissman, "The Importance of Being Ambiguous: Social Relations, Individualism, and Identity in Renaissance Florence," in *Urban Life in the Renaissance,* ed. Susan Zimmerman and Ronald F. E. Weissman (Newark, 1989), 269–80.

25. Kent, *Household and Lineage* (note 6 above).

26. Cf. my *Emancipation,* 6–7. Important critical perspectives on Kent's landmark book are offered by Anthony Molho, "Visions of the Florentine Family in the Renaissance," *Journal of Modern History* 50 (1978): 304–11.

27. Kent, *Household and Lineage,* 150–52.

28. On these matters, in addition to Kirshner, "Some Problems" (note 4 above), see my *Emancipation,* 1–9; Luigi Berlinguer, "Considerazioni su storiografia e diritto," *Studi storici* 15 (1974): 3–56; and the various papers and comments in Paolo Grossi, ed., *Storia sociale e dimensione giuridica: Strumenti d'indagine e ipotesi di lavoro,* Atti dell'Incontro di Studio, Firenze, 26–27 Aprile 1985 (Milan, 1986). A sensitive discussion of legal language is Peter Goodrich, *Legal Discourse: Studies in Linguistics, Rhetoric and Legal Analysis* (New York, 1987).

29. Most notably in his synthesis of medieval legal history: *Società e istituzioni in Italia dal Medioevo agli inizi dell'età moderna,* 3d ed. (Catania, 1982).

30. Manlio Bellomo, *Problemi di diritto familiare nell'età dei comuni: Beni paterni e "pars filii"* (Milan, 1968), 96–97.

31. Bellomo, *Società e istituzioni,* 462–80.

32. On *consilia,* see Ingrid Baumgärtner, "Consilia: Quellen für Familie in Krise und Kontinuität," in *Die Familie als sozialer und historischer Verband: Untersuchungen zum Spätmittelalter und zur frühen Neuzeit,* ed. Peter-Johannes Schuler (Sigmaringen, 1987), 43–66; Jacques Pluss, "Reading Case Law Historically," passim.

33. Here I part company to some degree with Lauro Martines, whose *Lawyers and Statecraft in Renaissance Florence* (Princeton, 1968) has been an essential tool for my own work, as can be seen from the frequency with which it is cited in the following pages.

34. Luciano Martone, *Arbiter-Arbitrator: Forme di giustizia privata nell'età del diritto comune,* Storia e Diritto (Naples, 1984).

35. These points are made more fully below, in chapter 2, where the anthropological literature is also cited extensively. One legal historian who has directly confronted the findings of anthropology is Peter Stein, *Legal Institutions: The Development of Dispute Settlement* (London, 1984). One anthropologist who has recently expressed discontent with the discipline's inability to come to grips with law in highly formal, institutionalized forms is Sally Falk Moore in her *Social Facts and Fabrications: "Customary Law" on Kilimanjaro, 1880–1980* (Cambridge, 1986).

36. Casey, *History of the Family* (note 7 above), 139–40; and, in addition to all his important works cited in the paper itself, see Paolo Grossi's "La proprietà e le proprietà nell'officina dello storico," in *La proprietà e le proprietà*, ed. Ennio Cortese (Milan, 1988), 205–72.

37. Casey, *History of the Family*, 74–79; Klapisch-Zuber, *Women, Family, and Ritual*, 117–31, 213–46; Maria Teresa Guerra Medici, *I diritti delle donne nella società altomedievale* (Milan, 1986); Julius Kirshner, "'Maritus lucretur dotem uxoris sue premortue' in Fourteenth- and Fifteenth-Century Florence," in *Zeitschrift der Savigny-Stiftung für Rechtsgeschichte (Kan. Abt.)* 77 (1991): 111–55; idem and Anthony Molho, "The Dowry Fund and the Marriage Market in Early Quattrocento Florence," *Journal of Modern History* 50 (1978): 403–38; Manlio Bellomo, *Ricerche sui rapporti patrimoniali tra coniugi: Contributo alla storia della famiglia medievale* (Milan, 1961); Laurent Mayali, *Droit savant et coutumes: L'exclusion des filles dotées, xiième–xvème siècles* (Frankfurt am Main, 1987).

38. Gene Brucker, *Giovanni and Lusanna: Love and Marriage in Renaissance Florence* (Berkeley, 1986); Thomas Kuehn, "Reading Microhistory: The Example of *Giovanni and Lusanna*," *Journal of Modern History* 61 (1989): 512–34.

39. For a suggestive anthropological perspective on personhood, see Marilyn Strathern, "Self-Interest and the Social Good: Some Implications of Hagen Gender Imagery," in *Sexual Meanings: The Cultural Construction of Gender and Sexuality*, ed. Sherry B. Ortner and Harriet Whitehead (Cambridge, 1981), 166–91.

40. Cohn, *Death and Property* (note 5 above); Steven Epstein, *Wills and Wealth in Medieval Genoa, 1150–1250* (Cambridge, Mass., 1984).

41. Cf. Thomas Kuehn, "Law, Death, and Heirs in the Renaissance: Some Meanings of the Repudiation of Inheritance," in *Renaissance Quarterly* 45 (1991): 484–516.

Chapter One

1. Francesco Calasso, *Medioevo del diritto*, vol. 1: *Le Fonti* (Milan, 1954); Manlio Bellomo, *Società e istituzioni in Italia dal Medioevo agli inizi dell'età moderna*, 3d ed. (Catania, 1982); Arthur Engelman et al., *A History of Continental Civil Procedure*, trans. and ed. Robert Wyness Millar (Boston, 1927;

reprint ed., New York, 1969); and Pietro Sella, _Il procedimento civile nella legislazione statutaria italiana_ (Milan, 1927).

2. John Larner, _Italy in the Age of Dante and Petrarch, 1216–1380_ (New York, 1980), 102–4, 110–11, 123–24; Lauro Martines, _Power and Imagination: City-States in Renaissance Italy_ (New York, 1979); Robert Davidsohn, _Storia di Firenze_, vol. 4: _I primordi della civiltà fiorentina_, Part 1: _Impulsi interni, influssi esterni e cultura politica_, trans. from German by Eugenio Dupré-Theseider (Florence, 1973).

3. Edward Powell, "Arbitration and the Law in England in the Late Middle Ages," _Transactions of the Royal Historical Society_, 5th ser., 33 (1983): 55. In addition, see Frederic L. Cheyette, "'Suum cuique tribuere,'" _French Historical Studies_ 6 (1970): 287–99; Stephen D. White, "'Pactum . . . Legem Vincit et Amor Judicium': The Settlement of Disputes by Compromise in Eleventh-Century Western France," _American Journal of Legal History_ 22 (1978): 281–308; Jenny Wormald, "Bloodfeud, Kindred and Government in Early Modern Scotland," _Past and Present_ 87 (1980): 54–97; J. A. Sharpe, "'Such Disagreement betwyx Neighbours': Litigation and Human Relations in Early Modern England," in _Disputes and Settlements: Law and Human Relations in the West_, ed. John Bossy (Cambridge, 1983), 167–87; Michael Clanchy, "Law and Love in the Middle Ages," in _Disputes and Settlements_, 47–67; William Ian Miller "Avoiding Legal Judgment: The Submission of Disputes to Arbitration in Medieval Iceland," _American Journal of Legal History_ 28 (1984): 95–134.

4. Powell, "Arbitration and Law," 50–51, and his "Settlement of Disputes by Arbitration in Fifteenth-Century England," _Law and History Review_ 2 (1984): 38–41; Nicole Castan, "The Arbitration of Disputes under the Ancien Regime," in _Disputes and Settlements_, 219–60; Richard L. Kagan, _Lawsuits and Litigants in Castile, 1500–1700_ (Chapel Hill, 1981), 82–84. One area of law producing pertinent examples was usury; cf. R. H. Helmholz, "Usury and the Medieval English Church Courts," _Speculum_ 61 (1986): 377, and his "Ethical Standards for Advocates and Proctors in Theory and Practice," _Proceedings of the Fourth International Congress of Medieval Canon Law, Toronto, 21–25 August 1972_, ed. Stephan Kuttner, Monumenta Iuris Canonici, Series C: Subsidia, vol. 5 (Vatican City, 1976), 291–93.

5. Sally F. Moore, "Law and Anthropology," _Biennial Review of Anthropology_ (1969): 252–300; J. F. Collier, "Legal Processes," _Annual Review of Anthropology_ 4 (1975): 121–44; Francis G. Snyder, "Anthropology, Dispute Processes and Law: A Critical Introduction," _British Journal of Law and Society_ 8 (1981): 141–80.

6. Even in modern societies there are relationships that cannot risk frequent handling by legal authorities. Cf. Klaus-Friedrich Koch, Soraya Altorki, Andrew Arno, and Letitia Hickson, "Ritual Reconciliation and the Obviation of Grievances: A Comparative Study in the Ethnography of Law," _Ethnology_ 16 (1977): 269–83.

7. Cf. Clifford Geertz, "Local Knowledge: Fact and Law in Comparative Perspective," in his *Local Knowledge: Further Essays in Interpretive Anthropology* (New York, 1983), 214–15; Vilhelm Aubert, "Law as a Way of Resolving Conflicts: The Case of a Small Industrialized Society," in *Law in Culture and Society,* ed. Laura Nader (Chicago, 1969), 282–303; P. H. Gulliver, *Disputes and Negotiations: A Cross-Cultural Perspective* (New York, 1979); and various studies by Richard L. Abel, "The Rise of Capitalism and the Transformation of Disputing: From Confrontation over Honor to Competition for Property," *UCLA Law Review* 27 (1979–80): 223–55; "Theories of Litigation in Society: 'Modern' Dispute Institutions in 'Tribal' Society and 'Tribal' Dispute Institutions in 'Modern' Society as Alternative Legal Forms," *Jahrbuch für Rechtssoziologie und Rechtstheorie* 6 (1979): 165–91; and "A Comparative Theory of Dispute Institutions in Society," *Law and Society Review* 8 (1973–74): 217–347. A typology in terms of modes of production is offered by Katherine S. Newman, *Law and Economic Organization: A Comparative Study of Preindustrial Societies* (Cambridge, 1983). And generally Sally Falk Moore, *Law as Process: An Anthropological Approach* (London, 1978). It should be acknowledged that some of the interest shown in methods of dispute settlement other than adjudication is undertaken with practical considerations in mind—finding ways to alleviate the crush on courts and improve the legal system. This concern appears in some of Abel's work and also in the volume *Access to Justice,* vol. 4: *The Anthropological Perspective: Patterns of Conflict Management: Essays in the Ethnography of Law,* ed. Klaus-Friedrich Koch (Milan, 1979), and the special issue on "Dispute Processing and Civil Litigation" of *Law and Society Review* 15 (1980–81).

8. Powell, "Settlement," 24.

9. Ibid., 35–36.

10. White, "'*Pactum . . . Legem Vincit,'*" 308; Powell, "Arbitration and Law," 55–56; Kagan, *Lawsuits and Litigants,* 17–18; Chris Wickham, "Comprendere il quotidiano: Antropologia sociale e storia sociale," *Quaderni storici* 60 (1985): 839–57; Janet L. Nelson, "Dispute Settlement in Carolingian West Francia," in *The Settlement of Disputes in Early Medieval Europe,* ed. Wendy Davies and Paul Fouracre (Cambridge, 1986), 45–64, who sees property issues as more suited for court processing; matters of relationship or honor more apt for feud or arbitration.

11. Davidsohn, *Storia di Firenze* (note 2 above), 536.

12. Cf. White, "'*Pactum . . . Legem Vincit'*"; Clanchy, "Law and Love".

13. On this theme, see the recent volume *The Settlement of Disputes in Early Medieval Europe* (note 10 above), especially the contributions of Chris Wickham, "Land Disputes and Their Social Framework in Lombard-Carolingian Italy, 700–900," 105–24, and Jenny Wormald, "An Early Modern Postscript: The Sandlaw Dispute, 1546," 191–205.

14. Cf. Powell, "Arbitration," 57–58; Richard L. Kagan, "A Golden Age of Litigation: Castile, 1500–1700," in *Disputes and Settlements,* 153–55.

15. Powell, "Arbitration," 62; Chris Wickham, "Land Disputes and Their Social Framework," 123–24; and "Conclusion," in *Settlement of Disputes in Early Modern Europe*, 233–35. Similar views of arbitration are found in Peter Stein, *Legal Institutions: The Development of Dispute Settlement* (London, 1984), which I have read in the Italian translation, *I fondamenti del diritto europeo: Profili sostanziali e processuali dell'evoluzione dei sistemi giuridici* (Milan, 1987).

16. Simon Roberts, "The Study of Disputes: Anthropological Perspectives," in *Disputes and Settlements*, 1–24, at 17.

17. "Conclusion," in *Settlement of Disputes in Early Medieval Europe*, 239.

18. Powell, "Settlement," 34.

19. Luciano Martone, *Arbiter-Arbitrator: Forme di giustizia privata nell'età del diritto comune* (Naples, 1984), 10–17, an excellent, comprehensive, and, at times, provocative examination of legal doctrines, statutes, and notarial practices, though not of litigation or even of actual arbitrations.

20. Roberts, "Study of Disputes," 14; cf. also Miller, "Avoiding Legal Judgement," 101.

21. Wormald, "An Early Modern Postscript," 192.

22. Cf. Powell, "Arbitration and Law," 60; and generally Carol J. Greenhouse, "Mediation: A Comparative Approach," *Man*, n.s. 20 (1985): 90–114.

23. Powell, "Arbitration and Law," 62; also see Kagan, *Lawsuits and Litigants*, 245; Miller, "Avoiding Legal Judgement," 97, notes that feud was also an alternative sanction to arbitration.

24. "Conclusion," in *Settlement of Disputes in Early Medieval Europe*, 234, 239.

25. Martone, *Arbiter-Arbitrator*, esp. 161–68, mounts an effective argument that it was precisely the admission of appeal to court of an inequitable *laudum* that solidified the place of arbitration in the legal order of Italian cities.

26. Powell, "Arbitration and Law," 66, for one, implies that on the Continent arbitration and law may have enjoyed a more fluid interaction.

27. The *arbiter* was thus dialectically assimilated to the *iudex* and followed an almost judicial procedure. The difference between the *arbiter* and the *iudex* was essentially that the former was chosen by the parties, at whatever stage in their dispute or litigation, whereas the latter held a jurisdiction giving him cognizance of the dispute without regard to the parties. Cf. Linda Fowler, "Forms of Arbitration," in *Proceedings of the Fourth International Congress of Medieval Canon Law, Toronto, 21–25 August 1972*, ed. Stephan Kuttner, Monumenta Iuris Canonici, Series C: Subsidia, vol. 5 (Vatican City, 1976), 133–47; Antonio Padoa Schioppa, *Ricerche sull'appello nel diritto intermedio*, vol. 2: *I glossatori civilisti* (Milan, 1970), 37, 80–88; Martone, *Arbiter-Arbitrator*, 29–34; Karl S. Bader, "'Arbiter, arbitrator seu amicabilis compositor,'" *Zeitschrift der Savigny-Stiftung für Rechtsgeschichte (Kan.*

Abt.) 77 (1960): 239–76; Karl-Hans Ziegler, "Arbiter, arbitrator und amicabilis compositor," *Zeitschrift der Savigny-Stiftung für Rechtsgeschichte (Rom. Abt.)* 84 (1967): 376–81.

28. For what follows, see Martone, *Arbiter-Arbitrator,* 74–79, 88–92.

29. Durante, *Speculum iudiciale* (Venice, 1566), Book I, Part I, 155.

30. Sella, *Il procedimento civile,* (note 1 above), 206.

31. *Tractatus de arbitris,* in *Opera omnia* (Venice, 1602), vol. 10, fol. 146va: "arbitrator est qui consilio suo tamquam bona fide, et bono motu, nulla iuris solemnitate servata absque iudiciorum strepitu litem decidit."

32. Generally, see Martone, *Arbiter-Arbitrator,* 36–56.

33. Fowler, "Forms of Arbitration," 139–40; Padoa Schioppa, *Ricerche sull'appello,* 2: 85–88.

34. In the metaphor of the thirteenth-century glossator Azzo, "cum arbitri sententia non liget plus quod aliquod filum tenuissimum ligaret hominem" (quoted in Padoa Schioppa, 2: 82–83).

35. Obviously there were, in fact, all sorts of consequences for others when their debtors' or creditors' property, for example, was allocated by arbitration. But this was no more nor less so than would have been the case from other private transactions (e.g., sale).

36. Padoa Schioppa, *Ricerche sull'appello,* 2: 85–87: Martone, *Arbiter-Arbitrator,* 58–60.

37. Durante, *Speculum iudiciale,* 154–55: "nam arbiter est quem partes eligunt ad cognoscendum de questione, vel lite: et sic sumitur super re litigiosa et incerta, ut ea cognoscatur: et debet iuris ordinem servare. Et sit semper cum poenae stipulatione. Non cogendum et statur eius sententia, aequa sit, sive iniqua. Nec ab eo appellatur. Nec ad arbitrium viri reducitur secundum quosdam. Arbitrator vero est amicabilis compositor. Nec sumitur super re litigiosa, vel ut cognoscat: sed ut pacificet, et quod certum est dividat: ut in societate, quam certum fuisse contractam. Sed eligitur, ut det cuilibet certam suam partem, quae ipsum ex societate contingit. Et hoc non dicitur arbitrium. Nec tenetur iuris ordinem observare; nec statur eius sententiae, si sit iniqua: sed reducitur ad arbitrium boni viri."

38. Bader, "'Arbiter, arbitrator seu amicabilis compositor,'" 272–73; Sella, *Il procedimento civile,* 206; Fowler, "Forms of Arbitration," 134–36.

39. On equity in this context, see Martone, *Arbiter-Arbitrator,* 111–19.

40. Ibid., 162–63.

41. Ibid., 127. In Baldo's terms, to C. 2.55(56).1 (Venice, 1577), fol. 104rb: "Ibi loquitur in arbitratore si inique laudat, reducitur ad bonum virum. Secus in arbitrio. Ratio haec est: quia arbiter assumitur ut sit finis litium. Et ideo etiam modica laesio tollatur. Sed arbitrator non assumitur ut sit finis litium: quia ut plurimus assumitur super contractibus. Et posito quod assumatur super lite: non videtur ei permissum nisi ut parum ledat." Baldo's sense of the matter certainly does not square with that of the legal anthropologists who would not see any such distinction.

42. Bader, "Arbiter, arbitrator seu amicabilis compositor," 275–76; Ziegler, "Arbiter, arbitrator und amicabilis compositor," 376–81.

43. Sella, *Il procedimento civile,* 206–8. The difference between *arbitrium* and *compromissum* lay in the fact that the latter carried stipulated penalties for a party's failure to follow through.

44. Fowler, "Forms of Arbitration," 143–45.

45. Martone, *Arbiter-arbitrator,* 94 n. 62.

46. Ibid., 133–44.

47. Sella, *Il procedimento civile,* 207–8.

48. Martone, *Arbiter-Arbitrator,* 139–59.

49. Ibid., 18.

50. The most eloquent evocation of the ethos of Renaissance families is Francis William Kent, *Household and Lineage in Renaissance Florence: The Family Life of the Capponi, Ginori, and Rucellai* (Princeton, 1977); see also Jacques Heers, *Family Clans in the Middle Ages,* trans. Barry Herbert (Amsterdam, 1977); and Gene A. Brucker, *Renaissance Florence,* rev. ed. (Berkeley, 1983), chap. 3. On familial conflict, see chapter 5.

51. This touches on a theme in histories of political thought. For now, in relation to legislation, litigation, and humanist rhetoric, see Julius Kirshner and Anthony Molho, "The Dowry Fund and the Marriage Market in Early Quattrocento Florence," *Journal of Modern History* 50 (1978): 435–36; Francesca Klein, "Considerazioni sull'ideologia della città di Firenze tra Trecento e Quattrocento," *Ricerche storiche* 10 (1980): 311–36; and chapter 7.

52. Martone, *Arbiter-Arbitrator,* 161–64.

53. ASF, Statuti del comune 16 (Statuti del Podestà del 1355), fols. 81r–82r. Also cf. *Statuti della repubblica fiorentina,* ed. Romolo Caggese, vol. 2: *Statuto del Podestà dell'anno 1325* (Florence, 1921), 168–69.

54. The terms used by the statute are *securitas* and *satisdatio.* Satisdatio reinforced a basic promise to pay damages and so forth by giving surety (cf. Max Kaser, *Roman Private Law,* 2d ed., trans. Rolf Dannenbring [Durban, 1968], 40).

55. Podestà 1355, fol. 81v: "Et possint dicti arbitri etiam eligere tertium predictum infra dictum tempus si discordes essent, qui tertius per inde habeatur et sit ac si in compromisso facto in eosdem arbitros esset expresse."

56. Martone, *Arbiter-Arbitrator,* 159.

57. Ibid., 147–59.

58. Ibid., 162–63.

59. *Statuta* 1415, 1: 162–64.

60. Also added was the curious provision that no one having six children could be forced to accept a compromise. Both 1355 and 1415 contained a clause to the effect that no *popularis* could be made to act as arbitrator for *magnates,* even if he were related.

61. BNF, Landau-Finaly 98, fols. 171r–75r. Bartolomeo da Saliceto (d. 1412) also had a hand in this first *consilium.*

62. Ibid., fols. 176r–v: "quod ergo a modo fiendum restat, concernit solum iuris executionem, quia de se certum est, et perito potest clare constare ex deductis hinc inde, qualis debeat sequi sententia, ergo non videtur posse allegare a modo questionem vel differentiam superesse inter partes, saltem talem que causare possit compromissum, quia dubietas solum iuris non aprat viam compromisso."

63. Ibid., fols. 176v–77r.

64. This statute ended with the observation, however, that "possit tamen talis in praedictis executionem, usu, allegatione, productione dicti laudi uti iure communi, et eius benefitio" (*Statuta* 1415, 168).

65. Slightly different terms applied to notifying those living outside Florence and outside her territory.

66. Cf. Christiane Klapisch-Zuber, "'Kin, Friends, and Neighbors': The Urban Territory of a Merchant Family in 1400," in her *Women, Family, and Ritual in Renaissance Italy,* trans. Lydia Cochrane (Chicago, 1985), 85–86, which examines in detail *Il libro degli affari proprii di casa di Lapo di Giovanni Niccolini de' Sirigatti,* ed. Christian Bec (Paris, 1969), which will hereafter be cited simply as Niccolini; and examples in Pierre Hurtubise, *Une famille témoin: Les Salviati* (Vatican City, 1985), 50, 85. Also see my *Emancipation in Late Medieval Florence* (New Brunswick, 1982), 72, 105–6, 110–22.

67. Niccolini, 142.

68. Cf. Lauro Martines, *Lawyers and Statecraft in Renaissance Florence* (Princeton, 1968), 406–8; Anna Maria Enriques, "La vendetta nella vita e nella legislazione fiorentina," *Archivio storico italiano* 91 (1933): 85–146, 181–223.

69. Niccolini, 131–32.

70. Ibid., 134.

71. Two examples: "Ricordo chome insino d'aghosto 1483 Ghuido di Francesco Baldovinetti per una parte, Giovanni e Piero di Ghuido Baldovinetti dal' altra parte feciono chonpromesso gienerale in quale chonpromesso si fecie in Ghuido Chanbi nostro parente, e il detto Ghuido Chanbi lodò di ditto mese e anno, e lodò in questo modo che poderi di Chalicharza fussono di Piero e di Giovanni per non divissi, e d'achordo Ghuido e Piero e Giovanni ratifichorno e Ghuido di Francesco Baldovinetti di nuovo donò ogni ragione avessi insu detti poderi e di tutto fu roghato ser Machario di ser Andrea Machalli ista al podestà di Firenze" (ASF, Acquisti e Doni 190/3, Ricordanze di Giovanni di Guido Baldovinetti [1476–96], fol. 13r).

"Onde che poi a dì 2 di dicembre 1409 per buon rispetti e per consiglio del detto ser Vanni, Giovanni di Maffeo sentenziò che il detto Barna non mi potesse chiedere né adomandare parte che gli tochasse o potesse gli pervenire della dota di monna Tessa sua madre e mia donna che fu né eziandio gli usufrutti alla mia vita tanto e piú che tutte chose e ragioni donateli per manceppagione o per altro modo, e non possa adomandare o altri per lui ma debbano ritornare al ceppo e nel mio albitrio e promisa la difesa etc. e non ven'incontro ec. e pienamente sa con ciò in questo effetto di tutto fu rogato il sopradetto ser Matteo Mazetti per ben di Barna e degli altri" (ASF, Manoscritti 77, Vari di casa Curiani, fol. 34v).

72. *Il libro di ricordanze dei Corsini,* ed. Armando Petrucci (Rome, 1965), 75–76. Only in 1428 did Neri finally die, and even then usufruct went to his illegitimate son Sandro by an agreement worked out with Matteo's sons and codified into the form of a *laudum* with two other Corsini as arbiters (ibid., 129).

73. ASF, Carte strozziane, 5th ser., 1750, Ricordanze di Bartolomeo di Tommaso di Federigo Sassetti, fol. 182r: "Ricordo come insino a dì vi di marzo 1436 Federigo di Tommaso Sassetti da una parte e io Bartolomeo dal' altra parte faciemo gienerale conpromesso in Domenicho di Filippo Tochini nostro cognato. . . .

"A dì 19 del detto mese di marzo 1436 il detto Domenicho lodò e giudicò che il podere da Nnobili di detto Federigo fusse di me Bartolomeo, presente il detto Federigo e ciascuno di noi notificò al detto lodo. . . .

"Il detto lodo si diede a cautela perché il detto Federigo avea debito assai in comune per li sue graveze e perché io lo difendessi et cosí feci mentre che io potei e delle volte gli assegnai conto come e sue cose sicome pe' nostri libri vecchi apariscie."

And fol. 204r: "In questo libro 182 e a 183 aparisce nel modo che io ebbi il podere da Nnobili et simile come di poi ancora mi fu confermato per uno lodo dato a dì 31 di luglo 1446, rogato per ser Agnolo di Piero da Terra Nuova, siché non me ne può essere dato piú inpaccio. Bene è vero che Federigo mio fratello me lo volle torre con dire che io avessi promesso di rendeglele a sua posta. Questo non fu mai vero né verisimile, in peró che avendoglele i'ò promesso v'arebbe voluto chiareze di mia mano come velle quando me ne fece carta nel anno 1436, perché io glele salvassi dalle graveze com' apare in questo 182 rogato. . . ."

Interestingly, Sassetti also noted that the property division worked out by arbitration between him and his other brother, Francesco, had to be revised a year later: "per la divisa fatta dirinpetto si restava a chiarire alchuna cosa fra noi" (fol. 181r).

74. *Ricordanze dei Corsini,* 125, 131–32.

75. Niccolini, 107–8.

76. Ibid., 121.

77. Cf. my "*Multorum Fraudibus Occurrere:* Legislation and Jurisprudential Interpretation Concerning Fraud and Liability in Quattrocento Florence," *Studi senesi* 93 (1981): 318, 325–29, 330–32.

78. Martone, *Arbiter-Arbitrator,* 135–36, 144–47.

79. Ibid., 92. Crucial pages presenting his views as given here are: 14–15, 17, 70, 76–79, 88, 107–12.

80. Ibid., 119–20, 166–68.

81. ASF, Notarile antecosimiano G 212, renumbered now as 9040. I have used this same cartulary to investigate another legal institution, the *mundualdus* (cf. Chapter 9). It will be referred to hereafter as Giacomini, with folio numbers and dates.

82. Martone, *Arbiter-Arbitrator,* 90–92, 117–18.

83. Giacomini also, as many other notaries, served as arbitrator, in which case the *lauda* appear in records of other notaries. Cf. Notarile B 491 (1418–26), 11 February 1419 [1420], 20 March 1423 [1424], 31 December 1426.

84. The Latin, from Giacomini, fol. 281v, can be found in the Appendix.

85. The same was true if they were not present at the *compromissum* but it was arranged by an agent with power of attorney (*procurator*).

86. Martone, *Arbiter-Arbitrator,* 68. Martone sees importance in patrimonial and familial terms in the terminological shift from Piacentino's *paterfamilias* to Azo's *vir bonus,* relating to exceptions allowing sons to operate in business without reference to their fathers. Such exceptions, however, had their limits. Cf. my *Emancipation in Late Medieval Florence,* 20–25, 42–48, 123–38, 144–52.

87. Cf. "Conclusion," in *The Settlement of Disputes,* 227.

88. As one situation is, in fact, revealed by a renunciation of arbitration that does not indicate who the arbitrators were to have been, there is a discrepancy between the first and second tables.

89. Giacomini, fols. 320v, 328v–32v (22 and 30 January 1427 [1428]). Other notaries may have encountered more institutional use of arbitration, notably on the part of ecclesiastical institutions. Cf. Notarile F 507 (1418–27), fols. 321v–22v (6 December 1427).

90. Of the eight, those recorded on fols. 2r, 11v–12r, 28r, 82v, 40v–41r, 63v–64v, involved urban folk as one party. On fols. 63v–64v (24 December 1422) Lando di Lorenzo degli Albizzi and his brother Antonio entered arbitration against twenty-nine men of Monte Lupo, with two Florentines as arbitrators. The subsequent *laudum* determined, on a basis not given, that all twenty-nine owed the Albizzi 350 florins and had one month to pay (a discount sum of 322 florins if paid by 10 January). On fol. 82v (13 March 1422 [1423]) Piero di Brancazio Rucellai, Giovanni di Bartolomeo di ser Spinello, and his two sons stood as one party against forty Pratesi, with nine Florentines as arbitrators. No *laudum* for this appears in Giacomini's book. The same parties renewed this *compromissum* a year later, 12 March 1423 [1424] (fol. 156r). The places of rural residence in that year—San Andrea a Botonaccio (twice), Prato, Gangalandi, Castrofiorentino, Monteficalli, Monte Lupo, Campoli indicate that Giacomini traveled north and west of Florence in that year.

91. Most continued to involve at least one Florentine. They include two arbitrations between women and the Camaldolese monastery of San Benedetto (fols. 214v, 217r–18v; 283v, 293r–96r), an arbitration between

Rinaldo and Luca degli Albizzi and seven men of Castro Franco (fols. 320v, 328v–32v). But there are some in which both parties inhabit the same community—Prato, Pistoia (twice), Rapoli—not all of which were truly "rural." For a sense of rural vs. urban in Tuscany, see David Herlihy and Christiane Klapisch-Zuber, *Les toscans et leurs familles* (Paris, 1978), 219–40 (English trans., *Tuscans and Their Families* [New Haven, 1985], 46–59).

92. Three involved business debts, most notably a complex interaction, requiring two arbitrations with different arbitrators, between Lodovico di Piero de' Ricoveri and Giovanni di Francesco Ferrantini—the *laudum* to one of which came one year later (fols. 340r, 403r–9r). Others involved settlement of dowry and inheritance issues (fols. 326v, 327r–28r; 281r–82v; 287r–88r), showing there was some relationship between the parties. One also involved a young man, come of age, recovering funds his *tutor* had loaned out as a dowry (fols. 321r–22r).

93. Giacomini, fols. 142r; 320v, 328v–32v; 283v, 284r–85r; 394v–95v; 438r. Other jurists appearing were Tommaso Salvetti (fol. 2r), Giuliano Davanzati (fols. 281r–82v), and Giovanni Buongirolami (fols. 443r, 447r–v). On all these jurists, see the profiles in Lauro Martines, *Lawyers and Statecraft in Renaissance Florence*.

94. The images, roles, and capacities of women in the Renaissance, and in Florence in particular, have been the object of increasing historical attention. See the relevant essays in Christiane Klapisch-Zuber, *Women, Family, and Ritual in Renaissance Italy*, as well as Manlio Bellomo, *La condizione giuridica della donna in Italia* (Turin, 1970), Julius Kirshner and Anthony Molho, "The Dowry Fund and the Marriage Market," 403–38, and chapters 9 and 10.

95. Giacomini, fols. 150r–51v (27 February 1423 [1424]).

96. Giacomini, fols. 255r–56v (5 August 1426).

97. Cf. Herlihy and Klapisch-Zuber, *Tuscans and Their Families*, 100.

98. Giacomini, fols. 214v, 217r–18v (22 and 31 October 1425). The arbitrator was Averardo, son of the canon lawyer messer Lapo da Castiglionchio.

99. Giacomini, fols. 338v–39v (28 February 1427 [1428]), Marco di Bernardo Bardi against his brothers Matteo and Jeronimo. The arbitrator was Niccolò di Lapo Falconi, who gave all property held in common by the three to Jeronimo. Giacomini, fols. 375r, 376r–v (21 and 26 January 1428 [1429]), contains the arbitration between Bardo di Francesco Bardi and his cousins, Bernardo and Jacopo di Giorgio Bardi. Two arbitrators sought to protect Bardo from the effects of a *fideiussio* for the other two.

100. Giacomini, fols. 258r, 259v–60r (17 and 21 September 1426), 260r–v (21 September). In effect a *podere* passed from daughter to mother to mother's brothers. The reason is not clear, but see the discussion of fraud and collusion below.

101. Giacomini, fols. 449v–50v (15 December 1429), fols. 451v–52v (21 December), 452r (21 December).

102. Giacomini, fols. 11v–12r (13 May 1422), fol. 28r–v (27 June), fol. 34r (31 August).

103. Giacomini, fols. 203v–5r (24 August 1425), fols. 225r–227r (6 January 1425 [1426]), fols. 257v–58r (13 September 1426). Another example from Giacomini is discussed in chapter 5 below.

104. Giacomini, fol. 340r (27 February 1427 [1428]), fols. 403r–9r (25 February 1428 [1429]).

105. Giacomini, fols. 360v, 361r–62r (26 August and 1 September 1428).

106. Giacomini, fols. 59v–61r (30 November 1422). Other examples are: fols. 6v–8v (6 May 1422), and fols. 321r–22r (19 September 1427).

107. Giacomini, fol. 4r (14 April 1422), fols. 12r–17v (14 May).

108. Giacomini, fol. 19r–v (4 June 1422), fols. 20r–24v (12 June).

109. Giacomini, fols. 219r–20v (13 November 1425). Another good example is fols. 250v–52r (3 August 1426), where a large supposed debt between Caterina, widow of messer Giovanni Gherardini, and her son Giovanni was settled immediately by transfering to her name a long list of credits in the son's banking firm. Reproduction of that list so quickly at least shows the settlement was worked out before the parties came to the notary—with or without the arbitrator's help.

110. Cf. my "*Multorum Fraudibus Occurrere,*" 325–32.

111. On this matter, see my *Emancipation,* 20–25, 42–48.

112. Giacomini, fols. 266r–67r (2 January 1426 [1427]).

113. In 1428 an arbitration between a brother and sister similarly reported that he had alienated to her "ad cautelam" a farm that "re vera habebat, tenebat vel possidebat." The (unspecified) reason for that alienation was now gone so ownership was returned to him by the arbitrator (Giacomini, fols. 347v, 380v–81r [18 May and 3 December 1428]).

114. Giacomini, fols. 154r, 155r–56r (5, 8, and 9 March 1423 [1424]), where Rinieri Peruzzi arbitrated between ser Lorenzo d'Antonio Cardi and his mother and determined that she owed her son 300 florins.

115. Giacomini, fol. 416r–v (15 July 1429), fols. 426r–v, 428r–29v (13 August). This case paralleled another in Giacomini's pages discussed in chapter 5.

116. But some of the worst vendettas were those within families. Divisions of patrimonies between siblings, a frequent function for arbitration, might be embroiled in bitterness. Giacomini's *lauda* rely on formulas to the effect that between brothers holding in common "occaxione dicte communicationis lix et questio oriri posset inter dictas partes et volentes materiam scandali tollere . . . " (Giacomini, fols. 219r–20v [13 November 1425]). More expressive of hostility between brothers is this *laudum* from the papers of ser Simone Grazzini: "Imprimis cum inveniamus et nobis constet inter dictas partes fuisse

litem et questionem occasione eorum bonorum, et maxime ex eo quia unus dicebat se deceptum ab altero et alius se multas utilitates et multa commoda domi attulisse, et alius dicebat sibi fructus esse restituendos et multa alia que de facili equa lance diffiniri et discerni non poterant" (Notarile G 616 [1460–62], fols. 123r–24r [20 February 1460 (1462)]).

117. Giacomini, fols. 281r–82v (29 March 1427).

118. Guicciardini, *Maxims and Reflections of a Renaissance Statesman*, trans. Mario Domandi (New York, 1965), 42, 69, 113.

119. Cf. Giacomini, fols. 19v–20r (6 June 1422), fol. 28r–v (27 June 1422), fols. 61r–62r (30 November 1422).

120. Giacomini, fols. 88r–89v (12 April 1423).

121. Giacomini, fols. 279v–80v (24 March 1426 [1427]).

122. As between Amerigo and Gherardo di messer Francesco Rucellai, where Gherardo got the paternal house where Amerigo was living (Giacomini, fol. 351r–v [6 June 1428]).

123. Giacomini, fols. 175r, 182r–v (13 February and 21 March 1424 [1425]). Interestingly, the arbitration text uses singular verbs to describe the second marriage: "Et considerantes quod noviter dicta domina Bice nupta est Tommaso Andree de Minerbectis civi florentino et sibi Tommaso pro dote ipsius domine dare promisit florenos sex centos auri predictos et non habet unde commode satisfacere posset dicta domina. . . ." The language thus implies that *she* arranged the marriage.

124. Giacomini, fols. 253v–54v (2 September 1426). Her aunt Bartolomea, widow of Domenico d'Andrea, was present as her *curatrix* and her brothers'. Following the *laudum,* Angelo, the older brother, made a *finis* regarding Ginevra's *dos* and *alimenta* to Bartolomea. Ginevra had apparently married with the dowry amount unsettled, and the arbitration only made clear that Angelo had to provide it.

125. Giacomini, fols. 179r, 181r–v (4 and 18 March 1424 [1425]).

126. The three arbitrations between unrelated parties seeking return of the dowry were all the work of one set of parties, monna Piera and the priest of San Giorgio de Ruballa, as reported above. One of the "miscellaneous" cases concerned recovering a wife's property by way of her father and mother, but it was nowhere termed *dos*. The other miscellaneous arbitration resulted in an order to go to arbitration again.

127. Giacomini, fols. 219r–20v (13 November 1425). Another example is fols. 52r, 73r–75r (13 November 1422 and 25 September 1425).

128. Giacomini, fols. 40v–41r (16 September 1422).

129. The Manelli case is in Giacomini, fols. 428v (18 August 1429), 431r–32v (3 September). Manelli was caught in Alexandria, "quapropter res et bona dicti Francisci periclitantur et in ruinam incurrunt propter dictam eius absentiam quin ymo potius carcerationem ut dici potest." Therefore, "locus fuit et est propter inopiam dicti Francisci consignationi dotis dicte olim domine Ginevre ut saltim dicte Papera et Tita si ex bonis dicti Francisci ali vel nubi

non possunt substententur et alantur ex bonis et dote dicte earum matris et ex inde dotes pro eis et quolibet earum constituantur." This was covered by transferring to the girls by arbitral order their father's share of the torre dei Manelli in Florence and a *podere*.

130. Giacomini, fols. 375r, 376r–v (21 January 1428 [1429]).

131. Giacomini, fols. 415r–16r (20 July 1429).

132. Giacomini, fols. 453r–54r (6 January 1429 [1430]).

133. Perhaps in a case like that mentioned above (Giacomini, fols. 266r–67r), with Paola, wife of Ridolfo Bardi, and her son Leonardo, the arbitrator was asked to establish the fact of the "debt"—in this case that Leonardo had used his funds to purchase a farm that he placed in her name. But this particular arbitration also has a collusive odor to it, and having the arbitrator establish the debt on paper in the *laudum* may have been a vital part of the collusion.

134. Giacomini, fols. 59v–61r (30 November 1422): "non est iustum atque conveniens quod aliquis ex facto alterius dampnum sentiat atque equissimum esse principalem conservare indempnes fideiussores qui pro eo obligati sunt."

135. Giacomini, fols. 287r–88r (30 April 1427).

136. As Giacomini, fols. 426v–28r (13 August 1429): "Et habito respectu ad statum et paupertatem dictorum Alexandri et Loysii et ad filios parvulos dicti Loysii qui sunt in maxima necessitate propter casus fallimenti et cessationis dicti Loysii. Et viso etiam quod dicta domina Nanna et dictus Laurentius eius vir et Crescius eius socer ex bona caritate quam habent erga dictum Alexandrum et filios dicti Loysii qui sunt parvuli et insontes. . . ."

137. Gene Brucker, *Giovanni and Lusanna: Love and Marriage in Renaissance Florence* (Berkeley, 1986), ix.

138. On these themes, see my comments in "Reading Microhistory: The Example of *Giovanni and Lusanna*," *Journal of Modern History* 61 (1989): 512–34.

139. Giacomini, fols. 373v–74v (2 November 1428). Salvi, like Giovanni, must have been emancipated.

140. Giacomini, fol. 283v (8 April 1427), fols. 293r–96r (29 May 1427). The parties all ratified the *laudum* later, Angnolo on 30 May (fol. 296r–v), Lisa on 2 June (fol. 297r–v), the monks on 16 June (fols. 299r–300r).

141. Giacomini, fols. 6v–8v (6 May 1422).

142. On property ownership vs. possession in this period, see chapter 4.

143. Giacomini, fols. 426v–28r (13 August 1429). Expressions I have in mind are: "plura alia allegabantur que causa brevitatis tacentur" and "alia hinc inde allegabantur que enarrare longum esset."

144. Giacomini, fols. 287r–88r (30 April 1427).

145. Giacomini, fols. 321r–22r (19 September 1427).

146. BNF, Principale, II, iv, 435.

147. Sella, *Il procedimento civile*, 210, notes that the rule was that there

could be no move to arbitration after formal *litis contestatio,* so Bencivenni must have had in mind an exchange of arguments prior to both parties agreeing to leave decision to a designated judge.

148. BNF, Principale, II, iv, 435, fols. 51v–52r.

149. BNF, Principale, II, iv, 435, fol. 53v: "In ver[bum] 'ac si instrumentum guarentigiatum.' Sed instrumentum guarentigiatum non potest executioni mandari in persona debitoris nisi post terminum certum in instrumento contentum et terminus expressus in laudo currit demum a die notificationis ut in precedenti statuto de notificatione laudi. Ergo videtur quod terminus contentus in laudo non sit certus et per consequens debeat fieri requisitio ut instrumento guarentigiato continente terminum incertum, et ita consuluit dominus Nellus in causa fratris cugini Francisci Neri sub aliis terminis. Sed contrarium fuit iudicatum per dominum Andream de Fulgineo collateralem domini Francisci de Ancona, et bene quia terminus laudi est declaratio compromissi guarentigiati."

150. BNF, Panciatichiano 138, fols. 205r–6v.

151. Sella, *Il procedimento civile,* chap. 11, treats the *consilium sapientis* and arbitration in the same chapter.

152. Here the consultative jurist was theoretically neutral, in distinction to composing a *consilium* "pro parte" for use by one party in bolstering its case.

153. The procedure of appointing a judicial (vs. advocatory) *sapiens* and rules governing him were laid out for Florence in the statute "De modo procedendi in civilibus" and others. Also cf. Luigi Lombardi, *Saggio sul diritto giurisprudenziale* (Milan, 1967), 79–199.

154. Cf. Helmholz, *Marriage Litigation in Medieval England* (Cambridge, 1974), 137, 162; Engelman et al., *History of Continental Civil Procedure,* 14–17; Guido Rossi, *Consilium sapientis iudiciale: Studi e ricerche per la storia del processo romano-canonico* (Milan, 1958).

155. In one instance, the parties to a very complex inheritance division enlisted the services of a jurist, Torello Torelli (fl. 1400), as arbitrator to oversee the division. With the aid of the parties and the text of the will in question, Torelli extracted a list of eight legal questions and submitted these to three colleagues, Paolo di Castro, Nello da San Gimignano, and Alessandro Bencivenni. On 10 October 1415 they wrote up a determination, relatively informal compared to a full-fledged *consilium,* and Torelli then simply embraced their findings as his *laudum.*

The case is copied in BNF, Landau Finaly 98, fols. 129r–39r. The three jurists' opinion utilizes legal citations, but it deals successively with the eight issues in a brief manner and without the pro-et-contra style that was so well suited to formal litigation.

156. BNF, Landau Finaly 98, fols. 355r–60r (new numeration). Quote on fol. 355r. This text will be referred to hereafter as Consilium.

157. As spelled out in "De modo procedendi in civilibus" (*Statuta* 1415,

1: 109–115) and Bencivenni's treatment of it, BNF, Principale, II, iv, 435, fols. 1r–9v.

158. Cf. Martines, *Lawyers,* 499, but also 107 and 302.

159. Ibid., 408–9, 416, 420 n. 47.

160. Gene Brucker, *The Civic World of Early Renaissance Florence* (Princeton, 1977), 313 n. 307, 484.

161. Consilium, fol. 356v.

162. Ibid., fol. 357r.

163. Bartolo to D. 4.8.2 (Venice, 1585), fol. 145ra.

164. Ibid., fol. 147rb; Consilium, fol. 357r.

165. Martone, *Arbiter-Arbitrator,* 166–67.

166. Ibid., 168.

167. Paolo di Castro, *Consilia* (Venice, 1580), vol. 1, *cons.* 462, fol. 237ra: "laudum tamquam iniquum, et enormem laesionem continens in dicta parte debet reformari non obstantibus renunciationibus et statutis."

168. Consilium, fol. 357v.

169. Baldo to D. 28.7.7 (Venice, 1577), fol. 102ra.

170. Ibid.

171. Consilium, fol. 358r.

172. Baldo, *Super pace Constantie,* in ver. sententie quoque, in *Super feudis restauratum comentum* (Pavia, 1495), fol. 93vb: "Respondeo tales sententie valent pro rebus compromissis sed extra compromissum non valent etiam si post compromissum nominatim emologetur laudum, nam expresse dicit decretalis quod non potest emologari laudum super quo non procedit compromissum, extra de confir. uti. vel inuti. c. examinata [X. 2.30.7] . . . nam ubi non procedit notio ibi sententia non procedit." Nello almost immediately cites the decretal *Examinata* also: Consilium, fol. 358r.

173. Angelo degli Ubaldi, *Consilia* (Frankfurt, 1575), *cons.* 42, fols. 26vb–28ra, *cons.* 218, fols. 146ra–47va. Angelo did concede latitude to deal with consequences of the resolution of the basic issue, as in setting performative conditions of compliance (*cons.* 42).

The "general" nature of arbitration was relied on, however, by Sallustio Buonguglielmi (1373–1461) and two colleagues in a later case (BNF, Magliabechiano xxix, 193, fols. 172r–78r). There the arbitrators had issued two *lauda,* one establishing a monetary compensation (termed *interesse*) for what seems to have been a murder, the other enjoining both sides to maintain peace. The second *laudum* was affirmed to be in the competence of the arbitrators because all parties were out to preclude vendetta, which had to be presumed (according to the subsequent unsigned *consilium,* fols. 281r–84v, which upheld the first *laudum* but not the second, on the ground that it had not been properly notified to the parties, "secundum comunem usum et comune vivere," persons who had suffered an offense considered vendetta, for not to do so would be to neglect their *fama,* and "qui negligit famam suam est sui interfector unde sicut non sunt domini suorum corporum" [fol. 284r]): "Further these words work the effect that it must be taken as if express mention was made of an article of peace, which is proved not only from the words of the *compromissum* but by reason. . . . it follows that the parties wanted to come into compromise; all of which should be arbitrated as if special mention was made. Therefore virtually it can be said that express mention was made of an article of peace." The establishment of a compensatory sum in the first *laudum* was also upheld: "This interpretation is to be followed as more benign and as favorable in practice to the republic and as avoiding that scandals might multiply, and even as customary in the city of Florence as is asserted to me."

174. Ibid., *cons.* 172, fols. 111rb–va.

175. Bartolo to D. 29.1.24 (Venice, 1581), fol. 140ra–rb.

176. Consilium, fol. 358v.

177. Baldo to D. 28.7.7 (note 99 above) and Bartolo to D. 28.7.8,4 (Venice, 1581), fol. 136va.

178. Consilium, fol. 359r.

179. Ibid.

180. (Venice, 1585), fols. 146va–47rb.

181. Consilium, fol. 359v.

182. Bartolo, fol. 147rb.

183. Consilium, fol. 360v.

184. Angelo, *cons.* 343, ed. cit., fol. 244rb: "quia natura arbitrii hoc est, quod libera arbitrii sit facultas, quam sententiam ferre velit."

185. Nelson, "Dispute Settlement in Carolingian West Francia," takes the opposite opinion as to what sorts of issues were more susceptible to processing in the different procedures. Here I would also point out, however, that this is also a false dichotomy in that one's claim to be a kinsman rests on and is embodied in property. Most any issue could be rendered, however arbitrarily, as a matter of property, so Nelson's distinction between property and relationship, though widely shared in social-legal analysis, is not totally meaningful in the end.

186. The problem with an anthropological approach that looks only at the structure of arbitration or litigation and derives its function therefrom is that it fails to mount a historical perspective, to observe the process work itself out. The process malfunctioned in the case we have been considering, or at least further steps were necessary after arbitration.

187. According to Rene David, *French Law: Its Structure, Sources, and Methodology*, trans. Michael Kindred (Baton Rouge, 1972), 46, arbitration currently precludes appeal based on "errors of law," by which he seems to mean procedural technicalities. The *laudum* Nello overturned was contested on wider issues of right and competence.

188. Sally F. Moore, "Political Meetings and the Simulation of Unanimity: Kilimanjaro, 1973," in *Secular Ritual*, ed. Sally F. Moore and Barbara G.

Myerhoff (Amsterdam, 1977), 153: "Formality in such contexts can convey the message that certain things are socially *unquestionable* (the secular equivalent of the sacred) and by so declaring in such a form, formality helps to make them unquestionable. The public making of choices implies a certain situational uncertainty, a degree of indeterminacy and openness in the social reality. Institutionalizing the settings in which the choices are made, and formalizing them decreases the amount of openness. It 'domesticates' the indeterminate elements in the occasion by surrounding them with fixed forms."

189. Martone, *Arbiter-Arbitrator,* 184: "L'attività dei giureconsulti pratici in questo campo fu in concreto sollecitata da prevalenti e pressanti interessi clientelari. Furono, in definitiva, le esigenze delle parti inadempienti a stimolare una linea interpretativa sempre più lontana dal dettato statutario. Di fronte alla rapidità irrituale imposta dal legislatore cittadino, i giuristi si provarono, così, ad introdurre tutti i gravami e tutte le lungaggini proprie dei riti ordinari."

190. Cf. Norbert Horn, *"Aequitas" in den Lehren des Baldus* (Cologne, 1968); Mario Sbriccoli, *L'interpretazione dello statuto: Contributo allo studio della funzione dei giuristi nell'età comunale* (Milan, 1969).

191. Andrew Arno, "A Grammar of Conflict: Informal Procedure on an Island in Lau, Fiji," in *Access to Justice,* vol. 4: *The Anthropological Perspective: Patterns of Conflict Management: Essays in the Ethnography of Law,* ed. Klaus-Friedrich Koch (Milan, 1979), 44. Also on this theme see John Comaroff and Simon Roberts, "The Invocation of Norms in Dispute Settlement: The Tswana Case," in *Social Anthropology and Law,* ed. Ian Hamnett (London, 1977), 77–112.

192. Cf. Roberts, "The Study of Dispute," 19.

193. Cf. John Comaroff and Simon Roberts, *Rules and Processes: The Cultural Logic of Dispute in an African Context* (Chicago, 1981). They also provide (221–24) an interesting discussion of intrafamilial disputes, especially between brothers, that has some resonance for the case we have discussed here.

194. Wickham, "Land Disputes," 123; see also Wormald, "The Sandlaw Dispute," 205.

195. Cf. Richard L. Kagan, "A Golden Age of Litigation," 145–66; Marc Galanter, "Why the 'Haves' Come Out Ahead: Speculation on the Limits of Legal Change," *Law and Society Review* 9 (1974): 95–160.

196. Comaroff and Roberts, "Invocation of Norms," 82–83.

197. Cf. Lynn Mather and Barbara Yngvesson, "Language, Audience, and the Transformation of Disputes," *Law and Society Review* 15 (1980–81): 775–821.

198. Cf. Miller, "Avoiding Legal Judgment," 101.

199. Ibid., 113–14.

200. Gene Brucker, *Renaissance Florence,* 2d ed. (Berkeley, 1983), 114–15. On the ideology of honor, see chapter 5.

201. Alberti, *De iciarchia,* in *Opere volgari,* ed. Cecil Grayson, 2 vols. (Bari, 1966), 2: 254–55.

202. Koch et al., "Ritual Reconciliation," 269.

203. As in the Machiavelli case analyzed in chapter 2.

204. In the next chapter I look at the case of Oderigo di Credi, which affords one of the few good insights into the potentially crippling costs of litigating in Renaissance Florence.

205. Arno, "A Grammar of Conflict," 43–44.

206. This is not to deny that arbitration was used at times to set the financial terms of spousal separations and, in that regard, came to affect marital status.

207. Cf. Comaroff and Roberts, *Rules and Processes,* 200: "The accepted designation of a kinship bond, in summary, entails a commitment to a specific property relationship and vice versa; the two are perceived as reciprocal, as transformations of each other."

208. Giacomini, fols. 255r–56v (5 September 1426).

209. Comaroff and Roberts, *Rules and Processes,* 138–40. The society they study is decidedly less "legalistic" in its definition of relationships than was any civil and canon law jurisdiction. But there is a more general validity, I think, to their view.

210. Martone, *Arbiter-Arbitrator,* 93–111.

211. Ibid., 130–42.

212. Ibid., 207–10, indicates that in the late sixteenth and seventeenth centuries arbitration allowed too many avenues of appeal to litigation, forestalling the creativity of arbitrators.

Chapter Two

1. On the relationship of anthropology to history and the use of the former in the latter, see Bernard Cohn, "Anthropology and History: The State of Play," *Comparative Studies in Society and History* 22 (1980): 198–221; Sydel Silverman, "On the Uses of History in Anthropology: The *Palio* of Siena," *American Ethnologist* 6 (1979): 413–36; Chris Wickham, "Comprendere il quotidiano: Antropologia sociale e storia sociale," *Quaderni storici* 60 (1985): 839–57.

2. For now, in addition to Cohn, "Anthropology and History," see Julius Kirshner, review of Jack Goody et al., eds. *Family and Inheritance, Journal of Modern History* 50 (1978): 320–22. Critiques of the objectivity of anthropology can be found in Pierre Bourdieu, *Outline of a Theory of Practice,* trans. Richard Nice (Cambridge, 1977), an especially important critique of anthropology's methods and assumptions in fieldwork which indicates that anthropologists' informants are not unbiased, unmotivated, or uninfluenced by the presence of the researcher and his questions. Also Marshall Sahlins, *Culture and Practical Reason* (Chicago, 1976); the essays in Victor W.

Turner and Edward M. Bruner, eds., *The Anthropology of Experience,* (Urbana, 1986); and for legal anthropology, Maureen Cain and Kalman Kulcsar, "Thinking Disputes: An Essay on the Origins of the Dispute Industry," *Law and Society Review* 16 (1981–82): 375–402.

3. This is most evident in a number of essays in *Disputes and Settlements: Law and Human Relations in the West,* ed. John Bossy (Cambridge, 1983), but also in the articles of legal historians like Edward Powell, "Arbitration and Law in England in the Late Middle Ages," *Transactions of the Royal Historical Society,* 5th ser., 33 (1983): 49–67, and "Settlement of Disputes by Arbitration in Fifteenth-Century England," *Law and History Review* 2 (1984): 21–43. He provides an excellent overview of the historical literature. Cf. also William Ian Miller, "Avoiding Legal Judgment: The Submission of Disputes to Arbitration in Medieval Iceland," *American Journal of Legal History* 28 (1984): 95–134.

4. In that dispute-oriented studies are most responsible for development of the notion of process versus structure: cf. Victor Turner, "Process, System, and Symbol: A New Anthropological Synthesis," *Daedalus* 106 (1977): 61–80. Among the best legal anthropology is: Sally Falk Moore, *Law as Process: An Anthropological Approach* (London, 1978); John Comaroff and Simon Roberts, *Rules and Processes: The Cultural Logic of Dispute in an African Context* (Chicago, 1981); Jane F. Collier, "Legal Processes," *Annual Review of Anthropology* 4 (1975): 121–44; Francis G. Snyder, "Anthropology, Dispute Processes and Law: A Critical Introduction," *British Journal of Law and Society* 8 (1981–82): 141–80, which is a very good introduction to the subject and the literature.

5. Classical formulation of dispute and the so-called extended case method belongs to Max Gluckman, "Limitations of the Case-Method in the Study of Tribal Law," *Law and Society Review* 7 (1973): 611–41; see also A. L. Epstein, "The Case Method in the Field of Law," in *The Craft of Social Anthropology,* ed. A. L. Epstein (London, 1967), 205–30; Carol J. Greenhouse, "Looking at Culture, Looking for Rules," *Man,* new series, 17 (1982): 58–73; and the important criticisms of Snyder, "Anthropology, Dispute Processes, and Law," 145–46.

6. Cf. Simon Roberts, *Order and Dispute: An Introduction to Legal Anthropology* (New York, 1979), 52, 168–82.

7. This has been a consistent conceptual theme of a vast literature (and perhaps a conceptual straightjacket): Richard L. Abel, "A Comparative Theory of Dispute Institutions in Society," *Law and Society Review* 8 (1973–74): 217–347, "Theories of Litigation in Society: 'Modern' Dispute Institutions in 'Tribal' Society and 'Tribal' Dispute Institutions in 'Modern' Society as Alternative Legal Forms," *Jahrbuch für Rechtssoziologie und Rechtstheorie* 6 (1979): 165–91, "The Rise of Capitalism and the Transformation of Disputing: From Confrontation over Honor to Competition for Property," *UCLA Law Review* 27 (1979–80): 223–55; P. H. Gulliver, *Disputes and Negotia-*

tions: A Cross-Cultural Perspective (New York, 1979); Katherine S. Newman, *Law and Economic Organization: A Comparative Study of Pre-industrial Societies* (Cambridge, 1983); Carol J. Greenhouse, "Mediation: A Comparative Approach," *Man,* new series, 20 (1985): 90–114; Laura Nader, "Styles of Court Procedure: To Make the Balance," in *Law in Culture and Society,* ed. Laura Nader (Chicago, 1969), 69–91; Vilhelm Aubert, "Law as a Way of Resolving Conflicts: The Case of a Small Industrialized Society," in ibid., 282–303; Klaus-Friedrich Koch, Soraya Altorki, Andrew Arno, and Letitia Hickson, "Ritual Reconciliation and the Obviation of Grievances: A Comparative Study in the Ethnography of Law," *Ethnology* 16 (1977): 269–83; Andrew Arno, "A Grammar of Conflict: Informal Procedure on an Island in Lau, Fiji," in *Access to Justice,* vol. 4: *The Anthropological Perspective: Patterns of Conflict Management: Essays in the Ethnography of Law,* ed. Klaus-Friedrich Koch (Milan, 1979), 41–68, and George E. Marcus, "Litigation, Interpersonal Conflict, and Noble Succession Disputes in the Friendly Islands," in ibid., 69–104. However, Kalman Kulcsar, "Social Aspects of Litigation in Civil Courts," in *Disputes and the Law,* ed. Maureen Cain and Kalman Kulcsar (Budapest, 1983), 85–118, for one, offers a more flexible approach to informal and formal means of resolution and, as always, Snyder, "Anthropology, Dispute Processes, and Law," 148, 155–57, has valuable insights.

8. In addition to those works cited above, in note 2, see Wendy Davies and Paul Fouracre, eds., *The Settlement of Disputes in Early Medieval Europe* (Cambridge, 1986), and the following papers: Osvaldo Raggio, "La politica nella parentela: Conflitti locali e commissari in Liguria orientale (secoli xvi–xvii)," *Quaderni storici* 63 (Dec. 1986): 721–57; Angelo Torre, "Faide, fazioni e partiti, ovvero la ridefinizione della politica nei feudi imperiali delle Langhe tra Sei e Settecento," ibid., 775–810, and Renata Ago, "Conflitti e politica nel feudo: Le compagne romane del Settecento," ibid., 847–74.

9. Cf. Comaroff and Roberts, *Rules and Processes,* 241–49; Ian Hamnett, Introduction, in *Social Anthropology and Law,* ed. Ian Hamnett (London, 1977), 1–13. The denial of special status to law as an analytical construct more recently flows from studies of language and invocation of norms during disputes. That is the core of Comaroff and Roberts' approach, as it is of Andrew Arno, "Structural Communication and Control Communication: An Interactionist Perspective on Legal and Customary Procedures for Conflict Management," *American Anthropologist* 87 (1985): 40–55. Above all, denying special status to law denies the difference between law and politics and asserts that law is inevitably political. This is the view espoused by those in the so-called critical legal studies, as David Kairys, Introduction, in *The Politics of Law: A Progressive Critique,* ed. David Kairys (New York, 1982), 1–7, and many of the articles therein, but also of anthropologists like Roberts, *Order and Dispute,* 182. On the other hand, Clifford Geertz, "Local Knowledge: Fact and Law in Comparative Perspective," in his *Local Knowledge: Further Essays in Interpretive Anthropology* (New York, 1983), 167–234, sees law as a

cultural process, a way of "imagining the real." So he cautions against over-politicizing analyses of legal processes.

10. Snyder, "Anthropology, Dispute Processes, and Law," 153–54.

11. Cf. Arno, "A Grammar of Conflict" and "Structural Communication"; Brenda Danet, "Language in the Legal Process," *Law and Society Review* 14 (1979–80): 445–564.

12. Comaroff and Roberts, *Rules and Processes,* 84–85.

13. The exceptions to this pattern are mainly "microhistories": Gene Brucker, *Giovanni and Lusanna: Love and Marriage in Renaissance Florence* (Berkeley, 1986); Natalie Zemon Davis, *The Return of Martin Guerre* (Cambridge, Mass., 1983); Judith Brown, *Immodest Acts: The Life of a Lesbian Nun in Renaissance Italy* (Oxford, 1985); Carlo Ginzburg, *The Cheese and the Worms: The Cosmos of a Sixteenth-Century Miller,* trans. John and Anne Tedeschi (Baltimore, 1980); Robert C. Palmer, *The Whilton Dispute, 1264–1380: A Social-Legal Study of Dispute Settlement in Medieval England* (Princeton, 1984), which, in comparison to the other works cited here, is much more thoroughly legal.

14. Comaroff and Roberts, *Rules and Processes,* 5–11; Snyder, "Anthropology, Dispute Processes, and Law," 142–44.

15. Cf. Peter Stein, *Legal Institutions: The Development of Dispute Settlement* (London, 1984).

16. Comaroff and Roberts, *Rules and Processes,* 16–17.

17. Snyder, "Anthropology, Dispute Processes, and Law," 163. Legal anthropology can thus fall into an ethnocentric and ahistorical trap (ibid., 163–64).

18. The presence of "legal pluralism" in a society is one of the innovative insights brought by anthropology; but there has been no spelling out of the relation of different legal forms to formal statist law (cf. ibid., 163).

19. On this theme, see Robert Bartlett, *Trial by Fire and Water: The Medieval Judicial Ordeal* (Oxford, 1986), esp. 158–64.

20. On this, see my *Emancipation in Late Medieval Florence* (New Brunswick, 1982), 38–45, and "*Multorum Fraudibus Occurrere:* Legislation and Jurisprudential Interpretation Concerning Fraud and Liability in Quattrocento Florence," *Studi senesi* 93 (1981): 309–50; more generally on Florentine *ricordi,* see Gian-Maria Anselmi, Fulvio Pezzarossa, Luisa Avellini, eds., *La "memoria" dei mercatores: Tendenze ideologiche, ricordanze, artigianato in versi nella Firenze del Quattrocento* (Bologna, 1980).

21. Cf. Anna Maria Enriques, "La vendetta nella vita e nella legislazione fiorentina," *Archivio storico italiano* 91 (1933): 85–146, 181–223. While Enriques saw state-regulated vendetta as an intermediate stage in a political evolution of a still weak state (190) on its way to becoming the all-encompassing state she would know, a conceptually anemic position, still she marshalls much useful evidence in a clear form. See also John Larner, *Italy in the Age of Dante and Petrarch, 1216–1380* (London, 1980), esp. 110–24.

22. Cf. my "Arbitration and Law in Renaissance Florence," *Renaissance and Reformation,* n.s. 11 (1987): 298–319 (incorporated in chapter 1 above); also Jacques Heers, *Family Clans in the Middle Ages: A Study of the Political and Social Structures in Urban Areas,* trans. Barry Herbert (Amsterdam, 1977), 105–7; Luciano Martone, *Arbiter-Arbitrator: Forme di giustizia privata nell'età del diritto comune* (Naples, 1984).

23. Enriques, "La vendetta," 223.

24. For example, Angelo degli Ubaldi, *Consilia* (Frankfurt, 1575), *cons.* 401, fols. 291ra–92rb.

25. Jacob Black-Michaud, *Cohesive Force: Feud in the Mediterranean and the Middle East* (New York, 1975), whose ideas are picked up by Wickham, "Comprendere il quotidiano," 852–53.

26. Leon Battista Alberti, *De iciarchia,* in *Opere volgari,* ed. Cecil Grayson, 2 vols. (Bari, 1966), 2: 254. Also cf. Enriques "La vendetta," 89.

27. Paolo da Certaldo, *Il libro di buoni costumi,* ed. Alfredo Schiaffini (Florence, 1945), 102–3. Further evidence on this theme is offered by Larner, *Italy in the Age of Dante and Petrarch,* 103–4. Heers, *Family Clans,* 108–9, corroborates this point, although he concludes that this lack of calculation and proportion demonstrates the lack of "even the most rudimentary code of honour." At the least this is a poor choice of words, for it was precisely a sense of honor that animated vendettas.

28. Reported in Francis William and Dale V. Kent, *Neighbours and Neighbourhood in Renaissance Florence* (Locust Valley, 1982), 49.

29. Paolo da Certaldo, *Libro di buoni costumi,* 159. See also Larner, *Italy in the Age of Dante and Petrarch,* 103.

30. Gene Brucker, *Renaissance Florence,* rev. ed. (Berkeley, 1983), 91–92, nuances his account of vendetta with the observation that the solidarity of powerful families provided vital support to individuals while giving pause to their enemies. Still, he indicates that "vendetta was slowly disappearing as a social institution" (92) and this development was accompanied by a "weakening" of familial bonds (98–99, 113) and increasing use and prominence of law and lawyers (102). He concludes generally that the patricians "learned to restrain their violent impulses over the course of the fifteenth century" (116). In his *The Society of Renaissance Florence: A Documentary Study* (New York, 1971), a collection of documents he used in writing *Renaissance Florence* (first published in 1969), Brucker seems to substantiate this trend in Florentine history when he labels the peaceful settlement in 1420 of a quarrel involving Antonio Rustichi "The Decline of the Vendetta" (119–20). Certainly Rustichi's willingness to settle for a public apology contrasts to the premeditated murder of revenge undertaken by Luca da Panzano in the previous selection (116–19, which is Carlo Carnesecchi, "Un fiorentino del secolo xv e le sue ricordanze domestiche," *Archivio storico italiano,* 5th series, 4 [1889]: 149–53). But terming Rustichi's response a "decline" of vendetta is, I think, misleading. For one thing, Luca da Panzano's bloody revenge

occurred in the same year and it is methodologically dubious to call it, as Brucker did, a relic of "a more primitive and uninhibited past" (*Renaissance Florence,* 117). Luca's own ancestors had concluded a *pace* after a long vendetta with their mortal enemies the Quaratesi as far back as 1395 (cf. Carnesecchi, 169–70), showing that making peace was simply part of the process of vendetta and not indicative of its "decline."

Secondly, Antonio Rustichi was by no means forgoing revenge. To cite from Brucker's own translation: "My relatives thought that this was a greater revenge than if we had assaulted him" (119–20). Brucker also notes (*Renaissance Florence,* 115) that the public apology was a "humiliation" that "more than compensated" Rustichi for his loss. The same Rustichi, says Brucker, "like many of his neighbors, thrived on lawsuits" (ibid., 114). A weighing of the costs of violence, lawsuit, and other means of settlement seems to have gone on. If, as Brucker maintains with some justification, there was less recourse to violence, it would seem to have been not because the impulse was not present but that the costs were too high relative to alternatives.

31. Cf. Enriques, "La vendetta," 98–102, 183.

32. Brucker, *Renaissance Florence,* 117. Yet even in the fourteenth century Paolo da Certaldo could give the general advice that peace was better than vendetta (*Libro di buoni costumi,* 205–6).

33. Marc A. Galanter, "Why the 'Haves' Come Out Ahead: Speculation on the Limits of Legal Change," *Law and Society Review* 9 (1974): 95–160.

34. See the previous chapter and the literature cited pertaining to the history of legal procedure.

35. Alberti, *De iciarchia,* 254–55.

36. Giovanni Boccaccio, *The Decameron,* trans. G. H. McWilliam (Harmondsworth 1972), Third Day, Seventh Tale; see also Eighth Day, Fifth Tale, in which a venal judge is "exposed" by some young pranksters.

37. Brucker, *Renaissance Florence,* 147–51.

38. Alberti, *De iciarchia,* 262–63.

39. Lauro Martines, *Lawyers and Statecraft in Renaissance Florence* (Princeton, 1968), 130–31.

40. Paolo da Certaldo, *Libro di buoni costumi,* 109–10, found it necessary to advise that one conduct himself honestly as a judge, rather than incur the enmities and penalties that would result. His advice may well have spoken to common practice.

41. Francesco Guicciardini, *Ricordi,* English translation as *Maxims and Reflections of a Renaissance Statesman,* trans. Mario Domandi (New York, 1965), 170–71.

42. Ibid., 69–70. This sense of the particularity of events became one of the central tenets of his approach to history in his most famous writings.

43. Ibid., 94–95. On the professional reasons for this tendency, see Luigi Lombardi, *Saggio sul diritto giurisprudenziale* (Milan, 1967).

44. Guicciardini, *Maxims,* 95 and 112.

45. Cf. Martines, *Lawyers,* 138, 163.

46. Guicciardini, *Maxims,* 124.

47. *Il libro degli affari proprii di casa di Lapo di Giovanni Niccolini de'*
Sirigatti, ed. Christian Bec (Paris, 1969), 141–43, 148–49. The description
of this arbitrator, ser Antonio di Niccolò di ser Pierozzo, with whom Lapo
had frequent dealings, as a friend occurs on 130. These events took place in
1418. On Lapo and his relations with kin and friends, see Christiane Klapisch-
Zuber, "Parenti, amici, vicini: Il territorio urbano d'una famiglia mercantile
nel xv secolo," *Quaderni storici* 33 (1976): 953–82, now translated in
Women, Family, and Ritual in Renaissance Italy, trans. Lydia Cochrane (Chicago, 1985), 68–93.

48. *Libro di Lapo Niccolini,* 125–28, detailing events of 1415.

49. See the previous chapter.

50. *Il libro di ricordanze dei Corsini,* ed Armando Petrucci (Rome, 1965),
42–44, 75–76.

51. Giovanni di Pagolo Morelli, *Ricordi,* ed. Vittore Branca (Florence,
1956), 154–55.

52. Brucker ed., *The Society of Renaissance Florence,* 218–22, this being .
Bernardo Machiavelli, *Libro di ricordi,* ed. Cesare Olschki (Florence, 1954),
15–23. Brucker's labeling treats this servant's pregnancy as an example of the
mistreatment of one of the *popolo minuto* by one of the *grassi.*

53. He also informed Niccolò that Giovanni wanted to speak with him.
Brucker, *Society of Renaissance Florence,* 219, renders this as the two Nelli
agreeing to talk with Niccolò, when the original clearly indicates "mi dissono
che trovassi Nicolò" (17).

54. The final clause containing the threat of paternal vendetta against
Niccolò was omitted by Brucker without ellipses in his translation.

55. The reference to a wife and "le sirocchie" is elliptical. Perhaps it means
he already had the shame of other women to worry about; perhaps it means
he bore a greater weight from those responsibilities and so could not feel the
weight of concern for a servant girl.

56. Machiavelli himself leaves a fuzzy chronology because he inserts November instead of October (which must be meant because he speaks of the
31st) in the first entry. This may also be an editorial mistake; I have not
consulted the manuscript.

57. Niccolò was also supposed to retrieve the *Monte* dowry Bernardo had
established for the girl and return the principal to Bernardo.

58. As reported in *Ricordi,* 35.

59. Machiavelli's inclusion of the incident in his *ricordi* likewise can be
seen as a claim to vindication of honor to be seen by his sons or other descendants who might read of it.

60. On the metaphoric status of the *casa,* see Julius Kirshner, *Pursuing*
Honor while Avoiding Sin: The Monte delle doti of Florence (Milan, 1978),
6–8.

61. Cf. Max Kaser, *Roman Private Law,* 2d ed., trans. Rolf Dannenbring (Durban, 1968), 152–54, 215; Barry Nicholas, *An Introduction to Roman Law* (Oxford, 1962), 215–22.

62. The semantic range of this term is much richer in a culture of honor: cf. J. Davis, *People of the Mediterranean: An Essay in Comparative Social Anthropology* (London, 1977), 89–101; J. G. Peristiany, ed., *Honour and Shame: The Values of Mediterranean Society* (Chicago, 1966).

63. What follows relies on the printed sections of Oderigo's *ricordanze* published by F. Polidori, "Ricordanze di Oderigo d'Andrea di Credi orafo, cittadino fiorentino, dal 1405 al 1425," *Archivio storico italiano,* 1st ser., 4 (1843): 53–110.

64. And as he elsewhere termed it (63) "cautamente sotto coverta," the same term used years later by Bernardo Machiavelli.

65. Jurists, however, could find ways around this statute. See chapter 10.

66. Cf. Francis William Kent, *Household and Lineage in Renaissance Florence: The Family Life of the Capponi, Ginori, and Rucellai* (Princeton, 1977), 124–49.

67. Cf. Comaroff and Roberts, *Rules and Processes,* 200. Florentine society, however, in contrast to the African context they studied, allowed jural prescription of relationships in advance of interaction to a good degree; but even for Florentines kinship had to be acted on to be socially meaningful.

68. "Ricordanze," 55–57.

69. This procedure is detailed in the statutes (Podestà 1355, fols. 72v–73v), and see chapter 3.

70. On the Sei and communal finances, see Anthony Molho, *Florentine Public Finances in the Early Renaissance, 1400–1433* (Cambridge, Mass., 1971), esp. 105–6. Also see David Herlihy and Christiane Klapisch-Zuber, *Les toscans et leurs familles* (Paris, 1978), 17–47; Charles de la Roncière, "Indirect Taxes or 'Gabelles' at Florence in the Fourteenth Century," in *Florentine Studies,* ed. Nicolai Rubinstein (London, 1968), 140–92.

71. With a legalistic thoroughness characteristic of his comportment in the affair, Oderigo lists the names of all the Sei and the notary.

72. Cf. Martines, *Lawyers,* 499.

73. This rationale and its counter are given later when Oderigo lists his expenses, for he clearly sees these children now becoming his problem: "Sicché ogni volta che fia di bisogno, come penso verrà ancora il caso, che a Dio piaccia sia tosto, mostreremo a Niccolò le falsità sue; e com'egli ha rubato Nofri e' figliuoli; e che non bisognava ch'i' dessi fiorini 20 per l'amore di Dio a chi n'avea di suo patrimonio piú di me. Fonne questa memoria per averlo sempre a mente, o chi di me romanesse, acciò che sappiano e possino mostrare le cattività di Niccolò, per qualunche caso bisognasse . . . pregando ciascuno, che, per l'amore di Dio e della ragione, chi dopo a me rimanesse, che sempre a ogni bisogno de' figliuoli di Nofri di Simone degli Agli, il quale ha nome Nanni e la femina Lora, gli debbino appresentare, concedere e prestare contro

a Niccolò di Lotto, in qualunche luogo di giudicio bisognasse, o caso accadesse" ("Ricordanze," 66–67).

74. "Ricordanze," 58: "e l'uficio loro non dà ch'eglino condannino persona, ma vendino de' beni di chi ha dare al Comune."

75. The numbers do not add up. It seems that, although the usually cited rate is 77 soldi di piccioli to the florin in 1405, Oderigo used 71 soldi to the florin. But that does not work out all the time, unless the transcriptions are in error. Using his 71 florins, the sum is 63 florins, 1 *lira*, 1 1/2 soldi. On the Florentine currency and moneys of account, see Carlo M. Cipolla, *The Monetary Policy of Fourteenth-Century Florence* (Berkeley, 1982).

76. ASF, Catasto 67, fols. 409v–10r. His assets total 765 florins, his debts total 391 (250 owed to his widowed sister) plus 1,000 for five *bocche*. There is no mention of sums owed to or from any of the Agli. The only house mentioned, which he had rented out, was in San Frediano, not the Agli neighborhood of San Michele Berteldi. Niccolò di Lotto degli Agli does not appear in the 1427 *catasto*.

77. BNF, Magliabechiano xxix, 174, fol. 185v: "Hereditatem maternam non aditam an filius transmictat ad filios videtur primo quod sic per casum l. penult. C. de legiptimis heredi. ubi dicitur quod queritur filiis ipso iure. Contrarium est verum quod non transmictitur et ita determinat expresse Bar. in l. ventre ff. de adquiren. her. per casum l. ii C. ad orfici., et per novellam § in novissimo de lege unica C. de cadu. toll. ad l. pe. C. de legip. heredi., respondet Bar. in loco preallegato quod filius succedit matri ipso iure. Intelligitur ipso iure scilicet si adeatur ab homine sicuti dicimus in compensatione ut C. de compensa. l. ii est ergo conclusio secundum Bar. quod hereditas matris non adita non transmictitur." This document, a copy from which headings, information, and signature were omitted, may in fact be an *allegatio pro parte* rather than a formal *consilium*. Still it shows this jurist at work in a setting of litigation. This manuscript contains some of the few extant examples of Antonio da Romena's work.

78. Simon Roberts, "The Study of Dispute: Anthropological Perspectives," in *Disputes and Settlements,* 20–22. Roberts' piece is an excellent introduction to legal anthropology for an audience of historians.

79. Brucker, *Renaissance Florence,* 140–42, reports on a similar prolonged dispute in 1381 and its politicization once beyond the courts. In a social scientific vein, see Jacek Kurczewski, "Dispute and Its Settlement," in *Disputes and the Law,* ed. Maureen Cain and Kalman Kulcsar (Budapest, 1983), 223–45.

80. Leon Battista Alberti, *The Family in Renaissance Florence,* trans. Renée Neu Watkins (Columbia, S.C., 1969), 118. The context of this statement is the first obtaining of a dowry, with the advice being that a smaller sum paid up front is better than a promise of a greater sum.

81. It is precisely here that the services of *procuratores* like ser Guido and of jurists like Antonio da Romena were most useful. This theme I have devel-

oped in other work: cf. *Emancipation in Late Medieval Florence*, 127–52; and chapters 3 and 10 below. For a succinct anthropological perspective on this issue, cf. John Comaroff and Simon Roberts, "The Invocation of Norms in Dispute Settlement: The Tswana Case," in *Social Anthropology and Law*, ed. Ian Hamnett (London, 1977), 77–112.

82. William L. F. Felstiner, Richard L. Abel, Austin Sarat, "The Emergence and Transformation of Disputes: Naming, Blaming, Claiming . . . ," *Law and Society Review* 15 (1980–81): 643.

83. So we are not left, as a simple process-oriented approach would have it, with maximizing actors looking to the material results of their transactions.

84. Conclusion, in Davies and Fouracre, eds., *The Settlement of Disputes in Early Medieval Europe*, 234.

85. Cf. ibid., 240.

Chapter Three

1. Hans Baron, "Franciscan Poverty and Civic Wealth as Factors in the Rise of Humanistic Thought," *Speculum* 13 (1938): 23. Too many pages would be needed to list all the studies that touch on humanistic views of property in light of Baron's work. Interesting treatments are: Walter Ullmann, *The Individual and Society in the Middle Ages* (Baltimore, 1966), 132–42; Lauro Martines, *Power and Imagination: City-States in Renaissance Italy* (New York, 1979), 211–17; Richard A. Goldthwaite, *The Building of Renaissance Florence* (Baltimore, 1980), 67–112; and Riccardo Fubini, "Poggio Bracciolini e San Bernardino: Temi e motivi di una polemica," in *Atti del simposio internazionale cateriniano-bernardiniano*, ed. Domenico Maffei and Paolo Nardi (Siena, 1982), 509–40.

2. Important are the following: Gene Brucker, *The Civic World of Early Renaissance Florence* (Princeton, 1977); David Herlihy and Christiane Klapisch-Zuber, *Les toscans et leurs familles* (Paris, 1978), chapters 1–3; Dale Kent, *The Rise of the Medici: Faction in Florence, 1426–1434* (Oxford, 1978); Nicolai Rubinstein, *The Government of Florence under the Medici (1434–1494)* (Oxford, 1965); Anthony Molho, *Florentine Public Finances in the Early Renaissance* (Cambridge, Mass., 1971); Lauro Martines, *The Social World of the Florentine Humanists, 1390–1460* (Princeton, 1963) and *Lawyers and Statecraft in Renaissance Florence* (Princeton, 1968); John M. Najemy, *Corporatism and Consensus in Florentine Electoral Politics, 1280–1400* (Chapel Hill, 1982); Alberto Tenenti, *Firenze dal Comune a Lorenzo il Magnifico, 1350–1494* (Milan, 1970).

3. In addition to the works cited in the previous note, Thomas Kuehn, *Emancipation in Late Medieval Florence* (New Brunswick, 1982), 37–39; Julius Kirshner and Anthony Molho, "The Dowry Fund and the Marriage Market in Early Quattrocento Florence," *Journal of Modern History* 50 (1978): 403–38; Thomas Kuehn, "*Multorum Fraudibus Occurrere:* Legisla-

tion and Jurisprudential Interpretation Concerning Fraud and Liability in Quattrocento Florence," *Studi senesi* 93 (1981): 314–25.

4. See below

5. BNF, Landau-Finaly 98, fols. 403r–14v, containing the formal original with seals and signatures. It is reproduced in the Appendix to the first version of this chapter, published in *Quaderni fiorentini per la storia del pensiero giuridico moderno* 14 (1985). This document will hereafter be referred to simply as Consilium.

6. ASF, Notarile antecosimiano G212 (1422–30), fols. 200r–v, edited in my "Women, Marriage, and *Patria Potestas* in Late Medieval Florence," *Tijdschrift voor Rechtsgeschiedenis* 49 (1981): 145–46, where it appears as an example of the use of a married woman by her father. This action is also reported in Consilium, fol. 408r. For an explanation of the emancipation gift, see *Emancipation*, 18–19.

7. ASF, Notarile G212, fol. 200v.

8. Consilium, fols. 408r–v.

9. The following discussion of the property's history is based on Consilium, fols. 408r–9r.

10. ASF, Notarile G212, fol. 200r. Cantini may have been related to Giovanni Cantini who had stood surety on the 1358 arbitration.

11. Information on Cantini's marriage and death comes from ASF, Notarile G212, fols. 269v–70v—about which document more will be said below.

12. Consilium, fol. 409v.

13. Quoted in Kent, *The Rise of the Medici*, 78.

14. Ibid., 51, 148, 170. The name Adimari occurs in the following notarial records: G212 (1422–29), fol. 360r; G212 (1430–32), fol. 18v; A672 (1432–40), fols. 294r–97v; A673 (1436–40), fols. 110v–12r.

15. Kent, *The Rise of the Medici*, 55, 60, 89, 174, 233, 316–17, 353.

16. In addition to information on the Bardi to be considered below, there are the following facts: Bardo di Francesco di messer Alessandro and Paolo di Giovanni d'Andrea Bardi were witnesses to the emancipation on 3 July 1425. Grezzo di Francesco and Andrea di Lipaccio Bardi, along with Giuliano di Francesco Sergini, witnessed the marriage vows six days later. Bernardo di Ciandrello and Paolo di Giovanni d'Andrea Bardi served as witnesses at the second emancipation of Checcha the following March, along with ser Niccolò Tinucci. Bandino di Buonaccorso Boscoli and Francesco di Tommaso de' Medici would be witnesses for Fraschi on 14 January 1427. Finally, Fraschi would name as his *procuratores* (temporarily) his son-in-law and Andrea and Larione di Lippaccio Bardi. Andrea and Larione Bardi would become supporters of the Medici (Kent, *Rise of the Medici*, 40n, 73, 292, 314–15, 352) and had old business ties with them, while Bardo di Francesco, who had business ties to the Medici in the 1420s, would appear among their enemies in 1434 (ibid., 166–67, 355). Ser Niccolò Tinucci was another Medici *amico*

who used his inside information on governmental operations to aid his patrons (ibid., 228–33, 354). Bardo, Andrea, and Larione Bardi commanded considerable wealth (Martines, *Social World*, 375–76).

17. Thus his Adimari connections were missed in the first (published) version of this paper, as was his marital connection to the Bardi, because it emerged clearly only in documentation uncovered later. It was as Fraschi that his son and descendants would be known. It may be that the cognomen he adopted derived from Franceschi (del Corso), a name taken by one Adimari branch when it became *popolano* in the 1380s. On name changes by magnate families in Florence, see Christiane Klapisch-Zuber, "Ruptures de parenté et changements d'identité chez les magnats florentins du xiv^c siècle," *Annales* 43 (1988): 1205–40.

18. ASF, Catasto 79, fols. 421v–22r. The total value of the farms, their fruits, the *Monte* credits, and other assets was given as 1,224 florins, 14 soldi, 5 denari. The only dependent Fraschi listed was his forty-eight-year-old wife Antonia. His marriage to her must have occurred about the time he returned to Florence after his eighteen-year absence, around 1398.

19. Kent, *Rise of the Medici*, 73, 167, 352.

20. Tani's assessed wealth placed him among the 600 wealthiest men in Florence in 1427 (cf. Martines, *Social World*, 371). He had been employed in the Rome branch of the Medici bank in 1402 with a salary of 40 florins (Raymond de Roover, *The Rise and Decline of the Medici Bank, 1397–1494* [Cambridge, Mass., 1963], 44). Tani's sons were active in trade and banking in the mid-fifteenth century, gaining substantial if not spectacular fortunes (ibid., 60, 87, 342, 344; and Martines, *Social World*, 136–37).

21. Cf. ASF, Notarile A672 (1432–40), fols. 294r–97v; A673 (1436–40), fols. 110v–12r; Kent, *Rise of the Medici*, 328, 335.

22. In the records of the *Conservatori delle Leggi* Fraschi's year of birth was given as 1365, making him sixty in 1425. But in the *catasto* two years later his age was given as sixty-four.

23. ASF, Notarile G212 (Testamenti, 1411–31), fol. 133r–v (1 May 1427), on which more below.

24. Examples of this practice in Martines, *Social World*, 120, and in chapter 8 below. In fact, in 1428, Fraschi appointed Tani and Andrea and Larione Bardi as his *procuratores* to settle a variety of his affairs, including those with the *Monte comune* and others, even after his death. Though he later revoked these appointments, they reveal a concern about his financial state. Cf. ASF, Notarile G212 (1422–29), fol. 360r.

25. As Checcha was a relatively old twenty-five at her marriage, and there is no firm evidence there were other children, the house may have been part of the dowry, despite the general preference among Florentines and others to keep real property in male hands.

26. Even with the house and a further settlement in his favor, the *catasto*

found his assets (f. 1689.0.1) less than his obligations (f. 1973.7.10), putting him f. 274.6.9 in arrears. That does not mean, however, that his situation was thoroughly desperate.

27. Important here is Francis William Kent, *Household and Lineage in Renaissance Florence: The Family Life of the Capponi, Ginori, and Rucellai* (Princeton, 1977), 125–49; also Richard Goldthwaite, *Private Wealth in Renaissance Florence* (Princeton, 1968), 270–71.

28. F. W. Kent, "Lorenzo de' Medici's Acquisition of Poggio a Caiano in 1474 and an Early Reference to His Architectural Expertise," *Journal of the Warburg and Courtauld Institutes* 42 (1979): 250–52. "Bardo di Lorenzo di Palla Strozzi was to take the view in 1496 that Poggio a Caiano, 'la nostra antichia', was still not Medici property which could be sold forcibly to strangers by the commune after the downfall of Piero in 1494"—even though it had been sold to them in 1477 by Giovanni Rucellai, who had first assembled the property with the approval of the exiled Palla Strozzi, "who was determined to win back, even indirectly, this prized property and certain other of his estates which had fallen into alien hands" (252). Also Kent's "Palaces, Politics and Society in Fifteenth-Century Florence," *I Tatti Studies: Essays in the Renaissance* 2 (1987): 41–70.

29. Jacob Black-Michaud, *Cohesive Force: Feud in the Mediterranean and the Middle East* (New York, 1975), esp. 24–27, 74–85, 93–103, 141–45, 172–207, 237–41. Anna Maria Enriques, "La vendetta nella vita e nella legislazione fiorentina," *Archivio storico italiano* 91 (1933): 85–146, 181–223.

30. Paolo da Certaldo, *Il libro di buoni costumi,* ed. Alfredo Schiaffini (Florence, 1945), 102–3, and his advice about property, 144–45: "Quando comperi possessioni, fa d'avere buoni mallevadori e sicuri, e le parole di donne e fanciulle o fanciulli de la casa, o d'altri stretti parenti, si che'nganno non ne potessi ricevere doppo la morte del venditore." Leon Battista Alberti, *I libri della famiglia,* ed. Ruggiero Romano and Alberto Tenenti (Turin, 1969), 402: "'Da ogni parte s'apre luogo a vendicarsi . . . purché tu aspetti el tempo.'"

31. See Giovanni Sercambi, *Novelle,* ed. Giovanni Sinicropi, 2 vols. (Bari, 1972), 522–23, 632–35; and Boccaccio, *Decameron,* Eighth Day, 7th and 10th tales.

32. Cf. ASF, Notarile, A680 (1459–62), fols. 187v–88r (16 February 1459 [1460]), where one finds a "domina Pippa vidua filia condam Francisci Cantini de Aldimaribus de Florentia."

33. ASF, Catasto 78, fols. 129v–31r.

34. Such manipulation of the law is most evident in Florentine *ricordi.* Note, for example, *Il libro di ricordanze dei Corsini,* ed. Armando Petrucci (Rome, 1965), 111–12, where (on the theme of possession as distinct from ownership) Giovanni di Matteo Corsini kept title to property bought in fact for his brother Niccolò.

35. At the statutory rate of 5 percent, with the surplus counted against the principal, Cantini (according to ser Loisio) had realized over 400 florins against the 350-florin dowry debt (Consilium, fol. 408v). The total was, in fact, close to 500 florins.

36. *De precepto de disgombrando*, in *Statuta* 1415, 1: 152–56 (Book 2, rubric 58), reproduced with no significant variations in Consilium, fols. 405r–7r. The version of 1355 is also reproduced in Consilium, fols. 404r–v, corresponding to Podestà 1355, fols. 72v–73v (Book 2, rubric 12).

37. These were the terms of the 1415 statute, which seem to back off from the 1355 statute's emphasis on title alone: "nec sufficiat solum allegare se possidere vel tenere pro se vel alio, sed titulum assignare ac probare debeat quare dimictere et disgombrare non debeat. . . ."

38. Her nephews figured among the wealthiest citizens of Florence in 1427 (cf. Martines, *Social World*, 376).

39. Consilium, fol. 408v.

40. Consilium, fols. 408v–9v.

41. ASF, Provvisioni registri 111, fols. 238r–39r; on which see Kuehn, *Emancipation*, 37–38. Archival documents support ser Davanzato. There is no entry for the emancipation of 3 July 1425 in ASF, Notificazioni di atti di emancipazione 1. However there is an entry in the registry kept by the Mercanzia: Mercanzia 10820bis, fol. 106v (7 July 1425).

42. Paolo Grossi, *Le situazioni reali nell' esperienza giuridica medievale* (Padua, 1968), 180. See also his "Usus facti: La nozione di proprietà nella inaugurazione dell'età nuova," *Quaderni fiorentini per la storia del pensiero giuridico moderno* 1 (1972): 302. These studies were preliminary to Grossi's landmark book, *"Un altro modo di possedere": L'emersione di forme alternative di proprietà alla coscienza giuridica postunitaria*, Per la Storia del Pensiero Giuridico Moderno 5 (Milan, 1977); English translation as *An Alternative to Private Property: Collective Property in the Judicial Consciousness of the Nineteenth Century*, trans. Lydia G. Cochrane (Chicago, 1981). His analysis, which avoids "the twin perils of idealist reductionism and mechanical materialism" (Julius Kirshner, Foreword, in *An Alternative to Private Property*, viii), provides an excellent framework for understanding the Florentine lawsuit. Grossi's historical account differs markedly from that of Charles Donahue Jr., "The Future of the Concept of Property Predicted from Its Past," in *Property*, ed. J. Roland Pennock and John W. Chapman (New York, 1980), 28–68, which offers a metahistorical position on the logic of property (esp. 45).

43. Grossi, *Situazioni reali*, 201, 205–6. For a succinct presentation of Grossi's views, see Kirshner, Foreword, in *An Alternative*, viii–ix, and his review of *Un altro modo di possedere* in the *American Journal of Legal History* 22 (1978): 342–46. A recent analysis of property within feudal relations, with relevant insights for this chapter, is Stephen D. White, *Custom, Kinship, and Gifts to Saints: The Laudatio Parentum in Western France, 1050–1150* (Chapel Hill: University of North Carolina Press, 1988), esp. 14–15, 139–42.

44. Grossi, *Un altro modo,* 379–80. As the phrase indicates, Grossi's analysis shares a great deal with that of C. B. Macpherson, *The Political Theory of Possessive Individualism* (Oxford, 1962) and *Property: Mainstream and Critical Positions,* ed. C. B. Macpherson (Toronto, 1978), 1–13, 199–207; and Michael E. Tigar with Madeleine R. Levy, *Law and the Rise of Capitalism* (New York, 1977), 197–206. But see also Donahue, "Future of the Concept of Property," 38–41. See also Otto Kahn-Freund, Introduction, in Karl Renner, *The Institutions of Private Law and Their Social Function,* trans. Agnes Schwarzschild (London, 1949), 22–23.

45. Grossi, *Situazioni reali,* 26–28. Also on the Roman notion of *dominium,* see Barry Nicholas, *An Introduction to Roman Law* (Oxford, 1962), 153–57; and, with an interesting presentation of distinctions between Roman and Anglo-Saxon common law, W. W. Buckland and Arnold D. McNair, *Roman Law and Common Law: A Comparison in Outline,* 2d ed. rev. F. H. Lawson (Cambridge, 1952), 62–82.

46. On the origins of the concept, Robert Feenstra, "Les origines du *dominium utile* chez les glossateurs (avec un appendice concernant l'opinion des Ultramontani)," in *Fata iuris romani: Etudes d'histoire du droit* (Leyden, 1974), 215–59. The characterization of *dominium utile* is drawn from Paolo Grossi, *"Locatio ad longum tempus": Locazione e rapporti reali di godimento nella problematica del diritto comune* (Naples, 1963), 18–19, 141–43, 155–56; idem, *Situazioni reali,* 173, 187–88: "Il dominio utile è caratterizzato da un elemento di godimento che ha una sua autonomia rispetto al proprietario formale del bene: o è l'ordinamento che costruisce, mediante rapporto a lunga durata, intorno al concessionario una sfera sufficientemente larga di poteri . . . o è la semplice durata del rapporto che, rendendo effettiva una situazione di fatto sul bene, gli conferisce per ciò stesso autonomia. . . .

"L'incidenza del tempo come fattore alterativo di situazioni giuridiche, la sua qualità di essere nel campo del reale strumento di partecipazione fra soggetto e cosa sono dati ricorrenti e riemergenti. . . ."

47. Grossi, *"Locatio ad longum tempus",* 64–77.

48. In reaction, several jurists, notably Baldo, declared that *dominium utile* was the only true ownership (cf. Feenstra, 258–59).

49. Bartolo to D. 41.2.17,1, *Si quis vi* § *differentia, De acquirenda possessione* (quoted in Grossi, *Situazioni reali,* 194–95 n. 31): "Quaero utrum utile dominium sit unicum vel plura? Respondeo: plura. Unum quod opponitur et contradicit vero dominio et est illud quod quaeritur ex prescriptione. . . . Aliud quod verum directum dominium recognoscit et est illud quod competit emphyteutae et superficiario et similibus."

50. Grossi, *Situazioni reali,* 188–89, notes that *usucapio,* on the other hand, was seen as "favorabilis." *Usucapio,* in contrast to prescription, concerned only *mobilia,* and resulted in full *dominium.* It was real property, then (such as the house in this dispute), that inhered in the owner's personality, and prescription of real property did not, strictly speaking, result in *domin-*

ium. Keeping to the sense of *dominium* in the Justinianic texts, but seeking to describe the right on which the action in prescription presumably rested, Bulgaro coined the term *effectus dominii*. Later Azo and Accursio applied the term *dominium utile* to the effect of prescription (cf. Feenstra, 224–28, 248–50).

51. Grossi, *"Locatio ad longum tempus"*, 166–70; idem, *Situazioni reali*, 203–4.

52. Grossi, *Situazioni reali*, 193–94, to the effect that in the language of canonists "proprietatis amittit effectum, in effectu et quo ad utilitatem, nam quo ad veritatem non amittit; quia iura proprietatis nimis inhaerent ossibus."

53. According to Grossi, the ideological moments behind modern subjectivism in property were constituted by Franciscan voluntary poverty, humanist individualism and historicism, and the voluntarism of sixteenth-century scholasticism: Paolo Grossi, "La proprietà nel sistema privatistico della seconda scolastica," in *La seconda scolastica nella formazione del diritto privato moderno* (Milan, 1973), 117–222; and "Usus facti," 350–55. Also pointing to voluntarism, mainly in the context of late medieval nominalism, is Dietmar Willoweit, "Dominium und Proprietas: Zur Entwicklung des Eigentumsbegriffs in der mittelalterlichen und neuzeitlichen Rechtswissenschaft," *Historisches Jahrbuch der Goerres-Gesellschaft zur Pflege der Wissenschaft im Katholischen Deutschland* 94 (1974): 154–55. On voluntarist and antivoluntarist views of usury, see Julius Kirshner, "Reading Bernardino's Sermon on the Public Debt," in *Atti del simposio internazionale cateriniano-bernardiniano* (note 1 above), 547–622.

54. Baron, "Franciscan Poverty and Civic Wealth," was so intent on drawing a distinction between Franciscan and civic humanist viewpoints—a distinction that could serve to mark the boundary between the medieval period and the Renaissance—that the differences among the Franciscans and the continuities between some of them and the humanists escaped his notice.

55. Requirements for prescription were reducible to the simple formula: "res habilis, titulus, fides, possessio, tempus" (cf. Enrico Besta, *I diritti sulle cose nella storia del diritto italiano* [reprint ed., Milan, 1964], 189). Law on prescription received a systematic summation in the sixteenth century from Giovanni Francesco Balbi, *Tractatus de praescriptionibus* (Venice, 1582).

56. Buckland and McNair, *Roman Law and Common Law*, 117–20; Nicholas, *Introduction to Roman Law*, 120–22.

57. Buckland and McNair, *Roman Law and Common Law*, 121–22.

58. Cf. Noel Vilain, "Prescription et bonne foi du Décret de Gratian (1140) à Jean d'André (d. 1348)," *Traditio* 14 (1958): 165–69.

59. Ibid., 121–42.

60. The crucial canonical text is X. 2.26.20, *Quoniam omne:* "Quoniam omne quod non est ex fide, peccatum est, synodali iudicio diffinimus, ut nullo valeat absque bona fide praescriptio tam canonica quam civilis, quum generaliter sit omni constitutioni atque consuetudini derogandum, quae abs-

que mortali peccato non potest observari. Unde oportet ut qui praescribit in nulla temporis parte rei habeat conscientiam alienae" (*Corpus iuris canonici,* ed. A. Friedburg, 2 vols. [Leipzig, 1874], 2: 394).

A succinct presentation of good faith regarding prescription is in *Enciclopedia del diritto,* s.v. "Buona fede (diritto canonico)," by Luigi Scavo Lombardo, 3: 368–70. Also Francesco Ruffini, *La buona fede in materia di prescrizione* (Padua, 1892); Urbano Navarrete, S.J., *La buena fe de las personas juridicas en ordén a la prescripcion adquisitiva: Estudio histórico-canonico* (Rome, 1959), esp. 319–25; Manuel Cuyas, S.J., *La buena fe en la prescripcion extintiva de deudas, desde el Concilio IV de Latrán (1215) hasta Bartolo (d. 1357)* (Rome, 1962), 1–25.

A brief definition of bad faith is provided by Antonio da Butrio, to X. 2.26.5, *Vigilanti, De praescriptionibus, Super secunda secundi decretalium* (Venice, 1578; reprint ed., Turin, 1967), vol. 4, fol. 107va: "No. quod male fidei possessor dicitur sciens rem alienam."

61. Podestà 1355, fols. 72r–v.

62. *Statuta* 1415, 1:169–170.

63. BNF, Principale II, iv, 435, fols. 54r–v, especially fol. 54v: "Nunquid debitor in quantitate male fidei prescribat adeo quod in ipsum incipiat prescriptio, dic quod non per d. Antonium de But. in c. fi. ex. de prescript. et sic hereditas eiusdem debitoris donec fuerit adita non incipit prescribere Ang. in d. l. adicit adde ver. ob. Casus in quibus non currit prescriptio vide. g[lossa] in l. sicut C. de prescript."

64. Consilium, fols. 409v–10r.

65. The text was clearly commissioned "pro parte dicte Checche" (Consilium, fols. 410r–v). In other words, it was not requested by the court nor by mutual agreement of the litigants, in either of which cases the judge would have been bound to frame his decision according to the determination of the jurists. On Florentine legal procedure and the place of *consilia* in it, see Robert Davidsohn, *Storia di Firenze,* vol. 4: *I primordi della civiltà fiorentina,* part 1: *Impulsi interni, influssi esterni e cultura politica,* trans. Eugenio Dupré-Theseider (Florence, 1973), 507–8; and Martines, *Lawyers and Statecraft,* 91–106, 130–69. On *consilia* themselves, see Luigi Lombardi, *Saggio sul diritto giurisprudenziale,* (Milan, 1967), 126–48; Guido Rossi, *Consilium sapientis iudiciale: Studi e ricerche per la storia del processo romano-canonico* (Milan, 1958), 113–238; Mario Ascheri, "'Consilium sapientis', perizia medica e 'res iudicata'," in *Proceedings of the Fifth International Congress of Medieval Canon Law,* ed. Stephan Kuttner (Rome, 1980), 533–79.

66. Martines, *Power and Imagination,* 217; Baron, "Franciscan Poverty and Civic Wealth," 19–26; Eugenio Garin, *L'umanesimo italiano: Filosofia e vita civile nel Rinascimento* (Bari, 1952), 54–58.

67. Francesca Klein, "Considerazioni sull'ideologia della città di Firenze tra Trecento e Quattrocento (Giovanni Villani-Leonardo Bruni)," *Ricerche storiche* 10 (1980): 311–36.

68. Cf. Giorgio Chittolini, "Ricerche sull'ordinamento territoriale del dominio fiorentino agli inizi del secolo xv," in his *La formazione dello stato regionale e le istituzioni del contado: Secoli xiv e xv* (Turin, 1979), 292–352; Martines, *Lawyers,* 220–45; Julius Kirshner, "Paolo di Castro on *Cives ex Privilegio:* A Controversy over the Legal Qualifications for Public Office in Early Fifteenth-Century Florence," in *Renaissance Studies in Honor of Hans Baron,* ed. Anthony Molho and John A. Tedeschi (Dekalb, 1971), 227–64.

69. *I libri della famiglia,* 216. Cf. Baron, "Franciscan Poverty," 23–24; Ruggiero Romano, *Tra due crisi: L'Italia del Rinascimento* (Turin, 1971), 139–50.

70. Alberti, *Libri della famiglia,* 204–11.

71. Ibid., 236–52.

72. Cf. Giovanni Ponte, "Etica ed economia nel terzo libro 'Della Famiglia' di Leon Battista Alberti," in *Renaissance Studies in Honor of Hans Baron,* ed. Anthony Molho and John A. Tedeschi (Dekalb, 1971), 302–3.

73. Grossi, *"Locatio ad longum tempus",* 143–58, distinguishes the transformative quality of time in *locatio ad longum tempus* from the indifferent, inert, neutral quantity of time in prescription. Cf. Jacques Le Goff, "Merchant's Time and Church's Time in the Middle Ages" and "Labor Time in the 'Crisis' of the Fourteenth Century: From Medieval Time to Modern Time," in his *Time, Work, and Culture in the Middle Ages,* trans. Arthur Goldhammer (Chicago, 1980), 29–52; Alberto Tenenti, "Temps et 'ventura' à la Renaissance: Le cas de Venise," in *Mélanges en l'honneur de Fernand Braudel,* vol. 1: *Histoire économique du monde méditerranéen, 1450–1650* (Paris, 1973), 599–610; Romano, *Tra due crisi,* 139–42.

74. Alberti, *Libri della famiglia,* 236–37: "ma in questo non so se fusse masserizia fare queste quali dite imprese su terreni altrui, le quali, benché sieno utili alla famiglia e grate ad acquistarsi benivolenza da chi sono le possessioni, pure stimo non troverresti chi poi non richiedesse le possessioni per godersele quando voi con quelle simili spese e opere così l'avesse bene migliorate. . . . [Giannozzo] Per questo proprio e per altre cagioni assai io mi comperrei la possessione de' miei danari, che fusse mia, poi e de' figliuoli miei, e così oltre de' nipoti miei, acciò che io con piú amore la facessi governare bene e molto coltivare, e acciò che e' miei rimanenti in quella età prendessono frutto delle piante e delle opere quali io vi ponessi." What was feared here was precisely what happened to Cantini.

75. Martines, *Power and Imagination,* 211–14 (on the nobility theme in humanist writings); Baron, "Franciscan Poverty," 25 n. 1, 22 n. 2, and his important *The Crisis of the Early Italian Renaissance* (Princeton, 1966), 420–21, 557 n. 22.

76. Donald Weinstein, "The Myth of Florence," in *Florentine Studies: Politics and Society in Renaissance Florence,* ed. Nicolai Rubinstein (Evanston, 1968), 36–37.

77. The humanist dialogue, especially one placed in an historical setting

(as was Montemagno's), could pose traditional views against counterargu- ments while keeping the issues insulated from adverse reaction in the present. The author could disavow full identification with any one of his speakers. The tendency in interpreting Montemagno's *De nobilitate*, however, has been to identify him fully with the second speaker who defends virtue. But the sym- metrical presentation of arguments and the failure to offer a firm resolution should warn one away from locating full truth in only one position. The strongest claim to nobility, after all, would still be one that contained refer- ence to birth and wealth, as well as virtue. Cf. David Marsh, *The Quattrocento Dialogue: Classical Tradition and Humanist Innovation* (Cambridge, Mass., 1980), 37, 48–49.

78. Montemagno, *De nobilitate*, in *Prosatori latini del Quattrocento*, ed. Eugenio Garin (Milan, 1952; reprint ed., Turin, 1976), 2: 142–65 (the sec- ond half of the dialogue). The entire work is in *Prose e rime de' due Buonaccorsi da Montemagno*, ed. G. Casotti (Florence, 1718). Alberti's sim- ilar conclusions about the moderate amount of wealth needed for a family are discussed by Ponte, "Etica ed economia," 294–95.

79. Montemagno, *De nobilitate*, 164–65.

80. Ibid., 164: "Quid enim beatius est in rebus humanis quam tranquillissima iocunditate, virtute ac moribus aetatem agere?"

81. Information on Montemagno and the other jurists is in Martines, *Lawyers*, 499–501. The date is given by Montemagno himself, Consilium, fol. 413v.

82. Consilium, fol. 410v. Indeed "facti proprii non est tolerabilis igno- rantia."

83. Ibid.

84. Bartolo, to D. 41.3.4,26(27), *Sequitur § si viam, De usucapionibus et usurpationibus, Opera omnia*, 10 vols. (Venice, 1570), vol. 5, fols. 99ra–rb: " . . . sed illa est vera ratio, quaedam est praescriptio, quae causatur ex possessione praescribentis, et tunc requiritur bona fides in praescriptione lon. temp. quaedam est praescriptio, quae causatur ex negligentia alterius, sine aliqua possessione praescribentis, ut in servitute viae, quae perditur non utendo, tunc non requiritur bona fides praescribentis. . . . Et per hoc consuevi multum dubitare. Nos habemus Decretalem, quae dicit quod malae fidei possessor ullo tempore non praescribit, ut extra eo. c. fin. et de reg. iu. in c. possessor lib. vi. Modo quaero utrum l. sicut et l. cum notissimi C. de prescr. xxx an. que dicunt quod tollitur actio spatio xxx an. hodie sint correctae et dico quod ille d. c. possessor malae fidei etc. non corriguntur, quia in pre- scriptionem actionibus personalibus non requiritur possessio. Ideo non requiritur bona fides, ut hic, et ex parte mea non est possessio sed praescribo per tuam negligentiam: vel potius tu perdis, quam ego praescribam."

85. Consilium, fols. 410v–11r. Cf. Vilain, "Prescription et bonne foi," 171–74; Cuyas, *La buena fe*, 93–139, 194–226.

86. Giovanni d'Andrea, to VI.[5.13].2, *Malaefidei possessor, De regulis*

iuris, Novella in titu. de regulis iuris (1536), fol. 134rb: "Possessor non praescribit, ratio secundum Inno. quia peccat et ex eo meretur penam."

87. Ibid., fol. 136rb: "Prescriptio est ius quoddam ex tempore congruens legum autoritate uni capiens penam negligentibus inferrens et finem litibus imponens." As such it was a matter of natural law to him, contrary to the opinions of some other canonists: ibid., fols. 136vb–37vb.

88. Ibid., fols. 139ra–rb: "Hoc autem non facit quia ius civile cum intendat pro ultimo fine conservare civilem societatem cui fini maxime deservit negligentia punitio et litium terminatio idcirco magis debet intendere ad hoc ut negligentes puniat et finem litibus imponat quam ut iniquitatem prescribentis corrigat vel removeat nam magis ad ipsum spectat illius duplicis finis equitas prosequenda quam ipsi prescribentis iniquitas corrigenda, ex quibus omnibus apparet immediate quare in prescriptione male fidei ius can. a iure civili discordat." This passage corresponds with his earlier assertion, fol. 135va, that "inquantum prescriptio respicit odium negligentis inducta fuit a iur. civili sed inquantum respicit prescribentem fuit permissa non inducta. . . ."

Also Antonio da Butrio, to X.2.26.20, *Quoniam omne,* ed. cit., fol. 115vb: "Dicit gl. quod lex civilis habuit respectum ad finem publicum conservandum, et canonica ad finem Dei: unde in eventu prescriptionis approbavit lex rationes que tendebant in finem suum: nam equum erat negligentiam punire contra publicam utilitatem, ex qua dubia remanebant in incerto, et lites continuabantur: sed lex canonica non tantum curavit de fine publico quantum et de anima: ideo cum aperto peccato non permisit prescriptiones: et peccatum non excusat negligentia non petentis. Per quae dicit, quod in utroque foro standum est legi canonice et non civili." Also Hostiensis, to X.2.26, *Aurea summa* (Venice, 1605), col. 706. In a similar vein, because it was not directed against the *dominus* and not contrary to *equitas,* the *actio publiciana* did not require *bona fides* according to many medieval jurists (cf. Robert Feenstra, "Action publicienne et preuve de la propriété, principalement d'après quelques romanistes du moyen âge," in *Fata iuris romani: Etudes d'histoire de droit* [Leyden, 1974], 135–36).

89. Giovanni d'Andrea, to VI.[5.13].2. ed. cit., fols. 135va–36ra, 140ra–vb.

90. Ibid., fol. 140vb: "homo non est dominus rerum exteriorum nisi pro quanto possunt venire ad suum usum et utilitatem hominis secundum ipsius arbitrium et voluntatem nunquam possunt cadere sub eius dominio sicut patet de corporibus celestis."

91. Ibid., fol. 141ra: "Tertia ratio ad idem est talis quia ille qui tacuit tanto tempore presumitur consentire."

92. In fact, in two of the commentaries cited by Montemagno, Baldo did not go as far as Giovanni d'Andrea had. Baldo, to C. 3.34.1, *Si quas actiones, De servitutibus et de aqua, In primos libros codicis commentaria* (Lyons, 1546), fols. 193vb–94ra, which dealt with rustic and urban praedial servitudes, and another commentary on fiefs, to § *siquis per triginta, Si de feudo fuerit controversia inter dominum et agnatum vasalli, Super feudis*

restauratum commentum (Pavia, 1495), fol. 49vb: "Tamen in foro iustiniani vera est opi. Bar. quia ius commune et statutum et consuetudo possunt statuere quod malefi. possessor prescribat non favore prescribentis sed odio negligentis . . . et est ista potius quedam pena legalis quam prescriptio." In his commentary (not cited by Montemagno), to X.2.26.20, *Quoniam omne, Super decretalibus* (1543), fol. 227va, Baldo equivocated on the issue: "Quero numquid hec decre. servetur in foro seculari. dicit Bar. quod non et verum est quod de facto non servatur. Sed cum sit equum et salutare debet servari vide in c. iii de reg. iur. lib. vi."

93. Consilium, fol. 411r. Baldo, to *C. 4.32.16, Auth. *Ad haec, De usuris, In quartum et quintum codicis libros commentaria* (Venice, 1577), fol. 92rb: "ideo questio prescribentis non procedit de iure canonico in debitore sciente se teneri, ut ext. de prescr. c. quoniam omne. Bar. tamen alias dicebat, quod illud cap. non loquebatur in prescriptione actionis, sed in prescriptione possessionis et dominii: quia ubi non requiritur bona fides, que est facti, ut ff. de acqu. re. do. l. bonae fidei. sed non dicebat verum, quia fortius obligat fides promissionis quam sola pos. ut insti. de ac. § i. sicut ergo obligatus ex possessione non prescribit mala fide: quoniam quod non est ex fide, peccatum est. . . ."

94. Ibid.: "Item alia ratio videtur multum vigore, nam fortius debet astringere bona fides promissoris quam bona fides possessoris, quia nichil tam naturale est quam ea que placuerit inter contrahentes servare." He also added a reference to Angelo degli Ubaldi, to D. 41.3.4,26(27), *In primam digesti novi commentaria* (1580), fols. 31vb–32ra: "nec credo eum [Bartolum] verum dixisse de iure civili: nam illa decretalis emanavit solum ad enervationem peccati, constat enim peccare, et in peccato nutriri omnem illum qui se tuetur iniquo praesidio praescrip. . . . Dixi enim et dico arbitramentum non esse iniquum si de mala fide praescribentis doceri potest: alias secus: cum praescriptio tam iure civili quam canonica sit inducta."

95. Such as the partial support of Antonio da Butrio, to X.2.26.20, ed. cit., fol. 115vb: "in prescriptionibus que currunt ex terminis residentibus in persona querentis ex prescriptione, ut in prescriptionibus que exigunt possessionem . . . quia cum tunc querat cum annexione peccati, non prescribit de iure canonico: quod servandum est in foro civili: et hoc planum secundum omnes. Ubi autem non exigitur possessio ex parte prescribentis, nec titulus sed prescriptio currit ex causa residente et concernente solam personam contra quam prescribitur: tunc dicit Inn. quod tunc prescribit: quia hoc cautum non est ex se acquirere: quia ille perdit ex negligentia sua, ut in personalibus obligationibus ad prescribendam libertatem contra eas, vel in prescriptione libertatis adversus servitutem rusticam."

96. An *absens* here would be "qui nullum habet domicilium vel habet plura" (Giovanni d'Andrea, to VI.[5.13].2, ed. cit., fol. 134va).

97. At least the observation of Bencivenni (BNF, Principale II, iv, 435, fol. 54v) "non prescribitur contra hereditatem iacentem quia mortuus pre-

summitur absens ex causa necessaria et probabili" seems to indicate that he agreed with ser Davanzato.

98. Baldo, to C. 9.9.27(28), *Ita nobis, De lege iulia de adulteriis, In vii, viii, ix, x, et xi codicis commentaria* (Venice, 1577), fol. 221ra. On these rules see the excellent work of Mario Sbriccoli, *L'interpretazione dello statuto: Contributo allo studio della funzione dei giuristi nell'età comunale* (Milan, 1969), 429–38.

99. Consilium, fol. 412r.

100. Cf. Buckland and McNair, *Roman Law and Common Law,* 314–19.

101. Baldo, to C. 4.29.5, *Si sine, Ad velleianum,* ed. cit., fol. 77va.

102. Consilium, fol. 412v.

103. Ibid., fols. 412v–13r.

104. Ibid., fols. 413r–v. This point had to be made because a debtor like Fraschi could not claim a prescription against the obligation to Cantini: *Glossa ordinaria,* to C. 7.39.3, *Sicut, De praescriptionibus* (Lyons, 1612), col. 1676.

105. Consilium, fol. 413v.

106. Ibid., fol. 414r.

107. Ibid., fol. 414v.

108. ASF, Notarile antecosimiano G212 (1422-29), fol. 236v; registered in Notificazioni di atti di emancipazione 1, fol. 63v (10 March) and in Mercanzia 10820bis, fol. 111v (12 March).

109. At the statutory 5 percent for "dampnis, expensis, et interesse" and the rest calculated against the principal, using the 22-florin rent on the house in 1427 as the revenue, the debt was paid off in 1420 and the subsequent earnings amounted to about 142 florins. Cf. Fraschi's *catasto* report, ASF, Catasto 79, fol. 422r, in the Appendix in *Quaderni fiorentini.*

110. ASF, Notarile G212 (1422-29), fols. 269v–70v.

111. Ibid., fol. 270v. On 13 March ser Loisio "substituted" Domenico as Checcha's *procurator* (ibid., fol. 278r). His stepping aside would seem to indicate that by that date the house had actually been reacquired. Moreover, by stepping aside he allowed Domenico to reacquire some control over property in Checcha's name.

112. ASF, Catasto 79, fol. 422r. It is also interesting that Fraschi was recorded in the *gonfalone* of Drago in the quarter of San Giovanni, where the house was, rather than Santo Spirito where he continued to reside.

113. Ibid., fol. 341r: "Domenicho di Zanobi, detto Frascha, f. cientocinquanta chome ciessonale della figliuola, per uno debito da qui dirimpetto di Matteo di Domenicho e compagni." Neither Fraschi nor Tani declared this asset.

114. Matteo di Domenico's debts to Martini came to 123 florins, and with the 26 from the sale, amounted to 149—only one less than the nominal value of the loan from Fraschi. Martini stood 150th in wealth among Florentines of the San Giovanni quarter, though his net assets of 2,286 florins would have put him higher in rank in any other quarter (cf. Martines, *Social World,* 372).

115. What follows is based on documents turned up in 1987 and was not included in the 1985 published version.

116. ASF, Notarile G212 (testamenti 1411–31), fol. 133r–v.

117. ASF, Notarile G212 (1430–32), fol. 18v (3 June 1430). It should be noted, however, that the description of the property in the sale varies from that given by the witnesses during litigation. The witnesses described it as "cum volta, curia, puteo et aliis rebus" and as bounded by *chiassi* on two sides, the piazza of the cathedral on one. The sale describes it as "cum voltis subtus terram et super terram, cameris et sala et aliis hedifitiis" bounded "dirimpecto al campanile cui a i° platea Sancti Johannis de Florentia, a ii° bona artis curazariorum de Florentia, a iii° Laurentii Johannis del Bullecta, a iiii° chiassus." Improvements could have been added to the house to change its descriptive components. One has some doubts about the *confines,* but it is also hard to see that Checcha could be selling any other house than that subject to litigation just four years before.

118. On the Spini, see Kent, *Rise of the Medici,* 163–64; Martines, *Social World,* 72–73, 78.

119. ASF, Notarile A762 (1432–40), fols. 294r–97v. In the legal formulas she gave to the notary, receiving on behalf of Zanobi, "omnia et singula iura et actiones reales et personales utiles et directas tacitas et expressas et alias quascunque dotis dicte condam domine Antonie olim matris sue. . . ."

120. Ibid., fols. 295v–96r: "omnia et singula iura et actiones reales et personales mixtas tacitas et expressas alias quascunque dotis domine Antonie filie olim Ligii de Quaratensibus et uxoris Francisci Daldi olim habite recepte et confessate per dictum Daldum, quas et que dicta domina Checha habet vel habiturus est contra Franciscum Daldi Francisci Cantini sibi domine Cheche cesse pro quantitate florenorum auri quatuorcentorum quadraginta-duorum. . . ."

121. All these acts are also recorded in a second copy in ASF, Notarile A673 (1436–40), fol. 18r–v.

122. ASF, Notarile A674 (1440–42), fols. 142v–47r. A later volume of the same notary's papers, A675 (1442–45), contains a *finis* by Lorenzo di Larione Bardi to Fraschi's estate (fol. 377v [23 March 1444 (1445)]).

123. ASF, Notarile N1 (1467–69), fol. 110r–v (10 June 1468). Four years later Zanobi's then emancipated son, appropriately named Domenico, ratified this sale: N1 (1472–74), fol. 29r–v (14 July 1472). According to Tratte records, Domenico was born in 1454, when his father was not much more than 20. Zanobi later had sons Bernardo (b. 1467) and Francesco (b. 1473).

124. For Zanobi, ASF, Catasto 826, fols. 77r–79r; for Tani, Catasto 821, fols. 130r–33v. Another indication of the social dimension of property was the requirement for owners like Zanobi to account for property held by his father earlier and since alienated. These lists of *beni alienati* dot *catasto* records for 1457, 1469, and 1480.

125. On this sense of norms, Sally Falk Moore, *Law as Process* (London,

1978); John L. Comaroff and Simon Roberts, *Rules and Processes: The Cultural Logic of Dispute in an African Context* (Chicago, 1981); Francis G. Snyder, "Anthropology, Dispute Processes and Law: A Critical Introduction," *British Journal of Law and Society* 8 (1981–82): 141–80.

126. Cf. Luigi Lombardi, *Saggio sul diritto giurisprudenziale* (Milan, 1967), 139–43.

127. Their situation, then, parallels that noted by Grossi (*"Locatio ad longum tempus"*, 295–96) about construing long-term rentals in actual cases.

128. BAV, Vat. Lat. 11605, fol. 148va–vb.

129. Grossi, *"Locatio ad longum tempus"*, 289, 304–5, 340. Similarly, Julius Kirshner, "Reading Bernardino's Sermon on the Public Debt," 563–64, points out that an antivoluntarist current ran through the writings of some Franciscan critics of usurious practices, including San Bernardino of Siena. A thoroughgoing voluntarism regarding property was certainly not completely in place in the fifteenth century.

130. As BNF, Panciatichiano 139, fol. 290r.

131. On whom, see Martines, *Lawyers,* 486–87.

132. ASF, Carte strozziane, 3d ser., 41/8, fols. 187r–89v. This case involved a statute of Pistoia. Crucial in his argument is the assessment that "et est advertendum quod ad causandam istam prescriptionem statutum non requirit quod vicinus sciverit rem esse venditam, quod esset difficilioris probationis, sed satis est quod sciverit quod sit possessa per annos decem per alium, qui actus possessionis facilius potest probari et oculis vicini magis innotescit. . . ." (fol. 188r). The statutory clause was overturned on the basis of its specific reference to events after 1301: "Item dum dicit *ad petendum rescindi venditionem factam* etc. et sic loquitur de venditionibus factis tempore quo fuit facta illa additio ad statutum et comprendit casus preteritos et sensus est quod statuentes voluerunt quando fuit facta illa additio, quod licet dictum esset superius quod emptor qui possedisset sciente vicino per annos decem esset tutus prescriptione annorum x, ne posset molestari a vicino vel consorte, tamen istam prescriptionem noluerunt habere locum statuentes in alienationibus factis ab anno mccci usque ad tempus facte dicte nove additionis ad statutum. Et ideo quo ad alienationes que fierent post additionem illam non loquitur, sed de illis nos remanemus in pristina dispositione dicti statuti. . . ." (fol. 189r).

133. Willoweit, "Dominium und Proprietas," 144–47, 153–54, provides an interesting discussion of the divergent views of Bartolo and Baldo on the meaning and nature of *dominium,* or *dominium* and *proprietas,* and the distance of each from the modern sense of ownership as "freie Verfügung und Ausschluss Dritter."

134. As Baldo, *repetitio* to D. 28.2.11, *In suis, De liberis et posthumis, In prima et secunda infortiati commentaria* (Venice, 1577), fols. 53vb–54ra: "dominium appellatur proprietas, et proprie proprium est illud, quod eadem consideratione non convenit pluribus, sed uni . . . non solum enim effectus,

sed prima causa hoc ostendunt, quod impossibilis est pluralitas plurium personarum ad idem dominium concurrentium." Cf. Manlio Bellomo, *Problemi di diritto familiare nell'età dei comuni: Beni paterni e "pars filii"* (Milan, 1968), 9.

135. This sense of ownership is most prominently associated with Bartolo, though it shared certain features with earlier definitions of *dominium* (cf. Willoweit, "Dominium und Proprietas," 142–46). Willoweit, 148–50, points to the fifteenth century as the era in which "diese geläufige Vorstellung des *libere disponendi* zu einem generellen Merkmal des Eigentums erklärt," notably with the use of the phrase "uti et abuti" in jurisprudential analyses.

136. Again, parallels exist in the more voluntaristic treatments of usury in the sale of shares in the public debt. These treatments argued that only the use of a share was sold, not ownership, and, therefore, no usury was involved. Cf. Kirshner, "Reading Bernardino's Sermon," 587–88.

137. Cf. Bellomo, *Problemi di diritto familiare*, 19 n. 25. Grossi, "Usus facti," 319–21, discusses the equivocal use of *habere* in Franciscan literature and, 337–39, their univocal treatment of the polyvalent term *usus*. He notes that they conceived of *usus*, and a corresponding sense of *habere*, as purely mechanical and economic—one image of which was a horse "using" the oats he eats. Antonio Roselli (1381–1466), a Florentine lawyer, used a similar image in arguing that an emancipated son did not own his father's property, even though he lived with his father (cf. Kuehn, *Emancipation*, 126, 221 n. 12). Similarly, Torello Torelli (fl. 1400), Bartolomeo Popoleschi (d. 1412), and Filippo Corsini (1334–1421) argued for Giovanni di Bicci de' Medici that his residence with his mother did not imply that he owned or even possessed the house that was in her name. At best only *tenere* could be predicated of such a *habitator,* and "tenere astractum est a iure et merum factum significat etiam nullo iuris adminiculo subsistente. Hinc est quod asinus tenet sellas [precisely Roselli's image] et servus qui iuris incapax est proprie tenet." And even *tenere* was denied in this case, for Giovanni was not in the house by any right (as would be true in his father's house) but merely "ex quadam patientia vel confidentia familiari" (cf. Phillips MS 8889, fols. 234r–36v).

138. Lombardi, *Saggio,* 144–46. This creativity should be contrasted to the views of those legal historians who see the fifteenth century, especially its consiliar activity, as evidence of rigidity and stasis in the law: Manlio Bellomo, *Società e istituzioni in Italia dal Medioevo agli inizi dell'età moderna,* 3d ed. (Catania, 1982), 479–80; Sbriccoli, *Interpretazione dello statuto,* 461; Francesco Calasso, *Medioevo del diritto* (Milan, 1954), 592–93, 597. In contrast, humanism is seen as the vital intellectual force of the fifteenth century: Domenico Maffei, *La donazione di Costantino nei giuristi medievali* (Milan, 1964), 290–96; Franz Wieacker, *Privatrechtsgeschichte der Neuzeit* (Göttingen, 1952), 38–45. In contrast, Lombardi, *Saggio,* 119–21.

139. Sbriccoli, *Interpretazione dello statuto,* 3–11, 462–65. Also Colin Sumner, *Reading Ideologies: An Investigation into the Marxist Theory of Ide-*

ology and Law (London, 1979); and with specific reference to property, Bernard Edelman, *Ownership of the Image: Elements for a Marxist Theory of Law*, trans. Elizabeth Kingdom (London, 1979).

140. On these themes, Martines, *Social World*, 18–39; Kent, *Household and Lineage*, 121–63; Christian Bec, *Les marchands écrivains: Affaires et humanisme à Florence, 1375–1434* (Paris, 1967), 50–63; and the important article of David Herlihy, "The Distribution of Wealth in a Renaissance Community: Florence 1427," in *Towns in Societies: Essays in Economic History and Historical Sociology*, ed. Philip Abrams and E. A. Wrigley (Cambridge, 1978), 131–57.

141. As Alberico da Rosciate, to the effect that a statute was erected for the common good "ut subditi conservent eorum res immobiles" and for public utility "ut familiarum dignitas et memoria conservetur, quae conservatur per divitias et per inopiam minuitur" (cited in Mario Sbriccoli, "Politique et interprétation juridique dans les villes italiennes du Moyen Age," *Archives de philosophie du droit* 17 [1972]: 109). The Florentine *catasto*, therefore, exempted family dwellings: David Herlihy, "Family and Property in Renaissance Florence," in *The Medieval City*, ed. Harry A. Miskimin, David Herlihy, and A. L. Udovitch (New Haven, 1977), 3–24, esp. 5. There was also the old distinction in civil law between rustic and urban praedial servitudes, the latter of which was associated with houses (and for prescription of which good faith was required): Baldo, to C. 3.34.1, ed. cit., fol. 193vb.

142. Guicciardini, *Maxims and Reflections*, 113.

143. Cf. Willoweit, "Dominium und Proprietas," 155.

144. Lombardi, *Saggio*, 107, notes that the medieval senses of *dominium* erected under the influence of Germanic constructs and economic realities "incontrino, sulla soglia delle facolta legali e del foro, un proibente filtro di tecnicismo. . . . E le *rationes* non propriamente 'giuridiche' continuano a fare un po' la figura di parenti povere nell'argomentazione giurisprudenziale." In the *consilium* itself, in addition, is the revealing comment by Montemagno (in the context of the problem of the witnesses) "calor iudicii est maioris auctoritatis quam actus extra iudiciales" (Consilium, fol. 413r).

145. Brucker, *Civic World*, 313 n. 307, 448 n. 235, 459 n. 290, 484.

146. Giovanni di Nello da San Gimignano was a humanist, as was Benedetto di Michele Accolti, a jurist who also rose to be a humanist chancellor of Florence. On them and Montemagno, see Martines, *Social World*, 330–31, 340, 343–44; and on Accolti, Robert Black, *Benedetto Accolti and the Florentine Renaissance* (Cambridge, 1985).

147. Grossi has pointed to humanism as influencing law on property, but he has not systematically investigated this point. For now, see Grossi, "Seconda scolastica," 189; *"Locatio ad longum tempus"*, 196.

148. The tendency of historians, however, has largely been to see the two as distinct and even antagonistic. An elegant summation of historians' views

of humanism and law was offered a number of years ago by Domenico Maffei, *Gli inizi dell'umanesimo giuridico* (Milan, 1956), 15–16.

149. Ibid., 34–62, 67–78. See also Roberto Abbondanza, "Jurisprudence: The Methodology of Andrea Alciato," in *The Late Italian Renaissance, 1525–1630*, ed. Eric Cochrane (New York, 1970), 72–90; Donald R. Kelley, "Civil Science in the Renaissance: Jurisprudence Italian Style," *The Historical Journal* 22 (1979): 777–94; Robert Black, "Ancients and Moderns in the Renaissance: Rhetoric and History in Accolti's *Dialogue on the Preeminence of Men of His Own Time*," *Journal of the History of Ideas* 43 (1982): 20.

150. Note the number of humanists who appear in Martines' profiles of Florentine lawyers, especially under the category of "outsiders," *Lawyers*, 482–508, and the legal training of various humanists profiled in his *Social World*. Also Jerrold E. Siegel, *Rhetoric and Philosophy in Renaissance Humanism: The Union of Eloquence and Wisdom, Petrarch to Valla* (Princeton, 1968) and his "'Civic Humanism' or Ciceronian Rhetoric? The Culture of Petrarch and Bruni," *Past and Present* 34 (July 1966): 3–48; Martines, *Power and Imagination*, 204.

151. Martines, *Lawyers*, 73–75, lists 22 "outsiders" and 11 men of "new" families, as against 13 of "old" families, in the period 1380–1430. The prominence of outsiders may have been due to their conventionally perceived impartiality, as much if not more so than to the existence of other outlets for the old elite (the reason cited by Martines for the relative paucity of "old" men in 1380–1430 vs. their relative abundance in 1480–1530). The outsiders of the earlier period were also a considerable array of talent, including (in addition to the five here) Paolo di Castro, Bartolomeo Vulpi, and Antonio Roselli. The outsiders were especially prominent in civil law, while several "old" family lawyers taught canon law. Among native Florentines, perhaps only Filippo Corsini, Alessandro Bencivenni, and Lorenzo Ridolfi could be said to have had good reputations. There seems a clear parallel to the reputation of outsiders among Florentine humanists in the same period: Bruni, Bracciolini, Marsuppini, Traversari.

Chapter Four

1. BNF, Fondo principale, II, v, 7, fols. 137r–38v. A transcription of the letter, along with letters from fols. 108r–v and 118r, appears in the first published version of this essay in *Ricerche storiche* 10 (1980): 305–10.

2. Gene Brucker, *The Society of Renaissance Florence: A Documentary Study* (New York, 1971), 64–66; idem, *Renaissance Florence*, 2d ed. (Berkeley and London, 1983), 114. I have generally relied on Brucker's translation for those passages quoted in the text (if Brucker translated the passage), although I have deviated from his renderings in the few instances where I thought it appropriate.

3. Francis William Kent, *Household and Lineage in Renaissance Florence: The Family Life of the Capponi, Ginori and Rucellai* (Princeton, 1977), 48.

4. Brucker, *Renaissance Florence,* 113.

5. Kent, *Household and Lineage,* 45.

6. Ibid., 48.

7. Ibid., 294.

8. Gene Brucker, *The Civic World of Early Renaissance Florence* (Princeton, 1977), 18.

9. Brucker, *Society of Renaissance Florence,* 28.

10. Ibid.

11. Lauro Martines, *The Social World of the Florentine Humanists, 1390–1460* (Princeton, 1963), 50. Studies that deal with the role of family and lineage in political affairs include Dale Kent, "The Florentine 'Reggimento' in the Fifteenth Century," *Renaissance Quarterly* 28 (1975): 575–638, and her *The Rise of the Medici: Faction in Florence, 1426–1434* (Oxford, 1978), as well as the works of Brucker cited above. See also Francis William Kent's characterization of the Florentine oligarchy in his review article, "A La Recherche du Clan Perdu: Jacques Heers and 'Family Clans' in the Middle Ages," *Journal of Family History* 2 (1977): 84.

12. Foremost in the demographic study of the family have been David Herlihy and Christiane Klapisch-Zuber, most notably in their study of the Florentine catasto of 1427, *Les toscans et leurs familles: Une analyse du catasto de 1427* (Paris, 1978). Important legal studies that have often served as the basis for other historians are: Manlio Bellomo, *Ricerche sui rapporti patrimoniali tra coniugi: Contributo alla storia della famiglia medievale* (Milan, 1961), and *Problemi di diritto familiare nell'età dei comuni: Beni paterni e "pars filii"* (Milan, 1968); Enrico Besta, *La famiglia nella storia del diritto italiano* (Milan, 1933: reprint ed., Milan, 1962); Nino Tamassia, *La famiglia italiana nei secoli decimoquinto e decimosesto* (Milan, 1910).

13. Cf. the following statement by Kent, *Household and Lineage,* 44, that in Florence *ottimati* households possessed "firm direction and a vision of the extended family which if idealized was nonetheless often attained." An important study of the problem of family continuity that recognizes, more so than Kent, the fragility of family relations is that of Paolo Cammarosano, "Aspetti delle strutture familiari nelle città dell'Italia comunale (*secoli* xii–xiv)," *Studi medievali,* 3d ser., 16 (1975): 417–35. An outlook similar to Kent's is that of Diane Owen Hughes, "Domestic Ideals and Social Behavior: Evidence from Medieval Genoa," in *The Family in History,* ed. Charles E. Rosenburg (Philadelphia, 1975), 115–43.

Kent's approach to the family is derived from that of the anthropologist Meyer Fortes (see Kent, *Household and Lineage,* 7, n. 17). Like Fortes Kent treats cultural observations "as facts of custom—as standardized ways of doing knowing, thinking, and feeling—universally obligatory and valued in a given group of people at a given time" (Fortes, "The Structure of Unilineal Descent Groups," *American Anthropologist* 55 [1953]: 21). Custom, in other words, can be seen as "symbolizing or expressing social relations." For a critique of Fortes, see J. A. Barnes, *Three Styles in the Study of Kinship* (Berkeley, 1971), 177–264.

14. Kent, *Household and Lineage*, 45.

15. See Kent's extremely valuable analysis of familial ideology, ibid., 43–62. For a similar approach to the figure of the father and the continuity and unity of the family, see Leonida Pandimiglio, "Giovanni di Pagolo Morelli e la ragion di famiglia," in *Studi sul medioevo cristiano offerti a Raffaello Morghen*, 2 vols. (Rome, 1974), 555–62, 575.

16. Kent, *Household and Lineage*, 77.

17. Ibid., 54. On the notion of the domestic development cycle, see J. Goody, "The Evolution of the Family," in *Household and Family in Past Time*, ed. Peter Laslett and Richard Wall, (Cambridge, 1972), 103–24.

18. *I libri di commercio dei Peruzzi*, ed. Armando Sapori, (Milan, 1934), 524–25 (translated in part by Brucker, *Society of Renaissance Florence*, 62–63).

19. My comments on the nature of honor in Florentine society owe a great deal to a reading of anthropological studies of honor. A good introduction is provided in J. G. Peristiany, ed., *Honour and Shame* (Chicago, 1966), and J. K. Campbell, *Honour, Family and Patronage* (Oxford, 1964). For a discussion of honor in specifically Italian contexts, see C. Cronin, *The Sting of Change: Sicilians in Sicily and Australia* (Chicago, 1970), 50–57, and J. Davis, *Land and Family in Pisticci* (London, 1973), 22–24. Extremely suggestive are the comments on honor offered by Pierre Bourdieu, *Outline of a Theory of Practice*, trans. Richard Nice (Cambridge, 1977), 60–61, 181–82.

20. An important anthropological contribution to the relation between cultural conceptions of honor and various forms of social conflict in an Italian context is the article of Peter Schneider, "Honor and Conflict in a Sicilian Town," *Anthropological Quarterly* 42 (1969): 130–54, especially his comments on pages 153–54, where he concludes that conflicts over honor are very real and important and that hostility occurs within certain limits and is expressed in certain forms. He does not treat conflict either as a purely emotional fact or as a result of failure to adhere to behavioral norms.

21. See the illuminating comments about honor in Southern Italy by J. Davis, "Morals and Backwardness," *Comparative Studies in Society and History* 12 (1970): 347–48.

22. Kent, *Household and Lineage*, 201.

23. Quoted from Leon Battista Alberti, *The Family in Renaissance Florence*, trans. Renée Neu Watkins (Columbia, S.C., 1969), 149–50.

24. Cf. Kent, *Household and Lineage*, 45–47, 55–61.

25. The points here summarized are presented at length in my *Emancipation in Late Medieval Florence* (New Brunswick, 1982), 55–71.

26. BNF, Fondo principale II, v, 7, fols. 108r–v.

27. See BNF, Fondo principale, II, v, 7, fol. 118r (13 April 1405).

28. The emancipation of Orsino and the subsequent arbitration are in ASF, Notarile antecosimiano A807 (ser Antonio di Niccolò Pierozzi), 31 October and 7 November 1412. The emancipation was recorded with the Mercanzia on 7 November (ASF, Mercanzia, 10820, fol. 240r). According to the arbitrator's *laudum,* Orsino had paid "de suis propriis" 80 florins for Lippa's dowry, plus other sums on Lanfredino's business affairs amounting in all to over 600 florins. In compensation he was awarded a large farm with all its appurtenances. By means of the emancipation and arbitration Orsino achieved a patrimonial separation that was less violent than that of his brother Remigio, but which equally brought him a measure of security and salvaged something from his father's chaotic economic state.

29. David Herlihy, "The Generation in Medieval History," *Viator* 5 (1974): 347–64, has offered an explanation for familial tension and conflict in terms of relative differences in age between fathers and sons and in terms of the life expectancies of the parent. A living parent, he says, stood in the way of sons who wanted to attain property and wives. Certainly such demographic variables must have played a part in quarrels between grown sons and their fathers, just as they would have in the intervention by mothers, who were often considerably younger than their husbands, between husband and off-spring (note Lanfredino's appeal to his wife to intercede). I would argue, however, that there is more to be considered than relative ages. Remigio was not prevented from marrying and holding property in the sense Herlihy implies. If anything, it may have been his relative independence that led him to quarrel with his father.

30. Paolo da Certaldo, *Il libro di buoni costumi,* ed. S. Morpurgo (Florence, 1921), 157.

31. Leon Battista Alberti, *De Iciarchia,* in *Opere volgari,* ed. Cecil Grayson, 2 vols. (Bari, 1960), 2: 275.

32. Kent, *Household and Lineage,* 55–57.

33. da Certaldo, *Libro di buoni costumi,* 165.

34. In this regard, note the analysis of kinship as a symbolic system by David Schneider, *American Kinship: A Cultural Account* (Englewood-Cliffs, N.J., 1968) and the comments of Pierre Bourdieu on the legalism of studies of kinship in "Les stratégies matrimoniales dans le système de reproduction," *Annales (E.S.C.)* 27 (1972): 1106–7.

35. Emancipation was a fact of life in the Lanfredini family. Orsino's emancipation has been mentioned. In 1419 and 1420 Orsino's brothers Salvatico and Salimbene (emancipated 20 June 1419, both "magiori d'anni diciotto," registered with the Mercanzia 27 June: ASF, Mercanzia 10820 bis, fol. 39r), Niccolò (emancipated 4 July 1419, also over eighteen, registered 6 July: ibid., fol. 39v), and Daniele (emancipated 9 May 1420, no indication of age, registered 13 May: ibid., fol. 56r) were emancipated in turn. I could find no indication in the Florentine emancipation registries of an emancipation of

Remigio, though that does not necessarily mean there was no emancipation. The reasons for these emancipations are not clear, but they may not have been the result of any friction within the family. I raise the point, however, to demonstrate one aspect of father-son relations ignored by Kent and others who have written on the family.

36. Anthony Molho has also advanced reservations about a too-static view of the family as patrilineage, which is incapable of fully contending with the manifold realities and changes experienced by Renaissance Florentine families, in his "Visions of the Florentine Family in the Renaissance," *Journal of Modern History* 50 (1978): 304–11.

37. Leon Battista Alberti, *I libri della famiglia*, ed. Ruggiero Romano and Alberto Tenenti (Turin, 1969), 3; Franco Sacchetti, *Le novelle*, 2 vols. (Florence, 1925), 1: 13.

38. Herlihy and Klapisch-Zuber, *Les toscans;* Julius Kirshner and Anthony Molho, "The Dowry Fund and the Marriage Market in Early Quattrocento Florence," *Journal of Modern History,* 50 (1978): 403–38.

Chapter Five

1. D. V. and F. W. Kent, "A Self-Disciplining Pact Made by the Peruzzi Family of Florence (June 1433)," *Renaissance Quarterly* 34 (1981): 337–55.

2. Ibid., 342.

3. Ibid., 354. Crimes in this case were described as "alcuna villania, danno o dispiacere ad alcuna persona, tanto ne' beni quanto nella persona, cioè di torre, sforzare, rubare quanto di battere, percuotere, fedire, uccidere alcun altro e cosí di villania, disonestà di parole si facessino fuori d'honestà. . . ."

4. Ibid., 337. Dale Kent is herself the foremost student of factionalism and politics in those eight years. See her, *The Rise of the Medici: Faction in Florence, 1426–1434* (Oxford, 1978). Also Gene Brucker, *The Civic World of Early Renaissance Florence* (Princeton, 1977), who substantially follows her lead, for the period 1426–34.

5. Kent and Kent, "Self-Disciplining Pact," 337–43.

6. Ibid., 345.

7. Ibid., 345–48.

8. Ibid., 349.

9. Ibid., 345 and n. 25.

10. On this area of late medieval law, see the masterful treatment of Luciano Martone, *Arbiter-Arbitrator: Forme di giustizia privata nell'età del diritto comune* (Naples, 1984).

11. ASF, Notarile antecosimiano G212 (1422–29) [renumbered as 9040], fol. 237r–v. This cartulary will be referred to hereafter as Giacomini (the notary's name).

12. Kent, *Medici*, 137, 153, and appendix.

13. On Fraschi, see chapter 3.

14. That is, he was married to Dianora di Piero di Banco degli Albizzi, according to his testament of 6 November 1437: ASF, Notarile antecosimiano C 475 (1437–42), fol. 23v. I owe this information to the kindness of Bill Kent.

15. Giacomini, fol. 398r–v.

16. Giacomini, fols. 417r–19v (11 May 1429).

17. Cf. Anna Maria Enriques, "La vendetta nella vita e nella legislazione fiorentina," *Archivio storico italiano* 91 (1933): "L'arbitrato riguarda le controversie in pendenza, la pace le offese passate" (197).

18. On the Serragli as anti-Mediceans and friends of the Peruzzi, see Kent, *Medici*, 138, 155, 188, 291; on Niccolò d'Agnolo, see Lauro Martines, *The Social World of the Florentine Humanists, 1390–1460* (Princeton, 1963), 230–37.

19. Giacomini, fols. 417r–18v.

20. Giacomini, fols. 418v–19r: "Et audito etiam et conperto quod dictus Pierus antequam dictum Johannem [sic] vulneraret in dicta civitate Barchinone percusserat cum uno bastone de ligno re acta ad maleficium commictendo Serotinum fratrem carnalem dicti Lipacci et filium dicti olim Bartholomei de Brancaccis, de qua offensione facta fuerat trehugua inter partes contra treugua et eius tempus ad huc durabat tempore quo dictus Pierus cum dicta dagha et seu cultello, ut prefertur, dictum Lippaccium vulneravit, et sic nedum dictus Pierus penitentiam de iam ceptis haberet vel penitentiam ageret sed mala malis addendo et treguam rumpendo dictum Lippaccium, ut prefertur, vulneravit. Et viso etiam et reperto et clare cognito quod dictus Pierus dictam scriptam et conventionem cuius tenor supra describitur non servavit in aliqua sui parte sed ipsam observare contempsit et sprevit in vilipendium iniuriam et preiudicium et dedecus dicti Lippacci et aliorum de dicta domo et familia de Brancaccis, et maxime quia dictus Pierus durante tempore et termino dicte scripte semper vel saltim pro maiori parte dicti temporis arma offendibilia palam detulit et deferebat contra formam et tenorem dicte scripte et conventionis cuius tenor supra describitur. Ac etiam non stetit nec habitavit continue in civitate Florentie prout debuit et tenebatur secundum formam et tenorem dicte scripte et absque aliqua licentia vel consensu dictorum arbitrorum et arbitratorum vel alicuius eorum se abstentavit plusquam debuit a civitate Florentie quin ymo Romane accessit et sepe sepius rus ivit et extra civitatem Florentie et ultra et plusquam debuit et ex forma dicte scripte poterat ivit et stetit, ac etiam non ivit solus vel inermis per civitatem Florentie nec se obstendit vel presentavit, et maxime in foro veteri temporibus et modis et prout debuit et tenebatur ex forma et tenore dicte scripte de qua supra fit mentio in dedecus et verecundiam dicti Lippacci et eius consortum et coniunctorum. Et audito et reperto qualiter de mense junii proximi preteriti et ante per plures menses et ultra quod dictus Bartholomeus frater dicti Pieri inmemor dictarum iniuriarum factarum per dictum Pierum in personam dicti Lippacci sepe sepius transibat ante domum habitationis dicti Lippacci et Johannis eius fratris, quod est contra usum et

bonos mores civitatis Florentie. Et cum dicatur quod dictus Johannes Bartolomei de Brancaccis et frater dicti Lippacci de mense junii proximi perteriti videns dictum Bartolomeum sic presentem ante domum habitationis dicti Johannis ita et calore iracundie motus cum quadam cultellessa de ferro percussit et vulneravit dictum Bartolomeum una percussione et vulnere in capite dicti Bartolomei cum sanguinis effuxione et fractura ossis super cilia, de qua percussione et vulnere formatum fuisse dicitur processum per proximum preteritum dominum executorem ordinamentorum iustitie civitatis Florentie, et ipsum processum ad huc pendere dicitur in curia presentis domini executoris civitatis Florentie. Et viso quod dictus Pierus non servavit per eum promissa in dicta scripta quapropter non intelligitur habere pacem a dicto Lippaccio et eius attinentibus de dictis iniuriis per dictum Pierum cum pro parte sua scriptam predictam non servavit et ipsam non servasse declaramus."

21. Kent and Kent, "Self-Disciplining Pacts," 342; Giacomini, fol. 418r.

22. Brucker, *Civic World,* 68, 245, 360–64.

23. For what follows, cf. Enriques, "La vendetta," but also Jacob Black-Michaud, *Cohesive Force: Feud in the Mediterranean and the Middle East* (New York, 1975); Christopher Boehm, *Blood Revenge: The Enactment and Management of Conflict in Montenegro and Other Tribal Societies* (Philadelphia, 1987); J. Davis, *People of the Mediterranean: An Essay in Comparative Social Anthropology* (London, 1977); Pierre Bourdieu, *Outline of a Theory of Practice,* trans. Richard Nice (Cambridge, 1977), 3–22, 33–43. Black-Michaud, xiii–xiv, sets out a distinction between feud and vendetta, the latter being characterized as limited to the perpetrator and victim and their direct heirs, therefore as a feature of sedentary village life. Feud he sees as appropriate in the unsettled conditions of Bedouin life where members of a corporate group face a feud equally. This issue of who is liable is clouded, however, by his later assertion that "the taking of vengeance always tends everywhere to be the affair of the close agnates of the victim rather than of the group as a whole" (50). There is indeed a matter of selection of whom to act vengeance upon—it need not be the perpetrator, as it was in the Peruzzi case—but the perpetrator is still the first choice. The desire of village authorities to limit acts of revenge to victims or immediate kin, the "ambiguity" that attaches to the one who must bring vengeance (136), likewise seem common to what Black-Michaud would call feud as well as to vendetta. In short, I am not convinced that feud and vendetta are not simply different names for the same thing, or at least that what we encounter with the Peruzzi in fifteenth-century Florence answers to his description of feud.

24. Cf. Black-Michaud, *Cohesive Force,* 80–85, who sticks with the language that the perpetrator has generated a "debt" that the victim must redeem. He sees the debtor here as the powerful party, who has the "funds" and must be made to pay them back. Creditors, however, obviously have their ways and it seems difficult to maintain, as he does, that they are *always* in an

inferior position. That debtors can be in the more powerful position is, none-theless, a valuable insight.

25. A point made in passing, without further elaboration of the logic behind it, in ibid., xiii–xiv.

26. On denial of the debt, see ibid., 237–41.

27. On this, ibid., 38–54. I draw attention here to two features of his discussion. One is the distinction between the passive solidarity of "the larger compensation-paying group" and the active "minimal lineage" directly con-cerned with vengeance (48). The other is the observation that recruitment to a vengeance group "is in the first place governed by contractual agreement and only subsidiarily by the principle of agnation"(46). Black-Michaud sees agnation as more primary in vengeance recruitment in sedentary societies where inherited property also follows agnatic lines (62). That feud constitutes a language is an insight powerfully developed by Angelo Torre, "Faide, fazioni e partiti, ovvero la ridefinizione della politica nei feudi imperiali delle Langhe tra Sei e Settecento," *Quaderni storici* 63 (Dec. 1986): 775–810.

28. Enriques, "La vendetta," 105–7, and on its expansiveness through solidary kin groups, 109–12.

29. Cf. Chapter 2, above; Black-Michaud, *Cohesive Force*, 63–80; En-riques, "La vendetta," 91; and Osvaldo Raggio, "La politica nella parentela: Conflitti locali e commissari in Liguria orientale (secoli xvi–xvii)," *Quaderni storici* 63 (Dec. 1986): 736.

30. Cf. Lauro Martines, *Power and Imagination: City-States in Renais-sance Italy* (New York, 1979), 76–77.

31. Enriques, "La vendetta," 181–191.

32. ASF, Statuti di Firenze 29, fols. 129r–30r, rubric De vindicta, in quibus casibus sit permissa, where the crucial passage is: "Et siquis aliquo modo quam aliquo ex supradictis offendiderit vel offendi fuerit in corpus aliquem de civitate, comitatu, vel districtu Florentie possit ab ipso sic offenso et ab eius coniunctis et de eadem domo et progenie et quolibet eorum cum ea comitiva quam habere voluerit etiam extraneorum, ut supra dictum est, impune offendi faciendo tamen competentem vindictam et sit in arbitrio rectoris coram quo penderet processus utrum intelligatur facta competens vindicta vel non."

33. Ibid., fols. 130r–31r, De pena facientis vindictam vel fieri facientis nisi in principalem personam.

34. For a description, see Lauro Martines, *Lawyers and Statecraft in Re-naissance Florence* (Princeton, 1968), 359–61.

35. Statuti di Firenze 29, fols. 130r, 393r. See Black-Michaud, *Cohesive Force*, 89–118, whose discussion of the sorts of men who are chosen as medi-ators in a feud compares in interesting ways with the men actually chosen by the Peruzzi and Brancacci, though in the Florentine situation the arbitrators did not stand alone in imposing penalties and so forth, the government and laws backed them.

36. Enriques, "La vendetta," 203; also Conclusion, in *The Settlement of Disputes in Early Medieval Europe*, ed. Wendy Davies and Paul Fouracre (Cambridge, 1986), 207–40.

37. Randolph Starn, *Contrary Commonwealth: The Theme of Exile in Medieval and Renaissance Italy* (Berkeley, 1982), 98–101; John Larner, *Italy in the Age of Dante and Petrarch, 1216–1380* (London, 1980), 109–33, uses the same terms, but in the earlier period he studies he sees the state, that is, the oligarchic elites, as relatively unsuccessful in curbing violence and divisions.

38. Raggio, "Politica nella parentela," 739. The arbitrators thus had to "elaborare un linguaggio di mediazione che tenesse conto anche del giudizio e delle esigenze piú ampie della comunità e di offrire soluzioni di reciproco vantaggio e 'soddisfatione' (con una particolare attenzione per l'onore) a tutte le parti."

39. Torre, "Faide, fazioni e partiti," 787. Martines, *Lawyers*, 373, notes the state's efforts to foster, mediate, and gain local settlement of trade disputes to avoid reprisals.

40. Enriques, "La vendetta," 98, 186.

41. As in this example, a *laudum* from 1493: "quia decet bonum Christianum remictere iniurias et vindictam deo relinquere, et in nos ea mente eaque intentione compromissum fuit ut pax fieret inter dictas partes . . . " (ASF, Notarile antecosimiano G 619 [1490–94], fols. 105r–6r [21 July 1493]).

42. At least as a rare example, I can mention a *laudum* (ASF, Notarile G 617 [1473–75], fols. 52v–54r [7 September 1473]) dealing with an enmity arising from the fact that one woman had hit another with a stone, breaking teeth and drawing blood. The woman who threw the stone and her husband were ordered to move out of their present habitation, away from the neighborhood and the possibility of frequent chance encounters with the other party and her husband. They were also ordered to stay away from the other's house and, most important, to pay 50 florins to the offended party. Interestingly, the period set for their dwelling away from the neighborhood was three years, the same period given the Brancacci to wound Piero Peruzzi.

43. The same notarial cartulary containing the Peruzzi texts has two examples of peace settlements (fols. 302v [15 July 1427] and 316r–v [11 November]). Their legal formulas carefully include all relevant kin of both parties, in addition to the principals. The operative language from one is "fecerunt et rediderunt sibi invicem, obsculo pacis interveniente, pacem perpetuam et bonam voluntatem etc. de omnibus et singulis offensionibus, iniuriis et delictis cum armis et sine et dicto vel facto seu aliter quomodocunque, qualitercunque et quandocunque per unam partem vel aliquem ex eis alteri parti vel alicui ex eis vel econverso factis personaliter vel in bonis vel in eorum personis etc."

44. There is, in contrast, no time limit on a vendetta sanctioned by the commune that is described by Martines, *Lawyers*, 406–8.

45. Such as the powerful Pitti (Brucker, *Civic World,* 360–64) or Benedetto di ser Guido di Tommaso Masi (Kent, *Medici,* 102–3, 282).

46. Note their honor was necessarily also implicated in his. For an example of such implication, see chapter 4.

47. Though they were not guarantors of it in a technical sense, at least in that there is no record of a formal declaration of *fideiussio.*

48. Kent and Kent, "Self-Disciplining Pacts," 347 n. 30.

49. Ibid., 347.

50. Ibid., 351.

51. Ibid., 349–50.

52. Ibid., 348 n. 38.

53. Ibid., 350.

54. Cf. Raggio, "Politica nella parentela," 739–40. The arbitration itself, however, could become a matter of dispute taken to court. One surviving example is a *consilium* of the later fifteenth century from a vendetta involving some of the Canacci is in BNF, Landau Finaly 98, fols. 277r–84v (new numeration). Its authors were Salustio Buonguglielmi, Abbot Niccolò da Sicilia, Benedetto Barzi, and a fourth jurist whose signature is missing. Among the findings of this *consilium* are that "partes reducantur ad concordiam et non veniant ad rissam nec capiant arma de hoc potest esse lix et ad hoc potest arbiter compellere partes nam per hoc res publica laederetur et sic est interesse rei publice et equissimum" (282v), while conceding that "est mos civitatis Italie non negligere famam suam quod enim est credendum quia qui negligit famam suam est sui interfector, unde sicut non sunt domini sue fame, ideo credendum ipsos cogitasse de vindicta fienda que poterat fieri licite et lege permictenti, nec est presummendum iniuriatis de vindicta non cogitasse que est dulcis medela iniuriato, quia iniuriam iniuriis repelle dulce refrigerium est iniuriati . . . " (284r).

55. Note Ridolfo's support for legislation against confraternities, justified as a measure to reduce dissension among citizens (Brucker, *Civic World,* 479).

56. Cf. Francis William Kent, *Household and Lineage in Renaissance Florence: The Family Life of the Capponi, Ginori, and Rucellai* (Princeton, 1977); and my *Emancipation in Late Medieval Florence* (New Brunswick, 1982), 6, 65–69. 109–12.

57. Kent, *Medici,* 193. At least one reviewer has pointed to insufficient stress on that point: Roberto Bizzocchi, review of *Rise of the Medici,* in *Journal of Modern History* 52 (1980): 339–41. Also Ronald F. E. Weissman, *Ritual Brotherhoods in Renaissance Florence* (New York, 1982), 26–41.

58. Kuehn, *Emancipation,* 161–63. Legalities also served to protect kin against outsiders, whether by legal or fraudulent means.

59. Cf. Enriques, "La vendetta," 117–18, and note how hard she finds it to account for these examples. Also chapter 4.

60. Raggio, "Politica nella parentela," 737.

61. Ibid., 734, 748. He points out (749) that poor can use feud, by

breaking the peace and so forth, as leverage to renegotiate their effective position in the lineage.

62. Kent and Kent, "Self-Disciplining Pacts," 353.

Chapter Six

1. Publication of an excellent critical edition has greatly promoted use of the dialogue: Leon Battista Alberti, *Opere volgari*, ed. Cecil Grayson (Bari, 1960), vol. 1. Grayson's edition was later reproduced as *I libri della famiglia*, ed. Ruggiero Romano and Alberto Tenenti (Turin, 1969)—the edition I have used here—and translated by Renée Neu Watkins as *The Family in Renaissance Florence* (Columbia, S.C., 1969).

2. Cf. Watkins, *Family*, 2–3, 16–20. Hers is a more careful formulation than that of Werner Sombart, which influenced Alfred von Martin, *The Sociology of the Renaissance* (New York, 1944), 66. Also interesting is Christian Bec, *Les marchands écrivains: Affaires et humanisme à Florence, 1375–1434* (Paris, 1967); Alberto Tenenti, "Famille bourgeoise et idéologie au bas moyen âge," in *Famille et parenté dans l'Occident médiéval*, ed. Georges Duby and Jacques Le Goff (Rome, 1977), 431–40.

3. Joan Gadol, *Leon Battista Alberti: Universal Man of the Early Renaissance* (Chicago, 1969); Cecil Grayson, "The Humanism of Alberti," *Italian Studies* 12 (1957): 37–56. Romano in his introduction to *I libri della famiglia*, xxv, xxx–xxxviii, convincingly contests the facile interpretations of it as either bourgeois or civic, but he does so also to erect a contrary sense of the feudal-aristocratic elements in Quattrocento society and in Alberti's ideological depiction of it.

4. Giovanni Ponte, "Etica ed economia nel terzo libro 'Della Famiglia' di Leon Battista Alberti," in *Renaissance Studies in Honor of Hans Baron*, ed. Anthony Molho and John A. Tedeschi (Dekalb, Ill., 1971), 297, 302–3. To Ponte the idealized character of the family depicted by Alberti and the emphasis on morality and honor preclude that "si può considerare in modo assoluto una manifestazione di spirito borghese" (308). Cf. also David Marsh, *The Quattrocento Dialogue: Classical Tradition and Humanist Innovation* (Cambridge, Mass., 1980), 96.

5. Ponte, "Etica ed economia," 308; Grayson, "Humanism of Alberti," 47; Romano, *Libri della famiglia*, xxv: "La famiglia albertiana si presenta a noi come una cellula chiusa, un microorganismo, un fattore aristocratico, la cui azione è fine a sé stessa."

6. Marsh, *Quattrocento Dialogue*, 78.

7. Gadol, *Alberti*, 215.

8. Grayson, "Humanism of Alberti," 49.

9. Tenenti, "Famille bourgeoise," 439.

10. Grayson, "Humanism of Alberti," 38. Marsh, *Quattrocento Dialogue*, 99, remarks "the world of Albertian dialogue is thus singularly idealized,

reflecting the isolation of its author who, though employed in the Roman Curia and noted among its humanist members, turned to the tradition of his own family for an exemplar of learned discussion . . . more closely concerned with the practical. . . ." See also Armando Sapori, "La famiglia e le compagnie degli Alberti del Giudice," in his *Studi di storia economica, secoli xiii–xiv–xv*, 2 vols. (Florence, 1955), 2: 1010–11.

11. Watkins, *Family*, 20; David Herlihy and Christiane Klapisch-Zuber, *Les toscans et leurs familles* (Paris, 1978), 549.

12. Watkins, *Family*, 4–5.

13. Romano, *Libri della famiglia*, xxvii.

14. Eugenio Garin, "Il pensiero di Leon Battista Alberti: Caratteri e contrasti," *Rinascimento* 12 (1972): 5–6.

15. Romano, *Libri della famiglia*, xxviii; Watkins, *Family*, 5–6; Grayson, "Humanism of Alberti," 39; Gadol, *Alberti*, 227.

16. My theoretical point of departure derives from a consideration of the problem of the "intentional fallacy" as discussed by Dominick LaCapra, "Rethinking Intellectual History and Reading Texts," *History and Theory* 19 (1980): 245–76, reprinted in his *Rethinking Intellectual History: Texts, Contexts, Language* (Ithaca, 1983), 23–71; David Couzens Hoy, *The Critical Circle: Literature, History, and Philosophical Hermeneutics* (Berkeley, 1978); David Silverman and Brian Torode, *The Material Word: Some Theories of Language and Its Limits* (London, 1980); and Raymond Williams, *Marxism and Literature* (Oxford, 1977).

17. Riccardo Fubini and Anna Menci Gallorini eds., "L'Autobiografia di Leon Battista Alberti: Studio e edizione," *Rinascimento* 12 (1972): 71–72.

18. On this sense of the Ciceronian dialogue, see J. R. Woodhouse, *Baldesar Castiglione: A Reassessment of The Courtier* (Edinburgh, 1978), 4.

19. Marsh, *Quattrocento Dialogue*, 14.

20. A point made by Garin, "Pensiero di Alberti," and echoed by Marsh, *Quattrocento Dialogue*, 83.

21. Cf., Garin, "Pensiero di Alberti," 3.

22. Marsh, *Quattrocento Dialogue*, 89.

23. Cf. Anke Leineweber, *Die rechtliche Beziehung des nichtehelichen Kindes zu seinem Erzeuger in der Geschichte des Privatrechts* (Königstein, 1978); Hermann Winterer, *Die rechtliche Stellung der Bastarden in Italien von 800 bis 1500* (Munich, 1978); Corrado Pecorella, "Filiazione (storia)," *Enciclopedia del diritto* 17: 449–56; Gabriella Airaldi, " . . . bastardos, spurios, manzeres, naturales, incestuosos . . . ," in her *Studi e documenti su Genova e l'Oltremare* (Genoa, 1974), 317–55.

Two important contemporary treatises by jurists who had connections to Florence provide a systematic presentation of civil law: Benedetto Barzi (fl. 1440s–50s), *Tractatus de filiis non legitime natis*, and Antonio Roselli (1381–1466), *Tractatus legitimationum*, both in *Tractatus universi iuris*, vol. 8: *De ultimis voluntatibus*, part 2 (Venice, 1584), fols. 24ra–29vb (Barzi), 75ra–

90va (Roselli). The distinction between *naturales* and *spurii* in inheritance carried through to Florentine statutory law: *Statuta* 1415, 1: 217–18.

24. Carlo Ceschi, "La madre di Leon Battista Alberti," *Bollettino d'arte* 33 (1948): 191–92. See also *Dizionario biografico degli Italiani,* s.v. "Alberti, Leon Battista," by Cecil Grayson, and the old but still valuable biography by Girolamo Mancini, *Vita di Leon Battista Alberti,* 2d ed. (Florence, 1911).

25. It was the wealthy who more frequently recognized and raised their bastards. Herlihy and Klapisch-Zuber, *Les toscans,* 434, found 81.6 percent of all acknowledged bastards in the 1427 *catasto* were in households whose assessed wealth exceeded 400 florins. In addition to wealth, one should note the argument of Lauro Martines, *Power and Imagination: City-States in Renaissance Italy* (New York, 1979), 239, that great families were so secure in their honor that they could trumpet their greatness by flaunting their transgressions of social norms and openly parading their bastards about. Infanticide and abandonment, practices widely associated in peoples' minds with illegitimacy, may have been a more common fate for others' bastards: cf. David Herlihy, "Medieval Children," in *Essays on Medieval Civilization: The Walter Prescott Webb Lectures,* ed. Bede Karl Lackner and Kenneth Roy Philip (Austin, 1978), 109–41; Richard C. Trexler, "The Foundlings of Florence, 1395–1455," *History of Childhood Quarterly* 1 (1973–74): 259–84.

26. Cf. Leineweber, *Rechtliche Beziehung,* 50; Barzi, *Tractatus de filiis non legitime natis,* fols. 25ra–vb; Baldo degli Ubaldi, to D. 1.6.6, *Filium diffinimus, De iis qui sunt sui vel alieni iuris, In primam digesti veteris partem commentaria* (Venice, 1577), fol. 35vb; Bartolo da Sassoferrato, to D. 1.6.1, *Item in potestate, De iis qui sunt sui vel alieni iuris, In primam ff. veteris partem commentaria* (Venice, 1585), fol. 24rb: "Item no. quod de hoc ut sit in potestate patris, oportet quod sit natus ex iustis nuptiis. Unde naturalis tantum non est in potestate patris, multominus spurius." On the related problem of the disagnation of sons on emancipation from *patria potestas,* see my *Emancipation in Late Medieval Florence* (New Brunswick, 1982), 18, 26–27, 32, 139, 146.

27. On the various forms of legitimation, see Pecorella, "Filiazione," 452–54; Winterer, *Rechtliche Stellung,* 60–73; Leineweber, *Rechtliche Beziehung,* 64–66; and Ferdinand Kogler, *Die legitimatio per rescriptum von Justinian bis zum Tode Karls IV* (Weimar, 1904). On the later marriage of Lorenzo and the terms of his will, see Mancini, *Vita di Alberti,* 27–52; Romano, *Libri della famiglia,* xli–xlii; Gadol, *Alberti,* 3–4. It is highly unlikely that Lorenzo was ignorant of legitimation, if only because so many Alberti were versed in law and notarial practices, including Battista. His failure to legitimate his sons must have been deliberate.

28. On Alberti's finances, see Lauro Martines, *The Social World of the Florentine Humanists, 1390–1460* (Princeton, 1963), 142–44; Mancini, *Vita di Alberti,* 51–53; Watkins, *Family,* 5; Roberto Cessi, "Gli Alberti di Padova," *Archivio storico italiano,* 5th ser., 40 (1907): 233–84.

29. "L'Autobiografia," 69–71. Note especially his comment "sensit iniquissimorum odia occultasque inimicitias sibi incomodas atque nimium graves; ac praesertim a suis affinibus acerbissimas iniurias intollerabilesque contumelias pertulit animo constanti." See also Mancini, *Vita di Alberti*, 54; Grayson, "Humanism of Alberti," 39; and Renée Watkins, "The Authorship of the *Vita anonyma* of Leon Battista Alberti," *Studies in the Renaissance* 4 (1957): 101–12.

30. "Affinium suorum gratia" ("L'Autobiografia," 70).

31. Grayson, "Alberti, Leon Battista," 703–4; Gadol, *Alberti*, 5–6; and Mancini, *Vita di Alberti*, 54ff. According to Grayson the dedicatory prologue of the third book was added in 1437; the fourth book, on "Friendship," was composed in that year, revised in 1440, and given to the city of Florence in 1441.

32. Watkins, *Family*, 6; Romano, *Libri della famiglia*, xxviii–xxix.

33. Cf. Tenenti, "Famille bourgeoise," 432.

34. Cf. Herlihy and Klapisch-Zuber, *Les toscans*, 548–49; Herlihy, "Medieval Children," 123–24; Kuehn, *Emancipation*, 63; Paolo Cammarosano, "Les structures familiales dans les villes de l'Italie communale, xiie–xive siècles," in *Famille et parenté dans l'Occident médiéval*, ed. Georges Duby and Jacques Le Goff (Rome, 1977), 193.

35. In the Romano-Tenenti version, the Prologue occurs on 3–14. I have used the Watkins translation to help clarify my reading of the text, but all translations offered here are my own (and tend to a more literal form). Quote here occurs on 12.

36. "L'Autobiografia," 71.

37. On the structure of the work and the nature of the interlocutors, see Watkins, *Family*, 9–15; Ponte, "Etica ed economia," 288–89.

38. The import of this theme in French *livres de raison* and French families in the sixteenth century has been elegantly treated by Natalie Zemon Davis, "Ghosts, Kin, and Progeny: Some Features of Family Life in Early Modern France," *Daedalus*, 106, n. 2 (1977): 87–114.

39. Romano ed., *Libri della famiglia*, 254–55.

40. Ibid., 131. This comment neatly contrasts with several in "L'Autobiografia," 73, 76, where the hatred of kin is opposed to the appreciation tendered by friends.

41. Marsh, *Quattrocento Dialogue*, 84–85, sees all four books moving from disagreement in initial debate to consensus laid out in exposition. While I agree with this for Book Two, I find he downplays the presence of consensus at the beginning of the other two. His discussion of the constant shift between debate and exposition is very valuable.

42. The undeniability of Lorenzo's points is cemented by the reverential reaction of Adovardo and Lionardo (Romano ed., *Libri della famiglia*, 33–36).

43. Ibid., 102–4.

44. Regarding Alberti's views on love, see Francis William Kent, *Household*

and Lineage in Renaissance Florence: The Family Life of the Capponi, Ginori, and Rucellai (Princeton, 1977), 91.

45. Cf. Jacob Black-Michaud, *Cohesive Force: Feud in the Mediterranean and the Middle East* (New York, 1975), 233 n. 12; J. K. Campbell, *Honour, Family and Patronage* (Oxford, 1964), 187.

46. Romano ed., *Libri della famiglia*, 124–25.

47. Ibid., 127–28.

48. Ibid., 128–29.

49. Ibid., 136–38. As David Herlihy, "The Making of the Medieval Family: Symmetry, Structure, and Sentiment," *Journal of Family History* 8 (1983): 122, points out, there is a tension between bilateral and agnatic systems of reckoning kinship. This is one tension, however, that Alberti minimizes—this section being the only place he touches on it—perhaps because in his experience as an illegitimate he had only agnatic kin and was only concerned to assert his belonging to the male line. His mother died when he was young and his father removed him from Genoa and any further contact with his mother's lineage.

50. Here, interestingly, Lionardo attributes the source of quarrels and divisions not to brothers fighting over inheritance but to fathers who jealously guard their position, who place their own interests above those of the whole family and cause it to fraction into two or more households (Romano ed., *Libri della famiglia*, 149). Can this be a veiled reference to the treatment Battista and Carlo received from the eventual executors of their father's will?

51. Ibid., 150.

52. Ibid., 150–51.

53. Ibid., 152.

54. Ibid., 152–53.

55. Ibid., 153–54 (my emphasis).

56. Cf editors' remarks, "L'Autobiografia," 43.

57. The rarity of adoption in practice is uniformly remarked on by legal historians. Cf. *Enciclopedia del diritto*, s.v. "Adozione (diritto intermedio)," by Giulio Vismara, 1: 583–84; Pietro Torelli, *Lezioni di storia del diritto italiano: Diritto privato* (Milan, 1947), 98; Antonio Pertile, *Storia del diritto italiano dalla caduta dell'impero romano alla codificazione*, 2d ed., 4 vols. (Turin, 1894), 3: 396.

Formal adoption, which created *patria potestas* and rights to inheritance, must be distinguished from the informal practices of raising another's child, including *trovatelli*, a practice "by no means uncommon" (Mary Martin McLaughlin, "Survivors and Surrogates: Children and Parents from the Ninth to the Thirteenth Centuries," in *The History of Childhood*, ed. Lloyd de Mause [New York, 1974], 122). Cf. also Herlihy and Klapisch-Zuber, *Les toscans*, 331; Christiane Klapisch-Zuber, "L'enfance en Toscane au début du xve siècle," *Annales de démographie historique* 9 (1973): 113.

58. ASF, Notificazioni di atti di emancipazione 16, fol. 81v, reveals one of the few instances of adoption I found. Matteo d'Antonio Adimari had previously arrogated Niccolò di Bernardo Bartolini and emancipated him on 28 July 1516. Practically the only other example I found could be termed the sort of exception that proves the rule. Andrea di Cresci di Lorenzo Cresci adopted not some stranger but Cresci, the son of his brother Migliore. Cresci had been expressly emancipated for this purpose (ASF, Notarile antecosimiano G 617 [1469–72], fols. 351r–v [24 December 1471]). Here there was also a blood connection as well as a legal adoption.

59. Technically this is the form of adoption known as *adrogatio,* the adoption of someone *sui iuris.* On adoption and legitimation in Roman law, see Barry Nicholas, *An Introduction to Roman Law* (Oxford, 1962), 76–79, 84–85.

60. On the history of legitimation in law, see the references cited above in note 23.

61. As Baldo degli Ubaldi to D. 1.7.1, *Filios, De adoptionibus, In primam digesti veteris commentaria* (Venice, 1577), fol. 38rb.

62. Bartolo to D. 41.3.15, *Si is qui, De usurpationibus et usucapionibus, In primam digesti novi commentaria* (Venice, 1580), fol. 95rb.

63. Baldo to D. 1.7.36, *Emancipari,* ed. cit., fol. 44ra, and Paolo di Castro, 2 *cons.* 252, *Consilia* (Frankfurt, 1582), 3 vols., vol. 1, fol. 123vb. In general, see Roselli, *Tractatus legitimationum,* fols. 79vb–81rb, 88va–89ra.

64. Cf. A. E. Astin, *Scipio Aemelianus* (Oxford, 1967), 12–13. Astin also argues, 322–24, from a fragment of Gellius that Scipio himself deplored the full legal equation of adopted with natural sons.

65. Cf. Marino Berengo, *Nobili e mercanti nella Lucca del Cinquecento* (Turin, 1965), 44. Lorenzo Alberti had obviously chosen to let his line lapse legally.

66. Cf. Davis, "Ghosts, Kin, and Progeny," 104–5.

67. Cf. Watkins, *Family,* 2.

68. Most probably by Benedetto, who continued to withhold his legacy: cf. Grayson, "Alberti," 705; Mancini, *Vita di Alberti,* 169.

69. ASF, Notarile antecosimiano S687 (1434–35), 14 May 1434 (no pagination). Angelino was less than four, Giovanni over twelve.

70. On the uses and advantages of emancipation, see my *Emancipation in Late Medieval Florence.*

71. "L'Autobiografia," 58.

72. Ibid., 69.

73. Kent, *Household and Lineage,* 5, 44–45.

74. Romano ed., *Libri della famiglia,* 226.

75. Ibid., 234: "Sí, Lionardo mio, sotto uno tetto si riducano le famiglie, e se, cresciuta la famiglia, una stanza non può riceverle, assettinsi almeno sotto una ombra tutti d'uno volere." Lionardo's response—"Sotto uno volere stiano *le famiglie*" (my emphasis)—recalls the earlier definition in its use of

the plural. Berengo, *Nobili e mercanti,* 32–33, notes a similar connection between *famiglia* and *casa* (*familia* and *domus*) in Lucca.

76. As in the interplay of *vecchi* and *padri,* Romano ed., *Libri della famiglia,* 25–26. Kent has generally affirmed the importance of the patriline as a median and mediating element between household and lineage. Cf. *Household and Lineage,* esp. 115–17, 294.

77. Ibid., 232–34.

78. Cf. ibid., 38–39. The two criteria, blood and family custom, come together in (among other passages) Lionardo's depiction of "l'antica usanza di casa nostra."

79. Ibid., 95.

80. Ibid., 94, Lionardo maintains that a diligent father will not have problems, but on the next page he gives advice on what to do if the sons turn out badly, for whatever reason. Sons' vices as a source of family division are also mentioned twice before in Book One: cf. ibid., 39, 69.

81. Ibid., 126–29.

82. Ibid., 149–50.

83. Watkins, *Family,* 4; Martines, *Social World,* 144.

84. This theme is set down at the beginning of *Della famiglia* by Lorenzo, supposedly quoting his father: "'Non è solo officio del padre della famiglia, come si dice, riempiere el granaio in casa e la culla, ma molto più debbono e' capi d'una famiglia [note the plural and the shift from *padre* with its biological overtones to *capi* with its sense of governance] vegghiare e riguardare per tutto . . .'" (Romano ed., *Libri della famiglia,* 20).

85. Cf. Ernst Kantorowicz, "The Sovereignty of the Artist: A Note on Legal Maxims and Renaissance Theories of Art," in his *Selected Studies* (Locust Valley, N.Y., 1965), 352–65.

86. Even as he contemplated the shape of the family, Alberti conducted optical experiments and began to formulate aesthetic theory closely connected to ethics, toward a single goal of "bene et beato vivere." On the connection between Alberti's ethics and aesthetics, see Gadol, *Alberti,* esp. 100–4, 215–16, 235–39; Grayson, "Humanism of Alberti," 49, 52–53. Grayson, "Alberti," 704, dates his optical experiments to the same period as the composition of *Della famiglia.*

87. It is this sense of a past and a center to the lineage that is Giannozzo's chief contribution to the dialogue, cf. Romano, ed., *Libri della famiglia,* 209–10.

Chapter Seven

1. BNF, Landau-Finaly 98, fols. 54r–66v, contains the case of Simone and some initial documentation and narrative of facts. This is the signed and sealed original. A copy, with a shorter explanatory introduction and without any attribution of authorship is in BNF, Magliabechiano xxix, 117, fols. 2r–5r.

This was the first of two legitimations of Simone. The lack of specificity in the source has forced me to be vague about the dates and other circumstances of this event. I tentatively place the legitimation in 1408 because Domenico clearly died in 1409 according to the testimony of the *consilium*.

The legal fiction "ac si ab initio de legitimo matrimonio procreatus" (or an equivalent phrase) was a set formula of legitimation charters. See, for example, ASF, Notarile antecosimiano G212 (1422–29), fol. 182r.

2. The statistical side of legitimation will be explored in subsequent work based on research I am currently engaged in. Firm statistics are difficult to generate, but legitimations from all sources (counts palatine, the bishops, the Signoria) seem to have averaged about two to three a year in Florence.

3. Christopher N. L. Brooke, "Marriage and Society in the Central Middle Ages," in *Marriage and Society: Studies in the Social History of Marriage*, ed. R. B. Outhwaite (New York, 1981), 26. For two contrasting views of the social function of legitimacy, see Max Weber, *Economy and Society*, ed. Guenther Roth and Claus Wittich, 2 vols. (Berkeley, 1978), 1: 357–74; Frederick Engels, *The Origin of the Family, Private Property, and the State* (New York, 1972), 125–34. Also see the important remarks of Jacques Donzelot, *The Policing of Families*, trans. Robert Hurley (New York, 1979), 24.

4. Cf. Gene Brucker ed., *The Society of Renaissance Florence: A Documentary Study* (New York, 1971), 162–66.

5. Edward Shorter, "Illegitimacy, Sexual Revolution, and Social Change in Modern Europe," *Journal of Interdisciplinary History* 2 (1971): 237–72, and in other papers. His position is comprehensively presented in his *The Making of the Modern Family* (New York, 1975).

6. W. R. Lee, "Bastardy and the Socioeconomic Structure of South Germany," *Journal of Interdisciplinary History* 7 (1977): 416; Peter Laslett, "Introduction: Comparing Illegitimacy over Time and between Cultures," in *Bastardy and Its Comparative History: Studies in the History of Illegitimacy and Marital Nonconformism in Britain, France, Germany, Sweden, North America, Jamaica, and Japan*, ed. Peter Laslett, Karla Oosterveen, and Richard M. Smith (Cambridge, Mass., 1980), 1–65; Cissie Fairchilds, "Female Sexual Attitudes and the Rise of Illegitimacy: A Case Study," *Journal of Interdisciplinary History* 8 (1978): 627–67; Alan Macfarlane, "Illegitimacy and Illegitimates in English History," in *Bastardy and Its Comparative History*, 75; Louise A. Tilly, Joan W. Scott, and Miriam Cohen, "Women's Work and European Fertility Patterns," *Journal of Interdisciplinary History* 6 (1976): 447–76. See also Sandra Cavallo and Simona Cerruti, "Onore femminile e controllo sociale della riproduzione in Piemonte tra Sei e Settecento," *Quaderni storici* 44 (1980): 346–83; Gianna Pomata, "Madri illegittime tra Ottocento e Novecento: Storie cliniche e storie di vita," in ibid., 497–542.

7. Peter Laslett, *Family Life and Illicit Love in Earlier Generations: Essays in Historical Sociology* (Cambridge, 1977), 102–3. That this narrowly func-

tionalist view of deviance cannot exhaust the phenomenon will, I hope, emerge from the following discussion.

8. Etienne van de Walle, "Illegitimacy in France during the Nineteenth Century," in *Bastardy and Its Comparative History*, 277. A problem with both Laslett and Shorter "is the notion that social structures are characterized by statistical regularities and have a low tolerance for deviance. . . . Otherwise, change would occur, installing the form with the greatest statistical incidence as the new societal norm" (William A. Douglass, "The South Italian Family: A Critique," *Journal of Family History* 5 [1980]: 355). Other historians of illegitimacy—Lee, Fairchilds, Tilly, et al.—have been, in my opinion, more successful in explaining the causes of illegitimacy (in terms of rule manipulation by social actors in given situations) and, in so doing, have indicated the path to be taken in examining the further assimilation of illegitimacy. Also interesting in the present context is the cautionary remark of van de Walle, "Illegitimacy in France," in *Bastardy and Its Comparative History*, 269, that legitimation by subsequent marriage is not a valid indicator of a lasting sexual relationship (as Laslett assumes) but of a serious intent of the father toward the child.

9. Typical here are the works of Leineweber, Winterer, and Pecorella cited herein, as well as Jean-Louis Flandrin, *Families in Former Times: Kinship, Household and Sexuality*, trans. Richard Southern (Cambridge, 1977). Telling criticisms of legal historical methodology can be found in Julius Kirshner, "Some Problems in the Interpretation of Legal Texts re the Italian City-States," *Archiv für Begriffsgeschichte* 19 (1975): 16–27; Luigi Berlinguer, "Considerazioni su storiografia e diritto," *Studi storici* 15 (1974): 3–56.

10. Lauro Martines, *Power and Imagination: City-States in Renaissance Italy* (New York, 1979), 239; Hermann Winterer, *Die rechtliche Stellung der Bastarden in Italien von 800 bis 1500* (Munich, 1978), 59–60; Anke Leineweber, *Die rechtliche Beziehung des nichtehelichen Kindes zu seinem Erzeuger in der Geschichte der Privatrechts* (Königstein, 1978), 71–98, wherein she argues generally, solely on the basis of legal doctrinal texts, that the legal lot of bastards improved from the fourteenth century. J. P. Cooper, "Patterns of Inheritance and Settlement by Great Landowners from the Fifteenth to the Eighteenth Centuries," in *Family and Inheritance: Rural Society in Western Europe, 1200–1800*, ed. Jack Goody, Joan Thirsk, and E. P. Thompson (Cambridge, 1976), 302, makes the same point about the nobility in France.

11. Robert Davidsohn, *Storia di Firenze*, vol. 4: *I primordi della civiltà fiorentina*, Part 3: *Il mondo della chiesa, spiritualità e arte, vita pubblica e privata*, trans. from the German by Eugenio Dupré-Theseider (Florence, 1973), 697–700, as well as those cited in the previous note. Davidsohn's vision of a modern and enlightened sense of childhood and illegitimacy prevailing in Florence does not stand up well before the facts of Simone's case.

12. The limited statistical evidence generated by Herlihy and Klapisch-Zuber is utilized below. The lack of consistent birth and marriage registration

for the fourteenth and fifteenth centuries in Florence will make full-scale statistical study of illegitimacy there impossible.

13. On Boccaccio, see Vittore Branca, *Boccaccio: The Man and His Works*, trans. and ed. Dennis J. McAuliffe (New York, 1976), 4–10, 53–54, 58, 71, 97, 119–22; Thomas G. Bergin, *Boccaccio* (New York, 1981). On Alberti, see Joan Gadol, *Leon Battista Alberti: Universal Man of the Early Renaissance* (Chicago, 1969), 3–4; *Dizionario biografico degli italiani*, s.v. "Alberti," by Cecil Grayson. Alberti, in fact, was deprived of his inheritance by paternal relatives because of his illegitimate birth. See Chapter 6.

14. *King Lear,* Act I, Scene ii, line 18.

15. The study of disputes through the so-called extended case method has been the hallmark of legal anthropology. This field has recently experienced a great deal of theoretical and methodological discussion, the reproduction of which is not possible in the present context. For now the reader is referred to the works cited in the first chapter.

16. BNF, Landau-Finaly 98, fols. 54r–57v. Simone's double legitimation was not that unusual, at least among cases that came to court. See other examples in Filippo Decio, *cons.* 698, *Consilia* (Venice, 1575), 2 vols., vol. 2, fols. 300va–301ra; Paolo di Castro, 2 *cons.* 22, *Consilia* (Frankfurt, 1582), 3 vols., fols. 12ra–vb, and 2 *cons.* 41, fols. 22ra–rb.

17. BNF, Landau-Finaly 98, fol. 54r.

18. Because the *consilium* serving as the source here reveals only the legal facts considered relevant to the case, it is not possible to determine precisely the material value of the estate at issue or any other socioeconomic data on the parties. It is likewise impossible to determine what sort of male help Lena may have had—beyond the male advocate she (as a woman) was required to have by law. It is possible that Lena was married, in which case her husband may have been instrumental. The hospital of San Francesco was also certainly an interested party and may have had a hand in the litigation.

19. On this theme, see Thomas Kuehn, *Emancipation in Late Medieval Florence* (New Brunswick, 1982), 55–71, and the literature cited therein.

20. BNF, Landau-Finaly 98, fols. 57v–59r, reproducing the 1355 statutes of the Podestà, Book 2, rubric 73: Qualiter mulier ab intestato succedat, fols. 97v–98v.

21. Franco Niccolai, *La formazione del diritto successorio negli statuti comunali del territorio lombardo-tosco* (Milan, 1940), 65–109.

22. Podestà 1355, Book 2, rubric 75: Quod commune Florentie ab intestato succedat. Quod generaliter succedant naturales et bastardi etc., fols. 98v–99r. The distinction between *naturales* and *spurii* was an important one in the law, for *naturales* were subject to fewer disabilities and had available legitimation by the possible subsequent marriage of their parents. *Spurii,* on the other hand, were the result of casual or illicit sexual unions: see Leineweber, *Rechtliche Beziehung,* 46–47; Corrado Pecorella, "Filiazione (storia)," *Enciclopedia del diritto,* 17: 453; and Benedetto Barzi, *Tractatus de filiis non*

legitime natis, in *Tractatus universi iuris* (Venice, 1584), vol. 8, part 2, fols. 24vb–25ra.

23. On these themes, see Chapters 8 and 9.

24. Hence marriage was described as *condurre ad onore* in contrast to fornication. See Julius Kirshner, *Pursuing Honor While Avoiding Sin: The Monte delle doti of Florence* (Milan, 1978), 10–11.

25. On this theme, *Prosatori minori del Trecento: Scrittori di religione del Trecento volgarizzamenti,* ed. Giuseppe de Luca (Milan, 1954; reprint ed., Turin, 1977), 3: 496–97; Giovanni Sercambi, *Novelle,* ed. Giovanni Sinicropi (Bari, 1972), novelle 30, 35, 60, 70, 83, 127, 149. Also Diane Owen Hughes, "From Brideprice to Dowry in Mediterranean Europe," *Journal of Family History* 3 (1978): 284–85; Leineweber, *Rechtliche Beziehung,* 55–59, 68. Among canonists the stain of birth was usually referred to as the *defectus natalium,* on which see Bernhard Schimmilpfennig, "*Ex Fornicatione Nati:* Studies on the Position of Priests' Sons from the Twelfth to the Fourteenth Century," *Studies in Medieval and Renaissance History,* n.s. 2 (1979): 23–25; and Winterer, *Rechtliche Stellung,* 58–59.

26. In addition to those mentioned below as applicable to Simone, there were also guild statutes prohibiting bastards from membership, as in the guild of lawyers and notaries: Lauro Martines, *Lawyers and Statecraft in Renaissance Florence* (Princeton, 1968), 28.

27. On these themes, David Herlihy, "Medieval Children," in *Essays in Medieval Civilization: The Walter Prescott Webb Lectures,* ed. Bede Karl Lackner and Kenneth Roy Philip (Austin, 1978), 109–41; Richard C. Trexler, "The Foundlings of Florence, 1395–1455," *History of Childhood Quarterly* 1 (1973–74): 259–84; idem, "Infanticide in Florence: New Sources and First Results," ibid., 96–116; and the important statistics garnered from the *catasto* of 1427 by David Herlihy and Christiane Klapisch-Zuber, *Les toscans et leurs familles* (Paris, 1978), 339, 434. Also Mary Martin McLaughlin, "Survivors and Surrogates: Children and Parents from the Ninth to the Thirteenth Centuries," in *The History of Childhood,* ed. Lloyd de Mause (New York, 1974), 120–22, 158–59 n. 110; James Bruce Ross, "The Middle-Class Child in Urban Italy, Fourteenth to Early Sixteenth Century," in ibid., 195–97. A revealing portrait of the dishonorable status of the bastard is offered by J. K. Campbell, *Honour, Family and Patronage* (Oxford, 1964), 187. The connection between honor and socially approved paternity is well drawn by Julian Pitt-Rivers, *The Fate of Shechem: Essays in the Anthropology of the Mediterranean* (Cambridge, 1977), 77–79.

28. Herlihy and Klapisch-Zuber, *Les toscans,* 434. As they acknowledge, however, the poorer classes may also have had a different view of marriage, so children in their homes may have been technically illegitimate. The wealthy, I would suggest, had more reason also to heighten and prolong the ambiguity of illegitimacy by hanging the tag on those whom it fit.

29. See Gian Savino Pene Vidari, *Ricerche sul diritto agli alimenti* (Turin,

1970), 153–72; Leineweber, *Rechtliche Beziehung*, 62–63; Barzi, *Tractatus*, fols. 24ra–29vb; Christiane Klapisch-Zuber, "Genitori naturali e genitori di latte nella Firenze del Quattrocento," *Quaderni storici* 44 (1980): 545. Not only was this support and identity confirmed in law, but such support and identity emerged in the treatment accorded illegitimates by their fathers, as revealed in domestic *ricordi:* as that of Luca da Panzano, ASF, Carte strozziane, 2nd ser., 9, fol. 22r, and Goro Dati, in *Two Memoirs of Renaissance Florence*, ed. Gene Brucker (New York, 1967), 112.

30. Florentine elite families in the fifteenth century had an acute sense of the precariousness of familial continuity resting on legitimate male descent: Herlihy and Klapisch-Zuber, *Les toscans*, 548–49; Paolo Cammarosano, "Les structures familiales dans les villes d'Italie communale, xiie–xive siècles," in *Famille et parenté dans l'Occident médiéval*, ed. Georges Duby and Jacques Le Goff (Rome, 1977), 193.

31. Schimmelpfennig, "*Ex Fornicatione Nati*," 27–29, 38–46; Iris Origo, "The Domestic Enemy: Eastern Slaves in Tuscany in the Fourteenth and Fifteenth Centuries," *Speculum* 30 (1955): 345.

32. Martines, *Power and Imagination*, 239.

33. It is not possible to tell if this occurred at the instigation of the parties or of the judge. The tone of the *consilium* and its balance, and the nature of some of the questions submitted to the jurists, would argue for its characterization as a judicial, rather than an advocatory, *consilium*. See Mario Ascheri, "'Consilium sapientis', perizia medica e 'res iudicata': Diritto dei dottori e istituzioni comunali," *Proceedings of the Fifth International Congress of Medieval Canon Law*, ed. Stephan Kuttner (Rome, 1980), 533–79.

34. Brief biographical data on Omodei and Fulgosio can be found in Domenico Maffei, *La donazione di Costantino nei giuristi medievali* (Milan, 1964), 210n, 261–62. Conti was teaching canon law in his native Padua ca. 1424–27 (see Jacques Le Goff, "Academic Expenses at Padua in the Fifteenth Century," in his *Time, Work, and Culture in the Middle Ages*, trans. Arthur Goldhammer [Chicago 1980], 101–6, 311–12 n. 3).

35. Martines, *Lawyers*, makes no mention of these three. Fulgosio was an advocate at the Council of Constance in 1414, and it is possible that he and the other two were in Florence in connection with the Council of Pisa of 1409. Certainly the council provoked a great deal of expert legal discussion and advice in Florence (as per ibid., 290–96). Use of traveling jurists was not unusual.

36. The signatures of Fulgosio and Conti even occupy a separate folio, BNF, Landau-Finaly, fol. 67r. I did not find this *consilium*, in any form, in Signorino degli Omodei, *Consilia* (Lyons, 1549) or in Raphaele Fulgosio, *Consilia* (Venice, 1575).

37. On these matters of legal history, Leineweber, *Rechtliche Beziehung*, 64–66; Pecorella, "Filiazione," 453–54; Winterer, *Rechtliche Stellung*, 74, 111; Ferdinand Kogler, *Die legitimatio per rescriptum von Justinian bis zum*

Tode Karls IV (Weimar, 1904), 44–45, 76–83; and especially Gabriella Airaldi, " . . . bastardos, spurios, manzeres, naturales, incestuosos . . . ," in her *Studi e documenti su Genova e l'Oltremare* (Genoa, 1974), 323, 333–37.

38. As per Antonio Roselli (a Florentine, 1381–1466), *Tractatus legitimationum,* in *Tractatus universi iuris,* vol. 8: *De ultimis voluntatibus,* part 2 (Venice, 1584), fols. 86va–vb; Baldo degli Ubaldi, to D. 1.7.36, *Emancipari, De adoptionibus, In primam digesti veteris partem commentaria* (Venice, 1577), fol. 44ra. On the imperial-papal jurisdictional issue, see Kenneth Pennington, "Pope Innocent III's Views on Church and State: A Gloss to *Per venerabilem,*" in *Law, Church, and Society: Essays in Honor of Stephan Kuttner,* ed. Kenneth Pennington and Robert Somerville (Philadelphia, 1977), 55.

39. As Roselli, *Tractatus legitimationum,* fol. 85ra: "istud ius legitimandi est quoddam officium inhaerens principali dignitati." See also his discussion of civic pretensions, fols. 86ra–va. Also Airaldi, " . . . bastardos," 320–22.

40. Manlio Bellomo, *Società e istituzioni in Italia dal medioevo agli inizi dell'età moderna,* 3d ed. (Catania, 1982), 413–83; Julius Kirshner, "Some Problems in the Interpretation of Legal Texts," 16–27.

41. BNF, Landau-Finaly 98, fol. 61r–v. Discussion of some of these jurisprudential positions can be found in Walter Ullmann, *The Medieval Idea of Law, as Represented by Lucas de Penna: A Study in Fourteenth-Century Legal Scholarship* (London, 1946), 176–78. Marc Bloch, *The Royal Touch: Sacred Monarchy and Scrofula in England and France,* trans. J. E. Anderson (Montreal, 1973), 126–27, explores the same theme, with the additional observation that, whereas monarchs and lawyers sought to refuse the capacity of coronation to constitute legitimacy, "common opinion in every country was reluctant to admit that a king was truly king, or an Emperor Elect truly head of the Empire, before the religious act had been performed." The election/coronation distinction in imperial or royal legitimacy had its echo in the birth/contract distinction in individual legitimacy, again as a result of "common opinion" (as will be seen below).

42. Roselli, *Tractatus legitimationum,* fol. 87ra; Antonio da Butrio, to X. 4.17.13, *Per venerabilem, Qui filii sint legitimi, In librum quartum decretalium commentaria* (Venice, 1578), fol. 52vb; Bartolo da Sassoferrato, to D. 1.6.11, *Inviti, De his qui sunt sui vel alieni iuris, In primam digesti veteris partem commentaria* (Venice, 1585), fol. 25rb. Analogously, consent of father and child was required to dissolve *patria potestas* in emancipation, on which see Kuehn, *Emancipation,* 12.

43. As Antonio da Butrio, to X. 4.17.13, ed. cit., fol. 52va. Roselli, himself mainly a canonist, records Hostiensis and Giovanni d'Andrea, *Tractatus legitimationum,* fols. 87vb–88ra.

44. BNF, Landau-Finaly 98, fol. 61v: "Est enim pater dominus bonorum suorum, ideo in eorum dispositione non requiritur consensus alterius quam ipsius patris." He echoes here Bartolo, to D. 28.2.29,5, *Gallus § et quid si*

tantum, De liberis et posthumis, In primam infortiati partem commentaria (Venice, 1581), fol. 95ra: "hoc principaliter tangit patrem qui potest disponere de bonis suis quomodo vult. . . ." Also Baldo degli Ubaldi, to D. 1.7.39, *Nam ita divus, De adoptionibus, In primam digesti veteris*, fol. 44va.

45. Decio, *Consilia*, 2 vols. (Venice, 1575), *cons.* 557, ed. cit., vol. 2, fol. 212rb: "quia tali casu non agitur de praeiudicio agnatorum, cum pater possit bona sua proicere in mari si velit."

46. BNF, Landau-Finaly 98, fol. 61v. On *infans* and other age categories in medieval civil law, see *Enciclopedia del diritto*, s.v. "Età (diritto intermedio)," by Ugo Gualazzini, 16: 80–85.

47. Important for Omodei's argument were Antonio da Butrio, to X. 4.17.13, *Per venerabilem*, ed. cit., fol. 52vb; and Bartolo, to C. 8.48(49).5, *Iubemus, De emancipationibus liberorum, In secundam codicis partem commentaria* (Venice, 1580), fol. 113va. These issues are summed up by Roselli, *Tractatus legitimationum*, fol. 87ra. On emancipation of *infantes*, see Kuehn, *Emancipation*, 16.

48. Omodei cites only D. 1.7.25,1, with an accompanying analogy to emancipation. While that was certainly the key text, he does not cite authoritative figures like Jacopo Bottrigari and Angelo degli Ubaldi, as does Roselli, *Tractatus legitimationum*, fol. 88rb.

49. BNF, Landau-Finaly 98, fol. 62r. The relevant passages are: Bartolo, to D. 28.2.29,8, *Gallus § forsitan*, ed. cit., fol. 96vb; Baldo, to D. 28.2.29,8, *In primam et secundam infortiati partes commentaria* (Venice, 1577), fols. 69ra–rb. Omodei cites these passages in his *consilium* only as support for an analogy in the use of a *procurator* in legitimation of a son and in manumission of a slave.

50. Omodei went on (BNF, Landau-Finaly 98, fol. 62v) to uphold a clause in that mandate of *procurationis* that enjoined Antonio from in any way revoking the legitimation. Because this issue is tangential to that of legitimation (though important to the case), it will not be discussed here.

51. BNF, Landau-Finaly 98, fols. 62v–63r.

52. Bartolo, to D. 28.2.29,5, *Gallus § et quid si tantum, De liberis et posthumis*, ed. cit., fols. 95ra–va; Roselli, *Tractatus legitimationum*, fols. 87vb–88ra.

53. And this although at the time of the legitimation Antonio still had the possibility of fathering his own children (BNF, Landau-Finaly 98, fol. 66r).

54. Ibid., fol. 63r: "In vita enim patris legiptimatio confert mixtum commodum et incommodum, commodum conferendo ius legiptimationis quo ad succedendum patri et aliis agnatis, incommodum quia subicitur patrie potestati. Ideo requiritur eius consensus . . . sed post mortem patris legiptimatio continet tantum commodum habilitando ad succedendum patri et aliis agnatis. Ideo adquiretur filio talis habilitatio sine consensu suo. . . . Ex predictis concludo primam legiptimationem validam esse et si ipsa non est valida secunda est valida sine dubio."

55. Ibid., fol. 59v: "Quarto nunquid iste Simon censeatur ficte vel vere legitimus et an comprendatur sub verbis statuti in fine, ita quod dici possit legitimus et naturalis ex legitimo matrimonio, ita quod excludat matrem Antonii a successione filii, et an dicta legitimatio et restitutio faciat eum vere legitimum quo ad omnia."

56. Ibid., fols. 63r–v. In so arguing, Omodei was echoing the assertions of Baldo, to D. 28.2.29,5, ed. cit., fol. 66va, who was also discussing this Florentine statute, as was Bartolo, to D. 36.1.2,47, *Sive ingenua, Ad Tertullianum, In secundam infortiati partem commentaria* (Venice, 1580), fols. 176va–vb.

57. BNF, Landau-Finaly 98, fol. 63v. The crucial texts he cites are D. 40.11.2 and 3 and 5, which can be found in *Corpus iuris civilis,* ed. T. H. Mommsen, W. Kroll, P. Krueger, and R. Schoell, 3 vols. (Berlin, 1928–29).

58. Ibid.: "Praeterea legiptimatus est restitutus antique nature et ingenuitati quo iure nature omnes nascebantur liberi. . . ."

59. Ibid.: "Et sic per legitimationem macula inlegiptimationis in totum extrepatur adeo quod taliter legiptimatus habetur per inde acsi esset per omnia legiptimus, ut dicta l. ii et iii et fi. ff. de na. resti. Unde magis dicitur redditus antique nature quam de novo legiptimus fieri ar. l. filio ff. de li. et po. Preterea sicut concupiscentia et inlicitus coitus fuit occaxio offuscandi antiquas legiptimas soboles ita legittimatio maculas extirpans reparat antiquam legiptimitatem."

60. See Winterer, *Rechtliche Stellung,* 71; Pecorella, "Filiazione," 453; Hostiensis, to X. 4.17, *Qui filii sint legitimi, Summa aurea* (Venice, 1605), cols. 1379–80; Innocent IV, to X. 4.17.13, *Commentaria in v libros decretalium* (Frankfurt, 1570; reprint ed., Frankfurt, 1968), fol. 481ra, repeated by Giovanni d'Andrea, to X. 4.17.13, *Novella super quarto et quinto decretalium* (Venice, 1504–5), fol. 37ra; Guglielmo Durante, *De successionibus ab intestato, Speculum iudiciale* (1479), fol. 205vb.

61. Jacopo Bottrigari, to *Prohemio codicis, Lectura super codice* (reprint ed., Bologna, 1973), fol. 1rb: "Cave tamen quod quis legitimando non facit quem legitimum sed iura legitimationis ei confert unde removet impedimentum et reddit eum iuri nature in qua non erat discretio in coitu."

62. BNF, Landau-Finaly 98, fol. 63v, citing the *Glossa ordinaria,* to D. 1.6.6, *Filium, De his qui sunt sui vel alieni iuris* (Lyons, 1612), vol. 1, col. 97.

63. BNF, Landau-Finaly 98, fol. 64r: "debet intelligi de legiptimis proprie et naturaliter et non de legiptimis civiliter per principis privilegium."

64. Baldo, to C. 2.44(45).4, *Si quis, De his qui veniam aetatis impetrant, In primos libros codicis commentaria* (Lyons, 1546), fol. 140ra, and to D. 31.[1].51,1, *Si ita quis, De legatis et fideicommissis ii, In primam et secundam infortiati,* ed. cit., fol. 151rb: "Civilis filius non implet conditionem fideicommissi. hoc dicit. Vel, sic, verbum prolatum simpliciter, intelligitur naturaliter, non secundum fictionem."

65. As he does, D. 1.7.1, *Filios, De adoptionibus,* ed. cit., fol. 38rb. With regard to legitimation, then, Baldo argued that what was restored was not a pristine nature so much as the *habitus* of acting in accord with that nature: *additio* to D. 1.7.36, *Emancipari,* ibid., fol. 44ra: "et cave quod legitimando non facit quem legitimum, si iura legitimorum ei confert, unde removet impedimentum, et reddit eum habilem, et restituit iuri nature. . . . Et dico quod legitimatus est restitutus iuri naturae, et ideo est legitimus vi restitutionis: quia auferre privationem nil aliud est quam conferre habitum . . . et aliud est removere obstaculum: quia obstaculum est velatio habitus. . . . Vel dic quod sicut aliud est ingenuus, aliud libertinus, sicut est legitimus, aliud est legitimatus per principem."

On fiction in medieval law, Ernst Kantorowicz, "The Sovereignty of the Artist: A Note on Legal Maxims and Renaissance Theories of Art," *Selected Studies* (Locust Valley, N.Y., 1965), 352–65. Specifically with regard to Baldo on the related theme of acquired citizenship, Kirshner, "*Ars imitatur naturam:* A Consilium of Baldus on Naturalization in Florence," *Viator* 5 (1974): 289–331 and idem, "Between Nature and Culture: An Opinion of Baldus of Perugia on Venetian Citizenship as Second Nature," *Journal of Medieval and Renaissance Studies* 9 (1979): 179–208; Joseph P. Canning, "A Fourteenth-Century Contribution to the Theory of Citizenship: Political Man and the Problem of Created Citizenship in the Thought of Baldus de Ubaldis," in *Authority and Power: Studies on Medieval Law and Government Presented to Walter Ullmann on His Seventieth Birthday,* ed. Brian Tierney and Peter Linehan (Cambridge, 1980), 197–212..

66. Paolo di Castro, *Consilia* (Frankfurt, 1580), 2 *cons.* 252, fol. 123vb: "cum enim legitimorum duae sint species, quia quidam originarii, quidam non, et inter eos in multis est differentia communis usus loquendi, ut singuli eorum singulis appellationibus distinguantur." See also Anna T. Sheedy, *Bartolus on Social Conditions in the Fourteenth Century* (New York, 1942), 73–74.

67. Bartolo, to D. 41.3.15, *Si is qui pro emptore, De usurpationibus et usucapionibus, In primam digesti novi partem commentaria* (Venice, 1580), fol. 95rb: "Pone ergo lex ex certa causa vult filium in potestate facere sui iuris, filium non legitimum vult facere legitimum, et servum liberum, potest ne hoc facere? Certe, sic, tamen non secundum fictionem sed secundum ipsam puram veritatem, quia vere erit sui iuris, vel legitimus, vel liber." This was consistent with Bartolo's view of acquired citizenship, as explained by Kirshner, "*Civitas Sibi Faciat Civem:* Bartolus of Sassoferrato's Doctrine on the Making of a Citizen," *Speculum* 48 (1973): 694–713.

68. Novel 89.9 in c. (=A. 7.1.9 in c.).

69. BNF, Landau-Finaly 98, fol. 64r: "Sublato ipso velamine per manumissionem detegitur sic et depulsio nubium non facit serenum sed detegit serenum quod inest celo naturaliter. Facit ad predicta quia discussio grani de spica non facit granum sed granum quod est naturaliter detegit. . . ."

Glossa ordinaria, to D. 1.1.4, *Manumissiones, De iustitia et iure* (Lyons, 1612), col. 57.

70. A succinct presentation and summation of this concept in relation to legitimacy is in Roselli, *Tractatus legitimationum,* fols. 76rb–va, 88vb; but see also Hostiensis, *Summa aurea,* ed. cit., cols. 1379–80; Angelo degli Ubaldi, to A. 7.1.1 in c, § *Natura, Quibus modis naturales efficiantur sui, Opus ac lectura autenticorum* (Venice, 1485), fol. 24ra; Paolo di Castro, 1 *cons.* 180, ed. cit., fol. 90rb; Winterer, *Rechtliche Stellung,* 71; Pecorella, "Filiazione," 453. On the political implications and the origins of the concept of *ius naturale primaevum,* see Bellomo, *Società e istituzioni,* 433–34.

71. Paolo di Castro, 2 *cons.* 467, ed. cit., fol. 226ra: "Legitimi vero dicuntur propter solennitatem mutui matrimonialis consensus coniunctam huic naturali coniunctioni, quae solennitas a iure civi. est inventa." Also A. Esmein, *Le mariage en droit canonique,* 2 vols. (Paris, 1891; reprint ed., New York, 1968), 2: 37–39.

72. BNF, Landau-Finaly 98, fol. 64r: "Sic legiptimitas in sui substantia inest spureo naturaliter cum ei insit a iure naturali primevo quod quidem ius naturale immutabile est, que legiptimitas propter spureitatem et inlegiptimum coitum offuscatur ut spureus non habeat exercitium legiptimitatis quo ad succedendum patri et agnatis et cognatis et quo ad honores. In hiis enim non reputatur pro filio nec pro agnato nec pro cognato. In hiis autem que sunt iuris naturalis primevi ut est defensio, coniungatio maris et femine, liberorum educatio. In hiis filius spureus habet exercitium legiptimitatis ei naturaliter inherentis."

73. Ibid., fol. 64v: "vel facit diversitatem inter legiptimum nullo tempore obumbratum et legiptimatum, qui erat legiptimus obumbratus a principio, tamen sublata obumbratione per legiptimationem legiptimus est naturaliter et in omnibus et per omnia ut legiptimus in principio non obumbratus." This passage was in fact an afterthought inserted in the margin.

74. As Paolo di Castro, 2 *cons.* 252, ed. cit., fol. 123vb; Antonio da Butrio, to X. 4.17.13, ed. cit., fol. 53rb; Roselli, *Tractatus legitimationum,* fol. 89va.

75. As Paolo di Castro, 2 *cons.* 343, ed. cit., fols. 171rb–va, where he rehearses arguments he attributes to Jacopo d'Arena; also Bartolomeo Sozzini, 3 *cons.* 63, *Consilia* (Venice, 1579), fols. 69vb–70rb.

76. Roselli, *Tractatus legitimationum,* fol. 89ra; Angelo degli Ubaldi, to A. 7.1.6, § *Si quis autem, Quibus modis naturales efficiantur sui, Opus ac lectura autenticorum,* fol. 20ra.

77. BNF, Landau-Finaly 98, fol. 65r.

78. Thus the statute directed attention to time of birth, while Francesco's will (by Omodei's implicit reckoning) referred to the time of death of Domenico and Antonio.

79. Ibid.: "In isto ergo capitulo in totum matris exclusivo non comprehendetur nepos ex fratre carnali legiptimatus cum non sit ex legiptimo matrimonio natus ut in c. innotuit extra de elec. [X. 1.6.20]." Also fol. 65v.

80. Along the same lines: Antonio da Butrio, to X. 4.17.6, *Tanta,* ed. cit., fol. 45rb; Roselli, *Tractatus legitimationum,* fol. 89rb; Decio, *cons.* 154, ed. cit., vol. 1, fol. 165ra; Paolo di Castro, 1 *cons.* 180, ed. cit., fol. 90va.

81. As Bartolo, to D. 38.17.2,47, *Sive ingenua § in videndum, In secundam infortiati,* ed. cit., fol. 176va.

82. BNF, Landau-Finaly 98, fols. 65v–66r. Omodei found no reason, as a result, to examine the question posed by the court as to whether Lena excluded Agnola.

83. Such use of a *consilium* was possible and became fairly frequent toward the end of the fifteenth century.

84. On this sense of "legitimate," see Pierre Bourdieu, *Outline of a Theory of Practice,* trans. Richard Nice (Cambridge, 1977), 19.

85. This sense of legal norms derives from a reading of Sally Falk Moore, "Descent and Legal Position," first published in 1972 in *Law in Culture and Society,* ed. Laura Nader (Chicago, 1972), now reprinted in Moore's *Law as Process* (London, 1978), esp. 152–53, 156–58, 162–64, 170.

86. Charles Donahue Jr., "The Case of the Man Who Fell into the Tiber: The Roman Law of Marriage at the Time of the Glossators," *American Journal of Legal History* 22 (1978): 1–53; Jean Dauvillier, *Le mariage dans le droit classique de l'église* (Paris, 1933); and John T. Noonan, Jr., "Power to Choose," *Viator* 4 (1973): 419–34.

87. This is a sense of nature that recurs in medieval and Renaissance medical literature. For a Florentine example of advice on how and when to have sex, so as to procreate the best possible nature in a child, see Leon Battista Alberti, *I libri della famiglia,* ed. Ruggiero Romano and Alberto Tenenti (Turin, 1969), 138–41. The sense that the circumstances of conception of bastards endowed them with a different nature was invoked in a humorous but satirical way by Ortensio Lando in his *Paradossi* (1544) and echoed by Shakespeare in Edmund's soliloquy in *King Lear,* Act I, Scene ii, lines 11–15.

88. Thus the juristic definitions of fiction: Bartolo, to D. 41.3.15, *Si is qui, De usurpationibus et usucapionibus, In primam digesti novi partem commentaria* (Venice, 1580), fol. 94vb: "Fictio est in re certa eius quod est possibile contra veritatem, pro veritate a iure facta assumptio. . . . Ars enim semper imitatur naturam, et id quod est impossibile secundum naturam est impossibile secundum artem." Baldo, to D. 1.7.1, *Filios, De adoptionibus,* ed. cit., fol. 38rb.

89. As Moore notes, *Law as Process,* 179, "Formal extension or loose interpretation [as in the *consilium*] does more lip-service to the exclusiveness of a patrilineal-patrilocal descent group ideology than would the open acknowledgement of legitimate alternative arrangements." Omodei's use of ontologically vague, as opposed to historically and factually precise, nature fits Moore's point. Bottrigari and Baldo, on the other hand, would seem more openly to have acknowledged the alternativeness of legitimation and thus to have made it more difficult to achieve.

90. On the ideological dimensions of jurists' work, the most forceful presentation is that of Mario Sbriccoli, *L'interpretazione dello statuto* (Milan, 1969), and his "Politique et interprétation juridique dans les villes italiennes du moyen âge," *Archives de philosophie du droit* 17 (1972): 99–113. More balanced views are those of Kirshner, "Some Problems," 22–23; Luigi Lombardi, *Saggio sul diritto giurisprudenziale* (Milan, 1967), 79–199; Colin Sumner, *Reading Ideologies: An Investigation into the Marxist Theory of Ideology and Law* (New York, 1979), 246–85.

91. The sense that this is what legitimation was all about was perhaps best expressed years later in another *consilium* by Bartolomeo Sozzini, 3 *cons.* 63, ed. cit., fol. 70rb: "sed ratio assignata, ne bona exeant, sed in familia remaneant, arguit quod cessantibus masculis de legitimo matrimonio, admittantur legitimati. . . . non est dubium quod videns quod nullo alio modo poterant in familia remanere, quod specifice disposuisset hunc legitimatum foeminis, et descendentibus ex foeminis praeferendum." Statutes excluding women from inheritance beyond their dowries were explained as safeguarding male descent and control of the patrimony, as by the late thirteenth-century jurist Guglielmo Durante, *Speculum iudiciale* (1479), fol. 202va: "familia proprie consistit in agnatis ff. de verbo. sig. pronuntiatio in prin. et § communi, et conservatur per masculinam prolem e. ti. l. familie. Ad publicam ergo utilitatem pertinet quod masculinam prolem concomitentur paterne et avite divicie nam huius avi per nepotem et eius prolem erit eterna memoria."

92. This insistence also paralleled that of contemporary humanists and others on the "natural," "rational," and "noble" aspects of domestic life that made them more functionally powerful. See Alberto Tenenti, "Famille bourgeoise et idéologie au bas moyen âge," in *Famille et parenté dans l'Occident médiéval*, 437; Natalie Z. Davis, "Ghosts, Kin and Progeny: Some Features of Family Life in Early Modern France," *Daedalus* 106, n. 2 (1977): 87–114; and Elizabeth Wirth Marvick, "Nature versus Nurture: Patterns and Trends in Seventeenth-Century French Child-Rearing," in *The History of Childhood*, 293.

Power in such a situation was not simply class-based, it was also gender-related: the power of father-husband without reference to wife (or Domenico's unnamed lover) over against female relatives like Lena. For remarks on the sexual political effects of the use of biological arguments, see M. Z. Rosaldo, "The Use and Abuse of Anthropology: Reflections on Feminism and Cross-Cultural Understanding," *Signs* 5 (1979–80): 389–417.

93. There were considerable differences between the two institutions, however, if only because legitimation did involve a degree of natural descent. With citizenship, then, performative conditions over a probationary period gave visibility to habits of comportment in accord with those of an original citizen: Kirshner, "Between Nature and Culture," 186, 190, 193, 198–201; idem, "*Ars Imitatur Naturam*," 320–21; idem, "Paolo di Castro on *Cives ex Privilegio*: A Controversy over the Legal Qualifications for Public Office in

Early Fifteenth-Century Florence," in *Renaissance Studies in Honor of Hans Baron,* ed. Anthony Molho and John A. Tedeschi (Dekalb, 1971), 252–55, 260–63. Equivalent habits were not demanded in legitimation, not that a legitimating father might not have taken account of the child's behavior and character. A further distinction between legitimation and acquired citizenship lies in the fact that, while the former could be spoken of in terms of "restored" legitimacy, the latter could be only termed contractual (Bartolo) or at best a *habitus* or "second nature" (Baldo).

94. For example, BNF, Magliabechiano xxix, 193, fols. 182r–91r, a *consilium* of Filippo Decio, a printed edition of which is in his *cons.* 383, ed. cit., vol. 2, fols. 42ra–43va.

Chapter Eight

1. Leon Battista Alberti, *I libri della famiglia,* ed. Ruggiero Romano and Alberto Tenenti (Turin, 1969), 265–95, quotation is on 266.

2. This ideological construct is nicely put by Alberti in the following passages: "Rispuose e disse che aveva imparato ubidire il padre e la madre sua, e che da loro avea comandamento sempre obedire me, e pertanto era disposta fare ciò che io gli comandassi" (ibid., 270). "Dissemi la madre gli avea insegnato filare, cucire solo, ed essere onesta ancora e obediente, che testé da me imparerebbe volentieri in reggere la famiglia e in quello che io gli comandassi quanto a me paresse d'insegnarli" (ibid., 271). Here the wife is not simply obedient, she has passed into the hands of a new teacher and is dependent on him even to learn her role.

3. Ibid., 132.

4. Poggio Bracciolini, *Oratio in laudem matrimonii,* ed. Riccardo Fubini, in *Opera omnia,* 4 vols., vol. 2: *Opera miscellanea edita ed inedita* (Turin, 1966), 914.

5. Ibid., 911–12: "Nullum quippe maius concordiae vinculum quam coniugium reperitur, quod duas voluntates, duos animos in unum coit, ut idem duorum sit velle atque idem nolle. Uxorem enim cum viro ita coniungit ut Veritatis testimonio duo in carne una esse censeantur."

6. Ibid., 912.

7. On the law of dowry, see the essential monograph of Manlio Bellomo, *Ricerche sui rapporti patrimoniali tra coniugi: Contributo alla storia della famiglia medievale* (Milan, 1961), especially 162–85; Julius Kirshner, "Wives' Claims against Insolvent Husbands in Late Medieval Italy," in *Women of the Medieval World,* ed. Julius Kirshner and Suzanne F. Wemple (Oxford, 1985), 256–303; Julius Kirshner and Jacques Pluss, "Two Fourteenth-Century Opinions on Dowries, Paraphernalia and Non-Dotal Goods," *Bulletin of Medieval Canon Law* 9 (1979): 64–77.

8. In addition to the works of Besta, Pertile, and Leicht cited below, the reader is referred to the following studies of Manlio Bellomo for a discussion

of the medieval *patria potestas: Problemi di diritto familiare nell'età dei comuni: Beni paterni e "pars filii"* (Milan, 1968), 2–7; *Enciclopedia del diritto*, s.v. "Famiglia (diritto intermedio)," 16: 749–50.

9. Enrico Besta, *La famiglia nella storia del diritto italiano* (Padua, 1933), 198. For a discussion of emancipation in the medieval civil law, see Thomas Kuehn, *Emancipation in Late Medieval Florence* (New Brunswick, 1982), 10–34.

10. Besta, *La famiglia*, 205. See also Antonio Pertile, *Storia del diritto itiliano dalla caduta dell'impero romano alla codificazione*, 2d ed. (Turin, 1894) 6 vols., 31: 383; P.S. Leicht, *Storia del diritto italiano: Il diritto privato*, vol. 1: *Diritto delle persone e di famiglia* (Milan, 1941; reprint ed., Milan, 1960), 229; Anna T. Sheedy, *Bartolus on Social Conditions in the Fourteenth Century* (New York, 1942), 52. Pietro Torelli, *Lezioni di storia del diritto italiano: Diritto privato - La famiglia* (Milan, 1947), 83–84, agrees with those cited above that "troviamo presto e più comunemente l'emancipazione della figlia per matrimonio," but, in opposition to them, he asserts that the doctrine of the schools held that women returned to subjection to paternal power at widowhood. In his words, "la potestà del padre è sospesa fin che il matrimonio duri." Torelli did not, however, analyze exactly what was the fate of the *patria potestas* at marriage, or he would not have confused the issue by equating marriage and emancipation.

11. Cf. Robert Davidsohn, *Storia di Firenze*, vol. 4: *I primordi della civiltà fiorentina*, part 3: *Il mondo della chiesa, spiritualità ed arte, vita pubblica e privata*, trans. Eugenio Dupré-Theseider (Florence, 1973), 679; Christiane Klapisch-Zuber, "L'enfance en Toscane au début du xv^c siècle," *Annales de démographie historique* 10 (1973): 99–122, esp. 111–12, 114, 116.

12. Lauro Martines, "A Way of Looking at Women in Renaissance Florence," *Journal of Medieval and Renaissance Studies* 4 (1974): 20–21. Martines' important observations rest largely on an analysis of the correspondence of Alessandra Macinghi Strozzi. See also David Herlihy and Christiane Klapisch-Zuber, *Les toscans et leurs familles* (Paris, 1978), 533; Paolo Cammarosano, "Aspetti delle strutture familiari nelle città dell'Italia comunale (secoli xii–xiv)," *Studi medievali*, 3d ser., 16 (1975): 417–35, esp. 420–23.

13. Cf. Francis William Kent, *Household and Lineage in Renaissance Florence: The Family Life of the Capponi, Ginori, and Rucellai* (Princeton, 1977), 92, 247, where he notes how men married to preserve the family and how the dispersal of women did not hurt the "solidarity" of the lineage. Also James C. Davis, *A Venetian Family and Its Fortune* (Philadelphia, 1975), 91. In this regard see also the important observations of Julius Kirshner, Review of Davis, *Journal of Modern History* 49 (1977): 506, and his *Pursuing Honor while Avoiding Sin: the Monte delle doti of Florence*, Quaderni di "Studi Senesi" 41 (Milan, 1978), 6 n. 19.

On the relationship between family wealth and the male members of the

family, see Bellomo, *Problemi,* 41–44; and Julius Kirshner and Anthony
Molho, "The Dowry Fund and the Marriage Market in Early Quattrocento
Florence," *Journal of Modern History* 50 (1978): 435–36.

14. Cf. David Herlihy, *The Family in Renaissance Italy* (St. Charles, Mo.,
1974), 10, but note also the comments of Kirshner, *Pursuing Honor,* 8 n. 23.
Also the essays of Christiane Klapisch-Zuber, "The 'Cruel Mother': Maternity, Widowhood, and Dowry in Florence in the Fourteenth and Fifteenth
Centuries," and "The 'Mattinata' in Medieval Italy," in *Women, Family, and
Ritual in Renaissance Italy,* trans. Lydia Cochrane (Chicago, 1985), 117–31,
261–82.

15. Diane Owen Hughes, "Domestic Ideals and Social Behavior: Evidence
from Medieval Genoa," in *The Family in History,* ed. Charles E. Rosenberg
(Philadelphia, 1975), 140, who speaks of aristocratic lineages. In this article
and in her "Urban Growth and Family Structure in Medieval Genoa," *Past
and Present* 66 (Feb. 1975): 3–28, she draws important distinctions in family
and marriage patterns between aristocratic and artisan families.

16. Herlihy and Klapisch-Zuber, *Les toscans,* 543–44.

17. Stanley Chojnacki, "Dowries and Kinsmen in Early Renaissance Venice," *Journal of Interdisciplinary History* 5 (1975): 597. See also Kent, *Household and Lineage,* 107–8.

18. For an enlightening discussion of the *parentado* in Florence, see Kent,
Household and Lineage, 93–99: also Christiane Klapisch-Zuber, "'Parenti
amici e vicini': Il territorio urbano d'una famiglia mercantile nel xv secolo,"
Quaderni storici 33 (1976): 956–82, esp. 963–68.

19. Alberti, *Della famiglia,* 134–35.

20. This ritual is described by Davidsohn, *Storia di Firenze* (note 11
above), 681–82, and by numerous contemporary *ricordanze.*

21. See Bellomo, *Ricerche,* and Pene Vidari (cited below, note 32). Another indication of a legal-institutional tie between a woman and her family
of origin is accorded parenthetically by the fact that, in discussing the law of
exiles and the *bannum* falling on whole families, the medieval civilians had to
find arguments as to why a wife should share the fate of her husband although
she was not part of his family. On this problem, see Desiderio Cavalca, *Il
bando nella prassi e nella dottrina giuridica medievale* (Milan, 1978), 114.
On another dimension of the same theme, see Sharon T. Strocchia, "Death
Rites and the Ritual Family in Renaissance Florence," in *Life and Death in
Fifteenth-Century Florence,* ed. Marcel Tetel, Ronald G. Witt, and Rona
Goffen (Durham, 1989), 120–45.

22. Filippo Decio to *Foeminae* (D. 50.17.2), *In titulum ff. de regulis iuris*
(Lyons, 1588), 32a–b: "quia mulier nupta retinet tamen originem et familiam
patris, ut not. Bar[tolus] in l. fi. § pen. ff. ad munici. [D. 50.1.37.5]. Et contra
Bartol[um] etiam tenet Alexa[nder] in l. cum quaedam puella col. fi. ff. de
iurisdi. omn. iudi. [D. 2.1.19]. Et late id concludit Cor[neus] Perus[inus] in
consil. clxxvij circa quod est primo videndum, col. fi. lib. iiii. Sed non est

laborandum: quia Bart[olus] in d. l. quoties [C. de privileg. schola., libr. xxi] [C. 12.29.3] non dicit illud ad quod allegatur. Et verissima conclusio videtur quod filia nupta gaudeat privilegio dato patri suo et filiabus: quia licet mulier nupta sit, remaneat tamen in potestate patris, ut no. per glos[sam] insti. ad Tertul. § i in versi. parentis [I. 3.3,2], et no. Bald[us] in l. si uxorem in princ. C. De cond. inser. [C. 6.46.5]. Et retinet originem et familiam patris ut not. Bart[tolus] in d. l. fin. § pen. ad municip. et Bald[us] in d. l. cum quaedam puella. Et ideo bona prohibita alienari extra familiam non prohibentur alienari in filiam nuptam, ut Alex[ander] concludit in consi. lvj consideratis verbis colum. penult. lib. i et late hoc tradit Soci[nus] in consi. ccxxvii praesens consultatio col. ix."

In the *consilium* cited by Decio, Bartolomeo Sozzini (1436–1507) makes no appeal to the fact that the *patria potestas* endures despite marriage. In order to deal with the problem that "filia videtur amictere genus et familiam patris et transire in familiam mariti secundum Bal[dum] in l. femine ff. de senator. [D. 1.9.8] et non videtur esse amplius de descendentibus patris, ut dicit Bar[tolus] no. per illum tex. in l. quotiens C. de privelig. sco. li.$ xii$ [C. 12.29 (30.3)]," Sozzini appealed not to the perduration of the *patria potestas* but to the closely related fact that "si filie femine sunt agnate patri et fratri, per matrimonium non tollitur agnatio. Igitur dicuntur de familia. Quod autem non tollatur agnatio tenent doct[ores] in l. voluntas [C. 6.42.4] et probatur in § item vetustas instit. de heredi. que ab intest. [I.3.1,15] ubi dicit tex. quod filie tanquam agnate succedunt sed eorum filii tanquam cognati, et sic vult quod filia nupta sit agnata, igitur de familia" (ASF, Carte strozziane, 3d ser., 41/2, fol. 221r).

23. Quoted in Bellomo, *Ricerche*, 192–93.

24. It is no accident that historians of Italian law have considered emancipation as the exclusive preserve of males. Since they do not concede that married women were still *in potestate,* they can find little opportunity, much less cause, for their emancipation. Note the treatment of emancipation in the only article devoted solely to it, by Bellomo, in *Enciclopedia del diritto,* s.v. "Emancipazione (diritto intermedio)," 14: 809–19.

25. Bartolo da Sassoferrato, *Tractatus de differentia inter ius canonicum et civile,* in *Opera omnia* (Venice, 1570), vol. 9, for. 153ra: "Item differunt quia iure civili durat patria potestas in omnem etatem filii, sed de iure canonico solvitur patria potestas adveniente adulta etate, quo ad matrimonium carnale et spirituale et quo ad iuramentum, xx q. ii c. puella, xxiii q. ii c. trib. et not. xxxii q. ii c. honorantur." For a discussion of this treatise, see Jean Portemer, "Bartole et les différences entre le droit romain et le droit canonique," in *Bartolo da Sassoferrato: Studi e documenti per il VI centenario,* ed. Università degli Studi di Perugia (Perugia, 1962–63), 2: 399–412. Portemer, however, appears to dismiss too easily the arguments against assignment of authorship of this treatise to Bartolo.

26. Alberico da Rosciate to *Divortii gratia* (C. 5.21.2), *Commentaria*

(Lyons, 1518), fol. 258va: "Item allegabam quod de iure lombardo, quod servatur Bergomi, uxor est in potestate mariti . . . et talis potestas equipararetur patriae potestati. . . . Sed iudicium vel lis non potest esse inter maritum et uxorem: nam filius etiam pro atroci iniuria non potest agere contra patrem, ut ff. de iniuriis l. hi tamen omnes § liberi [D. 48.2.11,1]." *Glossa ordinaria* to § i in ver. *parentis* (I. 3.3,2) [*Institutionum libri quatuor* (Venice, 1606), col. 355]: "scilicet mater. Et ita no. de iure Romanorum uxorem alicuius esse in potestate parentis, non mariti, nisi quo ad debitum carnis, aliud de iure Longobardorum, ut hic et C. De cond. inser. l. si uxorem tuam [C. 6.46.5], et in longobarda qualiter mulier alienare permissum sit l. i [Lomb. 2,10]. Tenetur tamen operari viro uxor ut l. sicut cum ibi notatis ff. de oper. libertorum [D. 38.1.48]."

27. Passage from Carlo di Tocco quoted in Torelli, *Lezioni di storia del diritto*, 46; see also Bellomo, *Problemi*, 5–6 n. 13.

28. Manlio Bellomo, *La condizione giurdica della donna in Italia: Vicende antiche e moderne* (Turin, 1970), 40.

29. Angelo degli Ubaldi to *Filiae* (C. 6.20.12), *Commentaria* (Lyons 1561), fol. 145ra: "Hic est casus quod filia nupta et dotata non exiit patris potestatem, in instit. ad Tertul. § i in fi. [I. 3.3,2], in de condi. inser. l. si uxorem [C. 6.46.5], quoad servitia tamen bene exiit: quia tenetur operari in domo viri, ut l. sicuti ff. de ope. liber. [D. 38.1.48] et ita tenet glo[ssa] in d. l. si uxorem."

A similar assertion is contained in the apparatus to the notarial formulary of Rolandino Passaggieri written by the Bolognese jurist Pietro de Unzola, where it is claimed that, with respect to the *ius civile*, "nihil enim quantum ad se obligandum et contrahendum habet facere cum marito, nec in eius potestate est tempore matrimonii, imo sui iuris est vel, si habet patrem, in patris potestate est vel avi paterni, ut C. De conditio, inser, l. si uxorem [C. 6.46.5] et instit. ad Tertu. § i in fi. [I. 3.3,2]. Operari tamen marito et in eius servitio esse debet, ut ff. de ope. liver. l. sicut [D. 38.1.48]" (Rolandino Passaggieri, *Summa totius artis notariae* [Venice, 1574], fol. 470vb).

30. Paolo di Castro to *Si uxorem tuam* (C. 6.46.5), *Commentaria in secundam partem codicis* (Lyons, 1548), fol. 119va: "allegatur ista lex quod mulier nupta non exit de potestate patris, licet transeat in potestatem mariti quo ad obsequia matrimonii, tamen quo ad effectum iuris et patriae potestatis remanet in eadem, et hoc in matrimonio carnali, sed in spirituali, ut si efficiatur episcopus vel ingrediatur monasterium, exit de patria potestate, ut in aut. si episcopalis dignitas supra de epi. et cle. [*C. 1.3.38(37)] et not. gl[ossa] in l. si ex causa § Papinianus ff. de minori [D. 4.4.20]."

31. *Obsequium* was that unclearly defined "duty of respectful conduct" that a *libertus* owed his *patronus*, which included the perfomance of *onera*. See W. W. Buckland, *A Textbook of Roman Law from Augustus to Justinian*, 3d ed., ed. Peter Stein (Cambridge, 1963), 88–89.

32. On the whole question of the law regarding *alimenta* and for the

opinions of Odofredo and Jacopo d'Arena, see Gian Savino Pene Vidari, *Ricerche sul diritto agli alimenti,* vol 1: *L'obbligo 'ex lege' dei familiari nel periodo della Glossa e del Commento* (Turin, 1970), 188–89, 364–88.

33. Baldo degli Ubaldi to *Si uxorem* (C. 6.46.5), *Opera omnia* (Venice, 1577), vol. 7, fol. 164va: "No. quod per nuptias filia non desinet esse in patris potestate, ut ff. solu. mat. l. ii § quod si in patris [D. 24.3.2,2] et l. quoties cum si. [D. 24.3.29]. Op. quod imo sit in potestate viri, cum vir vendicet eam a patre, ut infra de li. exhi. l. fin. [D. 43.30.5]. Sol. in tribus est in potestate viri, scilicet in residentia, quam debet facere cum viro. In operibus, quia debet operari viro. Item in iurisdictione quia ad forum et legibus et statutis viri debet esse obediens ut ff. de iudi. l. exigere dotem [D. 5.1.65]. In aliis autem est in potestate patris, unde non potest facere testamentum. Item non potest sibi eligere sepulturam nisi patre volente ut in c. licet de sepul. lib. vi. [VI. 3.12.4] Item non potest donare causa mortis, nisi patre corroborante, ut ff. de do. cau. mor. l. tam is [D. 39.6.25], quam donationem non potest facere ipsi patri, quia non posset interponere authoritatem in facto proprio."

34. The legal incapacities of a child *in potestate* were precisely concerned with those matters in which a child gained legal capacity if emancipated. As schematized for (and from) notaries by Guglielmo Durante (d. 1295), *Speculum iuris* (Venice, 1566), 690a, these capacities gained by an emancipated child were "ita ut absque patrie potestatis obtentu possit ex nunc testari, agere, contrahere, ac pascisci; et omnia et singula tam in iudicio quam extra facere ac libere exercere potest." See also Salatiele, *Ars notarie,* 2 vols., ed. Gianfranco Orlandelli (Milan, 1961), 2: 300–301; Rolandino Passaggieri, *Summa totius artis notariae* (Venice, 1574), fol. 178vb: Bencivenne, *Ars notarie,* ed. Giovanni Bronzino (Bologna, 1965), 72–73. Also see the documents in the Appendix to the original version of this essay in *Tijdschrift voor Rechtsgeschiedenis* 49 (1981): 145–47.

35. Baldo to *Soluto matrimonio* § *quod si in patris* (D. 24.3.2,2), vol. 3, fol. 4va–b: "Dos profectitia communis est patri et filie et in agendo et in delegando requiritur utriusque consensus, et factum solius patris non nocet filie, nec factum filiae patri, etiam si pater experiatur adiuncta filiae persona: ipsi tamen filiae morte patris vel emancipa[tione] sui iur[is] effectae proprium factum officit, hoc dicit."

36. Lauro Martines, *Lawyers and Statecraft in Renaissance Florence* (Princeton, 1968), 92.

37. *Statuta* 1415, Book 2, rubric 113: Quod filiae nuptae non teneatur pro debitis paternis, 1: 205.

38. Ibid., Book 2, rubric 110: De obligatione filii familias et qualiter pater pro filio conveniatur, 1: 201–3; Book 3, rubric 2: De filiis et aliis descendentibus, et de patribus et aliis ascendentibus, et de fratribus cessantium et fugitivorum et qualiter pro eis teneantur, 1: 520–21.

39. Ibid., Book 2, rubric 113, 1: 205.

40. Ibid., Book 2, rubric 111: De consensu et obligatione mulieris et de datione in solutum facta per virum de bonis suis, 1: 203–4.

41. Ibid., Book 2, Rubric 112: De mundualdis et quis possit tutores vel curatores et mundualdos dare, 1: 204–5: "Et nulla mulier possit se obligare modo aliquo sine consensu mundualdi, vel sine consensu sui viri, si virum haberet" (204). On this theme see the next chapter.

42. On the *munduladus,* see Ennio Cortese, "Per la storia del mundio in Italia," *Rivista italiana per le scienze giuridiche,* 3d.ser., 8 (1955–56): 323–474; Gigliola Villata di Renzo, *La tutela: Indagini sulla scuola dei glossatori* (Milan, 1975), 64–65; Carlo Guido Mor, "Capacità d'agire, comunioni familiari e consorzi nel diritto consuetudinario valdostano dei sec. xi–xiii," in *Studi di storia e diritto in onore di Enrico Besta,* 3 vols. (Milan, 1939), 3: 199–217.

43. ASF, Notarile antecosimiano (hereafter cited as Notarile) B697 (21 June 1324), no pagination.

44. ASF, Notarile B 775 (16 December 1450), fols. 94r–95v; S 455 (1380–89) (26 July 1383), no pagination.

45. ASF, Notarile N 4 (1494–97) (5 June 1497), fols. 227r–28v. The stipulation runs as follows: "considerans qualiter ipsa fuit a dicto suo patre dotata etc. et qualiter ex priori matrimonio [to Francesco d'Angelo Cavalcanti] etc. supervivit inter alios Cosa eius filia legitima et naturalis . . . et etiam habet aliam filiam, que est in monasterio Sancti Mactei de prope Florentia, que adhuc non est adita licet professa fuerit etc. nuncupata soror Alexandra. et qualiter ex dicto secundo matrimonio [to Ser Guglielmo di Garonte Bindi] etiam supervivit Franciscus, natus ex ea et dicto condam Guglielmo eius secundo marito . . . dat . . . dicto Francisco eius filio maschulo predicto legitimo et naturali pupillo et minoris etatis . . . salvis condictionibus infrascriptis dotem et iura quelibet dotis dicte domine Alexandre et creditum quelibet eidem competens . . . reservavit . . . sibi usumfructum . . . toto tempore sue vite et donec ipsa vixerit . . . quod dictus Franciscus . . . teneatur et obligatus sit dare et solvere Cose eiusdem domine donatarie filie florenos auri centum . . . et quando se nupxerit vel monacaverit . . . domine sorori Alexandre . . . florenos auri decem . . . inter octo dies post mortem dicte domine Agostine donatarie predicte facere et fieri facere unum offertum seu penitentiam pro anima sua fratribus Sancti Marci de Florentia . . . quandocunque decessit sine filiis maschulis legitimis et naturalibus . . . tunc et in dicta causa dicta iura dotis sue . . . devenire voluit pro una tertia parte totius dicte domine Cose . . . et pro aliis duabus partium devenire voluit etc. ad dictum dominum Simonem eius patrem et filios et descendentes dicti domini Simonis."

46. Note also the words of Baldo (above, note 33). Of course a father would not be consenting "in facto proprio" in the case of an emancipated daughter.

47. ASF, Notarile A 652 (15 March 1386), fol. 204r.

48. ASF, Notarile G 212 (1422–29), fols. 200r–v.

49. ASF, Notarile G 330 (1416–17) (25 April 1417): "reservato . . . quod ipse Tommasius non vult nec intendit quod per predicta vel aliquod predictorum nullum ius queritur vel queri intelligatur dicto Piero viro ipsius domine Belle . . . ac etiam reservavit sibi Tommasio toto tempore sue vite et donec advixerit dicte domus et bonorum et usumfructum." A similar stipulation is found in Notarile F 297 (1401–7) (28 December 1402), fols. 49v–50v.

50. On ages and aging in Florence in this period, see Herlihy and Klapisch-Zuber, *Les toscans,* 350–90.

51. ASF, Notarile G 329 (1397) (2 and 23 December 1397), fols. 146v–47v, 157r–59v. The *laudum* reads in part: "in primis quidem considerans infirmitatem incurabilem et perpetuo duraturam in persona sive corpore dicti Mactei, ex qua sive cuius occaxione [sic] nedum ipse Mactheus posset deinceps ex eius industria superare victum sed nisi domino nostro Yhesu Christo auxiliante vix poterit pannos aliquos pro suo dorso suis viribus inducere nec non respiciens ad etatem et modicam sanitatem dicte domine Care. Et etiam considerans quod conveniens est dictam dominam Lisabectam ipsorum filiam per omnibus debere ipsorum honera supporttare. Et adtendens ad promissionem per ipsam dominam Lisabectam in mei presentia de voluntate sive asensu dicti Piere [Nuccii de Miglioratis] eius viri factam dictis Mactheo et domine Care, videlicet inter alia promictentem eisdem Macteo et domine Care ut ex natura et honore tenetur ipsos Mactheum et dominam Caram et superviventem ex eis donec advixerint non deserere sed ut patrem et matrem semper honorare, tenere, alere, vestire, regere, et gubernare . . . considerans promissionem per ipsos Mactheum et dominam Caram eidem domine Lisabecte in remuneratione dicte sue promissionis factam, continentem inter cetera de dando eidem domine Lisabecte omnia eorum bona et iura . . . laudamus . . . quod dictorum Macthei et domine Care et cuiusque vel alterius ipsorum domus vetera cum palchis . . . ac etiam dos dicte domine Care . . . sint et esse intelligantur suprascripte domine Lisabecte . . . hiis quidem oneribus, modis, et condictionibus per nos dicte domine Lisabecte et eius heredes et [qui] habet ius ab ea teneatur et debeat et seu teneantur et debeant toto tempore vite dictorum Macthei et domine Care et cuiusque eorum et superviventis ex eis ipsos Mactheum et dominam Caram, et quemlibet eorum et superviventem ex eis et donec advixerint sive advixerit ipsius domine Lisabecte sumptibus et expensis et una cum ipsa domina Lisabecta et in sua habitatione tam in civitate quam in comitatu Florentie tenere, vestire, calciare, et nutrire et alimentare ac honorare et eis servire usque ad omnem ipsorum et cuiusque eorum indigentiam . . . et etiam post mortem ipsorum et cuiusque eorum facere et fieri facere omnes sumptus debitos et consuetos pro eorum funeribus racondendis secundum modum hactenus consuetum et ipsius domine Lisabecte facultatem."

52. ASF, Notarile G 429 (1494–96) (23 March 1496), fol. 317r. In the second half of the fifteenth century a number of women were emancipated

just before their marriages in order that they might renounce their rights to their mother's dowry in favor of their brothers or sisters. For examples, see Notarile N 3 (1482–84) (11 January 1483), fols. 263v–64r; B 832 (17 January 1479), fols. 226r–v.

53. As in the case of monna Francesca, daughter of Fruosino di Michele, who was given her dowry in *praemium emancipationis* and in return renounced any claim on her mother's dowry (ASF, Notarile C 430 [1397–1400] [22 December 1398], fols. 74v–75r). Similar cases are found in ibid., (29 June 1399), fols. 112v–13r, (24 July 1400), fol, 147r.

54. ASF, Notarile C 187 (1406–8) (5 September 1408), fols. 187r–v, where Nofri di Rogerio Federighi gave monna Felice "redditus, habitationem domus dicti Nofrii et eius filiorum et heredum toto tempore sue vite et viduetatis et quandocunque vidua steterit, ita quod dicto tempore libere et licite et sine ulla contradictione possit et sibi liceat redire et stare et habitare in domo habitationis dicti Nofrii."

55. ASF, Notarile G 211 (1412–16) (21 May 1412), fols. 14v–15r.

56. Note the case of monna Cella, daughter of Piero di Giovanni di messer Neri Tornaquinci, who was emancipated two months after her marriage to Luigi d'Immondini de' Vecchietti on the day her dowry was given to her husband. She then made the following promise: "quod si in quantum in casu ipsa domina Cella rehaberet dotes suas ab heredibus Luisii Immondini de Vecchiettis sue dotes que fuerint florenorum nonagenti auri ipsa domina Cella de dotibus suis dabit et solvet ipsi domine Lise sorori sue florenos centum auri si tunc ipsa domina Lisa vivet, alioquin fratribus carnalibus dicte domine Celle" (ASF, Notarile A 659 [21 November 1409], fols. 80v–81r; the marriage contract appears on fol. 76v [30 September 1409]).

57. To cite two overt examples where men admitted to using women, neither one, however, involving a father and married daughter, there is the instance recorded by Luca da Panzano in his *ricordanze,* where he tells us that his cousin Antonio emancipated his daughter Mea, who then took possession of her mother's estate "non instante vivento Antonio suo padre. E questo si fe' in verità per difendere i beni d'Antonio suo padre perchè fatti del suo bancho istavano male" (ASF, Carte strozziane, 2d ser., 9, fol. 3v [11 December 1414]). The other instance is that recorded by Giovanni di Matteo Corsini, who confessed in 1430 that he had given his sister Checha the family's house, "e la cagione si è che per rispetto del cattivo mio stato e parendomi meglio lasciare a' miei figluoli casa che non lasciargli sanza essa, perch' è i ritenimento della famiglia." He later also entered into arbitration with her and had her given his country estate in Castello "per cagione i miei creditori nollo potessono mai per nesuno tenpo averlo, pero ch' è il principale podere dela posesione e venduto quelo guasto ongni cosa, si che perchè mi parea il meglio a così fare per questo salvamento" (*Il libro di ricordanze dei Corsini (1362–1457),* ed. Armando Petrucci [Rome, 1965], 131).

58. ASF, Notarile G 210 (1405–7) (7 and 8 February 1407), fols. 203v–7r.

59. ASF, Notarile G 212 (1422–29) (12 May 1426), fols. 241v–42v.

60. Kirshner and Molho, "Dowry Fund," 435; Kirshner, *Pursuing Honor*, 2.

61. See note 57, above.

62. ASF, Notarile N 4 (1495–97) (20 May 1497), fols. 217r–18v.

63. ASF, Notarile N 125 (1400–1413) (28 and 30 April 1410), fols. 219r–21r. Another instance can be found in M 95 (1383–87) (7 June 1387), fol. 139v.

64. ASF, Notarile G 211 (1412–16) (1 June 1415), fols. 256v–57v. Certainly the law recognized that such an immediate declaration of an arbitrator was not his doing but that of the parties involved. Cf. a *consilium* of Antonio Strozzi in ASF, Carte strozziane, 3d ser., 41/3, fol. 375r: "compromissum iunctum simul cum laudo dicitur esse quedam transactio partium."

65. Note the following passages: Baldo to *Soluto matrimonio § quod si in patris* (D. 24.3.2,2), vol. 3, fol. 4vb: "Tertio no. quod factum solius patris non nocet filiae quantum ad substantiam debiti, sed bene nocet quoad exercitium dum est in potestate sed non postquam est sui iur[is]. . . . Sexto nota quod factum per filiam, dum est in potestate, nocet ei sui iur[is] effectae." Bartolo to the same *lex,* vol. 3, fol. 5ra: "Sed veritas est, ut dicit Io[hannis] in fi. quod si filia esset emancipata, tota actio remanet sua tam olim quam hodie. Ratio, quia per emancipationem actio, que est communis cum patre, solidatur in filiam, ut in § videamus de rei. uxo. act. [C. 5.13.1,11], multo magis efficitur propria filiae a principio, ut arg. l. acceptam iuncta gl[ossa] in ver. inhibetur in fi., l. si per te C. de usu. [C. 4.32.19 and 9]. . . ."

66. ASF, Notarile A 673 (8 August 1437), fol. 87r and (4 September 1437) fol. 97r. The central part of the *laudum* reports: "actributo et reperto quod dictus Taddeus recepit in dotem domine Cheche olim uxoris dicti Taddei et olim matris dicte domine Lise et filie olim Baronis Cappelli de Florentia florenos auri octingentos quadrigenta vel circa, et reperto quod dicta domina Lisa apprehendidit hereditatem domine Lise [sic] insolidum ab intestato sub die octavo mensis augusti . . . et reperto quod dictus Taddeus nupxit dictam dominam Lisam suprascripto Bernardo et dedit eidem in dotem florenos auri sexcentos, et quod leves expensas fecit in dotem domine Lise ascendentem ad summam florenorum auri trecentorum et ultra, et reperto quod dictus Taddeus habet quamplurimos filios et filias et pariter habet in bonis, et quod dicta dos fuit tradita et dicte expense fuerunt facte causa compensandi in dotem ipsuis domine Lise etc. . . . laudamus . . . in primis . . . dotem . . . domine Cheche et dictam dotem . . . per dictum Taddeum dicto Bernardo pro dicta domina Lisa et dictas expensas compensamus et pro compensatione esse volumus et mandamus et dictum Taddeum et eius heredes de dicta dote domine Cheche facemus et liberamus . . . et dictam dominam Lisam ad faciendum et liberandum et quietandum dictum Taddeum de dicta dote dicte domine Cheche dicti Taddei condempnamus etc."

67. ASF, Notarile A 670 (1428–30) (19 September 1428), fols. 33v–34v.

68. This hypothesis recalls the arrangements reported in note 45 above.

69. Cf. Davidsohn, *Storia di Firenze* (note 11 above), 680–81, where he describes the wedding procession, complete with armed escort, to the husband's house. Also Christiane Klapisch-Zuber, "Zacharias, or the Ousted Father: Nuptial Rites in Tuscany between Giotto and the Council of Trent," in *Women, Family, and Ritual in Renaissance Italy*, 178–212. In this context, see the remarks of Jane Schneider, "Of Vigilance and Virgins: Honor, Shame and Access to Resources in Mediterranean Societies," *Ethnology* 10 (1971): 1–24, esp. 21.

Chapter Nine

1. The text has been edited by Rab Hatfield, *Botticelli's Uffizi "Adoration": A Study in Pictorial Content* (Princeton, 1976), 126–28.

2. For a thorough history of the *mundium*, see Ennio Cortese, "Per la storia del mundio in Italia," *Rivista italiana per le scienze giuridiche*, 3d ser., 8 (1955–56): 323–474. See also Manlio Bellomo, *La condizione giuridica della donna in Italia: Vicende antiche e moderne* (Turin, 1970), 26–28.

3. On guardianship in medieval civil law, see Gigliola Villata di Renzo, *La tutela: Indagini sulla scuola dei glossatori* (Milan, 1975).

4. Cortese, "Storia del mundio," 436–42.

5. Ibid., 442–61.

6. Ibid., 453 n. 232 (quoting Biagio da Morcone): "quia cum ipsa non habeat legitimam personam standi in iudicio sine mundualdo."

7. Ibid., 436–40. See also Sergio Mochi Onory, "*Personam habere:* Studio sulle origini e sulla struttura della 'persona' nell'età del Rinascimento," in *Studi di storia e diritto in onore di Enrico Besta*, 3 vols. (Milan, 1939), 3: 417–39.

8. *Statuta* 1415, 1: 204, bk.2, rubric 112: "De mundualdis et quis possit tutores vel curatores et mundualdos dare."

9. As Ibid., 1: 206–7, bk. 2, rubric 115: "De aetate legitima, de obligatione minorum decem et octo annorum, et consensu mulierum super dotibus et restitutione in integrum."

10. Ibid., 1: 203, bk. 2, rubric 111.

11. Ibid., 1: 117, bk. 2, rubric 6. On the *procurator* in Florence see Lauro Martines, *Lawyers and Statecraft in Renaissance Florence* (Princeton, 1968), 38–40; Santi Calleri, *L'arte dei giudici e notai di Firenze nell' età comunale e nel suo statuto del 1344* (Milan, 1966), 49–53.

12. Cf. *Statutum potestatis comunis Pistorii anni mcclxxxxvi*, ed. Lodovico Zdekauer (Milan, 1888), 60–61, bk. 2, rubric 17: "De dandis tutoribus et inventario faciendo."

13. The professional training of Florentine lawyers is discussed by Martines, *Lawyers*, 33–34, 78–91. Generally on the legal profession, see Manlio Bellomo, *Società e istituzioni in Italia dal medioevo agli inizi dell'età*

moderna, 3d ed. (Catania, 1982), 413–70; and Luigi Lombardi, *Saggio sul diritto giurisprudenziale* (Milan, 1967), 79–199.

14. There is a vast literature on marriage in canon law and on the differences between canon and civil law in this regard. Cf. Adhemar Esmein, *Mariage en droit canonique,* 2 vols. (Paris, 1891); Jean Dauvillier, *Le mariage dans le droit classique de l'église* (Paris, 1933); and more recently, Charles Donahue, Jr., "The Case of the Man Who Fell into the Tiber: The Roman Law of Marriage at the Time of the Glossators," *American Journal of Legal History* 22 (1978): 1–53; Michael M. Sheehan, C.S.B., "Choice of Marriage Partner in the Middle Ages: Development and Mode of Application of a Theory of Marriage," *Studies in Medieval and Renaissance History* n.s. 1 (1978): 1–33; John T. Noonan, Jr., "Power to Choose," *Viator* 4 (1973): 419–34; René Metz, "Le statut de la femme en droit canonique médiéval," *Recueils de la société Jean Bodin pour l'histoire comparative des institutions,* vol. 12: *La femme* (1962): 86–89.

15. Metz, "Statut de la femme," 84.

16. Ibid., 88–89.

17. *Glossa ordinaria,* gl. *matrimonium* to C. 22 q. 4 c. 22; Guido de Baysio (d. 1313) to C. 31 q. 2, *Rosarium* (Venice, 1577); Giovanni d' Andrea (d. 1348) to X. 4.7.2, *Novella commentaria* (Venice, 1581): "Et copula facit hoc matrimonium propter voluntatem, quae inest sponsalibus contractis etiam per metum conditionalem." See also Noonan, "Power to Choose," 433.

Metz, "Statut de la femme," 80, makes the distinction between the order of grace and the order of nature in canon law's treatment of women. See also R. Metz, "Recherches sur le statut de la femme en droit canonique, bilan historique et perspectives d'avenir," *L'année canonique* 12 (1968): 85–113.

18. General statements in this regard were first incorporated by Gratian into the *Decretum.* See *Corpus iuris canonici,* ed. E. Friedberg, 2 vols. (Leipzig, 1879), vol. 1, II, C. 33 1. 5 cc. 12 and 17, also c. 7: "Feminae, dum maritantur, ideo velantur, ut noverint, se semper viris suis subditas esse et humiles." The legal implications garnered from these and other passages were that a wife was obligated to serve and work for her husband (Guglielmo Durante, *Speculum iuris,* IV, qui filii legitimi [Venice, 1578], fol. 194rb, and the *additiones* of Baldo and Giovanni d'Andrea; Baldo to X. 2.19.6, *Super decretalibus* [Lyons, 1551]) and to live with him (Hostiensis [d. 1271] to X. 4.1.5, *Summa aurea* [Venice, 1574]; and the decretal X. 3.28.7 allowing a woman to choose her own burial site because death is a state "in quo mulier solvitur a lege viri"). The obligation to serve her husband also, however, justified his legal obligation to feed and care for her (Hostiensis to X. 4.20.7 and Giovanni d'Andrea to X. 4.20.7).

19. See Metz, "Statut de la femme," 89. For a discussion of moral teachings on domestic life, see Raoul Manselli, "Vie familiale et éthique sexuelle dans les pénitentiels," in *Famille et parenté dans l'Occident médiéval,* ed. Georges Duby and Jacques Le Goff (Rome, 1977), 363–78.

20. Cf. Martines, *Lawyers*, 92, who says that problems of contracts and civil status were dealt with in terms of Roman law.

21. Bellomo, *Condizione guiridica della donna*, 30; P. S. Leicht, *Storia del diritto italiano: Il diritto privato*, 3 vols., vol. 1: *Diritto delle persone e di famiglia* (Milan, 1943), 95.

22. Rolandino Passaggieri, *Summa totius artis notariae* (Venice, 1574), fol. 470va–vb: "non quia mulier sit de illis personis, quae non possunt se obligare, quia ipsa suo nomine potest omnes contractus regulariter celebrare, ut infra patebit, nec ratione sexus prohibetur contrahere. . . . Unde venditiones, locationes, donationes et omnes contractus cum extraneo celebare potest nec exigitur consensus mariti, nihil enim quantum ad se obligandum et contrahendum habet facere cum marito."

23. On the *Velleianum*, see W. W. Buckland, *A Text-Book of Roman Law from Augustus to Justinian* 3d ed., ed. Peter Stein (Cambridge, 1966), 448–49. Canon law simply confirmed this feminine legal disability as contained in civil law (see *Glossa ordinaria*, gl. *nec fidem dare* to C. 33 1. 5 c. 17).

24. Bartolo to *Si unus § pactus* (D. 2.14.27,2), *Opera omnia*, 10 vols. (Venice, 1585), vol. 1, fol. 86rb: "Dicit auth. si qua mulier C. ad Velleianum quod mulier non potest obligari pro viro suo aliquo modo, nisi appareat quod in utilitatem mulieris convertatur. Ex hoc appareat quod mulier non potest liberare virum pacto, quia ex hoc obligatur naturaliter non petere. Quod facit pro statuto quod prohibet mulieres vel minores obligari nisi certis solemnitatibus servatis."

25. Bartolo to *Quamquam* (D. 26.5.1), vol. 3, fol. 59va: "Sunt enim per Italiam statuta quod minores et mulieres non possunt contrahere sine consensu aliquorum consanguineorum, quem sensum quis prestare non potest quando directo de acquirendo sibi tractatur."

26. Bartolo to *Si cum dotem § eo autem tempore* (D. 24.3.22,5), vol. 3, fol. 13ra.

27. Bartolo to *More* (D. 29.2.8), vol. 3, fols. 144vb–45ra.

28. See Susan Mosher Stuard, "From Women to Woman: New Thinking about Gender c. 1140," *Thought* 64 (1989): 208–19.

29. Baldo to *Qui iure* (D. 29.1.7), *Opera omnia*, 10 vols. (Venice, 1577), vol. 3, fol. 105rb: "Mulier tamen et minor propter eorum imbecillitatem et fragilitatem renunciare non possunt nisi certiorentur." Bartolo was as aware as Baldo of the arguments about female weakness, but he may have been more reluctant to make them his own (cf. Anna T. Sheedy, *Bartolus on Social Conditions in the Fourteenth Century* [New York, 1942], 53–54).

30. The teachings of Aquinas and other theologians are discussed by Metz, "Statut de la femme," 59–82, and Vern L. Bullough, "Medieval Medical and Scientific Views of Women," *Viator* 4 (1973): 485–501; Ian Maclean, *The Renaissance Notion of Woman: A Study in the Fortunes of Scholasticism and Medical Science in European Intellectual Life* (Cambridge, 1980). On the theme of the inherent weakness of women and minors in the law, see Bellomo, *Condizione guiridica della donna*, 37–39, and di Renzo, *La tutela*, 140–59.

31. Quoted in Leicht, *Storia,* 1: 100.

32. Paolo di Castro to *Si quis pro eo* (D. 46.1.56), *Super secundo digesto novo* (Lyons, 1548), fol. 80va–vb: "pone, dicit statutum quod mulier vel minor non possit se obligare vel alienare sine certa solemnitate, mulier vel minor non servata solemnitate se obligavit vel alienavit cum iuramento de non veniendo contra. Constat quod si non iurasset non valeret iure. Sed an iuramentum faciat valere vel cogatur ad ipsius observantiam, videtur quod sic, quia hic non sumus in aliquo de casibus praedictis. Ista enim prohibitio statuti nec est contra bonos mores nec contra publicam utilitatem, nec tendit in praeiudicium alterius, ergo iuramentum est observandum saltem de iure canonico. Contrarium determinat Bartolus, dicens quod sumus in primo casu, quia observantia iuramenti induceret peccatum iurantis, cum enim l. municipalis, cui tenetur parere dirigit prohibitionem in personam minoris vel mulieris si non parerent. . . . non sic quando provenit ex presumpta mente contrahentium sed mere ex dispositione statuti quod contractus presumatur simulatus vel dolo celebratus, et haec est veritas, licet assessores communiter nolint tales exceptiones admittere, imo de facto talia statuta observantur."

33. Bencivenni, *Commentaria statutorum,* BNF, Principale, II, iv, 435, fol. 12v: "Sed an hoc statutum habeat locum etiam in comitatu ubi est consuetudo opposita, et videtur quod non."

34. Salvetti, *Commentaria statutorum,* BNF, Principale, II, iv, 434, fol. 42r: "In comitatu autem videbatur habere locum . . . sed quia opposita est consuetudo in comitatu dicendum est contrarium. Alexander de rigore iuris videbatur contrarium eum per modum regule procedat, non referendo ad curias rectorum civitatis Florentie, ut dixit supra. . . . Unde indistincte videbatur ubique verificari, et presertim, cum sit statutum rationabile et inductum favore honestatis, sed quia hodiosum est et non servatum est in comitatu non loquitur nisi coram rectoribus civitatis, et sic est pratica quin imo est statutum in tertio."

35. *Statuta* 1415, 1: 205.

36. Bencivenni, *Commentaria* (n. 33 above), 435, fol. 62v.

37. Ibid., fol. 62r–v.

38. Ibid., fol. 52v.

39. Ibid., fol. 61v.

40. Ibid., fol. 61v: "In § consensus tamen, in ver[bo] in alienatione. Et sic non infringat alienationem factam per mulierem vel per alium nomine eius, immo nec consensum prestitum ex intervallo. Sed remanet dispositio iuris comunis."

41. Salvetti, *Commentaria,* fol. 20r: "Ad hoc facit quod notat Franciscus de Aretio . . . ubi ipse dicit quod in obligatione que inducitur a lege et non a consensu, mulier obligatur absque mundualdo, quamvis statutum disponat quod mulier non possit se obligare sine consensu mundualdi."

42. On alimentary obligations, see Gian Savino Pene Vidari, *Ricerche sul diritto agli alimenti* (Turin, 1970), 77–92, 197–276.

43. ASF, Carte strozziane, ser. 3, 41/18, fol. 106r: "Mulier est im-becillioris sexus quam masculus, l. i § i ff. ad velle. [D. 16.1.1,1], et leges minus de muliere confidunt, ut l. i § sexum ff. de postul. [D. 3.1.1,5], et maiorem debet servare castitatem et honestatem quam masculi."

44. Ibid., fol. 340r: "quoniam talium personarum simplicitas suadet potius hoc processisse ex facultate quam ex liberalitate."

45. Ibid., fol. 365v.

46. Ibid., fol. 375r.

47. Paolo da Certaldo, *Il libro di buoni costumi*, ed. A. Schiaffini (Florence, 1945), 105–6.

48. Leon Battista Alberti, *I libri della famiglia*, ed. Ruggiero Romano and Alberto Tenenti (Turin, 1969), 268.

49. For example, *Statuta* 1415, 1: 205–7, bk. 2, rubrics 113–15. Interesting with regard to the cultural perception of male dominance is an exchange among the female frame characters in the *Decameron*. Filomena responds to Pampinea's plan for the seven women to leave the plague-stricken city by saying "e non ce n'ha niuna sì fanciulla che non possa ben conoscere come le femine sieno ragionate insieme, e senza la provedenza d'alcuno uomo si sappiano regolare. Noi siamo mobili, ritrose, sospettose, pusillanime e paurose." Elisa adds the observation that "veramente gli uomini sono delle femine capo; e senza l'ordine loro, rade volte riesce alcuna nostra opera a laudevole fine" (Giovanni Boccaccio, *Il decamerone*, ed. Angelo Ottolini, 2d ed. [Milan, 1938], 16).

50. On these themes, see Julius Kirshner, *Pursuing Honor While Avoiding Sin: The Monte delle doti of Florence* (Milan, 1978), 2–9; idem and Anthony Molho, "The Dowry Fund and the Marriage Market in Early *Quattrocento* Florence," *Journal of Modern History* 50 (1978): 435; Christiane Klapisch-Zuber, "The 'Cruel Mother': Maternity, Widowhood, and Dowry in Florence in the Fourteenth and Fifteenth Centuries," and "The Griselda Complex: Dowry and Marriage Gifts in the Quattrocento," in her *Women, Family, and Ritual in Renaissance Italy*, trans. Lydia G. Cochrane (Chicago, 1985), 117–31, 213–46.

51. Cf. Bellomo, *Condizione guiridica della donna*, 41–43, and idem, *Ricerche sui rapporti patrimoniali tra coniugi* (Milan, 1961), 163–85. But see the next chapter.

52. Evidence concerning the negligent treatment of female children has been presented by David Herlihy and Christiane Klapisch-Zuber, *Les toscans et leurs familles* (Paris, 1978), 326–49; also the more concise treatment by Herlihy in "Life Expectancies for Women in Medieval Society," in *The Role of Women in the Middle Ages*, ed. Rosemarie Thee Morwedge (Albany, 1975), 14. On the importance of women as instruments in familial strategies, see the suggestive remarks of Anthony Molho, "Visions of the Florentine Family in the Renaissance," *Journal of Modern History* 50 (1978): 309–10.

53. Cf. Alberti, *Libri della famiglia*, 125–38. For an unusual example of

the utility of marriage alliances, see Melissa Meriam Bullard, "Marriage Politics and the Family in Florence: The Strozzi-Medici Alliance of 1508," *American Historical Review* 84 (1979): 668–87.

54. Kirshner, *Pursuing Honor*, 5–9.

55. Alberti, *Libri della famiglia*, 264–65. Kirshner, *Pursuing Honor*, 5–6, has pointed to the feminine nature of the *casa*. This association of the *casa* with women, it must be emphasized, does not rest on the gender of the word alone. Clearly Alberti makes a division of the social space—*casa* being the place for women and *piazza* (also feminine) the place for men (although, interestingly, Alberti immediately qualifies the feminine *piazze* with the masculine "in publico"). For anthropological insights into the nature of honor, see Julio Caro Baroja, "Honour and Shame: A Historical Account of Several Conflicts," in *Honour and Shame,* ed. J. G. Peristiany (Chicago, 1966), 42–46, 69; Pierre Bourdieu, "The Sentiment of Honour in Kabyle Society," in ibid., 216–28; Jane Schneider, "Of Vigilance and Virgins: Honor, Shame and Access to Resources in Mediterranean Societies," *Ethnology* 10 (1971): 1–24.

56. Alberti, *Libri della famiglia*, 269–70.

57. Ibid., 272–78.

58. Ibid., 280–89.

59. Ibid., 292.

60. Ibid., 265: "Ed è l'animo dell'uomo assai più che quello della femmina robusto e fermo. . . . Contrario le femmine quasi tutte si veggano timide da natura, molle, tarde, e per questo più utili sedendo a custodire le cose, quasi come la natura così provedesse al vivere nostro, volendo che l'uomo rechi a casa, la donna lo serbi. Difenda la donna serrata in casa le cose e sé stessi con ozio, timore e suspizione. L'uomo difenda la donna, la casa e' suoi e la patria sua, non sedendo ma esercitando l'animo, le mani con molta virtù per sino a spandere il sudore e il sangue."

61. If a woman married, her father did not lose his legal *potestas* over her. See Chapter 8.

62. Alberti, *Libri della famiglia*, 264: "Sarebbe poco onore se la donna traficasse fra gli uomini." On the *mundualdus* as a means of protecting patrimonial integrity, see Cinzio Violante, "Quelques caractéristiques des structures familiales en Lombardie, Émilie et Toscane aux xi^c et xii^c siècles," in *Famille* (n. 19 above), 114.

63. Hatfield, *Uffizi "Adoration,"* 26–29.

64. Giovanni Morelli, *Ricordi*, ed. Vittore Branca (Florence, 1956), 187–88.

65. *Il libro di ricordanze dei Corsini (1362–1457),* ed. Armando Petrucci (Rome, 1965), 131–32.

66. Francesco Guicciardini, *Ricordi, diari, memorie,* ed. Mario Spinelli (Rome, 1981), 39.

67. Cf. Julius Kirshner, "Wives' Claims against Insolvent Husbands in Late

Medieval Italy," in *Women of the Medieval World: Essays in Honor of John H. Mundy*, ed. Julius Kirshner and Suzanne F. Wemple (Oxford, 1985), 256–303.

68. Important studies of this period have been written by Herlihy and Klapisch-Zuber, Gene Brucker, Anthony Molho, and Dale Kent. Cartulary is ASF, Notarile antecosimiano G212 (1422–29), since renumbered as 9040 in the reorganization of this fondo at the time of the archive's relocation in 1988. This material will be cited hereafter simply by folio number.

69. Examples: monna Checca, daughter of Tommaso di Francesco di Neri Fioravanti (deceased), widow of Filippozzo di Lorenzo di Totto Gualterrotti, took as her *mundualdus* Dino di messer Guccio di Dino Gucci (fol. 90v); monna Margherita di fu Mori Rinaldini, widow of Angelo di Ugolino, and her daughter Mona, widow of Zenobi di Simone Rucellai, took Paperio di Chele of Prato, where they were staying in 1424, perhaps to escape the plague (fol. 162r); and five women took the son of the notary, whose connection to them was no more close and lasting than his father's (fols. 278v, 325r–v, 345v, 359r, 378r).

70. E.g., Francesca di fu Bozzo da Corella, wife of Jacopo di Giovanni Dini da Vetriceto, who took a *mundualdus* (ser Michele di Giovanni di Jacopo Banchi) in order to consent to a sale made by her husband (fol. 94r–v); or Vaggia di fu Filippo di Piero di Raniero, who took Agostino di Giovanni di Martino of Prato as *mundualdus* in order with his consent to appoint as her *procurator* her husband Francesco di Giovanni de' Bucelli (fol. 161r).

71. Three of the four who chose their fathers were widows. Of the thirteen who did not choose their fathers, five were married (one remarried) and chose their husbands (one took the husband's brother). In four of the eight cases in which a widow did not choose her father, the subsequent legal action involved either him or his son.

72. The one exception being Antonia di fu Benedetto di Lipaccio de' Bardi who, on the eve of her wedding to Niccolò di Domenico Giugni, struck by her brothers' generosity in adding 400 florins to the 1,200 set aside for her dowry in her father's will, "volens dictos suos fratres de dicta benivolentia remunerare et fraternaliter ac recipere cum amore conservare," made a *finis* "ulterius non petendi" from them on her father's estate (fols. 195r–96r [24 May 1425]).

73. An important and insightful recent study on the importance for widows of recovering their dowries is Isabelle Chabot, "Widowhood and Poverty in Late Medieval Florence," *Continuity and Change* 3 (1988): 291–311.

74. Fols. 391r–94r (18 January 1429).

75. Fol. 161r–v (8 June 1424). For a discussion of the situations in which return of the dowry was legally in order, see Bellomo, *Ricerche*, 187–222.

76. Fol. 178v (25 February 1425).

77. Fols. 252r–v (3 August 1426) and 278v–79r (21 March 1427). See also Kirshner, "Wives' Claims," passim.

78. Fols. 250v–52r (3 August 1426). Caterina was the daughter of messer Giovanni Gherardini.

79. Fols. 378r–79r (23 November 1428).

80. Fol. 382r–v (11 December 1428). Bonda and her brother made a number of appearances before this notary. Bonda was an exceptionally active widow whose activities always involved members of either the Bardi or the Brancacci. Among other things Bonda furnished property to her sons. The nature of the debt to Larione is not explained in the settlement; it may have been that he had given her the sum of her dowry or had taken over support of her widowhood.

81. Fols. 285v–86v (24 April 1427). One daughter was married to Buonaccorso di Niccolò de' Soldani, who served as Margherita's *mundualdus;* the other was the wife of Gherardo di messer Filippo Corsini, who served in the same capacity for both daughters. Not all women had their debts determined by arbitration, however, nor were female debtors only widows. The wife of Paolo di Piccardo Palesi borrowed 112 florins from a person outside the family (fol. 141r [24 November 1423]).

82. Fol. 42r (30 September 1422).

83. Fols. 90v–94r (23 April 1423).

84. For example, monna Nastasia's sale of a piece of land to Giovanni d'Antonio di Giovanni for 27 1/2 florins (fols. 115v–16r [5 May 1423]). Her father and husband were both dead.

85. Fols. 462r–63r (21 March 1430).

86. Fol. 148v (9 February 1424): "considerans et asserens suam iuvenilem etatem et pueritiam ipsius domine et quod honeste et commode tali tutele intendere non valet, ymo potius ad alias nuptias ire intendat."

87. Fols. 325v–26r (26 January 1428).

88. Fols. 448v–49r (30 November 1429).

89. Fols. 96v–97v (4 May 1423).

90. To cite one example of a *procuratio,* Paperia, widow of Lotto di messer Vanni Castellani, took three notaries, while her *mundualdus* was a Francesco di Giovanni. By my count married women received *procuratores* 18 times, in 4 of which neither the *mundualdus* nor the *procurator* was related. All 6 *fines* by married women involved a male relative as *mundualdus* or recipient. In contrast, 15 of 29 *procurationes* and 11 of 18 *fines* by widows saw no male kin.

91. Fol. 200r–v (3 July 1425). The lawyers' *consilia* are located in BNF, Landau-Finaly 98, fols. 403r–14v.

92. The *consilium* survives in a copy in ASF, Carte strozziane, 3d ser., 41/14, fols. 337r–39r. The relevant passage here is: "Ideo eius preiudicium et interesse non sunt in consideratione quia non passum uniuscuiusque potest interesse mulierem facere vel non facere contractum. Fuit igitur ratio imbecillitatis intellectus et ut eius persona, que presumitur a iure esse debilis et fragilis intellectus. . . ."

93. Ibid., fol. 337r–v.

94. Ibid., fol. 337v.

95. Ibid., fols. 337v–39r.

96. Ibid., fol. 339r: "nam statutum presumit quod mulier facilius decipi posset quando se deberet obligare quam quando ipsa actualiter deberet donare: cum mulierum genus sit avarissimum. . . ."

97. ASF, Carte strozziane, 3d ser., 41/9, fols. 84r–85v.

98. Ibid., fol. 84v: "Unde quando aliquo modo se obligaret ex donatione non videtur militari dispositio d. l. sed si ergo, neque consilium domini Aretii cuius decisio etiam in casu suo est valde dubitabilis, cum pariter et fortius militet ratio statuti in donatione que semper solet esse damnosa, quia in aliquibus contractibus qui possent non esse ita damnosi mulieribus." And again near the end, fol. 85v: "Et ista pars videtur magis rationabilis et consona menti statuentium que fuit succurrere fragilitatem mulierum, unde sicut statutum prohibuit mulierem obligari, eodem modo et fortiori debet prohibere donationem que est magis preiudicialis, quia quando alicui est concessa obligatio non tamen est concessa donatio que est maioris preiudicii, quia servus fugitivus potest obligare dummodo ignorantem l. cum fundum § servum si cer. pe., tamen non posset liberare debitorem etiam peculiarem. . . ."

99. BNF, Fondo panciatichiano 139, fols. 381r–82r, which is not a formal *consilium* but a *responsio* to questions or allegations put to him by another jurist.

100. An early assertion of this position can be found in Eileen Power, "The Position of Women," in *The Legacy of the Middle Ages,* ed. G. C. Crump and E. F. Jacob (Oxford, 1932), 433, reiterated in her *Medieval Women,* ed. M. M. Postan (Cambridge, 1975), 34. Important recent studies include those by David Herlihy, "Land, Family and Women in Continental Europe, 701–1200," *Traditio* 18 (1962): 89–113; Richard Goldthwaite, "The Florentine Palace as Domestic Architecture," *American Historical Review* 77 (1972): 1011; Susan Mosher Stuard, "Women in Charter and Statute Law: Medieval Ragusa/Dubrovnik," in *Women in Medieval Society,* ed. Susan Mosher Stuard (Philadelphia, 1976), 199–208; Stanley Chojnacki, "Patrician Women in Early Renaissance Venice," *Studies in the Renaissance* 21 (1974): 176–203; idem, "Dowries and Kinsmen in Early Renaissance Venice," *Journal of Interdisciplinary History* 4 (1975): 571–600; and Herlihy and Klapisch-Zuber, *Les toscans,* 604–6.

101. Cf. Lauro Martines, "A Way of Looking at Women in Renaissance Florence," *Journal of Medieval and Renaissance Studies* 4 (1974): 16–17.

102. My position differs somewhat from that taken by, among others, Chojnacki, who states "that women had a clear sense of their legal prerogatives and their economic significance, and were determined to exercise them," especially for the benefit of kin for whom they felt sympathy or responsibility ("Patrician Women," 197). In contrast, it would appear that the ever-informal influence of women was effective only to the degree that men failed to

make their formal control real. It was formal control that mattered in the types of activities (wills, sales, and so forth) by which women's rights were manipulated. In this connection see also Elizabeth S. Cohen and Thomas V. Cohen, "Camilla the Go-Between: The Politics of Gender in a Roman Household (1559)," *Continuity and Change* 4 (1989): 53–77.

103. Stuard, "Women in Ragusa," 200–203, has argued that such recognition was lacking in Ragusa, despite the fact that patrician women there were involved in important business activities.

104. Elaine G. Rosenthal, "The Position of Women in Renaissance Florence: Neither Autonomy nor Subjection," in *Florence and Italy: Renaissance Studies in Honour of Nicolai Rubinstein,* ed. Peter Denley and Caroline Elam, Westfield Publications in Medieval Studies 2 (London, 1988), 369–81, esp. 375–77, provides interesting examples, including women acting as *procurator* and *arbiter.* Cf. also Shulamith Shahar, *The Fourth Estate: A History of Women in the Middle Ages,* trans. Chaya Galai (London, 1983), 14–15, an often flawed book that presents the same general sense of a disjunction between norms and reality where women's legal abilities and actions are concerned.

105. Rosenthal, "Position of Women," 378, suggests on the basis of a notary's practice of leaving a space for the name of the *mundualdus* and filling it in later that women "acted without the presence or consent of a *mundualdo.*" There are other possible explanations for such scribal procedure, however, such as simply forgetting the man's name or moving on to the important core of the transaction first and coming back to the less important name. I can agree with Rosenthal that despite the *mundualdus* women could operate with a good degree of independence, but I also come back to the fact that the *mundualdus* was still there, that (to go back to her observations) the notary nonetheless *did* leave spaces and come back to fill in the names of *mundualdi.* Female independence in the face of law and ideology could be no more acknowledged or conceded than could taking interest in opposition to the usury prohibition.

106. This lacuna in the law was pointed out to me by Professor Richard Helmholz of the University of Chicago Law School.

107. For these aspects of the *tutela,* see di Renzo, *La tutela,* 345–98.

108. On this theme, see Kirshner, "Wives' Claims," passim.

109. Cortese, "Storia del mundio," traces the persistence of this patrimonial quality through the centuries (esp. 378, 382, 460–61). He notes also that an *extraneus* holding a woman's *mundium* could lose it for violating certain obligations (unlike paternal or marital power) (371–72) but says nothing about this in later law. Frederick II established a *restitutio in integrum* for women victimized by a *mundualdus's* fraud or negligence (456), but this provision for the kingdom of the south seems not to have been extended to the north.

110. Cf. Kirshner, *Pursuing Honor,* 5–9.

111. Of the thirty-six married and remarried women who took a

mundualdus other than husband or kinsman, twenty-one acted with the husband in some way, and one took her son as *procurator*. One must also admit the possibility that some, if not all, of the remaining fourteen acted at the husband's behest or in his interest, even if he was far away at the time. The wealthy merchant Francesco Datini, for example, was able to direct affairs at home through his wife by letter while absent on business. Cf. Iris Origo, *The Merchant of Prato: Francesco di Marco Datini* (New York, 1957), 172–80.

112. Herlihy and Klapisch-Zuber, *Les toscans,* 209, 402–4, 481–87. See also David Herlihy, "The Social and Psychological Roots of Violence in Tuscan Towns," in *Violence and Civil Disorder in Italian Cities, 1200–1500,* ed. Lauro Martines (Los Angeles, 1972), 129–54; idem, "Vieillir à Florence au Quattrocento," *Annales* 24 (1969): 1338–52; and Kirshner and Molho, "Dowry Fund," 432.

113. In contrast to the distinction established here, Chojnacki, who notes that over two-fifths of the cases he examines involved widows ("Patrician Women," 183), draws no distinction between their actions and those of married women.

114. Kirshner, *Pursuing Honor,* 9; and Martines's description of the activities of the wealthy patrician widow Alessandra Macinghi negli Strozzi, "Looking at Women," 19–28.

115. Cf. Giovanni Sercambi, *Novelle,* ed. Giovanni Sinicropi, 2 vols. (Bari, 1972), novelle 18, 30, 70. Also Herlihy, "Roots of Violence," 148–49; Martines, "Looking at Women," 23. For an anthropological perspective, see Juliet du Boulay, *Portrait of a Greek Mountain Village* (Oxford, 1974), 123–38.

116. Cf. Christiane Klapisch-Zuber, "Déclin démographique et la structure du ménage: L'exemple de Prato, fin xiv^c - fin xv^c," in *Famille* (n. 19 above), 225–68.

117. Herlihy and Klapisch-Zuber, *Les toscans,* 494–95, note how women as heads of households—meaning primarily widows—disposed of a disproportionately small share of wealth that decreased progressively with the age of women. One might add that even when a woman disposed of substantial economic rights, a legal action such as the appointment of a *procurator* may have been of little interest to men, because those rights would acquire effective content and become truly useful only after the *procurator* had done his job.

Chapter Ten

1. Jack Goody, *The Development of the Family and Marriage in Europe* (Cambridge, 1983), esp. 240–61. Goody's point is that vigorous action in the acquisition of new wealth or in the control of present resources was alone able to meet this threat. See also his *Production and Reproduction* (Cambridge, 1976) and "Inheritance, Property and Women: Some Comparative Consider-

ations," in *Family and Inheritance: Rural Society in Western Europe, 1200–1800*, ed. J. Goody, J. Thirsk, and E. P. Thompson (Cambridge, 1976), 10–36. What I have called simply dowry, but was actually the *dos* of civil law, Goody terms "direct dowry." This terminological precision allows him to make the point that what some historians have seen as a shift from "brideprice to dowry" in medieval Europe was instead a shift in emphasis in a series of interlinked property transfers at marriage and at death, a point elegantly made by Christiane Klapisch-Zuber, "Le complexe de Griselda: Dot et dons de mariage au Quattrocento," *Mélanges de l'Ecole Français de Rome* 94 (1982): 7–43 (English translation in *Women, Family, and Ritual in Renaissance Italy*, trans. Lydia G. Cochrane [Chicago, 1985], 213–46). However, in accordance with his more general position about the role of the Church in familial developments, Goody also rejects the link between this shift and the growth of agnatic kinship as "too specific." Goody's approach to dowry has been carefully criticized by John Comaroff, Introduction, in *The Meaning of Marriage Payments*, ed. J. L. Comaroff (New York, 1980), 7–11.

2. Franco Niccolai, *La formazione del diritto successorio negli statuti comunali del territorio lombardo-tosco* (Milan, 1940).

3. These provisions largely coincided with those of civil and canon law. Cf. Gian Savino Pene Vidari, *Ricerche sul diritto agli alimenti: L'obbligo 'ex lege' dei familiari nel periodo della Glossa e del commento* (Turin, 1970).

4. Generally women were not allowed to inherit real property on intestacy. Such was the case in Florence, as revealed by a reading of the relevant statute below.

5. On the assimilation of the legitim and the Falcidian portion of Roman law on the part of medieval jurists and legislators, see P. S. Leicht, *Storia del diritto italiano: Il diritto privato*, vol. 2: *Diritti reali e di successione* (Milan, 1960), 258–62.

6. Quoted in Niccolai, *Formazione del diritto successorio*, 104–5. Niccolai took these statutory principles as indicative of the subordination of individuals to familial imperatives, a subordination that in turn served as a workshop for subordination to communal political imperatives. For women this meant that marriage "broke every legal relation to her father's house; even every relation of succession" (ibid., 100). In contrast, on the legal effects of marriage, see Chapter 8. Also, the statutory treatment of dowry in the context of inheritance shows that it was considered to operate as part of the process of property devolution. The dowry was not simply a form of compensation for a woman's contribution to her natal household—in contrast to the situation analyzed by D. B. Rheubottom, "Dowry and Wedding Celebrations in Yugoslav Macedonia," in *The Meaning of Marriage Payments*, 221–49.

7. Manlio Bellomo, *Ricerche sui rapporti patrimoniali tra coniugi* (Milan, 1961), esp. 165, 184–85.

8. Ibid., 182.

9. Cf. Paolo Cammarosano, "Aspetti delle strutture familiari nelle città

dell'Italia comunale (secoli xii–xiv)," *Studi medievali,* ser. 3, 16 (1975): 417–35; Diane Owen Hughes, "From Brideprice to Dowry in Mediterranean Europe," *Journal of Family History* 3 (1978): 262–96 and "Struttura familiare e sistemi di successione ereditaria nei testamenti dell'Europa medievale," *Quaderni storici* 33 (1976): 929–52; Cinzio Violante, "Quelques caractéristiques des structures familiales en Lombardie, Émilie et Toscane aux xie et xiie siècles," in *Famille et parenté dans l'Occident médiéval,* ed. Georges Duby and Jacques Le Goff (Rome, 1977), 87–151; David Herlihy and Christiane Klapisch-Zuber, *Les toscans et leurs familles* (Paris, 1978), 532–33; John Larner, *Italy in the Age of Dante and Petrarch, 1216–1380* (London, 1980), 67–69; J. P. Cooper, "Patterns of Inheritance and Settlement by Great Landowners from the Fifteenth to the Eighteenth Centuries," in *Family and Inheritance,* 279–83; Julius Kirshner and Anthony Molho, "The Dowry Fund and the Marriage Market in Early Quattrocento Florence," *Journal of Modern History* 50 (1978): 403–38; Stanley Chojnacki, "Dowries and Kinsmen in Early Renaissance Venice," *Journal of Interdisciplinary History* 4 (1975): 571–600; Francis William Kent, *Household and Lineage in Renaissance Florence: The Family Life of the Capponi, Ginori, and Rucellai* (Princeton, 1977); Roberto Bizzocchi, "La dissoluzione di un clan familiare: I Buondelmonti di Firenze nei secoli xv e xvi," *Archivio storico italiano* 140 (1982): 3–45.

10. I take my theoretical point of departure here from, among others, Pierre Bourdieu, *Outline of a Theory of Practice,* trans. Richard Nice (Cambridge, 1977), esp. 36–37, and his "Marriage Strategies as Strategies of Social Reproduction," in *Family and Society,* ed. Robert Forster and Orest Ranum (Baltimore, 1976), 117–44; Bernard S. Cohn, "History and Anthropology: The State of Play," *Comparative Studies in Society and History* 22 (1980): 198–221; Julius Kirshner, Review of *Family and Inheritance: Rural Society in Western Europe, Journal of Modern History* 50 (1978): 320–22.

11. On this maxim and its effects, see Manlio Bellomo, *Problemi di diritto familiare nell'età dei comuni* (Milan, 1968), 41–44; Kirshner and Molho, "Dowry Fund," 435.

12. Anthony Molho, "Visions of the Florentine Family in the Renaissance," *Journal of Modern History* 50 (1978): 310; Goody, *Family and Marriage,* 258; Stanley Chojnacki, "Patrician Women in Early Renaissance Venice," *Studies in the Renaissance* 21 (1974): 176–203. Goody has argued that Western history was not marked by a replacement of patrilineal by bilateral inheritance, any more than the nuclear replaced the extended family, but that bilaterality was always present at the core of inheritance practices, even when most submerged in patrilineal emphasis and practices, as witnessed in the *dos* (Goody, *Family and Marriage,* 232–33).

13. Goody (ibid., 258), argues that dowry was both an instrument and a product of social stratification because a woman's father could prove he could support her. Indeed, a widow's father or brothers could be very eager to

arrange her remarriage, indicating that they still possessed some right to control her body and her dowry. Cf. Christiane Klapisch-Zuber, "La 'mère cruelle': Maternité, veuvage et dot dans la Florence des xive–xve siècles," *Annales* 38 (1983): 1097–1109 (English translation in *Women, Family, and Ritual,* 117–31).

14. I ingore here the distinctions between the different collections of statutes—those of the Podestà, the Capitano, Mercanzia, the Ordinances of Justice, not to mention the twenty-one guilds.

15. An introduction to the statutes and judiciary in Florence, though with little attention to private litigation, can be found in Lauro Martines, *Lawyers and Statecraft in Renaissance Florence* (Princeton, 1968), 91–106, 130–34. An interesting perspective on the relationship between the learned *ius commune* and statutes is provided by Charles Fried, "The *Lex Aquilia* as a Source of Law for Bartolus and Baldus," *American Journal of Legal History* 4 (1960): 142–72. See also the works of Mario Sbriccoli, Manlio Bellomo, and Luigi Lombardi cited below.

16. Cf. Goody, *Family and Marriage,* 257. Note also the statistical evidence from Genoese wills mustered by Steven Epstein, *Wills and Wealth in Medieval Genoa, 1150–1250* (Cambridge, Mass., 1984), 81–83.

17. Cf. Cooper, "Patterns of Inheritance," 242.

18. In other words, juristic interpretation as a process becomes part of the devolutionary process, which occupies the sort of pivotal position outlined by Comaroff in his Introduction, in *The Meaning of Marriage Payments,* 1–47.

19. *Statuti della repubblica fiorentina,* ed. Romolo Caggese, vol. 2: *Statuto del Podestà dell'anno 1325* (Florence, 1921), 139–141; Podestà 1355, fols. 97v–98v; *Statuta* 1415, 1: 223–25. Cf. Niccolai, *Formazione del diritto successorio,* 95–96, 143. The revisions were commissioned from Tommaso da Gubbio in the first instance and from Paolo di Castro (1360–1441) and Bartolomeo Vulpi (1359–1435) in the second. Cf. Lauro Martines, *Lawyers,* 186.

20. I exclude here any discussion of changes in word order, verb tense or mood, or similar matters.

21. The value of this fixed amount in *lire* was in steady decline relative to the gold florin in the course of the fourteenth and fifteenth centuries. Cf. tables in Richard Goldthwaite, *The Building of Renaissance Florence: An Economic and Social History* (Baltimore, 1980), 429–30, and the relevant sections of Charles M. de la Roncière, *Prix et salaires à Florence au xive siècle (1280–1380)* (Rome, 1982).

22. All versions gave special attention to half-brothers and stepbrothers also.

23. Regarding usufruct and property law in general, see Paolo Grossi, *Le situazioni reali nell'esperienza giuridica medievale* (Padua, 1968) and "Usus facti: La nozione di proprietà nella inaugurazione dell'età nuova," *Quaderni fiorentini per la storia del pensiero giuridico moderno* 1 (1972): 287–355.

24. Here is language from 1355, with the addition of 1415 in brackets and the omission in italics: "Et interim donec nuptui traderentur debeant habere alimenta de bonis patris, avi, vel proavi [vel cuiuslibet alterius ascendentis] de cuius successione ageretur. *Si ex defuncta persona filius vel filii vel descendentes per lineam masculinam existant. Si vero ipse filius et filii seu descendentes non extent et superessent frater vel fratres vel filius vel filii ex fratre carnalibus defuncte per tunc ipsa mulier habeat usumfructum omnium bonorum talis patris avi vel proavi defuncti.*" Also "Si vero filius, vel filii, vel descendentes masculi non extarent, et superesset frater, vel fratres, vel filius, seu filii ex fratre, vel fratribus carnalibus [vel pater, vel avus paternus] defunctae personae, eo casu ipsa mulier donec vidua steterit debeat habere *usumfructum omnium bonorum* [alimenta competentia et decentia in bonis] sui patris, avi, vel proavi [vel alterius ascendentis] mortui." This may have made more attractive to widows usufruct left them by husbands who died with concerns about care for their children. On this practice, cf. Klapisch, "La mère cruelle," 1100–1101.

25. Bartolo's role is well described by Filippo Corsini in his *consilium* discussed below.

26. Bartolo to D. 38.17.2,47 (Venice, 1580), fols. 176va–vb: "In contrarium quod excludatur avus maternus videtur ratio statuti que videtur velle quod hereditas remaneat apud agnatos. Preterea et si excluditur proximior in gradu, sequens videtur excludi. . . .

"Sed agnati excludunt matrem et omnes agnatos ex forma statuti: ideo concludo quod sive mater sit mortua sive vivat quod agnati admittantur exclusa matre, et omnibus sequentibus in gradu. Etiam puto si diceret statutum extantibus masculis filia foemina non succedat, quid de nepote ex filia? Certe idem quod in filia per ea que supra dixi. Tene ista menti et sic de facto consului in civitate Florentie."

27. See discussion of Deti's *consilium* below.

28. The following clause graced the end of the statute in 1325 but was omitted thereafter: "And this statute is precise and basic [*truncum*] and may not be disposed of or interpreted; and if some word in this statute should be obscure it is to be understood according to the reading of the assembly [*conventus*]." This clause's removal demonstrates how hopeless it was to keep jurists' hands off such an important and troublesome statute.

29. Bartolo to D. 38.4.1,8, ed. cit., fol. 164rb.

30. Baldo to D. 28.2.29,5 (Venice, 1577), fol. 66va: "Et hec faciunt ad quandam difficilem questionem super qua consului. Dictat statutum Florentiae quod filia dotata non succedit ab intestato existentibus filiis vel fratribus defuncti. Modo queritur, utrum si factum est testamentum, et est praeterita, utrum possit dicere testamentum nullum? Et videtur quod sic quia istud statutum disponit in casu testati. Ergo in casu intestati stamus iuri communi ut possit dicere testamentum nullum. . . . Bartolus tenet contra in l. ulti. infra ad Treb. nam cum in testamento sint instituti venientes ab intestato

quibus testator poterat tacite relinquere ab intestato moriendo . . . apparet quod nullam iniuriam fecit filiae et non culpandum si tacitum induxit in conditionem expressam secundum Bartolum. . . . quia cum ex legibus, id est ex lege municipali filia sit exclusa, intelligo quod sit exclusa a iure civili, et pretorio, quia istud ius novum, quod est posterius iure civili, et pretorio, derogat, ar. C. de li. pre. [l.] maximum vitium, et dicendo contrarium sequeretur absurdum quod imputaretur patri, cur non decesserit intestatus, et lex reputat hoc absurdum." On a different issue, Baldo to D. 24.3.22, ed. cit., fol. 11ra: "Statuto civitatis Florentiae cavetur quod non existentibus masculis succedant foeminae. Modo quaeritur si masculi sunt, utrum filiae succedant? Quidam dicunt quod sic: quia iste casus omissus. Cy. in d. civitate Florentiae consuluit contrarium. . . . et ista est veritas: quia videtur inducere tacitam prelationem masculorum. . . ."

31. BNF, Principale, II, iv, 435, fols. 71r–73v. Unfortunately no commentary on this statute survives in the later work of Tommaso Salvetti in BNF, Principale, II, iv, 434.

32. Ibid., fol. 71v. Another revealing passage, which also indicates a change in language in the statute: "In § et nulla mulier. in ver. ex filio vel filiis. Not. de nepote ex filio, nec de nepote ex fratre prout loquebatur statutum antiquum, et ideo si extat nepos ex fratre non excluditur filia sed remanet dispositio iuris communis ut in aut. in subcessione et ita respondi Dominico ser Filippi. Alex." (ibid., fol. 72v).

33. Ibid., fols. 71v–72r: "In § et si bona. in ver. etiam in avia. Scilicet materna, secus in paterna, que in totum excludit agnatum in vi gradu, ita consuluit d. Nellus in facto consanguinee ser Nicholai Galgani, quia in hac parte statuti est hodie per superiora, ubi loquitur de matre et non de patre. Sed not. quod hoc statutum vocat agnatos masculos tantum et sic alios excludit ut per Bar. in l. liberorum. Item dictum de avia habet locum etiam in paterna, in materna correctiva, ut in aut. matri et avie in prin. in favorem agnatorum masculorum emanavit et avia materna est sicut paterna, ideo eadem est ratio statuti, et ita respondi et ita reperio consuluisse d. Bartolomeus de Sali."

34. Ibid., fol. 72v.

35. Ibid., fol. 72r.

36. Ibid., fol. 72v.

37. This was a more complex process than merely filling in interstices, for a prior process of interpretation was required, at least, to identify the presence of a gap in the statute's coverage.

38. The rapid decease of the husband, wife, and daughter would seem to indicate a plague, either that of 1390 or 1400. No precise date is given. The form of the statute refered to is that of 1355, so it must date from before the redaction of 1415. The *consilium* survives in a copy in BNF, Panciatichiano 138, fols. 165v–66v.

39. Ibid., fol. 165v: "Finaliter tamen dominus Genitor meus tenuit avum excludi et personas in statuto nominatas ad subcessionem vocari. Et ita preterea consuluit dominus meus Bar. ex comissione de civitate Florentie sibi facta, dicens quod dictum statutum non solum habet virtutem exclusivam matris et avie, ut verba expresse dicunt, ut persone agnatorum in statuto nominatorum ad subcessionem admictantur." And fol. 166r: "Sed hodie videtur clarum quod patruus excludit avum maternum propter addictionem que fuit facta statuto post consilium genitoris mei et domini Bar., ut patet in statuto ibi 'et de anno m°ccc°li°, indictione xiiii , die xii januarii citra.'"

40. Which he had cited earlier as an analogy to the inclusion-exclusion process set up by the statute. Cf. my *Emancipation in Late Medieval Florence* (New Brunswick, 1982), 16.

41. The original *consilium* is preserved in BNF, Landau Finaly 98, fols. 89r–92v.

42. BNF, Principale, II, iv, 435, fol. 72r: "In ver. ex eis frater aut fratres. Intellige de fratre proprio, non autem de patrueli seu cugino quia ille est frater cum adictione et non simpliciter, ut per Bar. in l. Iutius § quesitum de leg. iii, unde respondi quod cum soror admictatur de iure comuni ad successionem ab intestato fratris per aut. cessante cum si. [non] perdit ius succedendi per existentiam filii patrui magis defuncti qui erat frater patruelis patris defuncti nec per existentiam fratris patruelis illius qui decessit. . . ."

43. Ibid., fol. 90r: "Statutum enim predictum est correptivum iuris communis quod ut supra dictum est inter cognatos et agnatos ultimo loco nullam fecit differentiam, ergo non ample sed stripte debet intelligi ut quam minus potest corrigat ius comune. . . ." The statute thus "corrected" civil law by altering it in accordance with a standard external to it.

44. Ibid., fol. 92v: "Puto clare tenendum quod ipsa debet habere quartam dimidie, non autem quartam respectu totius, cum nulla dispositio eius favore reperiatur que eius portionem augere videatur."

45. Cf. Mario Sbriccoli, *L'Interpretazione dello statuto: Contributo allo studio della funzione dei giuristi nell'età comunale* (Milan, 1969), 212–64.

46. Because Prato had no statute governing female inheritance, the Florentine statute applied. On the relation between Florence's statutes and those of the towns subject to her, see ibid., 220–45; also Giorgio Chittolini, *La formazione dello stato regionale e le istituzioni del contado: Secoli xiv e xv* (Turin, 1979), 292–352.

47. The original of this *consilium* is contained in BAV, Vat. Lat. 8067/1, fols. 20r–29v. The dating revolves around Accolti's matriculation into the Arte dei Giudici e Notai (he being the last of the four to do so) and Buongirolami's death in 1454. For information on these men and the other Florentine jurists mentioned here, see Martines, *Lawyers,* 481–509.

48. BAV, Vat. Lat. 8067/1, fol. 22r: "Unde si diceremus quod ex alio capite statuti dum loquitur de causa testati reservatum fuisset matri ius

dicendi nullum testamentum resultaret unum absurdum, videlicet quod mater ipsa rumperet testamentum et tamen testamento rupto ipsa non subcessisset. . . ."

49. Ibid., fol. 26v: "Unde ex istis verbis constat quod fundamentum illius partis fuit excludere feminas ex testamento et a iure dicendi nullum quando essent instituti descendentes, alias frustra repetisset hoc declarans de quibus descendentibus intelligat itaque ex hiis verbis declaratur mens statuentis." Also fol. 27r: "Nam statutum in dicto ver. si vero testatus semper loquitur et disponit quando supersunt filii et alii descendentes, sed iste non est casus noster sed casus diversus non tactus a statuto quia testator decessit nullis superexistentibus descendentibus et per consequens remanet in dispositione iuris comunis. . . ." This decision squares with the findings of Bartolo and Baldo mentioned above, in that they upheld a will against women when the *venientes ab intestato* were the designated heirs.

50. Ibid., fols. 28r–v.

51. Ibid., fols. 29r–v: "Quod cum compilatores maxime novorum statutorum, qui fuerunt pratichi causidici, et sciebant dubia huiusmodi per prius sepe fuisse et non aliter ampliaverint quam in casu illo ut iacet statutum, et detraxerunt de statuto antiquo verba a negativa iurisdictionis rectorum de intelligendo verba dubia secundum intentionem conventi, per que patet eos voluisse intelligi proprie ut verba important et non aliter, prout etiam dictat statutum in ordinamentis iustitie. . . ."

52. ASF, Carte strozziane, 3d series, 41/14, fols. 159r–69r, with the seals of Strozzi and Rucellai and a notation to the effect that Pepi and Amidei later signed the official copy. The case would seem to date from between 1500 (the year Rucellai matriculated into the Florentine guild) and 1513 (Pepi's death). On the *fideicommissum,* see Cooper, "Patterns of Inheritance," passim, and P. S. Leicht, *Il diritto privato,* 2: 249–56.

53. Strozzi's notation "pro illis de Squarcialupis" at the beginning of the *consilium* is a consistent indicator in his many surviving opinions that he was operating on behalf of one party.

54. Ibid., fols. 164r–65r. Strozzi seems to have been consistent in his views on this issue. In his legal glossary (Carte strozziane, 3d ser., 41/18, fol. 530r), on the basis of a *consilium* of Alessandro Tartagni da Imola, he said "onus dotandi pertinere ad patrem et non ad patruos."

55. Ibid., fols. 165r–v: "Sed adhuc casus noster est magis clarus quia presuponitur quod he neptes non fuerunt nate neque concepte tempore mortis avi et sic non fuerant coniuncte neque cognite avo, quo casu minus dici debet avum teneri ad dotandum neptem natam post mortem suam. Considero enim quod iste neptes concepte et nate post mortem avi nullo modo dicuntur coniuncte ipsi avo neque ad eius hereditatem tanquam incognite illi avo quo minus non dum animax erant, id est, non dum concepte."

56. The civil-law texts he alleges in support are § *si quis proximior, l. i, ff. unde cognati* (D. 38.8.1,8) and *l. titius, ff. de suis et legitimis* (D. 38.16.6).

D. 38.8.1,8, dealing with inheritance by pretorian *bonorum possessio* allows inheritance by those *in utero* when the *de cuius* died: "sed hoc ita demum erit accipiendum, si hic qui in utero esse dicitur vivo eo de cuius bonorum possessione agitur fuit conceptus, nam si post mortem, neque obstabit alii neque ipse admittetur, quia non fuit proximus cognatus ei, quo vivo nondum animax fuerit." D. 38.16.6, a fragment of the jurisconsult Julian, discusses the man who is disinherited but whose son (the grandson), in turn, seeks the estate because he was born after the grandfather's death: "respondit: qui post mortem avi sui concipitur, is neque legitimam hereditatem eius tamquam suus heres neque bonorum possessionem tamquam cognatus accipere potest, quia lex duodecim tabularum eum vocat ad hereditatem, qui moriente eo, de cuius bonis quaeritur, in rerum natura fuerit." In Strozzi's case, however, the girl's father was certainly not disinherited, and the impact of Ulpian's remarks in D. 38.8.1,8 is to eliminate those who were not conceived by the *de cuius* and, therefore, are unrelated to him—again not the case here. These citations to Roman law are to *Corpus iuris civilis*, ed. T. H. Mommsen. W. Kroll, P. Krueger, and R. Schoell, 3 vols. (Berlin, 1928–29).

57. BNF, Magliabechiano xxix, 193, fols. 182r–91r, the sealed original, also found in print in Filippo Decio, *Consilia*, 2 vols. (Venice, 1575), *cons.* 383, vol. 2, fols. 42ra–43va. Both Decio and Deti were teaching at Pisa when their *consilia* were rendered. According to Martines, *Lawyers*, 505, Decio taught in Pisa from 1484 to 89, most of the 1490s, 1500–1501, and 1515–21. Deti taught there in 1496 and subsequently, and again in 1515–22 (ibid., 488). Niccolini, the youngest of the three, matriculated into the Florentine guild in 1498 (ibid., 497). I suspect that Piero may not have been very old at the time, so I tend to an earlier date, say about 1498. Piero later had several sons (birth dates from Tratte evidence supplied by David Herlihy): Rinieri (b. 1509), Claudio (b. 1512), Giambattista (b. 1515), Priore (b. 1517), Ruberto (b. 1518), and Piero (b. 1520).

58. BNF, Magliabechiano, xxix, 193, fol. 182v: "Ista dubitatio in terminis statuti florentini cessat propter verba statuti que ulterius procedendo expresse dicunt quod statutum intelligatur de filiis legitimis et naturalibus legittimo matrimonio natis, quo casu cum appareat de mente statuti indubitanter concludendum est quod filie a Petro legittimato non excluduntur. . . ."

59. Ibid., fol. 186v: "Et concludo quod filie predicte a nepotibus ex fratre non succedentibus nullo modo excludantur quia privatio successionis facte propter masculos intelligitur casu quo masculi in quorum favorem fuit facta privatio admittantur, unde si alii instituti sint statutum non habet locum. . . ."

60. Ibid., fols. 1r–13v.

61. Ibid., fols. 5r–6r.

62. Ibid., fol. 8v: "in terminis statuti pater non potest filiam impune preterire sed beneficio filii legittimi vel agnatorum."

63. Ibid., fol. 190r: "et iste favor cessat ex quo agnati non admittuntur . . . exclusus privatur lucro quia illi non erat debita legitima sicut debetur filie de

iure comuni et in casu nostro extranei vocati sunt contra mentem statuti quod voluit vocare agnatos filia exclusa."

64. Bellomo, *Ricerhce,* 182-83.

65. Cf. Luigi Lombardi, *Saggio sul diritto giurisprudenziale* (Milan, 1975), 1-199; Mario Ascheri, "'Consilium sapientis', perizia medica e 'res iudicata': Diritto dei 'dottori' e istituzioni comunali," *Proceedings of the Fifth International Congress of Medieval Canon Law,* ed. Stephan Kuttner, Monumenta iuris canonici, ser. C, 6 (Rome, 1980), 533-79. Recently Jacques Pluss, "Baldus de Ubaldis of Perugia on Dominium over Dotal Property," *Tijdschrift voor Rechtsgeschiedenis* 52 (1984): 399-411, has reconstructed an interesting example of interpretive flexibility within a doctrinal framework that made law truly operative in Italian cities. Interesting insights on the pervasive nature of ambiguity in law are offered by Alan Watson, *Sources of Law, Legal Change, and Ambiguity* (Philadelphia, 1984).

66. In contrast to Sbriccoli, *Interpretazione,* and to a lesser degree Bellomo, *Società e istituzioni in Italia dal medioevo agli inizi dell'età moderna,* 3d ed. (Catania, 1982).

67. In this connection stand the comments of Angelo degli Ubaldi (1325-1400) echoing the conclusion of Francesco di Bici degli Albergotti (d. 1376) that a mother was not excluded from inheritance to her daughter in favor of the child's paternal aunt: "Mater habet pro se ipsam rerum naturam, et summam aequitatem, et coniecturas quasdam: amita habet pro se primam statuti figuram, scilicet statuti, cui tenacissime inhaerent homines, et maxime rudes [whose interpretation earlier was characterized as 'quaedam rudis et laicorum aequitas videtur, quod bona redeant ad stirpem, a qua profluxerunt'], qui mundi maximam partem id dicunt esse astutiam et cavillationem: de quorum tamen verbis parum curandum est, dum tamen non devietur a tramite rationis. Quid ergo finaliter dicendum est? Respondeo, servetur practica et interpretatio consueta: quae si non apparet, mater habet aequitatem, amita verborum ruditatem." Cf. Angelo degli Ubaldi, *Consilia* (Frankfurt, 1575), *cons.* 344 and 345, fols. 245ra-47va, (both his and Albergotti's) quotes on 247ra and rb.

68. Cf. Chojnacki, "Patrician Women," 187-93. Christiane Klapisch-Zuber, "Déclin démographique et structure du ménage," in *Famille et parenté dans l'Occident médiéval,* ed. Georges Duby and Jacques Le Goff (Rome, 1977), 255-68 (English translation in *Women, Family, and Ritual,* 23-35), argues that greater household complexity, based on patrilineal and patrilocal rules, made for greater subjection of wives and widows that coincided with a juridical antifeminism. But in actual operation legal institutions were not reticent about protecting women (as she herself notes, "La mère cruelle," 1100), perhaps precisely because they were so closely "controlled" by men. Also on legal control of women in Florence, see Chapter 9.

69. Grossi, *Situazioni reali.* In the last analysis, even the jurists' ideas dissolve into tangled relationships whose historical nature remains obscure.

As Julius Kirshner has warned, "*consilia* are constructed intertextually, that is, they are often little more than a concatenation of texts citing other texts; and they tend upon close examination to lose their historical specificity and disappear as discrete entities before one's eyes" (Review of Mario Ascheri, *I consilia dei giuristi medievali, Speculum* 58 [1983]: 842).

70. Kuehn, *Emancipation*, 26–27, 139.

71. Cf. Antonio Roselli, *Tractatus legitimationum*, in *Tractatus universi iuris* (Venice, 1584), vol. 8, part 2, fols. 75va–90ra; R. Génestal, *Histoire de la légitimation des enfants naturels en droit canonique* (Paris, 1905); Henri Regnault, *La condition juridique du bâtard au moyen âge* (Pont Audemer, 1922); Corrado Pecorella, "Filiazione (storia)," *Enciclopedia del diritto* 17: 450–54; Anke Leineweber, *Die rechtliche Beziehung des nichtehelichen Kindes zu seinem Erzeuger in der Geschichte des Privatrechts* (Königstein, 1978).

72. A point elegantly made by Sally Falk Moore, *Law as Process* (London, 1978), 149–80. Also John L. Comaroff and Simon Roberts, *Rules and Processes: The Cultural Logic of Dispute in an African Context* (Chicago, 1981), 175–215. On the other hand, I find that Goody's cross-cultural approach tends to take a construct like agnation as universal and unchanging, though not constructs like lineage or family. Cf. not only his *Development of the Family and Marriage*, and *Production and Reproduction* but also his theoretical essay, "Inheritance, Property and Woman: Some Comparative Considerations," in *Family and Inheritance*.

73. Cooper, "Patterns of Inheritance," 296, suggests that the trend after 1300 was "towards emphasis on a narrow definition of lineage, in turn fortified by policies of restrictive marriage," one aspect of which was "the preference of females over collateral males in inheritance." Also Richard Goldthwaite, *Private Wealth in Renaissance Florence* (Princeton, 1968), but see also Cooper, "Patterns of Inheritance," 279–80; Kent, *Household and Lineage* 3–15; Herlihy and Klapisch-Zuber, *Les toscans*, 511. There may indeed have been an increased emphasis on lineal succession, as in Bartolo's exclusion of the maternal line and the increased use of the *fideicommissum*.

74. Cf. Comaroff, Introduction, in *The Meaning of Marriage Payments*, 34–35: "it is with reference to the devolutionary process . . . that members acquire their rank and location within fields of relationships, that the social definition of linkages between them are negotiated and expressed, and that segmentary alignments gain their manifest shape." In a similar vein on the problem of succession, see his "Rules and Rulers: Political Processes in a Tswana Kingdom," *Man*, n.s. 13 (1978): 1–20.

75. A distinction between male and female senses of kinship is a valuable perspective raised by historians like Goody and Klapisch-Zuber, but see also Stanley Chojnacki, "Dowries and Kinsmen in Early Renaissance Venice," *Journal of Interdisciplinary History* 5 (1975): 571–600, and "Patrician Women in Early Renaissance Venice," *Studies in the Renaissance* 21 (1974): 176–203; Susan Mosher Stuard, "Women in Charter and Statute Law: Medi-

eval Ragusa/Dubrovnik," in *Women in Medieval Society,* ed. Susan Mosher Stuard (Philadelphia, 1976), 199–208; Lauro Martines, "A Way of Looking at Women in Renaissance Florence," *Journal of Medieval and Renaissance Studies* 4 (1974): 15–28.

76. Cf. Chapter 9 above.

77. It should be pointed out as well that it is not certain from case materials, least of all from *consilia,* exactly who was the moving force behind any given party. Female litigants may have been the pawns of male relatives, and conversely men might have been acting along lines laid out by mothers; or men may have worked through other men or women through women.

78. In his *Medieval Households* (Cambridge, Mass., 1985), 82–83, David Herlihy amplifies Goody's insights to insist that in the twelfth century the agnatic lineage began to overlay but not to replace the cognatic kindred.

BIBLIOGRAPHY

●

Primary Sources

Alberti, Leon Battista. *I libri della famiglia*. Edited by Ruggiero Romano and Alberto Tenenti. Turin: Einaudi, 1969.

———. "L'Autobiografia di Leon Battista Alberti: Studio e edizione." Edited by Riccardo Fubini and Anna Menci Gallorini. *Rinascimento* 12 (1972): 21–78.

———. *The Family in Renaissance Florence*. Translated by Renée Neu Watkins. Columbia, S.C.: University of South Carolina Press, 1969.

———. *Opere volgari*. Edited by Cecil Grayson. 2 vols. Bari: Laterza, 1966.

Balbi, Giovanni Francesco. *Tractatus de praescriptionibus*. Venice, 1582.

Bartolo da Sassoferrato. *In primam digesti novi partem commentaria*. Venice, 1580.

———. *In primam digesti veteris partem commentaria*. Venice, 1585.

———. *In primam infortiati partem commentaria*. Venice, 1581.

———. *In secundam codicis partem commentaria*. Venice, 1580.

———. *In secundam infortiati partem commentaria*. Venice, 1580.

———. *Opera omnia*. 10 vols. Venice, 1585.

———. *Opera omnia*. 10 vols. Venice, 1602.

Barzi, Benedetto. *Tractatus de filiis non legitime natis*, in *Tractatus universi iuris*. 29 vols. Venice, 1584. Vol. 8, Part 2, fols. 24ra–29vb.

Guido de Baysio. *Rosarium*. Venice, 1577.

Bencivenne. *Ars notarie*. Edited by Giovanni Bronzino. Bologna: Il Mulino, 1965.

Boccaccio, Giovanni. *Il decamerone*. Edited by Angelo Ottolini. 2d ed. Milan: Hoepli, 1938.

Bracciolini, Poggio. *Opera omnia*. Edited by Riccardo Fubini. 4 vols. Turin: Bottega d'Erasmo, 1966.

da Butrio, Antonio. *In librum quartum decretalium commentaria.* Venice, 1578.

———. *Super secunda secundi decretalium.* Venice, 1578. Reprint ed., Turin, 1967.

Carnesecchi, Carlo. "Un fiorentino del secolo xv e le sue ricordanze domestiche." *Archivio storico italiano,* 5th ser., 4 (1889): 147–73.

da Certaldo, Paolo. *Il libro di buoni costumi.* Edited by Alfredo Schiaffini. Florence: Le Monnier, 1945.

———. *Il libro di buoni costumi.* Edited by S. Morpurgo. Florence: Le Monnier, 1921.

Corpus iuris canonici. Edited by Emil Friedberg. 2 vols. Leipzig: Tauchnitz, 1879.

Corpus iuris civilis. Edited by T. H. Mommsen, W. Kroll, P. Krueger, and R. Schoell. 3 vols. Berlin: Weidmann, 1928–29.

Dati, Goro. "The Diary of Goro Dati." In *Two Memoirs of Renaissance Florence.* Edited by Gene Brucker. New York: Harper & Row, 1967. Pp. 107–41.

Decio, Filippo. *Consilia.* 2 vols. Venice, 1575.

———. *In titulum ff. de regulis iuris.* Lyons, 1588.

Durante, Guglielmo,*Speculum iudiciale.* Venice, 1566.

———. *Speculum iudiciale.* Venice, 1578.

———. *Speculum iudiciale.* 1479.

Fulgosio, Raphaele. *Consilia.* Venice, 1575.

Giovanni d'Andrea. *Novella commentaria.* Venice, 1581.

———. *Novella in titu. de regulis iuris.* 1536.

———. *Novella super quarto et quinto decretalium.* Venice, 1504–5.

Glossa ordinaria. Lyons, 1612.

Guicciardini, Francesco. *Maxims and Reflections of a Renaissance Statesman.* Translated by Mario Domandi. New York: Harper & Row, 1965.

———. *Ricordi, diari, memorie.* Edited by Mario Spinelli. Rome: Editori Riuniti, 1981.

Hostiensis. *Summa aurea.* Venice, 1574.

Innocent IV. *Commentaria in v libros decretalium.* Frankfurt, 1570. Reprint ed., Frankfurt, 1968.

Il libro di ricordanze dei Corsini. Edited by Armando Petrucci. Rome: Istituto Storico Italiano per il Medio Evo, 1965.

Machiavelli, Bernardo. *Libro di ricordi.* Edited by Cesare Olschki. Florence: LeMonnier, 1954.

da Montemagno, Buonaccorso. *De Nobilitate.* In *Prosatori latini del Quattrocento.* Edited by Eugenio Garin. 2 vols. Milan: Ricciardi, 1952. Reprint ed., Turin: Einaudi, 1976. Vol. 2: 142–65.

Morelli, Giovanni di Pagolo. *Ricordi.* Edited by Vittore Branca. Florence: LeMonnier, 1956.

Niccolini, Lapo di Giovanni. *Il libro degli affari proprii di casa di Lapo di Giovanni Niccolini de' Sirigatti.* Edited by Christian Bec. Paris: SEVPEN, 1969.

Omodei, Signorino degli. *Consilia.* Lyons, 1549.

Paolo di Castro. *Consilia.* 3 vols. Frankfurt, 1582.

———. *Commentaria in secundam partem codicis.* Lyons, 1548.

———. *Super secundo digesto novo.* Lyons, 1548.

Passaggieri, Rolandino. *Summa totius artis notariae.* Venice, 1574.

Polidori, F., ed. "Ricordanze di Oderigo d'Andrea di Credi orafo, cittadino fiorentino, dal 1405 al 1425." *Archivio storico italiano,* 1st ser., 4 (1843): 53–110.

Prosatori minori del Trecento: Scrittori di religione del Trecento volgarizzamenti. Edited by Giusseppe de Luca. 4 vols. Milan, 1954. Reprint ed., Turin: Einaudi, 1977.

da Rosciate, Alberico. *Commentaria.* Lyons, 1518.

Roselli, Antonio. *Tractatus legitimationum.* In *Tractatus universi iuris.* 29 vols. Venice, 1584. Vol. 8, Part 2, fols. 75ra–90va.

Sacchetti, Franco. *Le novelle.* 2 vols. Florence: Salani, 1925.

Salatiele. *Ars notariae.* Edited Gianfranco Orlandelli. 2 vols. Milan: Giuffrè, 1961.

Sercambi, Giovanni. *Novelle.* Edited by Giovanni Sinicropi. 2 vols. Bari: Laterza, 1972.

The Society of Renaissance Florence: A Documentary Study. Edited by Gene Brucker. New York: Harper & Row, 1971.

Statuta communis Florentie anno salutis mccccxv. 3 vols. Freiburg [Florence], 1778–83.

Statuti della repubblica fiorentina. Edited by Romolo Caggese. 2 vols. Vol. 2: *Statuto del Podestà dell'anno 1325.* Florence, E. Ariani, 1921.

Statutum potestatis comunis Pistorii anni mcclxxxxvi. Edited by Lodovico Zdekauer. Milan: Hoepli, 1888.

Ubaldi, Angelo degli. *Commentaria.* Lyons, 1561.

———. *Consilia.* Frankfurt, 1575.

———. *Opus ac lectura autenticorum.* Venice, 1485.

Ubaldi, Baldo degli. *In primam digesti veteris partem commentaria.* Venice, 1577.

———. *In primam et secundam infortiati partes commentaria.* Venice, 1577.

———. *In primos libros codicis commentaria.* Lyons, 1546.

———. *Opera omnia.* 10 vols. Venice, 1577.

———. *Super decretalibus.* Lyons, 1551.

———. *Super feudis restauratum commentum.* Pavia, 1495.

Secondary Sources

Abbondanza, Roberto. "Jurisprudence: The Methodology of Andrea Alciato." In *The Late Italian Renaissance, 1525–1630.* Edited by Eric Cochrane. New York: Macmillan, 1970. Pp. 77–90.

Abel, Richard. "A Comparative Theory of Dispute Institutions in Society." *Law and Society Review* 8 (1973–74): 217–347.

———. "The Rise of Capitalism and the Transformation of Disputing: From Confrontation over Honor to Competition for Property." *UCLA Law Review* 27 (1979–80): 223–55.

———. "Theories of Litigation in Society: 'Modern' Dispute Institutions in 'Tribal' Society and 'Tribal' Dispute Institutions in 'Modern' Society as Alternative Legal Forms." *Jahrbuch für Rechtssoziologie und Rechtstheorie* 6 (1979): 165–91.

Ago, Renata. "Conflitti e politica nel feudo: Le compagne romane del Settecento." *Quaderni storici* 63 (December 1986): 847–74.

Airaldi, Gabriella. " . . . bastardos, spurios, manzeres, naturales, incestuosos . . . " In *Studi e documenti su Genova e l'Oltremare*. Collana storica di fonti e studi, 19. Genoa: Università di Genova, Istituto di Paleografia e Storia Medievale, 1974. Pp. 319–55.

Anselmi, Gian-Maria, Pezzarossa, Fulvio, and Avellini, Luisa, eds. *La "memoria" dei mercatores: Tendenze ideologiche, ricordanze, artigianato in versi nella Firenze del Quattrocento*. Bologna: Patron, 1980.

Arno, Andrew. "A Grammar of Conflict: Informal Procedure on an Island in Lau, Fiji." In *Access to Justice*. Edited by Klaus-Friedrich Koch. 4 vols. Vol. 4: *The Anthropological Perspective: Patterns of Conflict Management: Essays in the Ethnography of Law*. Milan: Giuffrè, 1979. Pp. 41–68.

———. "Structural Communication and Control Communication: An Interactionist Perspective on Legal and Customary Procedures for Conflict Management." *American Anthropologist* 87 (1985): 40–55.

Ascheri, Mario. "'Consilium sapientis,' perizia medica e 'res iudicata': Diritto dei dottori e istituzioni comunali." *Proceedings of the Fifth International Congress of Medieval Canon Law*. Edited by Stephan Kuttner. Vatican City, 1980. Pp. 533–79.

Aubert, Vilhelm. "Law as a Way of Resolving Conflicts: The Case of a Small Industrialized Society." In *Law in Culture and Society*. Edited by Laura Nader. Chicago: Aldine, 1969. Pp. 282–303.

Bader, Karl S. "'Arbiter, arbitrator seu amicabilis compositor': Zur Verbreitung einer kanonistischen Formel in Gebieten nördlich der Alpen." *Zeitschrift der Savigny-Stiftung für Rechtsgeschichte (Kan. Abt.)* 77 (1960): 239–76.

Barbagli, Marzio. *Sotto lo stesso tetto: Mutamenti della famiglia in Italia dal xv al xx secolo*. Bologna: Il Mulino, 1984.

Barnes, J. A. *Three Styles in the Study of Kinship*. Berkeley: University of California Press, 1971.

Baroja, Julio Caro. "Honour and Shame: A Historical Account of Several Conflicts." In *Honour and Shame: The Values of Mediterranean Society*. Edited by J. G. Peristiany. Chicago: University of Chicago Press, 1966. Pp. 79–137.

Baron, Hans. "Franciscan Poverty and Civic Wealth as Factors in the Rise of Humanistic Thought." *Speculum* 13 (1938): 1–37.

———. *The Crisis of the Early Italian Renaissance.* Revised ed. Princeton: Princeton University Press, 1966.

Bartlett, Robert. *Trial by Fire and Water: The Medieval Judicial Ordeal.* Oxford: Oxford University Press, 1986.

Baumgärtner, Ingrid. "Consilia: Quellen für Familie in Krise und Kontinuität." In *Die Familie als sozialer und historischer Verband: Untersuchungen zum Spätmittelalter und zur frühen Neuzeit.* Edited by Peter-Johannes Schuler. Sigmaringen: Jan Thorbecke, 1987. Pp. 43–66.

Bec, Christian. *Les marchands écrivains: Affaires et humanisme à Florence, 1375–1434.* Paris: Mouton, 1967.

Bellomo, Manlio. "Erede e eredità (diritto intermedio)." In *Enciclopedia del diritto* 15: 184–95. Milan: Giuffrè, 1966.

———. "Famiglia (diritto intermedio)." In *Enciclopedia del diritto* 16: 744–79. Milan: Giuffrè, 1967.

———. *La condizione giuridica della donna in Italia.* Turin: Edizioni RAI, 1970.

———. *Problemi di diritto familiare nell'età dei comuni: Beni paterni e "pars filii".* Milan: Giuffrè, 1968.

———. *Ricerche sui rapporti patrimoniali tra coniugi: Contributo alla storia della famiglia medievale.* Milan: Giuffrè, 1961.

———. *Società e istituzioni in Italia dal medioevo agli inizi dell'età moderna.* 3d ed. Catania: Giannotta, 1982.

Berengo, Marino. *Nobili e mercanti nella Lucca del Cinquecento.* Turin: Einaudi, 1965.

Bergin, Thomas G. *Boccaccio.* New York: Viking, 1981.

Berlinguer, Luigi. "Considerazioni su storiografia e diritto." *Studi storici* 15 (1974): 3–56.

Besta, Enrico. *La famiglia nella storia del diritto italiano.* Padua, 1933. Reprint ed., Milan: Giuffrè, 1962.

———. *I diritti sulle cose nella storia del diritto italiano.* Milan: Giuffrè, 1935. Reprint ed., Milan: Giuffrè, 1964.

———. *Le successioni nella storia del diritto italiano.* Milan: Giuffrè, 1936.

Bizzocchi, Roberto. "La dissoluzione di un clan familiare: I Buondelmonti di Firenze nei secoli xv et xvi." *Archivio storico italiano* 140 (1982): 3–45.

Black, Robert. "Ancients and Moderns in the Renaissance: Rhetoric and History in Accolti's *Dialogue on the Preeminence of Men of His Own Time*." *Journal of the History of Ideas* 43 (1982): 3–32.

———. *Benedetto Accolti and the Florentine Renaissance.* Cambridge: Cambridge University Press, 1985.

Black-Michaud, Jacob. *Cohesive Force: Feud in the Mediterranean and the Middle East.* New York: St. Martin's Press, 1975.

Bloch, Marc. *The Royal Touch: Sacred Monarchy and Scrofula in England and France.* Translated by J. E. Anderson. Montreal: McGill/Queens, 1973.

Boehm, Christopher. *Blood Revenge: The Enactment and Management of Conflict in Montenegro and Other Tribal Societies.* Philadelphia: University of Pennsylvania Press, 1987.

Bossy, John, ed. *Disputes and Settlements: Law and Human Relations in the West.* Cambridge: Cambridge University Press, 1983.

Bourdieu, Pierre. "Marriage Strategies as Strategies of Social Reproduction." In *Family and Society.* Edited by Robert Forster and Orest Ranum. Baltimore: Johns Hopkins University Press, 1976. Pp. 117–44.

————. "The Sentiment of Honour in Kabyle Society." In *Honour and Shame: The Values of Mediterranean Society.* Edited by J. G. Peristiany. Chicago: University of Chicago Press, 1966. Pp. 191–241.

————. "Les stratégies matrimoniales dans le système de reproduction." *Annales* 27 (1972): 1105–25.

————. *Outline of a Theory of Practice.* Translated by Richard Nice. Cambridge: Cambridge University Press, 1977.

Branca, Vittore. *Boccaccio: The Man and His Works.* Translated and edited by Dennis J. McAuliffe. New York: New York University Press, 1976.

Brooke, Christopher N. L. "Marriage and Society in the Central Middle Ages." In *Marriage and Society: Studies in the Social History of Marriage.* Edited by Richard B. Outhwaite. New York: St. Martin's Press, 1981. Pp. 17–34.

Brown, Judith. *Immodest Acts: The Life of a Lesbian Nun in Renaissance Italy.* Oxford: Oxford University Press, 1985.

Brucker, Gene. *Giovanni and Lusanna: Love and Marriage in Renaissance Florence.* Berkeley and London: University of California Press, 1986.

————. *Renaissance Florence.* Revised ed. Berkeley and London: University of California Press, 1983.

————. *The Civic World of Early Renaissance Florence.* Princeton: Princeton University Press, 1977.

Buckland, W. W. *A Text-Book of Roman Law from Augustus to Justinian.* 3d ed. Edited by Peter Stein. Cambridge: Cambridge University Press, 1966.

Buckland, W. W., and McNair, Arnold D. *Roman Law and Common Law: A Comparison in Outline.* 2d ed. Edited by F. H. Lawson. Cambridge: Cambridge University Press, 1952.

Bullard, Melissa Meriam. "Marriage Politics and the Family in Florence: The Strozzi-Medici Alliance of 1508." *American Historical Review* 84 (1979): 668–87.

Bullough, Vern L. "Medieval Medical and Scientific Views of Women." *Viator* 4 (1973): 485–501.

Cain, Maureen, and Kulcsar, Kalman. "Thinking Disputes: An Essay on the Origins of the Dispute Industry." *Law and Society Review* 16 (1981–82): 375–402.

Calasso, Francesco. *Medioevo del diritto.* Vol. 1: *Le fonti.* Milan: Giuffrè, 1954.

Calleri, Santi. *L'arte dei giudici e notai di Firenze nell'eta comunale e nel suo statuto del 1344.* Milan: Giuffrè, 1966.

Cammarosano, Paolo. "Les structures familiales dans les villes de l'Italie communale, xiie–xive siècles." In *Famille et parenté dans l'Occident médiéval.* Edited by Georges Duby and Jacques Le Goff. Rome: Ecole Français de Rome, 1977. Pp. 181–94.

———. "Aspetti delle strutture familiari nelle città dell'Italia comunale (secoli xii–xiv)." *Studi medievali* 16 (1975): 417–35.

Campbell, J. K. *Honour, Family and Patronage.* Oxford: Clarendon Press, 1964.

Canning, Joseph P. "A Fourteenth-Century Contribution to the Theory of Citizenship: Political Man and the Problem of Created Citizenship in the Thought of Baldus de Ubaldis." In *Authority and Power: Studies on Medieval Law and Government Presented to Walter Ullmann on His Seventieth Birthday.* Edited by Brian Tierney and Peter Linehan. Cambridge: Cambridge University Press, 1980. Pp. 197–212.

Casey, James. *The History of the Family.* Oxford: Blackwell, 1989.

Castan, Nicole. "The Arbitration of Disputes under the Ancien Regime." In *Disputes and Settlements: Law and Human Relations in the West.* Edited by John Bossy. Cambridge: Cambridge University Press, 1983. Pp. 219–60.

Cavalca, Desiderio. *Il bando nella prassi e nella dottrina giuridica medievale.* Milan: Giuffrè, 1978.

Cavallo, Sandra, and Cerutti, Simona. "Onore femminile e controllo sociale della riproduzione in Piemonte tra Sei e Settecento." *Quaderni storici* 44 (1980): 346–83.

Ceschi, Carlo. "La madre di Leon Battista Alberti." *Bollettino d'arte* 33 (1948): 191–92.

Cessi, R. "Gli Alberti di Padova." *Archivio storico italiano* 40 (1907): 233–84.

Chabot, Isabelle. "Widowhood and Poverty in Late Medieval Florence." *Continuity and Change* 3 (1988): 291–311.

Cheyette, Frederic L. "'Suum cuique tribuere.'" *French Historical Studies* 6 (1970): 287–99.

Chittolini, Giorgio. *La formazione dello stato regionale e le istituzioni del contado: Secoli xiv e xv.* Turin: Einaudi, 1979.

Chojnacki, Stanley. "Dowries and Kinsmen in Early Renaissance Venice." *Journal of Interdisciplinary History* 5 (1975): 571–600.

———. "Patrician Women in Early Renaissance Venice." *Studies in the Renaissance* 21 (1974): 176–203.

Cipolla, Carlo. *The Monetary Policy of Fourteenth-Century Florence.* Berkeley and London: University of California Press, 1982.

Clanchy, Michael. "Law and Love in the Middle Ages." In *Disputes and Settlements: Law and Human Relations in the West.* Edited by John Bossy. Cambridge: Cambridge University Press, 1983. Pp. 47–68.

Cohen, Elizabeth S., and Cohen, Thomas V. "Camilla the Go-Between: The Politics of Gender in a Roman Household." *Continuity and Change* 4 (1989): 53–77.

Cohn, Bernard S. "History and Anthropology: The State of Play." *Comparative Studies in Society and History* 22 (1980): 198–221.

Cohn, Samuel K., Jr. *Death and Property in Siena, 1205–1800: Strategies for the Afterlife.* Baltimore: Johns Hopkins University Press, 1988.

————. "Donne in piazza e donne in tribunale a Firenze nel Rinascimento." *Studi storici* 22 (1981): 515–33.

Collier, Jane F. "Legal Processes." *Annual Review of Anthropology* 4 (1975): 121–44.

Comaroff, John L., ed. *The Meaning of Marriage Payments.* New York: Academic Press, 1980.

————. "Rules and Rulers: Political Processes in a Tswana Kingdom." *Man,* new ser., 13 (1978): 1–20.

Comaroff, John, and Roberts, Simon. "The Invocation of Norms in Dispute Settlement: The Tswana Case." In *Social Anthropology and Law.* Edited by Ian Hamnett. London and New York: Academic Press, 1977. Pp. 77–112.

————. *Rules and Processes: The Cultural Logic of Dispute in an African Context.* Chicago: University of Chicago Press, 1981.

Cooper, J. P. "Patterns of Inheritance and Settlement by Great Landowners from the Fifteenth to Eighteenth Centuries." In *Family and Inheritance: Rural Society in Western Europe, 1200–1800.* Edited by Jack Goody, Joan Thirsk, and E. P. Thompson. Cambridge: Cambridge University Press, 1976. Pp. 192–327.

Cortese, Ennio. "Per la storia del mundio in Italia." *Rivista italiana per le scienze giuridiche* 8 (1955–56): 323–474.

Cronin, Constance. *The Sting of Change: Sicilians in Sicily and Australia.* Chicago: University of Chicago Press, 1970.

Cuyas, Manuel, S.J. *La buena fe en la prescripcion extintiva de deudas, desde el Concilio IV de Latrán (1215) hasta Bartolo (d. 1357).* Rome: Università Gregoriana, 1962.

Danet, Brenda. "Language in the Legal Process." *Law and Society Review* 14 (1979–80): 445–564.

Dauvillier, Jean. *Le mariage dans le droit classique de l'église.* Paris: Recueil Sirey, 1933.

David, René. *French Law: Its Structure, Sources, and Methodology.* Translated by Michael Kindred. Baton Rouge: Louisiana StateUniversity Press, 1972.

Davidsohn, Robert. *Storia di Firenze.* 8 vols. Translated from the German by Eugenio Dupré-Theseider. Florence: Sansoni, 1973.

Davies, Wendy, and Fouracre, Paul, eds. *The Settlement of Disputes in Early Medieval Europe.* Cambridge: Cambridge University Press, 1986.

Davis, J. "Morals and Backwardness." *Comparative Studies in Society and History* 12 (1970): 340–53.

————. *Land and Family in Pisticci*. London: Athlone Press, 1973.

————. *People of the Mediterranean: An Essay in Comparative Social Anthropology*. London: Routledge, 1977.

Davis, Natalie Zemon. "Ghosts, Kin, and Progeny: Some Features of Family Life in Early Modern France." *Daedalus* 106 (1977): 87–114.

————. *The Return of Martin Guerre*. Cambridge, Mass.: Harvard University Press, 1983.

de la Roncière, Charles M. *Prix et salaires à Florence au xive siècle (1280–1380)*. Rome: Ecole Français de Rome, 1982.

————. "Une famille florentine au xive siècle: Les Velluti." In *Famille et parenté dans l'Occident médiéval*. Edited by Georges Duby and Jacques Le Goff. Rome: Ecole Français de Rome, 1977. Pp. 227–48.

————. "Indirect Taxes or 'Gabelles' at Florence in the Fourteenth Century." *Florentine Studies*. Edited by Nicolai Rubinstein. Evanston: Northwestern University Press, 1968. Pp. 140–92.

de Maio, Romeo. *Donna e Rinascimento*. Milan: Il Saggiatore, 1987.

de Roover, Raymond. *The Rise and Decline of the Medici Bank, 1397–1494*. Cambridge, Mass.: Harvard University Press, 1963.

Donahue, Charles, Jr. "The Case of the Man Who Fell into the Tiber: The Roman Law of Marriage at the Time of the Glossators." *American Journal of Legal History* 22 (1978): 1–53.

————. "The Future of the Concept of Property Predicted from Its Past." In *Property*. Edited by J. Roland Pennock and John W. Chapman. Nomos 22. New York: New York University Press, 1980. Pp. 28–68.

Donzelot, Jacques. *The Policing of Families*. Translated by Robert Hurley. New York: Pantheon, 1979.

Douglass, William A. "The South Italian Family: A Critique." *Journal of Family History* 5 (1980): 338–59.

du Boulay, Juliet. *Portrait of a Greek Mountain Village*. Oxford: Oxford University Press, 1974.

Duby, Georges. *The Knight, the Lady, and the Priest: The Making of Modern Marriage in Medieval France*. Translated by Barbara Bray. New York: Pantheon, 1983.

Edelman, Bernard. *Ownership of the Image: Elements for a Marxist Theory of Law*. Translated by Elizabeth Kingdom. London: Routledge, 1979.

Engelman, Arthur, et al. *A History of Continental Civil Procedure*. Edited by Robert Wyness Millar. Boston: Little, Brown, 1927. Reprint ed., New York: Augustus M. Kelley, 1969.

Engels, Friedrich. *The Origin of the Family, Private Property, and the State*. New York: International Publishers, 1972.

Enriques, Anna Maria. "La vendetta nella vita e nella legislazione fiorentina." *Archivio storico italiano* 91 (1933): 85–146, 181–223.

Epstein, A. L. "The Case Method in the Field of Law." In *The Craft of Social*

Anthropology. Edited by A. L. Epstein. London: Tavistock, 1967. Pp. 205–30.

Epstein, Steven. *Wills and Wealth in Medieval Genoa, 1150–1250.* Cambridge, Mass.: Harvard University Press, 1984.

Esmein, Adhémar. *Mariage en droit canonique.* 2 vols. Paris, 1891. Reprint ed., New York: Burt Franklin, 1968.

Fairchilds, Cissie. "Female Sexual Attitudes and the Rise of Illegitimacy: A Case Study." *Journal of Interdisciplinary History* 8 (1978): 627–67.

Feenstra, Robert. "Action publicienne et preuve de la propriété, principalement d'après quelques romanistes du moyen âge." In *Fata iuris romani: Etudes d'histoire de droit.* Leyden: Presse Universitaire de Leyde, 1974. Pp. 119–38.

———. "Les origines du *dominium utile* chez les glossateurs (avec un appendice concernant l'opinion des Ultramontani)." In *Fata iuris romani: Etudes d'histoire de droit.* Leyden: Presse Universitaire de Leyde, 1974. Pp. 215–59.

Felstiner, William L. F., Abel, Richard, and Sarat, Austin. "The Emergence and Transformation of Disputes: Naming, Blaming, Claiming . . . " *Law and Society Review* 15 (1980–81): 631–54.

Flandrin, Jean-Louis. *Families in Former Times.* Translated by Richard Southern. Cambridge: Cambridge University Press, 1979.

Fowler, Linda. "Forms of Arbitration." In *Proceedings of the Fourth International Congress of Medieval Canon Law, Toronto, 21–25 August 1972.* Monumenta Iuris Canonici, series C: Subsidia, vol. 5. Edited by Stephan Kuttner. Vatican City 1976. Pp. 133–47.

Fried, Charles. "The Lex Aquilia as a Source of Law for Bartolus and Baldus." *American Journal of Legal History* 4 (1960): 142–72.

Fubini, Riccardo. "Poggio Bracciolini e San Bernardino: Temi e motivi di una polemica." In *Atti del simposio internazionale cateriniano-bernardiniano.* Siena, 17–20 April 1980. Edited by Domenico Maffei and Paolo Nardi. Siena: Accademia Senese degli Intronati, 1982. Pp. 509–40.

Gadol, Joan. *Leon Battista Alberti: Universal Man of the Early Renaissance.* Chicago: University of Chicago Press, 1969.

Galanter, Marc A. "Why the 'Haves' Come Out Ahead: Speculation on the Limits of Legal Change." *Law and Society Review* 9 (1974): 95–160.

Garin, Eugenio. "Il pensiero di Leon Battista Alberti: Caratteri e contrasti." *Rinascimento* 12 (1972): 3–20.

———. *L'umanesimo italiano: Filosofia e vita civile nel Rinascimento.* Bari: Laterza, 1952.

Geertz, Clifford. *Local Knowledge: Further Essays in Interpretive Anthropology.* New York: Basic Books, 1983.

Génestal, R. *Histoire de la légitimation des enfants naturels en droit canonique.* Paris: Ernest Leroux, 1905.

Ginzburg, Carlo. *The Cheese and the Worms: The Cosmos of a Sixteenth-Cen-*

tury Miller. Translated by John and Ann Tedeschi. Baltimore: Johns Hopkins University Press, 1980.

Gluckman, Max. "Limitations of the Case-Method in the Study of Tribal Law." *Law and Society Review* 7 (1973): 611–41.

Goldthwaite, Richard. "The Florentine Palace as Domestic Architecture." *American Historical Review* 77 (1972): 977–1012.

———. *Private Wealth in Renaissance Florence.* Princeton: Princeton University Press, 1968.

———. *The Building of Renaissance Florence: An Economic and Social History.* Baltimore: Johns Hopkins University Press, 1980.

Goodrich, Peter. *Legal Discourse: Studies in Linguistics, Rhetoric and Legal Analysis.* New York: St. Martin's Press, 1987.

Goody, Jack. "The Evolution of the Family." In *Household and Family in Past Time.* Edited by Peter Laslett and Richard Wall. Cambridge: Cambridge University Press, 1972. Pp. 103–24.

———. "Inheritance, Property and Women: Some Comparative Considerations." In *Family and Inheritance: Rural Society in Western Europe, 1200–1800.* Edited by Jack Goody, Joan Thirsk, and E. P. Thompson. Cambridge: Cambridge University Press, 1976. Pp. 10–36.

———. *Production and Reproduction: A Comparative Study of the Domestic Domain.* Cambridge: Cambridge University Press, 1976.

———. *The Development of the Family and Marriage in Europe.* Cambridge: Cambridge University Press, 1983.

Grayson, Cecil. "Alberti, Leon Battista." *Dizionario biografico degli Italiani.* Vol. 1. Rome: Istituto della Enciclopedia Italiana, 1960. Pp. 702–9.

———. "The Humanism of Alberti." *Italian Studies* 12 (1957): 37–56.

Greenhouse, Carol J. "Looking at Culture, Looking for Rules." *Man,* new ser., 17 (1982): 58–73.

———. "Mediation: A Comparative Approach." *Man,* new ser., 20 (1985): 90–114.

Grossi, Paolo. *"Locatio ad longum tempus": Locazione e rapporti reali di godimento nella problematica del diritto comune.* Naples: Morano, 1963.

———. "La proprietà e le proprietà nell'officina dello storico." In *La proprietà e le proprietà.* Edited by Ennio Cortese. Milan: Giuffrè, 1988. Pp. 205–72.

———. "La proprietà nel sistema privatistico della seconda scolastica." *La seconda scolastica nella formazione del diritto privato moderno.* Milan: Giuffrè, 1973. Pp. 117–222.

———. *Le situazioni reali nell'esperienza giuridica medievale.* Padua: CEDAM, 1968.

———. ed. *Storia sociale e dimensione giuridica: Strumenti d'indagine e ipotesi di lavoro.* Atti dell'Incontro di Studio, Firenze, 26–27 Aprile 1985. Milan: Giuffrè, 1986.

———. *"Un altro modo di possedere": L'emersione di forme alternative di proprietà alla coscienza giuridica postunitaria.* Milan: Giuffrè, 1977. Translated as *An Alternative to Private Property: Collective Property in the Judicial Consciousness of the Nineteenth Century.* Translated by Lydia G. Cochrane. Chicago: University of Chicago Press, 1981.

———. "Usus facti: La nozione di proprietà nella inaugurazione dell'età nuova." *Quaderni fiorentini per la storia del pensiero guiridico moderno* 1 (1972): 287–355.

Gualazzini, Ugo. "Età (diritto intermedio)." In *Enciclopedia del diritto* 16: 80–85. Milan: Giuffrè, 1967.

Gulliver, P. H. *Disputes and Negotiations: A Cross-Cultural Perspective.* New York: Academic Press, 1979.

Hamnett, Ian, ed. *Social Anthropology and Law.* London and New York: Academic Press, 1977.

Hatfield, Rab. *Botticelli's Uffizi "Adoration": A Study in Pictorial Content.* Princeton: Princeton University Press, 1976.

Heers, Jacques. *Family Clans in the Middle Ages: A Study of the Political and Social Structures in Urban Areas.* Translated by Barry Herbert. Amsterdam: North Holland, 1977.

Helmholz, Richard. "Ethical Standards for Advocates and Proctors in Theory and Practice." *Proceedings of the Fourth International Congress of Medieval Canon Law, Toronto, 21–25 August 1972.* Monumenta Iuris Canonici, Series C: Subsidia, vol. 5. Edited by Stephan Kuttner. Vatican City, 1976. Pp. 283–99.

———. *Marriage Litigation in Medieval England.* Cambridge: Cambridge University Press, 1974.

———. "Usury and the Medieval English Church Courts." *Speculum* 61 (1986): 364–80.

Herlihy, David. "The Distribution of Wealth in a Renaissance Community: Florence, 1427." In *Towns in Societies: Essays in Economic History and Historical Sociology.* Edited by Philip Abrams and E. A. Wrigley. Cambridge: Cambridge University Press, 1978. Pp. 131–57.

———. "Family and Property in Renaissance Florence." In *The Medieval City.* Edited by Harry A. Miskimin, David Herlihy, and A. L. Udovitch. New Haven: Yale University Press, 1977. Pp. 3–24.

———. *The Family in Renaissance Italy.* St. Charles, Mo.: Forum Press, 1974.

———. "The Generation in Medieval History." *Viator* 5 (1974): 347–64.

———. "Land, Family, and Women in Continental Europe, 701–1200." *Traditio* 18 (1962): 89–113.

———. "Life Expectancies for Women in Medieval Society." In *The Role of Women in the Middle Ages.* Edited by Rosemarie Thee Morewedge. Albany: State University of New York Press, 1975. Pp. 1–22.

———. "The Making of the Medieval Family: Symmetry, Structure, and Sentiment." *Journal of Family History* 8 (1983): 116–30.

———. "Medieval Children." In *Essays on Medieval Civilization: The Walter*

Prescott Webb Lectures. Edited by Bede Karl Lackner and Kenneth Roy Philip. Austin: University of Texas Press, 1978. Pp. 109–41.

———. *Medieval Households.* Cambridge, Mass.: Harvard University Press, 1985.

———. *Opera Muliebria: Women and Work in Medieval Europe.* New York: McGraw Hill, 1990.

———. "The Social and Psychological Roots of Violence in Tuscan Towns." In *Violence and Civil Disorder in Italian Cities, 1200–1500.* Edited by Lauro Martines. Los Angeles: University of California Press, 1972. Pp. 129–54.

———. "Vieillir à Florence au Quattrocento." *Annales* 24 (1969): 1338–52.

Herlihy, David, and Klapisch-Zuber, Christiane. *Les toscans et leurs familles.* Paris: Fondation Nationale des Sciences Politiques, 1978.

———. *Tuscans and Their Families.* New Haven and London: Yale University Press, 1985.

Horn, Norbert. *"Aequitas" in den Lehren des Baldus.* Cologne: Böhlau, 1968.

Hoy, David Couzens. *The Critical Circle: Literature, History, and Philosophical Hermeneutics.* Berkeley and London: University of California Press, 1978.

Hughes, Diane Owen. "Domestic Ideals and Social Behavior: Evidence from Medieval Genoa." In *The Family in History.* Edited by Charles E. Rosenberg. Philadelphia: University of Pennsylvania Press, 1975. Pp. 115–43.

———. "From Brideprice to Dowry in Mediterranean Europe." *Journal of Family History* 3 (1978): 262–96.

———. "Struttura familiare e sistemi di successione ereditaria nei testamenti dell'Europa medievale." *Quaderni storici* 33 (1976): 929–52.

———. "Urban Growth and Family Structure in Medieval Genoa." *Past and Present* 66 (February 1975): 3–28.

Hurtubise, Pierre, O.M.I. *Une famille-témoin: Les Salviati.* Studi e Testi, 309. Vatican City: Biblioteca Apostolica Vaticana, 1985.

Kagan, Richard L. "A Golden Age of Litigation: Castile, 1500–1700." In *Disputes and Settlements: Law and Human Relations in the West.* Edited by John Bossy. Cambridge: Cambridge University Press, 1983. Pp. 145–66.

———. *Lawsuits and Litigants in Castile, 1500–1700.* Chapel Hill: University of North Carolina Press, 1981.

Kairys, David, ed. *The Politics of Law: A Progressive Critique.* New York: Pantheon, 1982.

Kantorowicz, Ernst. "The Sovereignty of the Artist: A Note on Legal Maxims and Renaissance Theories of Art." In *Selected Studies.* Locust Valley, N.Y.: J. J. Augustin, 1965. Pp. 352–65.

Kaser, Max. *Roman Private Law.* 2d ed. Translated by Rolf Dannenbring. Durban: Butterworth, 1968.

Kelley, Donald R. "Civil Science in the Renaissance: Jurisprudence Italian Style." *The Historical Journal* 22 (1979): 777–94.

Kent, D. V., and Kent, F. W. "A Self-Disciplining Pact Made by the Peruzzi Family of Florence (June 1433)." *Renaissance Quarterly* 34 (1981): 337–55.

Kent, Dale. "The Florentine 'Reggimento' in the Fifteenth Century." *Renaissance Quarterly* 28 (1975): 575–638.

———. *The Rise of the Medici: Faction in Florence, 1426–1434.* Oxford: Oxford University Press, 1978.

Kent, Francis William. *Household and Lineage in Renaissance Florence: The Family Life of the Capponi, Ginori, and Rucellai.* Princeton: Princeton University Press, 1977.

———. "A La Recherche du Clan Perdu: Jacques Heers and 'Family Clans' in the Middle Ages." *Journal of Family History* 2 (1977): 77–86.

———. "Lorenzo de' Medici's Acquisition of Poggio a Caiano in 1474 and an Early Reference to His Architectural Expertise." *Journal of the Warburg and Courtauld Institutes* 42 (1979): 250–57.

———. "Palaces, Politics and Society in Fifteenth-Century Florence." *I Tatti Studies: Essays in the Renaissance* 2 (1987): 41–70.

Kent, Francis William, and Kent, Dale. *Neighbours and Neighbourhood in Renaissance Florence.* Villa I Tatti, Harvard University Center for Italian Renaissance Studies, 6. Locust Valley, N.Y.: J. J. Augustin, 1982.

Kirshner, Julius. "*Ars Imitatur Naturam:* A Consilium of Baldus on Naturalization in Florence." *Viator* 5 (1974): 289–331.

———. "Between Nature and Culture: An Opinion of Baldus of Perugia on Venetian Citizenship as Second Nature." *Journal of Medieval and Renaissance Studies* 9 (1979): 179–208.

———. "*Civitas Sibi Faciat Civem:* Bartolus of Sassoferrato's Doctrine on the Making of a Citizen." *Speculum* 48 (1973): 694–713.

———. "'Maritus Lucretur Dotem Uxoris Sue Premortue' in Fourteenth- and Fifteenth-Century Florence." *Zeitschrift der Savigny-Stiftung für Rechtsgeschichte (Kan. Abt.)* 77 (1991): 111–55.

———. "Materials for a Gilded Cage: Non-Dotal Assets in Florence (1300–1500)." In *The Family in Italy from Antiquity to the Present.* Edited by David I. Kertzer and Richard P. Saller. New Haven and London: Yale University Press, 1991. Pp. 184–207.

———. "Paolo di Castro On *Cives Ex Privilegio:* A Controversy over the Legal Qualifications for Public Office in Early Fifteenth-Century Florence." In *Renaissance Studies in Honor of Hans Baron.* Edited by Anthony Molho and John A. Tedeschi. Dekalb: Northern Illinois University Press, 1971. Pp. 227–64.

———. *Pursuing Honor While Avoiding Sin: The Monte delle doti of Florence.* Milan: Giuffrè, 1978.

———. "Reading Bernardino's Sermon on the Public Debt." In *Atti del simposio internazionale cateriniano-bernardiniano.* Siena, 17–20 April 1980. Edited by Domenico Maffei and Paolo Nardi. Siena: Accademia Senese degli Intronati, 1982. Pp. 547–622.

———. Review of *Family and Inheritance: Rural Society in Western Europe, 1200–1800. Journal of Modern History* 50 (1978): 320–22.

———. Review of Mario Ascheri, *I consilia dei guiristi medievali. Speculum* 58 (1983): 841–42.

———. "Some Problems in the Interpretation of Legal Texts *re* the Italian City-States." *Archiv für Begriffsgeschichte* 19 (1975): 16–27.

———. "Wives' Claims against Insolvent Husbands in Late Medieval Italy." In *Women of the Medieval World: Essays in Honor of John H. Mundy.* Edited by Julius Kirshner and Suzanne F. Wemple. Oxford: Basil Blackwell, 1985. Pp. 256–303.

Kirshner, Julius, and Molho, Anthony. "The Dowry Fund and the Marriage Market in Early Quattrocento Florence." *Journal of Modern History* 50 (1978): 403–38.

Kirshner, Julius, and Pluss, Jacques. "Two Fourteenth-Century Opinions on Dowries, Paraphernalia and Non-Dotal Goods." *Bulletin of Medieval Canon Law* 9 (1979): 64–77.

Klapisch-Zuber, Christiane. "Le complexe de Griselda: Dot et dons de mariage au Quattrocento." *Mélanges de l'Ecole Français de Rome* 94 (1982): 7–43.

———. "Déclin démographique et la structure du ménage: L'exemple de Prato, fin xive–xve." In *Famille et parenté dans l'Occident médiéval.* Edited by Georges Duby and Jacques Le Goff. Rome: Ecole Français de Rome, 1977. Pp. 255–68.

———. "L'enfance en Toscane au début du xve siècle." *Annales de démographie historique* 9 (1973): 99–122.

———. *La famiglia e le donne nel Rinascimento a Firenze.* Bari: Laterza, 1988.

———. "La 'mère cruelle': Maternité, veuvage et dot dans la Florence des xive–xve siècles." *Annales* 38 (1983): 1097–1109.

———. "Genitori naturali e genitori di latte nella Firenze del Quattrocento." *Quaderni storici* 44 (1980): 543–63.

———. "'Parenti, amici, vicini': Il territorio urbano d'una famiglia mercantile nel xv secolo." *Quaderni storici* 33 (1976): 953–82.

———. "Ruptures de parenté et changements d'identité chez les magnats florentins du xive siècle." *Annales* 43 (1988): 1205–40.

———. *Women, Family, and Ritual in Renaissance Italy.* Translated by Lydia G. Cochrane. Chicago: University of Chicago Press, 1985.

Klein, Francesca. "Considerazioni sull'ideologia della città di Firenze tra Trecento e Quattrocento (Giovanni Villani-Leonardo Bruni)." *Ricerche storiche* 10 (1980): 311–36.

Koch, Klaus-Friedrich, ed. *Access to Justice.* Vol. 4: *The Anthropological Per-*

spective: Patterns of Conflict Management: Essays in the Ethnography of Law. Milan: Giuffrè, 1979.

Koch, Klaus-Friedrich; Altorki, Soraya; Arno, Andrew; and Hickson, Letitia. "Ritual Reconciliation and the Obviation of Grievances: A Comparative Study in the Ethnography of Law." *Ethnology* 16 (1977): 269–83.

Kogler, Ferdinand. *Die legitimatio per rescriptum von Justinian bis zum Tode Karls IV.* Weimar: Böhlaus, 1904.

Kuehn, Thomas. "Arbitration and Law in Renaissance Florence." *Renaissance and Reformation,* new ser., 11 (1987): 289–319.

———. "'As If Conceived within a Legitimate Marriage': A Dispute Concerning Legitimation in Quattrocento Florence." *American Journal of Legal History* 29 (1985): 275–300.

———. "Conflicting Conceptions of Property in Quattrocento Florence: A Dispute over Ownership in 1425–26." *Quaderni fiorentini per la storia del pensiero giuridico moderno* 14 (1985): 303–72.

———. "'Cum Consensu Mundualdi': Legal Guardianship of Women in Quattrocento Florence." *Viator* 13 (1982): 309–33.

———. "Il diritto e l'uso del diritto nelle famiglie fiorentine nel Rinascimento." In *Palazzo Strozzi: Metà Millenio, 1489–1989: Atti del Convegno di Studi.* Rome: Istituto della Enciclopedia Italiana, 1991. Pp.108-25

———. *Emancipation in Late Medieval Florence.* New Brunswick: Rutgers University Press, 1982.

———. "Honor and Conflict in a Fifteenth-Century Florentine Family." *Ricerche storiche* 10 (1980): 287–310.

———. "Law, Death, and Heirs in the Renaissance: Some Meanings of the Repudiation of Inheritance." *Renaissance Quarterly* 45 (1991): 484–516.

———. "*Multorum Fraudibus Occurrere*: Legislation and Jurisprudential Interpretation Concerning Fraud and Liability in Quattrocento Florence." *Studi senesi* 93 (1981): 309–50.

———. "Reading between the Patrilines: Leon Battista Alberti's *Della Famiglia* in Light of His Illegitimacy." *I Tatti Studies: Essays in the Renaissance* 1 (1985): 161–87.

———. "Reading Microhistory: The Example of Giovanni and Lusanna." *Journal of Modern History* 61 (1989): 512–34.

———. "Some Ambiguities of Female Inheritance Ideology in the Renaissance." *Continuity and Change* 2 (1987): 11–36.

———. "Women, Marriage, and *Patria Potestas* in Late Medieval Florence." *Tijdschrift voor Rechtsgeschiedenis* 49 (1981): 127–47.

Kulcsar, Kalman. "Social Aspects of Litigation in Civil Courts." In *Disputes and the Law.* Edited by Maureen Cain and Kalman Kulcsar. Budapest: Akademiai-Kiado, 1983. Pp. 85–118.

Kurczewski, Jacek. "Dispute and Its Settlement." In *Disputes and the Law.* Edited by Maureen Cain and Kalman Kulcsar. Budapest: Akademiai-Kiado, 1983. Pp. 223–45.

LaCapra, Dominick. "Rethinking Intellectual History and Reading Texts." *History and Theory* 19 (1980): 245–76.

———. *Rethinking Intellectual History: Texts, Contexts, Language.* Ithaca: Cornell University Press, 1983.

Larner, John. *Italy in the Age of Dante and Petrarch, 1216–1380.* New York and London: Longmans, 1980.

Laslett, Peter. *Family Life and Illicit Love in Earlier Generations: Essays in Historical Sociology.* Cambridge: Cambridge University Press, 1977.

———. "Introduction: Comparing Illegitimacy over Time and between Cultures." In *Bastardy and Its Comparative History: Studies in the History of Illegitimacy and Marital Nonconformism in Britain, France, Germany, Sweden, North America, Jamaica and Japan.* Edited by Peter Laslett, Karla Oosterveen, and Richard M. Smith. Cambridge, Mass.: Harvard University Press, 1980. Pp. 1–65.

Lee, W. R. "Bastardy and the Socioeconomic Structure of South Germany." *Journal of Interdisciplinary History* 7 (1977): 403–25.

Le Goff, Jacques. "Histoire médiévale et histoire du droit: Un dialogue difficile." In *Storia sociale e dimensione giuridica: Strumenti d'indagine e ipotesi di lavoro.* Edited by Paolo Grossi. Milan: Giuffrè, 1986. Pp. 23–63.

———. "Labor Time in the 'Crisis' of the Fourteenth Century: From Medieval Time to Modern Time." In *Time, Work, and Culture in the Middle Ages.* Translated by Arthur Goldhammer. Chicago: University of Chicago Press, 1980. Pp. 43–52.

———. "Merchant's Time and Church's Time in the Middle Ages." In *Time, Work, and Culture in the Middle Ages.* Translated by Arthur Goldhammer. Chicago: University of Chicago Press, 1980. Pp. 29–42.

Leicht, P. S. *Storia del diritto italiano, Il diritto privato.* 3 vols. Milan: Giuffrè, 1943–48. Reprint ed., Milan: Giuffrè, 1960.

Leineweber, Anke. *Die rechtliche Beziehung des nichtehelichen Kindes zu seinem Erzeuger in der Geschichte des Privatrechts.* Königstein: Peter Hanstein, 1978.

Lombardi, Luigi. *Saggio sul diritto giurisprudenziale.* Milan: Giuffrè, 1967.

Macfarlane, Alan. "Illegitimacy and Illegitimates in English History." In *Bastardy and Its Comparative History.* Edited by Peter Laslett and Karla Oosterveen. Cambridge, Mass.: Harvard University Press, 1980. Pp. 71–85.

McLaughlin, Mary Martin. "Survivors and Surrogates: Children and Parents from the Ninth to the Thirteenth Centuries." In *The History of Childhood.* Edited by Lloyd de Mause. New York: Harper & Row, 1974. Pp. 101–82.

Maclean, Ian. *The Renaissance Notion of Woman: A Study in the Fortunes of Scholasticism and Medical Science in European Intellectual Life.* Cambridge: Cambridge University Press, 1980.

MacPherson, C. B. *The Political Theory of Possessive Individualism.* Oxford: Oxford University Press, 1962.

———. ed. *Property: Mainstream and Critical Positions.* Toronto: University of Toronto Press, 1978.

Maffei, Domenico. *La donazione di Costantino nei giuristi medievali.* Milan: Giuffrè, 1964.

———. *Gli inizi dell'umanesimo giuridico.* Milan: Giuffrè, 1956.

Mancini, Girolamo. *Vita di Leon Battista Alberti.* Florence: Le Monnier, 1911.

Manselli, Raoul. "Vie familiale et éthique sexuelle dans les pénitentiels." In *Famille et parenté dans l'Occident médiéval.* Edited by Georges Duby and Jacques Le Goff. Rome: Ecole Français de Rome, 1977. Pp. 363–78.

Marcus, George E. "Litigation, Interpersonal Conflict, and Noble Succession Disputes in the Friendly Islands." In *Access to Justice,* vol. 4: *The Anthropological Perspective: Patterns of Conflict Management: Essays in the Ethnography of Law.* Edited by Klaus-Friedrich Koch. Milan: Giuffrè, 1978. Pp. 69–104.

Marsh, David. *The Quattrocento Dialogue: Classical Tradition and Humanist Innovation.* Cambridge, Mass.: Harvard University Press, 1980.

Martines, Lauro. *Lawyers and Statecraft in Renaissance Florence.* Princeton: Princeton University Press, 1968.

———. *Power and Imagination: City-States in Renaissance Italy.* New York: Knopf, 1979.

———. *The Social World of the Florentine Humanists, 1390–1460.* Princeton: Princeton University Press, 1963.

———. "A Way of Looking at Women in Renaissance Florence." *Journal of Medieval and Renaissance Studies* 4 (1974): 15–28.

Martone, Luciano. *Arbiter-Arbitrator: Forme di giustizia privata nell'età del diritto comune.* Storia e Diritto. Naples: Jovene, 1984.

Marvick, Elizabeth Wirth. "Nature versus Nurture: Patterns and Trends in Seventeenth-Century French Child-Rearing." In *The History of Childhood.* Edited by Lloyd de Mause. New York: Harper & Row, 1974. Pp. 259–302.

Mather, Lynn, and Yngvesson, Barbara. "Language, Audience, and the Transformation of Disputes." *Law and Society Review* 15 (1980–81): 775–821.

Mayali, Laurent. *Droit savant et coutumes: L'exclusion des filles dotées xiième-xvème siècles.* Ius Commune, Sonderhefte: Studien zur Europäischen Rechtsgeschichte 33. Frankfurt am Main: Klostermann, 1987.

Mazzi, Maria Serena, and Raveggi, Sergio. *Gli uomini e le cose nelle campagne fiorentine del Quattrocento.* Florence: Olschki, 1983.

Medici, Maria Teresa Guerra. *I diritti delle donne nella società altomedievale.* Milan: Giuffrè, 1986.

Metz, René. "Le statut de la femme en droit canonique médiéval." *Recueils de la Société Jean Bodin pour l'histoire comparative des institutions,* vol. 12: *La femme* (1962): 59–113.

Miller, William Ian. "Avoiding Legal Judgment: The Submission of Disputes to Arbitration in Medieval Iceland." *American Journal of Legal History* 28 (1984): 95–134.

Mitterauer, Michael, and Sieder, Reinhard. *The European Family: Patriarchy to Partnership from the Middle Ages to the Present.* Translated by Karla Oosterveen and Manfred Hörzinger. Chicago: University of Chicago Press, 1982.

Mochi Onory, Sergio. "*Personam habere:* Studio sulle origini e sulla struttura della 'persona' nell'età del Rinascimento." In *Studi di storia e diritto in onore di Enrico Besta.* 3 vols. Milan: Giuffrè, 1939. Vol. 3: 417–39.

Molho, Anthony. "Deception and Marriage Strategy in Renaissance Florence: The Case of Women's Ages." *Renaissance Quarterly* 41 (1988): 193–217.

———. *Florentine Public Finances in the Early Renaissance.* Cambridge, Mass.: Harvard University Press, 1971.

———. "Visions of the Florentine Family in the Renaissance." *Journal of Modern History* 50 (1978): 304–11.

Moore, Sally Falk. *Law as Process: An Anthropological Approach.* London: Routledge, 1978.

———. "Law and Anthropology." *Biennial Review of Anthropology* (1969): 252–300.

———. "Political Meanings and the Simulation of Unanimity: Kilimanjaro, 1973." In *Secular Ritual.* Edited by S. F. Moore and Barbara G. Myerhoff. Amsterdam: Van Gorcum, 1977. Pp. 151–72.

———. *Social Facts and Fabrications: "Customary Law" on Kilimanjaro, 1880–1980.* Cambridge: Cambridge University Press, 1986.

Mor, Carlo Guido. "Capacità d'agire, comunioni familiari e consorzi nel diritto consuetudinario valdostano dei sec. xi–xiii." In *Studi di storia e diritto in onore di Enrico Besta.* 3 vols. Milan: Giuffrè, 1939. Vol. 3: 199–217.

Nader, Laura, and Todd, Harry F., Jr., eds. *The Disputing Process: Law in Ten Societies.* New York: Columbia University Press, 1978.

Nader, Laura. "Styles of Court Procedure: To Make the Balance." In *Law in Culture and Society.* Edited by Laura Nader. Chicago: Aldine, 1969. Pp. 69–91.

Najemy, John J. *Corporatism and Consensus in Florentine Electoral Politics, 1280–1400.* Chapel Hill: University of North Carolina Press, 1982.

Navarrete, Urbano, S.J. *La buena fe de las personas juridicas en ordén a la prescripcion acquisitiva: Estudio histórico-canonico.* Rome: Università Gregoriana, 1959.

Nelson, Janet T. "Dispute Settlement in Carolingian West Francia." In *The Settlement of Disputes in Early Medieval Europe.* Edited by Wendy Davies and Paul Fouracre. Cambridge: Cambridge University Press, 1986. Pp. 45–64.

Newman, Katherine S. *Law and Economic Organization: A Comparative*

Study of Pre-industrial Societies. Cambridge: Cambridge University Press, 1983.

Niccolai, Franco. *La formazione del diritto successorio negli statuti comunali del territorio lombardo-tosco.* Milan: Giuffrè, 1940.

Nicholas, Barry. *An Introduction to Roman Law.* Oxford: Oxford University Press, 1962.

Noonan, John T., Jr. "Power to Choose." *Viator* 4 (1973): 419–34.

Origo, Iris. "The Domestic Enemy: Eastern Slaves in Tuscany in the Fourteenth and Fifteenth Centuries." *Speculum* 30 (1955): 321–66.

————. *The Merchant of Prato: Francesco di Marco Datini.* New York: Peregrine, 1957.

Padoa Schioppa, Antonio. *Ricerche sull'appello nel diritto intermedio.* Vol. 2: *I glossatori civilisti.* Milan: Giuffrè, 1970.

Palmer, Robert C. *The Whilton Dispute, 1264–1380: A Social-Legal Study of Dispute Settlement in Medieval England.* Princeton: Princeton University Press, 1984.

Pandimiglio, Leonida. "Giovanni di Pagolo Morelli e la ragion di famiglia." In *Studi sul medioevo cristiano offerti a Raffaello Morghen.* Rome: Istituto storico italiano per il Medio Evo, 1974. Pp. 553–608.

————. "Giovanni di Pagolo Morelli e le strutture familiari." *Archivio storico italiano* 136 (1978): 3–88.

Pecorella, Corrado. "Filiazione (storia)." *Enciclopedia del diritto,* 17: 449–56. Milan: Giuffrè, 1968.

Pene Vidari, Gian Savino. *Ricerche sul diritto agli alimenti.* Vol. 1: *L'obbligo 'ex lege' dei familiari nel periodo della Glossa e del commento.* Turin: Giappichelli, 1970.

Pennington, Kenneth. "Pope Innocent III's Views on Church and State: A Gloss to *Per Venerabilem.*" In *Law, Church, and Society: Essays in Honor of Stephan Kuttner.* Edited by Kenneth Pennington and Robert Somerville. Philadelphia: University of Pennsylvania Press, 1977. Pp. 49–67.

Peristiany, J. G., ed. *Honour and Shame: The Values of Mediterranean Society.* Chicago: University of Chicago Press, 1966.

Pertile, Antonio. *Storia del diritto italiano dalla caduta dell'impero romano alla codificazione.* 2d ed. 6 vols. Turin: Unione Tipografico, 1894.

Pitt-Rivers, Julian. *The Fate of Shechem: Essays in the Anthropology of the Mediterranean.* Cambridge: Cambridge University Press, 1977.

Plakans, Andrejs. *Kinship in the Past: An Anthropology of European Family Life, 1500–1900.* Oxford: Blackwell, 1984.

Pluss, Jacques. "Baldus de Ubaldis of Perugia on Dominium over Dotal Property." *Tijdschrift voor Rechtsgeschiedenis* 52 (1984): 399–411.

————. "Reading Case Law Historically: A *Consilium* of Baldus de Ubaldis on Widows and Dowries." *American Journal of Legal History* 30 (1986): 241–65.

Pomata, Gianna. "Madri illegittime tra Ottocento e Novecento: Storie cliniche e storie di vita." *Quaderni storici* 44 (1980): 497–542.

Ponte, Giovanni. "Etica ed economia nel terzo libro 'Della Famiglia' di Leon Battista Alberti." In *Renaissance Studies in Honor of Hans Baron*. Edited by Anthony Molho and John A. Tedeschi. Dekalb: Northern Illinois University Press, 1971. Pp. 283–310.

Portemer, Jean. "Bartole et les différences entre le droit romain et le droit canonique." In *Bartolo da Sassoferrato: Studi e documenti per il VI centenario*. Perugia: Università degli Studi di Perugia, 1962. Pp. 399–412.

Powell, Edward. "Arbitration and the Law in England in the Late Middle Ages." *Transactions of the Royal Historical Society* 33 (1983): 49–67.

———. "Settlement of Disputes by Arbitration in Fifteenth-Century England." *Law and History Review* 2 (1984): 21-43.

Power, Eileen. *Medieval Women*. Edited by M. M. Postan. Cambridge: Cambridge University Press, 1975.

———. "The Position of Women." In *The Legacy of the Middle Ages*. Edited by G. C. Crump and E. F. Jacob. Oxford: Oxford University Press, 1932. Pp. 401–34.

Raggio, Osvaldo. "La politica nella parentela: Conflitti locali e commissari in Liguria orientale (secoli xvi–xvii)." *Quaderni storici* 63 (December 1986): 721–57.

Regnault, Henri. *La condition juridique du bâtard au moyen âge*. Pont Audemer: Lescuyer, 1922.

Renner, Karl. *The Institutions of Private Law and Their Social Function*. Translated by Agnes Schwarzschild. London: Routledge, 1949.

Rheubottom, D. B. "Dowry and Wedding Celebrations in Yugoslav Macedonia." In *The Meaning of Marriage Payments*. Edited by John Comaroff. New York and London: Academic Press, 1980. Pp. 221–50.

Roberts, Simon. *Order and Dispute: An Introduction to Legal Anthropology*. New York: Penguin, 1979.

———. "The Study of Dispute: Anthropological Perspectives." In *Disputes and Settlements: Law and Human Relations in the West*. Edited by John Bossy. Cambridge: Cambridge University Press, 1983. Pp. 1–24.

Romano, Andrea, ed. *Le sostituzioni ereditarie nell'inedita 'Repetitio de substitionibus' di Raniero Arsendi*. Catania: Giannotta, 1977.

Romano, Ruggiero. *Tra due crisi: L'Italia del Rinascimento*. Turin: Einaudi, 1971.

Rosaldo, M. Z. "The Use and Abuse of Anthropology: Reflections on Feminism and Cross-Cultural Understanding." *Signs* 5 (1979–80): 389–417.

Rosenthal, Elaine. "The Position of Women in Renaissance Florence: Neither Autonomy nor Subjection." In *Florence and Italy: Renaissance Studies in Honour of Nicolai Rubinstein*. Edited by Peter Denley and Caroline Elam. London: Westfield College, University of London, 1989. Pp. 369–81.

Ross, James Bruce. "The Middle-Class Child in Urban Italy, Fourteenth to

Early Sixteenth Century." In *The History of Childhood*. Edited by Lloyd de Mause. New York: Harper & Row, 1974. Pp. 183–228.

Rossi, Guido. *Consilium sapientis iudiciale: Studi e ricerche per la storia del processo romano-canonico*. Milan: Giuffrè, 1958.

Rubinstein, Nicolai. *The Government of Florence under the Medici (1434–1494)*. Oxford: Oxford University Press, 1965.

Ruffini, Francesco. *La buona fede in materia di prescrizione*. Padua: n.p., 1892.

Sahlins, Marshall. *Culture and Practical Reason*. Chicago: University of Chicago Press, 1976.

Sapori, Armando. "La famiglia e le compagnie degli Alberti del Giudice." In *Studi di storia economica, secoli xiii–xiv–xv*. 2 vols. Florence: Sansoni, 1955. Vol. 2: 975–1012.

Sbriccoli, Mario. *L'Interpretazione dello statuto: Contributo allo studio della funzione dei giuristi nell'età comunale*. Milan: Giuffrè, 1969.

——. "Politique et interprétation juridique dans les villes italiennes du moyen âge." *Archives de philosophie du droit* 17 (1972): 99–113.

Scavo Lombardo, Luigi. "Buona fede." In *Enciclopedia del diritto*, 3: 369–70. Milan: Giuffrè, 1960.

Schimmelpfennig, Bernhard. "*Ex Fornicatione Nati:* Studies on the Position of Priests' Sons from the Twelfth to the Fourteenth Century." *Studies in Medieval and Renaissance History* 2 (1979): 1–50.

Schneider, David. *American Kinship: A Cultural Account*. Englewood-Cliffs, N.J.: Prentice-Hall, 1968.

Schneider, Jane. "Of Vigilance and Virgins: Honor, Shame, and Access to Resources in Mediterranean Societies." *Ethnology* 10 (1971): 1–24.

Schneider, Peter. "Honor and Conflict in a Sicilian Town." *Anthropological Quarterly* 42 (1969): 130–54.

Segalen, Martine. *Historical Anthropology of the Family*. Translated by J. C. Whitehouse and Sarah Matthews. Cambridge: Cambridge: University Press, 1986.

Sella, Pietro. *Il procedimento civile nella legislazione statutaria italiana*. Milan: Hoepli, 1927.

Shahar, Shulamith. *The Fourth Estate: A History of Women in the Middle Ages*. Translated by Chaya Galai. London: Metheun, 1983.

Sharpe, J. A. "'Such Disagreement betwyx Neighbours': Litigation and Human Relations in Early Modern England." In *Disputes and Settlements: Law and Human Relations in the West*. Edited by John Bossy. Cambridge: Cambridge University Press, 1983. Pp. 167–88.

Sheedy, Anna T. *Bartolus on Social Conditions in the Fourteenth Century*. New York: Columbia University Press, 1942.

Sheehan, Michael, C.S.B. "Choice of Marriage Partner in the Middle Ages: Development and Mode of Application of a Theory of Marriage." *Studies in Medieval and Renaissance History*, n.s., 1 (1978): 1–33.

Shorter, Edward. "Illegitimacy, Sexual Revolution, and Social Change in Modern Europe." *Journal of Interdisciplinary History* 2 (1971): 237–72.

———. *The Making of the Modern Family*. New York: Basic Books, 1975.

Siegel, Jerrold E. "'Civic Humanism' or Ciceronian Rhetoric? The Culture of Petrarch and Bruni." *Past and Present* 34 (July 1966): 3–48.

———. *Rhetoric and Philosophy in Renaissance Humanism: The Union of Eloquence and Wisdom, Petrarch to Valla*. Princeton: Princeton University Press, 1968.

Silverman, David, and Torode, Brian. *The Material Word: Some Theories of Language and Its Limits*. London: Routledge, 1980.

Silverman, Sydel. "On the Uses of History in Anthropology: The *Palio* of Siena." *American Ethnologist* 6 (1979): 413–36.

Snyder, Francis G. "Anthropology, Dispute Processes and Law: A Critical Introduction." *British Journal of Law and Society* 8 (1981–82): 141–80.

Starn, Randolph. *Contrary Commonwealth: The Theme of Exile in Medieval and Renaissance Italy*. Berkeley and London: University of California Press, 1982.

Stein, Peter. *Legal Institutions: The Development of Dispute Settlement*. London: Butterworth, 1984.

Strathern, Marilyn. "Self-Interest and the Social Good: Some Implications of Hagen Gender Imagery." In *Sexual Meanings: The Cultural Construction of Gender and Sexuality*. Edited by Sherry B. Ortner and Harriet Whitehead. Cambridge: Cambridge University Press, 1981. Pp. 166–91.

Strocchia, Sharon T. "Death Rites and the Ritual Family in Renaissance Florence." In *Life and Death in Fifteenth-Century Florence*. Edited by Marcel Tetel, Ronald G. Witt, and Rona Goffen. Durham: Duke University Press, 1989. Pp. 120–45.

Stuard, Susan Mosher. "From Women to Woman: New Thinking about Gender c. 1140." *Thought* 64 (1989): 208–19.

———. "Women in Charter and Statute Law: Medieval Ragusa/Dubrovnik." In *Women in Medieval Society*. Edited by Susan Mosher Stuard. Philadelphia: University of Pennsylvania Press, 1976. Pp. 199–208.

Sumner, Colin. *Reading Ideologies: An Investigation into the Marxist Theory of Ideology and Law*. London and New York: Academic Press, 1979.

Tamassia, Nino. *La famiglia italiana nei secoli decimoquinto e decimosesto*. Milan: Sandron, 1910.

Tenenti, Alberto. "Famille bourgeoise et idéologie au bas moyen âge." In *Famille et parenté dans l'Occident médiéval*. Edited by Georges Duby and Jacques Le Goff. Rome: Ecole Français de Rome, 1977. Pp. 431–40.

———. *Firenze dal comune a Lorenzo il Magnifico, 1350–1494*. Milan: Mursia, 1970.

———. "Temps et 'ventura' à la Renaissance: Le cas de Venise." In *Mélanges en l'honneur de Fernand Braudel*, vol. 1: *Histoire économique du monde méditerranéen, 1450–1650*. Paris: Privat, 1973. Pp. 599–610.

Tigar, Michael, with Madeleine R. Levy. *Law and the Rise of Capitalism*. New York: Monthly Review Press, 1977.

Tilly, Louise A., Scott, Joan W., and Cohen, Miriam. "Women's Work and European Fertility Patterns." *Journal of Interdisciplinary History* 6 (1976): 447–76.

Torelli, Pietro. *Lezioni di storia del diritto italiano: Diritto privato*. Milan: Giuffrè, 1947.

Torre, Angelo. "Faide, fazioni e partiti, ovvero la ridefinizione della politica nei feudi imperiali delle Langhe tra Sei e Settecento." *Quaderni storici* 63 (Dec. 1986): 775–810.

Trexler, Richard C. "The Foundlings of Florence, 1395–1455." *History of Childhood Quarterly* 1 (1973–74): 259–84.

————. "Infanticide in Florence: New Sources and First Results." *History of Childhood Quarterly* 1 (1973–74): 98–116.

Turner, Victor. "Process, System, and Symbol: A New Anthropological Synthesis." *Daedalus* 106 (1977): 61–80.

————. and Bruner, Edward M., eds. *The Anthropology of Experience*. Urbana and Chicago: University of Illinois Press, 1986.

Ullmann, Walter. *The Individual and Society in the Middle Ages*. Baltimore: Johns Hopkins University Press, 1966.

————. *The Medieval Idea of Law, as Represented by Lucas de Penna: A Study in Fourteenth-Century Legal Scholarship*. London: Metheun, 1946.

van de Walle, Etienne. "Illegitimacy in France during the Nineteenth Century." In *Bastardy and Its Comparative History*. Edited by Peter Laslett, Karla Oosterveen, and Richard M. Smith. Cambridge, Mass.: Harvard University Press, 1980. Pp. 264–77.

Vilain, Noel. "Prescription et bonne foi du Décret de Gratien (1140) à Jean d'André (d. 1348)." *Traditio* 14 (1958): 121–89.

Villata di Renzo, Gigliola. *La tutela: Indagini sulla scuola dei glossatori*. Milan: Giuffrè, 1975.

Violante, Cinzio. "Quelques caractéristiques des structures familiales en Lombardie, Emilie et Toscane aux xie et xiie siècles." In *Famille et parenté dans l'Occident médiéval*. Edited by Georges Duby and Jacques Le Goff. Rome: Ecole Français de Rome, 1977. Pp. 87–148.

Vismara, G. "Adozione (diritto intermedio)." In *Enciclopedia del diritto*, 1: 581–84. Milan: Giuffrè, 1958.

————. *Famiglia e successioni nella storia del diritto*. Rome: Editrice Studium, 1970.

Watkins, Renée Neu. "The Authorship of the *Vita anonyma* of Leon Battista Alberti." *Studies in the Renaissance* 4 (1957): 101–12.

Watson, Alan. *Sources of Law, Legal Change, and Ambiguity*. Philadelphia: University of Pennsylvania Press, 1984.

Weber, Max. *Economy and Society*. Edited by Guenther Roth and Claus Wittich. 2 vols. Berkeley: University of California Press, 1978.

Weinstein, Donald. "The Myth of Florence." In *Florentine Studies: Politics and Society in Renaissance Florence.* Edited by Nicolai Rubinstein. Evanston: Northwestern University Press, 1968. Pp. 15–44.

Weissman, Ronald F. E. "The Importance of Being Ambiguous: Social Relations, Individualism, and Identity in Renaissance Florence." In *Urban Life in the Renaissance.* Edited by Susan Zimmerman and Ronald F. E. Weissman. Newark: University of Delaware Press, 1989. Pp. 269–80.

———. *Ritual Brotherhoods in Renaissance Florence.* New York: Academic Press, 1982.

White, Stephen D. *Custom, Kinship, and Gifts to Saints: The Laudatio Parentum in Western France, 1050–1150.* Chapel Hill: University of North Carolina Press, 1988.

———. *"Pactum...Legem Vincit et Amor Judicium:* The Settlement of Disputes by Compromise in Eleventh-Century Western France." *American Journal of Legal History* 22 (1978): 281–308.

Wickham, Chris. "Comprendere il quotidiano: Antropologia sociale e storia sociale." *Quaderni storici* 60 (1985): 839–57.

———. "Land Disputes and Their Social Framework in Lombard-Carolingian Italy, 700–900." In *The Settlement of Disputes in Early Medieval Europe.* Edited by Wendy Davies and Paul Fouracre. Cambridge: Cambridge University Press, 1986. Pp. 105–24.

Wieacker, Franz. *Privatrechtsgeschichte der Neuzeit.* 2 vols. Göttingen: Vandenbroek & Ruprecht, 1952.

Williams, Raymond. *Marxism and Literature.* Oxford: Oxford University Press, 1977.

Willoweit, Dietmar. "Dominium und Proprietas: Zur Entwicklung des Eigentumsbegriffs in der mittelalterlichen und neuzeitlichen Rechtswissenschaft." *Historisches Jahrbuch der Goerres-Gesellschaft zur Pflege der Wissenschaft im Katholischen Deutschland* 94 (1974): 131–56.

Winterer, Hermann. *Die rechtliche Stellung der Bastarden in Italien von 800 bis 1500.* Munich: Arbeo, 1978.

Woodhouse, J. R. *Baldesar Castiglione: A Reassessment of The Courtier.* Edinburgh: Edinburgh University Press, 1978.

Wormald, Jenny. "Bloodfeud, Kindred and Government in Early Modern Scotland." *Past and Present* 87 (1980): 54–97.

———. "An Early Modern Postscript: The Sandlaw Dispute, 1546." In *The Settlement of Disputes in Early Medieval Europe.* Edited by Wendy Davies and Paul Fouracre. Cambridge: Cambridge University Press, 1986. Pp. 191–205.

Ziegler, Karl-Hans. "Arbiter, arbitrator und amicabilis compositor." *Zeitschrift der Savigny-Stiftung für Rechtsgeschichte (Rom. Abt.).* 84 (1967): 376–81.

INDEX

•

401